Routledge Handbook of Southeast Asian Economics

Edited by Ian Coxhead

D0073645

Routledge
Taylor & Francis Group

LONDON AND NEW YORK

First published in paperback 2018

First published 2015
by Routledge
2 Park Square, Milton Park, Abingdon, Oxon OX14 4RN

and by Routledge
711 Third Avenue, New York, NY 10017

Routledge is an imprint of the Taylor & Francis Group, an informa business

© 2015, 2018 selection and editorial matter, Ian Coxhead; individual chapters, the contributors

British Library Cataloguing in Publication Data
A catalogue record for this book is available from the British Library

Library of Congress Cataloging-in-Publication Data
Routledge handbook of Southeast Asian economics / [edited by] Ian Coxhead.
pages cm
Includes bibliographical references and index.
ISBN 978-0-415-65994-9 (hardback) -- ISBN 978-1-315-74241-0 (ebook) 1. Southeast Asia--Economic conditions. 2. Economic development--Southeast Asia. I. Coxhead, Ian A., editor. II. Williamson, Jeffrey G., 1935- Commodity export, growth and distribution connection in Southeast Asia, 1500-1940. Container of (work):
HC441.R68 2015
330.959--dc23

ISBN: 978-0-415-65994-9 (hbk)
ISBN: 978-1-138-31329-3 (pbk)
ISBN: 978-1-315-74241-0 (ebk)

Typeset in Bembo
by Integra Software Services Pvt. Ltd, Pondicherry, India

Routledge Handbook of Southeast Asian Economics

Now available in paperback, the *Routledge Handbook of Southeast Asian Economics* offers new insights into the rapidly developing economies of Southeast Asia. Despite widespread initial deprivation, Southeast Asia has achieved and sustained a remarkable rate of growth, in the course of which tens of millions have successfully escaped severe poverty. Though the economies of the region vary in many dimensions, integration into the wider East Asian network of production and trade is a notable common feature, one that continues a centuries-long history of engagement with global trade. A second striking feature is the pace and extent of transformation in the structure of production and in sources of household income in the region, which has undergone remarkably rapid industrialization and urban growth. However, the search for sustained and sustainable growth through and beyond middle-income continues to confront pressing economic and policy challenges.

This Handbook offers a timely and comprehensive overview of Southeast Asian economic development. Organized according to the logic of chronological and thematic unity, it is structured in these parts:

- Growth and development over the long term
- Food, agriculture, and natural resources
- Trade, investment, and industrialization
- Population, labor, and human capital
- Poverty and political economy
- Twenty-first-century challenges

This original Handbook, written by experts in their fields, is unique in the breadth and depth of its coverage. Its forward-looking perspective renders it relevant both now and in the future. This advanced-level reference work will be essential reading for students, researchers, and scholars of Asian Studies, Economics, and Southeast Asian Studies.

Ian Coxhead is a development economist at the University of Wisconsin–Madison, USA. He is a specialist in economic growth and development, international trade, labor markets and human capital, and household welfare and income distribution, with a strong regional emphasis on Southeast Asia.

Contents

Figures   viii
Tables   xii
Contributors   xvi
Foreword   xx
Map   xxii

PART I
Growth and development over the long term   1

1 Introduction: Southeast Asia's long transition   3
   Ian Coxhead

2 Trade, growth, and distribution in Southeast Asia, 1500–1940   22
   Jeffrey G. Williamson

3 A century of growth, crisis, war and recovery, 1870–1970   43
   Anne Booth

4 Lucky countries? Internal and external sources of Southeast Asian
   growth since 1970   60
   Tracy ThuTrang Phung, Ian Coxhead, and Chang Lian

PART II
Food, agriculture, and natural resources   87

5 The dynamics of agricultural development and food security in
   Southeast Asia: historical continuity and rapid change   89
   C. Peter Timmer

6 Natural resources, the environment and economic development in
   Southeast Asia   114
   Gerald Shively and Tim Smith

PART III
Trade, investment, and industrialization   137

7 Global production sharing, trade patterns, and industrialization in
Southeast Asia   139
Prema-chandra Athukorala and Archanun Kohpaiboon

8 Foreign direct investment in Southeast Asia   162
Fredrik Sjöholm

9 Regional trade agreements and enterprises in Southeast Asia   181
Ganeshan Wignaraja

PART IV
Population, labor, and human capital   199

10 The population of Southeast Asia   201
Gavin W. Jones

11 The determinants and long-term projections of saving rates in Southeast Asia   230
Charles Yuji Horioka and Akiko Terada-Hagiwara

12 Education in Southeast Asia: investments, achievements, and returns   245
Diep Phan and Ian Coxhead

13 Internal and international migration in Southeast Asia   270
Guntur Sugiyarto

PART V
Poverty and political economy   301

14 The drivers of poverty reduction   303
Peter Warr

15 The political economy of policy reform: insights from Southeast Asia   327
Hal Hill

PART VI
Twenty-first-century challenges   345

16 Dual-burdens in health and aging: emerging population challenges in
Southeast Asia   347
Jenna Nobles

17 Southeast Asian commercial policy: outward-looking regional
   integration   366
   Hal Hill and Jayant Menon

18 The global financial crisis and macroeconomic policy in Southeast Asia   385
   Bhanupong Nidhiprabha

19 Twenty-first-century challenges for Southeast Asian economies   408
   Ian Coxhead, Thee Kian Wie, and Arief Anshory Yusuf

Index   423

Figures

1.1 Growth of per capita income   4
1.2 Per capita income as percentage of world average   5
1.3 Export intensity relative to world average   6
1.4 Trends in sectoral structure of value added, 1970–2010   7
1.5 Long-run growth among resource-abundant economies   11
1.6 GDP growth rate deviations from long-run average (% per year), 1988–2012   14
2.1 Spice and coffee markups: Amsterdam vs. Southeast Asia, 1580–1939   24
2.2 Asian textile trade markups, 1664–1759   25
2.3 Explaining the world trade boom   26
2.4 The poor periphery: net barter terms of trade, 1796–1913   33
4.1 GDP growth rate weighted by share in world exports, four large economies   66
4.2 GDP growth rate weighted by share in world exports and distance from Singapore   67
4.3 Openness indexes for Southeast Asia (averages for half-decade periods beginning with date shown)   73
4.4 GDP growth spillovers from world economic growth, 1980s–1990s   78
4.5 GDP growth spillovers from Northeast Asian economic growth, 1980s–1990s   79
4.6 GDP growth spillovers from world economic growth, 2000s   79
4.7 GDP growth spillovers from Northeast Asian economic growth, 2000s   80
5.1 Regression 1 fit and residuals   92
5.2 Structural transformation in Japan and Indonesia, 1880–2010   96
5.3 Agricultural productivity change in Southeast Asia, 1961–2010, with comparisons   98
5.4 The dietary transformation   101
5.5 Per capita rice consumption by quintile over time, Indonesia, urban areas   103
5.6 Per capita rice consumption by quintile over time, Indonesia, rural areas   103
5.7 Engel curves over time for urban Indonesia   104
5.8 Annualized percentage change in rice consumption by quintile and location, Indonesia, India and Bangladesh   105

5.9	Ratio of rice to wheat consumption in Malaysia by age of household head, 1998/99	105
5.10	Modernizing food supply chains in Southeast Asia: the "10-wheeler" model	107
6.1	Agricultural expansion vs. deforestation in Southeast Asia, 1980–2010	117
6.2	Forest area vs. population density in Southeast Asia, 1990–2005	118
6.3	Ratio of rural to urban incomes for Southeast Asia, 1980–2010	121
6.4	Vulnerability and GDP per capita	124
6.5	PM_{10} vs. GDP	127
6.6	Electric power consumption and PM_{10} in Southeast Asia, 1989–2009	127
6.7	Genuine domestic savings as % of gross national income in Southeast Asia, 1980–2009	129
6.8	Primary export share and per capita growth, 1970–95	129
8.1	FDI inflows to Southeast Asia (1970–2011)	163
8.2	The share of foreign MNEs in Southeast Asian manufacturing (2006)	166
8.3	Foreign share of manufacturing export (2006)	175
10.1	Trends in total fertility rates, Southeast Asian countries	206
10.2	Thailand's age structure, 1990 and 2010	211
10.3	Philippines's age structure, 1970, 1990 and 2010	212
10.4	Total fertility rate and number of births in various Southeast Asian countries, 1960–2010	213
10.5	Population growth rates in Southeast Asia, 1970–75 to 2025–30	215
10.6	Southeast Asian countries: projected population growth, 2010–30	215
10.7	Index of projected population growth, 2010–50 – UN medium projection	216
10.8	Index of projected population growth, 2010–50 – UN low projection	217
10.9	Trends in dependency ratios, Southeast Asian countries, 1970–2040	219
10.10	Percentage of population aged over 65, 1970–2030	220
10.11	Trends in secondary school enrolment ratio, Southeast Asian countries	221
10.12	Index of projected population growth in different working age groups, 2010–30 – UN medium projection	222
11.1	Trends over time in domestic saving rates in developing Asia, 1966–2007	233
12.1	Primary school net enrollment rates	247
12.2a	Mean years of schooling for population age 15+	248
12.2b	Mean years of schooling for population age 15+ for comparable stage of development	249
12.3	Secondary school net enrollment rates	250
12.4	Tertiary gross enrollment rates	250
12.5	Total public education expenditure per pupil	252
12.6	Public education expenditure per pupil as percentage of GDP per capita	252
13.1	Urbanization rates in Southeast Asia region, 1990 and 2012	272
13.2	Urbanization rates in Asia compared with other regions	278

13.3	Urbanization rates in Southeast Asia region compared with other sub-regions	278
13.4	Main destinations of international migrants from Southeast Asia based on migrant stock, 2000–10	279
13.5	Remittance inflows to developing countries compared to other inflows	280
13.6	Aging in Southeast Asia countries as reflected in the shares of population aged 65+, 2000–10	284
13.7	Wages disparities across selected countries	285
14.1	Annual rates of poverty reduction	307
14.2	Annual rate of poverty reduction and economic growth	309
14.3	Southeast Asia: annual rates of poverty reduction	309
14.4	Southeast Asia: annual rate of poverty reduction and economic growth	310
14.5	Cambodia: poverty incidence, 1994 to 2010	310
14.6	Indonesia: poverty incidence, 1976 to 2010	311
14.7	Laos: poverty incidence, 1992 to 2007	311
14.8	Malaysia: poverty incidence, 1976 to 2009	311
14.9	Myanmar: poverty incidence, 2005 to 2010	312
14.10	The Philippines: poverty incidence, 1976 to 2008	312
14.11	Thailand: poverty incidence, 1969 to 2009	312
14.12	Vietnam: poverty incidence, 1993 to 2011	313
14.13	Indonesia: rural poverty reduction – data and counterfactual projections	323
14.14	Laos: rural poverty reduction – data and counterfactual projections	323
14.15	Malaysia: rural poverty reduction – data and counterfactual projections	323
14.16	Philippines: rural poverty reduction – data and counterfactual projections	324
14.17	Thailand: rural poverty reduction – data and counterfactual projections	324
14.18	Vietnam: rural poverty reduction – data and counterfactual projections	324
16.1	Total, child, and elderly dependency ratio, Southeast Asia, 1950–2050	353
16.2	Share of elderly among dependents by region and year	354
16.3	Loss of disability-adjusted life years	356
16.4	Prevalence of overweight and obesity in adult females, 1980–2008	358
16.5	Anthropometry in Southeast Asian countries, 2006–11	359
16.6	Animal products in food supply, Southeast Asia, 1980–2009	360
17.1	Intra-ASEAN trade shares, 1970–2012	372
18.1	GDP growth in the major ASEAN economies	387
18.2	Export growth in the major ASEAN economies	388
18.3	Estimated elasticity of exports with respect to China's imports	390
18.4	Bank loans to GDP, ASEAN economies	391
18.5	Banks' non-performing loans	392
18.6	Stock market capitalization	393
18.7	Stock market returns: correlation with Singapore	393
18.8	Output growth correlation: ASEAN-5	395
18.9	Business cycle synchronization: ASEAN-5 and CLMV	395
18.10	Consumption cycle in ASEAN-5	396
18.11	Corporate income tax rates in major ASEAN economies	397

18.12 Investment cycles in ASEAN-5 economies   398
18.13 Money market rate differentials relative to Singapore   400
18.14 Inflation synchronization in ASEAN   402
18.15 Trends in CLMV exchange rates   403
18.16 Exchange rate appreciation in ASEAN economies   404
19.1   Oil palm production and land area, 1961–2011   416
19.2   The impact of oil palm land moratorium on the GDP of Indonesia and
       Indonesia's oil-palm producing regions   417
19.3   The trend of number of climate-related disasters (flood, storm,
       and landslide) in Southeast Asia   418

Tables

1.1	Corruption perceptions and economic freedoms in Southeast Asian countries	12
2.1	Five centuries of European inter-continental and world trade growth, 1500–1992	23
2.2	Populations in Southeast Asia, 1820, 1913, and 1950	31
3.1	Trends in per capita GDP, 1870–1970	44
3.2	Percentage of total NDP/GDP accruing from non-agricultural sectors, 1900–38	45
3.3	Occupational distribution of the employed population, Japan, Thailand and colonies, c. 1930	47
3.4	Development indicators: East and South East Asia, late 1930s	53
4.1	Average GDP per capita growth rates by region (%)	61
4.2	GDP per capita growth rates in Southeast Asia (%)	64
4.3	Summary of regression data, by region and country	71
4.4	Unconditional spillovers with convergence (dependent variable: growth of per capita GDP)	74
4.5	Growth model with spillovers (dependent variable: growth of per capita GDP)	75
4.6	Growth model with spillovers and SE Asia interactions (dependent variable: growth of per capita income)	76
4.7	Maximum likelihood estimates (dependent variable: average annual growth rate of output per worker)	77
4.8	Countries with significantly high growth elasticity from spillovers	78
5.1	Comparative food security indicators	90
5.2	Relationship between the food security gap and the prevalence of undernutrition	91
5.3	Structural transformation in Southeast Asia	94
5.4	Agricultural transformation in Southeast Asia	100
5.5	Dietary transformation in Southeast Asia	101
5.A1	The changing role of rice in Indonesian food consumption	111
5.A2	Transforming the food of the poor to the fuel of the rich	111
6.1	Population and urbanization in Southeast Asia, 1970–2010	116
6.2	Forest cover and deforestation in Southeast Asia, 1980–2010	117

6.3 Biodiversity and species under threat in Southeast Asia, 2012   119
6.4 Cultivated area in Southeast Asia, 1979 and 2009   119
6.5 Urban environmental quality in Southeast Asia, 1980–2010   122
6.6 Fossil fuel consumption in Southeast Asia, 1980–2010   123
6.7 Carbon emissions and abatement programs in Southeast Asia, 2008–12   125
6.8 Primary export shares for Southeast Asia, 1965–2011   130
7.1 Shares of principal Asian exporters in total US imports of semiconductor devices, 1969–83   140
7.2 Geographic profile of world manufacturing trade: total trade and network trade   144
7.3 Share of network products in manufacturing trade, 1992–93 and 2009–10   147
7.4 Composition of network products exported from Southeast Asia, 2007–08   149
7.5 Direction of Southeast Asian manufacturing trade, 1996–2010   150
7.6 South Asia: share of parts and components in manufacturing trade flows, 1996–2010   150
7.7 Average annual compensation per production worker   152
7.8 Key indicators of manufacturing performance in Southeast Asian countries, 2000–01 and 2007–08   154
8.1 Shares of total FDI inflows to Southeast Asia, 1970–2011   164
8.2 The stock of inward FDI as percent of GDP   164
8.3 The main sources of FDI in Southeast Asia   165
8.4 The ranking of business climate in Southeast Asia and other regions (2005 and 2012)   172
8.A1 The share of foreign firms in a selection of countries   177
9.1 Characteristics of firms   184
9.2 Firms using and planning to use ASEAN RTAs   185
9.3 Benefits and costs of ASEAN RTAs   187
9.4 Impediments to using RTAs   188
9.5 Probit regressions of factors affecting the use of RTAs   191
9.6 Marginal effects of factors affecting the use of RTAs   192
10.1 Southeast Asian countries: population size, growth rates and population density   202
10.2 Urbanization levels in Southeast Asian countries, 1950–2030   203
10.3 Infant mortality rates and expectation of life at birth, Southeast Asian countries, 1965–70 to 2005–10   205
10.4 Maternal mortality ratios, Southeast Asian countries, 2010   205
10.5 Total fertility rates, percentage changes in rates, and percentage decline towards the replacement level, Southeast Asian countries, 1965–70 to 2005–10   207
10.6 Female labour force participation rates, 1990 and 2010   222
11.1 Trends over time in gross domestic saving rates in developing Asia   234

11.2	Population aging in developing Asia	239
11.3	Future trends in real domestic saving rates in developing Asia	240
11.A1	Variable definitions and data sources	241
11.A2	Descriptive statistics	242
12.1	Survival rate to grade 5, 2009	247
12.2	Pupil/teacher ratio in primary education	253
12.3	Mean years of schooling for population aged 17–22 by gender	255
12.4	Mean years of schooling for population aged 17–22 by rural/urban	255
12.5	Relative mean years of school for population aged 17–22 by income quintile	256
12.6	Public spending on education	261
13.1	Basic key indicators of countries in Southeast Asia	271
13.2	Level of urbanization and its percentage change across different regions	276
13.3	Level of urbanization and its percentage change across different countries in Southeast Asia	277
13.4	International labor migration within ASEAN, 2010	283
13.5	Dynamics of net international migration rate across countries and time periods, 1990–2015	283
13.A1	Migrant stock matrix, 2000 and 2010	288
13.A2	Migrant to population ratio, 2000 and 2010	290
13.A3	Regional share of migrant destination	292
14.1	Developing regions and countries: annual rates of poverty reduction, 1981 to 2008	308
14.2	Data decomposition: mean annual changes in poverty incidence	313
14.3	Average rates of poverty reduction, economic growth and variable correlations	315
14.4	National poverty and aggregate growth	319
14.5	National poverty and sectoral growth	320
14.6	Rural poverty and sectoral growth	321
14.7	Urban poverty and sectoral growth	322
16.1	Vertical and regional inequality, Southeast Asian countries	348
16.2	Duration of fertility transition	349
16.3	Children ever born to women age 40–49, by country, province, and period	350
16.4	Total fertility rate and associated growth by region, 1995–2011	352
17.1	Major intra-ASEAN trade flows, 2012	372
17.2	Intra- and extra-regional FDI flows, 2010–12	375
17.3	FTA status, ASEAN by country, as of July 2013	376
17.4	Indicators of economic integration	381
18.1	Post-GFC current account surplus in ASEAN-5 economies	389
18.2	Post-GFC current account deficit in CLMV economies	389

18.3 Impact of the GFC on ASEAN export growth, 2009–11 390
18.4 Aggregate demand: structural differences and similarities 390
18.5 Budget deficit after the GFC 399
18.6 Growth rate of broad money, ASEAN-5 economies 401
18.7 Growth rate of broad money: CLMV economies 401
19.1 Summary measures of inequality for Southeast Asian countries 412

Contributors

Prema-chandra Athukorala is Professor of Economics at the Arndt-Corden Department of Economics, Crawford School of Public Policy, College of Asia and the Pacific, Australian National University, and Honorary Professorial Research Fellow, School of Environment and Development, University of Manchester, UK.

Anne Booth has recently retired from SOAS, University of London, UK, where she has been Professor of Economics (with reference to Asia) since 1991. In recent years her research has concentrated on the economic history of Southeast Asia, and comparative colonial legacies across East and Southeast Asia.

Ian Coxhead is Professor and Chair of the Department of Agricultural and Applied Economics at the University of Wisconsin-Madison, USA. He is a specialist in economic growth and development, international trade, labor markets and human capital, and household welfare and income distribution, with a regional focus on Southeast Asia. At Wisconsin he teaches development economics at both graduate and undergraduate levels.

Hal Hill is the H.W. Arndt Professor of Southeast Asian Economies at the Australian National University. His research interests are the economies of ASEAN, including country case studies and thematic, comparative work; industrialization and foreign investment in East Asia; regional development; and the political economy of development. He is the author or editor of 18 books and has written about 150 academic papers and chapters.

Charles Yuji Horioka is Research Professor in the Asian Growth Research Institute in Kitakyushu City, Japan, and Research Associate of the National Bureau of Economic Research. In 2001, he was awarded the Japanese Economic Association/Nakahara Prize, which is given annually to the most outstanding Japanese economist aged 45 or younger. His specialties are the Japanese economy, Asian economies, household economics, and macroeconomics.

Gavin W. Jones is Director of the JY Pillay Comparative Asia Research Centre at the National University of Singapore. His research interests focus on Southeast and East Asia, and range widely, including marriage and the family, determinants of fertility, education and human capital, urbanization and population policy.

Archanun Kohpaiboon is an Assistant Professor in the Faculty of Economics, Thammasat University, Bangkok, Thailand. He is also the chief editor of *Thammasat Economic Journal*. He won the best paper award in industrial economics 2003 at the Annual Conference of PhD

Students in Economics in Australian Universities and the best young economist of Thailand prize in 2006.

Chang Lian is a PhD candidate in the Department of Agricultural and Applied Economics at the University of Wisconsin-Madison, USA. His current research focuses on development economics, international trade, and political economy with a regional interest in China and India. In the spring of 2014, he was a visiting scholar at the International Monetary Fund (IMF).

Jayant Menon is Lead Economist in the Office for Regional Economic Integration at the Asian Development Bank (ADB), where he works on trade, international finance and development issues. Prior to this he worked at the Center of Policy Studies at Monash University, Australia. He is the author or co-author of more than a 100 academic publications, mostly on trade and development, and their relation to Asia.

Bhanupong Nidhiprabha is Associate Professor at the Faculty of Economics, Thammasat University, Bangkok, Thailand. He served as Vice Rector for Academic Affairs of Thammasat University between 1999 and 2004. From 2011 to 2014, he was the Dean of the Faculty of Economics, Thammasat University.

Jenna Nobles is an Associate Professor of Sociology and an affiliate of the Center for Demography and Ecology at the University of Wisconsin-Madison, USA. She studies aspects of health, development, and family processes in Southeast Asia and Latin America. Her current research investigates fertility decisions and the process of population rebuilding in Aceh, Indonesia, after the 2004 Indian Ocean tsunami.

Diep Phan teaches international economics, globalization, and development in the Department of Economics at Beloit College, USA. She currently studies Vietnam's labor market, wages, labor demand, labor migration, and human capital. Her primary research interest is in the economic growth and development of East and Southeast Asia.

Tracy ThuTrang Phung is an Honorary Research Fellow in the Department of Agricultural and Applied Economics, University of Wisconsin-Madison, USA. Her research interests include economic growth and development, poverty reduction and education. She received several awards during her study at the University of Wisconsin, including the Center for Southeast Asian Studies Fellowship and the Academic Achievement Award.

Gerald Shively is Professor of Agricultural Economics at Purdue University, USA, and an Adjunct Professor in the School of Economics and Business at the Norwegian University of Life Sciences. In 2007 he received Purdue's Agricultural Research Award and in 2008 was named a Purdue University Faculty Scholar. He is editor-in-chief of *Agricultural Economics*, the flagship journal of the International Association of Agricultural Economists.

Fredrik Sjöholm is a Professor of International Economics at Lund University, Sweden, and an affiliated researcher at the Research Institute of Industrial Economics (IFN). His research focuses on the role of multinational companies in the global economy and the home and host country effects of foreign direct investment. His current research includes work on labor market effects of globalization, and on economic development in East Asia.

Tim Smith is a graduate student at Purdue University, USA, working toward his PhD in Agricultural Economics. He received his BA in Public Policy and International Studies from the University of North Carolina at Chapel Hill in 2011 and his MS degree in Agricultural Economics from Purdue University in 2014.

Guntur Sugiyarto is a Senior Economist at the Economics and Research Department, Asian Development Bank (ADB). He has published a significant number of works on a wide range of development issues, including competitiveness, investment, tourism economics, labor markets, poverty, computable general equilibrium (CGE) modeling, trade liberalization, taxation, commodity prices, biofuel and food security, education, infrastructure, fragility, and migration.

Akiko Terada-Hagiwara is a Senior Economist at the Macroeconomics and Finance Research Division (Economics and Research Department) of the Asian Development Bank (ADB). From 2005 to 2008, she was also an economist at the Institute for Monetary and Economic Studies of the Bank of Japan. Her areas of expertise are in international finance, development economics, and macroeconomic policies.

Thee Kian Wie devoted his entire professional life to research, teaching, and public affairs in Indonesia. He was a staff member of the Indonesian Institute of Sciences (LIPI) for 55 years. His academic output was prodigious: he authored or edited over 20 books and monographs, and more than 80 book chapters and journal articles. He served for several years as chairman of the Board of Governors of the SMERU Research Institute, Indonesia's leading academic think tank for research on poverty and social issues. Dr. Thee passed away in February 2014.

C. Peter Timmer is a leading authority on agricultural development and structural transformation during the process of economic growth, as well as on the causes and impact of food price volatility. He has served as a professor at Stanford, Cornell, Harvard, and the University of California, San Diego, USA, and is Thomas D. Cabot Professor of Development Studies, *emeritus*, Harvard University, and Adjunct Professor, Crawford School of Economics and Government, Australian National University. In 1992, he received the Bintang Jasa Utama (Highest Merit Star) from the Republic of Indonesia, and in 2012, he received the Leontief Prize from Tufts University.

Peter Warr is Head of the Arndt-Corden Department of Economics, John Crawford Professor of Agricultural Economics and founding Director of the Poverty Research Centre at the Australian National University. He is President of the Australian Agricultural and Resource Economics Society and a Fellow of the Academy of Social Sciences in Australia.

Ganeshan Wignaraja is the Director of Research of the Asian Development Bank Institute (ADBI). He has held positions with Oxford University, the OECD, the United Nations Institute for New Technologies, the Asian Development Bank, the Commonwealth Secretariat, and the private sector. His recent books include *A WTO for the 21st Century: The Asian Perspective* (forthcoming) and *Patterns of Free Trade Areas in Asia* (2013).

Jeffrey G. Williamson is Laird Bell Professor of Economics, *emeritus*, Harvard University, and Honorary Fellow, Department of Economics, University of Wisconsin-Madison, USA. Past president of the Economic History Association, chairman of the Harvard Economics Department, and Master of Harvard's Mather House, his most recent books are: *Trade and*

Poverty: When the Third World Fell Behind (2011) and *Globalization and the Poor Periphery before 1950 (2006).*

Arief Anshory Yusuf is the Director of the Center for Economics and Development Studies of Universitas Padjadjaran, Indonesia. He is also a Senior Economist of the Economy and Environment Program for Southeast Asia and an Adjunct Fellow at the Australian National University. He serves as the Secretary-General of the Indonesian Regional Science Association. His research is on natural resource and environmental economics, poverty and inequality, and economy-wide modeling.

Foreword

On reading the email inviting me to edit a *Handbook of Southeast Asian Economics*, my first reaction was "delete." Too much work, too little reward. After more thought, however, I decided that the benefits of a project like this could be substantial under some conditions. A volume structured as a set of thematic studies might create an opportunity to obtain insights that are not normally accessible in a set of single-country chapters. Involving a top-class set of contributing authors would help ensure high quality analyses. Finally, bringing the authors together to present and discuss their work in draft form would surely generate synergistic interactions and so help make the whole book more valuable than the sum of its component chapters. With some effort, a lot of cooperation, and a pinch of luck all three conditions were ultimately met.

Bringing this volume to completion has been an enormously satisfying experience. Thanks are due to many for their help along the way.

Above all else, this volume owes its existence and the quality of its contents to the enthusiastic participation of a terrific set of contributing authors. All have been very gracious, constructive and cooperative. These qualities—along with an equally desirable dose of sharp-edged attention to scholarly rigor—were all on display when we convened in Bangkok, Thailand in March 2013 for a mini-conference. I am very grateful to the Henry Luce Foundation and in particular to Helena Kolenda, its Asia program director, for a generous grant making that meeting possible. Bhanupong Nidhiprabha, Dean of the Faculty of Economics at Thammasat University and his staff gave very generously of their time and energy to provide a conference secretariat and logistical support. In addition to the authors themselves, several discussants and participants also deserve thanks for contributing to a lively interaction, notably Corbett Grainger, Sisira Jayasuriya, Mingsarn Kaosa-ard, Sirilaksana Khoman, and Yoko Niimi.

At the University of Wisconsin, Tracy Phung did a great job of building and maintaining the project website. Mary Jo Wilson at the Center for Southeast Asian Studies managed the conference grant, and both she and the Center's Associate Director, Mike Cullinane, provided valuable moral support. In the UK, the Routledge editorial team (Dorothea Schaefter, Jillian Morrison, and Becky Lawrence) have provided abundant guidance and encouragement, and I speak for all the authors in expressing our sincere gratitude to copy editor Liz Dawn.

This volume is dedicated to the memory of our colleague Thee Kian Wie (1935–2014). Kian Wie was an observer, commentator, analyst and participant in Indonesian economic life for over half a century, during which time his native country emerged from the chaos of war and decolonization to become the world's 16th largest economy. With his intellect, experience, insight and sly wit he guided and inspired a generation of scholars of economic development in

Indonesia and the region. We were fortunate to have him participate in the Bangkok conference and to have his input as contributor to a chapter in this volume. His passing leaves an empty chair at all such meetings in the future.

Ian Coxhead
Madison, Wisconsin, USA
Summer 2014

Map

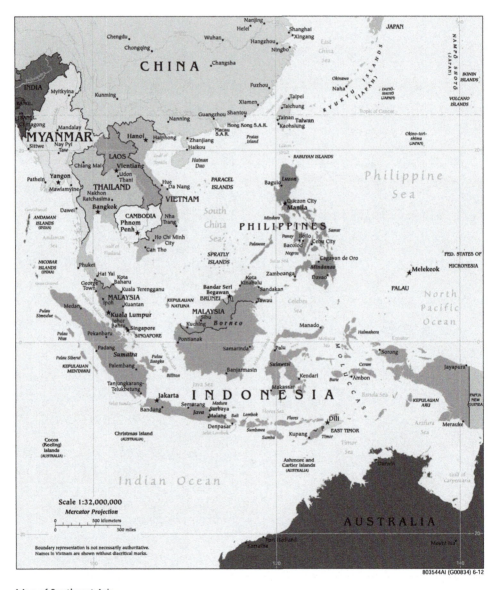

Map of Southeast Asia
Source: University of Texas Libraries.

Part I

Growth and development over the long term

1

Introduction

Southeast Asia's long transition

Ian Coxhead

UNIVERSITY OF WISCONSIN-MADISON

Introduction

As of 2014 Southeast Asia is home to 620 million people, or 8.6 percent of world population. Its six large economies (Indonesia, Singapore, Thailand, Malaysia, the Philippines, and Vietnam) and five smaller ones (Cambodia, Laos, Myanmar, Brunei, and East Timor) together account for one-tenth of the income generated in all low- and middle-income economies worldwide. Less than two generations ago the vast majority of Southeast Asians were very poor. Since the 1980s, however, the region as a whole has achieved and sustained a remarkable rate of growth (Figure 1.1), in the course of which tens of millions of its citizens have successfully escaped severe poverty. This growth experience sets the region as a whole apart from other developing areas (only China can claim a consistently higher growth rate of per capita gross domestic product [GDP]) and has seen incomes in most Southeast Asian countries lifted well above the developing country average (Figure 1.2).

Despite this remarkably convergent growth, however, the countries of the region display a great variety of development experiences. This is due in large part to differences in initial resource endowments, systems of government and development strategies, and the pace and extent of their integration with external markets. Today's high degree of international market integration in the region is a phenomenon with deep roots in the region's historical role both as a unique supplier of spices and other natural resource products, and as an entrepôt on maritime trade routes linking the world's largest economies. In recent decades, Southeast Asia's outward orientation has been reinforced by adoption of growth and development strategies that exploit trade-based opportunities created by its abundance of labor and natural resources and by its geographic, cultural, and economic proximity to large, fast-growing economies in Northeast Asia. Countries of the region (Myanmar excepted) display high and/or rising trade intensity relative to the world average (Figure 1.3). The nature of Southeast Asia's contemporary economic development experience is increasingly dominated by its ever-closer integration into the wider Asian and global production and trade networks for agriculture, resources, manufactures – and, increasingly, of services.

Another striking feature of the region's recent development is the pace and extent of transformation of production and sources of household income. Fifty years ago, nearly all

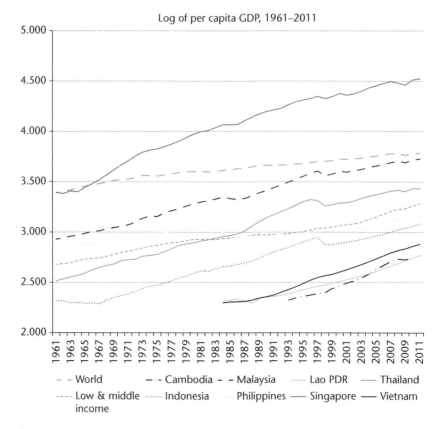

Figure 1.1 Growth of per capita income
Source: World Bank: World Development Indicators Online.

inhabitants of this region lived in rural areas and relied on their own labor to supply food, shelter, and other necessities of life. But in less than three decades from the early 1970s, the region's economic center of gravity moved from primary industries (agriculture, fisheries, mining, and forestry) to manufacturing – initially, raw materials processing and simple assembly operations, but becoming more technologically sophisticated over time (Figure 1.4). This sectoral transformation occurred at a rate far higher than comparable changes in Western Europe, the United States, and Japan, and matched or exceeded rates achieved a generation earlier by the Northeast Asian "tiger" economies, Taiwan and South Korea. It has been accompanied by urbanization, rising labor productivity, and the emergence of a sizable middle class, and has to most observers been the region's most visible manifestation of economic growth. It has resulted in Southeast Asia's economies achieving a far more diversified pattern of production and trade than is found in other regions of the developing world. Within Southeast Asia, later starters such as Vietnam and Laos now show signs of making the transformation even more rapidly than their neighbors.

This rate and pattern of growth has proved remarkably robust despite severe setbacks (notably the Asian Crisis of 1997–99 and the global Great Recession of 2008–10), and periods of great volatility in world markets for important regional commodity exports such as oil and gas, rice, coffee, and rubber. In resonance with the structural transformation, the sectoral basis for growth

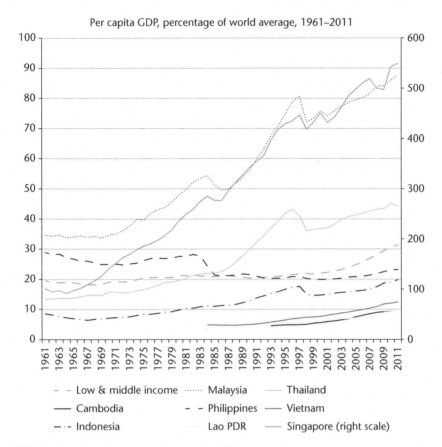

Per capita GDP, percentage of world average, 1961–2011

Legend:
- – Low & middle income ⋯⋯ Malaysia —— Thailand
—— Cambodia – – Philippines —— Vietnam
—·– Indonesia Lao PDR —— Singapore (right scale)

Figure 1.2 Per capita income as percentage of world average
Source: World Bank: World Development Indicators Online.

has changed over time. So too has the distribution of gains from growth among factors such as land, labor, and capital, and of course among households as owners of those factors. As a consequence, the region continues to provide a fertile ground for theorizing about economic development, just as it has since the end of the colonial era.

Although the foregoing description suggests a group of countries that are homogeneous relative to the rest of the developing world, it goes without saying that each country's development path has been shaped by unique features and conditions. In fact, the divergent features of country experience are as noticeable as their similarities, and understanding these after controlling for inherited factors such as natural resource wealth is an important task for scholars of Southeast Asian development. The Philippines, a promising early leader in development, experienced decades of growth at rates much lower than its neighbors, and in so doing slipped on many measures of economic wellbeing from regional leader toward the middle of the pack. In contrast Vietnam, a much later initiate to modern economic growth, has displayed remarkably rapid convergence on all key measures of wellbeing during its transition from command to semi-market economy. Meanwhile, increasingly close regional economic integration, through institutions such as the Association of Southeast Asian Nations (ASEAN) as well as through adoption of a broadly common regional stance in relation to the Asian and world economies, surely accounts for much of the growth catch-up that can be observed in

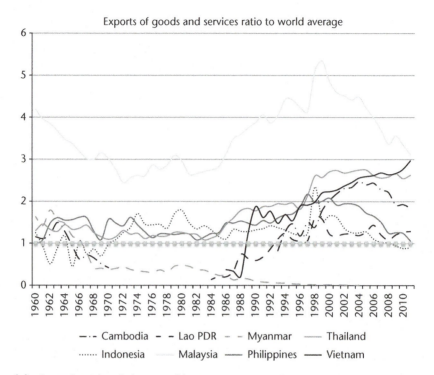

Exports of goods and services ratio to world average

- · - Cambodia   - - Lao PDR   - - - Myanmar   ——— Thailand
······ Indonesia   ——— Malaysia   ——— Philippines   ——— Vietnam

Figure 1.3   Export intensity relative to world average
Source: World Bank: World Development Indicators Online.

Vietnam as well as in Laos, Cambodia, and Myanmar, the region's most recent arrivals to market-based development.

The goal of this chapter is to provide an overview of Southeast Asian economics and to introduce some of the key themes to be explored in later chapters. The next two sections offer a brief historical survey of regional economic development since about 1970. The emphasis is on comparisons between "then" and "now," especially those phenomena that can be linked to outcomes such as the divergent economic growth rates of the early decades in this era, or the convergence that has occurred more recently. The chapter's focus is more broad, however, than aggregate growth alone. Both the reality and perceptions of the distribution of the costs and the gains from growth are increasingly important political economy issues. And arguably the main point of any survey of development is to identify challenges and opportunities that the future will bring; this is the subject of the fourth section of this chapter. Finally, a concluding section provides an overview of chapters making up the remainder of the volume.

Initial conditions

In order to interpret the present, let alone to predict the future, it is necessary first to understand the past. In the generation that followed World War II, as colonialism gave way to modern states and as the geopolitical theater of the Cold War began to take shape, Southeast Asia became the subject of a wealth of studies by economists and other social scientists. Some focused tightly in on local institutions and the behaviors of farm and village communities, which they identified as organizationally distinct from urban (or "modern") populations

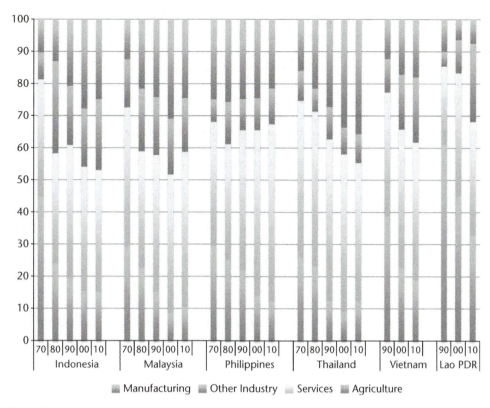

Figure 1.4   Trends in sectoral structure of value added, 1970–2010
Source: World Bank: World Development Indicators Online.

(Boeke 1953; Geertz 1963). Others traced the birth and early development of individual nations. Only a few chose to examine the region as an entity. By far the most famous among regional surveys is Gunnar Myrdal's *Asian Drama: An Inquiry into the Poverty of Nations* (Myrdal 1968a), which meticulously documented and compared levels of living and progress in economic growth across South and Southeast Asia. The data and analyses in this landmark work of early scholarship in development economics still provide a baseline for measuring regional progress in economic development.[1]

Possibly the most articulate and insightful appraisal of early economic life in the region, however, comes not from an economist but from a journalist-turned historian: the late Stanley Karnow, in his contribution to the *Life World Library*, a popular American series of coffee-table books. Karnow's volume, *Southeast Asia*, was published in 1962. To revisit it 50 years later is to discover a fascinating mix of continuity and contrast. Karnow documents a region united by geography (he likened the map of Southeast Asia to "a huge jigsaw puzzle") and history, and yet fractured by deep social and economic divisions. Some, such as the dichotomies between countryside and city and between wealthy and impoverished, are as familiar today as they were obvious to observers like Karnow, through the lenses of the *Life* photographers, or in Myrdal's careful tables of data. For confirmation, one need only consider the sharp rural–urban divisions that define opposing factions in Thai politics since 2001, a gulf so wide that it now threatens to bring growth in this otherwise successful regional economy to a halt.

Some other divisions recorded by Karnow are much more surprising to a twenty-first-century witness. These are notably the economic and cultural chasms that seemed to divide the region's states from one another,[2] and the contrast between entrepreneurial, development-oriented states and institutions and those seemingly committed to a lethargic, inwardly-oriented status quo.[3] Lastly, without the depth of perspective that history provides, it is difficult today to comprehend the theme, pervasive in Karnow's writing and that of most of his Western contemporaries, of an unstable, hungry, and avaricious "Red" China posing an existential challenge to Southeast Asian states and threatening the wellbeing of their peoples. China remains a daily preoccupation for the region, but it is a very different China and a very different set of issues – far more economic than geopolitical – that now command regional attention.[4]

Economically, the early postcolonial regimes typically rendered economic policies subservient to the seemingly more pressing political tasks of state formation and nation-building. Most of these regimes harbored deep suspicions of capitalism, an economic system that they associated with colonial subjugation. To the leaders of newly independent nations, some of the most appealing alternatives were to be found in the experiences of the Soviet Union and Maoist China, whose quasi-autarkic strategies for the transition from peasant agriculture to industrialization appeared to offer an alternative to the "unequal exchange" of raw materials for manufactures imported from the West. There was also, of course, a more pragmatic motive for mistrust of trade, as Karnow realized in 1962: "As producers of raw materials, Southeast Asians have come to recognize the dangers of dependence on whimsical world markets" (p. 147). During the early postcolonial years, the intensity of Southeast Asia's reliance on trade diminished to historically low levels (Booth 2004).

As the curtain rose on the era of modern economic development, the states of Southeast Asia were (mostly) new, their governments inexperienced, their policies ill-informed and untested, and their basic human needs very great.

The long transition

As recently as 1970 (and far later in some countries and areas) the typical Southeast Asian was rural, agrarian, undernourished, unlettered, unbanked, and unconnected to the broader world whether through markets, media, or migration. Miserable as these conditions were, however, they did not clearly distinguish this region from other developing areas. There were two phenomena, however, that set Southeast Asia apart. First, as home of the fabled Spice Islands and for centuries a key waypoint on global East–West trade routes, Southeast Asia had had a precolonial economy that was far more heavily trade-dependent than can be said for most other countries. Second, according to experts of the day the region's development prospects, along with those of the rest of Asia other than Japan, were globally dim.

One contemporary assessment ranked "Southeast Asia" (meaning the regions we now call South, East, and Southeast Asia) below the Middle East, Sub-Saharan Africa, and Latin America on measures of per capita income, population pressure, and economic culture, concluding that "while some of the intermediate rankings are uncertain … in general the degree of poverty and general backwardness is greatest in Southeast Asia and smallest in Latin America" (Enke 1963: 61).[5]

Within the region, Malaysia (including Singapore before 1965) was undeniably better off than most. However, even these countries' growth prospects were not uniformly seen as promising, and those of some other regional states such as the Philippines and Burma (now Myanmar) were judged – inaccurately, as it turns out – to be much brighter. One key growth ingredient found to be missing in much of the region was an entrepreneurial spirit. Enke (1963: 61) dismissed Asia as having "an uneconomic culture." Finally, the entire region was highly susceptible to economic collapse, whether precipitated by crop failure, government failure, internal conflict, or Cold

War-related external aggression. Myrdal, in *Asian Drama*, saw Southeast Asia in the late 1960s as a region in which turmoil was pervasive – except in the mainland kingdoms of Thailand and Cambodia, where, as he saw it, "complacent authoritarian regimes administer[ed] a lethargic peasantry."

On international economic integration in about 1970, the region also scored poorly (Booth 2004; Thee 2012). Foreign investment other than in extractive industries was virtually nonexistent. As late as 1980, the exports of every country for which adequate data exist were dominated by natural resources and agricultural products. For Indonesia, these contributed 97 percent of 1980 merchandise exports; for Malaysia 80 percent, Thailand 72 percent, and the Philippines 63 percent.[6]

This pattern of trade reflects comparative advantage of course: the region had for centuries served as a source for exports of natural resource wealth to the larger, more technologically advanced economies of India, China, and Japan. But this trade pattern is also a consequence of development policies. In the early postcolonial era most nations of the region pursued development strategies that embodied a substantial anti-trade bias, with tariffs and other barriers that greatly restricted trade in manufactures. As Athukorala (2006) has shown for Vietnam (one of the later-transitioning economies), anti-export bias in trade and domestic policy is a significantly negative predictor of prospects for growth. In Southeast Asia, differential rates of progress in the transition back to global market integration – what Booth (2004) has called "re-linking" – serve to demarcate divergent growth and development experiences.

Among international experts, prognoses of growth were almost uniformly negative in the 1960s, and even much later. Myrdal, in *Asian Drama*, saw the countries of the region (with the possible exceptions of Malaysia and Singapore) as backward, agrarian, and institutionally unprepared for modern economic development, confronting potentially devastating problems of population growth, poverty, and food supply. His concerns about Malthusian limits to growth were echoed by numerous influential commentators of the era. These included such influential contributions as Paul Erlich's *The Population Bomb* (1968) and William and Paul Paddock's *Famine 1975!* (1967), which, among other things, dismissed Indonesia as a state that "could not be saved." Yet grow the region did, and through a combination of agricultural modernization, industrial transformation, and the relatively sensible application of windfall earnings from oil and other natural resources managed both to increase food supply growth and to maintain the productivity of labor so as to ensure stable or even rising material living standards for their populations.

Breaking out of the Malthusian trap was in large part a consequence of the massive technological breakthrough in the production of rice, the regional staple, known as the Green Revolution (ADB 1969; Timmer 1988). New plant types, together with complementary inputs such as fertilizer, irrigation, and improved pest management methods made it possible for per capita food supply to grow much faster than land area. Rising yields also increased labor productivity, thereby freeing up a larger part of the workforce for non-farm employment at a historical moment when global demand for labor-intensive manufacturing was poised to boom. And higher and more stable incomes, among other factors, helped spark a rapid decline in fertility, lowering population dependency ratios.

Of course, this historical process exhibited plenty of variation. The Philippines enjoyed far less success in agricultural development and also a much slower decline in fertility. The Mekong countries (Cambodia, Laos, and Vietnam) started down the path of sustained growth a generation later than their regional counterparts, and Myanmar, after half a century of self-imposed isolation and poverty, has only just begun to build the institutional and policy foundations for a modern economy. Overall, however, the region has pulled off a spectacular escape from the Malthusian trap. Twenty-first century students of this part of the world are hard-pressed to reconcile the doomsday predictions of the 1960s with the thriving populations they can see today.

Another more subtle but hardly less negative prediction emerged, ironically, at the peak of the region's growth boom of the late 1980s and early 1990s. With GDP growth rates hitting double-digit levels, Southeast Asia's four largest economies (Indonesia, Thailand, Malaysia, and Singapore) were labeled (along with Taiwan, Korea, Japan, and Hong Kong) as "high-performing Asian economies" in the landmark World Bank study, *East Asian Miracle* (World Bank 1993). Countries like Thailand and Singapore enjoyed a brief existence as global poster children for economic growth.

In the same years, however, many economists observed that this "miracle" growth was almost entirely due to rather more prosaic processes: the accumulation of new capital and the workforce "gift" of the demographic transition. Krugman (1994) observed that Asian growth of the foregoing two decades could be accounted for almost entirely in terms of increased rates of capital investment, labor force participation, and educational achievement, with little or no additional gain due to productivity growth.[7] As he succinctly put it, the "miracle" depended on "perspiration, not inspiration."[8] As such, he argued, regional growth "has been based largely on one-time changes in behavior that cannot be repeated" (p. 71), and diminishing returns to further factor accumulation would ensure that the miracle could not be sustained. As a result, Krugman concluded, "popular enthusiasm about Asia's boom deserves to have some cold water thrown on it … the future prospects for that growth are more limited than almost anyone now imagines."

At the time, this seemed not inaccurate as a look in the rearview mirror of regional development. However, Krugman's prediction of slowing growth rates has not stood the test of time – in spite of mixed results on total factor productivity growth. Rather, the East and Southeast Asian experiences helped to redirect thinking among economists towards new paradigms in which the modalities of international integration – including lower tariffs and transport costs, international factor flows, and, above all, rapid movement up the industrial product ladder – help to forestall the onset of diminishing returns to capital investment (Ventura 1997; Schott 2003). Participation in an expanding and dynamically changing regional economy has sustained growth in these very trade-dependent economies, even in the absence of demonstrable contributions from productivity growth, whether extrinsic or intrinsic (that is, arising endogenously from increasing returns or industry-scale productivity spillovers).

A third pessimistic prediction was based on extrapolation from the 1980s transitions of post-Soviet Eastern European economies. Adjustment from command to market economy involves a so-called J-curve transition in which output, jobs, and productivity must all fall (sometimes by a great deal) before the effects of economic restructuring take hold and they begin to rise again. This phenomenon, so clearly observed in the 1990s in Eastern Europe and the states of the former USSR, did not transpire during analogous Asian transitions – those of China and Vietnam in particular. Why this is so remains a subject for more detailed research, but clearly the Asian economies' rapid and decisive reintegration with thriving regional and global markets was a major contributing factor. In the Chinese and Vietnamese command-to-market transitions, elastic world supplies of intermediate goods, rapidly growing world demands for final goods, and abundant inflows of global investment all helped to cushion economic losses due to obsolescence and facilitated expansion of new, internationally competitive industries.

Fourth, we also know that Southeast Asian resource exporters achieved far greater success in economic growth than is predicted by theories of the so-called curse of natural resource wealth. The curse is said to be of slow economic growth due to a failure to sustain efficient factor use, especially in industrial sectors where the potential for productivity gain is highest. According to Sachs and Warner (2001: 828), "there is virtually no overlap between the set of countries with large natural resource endowments – and the set of countries that have high levels of GDP … resource intensity tends to correlate with slow economic growth." Since resource abundance has economic meaning only in relation to a country's trading partners (and, indeed, is frequently measured as the ratio of resource-based exports to GDP or total trade), the implication is that for a developing economy, possessing and exploiting comparative advantage in natural resource products can be harmful to growth.

Among resource-rich countries, those in Southeast Asia exhibit the least close fit with the resource curse model. Indonesia, Thailand, and Malaysia are almost unique in the developing world for having both high levels of initial resource dependence and also high rates of long-run economic growth (Figure 1.5). There are many possible explanations, of which the most persuasive is a high rate of success in converting the earnings from natural resource exports into other forms of capital, such as infrastructure, education, and the less tangible asset of macroeconomic stability, that create fertile conditions for a transition to industry and thus reduced dependence on resources as an income source (Coxhead 2007). This is not to say that the region's economies, and especially Indonesia's, have not experienced Dutch Disease, the attenuation of growth in non-resource tradable sectors that often follows a commodity export boom (Warr 1986) – nor that they will not experience it again in the future. They have simply been more adept at recognizing the symptoms and addressing them in a timely way through policy. And they have avoided (for the most part) a major corollary of the resource curse: military conflict over oil, diamonds, and other mineral deposits and the revenue flows they engender. In Sub-Saharan Africa, by contrast, 28 of 50 countries have been involved in war or civil war (or in some cases, both) since 1980, generating over 9 million refugees or internally displaced persons and accounting for 88 percent of conflict fatalities worldwide since 1990.[9] The costs of war, in terms of foregone growth, are massive.

A fifth pessimistic prediction about Southeast Asian growth, and one that remains moot, comes from contemporary analysts such as the Malaysian economist Jomo K.S. (2003). This

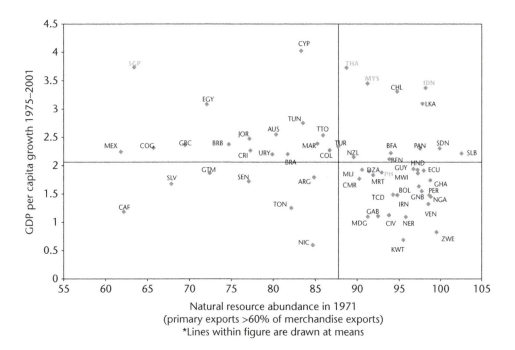

Figure 1.5 Long-run growth among resource-abundant economies
Source: Coxhead 2007.

view regards regional growth booms as driven largely by external factors, especially trade and foreign direct investment (FDI), and as lacking the internal dynamics and governance capacity required to sustain them in the longer run. Jomo's discussion of regional development through the early 2000s concluded that

> the Southeast Asian component of the East Asian Miracle … was inferior to the rest of the region's economic achievements in terms of growth, inequality, industrialisation, policy formulation and implementation, human resource development, as well as development of industrial and technological capabilities. … Unless adequately addressed, these failings will limit the likelihood of rapid future growth and structural transformation associated with the East Asian Miracle.
>
> (Jomo 2003: 17)

The core of this argument is pessimism about institutional capacity for good economic governance, a broad term used to capture the essential qualities of economic and political institutions required to support long-run growth.[10] This idea reflects an important branch of thinking among development economists in which institutions, rather than geography, culture, or "luck," are primarily responsible for differences in comparative growth (Acemoglu et al. 2005). Though measures of institutional quality by their nature are very imprecise, no Southeast Asian country other than Singapore displays any special institutional strengths in international comparisons. Corruption, for example, is thought to have a strongly negative effect on potential for economic growth, yet all Southeast Asian countries except Singapore rank low in international comparisons of corruption perceptions (Table 1.1). As Table 1.1 also shows, other than Singapore the region generally receives poor scores and rankings on institutions for economic governance. Yet, as we have seen, Southeast Asia has succeeded in achieving and maintaining a truly impressive rate of economic growth. If corruption is so high and measures of the quality of economic institutions so low, how is it that large, low-income countries like Indonesia and Vietnam have outperformed the rest of the developing world on growth?

Table 1.1 Corruption perceptions and economic freedoms in Southeast Asian countries

Country	Corruption[a] (0–100 scale)		Indices of economic freedoms[b] (1–10 scale)					
	Score 0–100	Rank (N = 177)	Legal system & property rights	Rank (N = 144)	Freedom to trade internationally	Rank (N = 144)	Government regulation	Rank (N = 144)
Cambodia	20	160	4.6	95	7.3	65	6.5	101
Indonesia	32	114	4.5	105	6.8	93	6.3	112
Lao PDR	26	140						
Malaysia	50	53	6.9	34	7.3	66	8.0	20
Myanmar	21	157	3.2	134	1.8	144	4.4	143
Philippines	36	94	4.4	110	6.7	96	6.9	74
Singapore	86	5	8.4	6	9.4	1	8.9	4
Thailand	35	102	5.4	79	6.8	88	7.0	65
E. Timor	30	119						
Vietnam	31	116	5.9	59	6.3	109	6.5	105

Sources: [a]Transparency International 2013. [b]Gwartney et al. 2012 .

The institutions argument certainly raises puzzles about the rate and persistence of past growth in the region. Perhaps the commonly used measures of institutional strength do not capture essential qualities relevant to growth and stability. Or perhaps there are interactions among institutions, culture and geography in which weaknesses in the former are compensated by advantages in the latter. These interactions would not necessarily appear in the kinds of global-scale cross-country analyses favored by those seeking generalized or global explanations for economic growth and development.

Finally, we know that economic and political institutions evolve over time and under changing conditions, so what predictions for the future, if any, can be made with confidence? One possibility is that rapid growth creates its own compensating circumstances, for example by reducing pressure on the distribution of resources, which in turn affects de jure and de facto political power, the drivers of change in economic and political institutions (Acemoglu et al. 2005). If so then the region is poised to enter a crucial period in the early twenty-first century, in which lower GDP growth rates generate greater tension between competing policy and political economy goals. We outline some of these possibilities in the next section.

In its transition from poverty to middle income over a half-century, Southeast Asia has managed to avoid many of the economic growth traps that have impeded progress in other parts of the developing world. There is, however, tremendous variation around this overall trend, and, moreover, successes in the past do not guarantee continued progress through middle income in the future. These two concerns are central to much of the content of this handbook.

Southeast Asian economies today

Contemporary Southeast Asian economics is an encouraging mix of growth, economic stability, and improving standards of living. The Philippines, for many years the laggard among the large regional economies, has registered solid growth since the mid-2000s. Even Myanmar, one of the world's poorest economies after 50 years of self-imposed isolation, has begun making rapid strides toward reintegration and growth. The region's long transition continues.

In the evolution of today's Southeast Asian economies, the regional economic crisis of 1997–99 was a turning point. The "miracle" years had seen all the region's large economies except the Philippines growing at well above their trend rates (Figure 1.6a). Increasing confidence in the continuity of growth had encouraged governments to relax rules on capital inflows. As a result, ever-larger injections of short-term capital into domestic financial systems helped fuel speculative booms in stock markets, property, and construction. These inflows of portfolio capital and foreign loans were largely unhedged because they were "insured" by buoyant growth and by public commitments to fixed (or at least predictable) exchange rates. The latter were promises that were relatively easy to keep during a period of rapid growth with stable domestic prices. By the mid-1990s, however, export-oriented manufacturing booms began to drive up labor costs and create costly infrastructural bottlenecks, causing expectations of profit margins to decline. This trend, plus current account deficits due to the capital inflows, undermined confidence in exchange rate stability, and, starting in early 1997, liquid capital began to exit the region. With foreign reserves nearing exhaustion, exchange rate anchors began to drag, and the collapse of regional asset price bubbles was accompanied by a brief but intense liquidity crisis in which many thousands of jobs and livelihoods were lost. As Figure 1.6a reveals, the crisis was a sudden stop for all economies, although in the Philippine case low rates of prior capital inflow and growth meant a correspondingly shallow recession.[11]

The recession was unprecedented in nature and depth for much of the region (Indonesia and Thailand had not experienced even one year of recession in three prior decades). It exposed

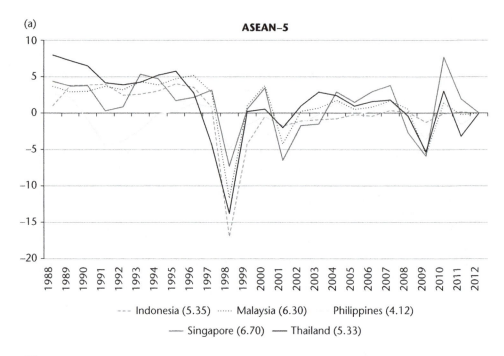

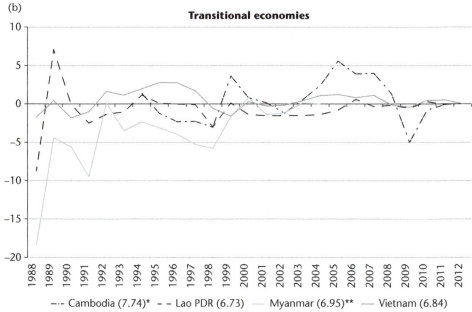

Figure 1.6   GDP growth rate deviations from long-run average (% per year), 1988–2012
Source: World Bank: World Development Indicators Online.
Notes: Average growth rates shown next to country names.
*Cambodia data 1994–2012; **Myanmar data 1988–2004.

internal vulnerabilities that had been disguised by years of rapid growth. These included policy failures as well as inherent weaknesses in economic institutions, especially where the will and capacity to respond to a sudden external shock were concerned.[12] The crisis also precipitated political upheavals, most catastrophically in Indonesia, where *krismon* ("monetary crisis") quickly spilled over to *kristal* ("total crisis"), a period of chaos and violence culminating in the collapse of the 32-year New Order regime and the beginnings of a transition to democratic governance.

The crisis also led governments of the region to rethink economic policies, especially although not exclusively in the areas of exchange rate and monetary policy and governance of financial systems (Corden 2007). It stimulated moves toward greater regional economic and financial integration, and to the extent that it was fueled by loss of competitiveness in labor-intensive manufacturing, the crisis also brought into sharp relief the challenge posed by a rising Chinese economy (Eichengreen and Tong 2006; Coxhead 2007).

The later-developing Mekong economies were never as open to international capital flows as their larger and more advanced neighbors. This afforded them a degree of insulation from the capital market shocks that precipitated regional recessions (Figure 1.6b). Their GDP growth rates fell briefly below trend, but as quickly recovered again. Overall, these economies have experienced far smaller variation in GDP growth (and higher overall growth rates) since beginning their economic reforms.

The decade following the crisis, from about 2000 until the onset in 2009 of the global Great Recession, saw a gradual but steady recovery throughout the region. However, the largest ASEAN economies have never returned to the heady GDP growth rates of the Asian Miracle years (Figure 1.6a). Lower growth rates have had fiscal and political implications. With leaner economic times, budgetary "fat" such as subsidies on fuel prices have become unsustainable, and attempts to lower subsidy rates have been the cause of political unrest. And in Thailand, the combination of constitutional changes leading to populist politics based on generous subsidies to rural constituencies, together with reduced tax revenues from lower rates of economic growth, has exposed deep societal divisions over the distribution of income and opportunity. This has brought with it increasing levels of extraparliamentary protest, conflict, violence, and political instability.

More positively, ASEAN economies now see more clearly the benefits of internal and external coordination in trade, capital markets, and external economic relations. ASEAN, the primary vehicle for regional cooperation, has taken on a far more prominent and proactive role in Southeast Asian economic life.

In the second decade of the twenty-first century, nearly nine out of ten Southeast Asians live in countries classed as "middle income." Compared with their grandparents they are immeasurably healthier, wealthier, better educated, and more secure. Despite this great progress, however, many still live just one missed paycheck or one major medical bill above the poverty line – and in societies whose social safety nets cannot guarantee to catch them if they fall. Looking to the future, most can see continuing improvements in their levels of living. But how fast this improvement will be, and over what period of time it will extend, is much less certain.

Overview of this volume

Why have a book on Southeast Asian economics? The very term "Southeast Asia" is a recent creation, a convenient catchall for an Allied theater of war in World War II (Karnow 1962: 11). However, the last four decades have seen a strongly increasing trend in regional economic integration and policy coordination, and provide increasing evidence of positive spillovers in growth, public administration, political systems, and more.

Is there a specifically *Southeast Asian* economics? Strictly speaking, the answer must be "no." However, there is a case that the regional experience embodies an important and interesting specific *configuration* of factors: resources, geography, and history, trade and international investment, and the proximity of large, dynamic neighbors. This configuration naturally brings certain themes to the fore, and in this respect Southeast Asia does seem sharply different, if not unique, among developing regions. Most prominent among these themes are those relating to the region's unusually long and deep levels of global and market integration and unusually high proximity to large, dynamically growing economies. Global market integration, beginning long before the great European voyages of discovery, exposed Southeast Asia from very early on to interactions with economies that differed dramatically from it in terms of endowments, technology, and tastes. This meant that prices for commodities and services produced and consumed in the region have changed greatly with changes in its exposure to trade with other world regions.[13] Proximity to the world's largest (at times) and (at times) most dynamic economies further reinforced the importance of trade, which fluctuates with greater volatility than underlying economic conditions. Hence, at some points in history the region's giant neighbors have catapulted the Southeast Asian economies onto "miracle" growth paths, and at others plunged them deep into recession.

These themes pervade the story of Southeast Asian economic development. Williamson (Chapter 2) surveys half a millennium of regional interaction with the world, primarily through trade, and explores the ways in which precolonial and colonial-era trade affected incomes and development. Booth (Chapter 3) picks up the thread in the colonial era, which affected every country except Thailand, and follows it through postwar decolonization and the establishment of modern nation-states. Her chapter stresses both the late colonial-era mechanisms of economic growth, and the difficult transition to postcolonial policies when trade and foreign investment, the long-run keys to regional growth, came to be regarded by newly minted regimes with deep suspicion, ushering in a brief era of "delinking" from the world economy.

In Chapter 4, Phung, Coxhead, and Lian present a quantitative exploration of the sources of modern Southeast Asia's contemporary economic growth. As is standard in this type of research, their analysis identifies contributions from growth of endowments of capital, labor, and skills. However, they also identify important spillovers from growth booms in the region's large and dynamic neighbors in Northeast Asia. These Northeast Asian booms conferred positive growth externalities on the region, in addition to serving as powerful stimuli to investment and growth-enhancing structural changes in employment and output. Proximity to Northeast Asia, in both a geographic and an economic sense, was an advantage not shared by other regions of the developing world.

The next nine chapters in this volume address factor endowments and economic organization and their contributions to economic growth. Appropriately for a region that was almost entirely agrarian just two generations ago, we begin with a survey of agricultural development (Timmer, Chapter 5). Also appropriately, for a region whose largest country was dismissed two generations ago as structurally unable to feed its own population, this survey views agricultural development primarily through the lens of food security. Timmer documents the region's convincing escape from imminent Malthusian disaster, mainly though not wholly by means of the Green Revolution technologies that so greatly increased the productivity of rice cultivation. Looking at the present and the future, Timmer notes large ongoing changes in demand (through income-driven dietary transformations) and markets, especially the rise of corporate distribution channels such as supermarkets. While food supply is no longer the pressing issue that it once was, the future holds significant challenges from climate change and from competition for land from industrial crops, such as oil palm.

Shively and Smith (Chapter 6) address the natural resource and environmental basis for growth. In spite of rapid industrialization, Southeast Asia's poor remain heavily reliant on land and other natural resources. It is logical for poor countries to exploit their comparative advantage in natural resources in order to get started on growth, but the momentum of resource depletion and damages to environmental quality may be virtually unstoppable, especially when foreign demand is strong and domestic regulatory institutions are weak. Their chapter concludes by emphasizing the synergistic interaction of economic growth with institutional innovations to regulate resource depletion and environmental damages. Success in economic growth relieves some of the pressures to exploit the resource base, and this in turn can support the move to a more sustainable growth trajectory.

Rapid and pervasive industrial growth is one of the most visible and unusual features of Southeast Asian development. The origins of industrialization in the region are well known, but in Chapter 7, Athukorala and Kohpaiboon pick up a more contemporary account of the transition from "traditional" manufactures of final goods to participation in regional and global networks of vertically fragmented producers. Trade in parts and components, mainly of electronic, electrical and machinery products, is the fastest-growing category of trade in East Asia, and brings with it new forms of industrial organization and sources of dynamic economic growth. However, not all countries in the region are equally well prepared to take advantage of the new patterns of production and trade, and this raises interesting questions about future divergence along the industrial growth path. A similar story emerges on the counterpart flow, of investment capital (primarily, though not entirely, into the region). Sjöholm (Chapter 8) appraises the sources and impacts of FDI flows. Among his findings is an important political economy observation, that of synergies between policies and institutions relevant to FDI and economic growth. Once again, country-level differences in attitudes toward FDI – some of them the enduring legacies of the fight against colonialism – introduce much heterogeneity within the region.

Wignaraja (Chapter 9) takes the account of industrialization down to firm level, with an empirical study of firms' use of regional trade agreements (RTAs) in their business dealings. RTAs have been among the key vehicles for reducing trade barriers both within Southeast Asia and to the region's major trade partners. The study of firms in three large countries – Indonesia, the Philippines, and Malaysia – asks quantitatively how valuable these RTAs are as stimuli to commercial activity. He finds surprisingly low take-up rates of RTA concessions, with a variety of reasons emerging across the surveyed firms and countries.

Attention in the book then turns to the region's most important asset, its labor. Jones (Chapter 10) provides a masterful and very thorough survey of population and demographic trends. His study highlights the momentum imparted by years of rapid population growth, even as fertility rates in the region have declined, in almost every case, to less than replacement rate. Horioka and Terada-Hagiwara (Chapter 11) explore how demographic trends (mainly) have determined variation in domestic savings rates. As populations age (led by Singapore and Thailand, the countries with the lowest birth rates), savings rates can also be expected to decline, and this will in turn have macroeconomic implications as current account surpluses diminish and dependence on imported capital (FDI) increases.

In Chapter 12, Phan and Coxhead document progress in increasing educational attainment. It is widely believed that Southeast Asian economies owe much of their success to human capital investments. This chapter finds, however, that the region is not exceptional in that regard – and, indeed, by comparison with Northeast Asian economies such as Taiwan and Korea at comparable stages of their own development, most of Southeast Asia lags behind. Education and human capital are perhaps the strongest predictors of escape from the middle-income trap, so these findings are not encouraging for the region as a whole. Finally, Sugiyarto (Chapter 13) turns attention to the all-important topic of labor mobility. Capital investments that sustain industrial and urban growth are of course highly location-specific; therefore, if a country is to take advantage of the opportunities created by capital, its labor force must move. Urbanization is the most common expression of labor mobility, but the region has also become a significant exporter of labor to other world regions, and the remittance flows from both types of labor movement have helped distribute the gains from spatially unequal growth more broadly throughout national populations.

Sustained poverty alleviation is arguably the most significant indicator of progress in economic development, and in this respect Southeast Asia's achievements have been dramatic. In Chapter 14, Warr documents poverty trends in the region. He notes in particular the strong relation between overall growth and poverty reduction. More surprisingly, he finds that in this region the principal sectoral driver of poverty reduction has been agricultural growth, not industrial development. This, he concludes, is due to the extreme labor-intensity of agriculture relative to industry, even in the latter's more labor-intensive forms. These findings are a reminder that despite much progress in economic growth, labor, mostly in its raw (unskilled) form, remains the primary income source for virtually all of Southeast Asia's poor.

The quality and timeliness of policy innovations and reforms as drivers of economic growth are often underappreciated in the developing world. Hill (Chapter 15) effectively dispels that notion for this region. With the support of several well-chosen case studies, he documents the interactions of policies (both good and bad), the institutions that underpin them, and the outcomes they engender. His chapter concludes with a number of general conclusions on the political economy of economic development in this part of the world.

The final four chapters of this volume address issues of increasing importance in the region for the foreseeable future. Nobles (Chapter 16) picks up the demographic thread once more. She notices that alongside the demographic transition through which most of the region is rapidly passing, there is an accompanying transition in disease and health demands. She notes in particular the dyssynchrony of development at a subnational level: within countries, some regions are aging fast while others continue to experience high fertility and population growth, creating a dual burden of demands for both old and young populations. At the same time, the very rapid growth of regional incomes means that countries that still suffer from "third world" diseases like tuberculosis and under-nutrition are simultaneously experiencing rapidly rising rates of "first world" ailments like diabetes and cancer. This places even more stresses on the design, funding, and delivery of health services, creating a second, fiscal type of health-related "dual burden."

Returning to the regional economy, Hill and Menon (Chapter 17) explore the recent and emerging pressures for greater regional integration. In a world of network trade and covariate macroeconomic shocks there is a large premium on lowering barriers to cross-border trade, investment, and financial services. Yet these are among the most difficult deals to make. Hill and Menon zero in on the role of ASEAN, an entity that has matured from a primarily political mandate toward a much broader and far-reaching set of goals for economic integration, including the formation of a regional financial safety-net.

In Chapter 18, Nidhiprabha documents the impacts and policy responses to the Great Recession, also known as the global financial crisis (GFC). Coming just a decade after the onset of the Asian crisis (1997–99), the GFC tested the robustness of macroeconomic policies adopted in response to the earlier crisis. In general, the GFC had a much smaller impact on Southeast Asian economies, although whether this was due to their policy innovations, or the stabilizing influence of continued expansion in the Chinese economy, or because the GFC (unlike the Asian Crisis) was an external shock, is as yet unclear. What is sure is that the nature of the region's macroeconomic environment is constantly changing, most recently with the rise of China not only in trade, but also as an influence over financial markets and exchange rates.

Finally, in Chapter 19, Coxhead, Thee, and Yusuf draw together some thematic threads of the volume and discuss some key areas in which Southeast Asia will continue to face growing economic and policy challenges in the future. These include continued labor force and human capital development, finding new and efficient ways to cope with global economic volatility, managing the tensions between economic growth and inequality, and formulating responses to global climate change and especially its regional expressions in rising sea levels and greater intensity of severe weather. Although the region has achieved great progress in economic growth and development, the path ahead to sustained, and sustainable, improvements in human welfare is by no means clear. There is much that remains to be learned.

Notes

1 Myrdal memorably described governments of the region as "soft" states, meaning that they were characterized by "indiscipline" in legislation, public administration, law enforcement, and the tolerance of corruption. These arise from and reinforce colonial-era weakening of social and political institutions, and give rise to social and economic inequalities which "constitute severe obstacles to development" (Myrdal 1968b: 1129).

2 In the early 1960s the historian George Kahin is said to have likened the region to a Manhattan apartment building: "the tenants occupy adjoining apartments but rarely speak to one another, and their friends are elsewhere."

3 "Centered in their capitals and remote from the mass of their population, many governments of Southeast Asia are like heads without bodies. In ancient times, these lands had two associated classes, aristocrats and peasants. Today the division is between urban and rural folk, and there is scant connection between the two" (Karnow 1962: 77). Myrdal (1968a) documents a similar set of impressions in his descriptions of 1960s Thailand, Laos, and Cambodia.

4 Geopolitical issues also persist, however, in ongoing conflicts over ownership and access to large swathes of the South China Sea.

5 I am indebted to Easterly (1995) for identifying this source.

6 Source: World Development Indicators Online.

7 The latter claim is largely borne out in empirical analyses of regional growth (Collins and Bosworth 1996; Radelet et al. 1997).

8 NB: This was also the logical outcome of "vent-for-surplus" growth described by the noted Burmese economist Hla Myint (1965).

9 http://www.globalissues.org/article/84/conflicts-in-africa-introduction (accessed 8 June 2014).

10 Institutional pessimism is an enduring theme. In 1978 the Asian Development Bank's review of prospects for regional success in agricultural development bemoaned the "growth-retarding effects of production technologies and the institutions serving agriculture when these are not properly aligned with each other" (pp. 319–20). This report called for strong and pervasive state actions, yet condemned states as elite-dominated, incompetent, and possibly corrupt, and capable only of "responses to short-term situations ... insufficient consideration was given to assessing the implications for long-run orientation of policy" (p. 9).

11 To paraphrase one Filipino commentator, "we only had a little boom, so we only had a little bust."

12 There have been many excellent economic accounts of the crisis and its immediate aftermath. See, for example, Corden 1999, McLeod and Garnaut 1998, and for Thailand, Warr 2005.

13 Compare Hansen (2012)'s revisionist history of the overland Silk Road, in which the author argues that paper, not silk, may have been the most important commodity traded – and emphasizes the concomitant spread of metals and metallurgy, technologies, and ideas. Southeast Asia sits astride the maritime silk route and experienced the same rich mix of commodity trade items (Reid 1993).

Bibliography

Acemoglu, D., S. Johnson, and J.A. Robinson, 2005. "Institutions as a fundamental cause of long-run growth," in P. Aghion and S. Durlauf (eds), *Handbook of Economic Growth*. Amsterdam: North-Holland, pp. 385–472.

Asian Development Bank (ADB), 1969. *Asian Agricultural Survey*. Manila: University of Tokyo Press and University of Washington Press for the ADB.

Asian Development Bank (ADB), 1978. *Rural Asia: Challenge and Opportunity*. New York: Praeger Publishers.

Athukorala, P., 2006. "Trade policy reforms and the structure of protection in Vietnam." *World Economy* 29(2): 161–87.

Bloom, D.E., and J.G. Williamson, 1998. "Demographic transitions and economic miracles in emerging Asia." *World Bank Economic Review* 12(3): 419–55.

Boeke, J.H., 1953. *Economics and Economic Policy of Dual Societies as Exemplified by Indonesia*. New York: Institute of Pacific Relations.

Booth, Anne, 2004. "Linking, de-linking and re-linking: Southeast Asia in the global economy in the twentieth century." *Australian Economic History Review* 44(1): 35–51.

Collins, S.M., and B.P. Bosworth, 1996. "Economic growth in East Asia: accumulation versus assimilation." *Brookings Papers* 27(2): 135–203.

Corden, W.M., 1999. *The Asian Crisis: Is There a Way Out?* Singapore: Institute of Southeast Asian Studies.

Corden, W.M., 2007. "The Asian crisis: a perspective after ten years." *Asian-Pacific Economic Literature* 21(2): 1–12.

Coxhead, Ian, 2007. "International trade and the natural resource 'curse' in Southeast Asia: does China's growth threaten regional development?" *World Development* 35(7): 1099–119.

Easterly, W., 1995. "Explaining miracles: growth regressions meet the Gang of Four," in A.O. Kreuger and T. Ito (eds), *Growth Theories in Light of the East Asian Experience*. Chicago, IL: University of Chicago Press.

Eichengreen, B., and Hui Tong, 2006. "Fear of China." *Journal of Asian Economics* 17: 226–40.

Enke, S., 1963. *Economics for Development*. London: Prentice-Hall.

Erlich, P., 1968. *The Population Bomb*. New York: Sierra Club/Ballantine.

Geertz, C., 1963. *Agricultural Involution: The Processes of Ecological Change in Indonesia*. Berkeley: University of California Press.

Grosskopf, S., and S. Self, 2006. "Factor accumulation or TFP? A reassessment of growth in Southeast Asia." *Pacific Economic Review* 11(1): 39–58.

Gwartney, J., R. Lawson, and J. Hall, 2012. *Economic Freedom of the World: 2012 Annual Report*. Vancouver: Fraser Institute.

Hansen, V., 2012. *The Silk Road: A New History*. Oxford: Oxford University Press.

Jomo, K.S., 2003. "Southeast Asia's ersatz miracle," in K.S. Jomo (ed.), *Southeast Asian Paper Tigers: From Miracle to Debacle and Beyond*. London: RoutledgeCurzon.

Karnow, S., 1962. *Southeast Asia*. Life World Library. New York: Time Inc.

Krugman, P., 1994. "The myth of Asia's miracle." *Foreign Affairs* Nov./Dec., pp. 62–78.

McLeod, R.H., and R. Garnaut (eds), 1998. *East Asia in Crisis: From Making a Miracle to Needing One?* New York: Routledge.

Myint, Hla, 1965. *The Economics of the Developing Countries*. New York: Praeger.

Myrdal, G., 1968a. *Asian Drama: An Inquiry into the Poverty of Nations*. New York, Pantheon.

Myrdal, G., 1968b. "The 'soft state' in underdeveloped countries." *UCLA Law Review* 15: 1118–34.

Paddock, W., and P. Paddock, 1967. *Famine 1975! America's Decision: Who Will Survive?* Boston, MA: Little, Brown.

Radelet, S., J. Sachs, and J-W. Lee, 1997. "Economic growth in Asia." Manuscript, Harvard Institute for International Development.

Reid, A., 1993. *Southeast Asia in the Age of Commerce, 1450–1680*. New Haven, CT: Yale University Press.

Sachs, J.D., and A.M. Warner, 2001. "The curse of natural resources." *European Economic Review* 45: 827–38.

Schott, P., 2003. "One size fits all? Heckscher–Ohlin specialization in global production." *American Economic Review* 93(3): 686–708.

Thee, K.W., 2012. *Indonesia's Economy since Independence*. Singapore: ISEAS.

Timmer, C.P., 1988. "The agricultural transformation," in H. Chenery and T.N. Srinivasan (eds), *Handbook of Development Economics*, Volume I. Amsterdam: North-Holland, pp. 276–331.

Transparency International, 2013. *Corruption Perceptions Index 2013*. www.transparency.org (accessed 1 June 2014).

Ventura, J., 1997. "Growth and interdependence." *Quarterly Journal of Economics* 112(1): 57–84.

Warr, P.G., 1986. "Indonesia's other Dutch disease: economic effects of the petroleum boom," in J.P. Neary and S. van Wijnbergen (eds), *Natural Resources and the Macroeconomy*. London: Basil Blackwell, pp. 288–320.

Warr, P.G., 2005. "Boom, bust and beyond," in P.G. Warr (ed.), *Thailand beyond the Crisis*. London: RoutledgeCurzon, pp. 3–65.

World Bank, 1993. *The East Asian Miracle*. Policy Research Report. Washington, DC: World Bank.

Yusuf, A.A., and B. Resosudarmo, 2007. "On the distributional effect of carbon tax in developing countries: the case of Indonesia." Padjadjaran University, Working Papers in Economics and Development Studies, no. 200705.

2

Trade, growth, and distribution in Southeast Asia, 1500–1940

Jeffrey G. Williamson

HARVARD UNIVERSITY AND UNIVERSITY OF WISCONSIN

Why has world trade grown and has Southeast Asia always been part of it? This fundamental question has been posed by economists like Nobel laureate Paul Krugman, who said "Most journalistic discussion of the growth of world trade seems to view growing integration as driven by a techno-logical imperative – to believe that improvements in transportation and communication technology constitute an irresistible force dissolving national boundaries" (1995: 328). An alternative explanation might stress instead declining political barriers to trade, which help link distant markets and erase commodity price gaps between them. A third potential explanation seems to have been even more powerful in practice – unusually fast world income growth during those epochs of trade booms.

This historical debate should have powerful resonance for modern Southeast Asia. What this chapter will explore are the sources of the region's trade growth and its impact in three quite distinct periods: the anti-global mercantilist epoch, 1500–1800; the pro-global liberal epoch, 1815–1913 (sometimes called the *first global century*); and the anti-global collapse, 1914–40. Having done so, it asks how history speaks to modern pro-global Southeast Asia since World War II.

Southeast Asia's first trade boom, 1500–1800

For some time, scholars have written of a secular Euro-Asian and Euro-American trade boom following the Voyages of Discovery led by Christopher Columbus heading west and Vasco da Gama heading east. With the early importance of the spice trade, particularly in the Moluccas, and later the galleon trade, Southeast Asia was very much part of this world trade boom. The most obvious explanation for the post-1500 trade boom would seem to be declining trade costs between Europe – where GDP and the demand for tradables was growing fastest – and the overseas continents with whom it traded. However, the evidence is inconsistent with this view. This section offers the economics and the evidence which allows us to decompose the sources of the inter-continental trade boom into the demand and supply fundamentals that mattered most. We then explain its impact on Southeast Asia.

The European inter-continental trade boom after 1500

Table 2.1 documents the Euro-Asian and Euro-American trade booms between 1500 and 1800, as well as the world trade boom which occurred thereafter.[1] The table reports two notable facts.

Table 2.1 Five centuries of European inter-continental and world trade growth, 1500–1992 (% per annum)

1500–1599	1.26	(volume only: 1.26)
1600–1699	0.66	(volume only: 0.11)
1700–1799	1.26	(volume only: 0.90)
1500–1799	1.06	(volume only: 0.76)
1820–1899	3.85	(1990 US$)
1900–1992	3.65	(1990 US$)
1820–1992	3.70	(1990 US$)

Source: O'Rourke and Williamson (2002: table 1, p. 421).

First, the growth of world trade was pretty much the same in the nineteenth and twentieth centuries, roughly 3.7 or 3.8 percent per annum. This is surprising, given that world GDP growth doubled from 1.5 to 3 percent per annum between 1820 and 1913, and 1913 and 1992 (Maddison 1995: 227). Since the growth of world trade was almost identical in the two centuries, it follows that world trade shares rose much faster in the nineteenth than in the twentieth century. So far, it looks as though the nineteenth century is the canonical globalization epoch, not the twentieth century. Second, European inter-continental trade growth prior to 1800 was much slower, about 1.1 percent per annum. Of course, everything grew much slower in this pre-industrial period, including GDP, so a 1.1 percent per annum growth rate was plenty fast enough to ensure that European trade shares increased in the wake of da Gama and Columbus.

The trade boom was not driven by declining trade barriers and market integration!

The most obvious explanation for the inter-continental trade boom is that it was caused by discovery, declining transport costs, and/or some fall in man-made barriers to trade. Call this the *market integration hypothesis*, and it implies that discovery and declining transport costs converted potential trading partners into actual trading partners by lowering the cost of doing business between them. If this market integration hypothesis is correct, then we should be able to document commodity price convergence between Europe and Asia (and the Americas) over the three centuries. After all, a decline in the costs of doing business between two markets has got to be reflected by a decline in price gaps between them. If we cannot document commodity price convergence, then the market integration hypothesis must be rejected and we will have to search for other explanations of the trade boom.

Where, then, should we look for evidence of inter-continental market integration? Initially, only goods with very high value to bulk ratios were shipped, like silk, ceramics, exotic spices, and precious metals. Indeed, European long distance trade in the pre-nineteenth century period was strictly limited to what international economists call non-competing goods: Europe imported spices, silk, sugar, and gold, items which were not produced there at all, or at least were in very scarce supply; Asia imported silver, linens, and woolens, which were not found there at all (with the important exception of Japanese silver before 1668). The imports of the Dutch East India Company (hereafter, VOC: Vereenigde Oostindische Compagnie, 1602–1796) were dominated by spices, tea, coffee, drugs, perfumes, dye-stuffs, sugar, and saltpeter. Indeed, these were 84 percent of the VOC import total in 1619/1621, 73 percent in 1698/1700, and still 64 percent as late as 1778/1780. Portuguese imports from Asia were almost all spices in 1518. Textiles came to take a larger share of that total, but spices were still 88 percent of Asian imports into Lisbon by 1610. Even the English (later British) East India Company (founded 1591), famous for its gamble

23

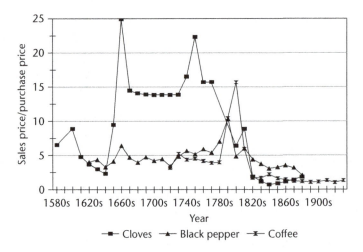

Figure 2.1 Spice and coffee markups: Amsterdam vs. Southeast Asia, 1580–1939

to focus on the Indian textile trade, had imports heavily weighted by spices and other luxuries: the figure is 43.4 percent in 1668/1670 and 46.5 percent in 1758/1760. These non-competing Asian commodities were very expensive luxuries in European markets, and thus could bear the very high cost of transportation from their (cheap) sources.[2]

So what is the evidence of price convergence for those commodities that were traded during the Age of Commerce between Europe and Asia? We have the price data for spices and coffee, items which combined were 68 percent of Dutch homeward cargoes in the mid-seventeenth century (Reid 1993: 288–9). Figure 2.1 plots markups for cloves, pepper, and coffee, where markups are defined as the ratio of European to Southeast Asian price (Bulbeck et al. 1998). There is plenty of evidence of price convergence for cloves from the 1590s to the 1640s, but it was short-lived, since the spread soared to a 350-year high in the 1660s, maintaining that high level during the VOC monopoly and up to the 1770s. The clove price spread did not fall until the end of the Napoleonic Wars (1803–15), and by the 1820s was one-fourteenth of the 1730s level. Between the 1620s and the 1730s, the pepper price spread showed no trend, after which it soared to a 250-year high in the 1790s. After that peak, a new era of price convergence took place. While there is some modest evidence of price convergence for coffee during the half-century between the 1730s and the 1780s, everything gained was lost and more so during the Napoleonic Wars. Thus, there is absolutely no evidence of long-term price convergence of Southeast Asian commodities in their port of export and their prices in Amsterdam markets. Was English trade with South Asia any different? Apparently not, at least based on the Anglo-Indian trade in pepper, tea, silk, coffee, and indigo (O'Rourke and Williamson 2002).

Why no price convergence and market integration? The answer is simply that the price spread on pepper, cloves, coffee, tea, and other non-competing goods was not driven by the costs of shipping, but rather by monopoly,[3] international conflict, predatory pirates, and mercantilist restrictions. *Ceteris paribus*, anything that lowers price gaps between markets encourages trade, but there is no evidence of a secular erosion in Euro-Asian commodity price gaps before the 1810s. The *ceteris paribus* qualification is, of course, important since something else must have accounted for the inter-continental trade boom if it was not declining trade barriers.

Is there any reason to expect the price spread on *competing* goods between Europe and Asia to have behaved differently, as opposed to the *non-competing* "exotics" we have just examined? It

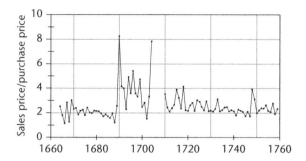

Figure 2.2   Asian textile trade markups, 1664–1759

seems very unlikely, especially if we cannot find it for the important East Indian cloth trade. Figure 2.2 plots the average prices received by the British East India Company on its Asian textile sales in Europe, divided by the average prices it paid for those textiles in Asia. Again, there is no sign of a secular decline in markups (where markups include all trade costs, as well as any East India Company monopoly profits) over the century between 1664 and 1759.[4] This textile trade was extremely large and it was on the rise. Yet, the evidence on freight rates and markups suggests that growing trade volumes in the late seventeenth century were almost certainly driven by the outward expansion of European import demand or Asian export supply rather than by declining inter-continental trade barriers and market integration per se: there is no evidence of commodity price convergence.

So, what did *drive the trade boom? Theory*

The boom in European imports from Asia must have had its source in some combination of three factors: a boom in European demand for tradables, a boom in tradable supply from Asia, and/or a decline in the barriers to trade between them. If a decline in trade barriers had accounted for the European overseas trade boom over the three centuries, then market integration would have been the driving force. We are not searching for perfect market integration and evidence supporting the Law of One Price, but we *are* searching for evidence of *greater* market integration and *smaller* price gaps through time. Since there is no evidence of secular decline in trade barriers, Euro-Asian trade must have boomed *in spite of* barriers to trade and anti-global mercantilist institutions. There would have been a bigger boom without these anti-global forces.

Figure 2.3 presents a stylized view of trade between Europe and the rest of the world (the latter denoted by an asterisk). MM is the European import demand function (that is, domestic demand minus domestic supply), with import demand declining as the home market price (p) increases. SS is the foreign export supply function (foreign supply minus domestic demand), with export supply rising as the price abroad (p^*) increases. It is worth emphasizing that SS is foreign supply less domestic demand; thus calling SS a "foreign export supply function" does *not* exclude the possibility that demand conditions in Asia could help account for the inter-continental trade boom, as we shall see below.

In the absence of transport costs, monopolies, and other trade barriers, international commodity markets would be perfectly integrated: prices would be the same at home and abroad, determined by the intersection of the two schedules. Trade costs drive a wedge (t) between export and import prices: higher tariffs, transport costs, war embargoes, and monopoly rents increase the wedge while lower trade costs reduce it. Global commodity market integration is

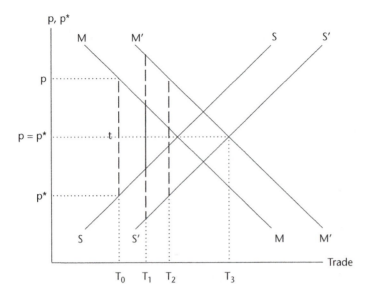

Figure 2.3   Explaining the world trade boom

represented in Figure 2.3 by a decline in the wedge: falling trade barriers and trade costs lead to falling import prices in both places, rising export prices in both places, an erosion of price gaps between them, and an increase in trade volumes connecting them.

The fact that trade should rise as trade barriers fall is, of course, the rationale behind using trade volumes or the share of trade in GDP as a proxy for trade "openness." However, Figure 2.3 makes it clear that global commodity market integration is not the only reason why trade volumes, or trade's share in GDP, might increase over time. Just because we see a trade boom does not necessarily mean that more liberal trade policies or transport revolutions are at work. After all, outward shifts in either import demand (to MM') or export supply (to SS') could also lead to trade expansion, and such shifts could occur as a result of population growth, the settlement of frontiers, capital accumulation, technological change, a shift in income distribution favoring those who import luxuries, and a variety of other factors. Thus, Figure 2.3 argues that the *only* irrefutable evidence that global commodity market integration is taking place is a decline in the international commodity price gaps, or commodity price convergence.[5] However, we cannot find it.

The post-1500 trade boom is represented as a rise from T0 to T1, T2 or T3. If t remained constant, then outward shifts in either MM or SS, but not both, would generate a trade boom to T1 (where the price gap, t, remains the same, although prices change in both markets). An outward shift in *both* MM and SS would generate a bigger trade boom to T2 (still holding t constant). If at the same time t evaporated (complete global commodity market integration), we would observe an even bigger trade boom to T3. Figure 2.3 has been translated into an explicit sources-of-trade equation, estimated, and then, given commodity prices in European markets, used to decompose the secular trade boom in European import demand and Asian export supply (O'Rourke and Williamson 2002).

Let's begin with the fact that the vast majority of the imports from Asia (except for cotton textiles) were out of reach of all but the rich: changing living standards of the workers in cities and villages would have had only a trivial impact on European import demand; changing incomes of those at or near the top of the income pyramid would have had a big impact. The rich consisted mainly of landowning elite, urban merchants dealing with this overseas trade, and those serving the rich and controlling the poor. Thus, the growth of the European "surplus" between 1500 and 1800 can be estimated by the behavior of European land rents over the three centuries. The results are these. European surplus income fell in the sixteenth century, so it could not have contributed anything to the trade boom; surplus income grew vigorously in the seventeenth and eighteenth centuries, when its contribution to the trade boom must have been much more important; and surplus income boomed in the nineteenth century, when it must have contributed very importantly to the trade boom.

What drove the trade boom? Fact

As we just saw, European income growth can explain none of the sixteenth century trade boom: it must therefore be explained either by rising overseas supply, falling overseas demand, or by some combination of the two. In contrast, the seventeenth century trade boom is explained entirely by European income growth, as evidenced by the rising relative prices of non-competing imports during the period. The eighteenth century trade boom is explained by a mix of demand and supply: between 59 and 75 percent of the trade boom can be explained by European income growth. Over the three centuries as a whole, European income growth explains between 50 and 65 percent of the inter-continental trade boom. The average of these two figures is 57 percent, exactly the same as that calculated for the Organization for Economic Cooperation and Development (OECD) trade boom from the late 1950s to the late 1980s (Baier and Bergstrand 2001), while the figure is similar for the world trade boom between 1870 and 1913 (Estevadeordal et al. 2003: table III).

A European population and trade boom connection?

What determined growth of this economic surplus, a surplus which in pre-industrial times consisted mostly of land rents? Since west European land acreage changed only very slowly, or not at all, the surplus must have grown at about the same rate as did rents per acre. In the sixteenth and seventeenth centuries, total factor productivity growth was very slow in European agriculture, so land rents must have been driven primarily by land/labor ratios – periods of rising population pressure on the land being periods of rapid increase in the ratio of land rents to the wages of landless laborers, as well as rising land rents themselves. Thus, European population pressure on the land and soaring land rents must have contributed mightily to the trade boom after 1600. Rising European inequality caused the boom in Euro-Asian trade in the three centuries after 1500. As we shall see below, the nineteenth century trade boom caused rising inequality in Southeast Asia. That inequality caused trade before 1800 offers a nice contrast with the more modern post-1800 globalization era when trade caused inequality.

Did Chinese autarkic policy crowd in Europe?

It appears that overseas export supply explained the sixteenth century trade boom while European import demand explained most of the seventeenth and eighteenth century booms. But did European demand drive *Southeast Asian* trade over those centuries? The answer is yes and no. First, although we do not know the magnitudes, intra-regional trade obviously must have been important in Southeast Asia. Yet, "transport impediments" and the fact "that local communities were self-sufficient" implies that intra-regional trade must have been modest (van der Eng 2004a: 1343). More to the point, there was not enough growth in regional GDP to have warranted an intra-regional-driven trade boom in Southeast Asia. Second, Southeast Asia certainly "benefitted from its location in between the main centres of economic activity in Asia" (van der Eng 2004a: 1343), but GDP was not growing fast in East Asia or South Asia either. What mattered most was the willingness (or unwillingness) of these powerful empires to trade with each other and with Southeast Asia. In fact, could China explain those special sixteenth century Asian export supply conditions?

Southeast Asian export supply to Europe equaled total Southeast Asian supply *minus* South and East Asian demand. There is a traditional view that suggests that East Asian demand declined sharply from the fifteenth century onward, as China went increasingly autarkic. This would have had a major impact on the demand for internationally traded commodities, since China represented as much as a quarter of global GDP at that time. If true, this move would have represented a profound switch from what appears to have been previously a fairly open trade policy. Between 1405 and 1430, seven great junk armadas sailed as far as Zanzibar, and Chinese trade with East Africa was sizable. Chinese envoys went to Mecca, and kings from Ceylon and Sumatra were brought back to China. Trade followed in their wake: "The emperor Yung-lo … had found the imported goods [of] horses, copper, timber, hides, drugs, spices, gold, silver, even rice … to be well worth acquiring. He had sent in return … silk, ceramics and tea. … In addition, private trade was growing" (Jones 1981: 204). But the last great Chinese fleet was sent abroad in 1433, and soon afterwards private maritime trade was declared illegal. While the resumption of the imperial voyages was proposed in 1480, the idea went nowhere and by 1553 the art of building large ships had, according to the traditional view, been forgotten (Jones 1981: 203–5). While smuggling and piracy filled a bit of the vacuum, the traditional view holds that the withdrawal continued and intensified: the Ming authorities (1368–1644) eventually banned all trade and the Manchu authorities (1644–1911) pushed the autarkic policy still further across the seventeenth century. Thus, the official imperial policy of shutting China's doors to external trade was already in place by the time of the European Voyages of Discovery. And, so the argument goes, China kept its doors tightly closed until it lost the Opium Wars to British gunboats, and the Treaty of Nanking (1842) opened China up to all comers.

More modern scholarship challenges the traditional view and suggests that imperial trade policy varied considerably between 1433 and 1842, that private interests found ways to overcome imperial anti-trade decrees, and that China's trade with the rest of the world flourished (Marks 1997; Pomeranz 2000: 114–65, 189–94). After all, what else can explain the growth of China's exports of porcelain, tea, and silk to foreign markets (including Europe)? Furthermore, didn't those exports make it possible for China to import all that silver that was being mined in the Americas?[6] Still, the new "partially open" view of China does not necessarily exclude the possibility that official policy had *some* effect. For example, Robert Marks wrote that "the explosive growth of Chinese coastal and foreign trade immediately follow[ed] the lifting in 1684 of the ban on coastal shipping" (Marks 1999: 104). If explosive growth followed in the wake of going partially open in 1684, policy must have had a powerful closing effect before. How much before? How closed? And if the Nanking Treaty of 1842 marked a "breakthrough for the history of the silk trade," after which there was "the evolution of a single global market" for silk, restrictive trade policy must again have had some trade-suppressing effect prior to 1842 (Ma 1999: 52). There is an abundant literature that deals with this issue, but nowhere is there satisfactory evidence offered to tell us how open or closed China was to foreign trade at various points in time. Such evidence should be price-based rather than quantity-based: while goods may have continually flowed across Chinese borders, despite official restrictions, the real test of policy effectiveness is whether the relative price of importables rose and the relative price of exportables fell.

We do not have the price evidence which could discriminate between the hypotheses that China was relatively closed or open between 1500 and 1842. But suppose it *was* closed: China's anti-trade policy move in the fifteenth century would have crowded in European trade with the rest of Asia. The phrase "rest of Asia" means South and Southeast Asia since Korea and Japan joined China's move towards greater autarky until American gunboats opened up Japan to trade in 1858 after more than two centuries of relative economic isolation under Tokugawa rule. We stress *relative* in all three East Asian cases since the issue is only whether restrictions on the external trade of China, Korea, and Japan *rose* between 1450 and 1852. The issue is not whether policy *eliminated* inter-continental or intra-continental trade involving East Asia. Rather, it is whether policy significantly *reduced* it.

A withdrawal of China from Asian markets would only have had an impact during the *transition* from an open to a closed trade policy which we take to be during the late fifteenth and sixteenth centuries. Once China had completely withdrawn, it would, of course, have had no further impact on world markets. But *while* it withdrew, the prices of exportables in Southeast Asia would have fallen as demand in a previously major market dried up. At the same time, the price of importables in Southeast Asia would have risen as supply from a previously major producer dried up. Did relative prices in Southeast Asia exhibit these trends from the late fifteenth century onwards? Better yet, did the price of exportables in *China* fall relative to the price of its importables? We do not yet know.

Why did Southeast Asia gain so little from the European trade boom?

Just because Europe had a trade boom, does not necessarily imply that Southeast Asia did, or that the boom was good for the region.

Anthony Reid divides Southeast Asian pre-modern and post-de Gama experience in to three epochs: economic growth across the sixteenth century up to the 1620s, economic decline across the seventeenth century and up to the 1740s, and economic growth from about 1750 onwards (Reid 2001: 46–58). Why the economic decline in the sixteenth and early seventeenth centuries? Why the strong recovery after about 1750? During the first century or so of European contact, centralized states flourished and urbanization rose everywhere in the region: Hanoi, Ayutthaya, and Mataram reached 150,000; the port cities of Banten, Aceh, and Makassar reached 100,000; and the whole region reached urbanization rates of 5 percent or more, levels equal to or greater than Europe at this time (Reid 1993: 73–5; de Vries 1976: 154). The region was sufficiently specialized in commodity exports so that most of these cities and their hinterlands were net importers of rice. After a secular prosperity peak in the early seventeenth century, the region underwent economic decline: the cities dwindled in size and numbers, trade indicators fell, and mortality rates rose (Reid 2001: 48–50). And it appeared everywhere in the region, not just in the Indonesian archipelago, but also in Luzon, the Visayas, and the Red River delta of Vietnam.

What accounts for the economic decline? Although absent evidence will make them hard to confirm, two plausible trade-related hypotheses suggest themselves. First, when China withdrew from trade with Southeast Asia, perhaps the Europeans took up some, but not all, of the slack. If so, there would have been no net gain for Southeast Asia, and perhaps even a loss. Thus, the issue of when and how much China withdrew becomes crucial. Second, the Europeans had brutally effective trading monopolies and monopsonies which one assumes lowered the price of exportables received by local Southeast Asian suppliers and raised them to local European buyers. Figure 2.1 cannot document the likely rise in markups across the sixteenth century – when European trade monopolies replaced competitive Chinese traders – but by the late sixteenth and early seventeenth centuries those markups on spices and coffee were huge. This evidence does not prove the point, but it is consistent with a large deterioration in Southeast Asia's terms of trade. Furthermore, the most rapacious monopoly was the Dutch VOC (founded in 1602), so the timing of some Southeast Asian terms of trade decline seems about right.

One supposes that these hypothesized offsets to the European trade boom were centered on the seventeenth and early eighteenth centuries. These offsetting forces could have been reinforced by other negative seventeenth century shocks, and apparently climate is likely to have been one (Boomgaard 1989). Everything appears to have turned around in the eighteenth century. First, climate conditions became more favorable with the end of the "little ice age." Second, there was the decline and fall of the Dutch VOC, and the appearance of more benign British and Chinese traders. Third, China re-emerges as a trade force: "China experienced a period of remarkable economic and demographic growth in the eighteenth century, stimulating both trade and emigration on a large scale to Southeast Asia" (Reid 2001: 50–1).

Southeast Asia's second trade boom, 1815–1913

Four things happened to the world economy from the early nineteenth century to World War I which had never happened before and which would not happen again until after World War II. First, the richest and fastest growing European economies went open, removing long-standing mer-cantilist policies, lowering tariffs, and removing non-tariff barriers. Their colonies in Africa and Asia did the same, and many of the others were forced to follow suit in response to gunboat diplomacy. In addition, much of the world integrated their currencies by going on the gold standard and other currency unions, lowering exchange risk. Thus, liberal commercial and exchange rate policy gave world trade one good reason to boom. Second, led by new steam engine technologies, the world underwent a pro-trade transport revolution. As transportation costs fell dramatically, the ancient barrier of distance was broken, and all forms of global commu-nication boomed, especially trade and migration. Southeast Asia was very much part of this revolution in transport (especially after the completion of the Suez Canal in 1869), and the ports of Rangoon, Belawan, Penang, Singapore, Bangkok, Cholon, Danang, Haiphong, Makassar, Banjarmasin, Tanjung Perak, and Manila boomed (van der Eng 2004a: 1344). The revolution was given added impetus by the appearance of the telegraph, another pro-trade technology that lowered uncertainty about prices in distant markets. Third, and carried by an industrial revolution in Europe and its offshoots, economic growth rose steeply to rates many times faster than what had been common over the previous two millennia. As a consequence, the demand for everything soared, especially imports of manufacturing intermediate inputs (cotton, wool, tin, rubber), fuel (coal, petroleum), and luxury foodstuffs (sugar, tea, coffee, meat). Fourth, *pax Britannica* reigned, and a trade-stimulating peace prevailed for a century.

Thus, trade had four reasons to boom during this first global century and Southeast Asia took good advantage of it. And while the region's trade growth may not always have been dominated by European demand before 1800, it certainly was afterwards.[7] Table 2.2 gives some sense of which parts of this diverse regional economy mattered most. The biggest by far was Indonesia, but its share of total Southeast Asian population slowly fell, from 47.6 percent in 1820 at the start of the first global century to 45.5 percent in 1950. Next in size was Vietnam, but whose population shares also fell, from 17.4 to 14 percent. Third in size (in 1820) was Siam, whose share also fell, from 12.4 to 11 percent. The next two, Cambodia and Laos combined fell from 6.8 to 5.5 percent. The remaining regions, while smaller in 1820 (except for Burma), all increased their relative size since they were the most active participants in the regions' great commodity export boom: Malaya, 0.8 to 3.5 percent; Burma, 9.3 to 10.7 percent; and, most spectacularly, the Philippines, 5.8 to 11.6 percent. Export values per capita (in current US dollars) from the 1870s

Table 2.2 Populations in Southeast Asia, 1820, 1913, and 1950

	1820	*1913*	*1950*
	000 (%)		
Malaya	287 (0.8)	3,084 (2.8)	6,434 (3.5)
Cambodia & Laos	2,560 (6.8)	4,467 (4.1)	6,357 (5.5)
Philippines	2,176 (5.8)	9,384 (8.6)	21,131 (11.6)
Siam	4,665 (12.4)	8,689 (8.0)	20,042 (11.0)
Burma	3,506 (9.3)	12,326 (11.3)	19,488 (10.7)
Vietnam	6,551 (17.4)	19,339 (17.8)	25,348 (14.0)
Indonesia	17,927 (47.6)	51,637 (47.4)	82,612 (45.5)
Total	37,672	108,916	181,412

Source: Angus Maddison horizontal-file_02–2010.

to the 1920s document the booms well enough (van der Eng 2004a: table 1): Burma 4 to 16 (an increase of 4 times); Thailand 1 to 8 (8 times); Indonesia 2 to 10 (5 times), Malaya 16 to 119 (7.5 times), Indochina 1 to 6 (6 times), and the Philippines 3 to 11 (3.7 times). According to this index, the most export-intensive were Burma, Indonesia, Malaya, and the Philippines.

The great commodity exporters' terms of trade boom

Since falling trade costs from all sources accounted for more than half of the trade boom between 1870 and 1914 (Jacks et al. 2008: 529), it must have accounted for even more before 1870 when the fall in transport costs was more dramatic and the move to free trade was in full swing. In any case, it is clear that falling trade costs played a major role in fueling the trade boom between core and periphery. By raising every country's export prices and lowering every country's import prices, it also contributed to a rise in every country's external terms of trade, especially, as it turned out, in Southeast Asia.

The accelerating growth in world GDP, led by industrializing Europe and its offshoots, was the second force driving the trade boom. The derived demand for industrial intermediates – like fuels, fibers, and metals – soared as manufacturing production led the way. Thus, as the European core and its offshoots raised their industrial output shares, manufacturing output growth raced ahead of GDP growth. This rapid manufacturing productivity growth lowered supply costs and output prices, demand for factory-made manufactures expanded, and by so doing generated a soaring derived demand for raw material inputs. This was reinforced by accelerating GDP per capita growth and a high income elasticity of demand for luxury consumption goods like meat, dairy products, fruit, sugar, tea, tobacco, and coffee. Since industrialization was driven by productivity advance favoring manufacturing, the relative price of manufactures fell everywhere.

All of these forces produced a powerful and sustained terms of trade boom in the commodity exporting periphery, an event that stretched over almost a century. Some parts of the periphery had much greater terms of trade booms than others, and some reached a secular peak later than others, but all (except China and Cuba) underwent a secular terms of trade boom. Factor supply conditions facilitated the periphery's response to these external demand shocks, carried by South–South migrations from labor-abundant to labor-scarce regions within the periphery – Chinese migrating to Luzon, Indochina, Siam, the Dutch East Indies, and the rest of Southeast Asia, Indians to Burma – and by financial capital flows from the industrial core – the French, Dutch, and British

31

colonists in the case of Southeast Asia. Like the others in the periphery, the Dutch East Indies, the Philippines, Indochina, and the rest of Southeast Asia increasingly specialized in a few primary products, reduced their production of manufactures and imported them in exchange. Many also reduced foodstuff production: the Dutch East Indies, Malaya, and the Philippines were often net importers of rice during these years.

Thus, the periphery shared some of the fruits of the industrial revolution taking place in the core by the gift of a terms of trade boom, although a Great Divergence still emerged. That is, the income per capita gap between core and periphery widened sharply. On average, Southeast Asian GDP per capita was 47 percent of western Europe in 1820 (Maddison 2008). In 1870, the figure had fallen to 29 percent, and to 22 percent in 1913. We are less confident as to which country was richest in this poor region, but in 1920 real wages (in US dollars: Japan = 100) were the following: the Philippines 57, Thailand 44, Indonesia Outer Islands 42, Malaya 33, Java 25, and South Vietnam 18.[8]

All of these pro-global forces eventually abated. A protectionist backlash swept over continental Europe and Latin America (Williamson 2006). The rate of decline in real transport costs along sea lanes slowed down before World War I, and then stabilized for the rest of the twentieth century (Williamson 2011: chapter 2). Most of the railroad networks were completed before 1913, even those connecting interior to port in Southeast Asia (van Zanden and Marks 2012: 90–1). The rate of growth of manufacturing slowed down in the core as the transition to industrial maturity was completed. As these forces abated, the resulting slowdown in commodity demand growth was reinforced by resource-saving innovations in the industrial core, induced, in large part, by those high and rising commodity prices during the century-long terms of trade boom.[9] Thus, the secular boom faded. Exactly when and where the boom faded depended on the export commodity, but throughout the poor periphery each region's terms of trade peaked somewhere between the 1860s and World War I.

Figure 2.4 documents the terms of trade boom. Excluding China and the rest of East Asia (more on that below), the terms of trade in the poor periphery soared from the late eighteenth century to the late 1880s and early 1890s, after which it underwent a modest decline up to 1913, before starting the interwar collapse. The secular price boom was huge: between the half-decades 1796–1800 and 1856–60, the terms of trade increased by almost two and a half times, or at an annual rate of 1.5 percent, a rate which was vastly greater than per capita income growth in Asia (0.1 percent per annum 1820–70; Maddison 1995: 24), and even greater than per capita income growth in the United Kingdom 1820–70 (1.2 percent per annum; Maddison 1995: 23).

Not every part of the poor periphery underwent the same terms of trade boom since what a region traded mattered. The best counter-example is China, which did not undergo a terms of trade boom over the century before 1913, but rather underwent a secular slump! As the rest of the periphery began the boom between 1796 and 1821, China underwent its first big *collapse*, with its terms of trade falling to one-fifth (*sic!*) of the 1796 level. When China finally joined the boom taking place in the rest of the periphery, it was very brief since its terms of trade peaked out much earlier than the rest, in 1840 after only a two decade boom. Following the early 1860s, China underwent the same slow secular decline in its terms of trade that was common across much of the late nineteenth century poor periphery. China's terms of trade *exceptionalism* was driven by its unusual country-specific mix of imports and exports. On the import side, what distinguished China from the rest was opium. The price of imported opium rose sharply from the 1780s to the 1820s, partly because of a successful monopoly by the East India Company (Chaudhuri 1978; Farrington 2002; Bowen et al. 2003), and it maintained those high levels until the 1880s (Clingingsmith and Williamson 2008). Since opium imports rose from about 30 to 50 percent of total Chinese imports over the period, the rise in the opium price played a key role in pushing

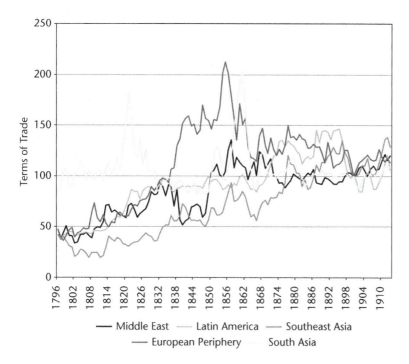

Figure 2.4   The poor periphery: net barter terms of trade, 1796–1913

China's terms of trade downwards. Reinforcing that secular fall was the fact that it also exported the "wrong" products since the price of silk and cotton fell dramatically over the century between the 1780s and 1880s, by 60 and 71 percent, respectively (Mulhall 1892: 471–8).

Japan was exceptional as well, but in a different way. When it was forced to go open in 1854 by the threat of American gunships, it underwent the biggest nineteenth century terms of trade boom by far: the price of its exportables boomed and the price of its importables slumped, just when the rest of the poor periphery had completed much of its secular boom.

While each region in the poor periphery had much the same import mix (except for China and its opium), each specialized in quite different commodities on the export side. Endowments and comparative advantage dictated the export mix, and different commodity price behavior implied different terms of trade boom magnitudes. Figure 2.4 documents terms of trade performance in each of the five poor periphery regions, some series starting as early as 1782. Southeast Asia had a bigger terms of trade boom than most. It persisted much longer than the periphery average – up to 1896, and the size of the century-long boom was double the periphery average. Still, there was immense variance within Southeast Asia: terms of trade for Siam (a rice exporter) grew at "only" 0.4 percent per annum over the century up to 1885–90, but it grew almost twice as fast in the Philippines (an exporter of copra, hemp, sugar, and tobacco) at 0.7 percent per annum, and more than *eight* times as fast in the Dutch East Indies at 3.3 percent per annum (an exporter of coffee, copra, sugar, tea, tin, tobacco, and, towards the end of the period, rubber and petroleum), the highest in the periphery. Due to its size, Indonesia dominates the Southeast Asian weighted average, and the terms of trade experience suggests that globalization must have had a bigger impact on the region than anywhere else in the non-European periphery. Southeast Asia illustrates nineteenth century export-led growth *par excellence*.

De-industrialization

The terms of trade boom encouraged the periphery to increase its specialization in commodity exports. The production of manufactures and even food crops was reduced to release labor, land, and other resources for use in the booming commodity-producing sectors. De-industrialization was one manifestation of this process, and it happened everywhere in the periphery. Productivity gains in west European manufacturing, first in cottage industry and then in factory goods, led to declining world prices of manufactures, making production in Mexico, São Paolo, Catalonia, Russia, Anatolia, Bengal, Madras, Java, Luzon, and elsewhere increasingly unprofitable. These forces were reinforced by declining sea freight rates, which served to foster trade and specialization for both Europe and its trading partners. As a result, Europe first won over world export markets in manufactures and eventually took over much of the periphery's domestic markets as well. This is simply the other side of the terms-of-trade-boom coin: relative to textiles, metal products and other manufactures, the periphery's commodity export sector saw its terms of trade improve and thus drew workers away from manufacturing. We call it the *Dutch disease*, and it was powerful.

Was there really any manufacturing there to de-industrialize? Early manufacturing, even in Europe, has always been small scale, labor intensive, animal or hand-powered, and often organized partly by the putting-out cottage system. But still, the business of making textiles, ceramics, furniture, building materials, metal products, and primitive machines employed large numbers and had high value added. In 1750, the Indian subcontinent and China together produced more than 57 percent of world manufacturing (Bairoch 1982). In addition, China and the Indian subcontinent claimed about 47 percent of world GDP (Maddison 2007). These two figures imply that most of Asia had higher manufacturing output shares in domestic GDP than did the rest of the world. The developed core produced 27 percent of world manufacturing output, more than its 22 percent share of world GDP, also implying a higher manufacturing output share than the global average. The amazing implication of these numbers is that China and India were just as "industrialized" as was the European core in 1750 (57/47 = 1.21 is about the same as 27/22 = 1.23).

And then the industrial revolution arrived! By 1830, the regional shares in world manufacturing output were moving everywhere towards what W. Arthur Lewis (1978) called the *new economic order*: the developed core manufacturing share rose to 40 percent, and it fell everywhere else. Indeed, by the 1830s the share of United Kingdom manufacturing exports in world manufactures exports was 91 percent, and the share of poor periphery commodity exports was 92 percent of world commodity exports (O'Brien 2004: table 3). All that was left to dominate were domestic markets in the periphery. By the 1880s, de-industrialization in the poor periphery was about complete.

Take India first. By 1833, it had lost *all* of its very large (net) export market *and* 5 percent of its domestic market. By 1877, the de-industrial damage was done, with domestic producers claiming only 35–42 percent of their own home market. Although the Ottoman Empire did not have a large foreign market to lose, it underwent a similar dramatic collapse in its home market, domestic producers undergoing a huge fall in their home market share from 97 to 11–38 percent over the half-century between the 1820s and the 1870s. In the Dutch East Indies, local production fell from 82 to 38 percent of the home market between 1822 and 1870. But de-industrialization persisted much longer there, with the local producer share falling still further to 11 percent in 1913.[10]

Indonesian textile manufacturing was an important economic activity in the early 1800s. Indeed, Jan Luiten van Zanden estimates that textiles were about 15 percent of GDP in the 1820s (van Zanden 2002), a figure implying that manufacturing may have been as much as a fifth or even a quarter of total Indonesian GDP at that time. By the early 1850s, textiles had fallen by more than half, to 6–7 percent of GDP. And the share of the home textile market supplied by Indonesian producers dropped from about 82 to 38 percent from 1822 to 1870, before falling still further to about 11 percent in 1913. Pierre van der Eng, who derived these estimates, points out that value added in textile manufacturing increased between 1820 and 1871 (van der Eng 2007: 1). But in a growing economy, it is the sector's performance *relative* to the overall economy that matters (Booth 1998: 96–7). Although per capita income hardly grew at all over the half-century following 1820 (only 0.1 percent per annum according to Maddison 2007), population grew at 1.2 percent and GDP at 1.3 percent per annum. Thus, it is the relative de-industrialization measure that matters in judging the impact of Dutch disease effects, and they were enormous in Indonesia.

Indonesia was not alone in suffering de-industrialization, since it happened to all its Southeast Asian neighbors. By the late 1890s, Burma's "textile industry had suffered a serious decline and it was finally … destroyed by the 1920s" and "weaving … spinning, iron and metal making, pottery … and paper making" had declined in Siam (Resnick 1970: 57, 60). Like Indonesia, the Philippines started the nineteenth century with a well-developed textile industry. Indeed, by 1818 local cloth accounted for 8 percent of Manila's exports with much of it produced in the province of Iloilo which "sucked in migrants from far and wide … selling as far afield as Europe and the Americas" (Clarence-Smith 2005: 8). But the Dutch disease spelled trouble for Philippine industry too. By 1847, almost 60 percent of Philippine imports were textiles, and they increased nine-fold over the half-century that followed (Legarda 1999: 149–50). By the 1880s, "native textiles were in a sad state, especially in southern Panay (around Iloilo) and Ilocos" (Legarda 1999: 155).

In short, it does indeed appear that the biggest terms of trade boom between 1800 and 1913 – that of Southeast Asia – produced the biggest Dutch disease and thus the biggest de-industrialization in the poor periphery.

Rising inequality, strengthening colonial rule

In judging the impact of globalization on any economy, we can focus on the income gains for the average resident (the so-called gains from trade), the distributional impact of those gains (who gains and who loses), and the long run growth impact. So far, we have focused on per capita income and the average resident. Social fairness, however, argues that we should explore the extent to which these gains are shared across all income classes, social groups, and regions. In addition, if the distribution of income is thought to have an impact on long run growth performance (Acemoglu et al. 2001, 2002; Engerman and Sokoloff 1997, 2012), we have even more reason to see who gained from globalization in Southeast Asia during the first global century. Finally, rising mineral rents, land rents, and tax revenues from commodity-boom-generated incomes, all favored the colonialists, their bureaucracy, the financial condition of the colonial system, and their policies.

What happened to income distribution in the poor periphery when these pre-industrial societies were exposed to global forces? In the absence of comprehensive inequality information,[11] this question can be answered by focusing on the returns to labor relative to land and mineral resources, or the wage–rental ratio. Where agriculture and mining are "big" in pre-industrial economies, the changing wage–rental ratio can be a very effective proxy for trends in inequality (Williamson 1997, 2002; Lindert and Williamson 2003). A "big" agriculture-cum-mining sector is one in which the share of land and mineral resources in total economy-wide tangible wealth is more than a third and/or in which the employment share is more than a half. Around the turn of the last century, the agriculture employment share (percent) in Asia was certainly "big": India 67.3, Indonesia 73.1, and Taiwan 70.3 (Mitchell 1998: 91–101).

The denominator "rental" in the wage–rental ratio does *not* refer to the returns to capital. Indeed, a well-integrated world capital market insured that risk-adjusted financial capital costs were pretty much equated the world around by 1913 (Obstfeld and Taylor 2004). Thus, while terms of trade shocks should have influenced the returns to internationally immobile land, mineral resources, and labor, they should not have influenced returns to internationally mobile capital. Furthermore, the distribution of income in the nineteenth century periphery was determined just as the classical economists modeled it, namely, by the relative shares of rents and wages in national income. To assess the distributional impact of world commodity markets on the periphery, we should, therefore, focus on labor and land, and thus on the wage–rental ratio.

Ever since Eli Heckscher, Bertil Ohlin, Wolfgang Stolper, and Paul Samuelson wrote about the problem, world trade booms have been associated with relative factor price changes. With a commodity price boom, the wage–rental ratio (w/r) should fall in the poor resource-abundant commodity exporter (since the export boom raises the relative demand for land and mineral resources). Since land and other natural resources were held by the colonial and domestic elite, the pre-World War I world trade boom implied lesser inequality in resource-scarce economies like those in East Asia, where land rents (and land values) fell, wages rose, and w/r rose even further. For the commodity exporters, the pre-World War I terms of trade boom induced a rise in resource rents, and an even greater fall in w/r, implying greater inequality, especially where the ownership of land and mines dictated the ownership of wealth.[12]

This narrative that goes from commodity price booms to rising r/w and to rising inequality might well be weakened in any Southeast Asian country with a frontier, that is where land was still in elastic supply and available to smallholders, like Burma and Malaya. But in those countries of small holdings, globalization appears to have helped to increase land concentration, thus adding to inequality trends. Smallholders moving into cash crops accumulated debt to finance the increased use of purchased inputs, more extensive irrigation systems, and better transportation, all of which were essential to supply booming world markets. It also exposed them to greater price volatility. Thus, default during slumps converted many of these smallholders into tenants or wage labor on large estates. Thus, cash tenancy on rice-producing land rose in Burma from 25 to 58 percent between the 1900s and 1930s, and similar trends took place in Indochina, Assam, and Tonkin (Steinberg 1987). The move to large sugar plantations in the Philippines had the same impact on land concentration there (Corpuz 1997).

So much for theory. What about the facts? Export prices boomed in the commodity-specializing countries throughout most of the nineteenth century, while, as we shall see in the next section, they collapsed in the interwar years. Thus, the relative rewards to land and labor – and overall income distribution – should have moved in very different directions on either side of World War I. Exactly how they were affected depended, of course, on whether a country's abundant factor was land or labor.

In contrast with land-scarce East Asia, the Punjab was relatively land abundant, a characterization that is confirmed by the fact that agricultural exports from the Punjab to Europe boomed after the early 1870s, while irrigation investment, immigration, and new settlement made it behave like a frontier region.[13] Globalization should have had the opposite effect on the wage–rental ratio in land-abundant Punjab compared with land-scarce East Asia: it should have fallen in the former, and fall it did. Between 1875/79 and 1910/14, the wage–rental ratio in the Punjab fell by 60 percent. The Punjab wage–rental ratio experience was not so different from that of other land-abundant parts of the poor periphery. Between 1880/84 and 1910/14 the wage–rent ratio fell by 85 percent in the combined pair of Argentina and Uruguay. Riding a cotton boom, the

Egyptian wage–rental ratio fell by 54 percent from the late 1870s to World War I, and by 85 percent from the late 1880s to World War I.

The recorded decline in wage–rental ratios in the land-abundant Southern Cone, the Punjab and Egypt prior to World War I is simply enormous. But they were even bigger in land-abundant and labor-scarce Southeast Asia: the wage–rental ratio fell by 44 percent in Burma over the 20 years between 1890/94 and 1910/14; in Siam, it fell by 98 percent between 1870/74 and 1910/14. These trends had obvious inequality implications in resource-abundant regions as the landed local and colonial elite gained dramatically relative to labor. As noted above, globalization also served to increase the concentration of landholdings in much of Southeast Asia due to rising smallholder indebtedness as they shifted to commercial export crops and exposed themselves to greater price volatility associated with many of those crops, resulting in subsequent default for the poorly insured. Smallholders evolved into tenant or wage labor on large estates (e.g. plantations in the Dutch East Indies: van Zanden and Marks 2012: 74), inducing more land and wealth concentration, and even more income inequality as a consequence.

In Southeast Asia, Indonesia's inequality trends are documented best. Economy-wide labor productivity rose by 1.5 percent per annum between 1860 and 1914 in Java (van Zanden and Marks 2012: table 2.1, p. 16), while real wages hardly changed at all (Allen et al. 2011: figure 6.4). This is, of course, consistent with soaring rent/wage ratios. But Java offers even better inequality evidence: between 1880 and 1925, the Gini coefficient there rose from 0.39 to 0.48, and the ratio of average incomes (including foreigners – mainly Chinese and Europeans) to that of natives rose from 1.12 to 1.34 (van Zanden and Marks 2012: table 6.3, p. 118). In short, inequality soared during the commodity price boom, and European colonists raised their share of the spoils. It seems unlikely that things were any different in Burma, Indochina, Malaya, Siam, and the Philippines.

Southeast Asia's trade bust, 1914–1940

The bad news: commodity price volatility and export-led collapse

Commodity price, export revenue, and income volatility was hardly unfamiliar to the poor periphery before the interwar decades and the Great Depression. Indeed, commodity prices have always been far more volatile than manufactures or services (Jacks et al. 2011) and they had a powerful negative impact on GDP and its growth in the poor periphery between 1870 and today (Blattman et al. 2007; Poelhekke and van der Ploeg 2009; Williamson 2012). Over the seven decades before World War II, the average terms of trade volatility in the periphery was 78 percent higher than the industrial leaders, and it was 83 percent higher in South and Southeast Asia. Before the Great Depression, the really big commodity price busts were in the 1840s, the late 1860s, the mid 1880s, and the late 1890s (Figure 2.4). Thus, the experience of Southeast Asia during the 1930s should come as no surprise. Between 1929 and 1932, the terms of trade fell by: Burma 24 percent; Indonesia 20 percent; the Philippines 38 percent; and Siam 32 percent (data underlying Blattman et al. 2007).

But the long run secular decline in their terms of trade started well before the 1930s: in Southeast Asia, the secular peak was 1896, eventually turning into a twentieth century secular bust during the interwar slowdown and the Great Depression of the 1930s. For example, between 1896 and 1932, the terms of trade for Indonesia fell by 48 percent while that of the Philippines fell by 65 percent. Experience like this persuaded many economists to advise newly independent post-war Third World nations everywhere to adopt anti-global and pro-industrial policies (Prebisch 1950; Singer 1950).

Some good news: emerging industrialization

But when their commodity terms of trade fell, the relative price of imported manufactures rose, thus offering some stimulus to domestic industry in the poor periphery. While there were other stimulating forces at work, this one left its mark before the post-war import-substitution industrialization (ISI) policies were introduced by most of the Third World. Although hardly double-digit performance, constant price manufacturing output was growing faster than constant price GDP in Southeast Asia between 1920 and 1938, at least for four countries that can be documented (percent per annum): Indonesia 2.7 vs 2.6; the Philippines 3.4 vs 2.9; Siam 2.3 vs 2.1; and Burma 2.6 vs 1.4 (Bénétrix et al. 2012; Maddison 2007). If these "emerging industrializer rates" seem low, note that they were higher than the leaders' 1.9 percent per annum (the weighted average of Germany, the USA, and UK); while only modest, they were catching up growth rates just the same and a hint of what was to come after World War II. Furthermore, it appears to have left its mark on relative GDP per capita growth. Angus Maddison (2008) shows that the century of Southeast Asia's Great Divergence 1820–1913 stopped in the interwar years. Between 1913 and 1940, Southeast Asian GDP per capita relative to western Europe remained steady at 0.22, this after the spectacular fall of 1820–1913. The Philippines did the best while Burma and Thailand did the worst, but on average Southeast Asia held its own.

More good news: falling inequality, weakening colonial rule

Rental/wage ratios followed the terms of trade collapse – they fell as commodity-price-driven mineral and land rents drifted downward throughout Southeast Asia. Between 1890/94 and 1920/24, they fell by 40 percent in Burma and 88 percent in Siam. Up to 1935/39, they fell by 91 percent in Siam. Falling mineral rents, land rents, and tax revenues from commodity-boom-generated incomes certainly did not favor the colonialists, their bureaucracy, and the financial condition of their system. Once again, Indonesia offers the most comprehensive inequality information, but only for the top income shares and only for 1921 onwards (Leigh and van der Eng 2010: figures 4.1–4.3): from a peak in the 1920s, the top income shares fell (or at least stopped rising) into the 1930s, and are much lower in 1980; and, as predicted, inequality was much lower in resource-scarce East Asia than in resource-abundant Indonesia. Colonialism was losing its *raison d'être* in Southeast Asia.

History lessons?

This chapter has explored Southeast Asia's trade performance in a global context over the four and a half centuries from 1500 to 1940. It appears that income growth and trade policy of its trading partners determined most of its commodity export performance, while falling trade costs were much less important. It also identified the impact of trade on Southeast Asia's growth performance: trade specialization in commodities generated de-industrialization 1500–1913 (when commodity prices boomed), but it generated some re-industrialization forces 1913–1940 (when commodity prices underwent a secular collapse). Throughout, commodity price volatility inhibited growth. The chapter also identifies the distributional impact of commodity export booms and slumps throughout the last century: when commodity prices boomed, inequality rose and colonial power waxed; when commodity prices slumped, equality rose and colonial power waned.

To the extent that industrialization has transformed Southeast Asia since World War II, and to the extent that Southeast Asia now specializes in labor-intensive manufactures, the historical links between commodity exports, growth, and inequality – forged over 450 years – seem to have been broken.

Acknowledgments

This chapter draws heavily on my *Trade and Poverty: When the Third World Fell Behind* (MIT 2011) and "Land, Labor and Globalization in the Third World 1870–1940," *Journal of Economic History* 62 (March 2002): 55–85; as well as K. H. O'Rourke and J. G. Williamson, "After Columbus: Explaining Europe's Overseas Trade Boom, 1500–1800," *Journal of Economic History* 62 (June 2002): 417–56; and finally A. Bénétrix, K. H. O'Rourke, and J. G. Williamson, "The Spread of Manufacturing to the Periphery 1870–2007: Eight Stylized Facts," *NBER Working Paper 18221*, National Bureau of Economic Research, Cambridge, MA (July 2012). I am grateful for the contributions of my past two collaborators, the suggestions from the March 22–23, 2013, Bangkok conference participants and for those from Jean-Pascal Bassino, Gregg Huff, Wolfgang Keller, and, especially, Anne Booth, Ian Coxhead, Pierre van der Eng, and (*pacem*) Thee Kian Wie. The usual disclaimer applies.

Notes

1 The focus here is on commodities other than silver and gold, since these precious metals played a monetary role as well as a more standard commodity role, and different factors thus explain their large and growing importance in international trade during the period. This chapter is solely interested in the growth of non-monetary commodity trade, and as such the large literature on the impact of inter-continental silver flows on aggregate price levels, while important, is not relevant here.

2 The Dutch, Portuguese, and English import mix data all come from Prakesh (1998: tables 2.2, 2.3, 4.1, and 4.2, pp. 35, 36, 115, 120).

3 Douglas Irwin (1991: especially p. 1297) suggests that pretty much *all* of the inter-continental trade at this time was by state-chartered monopolies. Like most monopolies, they raised prices paid by consumers (in Europe), lowered prices paid to suppliers (in Asia), restricted output, and limited trade. This is hardly the stuff that globalization is made of!

4 All these import price data come from Chaudhuri (1978: tables A.13 and C.24), who also provides data on sales prices and markups.

5 Figure 2.3 offers another reason why trade volumes or trade shares in GDP can be very poor proxies for "openness." The points of intersection at (M,S), (M,S'), and (M',S') represent rising trade volumes, but each one is just as "open" (e.g. $t = 0$) as the next.

6 See von Glahn (1996), Flynn (1995), and Flynn and Giraldez (1997).

7 That is not to say that there was no "dynamic" intra-Asian trade up to World War I. See Latham (1994) for an excellent account. But the more important point is that China was a much smaller player in Southeast Asian trade.

8 Van der Eng 2004b: table 4. Exchange rates will bias the Southeast Asian real wages downward relative to Japan, but the problem must be greatly diminished when comparing the Southeast Asian countries with each other.

9 This should have a modern resonance for the reader, as we have watched commodity prices boom in recent years, driven by the industrialization of China, India, and other BRICs (i.e. Brazil, Russia), just as we saw in the nineteenth century for Europe and its offshoots.

10 These figures are from Dobado et al. (2008: table 4).

11 But see the still-useful survey of the colonial Indonesia inequality evidence in Booth (1988), and the comparative pre-industrial evidence in Milanovic et al. (2011).

12 Where w/r and full inequality data are both available in the nineteenth and early twentieth centuries, their trends are highly correlated (Williamson 2002).

13 All the w/r figures that follow are from Williamson (2011: table 9.4).

Bibliography

Acemoglu, Daron, Simon Johnson, and James Robinson. 2001. "The colonial origins of comparative development," *American Economic Review* 91(5): 1369–401.

Acemoglu, Daron, Simon Johnson, and James Robinson. 2002. "Reversal of fortune: geography and institutions in the making of the modern world income distribution," *Quarterly Journal of Economics* 117 (November): 231–94.

Allen, Robert C., Jean-Pascal Bassino, Debin Ma, Christine Moll-Murata, and Jan Luiten van Zanden. 2011. "Wages, prices and living standards in China, Japan, and Europe," *Economic History Review* 64(1): 8–38.

Baier, Scott L. and Jeffrey H. Bergstrand. 2001. "The growth of world trade: tariffs, transport costs, and income similarity," *Journal of International Economics* 53(1): 1–27.

Bairoch, P. 1982. "International industrialization levels from 1750 to 1980," *Journal of European Economic History* 11 (Fall): 269–333.

Bénétrix, Agustín, Kevin H. O'Rourke, and Jeffrey G. Williamson. 2012. "The spread of manufacturing to the periphery 1870–2007: eight stylized facts," *NBER Working Paper* 18221, National Bureau of Economic Research, Cambridge, MA (July).

Blattman, Chris, J. Hwang, and Jeffrey G. Williamson. 2007. "The impact of the terms of trade on economic development in the periphery, 1870–1939: volatility and secular change," *Journal of Development Economics* 82 (January): 156–79.

Boomgaard, Peter. 1989. *Children of the Colonial State: Population Growth and Economic Development in Java, 1795–1880.* Amsterdam: Free University Press.

Booth, Anne. 1988. "Living standards and the distribution of income in colonial Indonesia: a review of the evidence," *Journal of Southeast Asian Studies* 19: 310–43.

Booth, Anne. 1998. *The Indonesian Economy in the Nineteenth and Twentieth Century.* New York: St. Martin's Press.

Bowen, H.V., M. Lincoln, and N. Rigby (eds). 2003. *The World of the East Indian Company.* Rochester, NY: Brewer.

Bulbeck, David, Anthony Reid, Lay Chengtan, and Yi Qi Wu. 1998. *Southeast Asian Exports since the 14th Century: Cloves, Pepper, Coffee, and Sugar.* Leiden, the Netherlands: KITLV Press.

Chaudhuri, Kirti N. 1978. *The Trading World of Asia and the English East India Company 1660–1760.* Cambridge: Cambridge University Press.

Clarence-Smith, W.G. 2005. "Cotton textiles on the Indian Ocean periphery, c1500–c1850." Paper presented at the Global Economic History Network, Conference 8, Pune, India (18–20 December).

Clingingsmith, David and Jeffrey G. Williamson. 2008. "Deindustrialization in 18th and 19th century India: Mughal decline, climate shocks and British industrial ascent," *Explorations in Economic History* 45 (July): 209–34.

Corpuz, O.D. 1997. *An Economic History of the Philippines.* Quezon City: University of the Philippines Press.

de Vries, Jan. 1976. *Economy of Europe in an Age of Crisis, 1600–1750.* Cambridge: Cambridge University Press.

Dobado Gonzáles, R., A. Gómez Galvarriato, and J.G. Williamson. 2008. "Mexican exceptionalism: globalization and de-industrialization 1750–1877," *Journal of Economic History* 68 (September): 1–53.

Engerman, Stanley L. and Kenneth L. Sokoloff. 1997. "Factor endowments, inequality, and differential paths of growth among New World economies," in S. Haber (ed.), *How Latin America Fell Behind.* Stanford, CA: Stanford University Press, pp. 260–304.

Engerman, Stanley L. and Kenneth L. Sokoloff. 2012. *Economic Development in the Americas since 1500: Endowments and Institutions.* New York: Cambridge University Press.

Estevadeordal, A., B. Frantz, and A.M. Taylor. 2003. "The rise and fall of world trade, 1870–1939," *Quarterly Journal of Economics* 118 (May): 359–407.

Farrington, A. 2002. *Trading Places: The East Indian Company and Asia, 1600–1834.* London: British Library.

Ferguson, N. 2003. *Empire: How Britain Made the Modern World.* New York: Penguin.

Flam, H. and M.J. Flanders. 1991. *Heckscher–Ohlin Trade Theory.* Cambridge, MA: MIT Press.

Flynn, Dennis O. 1995. "Arbitrage, China, and world trade in the early modern period," *Journal of the Economic and Social History of the Orient* 38(4): 419–48.

Flynn, Dennis O. and Arturo Giraldez. 1997. "Introduction," in Dennis O. Flynn and Arturo Giraldez (eds), *Metals and Monies in an Emerging Global Economy.* Aldershot: Variorum.

Irwin, Douglas A. 1991. "Mercantilism as strategic trade policy: the Anglo-Dutch rivalry for the East India trade," *Journal of Political Economy* 99(6): 1296–314.

Jacks, David S., Chris M. Meissner, and D. Novy. 2008. "Trade costs, 1870–2000," *American Economic Review* 98 (May): 529–34.

Jacks, David S., Kevin H. O'Rourke, and Jeffrey G. Williamson. 2011. "Commodity price volatility and world market integration since 1700," *Review of Economics and Statistics* 93(3): 800–13.

Jones, Eric L. 1981. *The European Miracle*. Cambridge: Cambridge University Press.

Krugman, Paul. 1995. "Growing world trade: causes and consequences." *Brookings Papers on Economic Activity*, no. 1: 327–77.

Latham, A.J.H. 1994. "The dynamics of intra-Asian trade, 1868–1913: the great entrepots of Singapore and Hong Kong," in A.J.H. Latham and H. Kawakatsu (eds), *Japanese Industrialization and the Asian Economy*. London: Routledge.

Legarda, Benito J. 1999. *After the Galleons: Foreign Trade, Economic Change and Entrepreneurship in the Nineteenth-Century Philippines*. Madison: University of Wisconsin Press.

Leigh, Andrew and Pierre van der Eng. 2010. "Top incomes in Indonesia, 1920–2004," in A.B. Atkinson and T. Piketty (eds), *Top Incomes: A Global Perspective*. Oxford: Oxford University Press.

Lewis, W.A. 1978. *The Evolution of the International Economic Order*. Princeton, NJ: Princeton University Press.

Lindert, Peter H. and Jeffrey G. Williamson. 2003. "Does globalization make the world more unequal?" in M. Bordo, A.M. Taylor and J.G. Williamson (eds), *Globalization in Historical Perspective*. Chicago, IL: University of Chicago Press, pp. 227–71.

Ma, Debin. 1999. "The Great Silk exchange," in Dennis O. Flynn, L. Frost, and A.J.H. Latham (eds), *Pacific Centuries*. London: Routledge, pp. 38–69.

Maddison, Angus. 1991. *Dynamic Forces in Capitalist Development: A Long-Run Comparative View*. Oxford: Oxford University Press.

Maddison, Angus. 1995. *Monitoring the World Economy 1820–1992*. Paris: OECD.

Maddison, Angus. 1998. *Chinese Economic Performance in the Long Run*. Paris: OECD.

Maddison, Angus. 2001. *The World Economy: A Millennial Perspective*. Paris: OECD.

Maddison, Angus. 2007. *World Population, GDP and Per Capita GDP, 1–2003AD* (August 2007 update), www.ggdc.net/Maddison.

Maddison, Angus. 2008. 03_PerCapitaGDPLevels,1AD-2008AD[1].

Marks, Robert B. 1997. *Tigers, Rice, Silk, and Silt: Environment and Economy in Guangdong, 1250–1850*. New York: Cambridge University Press.

Marks, Robert B. 1999. "Maritime trade and the agro-ecology of South China, 1685–1850," in Dennis O. Flynn, L. Frost, and A.J.H. Latham (eds), *Pacific Centuries*. London: Routledge, pp. 85–109.

Meissner, C. 2005. "A New World order: explaining the emergence of the classical gold standard," *Journal of International Economics* 66 (July): 385–406.

Milanovic, B., P.H. Lindert, and J.G. Williamson. 2011. "Pre-industrial inequality," *Economic Journal* 121 (551): 255–72.

Mitchell, Brian R. 1998. *International Historical Statistics: Africa, Asia and Oceania 1750–1993*. 3rd ed. London: Macmillan.

Mitchener, Kris J. and Marc Weidenmier. 2008. "Trade and empire," *Economic Journal* 118 (November): 1805–34.

Mulhall, M.G. 1892. *The Dictionary of Statistics*. London: Routledge.

O'Brien, Patrick K. 2004. "Colonies in a globalizing economy 1815–1948." *LSE Working Paper 08/04*, Global Economic History Network, London School of Economics (December).

Obstfeld, Murray and Alan M. Taylor. 2004. *Global Capital Markets: Integration, Crisis, and Growth*. Cambridge; Cambridge University Press.

O'Rourke, Kevin H. and Jeffrey G. Williamson. 2002. "After Columbus: explaining Europe's overseas trade boom, 1500–1800," *Journal of Economic History* 62(2): 417–56.

Poelhekke S. and F. van der Ploeg. 2009. "Volatility and the natural resource curse," *Oxford Economic Papers* 61(4): 727–60.

Pomeranz, Kenneth. 2000. *The Great Divergence: Europe, China, and the Making of the Modern World Economy*. Princeton, NJ: Princeton University Press.

Prakesh, Om. 1998. *The New Cambridge History of India: Volume II (5): European Commercial Enterprise in Pre-Colonial India*. Cambridge: Cambridge University Press.

Prebisch, Raoul. 1950. *The Economic Development of Latin America and Its Principal Problems*. Lake Success, NY: United Nations, Department of Economic Affairs.

Reid, Anthony. 1987. "Low population growth and its causes in pre-colonial Southeast Asia," in N.G. Owen (ed.), *Death and Disease in Southeast Asia: Explorations in Social, Medical and Demographic History*. Oxford: Oxford University Press, pp. 33–47.

Reid, Anthony. 1993. *Southeast Asia in the Age of Commerce 1450–1680: Volume Two: Expansion and Crisis*. New Haven, CT: Yale University Press.

Reid, Anthony. 2001. "South-East Asian population history and the colonial impact," in T-J. Liu, J. Lee, D.S. Reher, O. Saito, and W. Feng (eds), *Asian Population History*. Oxford: Oxford University Press, pp. 45–62.

Resnick, S.A. 1970. "The decline of rural industry under export expansion: a comparison among Burma, Philippines, and Thailand, 1870–1938," *Journal of Economic History* 30 (March): 51–73.

Singer, Hans W. 1950. "The distribution of gains between investing and borrowing countries," *American Economic Review* 40(2): 473–85.

Steinberg, D.J. 1987. *In Search of Southeast Asia*. Honolulu: University of Hawaii Press.

van der Eng, Pierre. 2004a. "Trade and commerce of Southeast Asia," in O.K. Gin (ed.), *Southeast Asia: A Historical Encyclopedia*. Santa Barbara, CA: ABC-CLIO, pp. 1343–50.

van der Eng, Pierre. 2004b. "Productivity and comparative advantage in rice agriculture in South-East Asia since 1870," *Asian Economic Journal* 18(4): 345–69.

van der Eng, Pierre. 2007. "De-industrialization and colonial rule: the cotton textile industry in Indonesia, 1820–1941." Unpublished manuscript, Australian National University, Canberra.

van Zanden, J.L. 2002. "Colonial state formation and patterns of economic development in Java, 1800–1913." Unpublished manuscript, Utrecht University, the Netherlands.

van Zanden, Jan Luiten, and Daan Marks. 2012. *An Economic History of Indonesia 1800–2010*. London: Routledge.

von Glahn, Richard. 1996. *Fountain of Fortune: Money and Monetary Policy in China, 1000–1700*. Berkeley: University of California Press.

Williamson, Jeffrey G. 1997. "Globalization and inequality, past and present," *World Bank Research Observer* 12(2): 117–35.

Williamson, Jeffrey G. 2002. "Land, labor and globalization in the Third World 1870–1940," *Journal of Economic History* 62(1): 55–85.

Williamson, Jeffrey G. 2006. "Explaining world tariffs 1870–1938: Stolper-Samuelson, strategic tariffs and state revenues," in R. Findlay, R. Henriksson, H. Lindgren, and M. Lundahl (eds), *Eli Heckscher, 1879–1952: A Celebratory Symposium*. Cambridge, MA: MIT Press.

Williamson, Jeffrey G. 2011. *Trade and Poverty: When the Third World Fell Behind*. Cambridge, MA: MIT Press.

Williamson, Jeffrey G. 2012. "Commodity prices over two centuries: trends, volatility and impact," *Annual Review of Resource Economics* 4: 185–207.

3

A century of growth, crisis, war and recovery, 1870–1970

Anne Booth

SCHOOL OF ORIENTAL AND AFRICAN STUDIES, UNIVERSITY OF LONDON

Introduction

This chapter surveys the economic development of Southeast Asia over the century from 1870 to 1970, a century which saw the rapid integration of many parts of the region into the world economy, followed by the great depression of the 1930s, the Japanese occupation from 1942 to 1945, and the transition to independence, which was in some former colonies peaceful and in others violent and prolonged. Although many economic historians consider that the first era of globalization came to an end in 1913, I suggest that in Southeast Asia it continued until 1929, when the world depression had a serious effect on many parts of the region. Not only did Southeast Asia's commodity trade grow rapidly between 1870 and 1930, but there were substantial movements of people, both within the various colonies, and between them and the two huge population reservoirs of India and China. Last but by no means least, there were considerable flows of capital, both public and private, into Southeast Asia. These increased flows of goods, people and capital left deep and lasting legacies to the independent governments in the region.

When the Suez Canal was just completed in 1870, and Southeast Asia's trading links with rapidly industrializing Europe and North America were expanding, the various parts of the region were not greatly dissimilar in economic structure and in the level of their economic development. In contrast to the ancient civilizations of China and India, which had larger populations and, especially in the case of China, much higher agricultural densities, densities were still quite low in most parts of Southeast Asia. Only the "inner core" of the Netherlands Indies, comprising the islands of Java and Bali, and the delta region of North Vietnam could be considered densely settled.[1] Although trading links with the outside world had been established for many centuries and an urban and commercial tradition certainly existed in most parts of the region, most of the population of Southeast Asia was predominantly rural and agricultural, with their basic needs of food, shelter and clothing and other manufactures being satisfied from their own labour, or that of their immediate family and neighbours.[2] There was considerable economic change after 1870, but the fundamentally agrarian nature of much of the region persisted until 1942, and into the post-1950 era.

Economic growth and structural change

By 1870, most of Southeast Asia was under the control of European powers, and even nominally independent Siam (as Thailand was known until 1939) had conceded considerable autonomy in economic policy-making under the provisions of the Bowring Treaty which went into effect in 1856, and subsequent treaties with other foreign powers.[3] Between 1870 and 1913, rapid world trade expansion led to an increase in exports from many parts of Southeast Asia. The region followed the classic colonial pattern of exporting a few primary commodities and importing consumption and capital goods from the colonial power and from other developed countries, although there was also some intra-regional trade, especially in rice. By the early twentieth century, the Philippines, British Malaya and the Netherlands Indies had all become net rice importers, dependent on supplies from surplus regions in Thailand, Burma and South Vietnam.

For 1870 to 1913, estimates of per capita GDP show growth for most of Southeast Asia. Thailand apart, growth continued until 1929 (Table 3.1). The most rapid growth was in Singapore where per capita GDP more than trebled between 1870 and 1929, and in modern Malaysia (until 1942 the federated and unfederated states plus North Borneo and Sarawak, together with Malacca and Penang), where per capita GDP more than doubled. Elsewhere growth rates were lower but only in Thailand was there little progress in per capita terms after 1913. All the main Southeast Asian economies suffered some decline in per capita GDP after 1929 as a result of the global depression, which severely affected demand for tropical exports. But by 1938 per capita GDP was still well above 1913 levels everywhere except Thailand.[4]

The growth in output that took place in most parts of Southeast Asia between 1870 and 1930 was driven mainly by agricultural growth, both for domestic consumption and for export. By 1930, Southeast Asia was exporting ever larger quantities of a number of traditional agricultural staples with which the region had long been associated, including sugar, rice, coffee, tea, spices, hard fibres and coconut oil. In addition, the cultivation of new crops such as rubber and palm oil was expanding rapidly, and by the 1930s, smallholder producers in Indonesia were accounting for almost half of total production of rubber (Creutzberg 1975: 94). The increase in agricultural output was associated with considerable expansion of cultivated land, although only in a few cases, such as sugar in Java, did increased yields per unit of land contribute to growth in output.[5] For the most part, the growth in agricultural output occurred by replicating known production

Table 3.1 Trends in per capita GDP, 1870–1970

Year	Burma	Indonesia	Philippines	Thailand	Malaysia	Singapore
1870	4	72	74	85	74	53
1913	100	100	100	100	100	100
1920	104	105	124	n/a	123	110
1929	132	129	133	94	187	170
1934	122	111	127	n/a	171	136
1938	108	130	136	98	151	149
1950	58	93	106	97	173	159
1960	82	113	146	128	170	141
1970	94	132	175	201	231	269
GDP per capita (1990 International Geary–Khamis Dollars)						
1913	685	904	1053	841	900	1,279
1970	642	1,194	1,764	1,694	2,079	4,439

Sources: Maddison (2003: 180–5) with data for Singapore after 1913 from Sugimoto (2011: 185) and for the Philippines after 1913 from Hooley (2005).
Notes: Index: 1913 = 100. The estimates for Malaysia and Singapore refer to the modern states of Singapore and Malaysia, which includes Sarawak and Sabah. The figures for Burma after 1913 refer to 1921, 1931 and 1936 respectively.

technologies over more land. In some regions, such as the delta region of lower Burma, the expansion in rice production was the result of considerable migration of people from the densely settled rural heartlands to frontier regions.[6]

Non-agricultural sectors of the economies of Southeast Asia also grew over these decades. This was partly due to the growth of export production, including mining as well as agriculture, which brought with it rapid expansion in transport, trade and financial services, as well as in processing industries. This diversification led to a considerable change in the economic structure of the various national economies. By the late 1930s, the agricultural sector accounted for at most around half the national product in those countries for which figures are available (Burma, Thailand, Indonesia, the Philippines). In Indonesia, 66 per cent of total output is estimated to have originated from non-agricultural activities (Table 3.2).

It is often asserted that, up to 1940, industrialization in Southeast Asia was largely restricted to agricultural and mineral processing for export, but this is not strictly correct. While there can be little doubt that processing activities had an important impact on the growth of industry and on the formation of a wage labour force in many parts of the region, there was also some growth in manufacturing for local consumption. The increase in incomes that occurred in the latter part of the nineteenth and the early twentieth centuries gave rise to demand for new consumption goods which could be produced locally such as processed foodstuffs (including beer and other alcoholic drinks), cigarettes, newsprint and western clothing. Although little positive encouragement was given to local production before the 1930s, through tariffs or other forms of protection, those manufactures that enjoyed some measure of natural protection through high transport costs began to be locally produced, often by Chinese or Indian entrepreneurs.

However it was with the depression of the 1930s that colonial governments in various parts of Southeast Asia began seriously to consider industrialization as a policy goal. As Shepherd pointed out, the collapse of export markets in the early 1930s resulted in a widespread conviction among many colonial civil servants, especially in Indonesia and Indochina, that the colonial economies

Table 3.2 Percentage of total NDP/GDP accruing from non-agricultural sectors, 1900–38

Year	Taiwan	Malaysia	Indonesia	Burma[b]	Thailand	Philippines[d]
1900	34.4[a]	n/a	55.5	36.4	56.3	60.2
1913	46.2	n/a	59.5	36.6	55.3	61.5
1916	55.4	n/a	59.6	35.3	n/a	61.1
1921	56.0	n/a	63.1	49.6	n/a	61.0
1926	55.0	n/a	62.1	49.0	n/a	61.4
1931	55.6	n/a	62.7	42.4	56.2[c]	60.5
1936	60.3	n/a	64.6	45.6	n/a	60.0
1938	58.8	n/a	66.3	48.7	55.7	61.9
1960	73.6	66.6	67.1	64.2	60.4	70.0
1970	85.0	73.5	70.1	62.0	71.7	71.8

Sources: Taiwan: Mizoguchi and Umemura (1988: 234–8); Indonesia: van der Eng (2002: 171–2); Philippines: Hooley (2005); Burma: Saito and Lee (1999); Thailand: Sompop (1989: 251). Data for 1960 and 1970 for Taiwan, Malaysia, Burma and Thailand from World Bank (1976).
Notes:
[a] 1903.
[b] Figures for Burma refer to fiscal years 1901–2, 1911–12, 1916–17, 1921–22, 1926–27, 1931–32, 1936–37 and 1938–39 respectively.
[c] 1929.
[d] Figures for the Philippines refer to 1902, 1918, 1928 and 1938.

must be diversified, in order to reduce dependency on a narrow range of primary commodities which were extremely vulnerable to world market fluctuations. "Among the solutions offered none was seized upon with more enthusiasm than industrialization" (Shepherd 1941: 5). Apart from the impact of the world slump on markets for tropical primary products, the other factor that goaded colonial governments in Southeast Asia into greater concern about industrial development was the extraordinary success of Japan's great export drive during the early 1930s.[7] Most colonial governments reacted to the flood of cheap Japanese manufactures by increasing tariffs and quotas, particularly on textile goods. The main intention of these measures was to provide protection for exports from the mother countries, but a secondary consequence was to encourage local production of manufactures. Increasingly colonial officials reasoned that if Japan could industrialize using its abundant supplies of cheap labour, why not Java, or Indochina?[8]

The decade of the 1940s saw the Japanese Imperial Army sweep through the region, inflicting humiliating defeats on the colonial powers in Burma and British Malaya, and in the Philippines and the Netherlands Indies. Although the Japanese were initially greeted as liberators in some parts of Southeast Asia, disillusion rapidly set in as food supplies were requisitioned and local people were forced to work on various government projects; young men in particular were often forced to move far from their home regions, and mortality rates were high. After Japan's defeat in 1945, the returning colonial powers had to deal with nationalist movements which were in some places inspired by communist ideology. The Americans honoured previous pledges to grant the Philippines full independence in 1946, and Burma was granted independence shortly after the rest of British India in early 1948. After the Americans exerted pressure, the Indonesian declaration of independence, signed by Sukarno and Hatta on 17 August 1945, was finally recognized by the Dutch in late 1949. In all three countries per capita GDP in 1950 was below 1938 levels (see Table 3.1).

In Burma and Indonesia, per capita GDP recovered only slowly in the two decades from 1950 to 1970; in Burma it was still lower in 1970 than in 1938, while in Indonesia it was only slightly higher. Paauw (1960: 209) argued that in Indonesia there had been structural retrogression after 1950, in the sense that the share of the labour-intensive sectors, including smallholder agriculture, and small-scale manufacturing and services in total output had increased. In other parts of the region, these two decades saw some growth. Particularly striking was the accelerated growth in Thailand, where after decades of economic stagnation, per capita GDP more than doubled between 1950 and 1970. After slow growth in per capita terms through the 1950s, growth also accelerated in the 1960s in both Singapore and Malaysia. By 1970, marked inequalities in per capita GDP were already obvious across the region. There were also differences in economic structure. In both the Philippines and Thailand, the non-agricultural sectors of the economy grew quite quickly after 1950, and accounted for more than 70 per cent of total GDP by 1970. The share was also over 70 per cent in Malaysia. But although by the 1960s, the industrial and service sectors were expanding, with the exception of Singapore the pace of growth was slower than in Taiwan and South Korea, let alone Japan. It was only when foreign, and particularly Japanese, investment in manufacturing in Southeast Asia accelerated after 1970 that the manufacturing sector not only grew more rapidly but also began to account for a growing share of exports.

Diversification of employment

In spite of the growth of output of non-agricultural sectors in many parts of Southeast Asia after 1900, agriculture still employed at least 60 per cent of the labour force in most colonies in the latter part of the 1930s (Table 3.3). With the exception of British Malaya, and especially the Federated Malay States, most agricultural employment was on smallholdings; large-scale estate agriculture

Table 3.3 Occupational distribution of the employed population, Japan, Thailand and colonies, c. 1930

Country/Year	Agriculture	Industry	Other	Total
Japan (1930)	49.6	20.1	30.3	100.0
Taiwan (1930)	73.0	8.6	18.3	100.0
Korea (1930)	79.6	6.3	14.1	100.0
Thailand (1929)	84.2	2.2	13.6	100.0
Burma (1931)	69.6	11.0	19.4	100.0
British Malaya (1930)	60.8	12.3	26.9	100.0
Philippines (1939)	69.0	12.2	18.8	100.0
Indonesia (1930)	68.0	10.4	19.6	100.0

Sources: Japan: Grajdanzev (1944); Korea: Suh (1978, table 2); Taiwan: Grajdanzev (1942: 33); British Malaya: Vlieland (1932: 99); Burma: Saito and Lee (1999 table 1.6); Indonesia: Mertens (1978, appendix table 1.5); Philippines: Kurihara (1945: 16); Thailand: Ingram (1971: 57, 144).

offered full-time employment to only a small proportion of the total labour force. Much of the non-agricultural employment was in small-scale industries and petty trade. The "modern" or large-scale manufacturing sector employed only about 300,000 people in Indonesia in 1939, from an estimated labour force of 24 million. In Burma, Spate (1941) estimated that employment in the "factory" sector (including ricemills) was around 100,000 in the late 1920s, but contracted in the 1930s. In Indochina, Robequain (1944) estimated that a maximum of 120,000 workers was employed in modern industry by the late 1930s.[9] Even if a rather larger share of the 601,000 workers employed in manufacturing in the Philippines in 1939 was in large-scale enterprises, compared with Indonesia or Burma, it is unlikely that more than one million people were employed in the factory sector in the whole of Southeast Asia in the late 1930s.[10]

Most workers enumerated as "employed in manufacturing" in censuses were occupied in producing manufactures either in the home or in small workshops, typically employing fewer than 10 people. Rural manufacturing was often dominated by women workers. In Thailand weaving, cookery and pottery were considered female jobs; this was also the case in Burma and Indonesia. In the Philippines, the 1939 census found that manufacturing employed 7.9 per cent of the male labour force but almost 25 per cent of all female workers. Embroidery, dressmaking and native textile manufacture together employed more workers than any other sub-sector of manufacturing, and almost all were women. Women also dominated in hat and mat manufacture. These occupations were often contracted out to home-workers, and this could be combined with child care and other domestic chores. Critics such as Kurihara (1945: 19–22) pointed to the low wages typically received by women workers, and the lack of any worker protection. But clearly many thousands of women were prepared to work under "bad" conditions in order to supplement household incomes, as indeed they continued to do after independence.

The persistence of a large handicraft sector in Southeast Asia up till the end of the colonial period and beyond is surprising in that it runs counter to the "de-industrialization" hypothesis which has had much attention in Southeast Asia, as well as in South Asia and Africa. Resnick (1970: 58) argued in the case of Burma, Thailand and the Philippines that, as these economies became more involved in producing agricultural products for the world market in the last part of the nineteenth century, and as imports from industrial Europe and North America increased, many indigenous industries "were fragmented and displaced". Quoting authorities such as Homan van der Heide and Ingram, Resnick argued that traditional industries such as weaving and spinning, iron and metal making, pottery and earthenware, paper making, and sugar manufacturing all declined, although the regional impact was uneven because of poor transport. While this might have been true, there can be little doubt that, even allowing for the demise of some cottage industries, by the early twentieth century, the labour force in several Southeast Asian economies was becoming more diversified in terms of sources of income. By the 1930s, over 30 per cent of the labour force was employed in non-agricultural occupations everywhere except in Thailand (Table 3.3). In British Malaya a large proportion of the non-agricultural labour force consisted of migrant workers from China and India but this was not the case elsewhere.

In Indonesia, Burma and the Philippines, indigenous workers accounted for well over 85 per cent of the total labour force and many of these had found employment in both manufacturing industry and a range of service occupations, including trade and transport, and government service. Although Chinese workers were important in both trade and the professions in Indonesia by the 1930s, they only comprised a minority of the labour force in these occupations.[11] Many workers who were still mainly employed in agriculture would have taken on other jobs in the off-season, and certainly would have been familiar with the cash economy as sellers of output and buyers of inputs, and as wage workers, creditors or debtors.[12] Only a minority, even outside Java, would still have been living in a traditional subsistence economy. Increasingly, this was true of other parts of Southeast Asia as well.[13]

Thus people in many parts of Southeast Asia were already familiar with the monetized economy by the 1950s when political independence arrived. But, largely as a result of the slow growth, or even declines in per capita GDP in the 1960s and 1970s, changes in the structure of employment took place only slowly. By 1970, the proportion of the labour force employed in agriculture was still around 65 to 70 per cent in most parts of the region. The role of migrant Chinese and Indians in the economies of Southeast Asia also remained important after independence, although in Burma the military government which assumed power in the early 1960s adopted an aggressive policy which resulted in the departure of most Indians. In Indonesia, over 100,000 Chinese left for China, and others decided to move to other parts of the region or to other parts of the world. By 1970 it is likely that Chinese comprised less than 2 per cent of the population, although questions regarding ethnic origin were no longer asked in the post-independence censuses.

Demographic change, urbanization and the emergence of the plural economy

The countries of Southeast Asia experienced much faster population growth in the latter part of the nineteenth century and the early decades of the twentieth century than either China or India.[14] In all cases the annual average growth in population was well over 1 per cent, and in those regions that attracted substantial in-migration such as British Malaya it was over 2 per cent per annum. This rapid growth was due to a combination of high fertility, falling mortality compared with other parts of Asia and Africa, and especially in Burma and Malaya, high in-migration. It seems probable that an important explanation for lower mortality in nineteenth century Southeast Asia compared with either India or China was the greater abundance of land and food supplies relative to population, although by the 1920s colonial governments were also taking greater responsibility for public health measures, including programmes to promote the health of babies and young children.[15] In addition, the colonial regimes in most parts of Southeast Asia prevented the kind of recurrent wars and rebellions that took a heavy toll of human life in China in the middle decades of the nineteenth century.

Much of the foreign in-migration to Southeast Asia in the colonial era was from the vast population reservoirs of India and China; by the 1930s these "foreign Asians" comprised more than half the population of British Malaya, including Singapore, and around 10 per cent of Burma. In comparison with migration streams across the Atlantic to the USA, the numbers moving into

Southeast Asia were quite large. Huff and Caggiono have estimated that, between 1911 and 1929, gross migration into Burma, British Malaya and Thailand was over twice as high as gross migration into the USA.[16] Although net migration was much lower than in the USA, reflecting the fact that a high proportion of the migrants into Southeast Asia returned home again, net inward migration still amounted to around 1.55 million over these years. Migrant Asians were a much smaller percentage of the total population in Indonesia, where the Dutch had imposed controls in the early twentieth century, although Chinese migrants were important in particular regions, such as the East Coast of Sumatra, where they comprised a considerable part of the estate labour force. In Thailand and the Philippines, Chinese migrants integrated themselves into the local community more successfully and usually took Thai and Spanish names, as well as adopting local religious practices. Thus they were not always enumerated separately in censuses.

In addition to foreign in-migration, there is abundant evidence that indigenous populations moved out of densely settled agricultural areas to colonize new lands everywhere in the region and that this movement was in some cases facilitated by the introduction of individual land rights in the latter part of the nineteenth century. Much of this population movement was unassisted by government, although the Dutch in Indonesia after 1900 began a programme of officially sponsored migration from Java to the outer islands, especially Sumatra. This policy continued into the post-independence era. Both Dutch and French officials also facilitated the movement of workers from densely settled regions in Java and North Vietnam to estates areas in Sumatra and South Vietnam respectively.[17] Most colonial governments in Southeast Asia wanted to establish a rural economy based on landowning smallholders, but as the demand for tropical agricultural products boomed in the early twentieth century, conflicts over land between large commercial estates and smallholders became more frequent. While colonial regimes did not always side with the former, they were often under pressure from powerful metropolitan interests to ensure that commercial estates did get access to land.[18]

Thus by the early twentieth century, Southeast Asia was characterized by an increasingly mixed and mobile population, and the contours of the "plural society" plain to see. As Furnivall (1948: 304–5) pointed out, the various ethnic groups in Southeast Asia mixed but did not combine. Each group had its own economic role, and very often also a separate language and religion. They came together in the marketplace, but socially they remained distinct. Furnivall admitted that traces of a plural society were evident in several societies outside the tropical world including Canada, the United States and South Africa. But he thought that the process of differentiation had gone further in Southeast Asia than elsewhere. In spite of some attempt to impose controls on in-migration from China in particular, by the 1930s, when the severe economic downturn reduced in-migration in most parts of Southeast Asia, the plural society and economy were well entrenched. Post-colonial governments were to wrestle with its legacy for most of the last half of the twentieth century.

The extent of urbanization itself varied considerably in Southeast Asia by the early twentieth century. Huff (2012: table 1) finds that by 1930, Batavia (as Jakarta was then known) was the largest city in the region, with a population of 533,000, followed by Singapore, Manila, Bangkok and Rangoon, all with populations in excess of 400,000. British Malaya was the most urbanized colony with 18 per cent of the population living in the largest five towns. Elsewhere the proportion was considerably smaller. A further feature of most colonial cities in Southeast Asia was that they often contained a high proportion of non-indigenous peoples. For example only 60 per cent of the urban population of Burma in 1931 were indigenous Burmese; the percentage for Rangoon was even lower.[19] In the four largest cities of Java (Batavia, Surabaya, Semarang and Bandung), over 20 per cent of the population in 1930 were European, Chinese or other foreign Asians, while in Medan indigenous Indonesians were only 54 per cent of the population.

In Malaya, where the urban population comprised 35 per cent of the total in 1947, the Chinese predominated in most urban areas.[20]

As well as having better access to infrastructure, urban populations usually got better access to educational and health facilities. It is widely held that colonial governments in most parts of Asia and Africa neglected education except to the extent that it was necessary to provide clerks for the civil service and the private sector. In India in particular, but also in parts of Southeast Asia, the colonial authorities by the early years of the twentieth century were already alarmed at the growing "educated unemployment", as well as the evidence that increased education went hand in hand with the growth of nationalism, and in some cases crime. The reason that parents scrimped and saved to educate their children in most colonies was not a belief in the virtues of a "western" education for its own sake, but rather a conviction that such education was the only means to social and economic advancement in a colonial society, although as more young people gained access to such education the value of their qualifications as a passport to "modern" employment inevitably declined.

Nationalists in many parts of Southeast Asia saw education in vernacular languages as a means of encouraging national consciousness, but also wanted more scientific and technical education in order to catch up with the industrial economies (Furnivall 1943: 51–2). After 1950, there was rapid expansion in both secondary and tertiary education in most parts of the region, albeit usually from a low base. The former British colonies, and the Philippines continued to teach in English, although this often disadvantaged indigenous students, especially from rural backgrounds. Because of the American legacy, the Philippines had more university-educated people than most other parts of Asia; in 1955, numbers of science and technology graduates relative to population was higher than in South Korea and Taiwan, and only slightly below Japan (Booth 2007a: 194).

Increasing links with the international economy

From 1830 to 1938, the share of Southeast Asia in total exports from Asia (excluding Japan) grew steadily while that of both China and India fell.[21] This reflected both the rapid growth of large-scale production of export crops by estates, and the growth of smallholder production. In addition foreign investors began to invest not just in agricultural estates, but also in the extraction of mineral resources including coal and petroleum. By 1938 Southeast Asian economies accounted for over half of all foreign direct investment in Asia. Colonial Indonesia was the largest recipient of foreign investment in absolute terms although in per capita terms it was surpassed by both British Malaya and the Philippines (Booth 2004: table 6; Lindblad 1998: 12–23).

It has frequently been argued that most colonies tend to trade disproportionately with the metropolitan power, and that most foreign investment also originates from the metropole. This "colonial" pattern of trade is supposed to have imposed a considerable cost on the colony in that it was not able to buy imports (usually manufactured consumer goods and capital equipment) in the cheapest market and sell their exports (usually primary products) in the dearest. While some colonies in Southeast Asia did trade extensively with the metropole, important changes were taking place by the early twentieth century. The Netherlands' share of Indonesia's export trade was under 40 per cent, as was France's of Indochinese trade (Booth 2007a: table 5.2). By 1939, only 14 per cent of Indonesia's exports were going to the Netherlands. Among the Southeast Asian colonies, only the Philippines had the expected high percentage of total trade with the USA by 1939. Even allowing for the fact that the Netherlands was not a major trading nation, and its industries were relatively undeveloped, its low and declining share of Indonesia's trade between 1900 and 1940 is rather remarkable. The major source countries for Indonesia's imports after 1900 were the UK, the USA, Germany and, increasingly, Japan. Japanese imports of cheap manufactures to most parts of Southeast Asia grew rapidly after 1920, with the notable exception of Indochina, where apparently it was deliberate French colonial policy to keep out Japanese products and increase France's share of the colony's imports.[22]

A frequent criticism of the export-led growth which occurred over the decades from 1870 to 1930 was that it did not lead to any appreciable improvement in living standards for the great majority of the population. This was in spite of the fact that in many parts of Southeast Asia indigenous populations responded vigorously to the opportunities that international trade presented, and rapidly increased their production of export crops as diverse as rice, corn, coffee, copra, rubber, pepper and spices. In some regions, real incomes and living standards did probably improve, but in some places per capita consumption of basic staples such as rice appears to have declined, especially in the interwar years (Booth 2007a: table 7.1). In addition many smallholder producers became increasingly indebted to rural money lenders, often Indian or Chinese.

There would appear to be several reasons for this paradox. In the first place, most Southeast Asian economies were penalized by deteriorating commodity terms of trade after 1913; the deterioration appears to have been especially severe in Indonesia, where the income terms of trade (the purchasing power of export earnings in terms of imports) also declined after 1928 (Booth 1998: table 2.1). A second reason for the failure of trade to promote more broadly based development in Southeast Asia concerns the size of the so-called "drain", or unrequited export surplus. It has been argued that this was unusually large in several parts of Southeast Asia after 1900, and was sustained at a high level in Indonesia for an entire century, from 1831–40 to 1931–40.[23] A third reason for the failure of trade to lead to growth concerns the investment policies of the government and the private sector. To the extent that both governments and private individuals preferred to use the increased income accruing from trade for consumption or for low-yielding investment, the longer run impact of trade on growth would be reduced.

I look at the issue of government investment expenditures in more detail below. As far as the drain argument is concerned, in many parts of the region the ratio of commodity imports to exports fell sharply after 1900, and in most countries were less than 75 per cent of exports. These export surpluses were used to fund considerable outward flows of profits. The standard colonial defence was that these profits represented a "fair return" on the foreign resources, both capital and expertise, which the undeveloped colonies had to import if they were to develop. The nationalist response was that they represented the monopoly profits of enterprises from the metropolitan countries which were granted protection from both domestic and foreign competitors, as well as payments to the civilian and military colonial bureaucracies whose presence benefited the colonies little, if at all.[24] In the rather special case of Burma, it has been argued that the "phenomenal" trade surplus was due, in part at least, to the very large population of Indian labourers, money lenders and other businessmen, who repatriated their earnings to India (Andrus 1948: 182). In addition the Burmese government made large contributions to the British Indian budget in Delhi which were not balanced by expenditures in Burma.[25]

After 1950, the share of Southeast Asia in all exports from the tropical world fell compared with 1937, and only began to increase again after 1980. The share of Burma, Indochina and Indonesia in total exports from Southeast Asia fell after 1950 while the share of British Malaya and Singapore, Thailand and the Philippines increased (Booth 2004: tables 3 and 4). These figures support Myint's assertion that after 1950, the countries of Southeast Asia divided into the inward-looking and the outward-looking groups (Myint 1967). The former reacted to what many nationalists saw as a colonial trade regime by adopting policies that penalized exporters and deterred foreign investment in export sectors. The latter group, while taxing exports, pursued exchange rate and investment policies which were more supportive of export production on the part of both smallholders and large foreign-owned companies.

The changing role of government

By the early years of the twentieth century, most Southeast Asian governments were deriving the bulk of their revenues from land taxes, and non-tax sources such as government charges and royalty payments and revenues from state monopolies, including opium. While some governments tried to reduce reliance on "vice taxes" such as those derived from sales of alcohol and narcotics, others continued to rely on them for a substantial part of government revenues.[26] The three components of British Malaya (Straits Settlements, Federated States, Unfederated States) were deriving a substantial proportion of all their revenues from opium and alcohol in the early decades of the twentieth century, although reliance did fall after 1920, and by 1938 the proportion of total revenues derived from opium revenues in the Straits Settlements and the Federated Malay States had fallen to under 10 per cent (Booth 2007b: table 1). Direct taxes on personal and corporate incomes were a small part of total revenues everywhere except in Indonesia and Burma, and to a lesser extent the Philippines.[27] Land taxes were important in some territories, although they required accurate cadastral information which was not available in many parts of Southeast Asia. Elsewhere cruder taxation devices such as head taxes remained important.[28]

The traditional view of the colonial state was that of a "nightwatchman", whose main functions were the collection of revenues and the maintenance of law and order. But by the early twentieth century, several governments in Southeast Asia were taking a much more proactive view of their responsibilities. The Dutch launched the "ethical policy" in 1901, which emphasized the development of rice agriculture through improved irrigation, expanded access to education and greater movement of people from the densely settled islands of Java and Bali to land settlement projects in Sumatra and Sulawesi.[29] French policy in Indochina placed great emphasis on *mise en valeur* through infrastructure development, while in the Philippines, the American government saw "native upliftment" as the main justification for its colonial mission, a mission which was far from popular in the USA.[30] The Americans saw their role as preparing the Philippines for self-government, and placed special emphasis on expanding access to education. Even the supposedly laissez-faire British recognized that the full development of the agricultural potential of Peninsular Malaysia would require heavy investment in roads, railways, ports and electrification, and substantial sums were spent on these sectors after 1900.

By 1930, there was considerable variation both in government expenditures per capita, and in the breakdown of government expenditures by sector. In 1929, government expenditures per capita (in dollar terms) ranged from 29 dollars in the Federated Malay States to three dollars in Vietnam (Booth 2007b: table 4). A comparative study carried out by an American official in the Philippines in 1931 found that the Philippines was devoting around one-third of total expenditures to education and health, and around 18 per cent to public works and agriculture, and most of the balance to administration and debt service. In the Netherlands Indies a much greater share, around 77 per cent, was going on administration, defence and debt service, and a correspondingly small proportion on health and education. The Federated Malay States, which had by far the largest expenditure in per capita terms, was devoting around half the budget to education, health, public works and agricultural development.[31]

The very different patterns of budgetary allocation that were clear by the 1920s in Southeast Asia were reflected in very different out-turns regarding expenditure on both infrastructure and social welfare. By the 1930s, Java and Peninsular Malaya had extensive road and rail networks; in terms of kilometres of road per unit of area these two regions compared very favourably with the Japanese colonies of Taiwan and Korea. Other parts of Southeast Asia, including independent Thailand, were by the 1930s less well endowed with infrastructure.[32] In Thailand the government devoted considerable resources to railway construction, mainly for defence purposes, but largely neglected road building. In the Philippines, more emphasis was given to road development. But the roads and railways which were constructed were often designed to benefit foreign enterprises, and their benefits to local populations were limited, especially when feeder roads linking settlements to railheads and main roads were not constructed.[33] Virtually everywhere, provision of electricity and piped water was restricted to urban areas, and usually only to large-scale industry and to the more affluent residential neighbourhoods.

By the late 1930s, there was also considerable variation among the various colonies in Southeast Asia, and in independent Thailand, in infant mortality, and crude death rates, as well as in educational enrolments and per capita GDP (Table 3.4). Infant mortality remained high in Burma, Java and Indochina, although in all these colonies there had been some decline since the turn of the twentieth century, mainly due to government public health initiatives. It was lower in the Philippines and British Malaya; in both these colonies it was little different from Taiwan.[34] But government health programmes often tended to be limited in terms of geographical reach, and also in terms of ethnic group (Booth 2012: 162–71). Typically, by the latter part of the 1930s, infant mortality rates among European children in Southeast Asia were only slightly higher than those in West Europe and the USA. Among babies and children of the Chinese, mortality rates were considerably higher than among Europeans, but lower than among the indigenous populations. While babies and children in urban areas usually had better access to medical care than those in rural areas, in some urban areas infant mortality rates remained very high. On the basis of the 1931 census in British Malaya, Vlieland (1932: 110) found that infant mortality rates in urban Singapore were considerably higher than in the more rural Federated Malay States. This reflected the poor housing and overcrowding which increased the risk of premature death for many babies and children in Singapore at that time. Overcrowding and poor housing in Singapore, and most other cities in the region, became a major challenge for most governments in the post-1950 era.

The advent of political independence inevitably raised expectations on the part of indigenous populations across Asia, who looked to their governments to provide improved infrastructure and

Table 3.4 Development indicators: East and South East Asia, late 1930s

Country	Per capita GDP, 1938 (1990 inter national dollars)[a]	Infant mortality rates	Crude death rates	Educational enrolments as % of total population
Philippines	1,542	139	23	11.54
Malaya[b]	1,426	147	21	7.76
Taiwan	1,318	142	21	11.36
Indonesia	1,171	225–250	28	4.01
Thailand	826	n/a	22	10.65
Burma	740	232	30	5.45
Indochina	n/a	190	24	2.47

Sources: GDP data: Maddison (2003: 182–3). Educational enrolments: Furnivall (1943: 111). Data on infant mortality rates and crude death rates for Indonesia: Nitisastro (1970: 113, table 39) and refer to Java only; Philippines: Zablan (1978: 100–5); Taiwan: Barclay (1954: 146, 161); Thailand: Sompop (1989: 35); Vietnam: Banens (2000: 36–7); crude death rates refer to Cochinchina; infant mortality rates refer to Hanoi only. Burma: Sundrum (1957: 20, 52); British Malaya: Evans (1939: table XV); crude death rates: Palmore et al. (1975: table 4.1). Educational enrolments from Furnivall (1943).

Notes:

[a] For the Philippines, Malaya, Taiwan and Indonesia, GDP data are three-year averages centered on 1938. For Thailand and Burma the data refer to 1938 only.

[b] GDP and crude death rate data refer to the territory covered by modern Malaysia (British Malaya plus Sabah and Sarawak less Singapore). Infant mortality rates refer to the Federated Malay States only. Educational enrolments refer to British Malaya including Singapore.

better services including health and education. In many parts of the region, infant mortality rates did decline after 1950 and educational enrolments improved.[35] Socialist ideas had considerable influence, and economic planning in some form or other was adopted by most governments. But it often proved difficult to raise sufficient revenues to fund ambitious government spending programmes, especially after the impact of the Korean War on commodity prices subsided in the mid-1950s. By 1954 government revenues per capita in real terms were lower in both Indonesia and the Philippines than in 1938, and they were only slightly higher in Burma and the Malayan Federation (Booth 2013: table 7). The problem was especially acute in Indonesia, where per capita GDP still had not returned to its pre-1942 peak by 1960, and successive governments had difficulty increasing tax and non-tax revenues. Persistent government deficits were funded by borrowing from the central bank, with inevitable consequences for inflation.

Conclusions

A number of conclusions can be drawn from this survey. The first is that economic growth, in the sense of increasing per capita GDP, does appear to have occurred in Southeast Asia between 1870 and 1940. Paradoxically, the slowest growth was in Thailand, the country that managed to remain free of direct colonial control. The second conclusion is that the growth that occurred did lead to structural change in the economies of the region. Industrial growth did occur, as did growth in trade, transport, financial services and public services. To a limited extent, employment opportunities outside agriculture did increase for the indigenous populations of the region even though many managerial, technical and administrative jobs were monopolized by nationals of the colonial power, other Europeans and Americans, and migrant Asians, who were mainly Chinese and Indians. The third main conclusion is that export growth played a crucial role in driving economic growth. Increasingly, not only large foreign-owned companies but also millions of smallholder producers became involved in the production of crops for export. While this did increase their cash incomes, it also made them more vulnerable to the vagaries of world markets for tropical products.

A fourth conclusion is that governments, far from adopting a laissez-faire, or "nightwatchman", role, were, by the early twentieth century, taking a more proactive role in building infrastructure and in the provision of educational and health facilities for the indigenous populations. The extent to which government raised revenues and spent those revenues on activities that would now be thought of as developmental varied considerably, both over time and between colonies. But there can be no doubt that governments did take an increasing role in taxing and spending in the first part of the twentieth century, and that the results were obvious not just in terms of infrastructure but also in terms of access to educational and health facilities. By the 1930s, several governments were taking a more activist role in promoting industrial growth.

A fifth conclusion relates to the impact of economic growth and structural change on living standards in Southeast Asia. Here the evidence suggests that the outcomes varied considerably. In the Philippines the emphasis of the American administration on "uplifting the natives" paid off in terms of access to education, and to health care. By the late 1930s infant mortality rates were lower than in most other parts of Southeast Asia, and probably lower than in most other parts of Asia and Africa, and literacy rates were higher The record in other parts of Southeast Asia was much more patchy. By the 1930s, migrants from China and India comprised the majority of the population in British Malaya, and were a significant minority elsewhere. The Chinese in particular often had better access to both educational and health facilities, which gave them considerable advantages in the post-independence era.

The last conclusion relates to the legacy of colonialism for post-colonial governments. After independence most countries in Southeast Asia had to struggle with rising expectations from their populations in terms of provision of public goods, while at the same time dealing with the consequences of the 1940s on economic output. Per capita GDP was lower in most parts of the region in 1950 than a decade earlier and in several countries recovery was slow. In Burma and Indonesia, governments responded to the economic challenges of independence by adopting policies that discriminated against exports and discouraged investment, both foreign and domestic. It was hardly surprising that popular resentments boiled over into social unrest and open rebellion. They were usually suppressed by military force, but the consequences of these tensions persist until the present day.

Notes

1 These densely settled regions often accounted for a high proportion of the total population; for example in 1930 Java's population was estimated to be over 40 million, compared with only 19 million in the rest of the Netherlands Indies, although Java had only 7 per cent of the land area.

2 For an account of Southeast Asian development in the "age of commerce" see Reid (1993). In another essay, Reid (2001) has argued that after 1700, the percentage of the population in urban and non-agricultural occupations in Southeast Asia probably contracted.

3 For a discussion of the Bowring Treaty in the context of the Thai economy in the 1850s see Ingram (1971: 33–5) and Phongpaichit and Baker (1995: 98–9).

4 Maddison's figures on economic growth in Thailand are taken from Sompop (1989: 251).

5 A valuable discussion of growth and technical change in the world sugar industry is given in Evenson and Kislev (1975: chapter 3). After the mid-1920s, falls in world prices meant that the real value of yields per hectare fell compared with the 1921–5 peak (Booth 1988: 222–3). For a discussion of the evolution of the sugar industry in Java in the Dutch colonial period, see Boomgaard (1988).

6 The classic discussion of the expansion of rice cultivation in Burma is by Adas (1974). See also Owen (1971) and Siamwalla (1972).

7 For an extensive discussion of the reasons for the increase in Japanese exports to Asia, and the response by colonial governments, see the papers in Sugiyama and Guerrero (1994). See also Booth (2003).

8 Industrialization was harder to achieve in open and land-abundant economies such as peninsular Malaysia, where exports of natural resource exports kept the exchange rate too high to make most domestic manufacturing profitable (Huff 2002). In Indonesia, a cotton textile industry only developed in the 1930s after controls were placed on imports from Japan (van der Eng 2013).

9 Useful overviews of industrialization in Southeast Asia before 1940 can be found in Shepherd (1941) and Mitchell (1942). For additional material on Indonesia, see van Oorschot (1956: 856), for Burma, see Spate (1941: 78), and for Indochina see Robequain (1944: 303). Norlund (1991) discusses the case of Vietnam.

10 An analysis of the 1939 census data for the Philippines is given in Kurihara (1945: 15–22). A valuable analysis of the 1930 census data on employment can be found in Mertens (1978).

11 See Booth (2007a: tables 6.2, 6.3 and 6.4). It is striking that indigenous workers comprised a larger proportion of the labour force employed in government and the professions in Indonesia, the Philippines and Burma than was the case in Korea and Taiwan in the 1930s, where Japanese nationals were more dominant.

12 For an analysis of agricultural "by-employment" in colonial Java, see in particular Boomgaard (1991).

13 Given the increasing importance of wage labour as a source of income after 1900 for the indigenous populations, as well as for migrants, one might ask why worker organizations were so slow to form in colonial Southeast Asia. For a discussion of this see Thompson (1947), especially chapter 1.

14 The population of China actually fell between 1850 and 1870 as a result of wars and civil strife; the estimated population in 1850 of 412 million was only regained in 1905; in India population grew but at a slow rate. See Maddison (2003: 160).

15 For a comprehensive discussion of health policies in colonial Malaya, see Manderson (1996).

16 See Huff and Caggiano (2007: table 1). On the impact of labour migration on labour markets in British Malaya and the Netherlands Indies, see Kaur (2004: part 2).

17 The methods used by estates companies to induce labour to move, and the impact on the welfare of workers, were highly controversial especially in colonial Indonesia. For a review of the issues in Indonesia, see Houben et al. (1999) and Kaur (2004: chapters 4 and 5).

18 A classic discussion of land tenure issues in Southeast Asia at the end of the colonial era is given by Pelzer (1945). See also Booth (2007a: chapter 3). Valuable discussions of land tenure issues in colonial Malaya are given in Lim (1977: chapter 4) and Sundaram (1988: chapter 4).

19 Sundrum (1957: 121) and Baxter (1941: 21).

20 An overview of urbanization in Southeast Asia before 1950 is given in Huff (2012).

21 See Booth (2004: table 2). The growth of exports from British Malaya was particularly rapid; see Drabble (2000: 39).

22 For further discussion of Japanese exports to Southeast Asia in the interwar years, and of the response of different colonies see Booth (2003).

23 See Booth (1998: 210–14) for a discussion of the Indonesian current account surplus. For an alternative view which argues that current account surpluses were less damaging to the Indonesian economy, see van der Eng (1993). Further discussion of the drain in Southeast Asia can be found in Golay (1976).

24 For an argument along these lines in the case of British Malaya, see Khor (1983), especially chapters 4 and 5.

25 On the provincial contract system see in particular Shein Maung et al. (1969). For an estimate of the "imperial drain" as a proportion of national income in Burma, see Booth (2007b: table 9).

26 An account of the differing attitudes to revenues from opium in different colonial regimes can be found in Foster (2003). Further discussion of the role of opium in government revenues in colonial Southeast Asia is given in Booth (2013).

27 For a discussion of the evolution of the fiscal system in Indonesia in the last part of the Dutch colonial era, see Booth (1990). An overview of the attempts by the American administration to reform the fiscal system in the Philippines is given in Luton (1971).

28 In the Philippines, the *cedula* was a head tax levied in the Spanish era which became a "kind of personal registration and identity certificate" in the American period. Like most head taxes it was regressive in its incidence (Doeppers 1984: 57). In Vietnam, the French implemented a mixture of head taxes and land taxes in rural areas; most authorities considered the resulting system to be highly regressive. See Popkin (1979: 142–9).

29 The literature on the ethical policy is extensive; good introductions are given in Boomgaard (1993) and Cribb (1993).

30 On the motivations of American policy in the Philippines see Hutchcroft (2000). Also useful are May (1980) and Adas (1998).

31 Schwulst (1932: 42–59). Schwulst's main findings are summarized in Booth (2007b: table 7). In spite of the evidence that both the Straits Settlements and the Federated Malay States had higher per capita expenditures than other colonies, critics argued that the British authorities were running what were still in effect nightwatchman states. Emerson (1964: 306) argued that in the Straits Settlements "the government has not interpreted its function more broadly than in terms of the police power". Emerson was especially critical that the government did not assume "any responsibility for the adequacy of the lives of its subjects", beyond basic sanitation and "a minor degree of education". Huff's more recent study argued that the colonial government in Singapore "conceived of its role as primarily to enforce law and order and secure property rights" (Huff 1994: 168).

32 Booth (2007a: table 4.7). For an analysis of Thailand's road and rail building programmes, see Andrews (1935: 390).

33 For a critical discussion of infrastructure development in colonial Malaya, see Kaur (1985), especially chapter 6.

34 An attempt to construct a Human Development Index for the 1930s is given in Metzer (1998: 57). Of the 36 countries which he ranked in terms of per capita GDP, literacy, educational enrolments and life expectancy, the Philippines was twenty-second. This was higher than Thailand and India (the only other Asian countries ranked), and higher than any Latin American country except Chile.

35 In Indonesia, many local governments built schools and health clinics from local taxes in cash, kind and labour. People were willing to pay taxes for specific projects whose benefit accrued to local people. Paauw (1960) discusses these local revenues in more detail.

References

Adas, Michael (1974) *The Burma Delta: Economic Development and Social Change on an Asian Rice Frontier, 1852–1941*, Madison: University of Wisconsin Press.

Adas, Michael (1998) "Improving on the civilising mission? Assumptions of United States exceptionalism in the colonisation of the Philippines", *Itinerario*, 22(4): 44–66.

Andrews, James M. (1935) *Siam: 2nd Rural Survey 1934–1935*, Bangkok: Bangkok Times Press.

Andrus, J.R. (1948) *Burmese Economic Life*, Stanford, CA: Stanford University Press.

Banens, Maks (2000) "Vietnam: a reconstruction of its 20th century population history", in Jean-Pascal Bassino, Jean-Dominique Giacometti and K. Odaka (eds), *Quantitative Economic History of Vietnam 1900–1990*, Tokyo: Hitotsubashi University, Institute of Economic Research.

Barclay, George (1954) *Colonial Development and Population in Taiwan*, Princeton, NJ: Princeton University Press.

Baxter, James (1941) *Report on Indian Migration*, Rangoon: Government Printing and Stationery.

Boomgaard, Peter (1988) "Treacherous cane: the Java sugar industry between 1914 and 1940", in Bill Albert and Adrian Graves (eds), *The World Sugar Economy in War and Depression 1914–40*, London: Routledge.

Boomgaard, Peter (1991) "The non-agricultural side of an agricultural economy Java, 1500–1900", in Paul Alexander, Peter Boomgaard and Ben White (eds), *In the Shadow of Agriculture: Non-farm Activities in the Javanese Economy, Past and Present*, Amsterdam: Royal Tropical Institute.

Boomgaard, Peter (1993) "Upliftment down the drain? Effects of welfare measures in late colonial Indonesia", in Jan-Paul Dirkse, Frans Husken and Mario Rutten (eds), *Development and Social Welfare: Indonesia's Experiences Under the New Order*, Leiden: KITLV Press.

Booth, Anne (1988) *Agricultural Development in Indonesia*, Sydney: Allen and Unwin.

Booth, Anne (1990) "The evolution of fiscal policy and the role of government in the colonial economy", in Anne Booth, W.J. O'Malley and Anna Weidemann (eds), *Indonesian Economic History in the Dutch Colonial Era*, New Haven, CT: Yale University Southeast Asia Studies, Monograph Series 35.

Booth, Anne (1998) *The Indonesian Economy in the Nineteenth and Twentieth Centuries: A History of Missed Opportunities*, London: Macmillan.

Booth, Anne (2003) "Four colonies and a kingdom: a comparison of fiscal, trade and exchange rate policies in South East Asia in the 1930s", *Modern Asian Studies*, 37(2): 429–60.

Booth, Anne (2004) "Linking, de-linking and re-linking: Southeast Asia in the global economy in the twentieth century", *Australian Economic History Review*, 44(1): 35–51.

Booth, Anne (2007a) *Colonial Legacies: Economic and Social Development in East and Southeast Asia*, Honolulu: University of Hawaii Press.

Booth, Anne (2007b) "Night watchman, extractive or developmental state? Some evidence from late colonial South East Asia", *Economic History Review*, 60(2): 241–66.

Booth, Anne (2012) "Measuring living standards in different colonial systems: some evidence from South East Asia, 1900–1942", *Modern Asian Studies*, 46(5): 1145–81.

Booth, Anne (2013) "Colonial revenue policies and the impact of the transition to independence in South East Asia", *Bijdragen tot de Taal-, Land- en Volkenkunde*, 169: 1–31.

Creutzberg, P. (1975) *Changing Economy in Indonesia, Volume 1, Indonesia's Export Crops, 1816–1940*, The Hague: Martinus Nijhoff.

Cribb, Robert (1993) "Development policy in the early 20th century", in Jan-Paul Dirkse, Frans Husken and Mario Rutten (eds), *Development and Social Welfare: Indonesia's Experiences under the New Order*, Leiden: KITLV Press.

Doeppers, Daniel F. (1984) *Manila 1900–1941: Social Change in a Late Colonial Metropolis*, Manila: Ateneo de Manila University Press.

Drabble, John H. (2000) *An Economic History of Malaysia c.1800–1990: The Transition to Modern Economic Growth*, Basingstoke: Macmillan.

Emerson, Rupert (1964) *Malaysia, A Study in Direct and Indirect Rule*, Kuala Lumpur: University of Malaya Press, reprint of 1937 edition.

Eng, Pierre van der (1993) "Southeast Asia: the colonial drain from Indonesia", *Economics Division Working Papers 93/1*, Canberra: Australian National University.

Eng, Pierre van der (2002) "Indonesia's growth performance in the 20th century", in A. Maddison, D. Rao and W. Shepherd (eds), *The Asian Economies in the Twentieth Century*, Cheltenham: Edward Elgar.

Eng, Pierre van der (2013) "Why didn't colonial Indonesia have a competitive cotton textile industry?", *Modern Asian Studies*, 47(3): 1019–54.

Evans, L.W. (1939) *Federated Malay States, Report of the Registrar General of Births and Deaths for the Year 1938*, Kuala Lumpur: FMS Government Press.

Evenson, Robert E. and Y. Kislev (1975) *Agricultural Research and Productivity*, New Haven, CT: Yale University Press.

Foster, Anne L. (2003) "Models for governing: opium and colonial policies in Southeast Asia, 1898–1910", in Julian Go and Anne L. Foster (eds), *The American Colonial State in the Philippines: Global Perspectives*, Durham, NC: Duke University Press.

Furnivall, J.S. (1943) *Educational Progress in Southeast Asia*, New York: Institute of Pacific Relations.

Furnivall. J.S. (1948) *Colonial Policy and Practice: A Comparative Study of Burma and Netherlands India*, Cambridge: Cambridge University Press.

Golay, Frank (1976) "Southeast Asia: the 'colonial drain' revisited", in C.D. Cowan and O.W. Wolters (eds), *Southeast Asian History and Historiography*, Ithaca, NY: Cornell University Press.

Grajdanzev, Andrew J. (1942) *Formosa Today: An Analysis of the Economic Development and Strategic Importance of Japan's Tropical Colony*, New York: Institute of Pacific Relations.

Grajdanzev, Andrew J. (1944) *Modern Korea*, New York: Institute of Pacific Relations.

Hooley, Richard (2005) "American economic policy in the Philippines, 1902–1940: exploring a dark age in colonial statistics", *Journal of Asian Economics* 16: 464–88.

Houben, Vincent J.H., J. Thomas Lindblad and others (eds) (1999) *Coolie Labour in Colonial Indonesia: A Study of Labour Relations in the Outer Islands, c. 1900–1940*, Wiesbaden: Harrassowitz Verlag.

Huff, W.G. (1994) *The Economic Growth of Singapore: Trade and Development in the Twentieth Century*, Cambridge: Cambridge University Press.

Huff, W.G. (2002) "Boom-or-bust commodities in pre-World War II Malaya", *Journal of Economic History*, 62: 1074–115.

Huff, Gregg (2012) "Export-led growth, gateway cities and urban systems development in pre-World War II Southeast Asia", *Journal of Development Studies*, 48(10): 1431–52.

Huff, Gregg and Giovanni Caggiano (2007) "Globalization, immigration and Lewisian elastic labor in pre-World War II Southeast Asia", *Journal of Economic History*, 67(1): 1–36.

Hutchcroft, Paul D. (2000) "Colonial masters, national politicos, and provincial lords: central authority and local autonomy in the American Philippines, 1900–1913", *Journal of Asian Studies*, 59(2): 277–306.

Ingram, J. (1971) *Economic Change in Thailand, 1850–1970*, Kuala Lumpur: Oxford University Press.

Kaur, Amarjit (1985) *Bridge and Barrier: Transport and Communications in Colonial Malaya 1870–1957*, Singapore: Oxford University Press.

Kaur, Amarjit (2004) *Wage Labour in Southeast Asia since 1840: Globalisation, the International Division of Labour and Labour Transformations*, Basingstoke: Palgrave Macmillan.

Khor, Kok-Peng (1983) *The Malaysian Economy: Structures and Dependence*, Kuala Lumpur: Marican.

Kurihara, Kenneth (1945) *Labor in the Philippine Economy*, Stanford, CA: Stanford University Press.

Lim, Teck-Ghee (1977) *Peasants and their Agricultural Economy in Colonial Malaya 1874–1941*, Kuala Lumpur: Oxford University Press.

Lindblad, J. Thomas (1998) *Foreign Investment in Southeast Asia in the Twentieth Century*, Basingstoke: Macmillan.

Luton, Harry (1971) "American internal revenue policy in the Philippines to 1916", in Norman G. Owen (ed.), *Compadre Colonialism: Studies on the Philippines under American Rule*, Ann Arbor: Michigan Papers on South and Southeast Asia, Number 3.

Maddison, Angus (2003) *The World Economy: Historical Statistics*, Paris: OECD Development Centre.

Manderson, Lenore (1996) *Sickness and the State: Health and Illness in Colonial Malaya, 1870–1940*, Cambridge: Cambridge University Press.

May, Glenn Anthony (1980) *Social Engineering in the Philippines: The Aims, Execution, and Impact of American Colonial Policy, 1900–1913*, Westport, CT: Greenwood Press.

Mertens, Walter (1978) "Population census data on agricultural activities in Indonesia", *Majalah Demografi Indonesia*, No. 9: 9–53.

Metzer, Jacob (1998) *The Divided Economy of Mandatory Palestine*, Cambridge: Cambridge University Press.

Mitchell, Kate L. (1942) *An Economic Survey of the Pacific Area, Part III, Industrialization of the Western Pacific Area*, New York: Institute of Pacific Relations.

Mizoguchi, Toshiyuki and Mataji Umemura (eds) (1988) *Basic Economic Statistics of Former Japanese Colonies, 1895–1938, Estimates and Findings*, Tokyo: Toyo Keizai Shinposhain.

Myint, Hla (1967) "The inward and outward-looking countries of Southeast Asia", *Malayan Economic Review*, 12: 1–13.

Nitisastro, Widjojo (1970) *Population Trends in Indonesia*, Ithaca, NY: Cornell University Press.

Norlund, Irene (1991) "The French Empire, the colonial state in Vietnam and economic policy: 1885–1940", *Australian Economic History Review*, 21(1): 72–89.

Oorschot, H.J. van (1956) *De Ontwikkeling van de Nijverheid in Indonesie*, Den Haag and Bandung: W. van Hoeve.

Owen, Norman (1971) "The rice industry in mainland Southeast Asia, 1850–1914", *Journal of the Siam Society*, 59(2): 79–143.

Paauw, Douglas S. (1960) *Financing Economic Development: The Indonesian Case*, Glencoe, IL: The Free Press.

Palmore, James A., Ramesh Chander and Dorothy Fernandez (1975) "The demographic situation in Malaysia", *East–West Population Institute, Reprint Series 70*, Honolulu: University of Hawaii.

Pelzer, Karl (1945) *Pioneer Settlement in the Asiatic Tropics*, New York: American Geographical Society.

Phongpaichit, Pasuk and Chris Baker (1995) *Thailand: Economy and Politics*, Kuala Lumpur: Oxford University Press.

Popkin, Samuel L. (1979) *The Rational Peasant: The Political Economy of Rural Society in Vietnam*, Berkeley: University of California Press.

Reid, Anthony (1993) *Southeast Asia in the Age of Commerce 1450–1680, Volume 2: Expansion and Crisis*, New Haven, CT: Yale University Press.

Reid, Anthony (2001) "South-East Asian population history and the colonial impact", in T.J. Liu, James Lee, David Sven Reher, Osamu Saito and Wang Feng (eds), *Asian Population History*, Oxford: Oxford University Press.

Resnick, Stephen A. (1970) "The decline of rural industry under export expansion: a comparison among Burma, Philippines and Thailand, 1870–1938", *Journal of Economic History*, 30(1): 51–73.

Robequain, Charles (1944) *The Economic Development of French Indo-China*, London: Oxford University Press.

Saito, T. and Lee Kin Kiong (1999) *Statistics on the Burmese Economy: The 19th and 20th Centuries*, Singapore: Institute of Southeast Asian Studies.

Schwulst, E.B. (1932) "Report on the budget and financial policies of French Indo-China, Siam, Federated Malay States and the Netherlands East Indies", in *Report of the Governor General of the Philippine Islands 1931*, Washington, DC: United States Government Printing Office.

Shein Maung, Myint Myint Thant and Tin Tin Sein (1969) "'Provincial Contract System' of British Indian Empire, in relation to Burma – a case of fiscal exploitation", *Journal of the Burma Research Society*, LIII: 1–27.

Shepherd, Jack (1941) *Industry in South East Asia*, New York: Institute of Pacific Relations.

Siamwalla, Ammar (1972) "Land, labour and capital in three rice-growing deltas of Southeast Asia 1800–1940", *Centre Discussion Paper No, 150*, New Haven, CT: Yale University Economic Growth Center.

Sompop Manarungsan (1989) "Economic development of Thailand, 1850–1950", PhD Dissertation, State University of Groningen.

Spate, O.H. (1941) "Beginnings of industrialisation in Burma", *Economic Geography* 17: 75–92.

Statistics Department (1939) *Malayan Yearbook 1939*, Singapore: Straits Settlements and FMS Department of Statistics.

Sugimoto, Ichiro (2011) *Economic Growth of Singapore in the Twentieth Century: Historical GDP Estimates and Empirical Investigations*, Singapore: World Scientific Publishing.

Sugiyama, Shinya and M.C. Guerrero (eds) (1994) *International Commercial Rivalry in Southeast Asia in the Interwar Period, Monograph 39*, New Haven, CT: Yale Southeast Asian Studies.

Suh, Sang-Chul (1978) *Growth and Structural Changes in the Korean Economy, 1910–1940*, Cambridge, MA: Harvard University Press.

Sundaram, Jomo Kwame (1988) *A Question of Class: Capital, the State, and Uneven Development in Malaya*, New York: Monthly Review Press.

Sundrum, R.M. (1957) "Population statistics of Burma", *Economics Research Project, Statistical Paper No. 3*, Rangoon: Economics, Statistics and Commerce Departments, University of Rangoon.

Thompson, Virginia (1947) *Labor Problems in Southeast Asia*, New Haven, CT: Yale University Press.

Vlieland, C.A. (1932) *British Malaya: A Report on the 1931 Census and on Certain Problems of Vital Statistics*, London: Crown Agents.

World Bank (1976) *World Tables 1976*, Baltimore, MD: Johns Hopkins University Press for the World Bank.

Zablan, Z.C. (1978) "Trends and differential in mortality", in *Population of the Philippines, Country Monograph Series No. 5*, Bangkok, United Nations Economic Commission for Asia and the Pacific.

4

Lucky countries?

Internal and external sources of Southeast Asian growth since 1970

Tracy ThuTrang Phung, Ian Coxhead, and Chang Lian

UNIVERSITY OF WISCONSIN-MADISON

Economic growth in East and Southeast Asia

Among developing economies, East and Southeast Asia stand out as the most dynamically growing regions. With just a few exceptions, incomes in the region have risen sharply relative to world averages over the course of several decades (Table 4.1).

This remarkable performance has inspired many explanations.[1] Growth of labor and capital endowments has clearly played an important role (Young 1994, 1995; Krugman 1994; Collins and Bosworth 1996), as has human capital accumulation. Macroeconomic stability has attracted much attention, and so has the degree to which the region's economies have been open to international trade and factor flows. Other studies (including the World Bank's influential 1993 study *East Asian Miracle*, hereafter *EAM*) assert that governments in the region have intervened systematically and through multiple channels to foster development. Finally, there is widespread, though informal, recognition that the exceptional performance of Asia's "miracle" economies has been exported to other regional countries through trade, factor market linkages, and less tangible influences such as the demonstration effects of apparently successful development policies.

A number of prominent studies have used growth accounting or regression techniques to infer sources of Asian growth. *EAM* regressed growth from 1965 to 1990 on primary factor and human capital endowments and found that for the eight "high-performing Asian economies" (HPAEs),[2] physical capital accumulation and primary education contributed the most to explained growth rates. Collins and Bosworth (1996) found that most growth in developing Asia was accounted for by factor accumulation and policies, with virtually no role for productivity growth. Radelet et al. (2001) found that a combination of initial conditions, economic policies and demographic changes account for East Asia's rapid growth, with an especially important role played by success in export growth, especially of labor-intensive manufactured products. In a significant advance for the quality of inference, Lee and Hong (2010) accounted for endogeneity in key explanatory variables of the standard growth model (their paper also supplies a good survey of earlier work). They found that capital accumulation has been the key driver of regional growth, with much more modest contributions from labor force, human capital and TFP growth. In simulations based on their econometric results they also found that policy reforms relating to property rights,

Table 4.1 Average GDP per capita growth rates by region (%)

Region	1970–89	1990–2010	1970–2010
East Asia and Pacific (developing only)	5.45	7.47	6.48
Europe and Central Asia (developing only)	n/a	1.34	n/a.
Latin America and Caribbean (developing only)	1.49	1.65	1.57
Middle East and North Africa (developing only)	1.46	2.25	1.85
Sub-Saharan Africa (developing only)	0.31	0.78	0.55
South Asia	1.84	4.25	3.08
Southeast Asia (exc. Brunei, East Timor and Myanmar)	4.01	3.77	3.89
Cambodia, Laos, Vietnam	*2.09*	*5.75*	*5.05*
Northeast Asia (China, Hong Kong, Japan, Korea)	6.39	8.32	7.38
Hong Kong, Japan, Korea	*4.09*	*2.02*	*3.03*
China	*6.76*	*9.22*	*8.02*

Source: World Development Indicators.

research and development (R&D) and education have the potential to raise growth rates significantly among currently lagging economies.

These studies, along with many others, are built upon modifications to the standard Solow aggregate growth model with human capital (Mankiw et al. 1992). They also share some common features. First, in regression analyses from cross-country data they typically find an "East Asia" (i.e., Northeast and Southeast Asia) dummy variable to be positive and significant. This indicates a higher *ceteris paribus* rate of growth in developing Asia, but does not explain it.[3] Second, none of them explore more deeply the possibility that growth in Asian economies might differ in a more structural fashion – that is, they do not test the assumption of homogeneity in slope parameters. Third, although narratives of East Asian growth invariably focus on international trade and factor flows as perhaps the most distinctive features of the region's experience, empirical treatment of openness remains quite cursory. Most studies that do address openness measure it by the Sachs–Warner index (Sachs and Warner 1995).[4] An earlier literature, and a minority of contemporary studies, relies on the ratio of trade to GDP, an obviously endogenous variable.[5] Although strongly associated with growth, this index has been criticized as a weak measure of underlying trade policies (Rodriguez and Rodrik 2001). Fourth, to our knowledge no existing study takes account of potential growth spillovers among countries, in spite of the prominent role these play in regional growth narratives.[6] All in all, these limitations suggest that despite much prior empirical work, there is still scope to learn more about the Asian growth experience.

The value of another empirical growth exercise lies in the lessons it might convey. Although they are often treated as a single region in global growth studies, Northeast and Southeast Asian economies have followed quite distinct growth trajectories. Growth rates in Northeast Asia have slowed in the last two decades, while in Southeast Asia – and notably in the poorest transitional economies of Vietnam, Laos and Cambodia – growth has accelerated. Does the same model that explained Northeast Asian growth also account for that of the later-emerging economies? The rapid growth of the Southeast Asian economies is all the more surprising when considered in light of predictions from globally prominent cross-country studies of growth. Tropical locations and natural resource wealth, both features of Southeast Asian economies, were identified as having a strong negative association with growth in a series of studies by Sachs and Warner (1995, 2001). Weaknesses in the institutions of political and economic governance have likewise received notable attention as restraints on growth (Acemoglu et al. 2005; Acemoglu and Robinson

2012), and the Southeast Asian economies other than Singapore receive only fair to poor scores in international rankings of institutional quality. What factors helped the region's economies to overcome these impediments?

To answer questions of this kind, we estimate a growth model on international data and then test for differences in parameters for countries within and outside Southeast Asia. Rather than conduct a completely open-ended search, we consider determinants of Southeast Asian growth that have received the greatest attention in past debates. These are capital and human capital accumulation, macroeconomic stability, openness to trade and investment, and the spillover effects of growth, both in the global economy and during booms in two large regional economies: Japan in the 1980s, and China since the 1990s.

We use data from 1971 to 2010 covering a sample of 139 countries. Eight out of 11 Southeast Asian countries are included: Cambodia, Indonesia, Laos, Malaysia, Philippines, Singapore, Thailand and Vietnam. The other three, Brunei Darussalam, East Timor and Myanmar are excluded for lack of reliable data. In a departure from existing studies, we use an index of openness that is explicitly based on trade and other closely related policies, we incorporate measures of growth spillovers as described above, and we test the interaction of openness and spillovers. Finally, we evaluate the robustness of our results in different model specifications and subsets of the data. Based on these estimates, we draw implications and policy lessons for the region's future development, especially the contributions to growth of openness to international trade and investment.

The remainder of the chapter is organized as follows. The following section provides a very brief review of the role of openness in growth theory and empirical applications. The next section then surveys the Asian economic growth experience and discusses possible determinants of Southeast Asia's rapid growth. This is followed by a presentation of the data, growth models and estimation results, and interpretation of the findings. The study concludes with a summary of the analysis and implications of our findings.

Openness and economic growth

Openness

The measurement of openness, and of the links between openness and growth, has always been controversial. This is partially due to the variation in the ways economists define and measure openness (Baldwin 2003). Of many measures, the Sachs–Warner index referred to above has proved most popular in empirical work. As a measure of trade policy interventions, however, it is both very blunt and also demonstrably flawed. Rodriguez and Rodrik (2001) have shown that just two of the index's five components – the existence of a state monopoly on the country's main exports, and a black market premium of more than 20 percent – are responsible for nearly all of its explanatory power in cross-country regressions. These two variables do not cover variation in tariff and non-tariff barriers, let alone in a way that connects to growth theory.

Another problem for empirical growth studies is that the Solow growth model has no explicit role for trade and other international interactions. There were substantial theoretical advances on this front in the early 1990s (e.g., Rebelo 1992; Lee 1993), but while these models identified *ex ante* mechanisms, they were not linked to empirical tests. More recently, Estevadeordal and Taylor (2008) have integrated openness into the Solow model in a manner that is both consistent with neoclassical growth theory and also rich in empirically testable propositions. The main features of their model can be summarized as follows. Assume that the aggregate production function is of Cobb–Douglass form and includes intermediate inputs, which are combined with a primary factor composite such that $Y = A(K^\alpha L^{1-\alpha})^{1-\sigma} X^\sigma$, where Y is output and K, L and X are capital, labor and intermediate inputs respectively. An open developing economy is a net exporter of its output and a net importer of intermediate goods. It is also a net importer of capital (investment) goods, so that the equation of growth of net capital stocks, $\Delta K = I - \delta K$ (where I is investment, Δ a change operator, and δ the depreciation rate) is augmented to allow for imported capital. Demand for each type of import is a declining function of its price, which depends both on world prices and also on trade policies such as tariffs. Hence lowering tariffs (or equivalent barriers to imports) on intermediates increases their demand, and similarly, lowering the domestic cost of capital goods increases the stock of savings available for domestic investment.[7]

This model yields two interesting implications. First, a lower cost of intermediate imports is analogous to higher total factor productivity (TFP) growth, and second, since savings (the inputs to production of capital goods) can come from either domestic or foreign sources, any policy that lowers the cost of imported capital is isomorphic to a higher domestic savings rate. It follows that lowering tariffs on capital goods and intermediates can generate faster growth both along the transitional path and in the steady state.[8]

Empirically, the Estevadeordal and Taylor model also implies a focus not on tariffs in general, but specifically on those applied to intermediates and capital goods. As such it overcomes an important limitation in previous studies in which all forms of tariff data were combined, thereby imposing the (unreasonable) assumption that protection on all types of goods has equivalent growth effects. Using disaggregated tariff data in a difference-in-difference model, the authors find robust evidence that lower tariffs on imported capital and intermediate goods are associated with significantly faster income growth in a large panel of countries. The effects are weaker for the case of average tariffs, which reinforces their case.[9]

By incorporating openness into the Solow model, this study has advanced our theoretical and empirical understanding of the openness–growth nexus. It provides a theoretically defensible mechanism through which openness can be related to growth. This in turn motivates hypotheses not only about the direct impact of openness on growth, but also about its role in transmitting growth booms (or busts) among economies.

Southeast Asian growth in global context

Regional growth rate comparisons

From 1965 to the 1990s, the eight HPAEs identified in *EAM* were able to maintain income per capita growth rates averaging more than 5 percent.[10] More recently, China has joined this group, having emerged in the early 1990s as the world's most rapidly growing economy.

Since the 1970s these economies have grown faster than any other developing region. As seen in Table 4.1, developing countries in East Asia and Pacific achieved the highest average growth rates of per capita GDP (6.5 percent) in the last four decades. The Southeast Asian economies are now growing faster than all their counterparts in Northeast Asia except China. While the former region has enjoyed per capita income growth at approximately 4 percent since the 1970s, growth rates in the latter region have decelerated. In 1990–2010, Northeast Asian economies other than China grew at less than half the rate they had achieved in the 1970s and 1980s.

As a result, after China, Southeast Asia stands out among regions in the developing world. Its economies achieved on average 3.89 percent per capita income growth in the last four decades, significantly higher than Sub-Saharan Africa (0.55 percent), Latin America and Caribbean (1.57 percent), Middle East and North Africa (1.85 percent) and South Asia (3.08 percent). If we had invested $100 in each region in 1970, then by 2010 this would have returned $124 from

Table 4.2 GDP per capita growth rates in Southeast Asia (%)

Country	1970–89	1990–2010	1970–2010
Indonesia	4.71	3.63	4.15
Malaysia	4.12	3.72	3.92
Singapore	6.66	3.90	5.24
Thailand	5.01	3.80	4.39
Cambodia	n/a.	5.97	5.97
Lao PDR	1.31	4.58	3.95
Vietnam	2.14	5.82	5.11
Philippines	1.05	1.65	1.36
Southeast Asia	**4.01**	**3.77**	**3.89**

Source: World Development Indicators.

Sub-Saharan Africa, $187 from Latin America and Caribbean, $209 from Middle East and North Africa, $336 from South Asia, and $468 from Southeast Asia.

While the inter-regional comparison is illuminating, there is also variation in within-region growth rates. Table 4.2 shows income per capita growth rates of eight major Southeast Asian economies (Myanmar, Brunei and East Timor are again excluded). From 1970 to 2010 all countries except the Philippines grew faster than the averages for Sub-Saharan Africa, Latin America and Caribbean, Middle East and North Africa and South Asia. In 1991–2010, Southeast Asian high-performing countries including Indonesia, Malaysia, Singapore and Thailand continued to grow rapidly, though at a slightly lower pace, down from 4.7–6.6 percent in 1971–90 to 3.6–3.9 percent.[11] In contrast, poorer economies in Southeast Asia including Cambodia, Laos and Vietnam accelerated to growth rates ranging from 4 percent to 6 percent. Significant differences in real income between the region's earlier and later developers remain, but the gap is closing.

Determinants of growth

East Asian Miracle showed that factor accumulation matters in the East Asian growth experience. For the HPAEs, primary education and investment were found to make the largest contributions to growth. However, different rates of factor accumulation explain only part of the variation in income growth rates between HPAEs and other regions, and overall, the *EAM* regression model predicted only about two-thirds of observed HPAE growth. Moreover, there is reason to suspect that the most important factors explaining growth in 1965–90 are not necessarily those that dominate in later years and/or for later-developing economies.

In studies of Southeast Asian growth success, four main factors are usually identified.[12] First, saving and investment rates rose early and have been maintained at high levels by global standards (Horioka and Terada-Hagiwara 2011). Second, countries in the region are said to have allocated significant resources to education and human capital, and this, it is claimed, has facilitated the shift from labor-intensive exports to products of higher value. Third, after early experiments with import substitution most regional governments moved to liberalize trade and capital flows, for example by lowering tariff rates, creating export processing zones and imposing duty exemption schemes. Last but not least, Southeast Asian policymakers have played an important role in maintaining macroeconomic stability, something that is clearly of great importance when the bulk of new capital investment occurs in industries, such as assembly and other light manufacturing, that are internationally footloose. Of course no regional country other than Singapore comes close to an ideal on these criteria, and in particular, the poorer Southeast Asian countries are especially weak. However, Cambodia, Laos and Vietnam have also made great progress in liberalization since the 1990s; there are now signs that even Myanmar, the region's perennial laggard, may be catching up.

Another significant factor facilitating Southeast Asian development is its geographic proximity to the large booming economies of Northeast Asia. The gravity model literature asserts that proximity enhances trade (Bergstrand 1985; Deardorff 1998; Mátyás 1997; Frankel et al. 1996), and a subset of contributions to the empirical growth literature have examined growth spillovers from neighboring countries.[13] The proximity of Southeast Asia to the large and dynamic economies of Northeast Asia has presumably brought critical opportunities for development through this channel. Trade connections between the two sub-regions have deep historical roots, but the modern history begins at the start of the 1970s with three-way trade in which electronic components were shipped from Japan to Malaysia and Singapore for assembly into radios and other appliances to be sold in the US market. These trade linkages were accompanied by FDI inflows from Japanese, US and European firms, and those in turn paved the way for a massive surge in inward FDI to Southeast Asia from Japan and its Northeast Asian neighbors following the 1985 Plaza Accord, under which the Japanese yen (and the Korean won and New Taiwanese dollar, two currencies closely linked to the yen) appreciated sharply against the US dollar. Currency appreciation accelerated the outsourcing of Northeast Asia's most labor-intensive industries, and producers of textiles, apparel, footwear, simple electronics and other light manufacturing found Southeast Asia to be an attractive host for offshore production due to its geographical proximity, abundant low-wage labor, relatively stable political systems and macroeconomic stability.[14]

In the decade after the Plaza Accord, trade and FDI flows between Northeast Asia and Malaysia, Singapore, Indonesia and Thailand increased dramatically. By this means the Southeast Asian economies became established as producers of manufactures for the global market – and this provides a clue to their continued high GDP growth. Southeast Asian economies were able to turn trade and FDI into productivity growth through technology transfers, licensing or joint ventures with foreign companies. Rapid investment growth together with improvements in labor skills and technology caused rises in both output and productivity. Export industries were promoted by creating export-processing zones, lowering input tariffs and removing other barriers to international trade and payments. Allocative efficiency improved as a result, and gradually, with improvements in both skills and wages, investment shifted to high-skill and capital-intensive products such the manufacture of parts and components for electronics and machinery (Dowling 1997; Athukorala and Yamashita 2006).

More recently, China's rapid emergence as the "the world's factory" has significantly affected the global economy and the structure of international trade. China's growth has presented challenges as well as opportunities to Southeast Asian development – the former through competition in sales to third markets, the latter through complementarities in production (Ianchovichina and Walmsley 2003; Ianchovichina et al. 2004; Ravenhill 2006; Eichengreen and Tong 2005; Coxhead 2007). All these phenomena operate directly and indirectly through trade and international factor flows. Intra-regional exports of raw materials and electronic parts and components to China have boomed, while Southeast Asian producers of labor-intensive goods such as textiles, clothing and footwear have suffered due to direct competition from Chinese exporters. In a study limited to trade in manufactures, Eichengreen and Tong (2005) estimated that the impact of China's growth is positive on exports from high- and middle-income Southeast Asian economies (Singapore, Malaysia, Indonesia, Philippines and Thailand) and negative for low-income countries such as Cambodia that depend heavily on labor-intensive assembly. For resource-rich lower-income countries like Indonesia, Vietnam, Laos, Cambodia and Myanmar, short-term gains from exports of primary and agricultural products have been accompanied by concerns over their long-term welfare due to diminished profitability in labor-intensive manufactures and the negative consequences of natural resource export booms (Coxhead 2007; Thee 2011).

This account of the growth of Northeast Asian influences on developing Asian economies motivates tests of spillover effects on growth. In the 1980s, the Japanese economy accounted for an average 16 percent of world GDP and its GDP growth rate, which averaged 4.4 percent, was 1.75 times greater than in the rest of the world and 1.9 times greater than in the rest of the OECD (which accounted for 83 percent of world GDP at the time).[15] Japan's share in global trade was about 10 percent in the 1980s – second only to the USA, which grew much less quickly during this decade. China's shares in global GDP and trade in the 1990s and 2000s were both smaller than Japan's in the 1980s, but its GDP growth rate in the 1990s was on average 3.7 times greater than the world average in the 1990s, and over four times greater in the 2000s. By the end of the decade China had become the world's second-largest economy with 8 percent of world trade. Therefore, it is reasonable to expect that these booms in the Japanese and Chinese economies influenced growth among their neighbors, and for that matter in the global economy as a whole.

Figure 4.1 provides one (admittedly informal) way to see the magnitudes of these booms. It shows annual GDP growth rates of the world's four largest economies multiplied by each economy's share in global merchandise exports. The Japanese boom of the late 1970s through 1991 is clearly evident, as is the United States' "long expansion" from the mid-1980s to 2000.

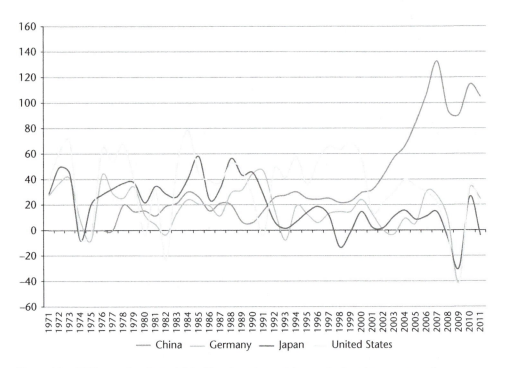

Figure 4.1 GDP growth rate weighted by share in world exports, four large economies
Source: WDI Online.

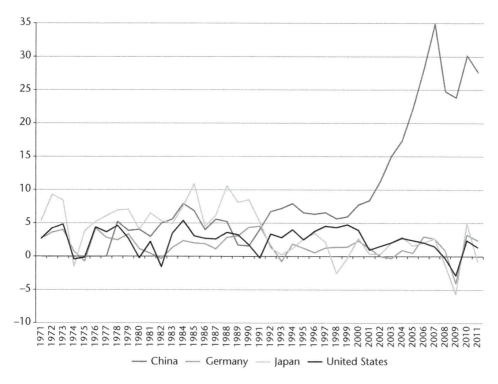

Figure 4.2 GDP growth rate weighted by share in world exports and distance from Singapore
Source: WDI Online.

China's growth rate is high almost throughout this period; however, what brings it to global prominence is the huge increase in its global export share after the early 1990s.

If geographic proximity is correlated with trade and other international linkages, then these booms in large economies appear quite different in different parts of the world. Figure 4.2 illustrates this by dividing the data in Figure 4.1 by distance from Singapore, which is located near the geographic center of Southeast Asia. In the "view from Singapore," the Japanese and Chinese booms acquire far greater prominence, while export-weighted growth in the USA and Germany is diminished, despite those countries' size and global trade shares.

Model, estimation and discussion

Model specification

The literature on East Asian and Southeast Asian growth experience provides very limited empirical evidence to distinguish those countries from other developing regions due to either restricted data or methodologies. As noted, a common approach is to introduce an "Asia" dummy variable to test for any deviation from a common intercept (Collins and Bosworth 1996; Radelet et al. 2001). This approach assumes that the underlying growth model is identical everywhere. Radelet et al. (2001) go one step further to point out Southeast Asian distinctiveness by examining "controlled" averages of various variables for Southeast Asia and other regions. They estimate a cross-country gravity model controlling for a number of structural and geographic variables where dependent variables are the variables under consideration like trade ratios, government spending, etc. They include a dummy variable to represent high-performing countries in East Asia and Southeast Asia. Higher shares of imports, total exports and manufactured exports, higher savings and investment, and slightly larger central government budget shares are aspects in which Southeast Asia differed from other countries in 1990 as the Southeast Asian dummy is positive and significant in those regressions. Despite being more informative than the comparison of simple averages, this approach does not reveal the mechanisms by which Southeast Asian distinctiveness contributes to its growth. To the best of our knowledge, no empirical study has employed a method that is well suited to address this.

We augment the Solow growth specification made popular by Mankiw et al. (1992), which includes initial income, physical and human capital and labor force as contributors to GDP growth. Our modifications to this basic model take three forms. First, we introduce variables intended to capture macroeconomic stability and openness. Second, we introduce a measure of economic growth in the world economy, and additional measures of the East Asian growth booms discussed in the previous section. As described below, these measures are based on geographic distance but take account also of economic "distance" via the relative sizes and growth rates of economies, taking account of openness as discussed in the second section. Third, we test whether the parameters of this model are equal for Southeast Asian economies relative to the rest of the world.

The basic growth model makes use of the standard Mankiw et al. variables augmented by policy indicators as described above. Its elements are:

- – The logarithm of per capita GDP in the initial year of the period
- – Capital investment (Investment/GDP)
- – Human capital (Secondary school enrollment)
- – Demographic development (Working-age population)
- – Macroeconomic stability (Average annual inflation rate)
- – Openness (Freedom to Trade Internationally index).[16]

An important modification is to allow for growth spillovers among countries. Early tests of external effects in growth models took the form of spillovers from growth shocks in adjacent countries (e.g., Easterly and Levine 1998). This approach is conceptually limited in that a country's international interactions may extend far more broadly than to its immediate neighbors. It is also methodologically difficult since growth among immediate neighbors raises issues of endogeneity and simultaneity. Our approach is closer in spirit to studies that examine spillovers according to data-rich measures of "economic distance" (Moreno and Trehan 1997; Conley and Ligon 2002; Roberts and Deichmann 2011). These measures take account not only of geographic proximity, but also of the relative size and/or growth rates of other economies.

Our estimation framework of the spatial spillover model follows Moreno and Trehan (1997) and Erter and Koch (2007). We extend their work in two important ways: we take account of a country's openness as a factor conditioning its receptiveness to growth spillovers, and we examine spillovers not only from the world economy as a whole, but also from a specific subset, the Northeast Asian economies.

The model to be estimated is given by:

$$g_i = \rho \sum_{j=1}^{n} w_{ij} g_j + X_i \beta + e_i, \ i = 1 \ldots n \tag{1}$$

or in matrix form,

$$G = \rho WG + X\beta + e, \tag{2}$$

where g_i is the per worker income growth rate in country i over some period. Following Ertur and Koch (2007), it is computed as:

$$g_i = \frac{\ln y(ending\ period) - \ln y(starting\ period)}{T};$$

Income within starting/ending period is simply an average of per worker GDP of its first and last year. T is the number of years between the beginning years of starting and ending periods. w_{ij} is the (i,j) element of weighting matrix W which essentially characterizes the "influence" of country j on country i (construction of the weight matrix will be explained later). Regressor X_i includes the commonly used cross-country growth regression variables such as logged investment rate, logged effective depreciation rate, logged secondary school enrollment rate, and inflation. In order to explore how a country's trade liberalization policy directly affects its own growth, we also include an index of logged openness (between 0 and 1) in X_i. The error term, e_i, is assumed to be distributed $N(0, \sigma^2)$. Following Ertur and Koch (2007) and papers cited therein, the effective depreciation rate is defined as the population growth rate plus 0.05 (the latter number is assumed to be the sum of capital depreciation rate and steady state capital growth rate).

It can be shown that in Eq. (2), the spatially lagged variable WG is correlated with the error term. Therefore, the Ordinary Least Squares (OLS) estimator will be biased and inconsistent. Following Moreno and Trehan (1997) and Ertur and Koch (2007), such a spatial autoregressive model (SAR) can be estimated in a maximum likelihood framework. We provide details in Appendix A at the end of this chapter.

The spatial weight matrix

We use four types of weight matrices.

TYPE 1: INVERSE OF DISTANCE

$$w_{ij} = \frac{1/d_{ij}}{\sum_k d_{ik}} (i \neq j) \quad w_{ii} = 0,$$

where d_{ij} is the Great Circle distance between country i's capital and country j's capital. This method is used in Moreno and Trehan (1997) and Ertur and Koch (2007). Diagonal elements are all 0.

TYPE 2: INVERSE OF DISTANCE SQUARED

$$w_{ij} = \frac{1/(d_{ij})^2}{\sum_k (d_{ik})^2} (i \neq j) \quad w_{ii} = 0$$

This method is used in Ertur and Koch (2007).

TYPE 3: TYPE 1 WEIGHTED BY GDP_j

$$w_{ij} = \frac{GDP_j/d_{ij}}{\sum_k GDP_j \cdot d_{ik}} (i \neq j) \quad w_{ii} = 0$$

This matrix not only takes geographical distance into account, but also the size of the foreign economy relative to the total sample of countries. Within-period GDP is a simple average of annual aggregate GDP from the five years involved. A variant on this weighting scheme uses growth rates instead of GDP levels (Moreno and Trehan 1997). Note that for the first three types of weight matrix, the sum of each row is equal to 1.[17]

Finally, we have hypothesized that the influence of growth elsewhere in the world will be greater for more open economies.

TYPE 4: TYPE 3 WEIGHTED BY OPENNESS

$$w_{ij} = Open_i * \frac{GDP_j/d_{ij}}{\sum_k GDP_j \cdot d_{ik}} \ (i \neq j) \quad w_{ii} = 0$$

This weight matrix further weaves a country's own openness into the spillover effect. Singapore and Indonesia, for example, are roughly the same distance from the USA, but since the former country is more open than the latter, it is expected that the USA will have a greater influence on Singapore than on Indonesia. Note that in this type of weight matrix, row sums do not add to 1.

Estimation

Do Southeast Asian economies grow differently?

Even though OLS estimates are likely to be biased, it is still feasible to use an OLS or fixed effects model to test for the significance of individual regressors. This is valuable in the first tests that we conduct, which are aimed at discovering whether the Southeast Asian economies as a group grow "differently." We test for structural breaks between the Southeast Asian economies and others in the dataset. We do this by interacting a Southeast Asia dummy variable with all explanatory variables (other than regional fixed effects). This approach draws from Block (2001), who used an equivalent method and found some significantly different slope parameters for Sub-Saharan Africa relative to the rest of the world. The regressors include measures of the size and/or growth of the big Northeast Asian economies, China and Japan.

A fixed-effects approach allows us to exploit the panel data dimensions of the dataset. Panel data methods endow regression analysis with both spatial and temporal dimensions. This approach also eliminates any short-run business cycle effects by using five- or ten-year averages instead of annual data. In addition, fixed-effects methods control for unobserved heterogeneity across countries and provide unbiased and efficient estimates compared to simple OLS regressions. Empirically, the fixed effects estimator is justified by a Hausman test, which rejects the null hypothesis that the error terms are uncorrelated with other regressors. A disadvantage of the fixed-effects model is that it does not allow consideration of time-invariant variables such as natural resource endowments. However, its advantages are sufficient to prefer it despite this constraint. In a final OLS exercise we restrict the dataset to the Southeast Asian countries only, and once again test hypotheses on existence of spillovers controlling for openness.

How influential are inter-country spillovers?

In the second part of the analysis we seek to quantify the spillover effects. As discussed above, this is infeasible with OLS. In moving to a maximum likelihood model with spatial spillovers, we are unable to retain the nested tests of separate parameter values for Southeast Asia. Therefore we pool all country data. To obtain more detail on the effects of spillovers we divide the data into two periods. The first spans 1981–2000, the years prior to and up until the onset of the Asian financial crisis (AFC), which marked a sharp break in the development of the Southeast Asian economies. The second is the decade 2001–2010. This division allows for the possibility of a structural break around 2000, though in the estimates we see relatively little evidence for this. For pre- and post-AFC periods analysis, GDP weights used to construct the matrix of distance measures are the average of 1996–2000 in the first period, and of 2006–2010 in the second. In constructing the Type 4 weight matrix, the openness index of country i is the average of 1981–85 in the early period, and of 2001–05 in the later period.[18]

Data

The sample includes all economies with available data, a total of 139 economies. The dataset covers 1971 to 2010 in five-year sub-periods. Most data are from the World Bank's World Development Indicators, except for GDP and investment data (Penn World Tables) and the openness measure, which is from the Economic Freedom of the World project (Gwartney et al. 2011). Table 4.3 presents a summary of regional and country averages.

Table 4.3 Summary of regression data, by region and country

Region and country	PC GDP growth (%)	Initial GDP per capita ($)	Investment (% GDP)	Labor force (m)	Enrollment rate (%)	Inflation (%)	Openness
Southeast Asia	3.74	3,055	29.9	57.2	51.4	8.2	6.6
Cambodia	1.21	924	11.8	5.6	24.0	4.3	2.3
Indonesia	3.95	2,269	28.5	112.1	44.1	12.2	6.5
Lao PDR	3.69	1,168	14.2	2.4	25.3	26.4	2.1
Malaysia	4.03	6,407	31.2	11.5	57.2	3.8	7.7
Philippines	1.31	2,110	20.7	35.9	69.5	10.7	6.1
Singapore	5.34	23,534	42.2	2.3	68.8	3.1	9.3
Thailand	3.91	4,242	35.1	35.8	42.8	5.4	6.7
Vietnam	4.09	1,165	22.9	39.4	56.9	6.4	3.1
China	8.17	1,827	37.5	732.3	53.7	6.2	6.0
NE Asia and Pacific*	1.70	2,220	24.2	1.8	43.0	17.2	6.8
Europe and Central Asia	1.69	8,097	22.0	62.2	83.6	139.4	6.1
Latin America and Caribbean	1.29	5,544	21.3	11.6	57.7	75.6	5.9
Middle East and N. Africa	1.40	4,688	27.9	25.1	56.2	13.1	5.1
South Asia	3.38	1,370	22.1	426.1	38.0	8.2	4.7
Sub-Saharan Africa	0.97	2,045	18.7	21.3	42.9	45.2	5.8
High-income economies	1.82	25,181	21.3	87.6	95.8	5.4	7.4

Source: Penn World Table, World Development Indicators and Economic Freedom of the World project.
Notes: Panel data covers 8 five-year sub-periods from 1971 to 2010 for the 139 country sample. Regional averages are weighted averages where the weights are total GDP.
GDP per capita growth for each period is calculated based on geometric average.
Except for the initial GDP per capita which takes the value of the first year of each five-year period, all other explanatory variables are the five-year averages for the time period 1971–2010.
* Includes countries in East Asia and Pacific other than China and Southeast Asia.

Income in this table is measured as real GDP per capita in constant 2000 purchasing power parity (PPP) dollars. The dependent variable for the OLS model is the GDP per capita growth rate measured by the geometric average of each sub-period. The use of geometric rather than simple averages eliminates any bias caused by outliers in GDP data. Thus, the regional and country GDP per capita growth rates presented in Table 4.3 differ slightly from those in Tables 4.1 and 4.2. Southeast Asian growth still remains higher than that of other developing economies except China (8.17 percent) and Europe and Central Asia (1.69 percent). Most economies in Europe and Central Asia were in recession during the first half of the 1990s; hence the simple average growth rate of 1.34 percent presented in Table 4.1 underestimates their real growth.

All other explanatory variables are the five-year averages of each sub-period. Southeast Asia's average investment share of GDP is similar to other regions, but investment rates have been consistently high (ranging from 28 percent to 42 percent of GDP) in the high-performing regional subgroup of Indonesia, Malaysia, Singapore and Thailand. Differences in labor force size reflect population differences. Secondary school enrollment is highest in Eastern Europe and Central Asia and high-income economies, and lowest in South Asia and Sub-Saharan Africa. Southeast Asia as a region is by no means exceptional on this measure of human capital. The Philippines and Singapore have very high enrollment rates, consistent perhaps with high expectations of employment outside of agriculture.[19] But enrollments in Malaysia, Thailand and Indonesia are quite low relative to per capita incomes.

We proxy for macroeconomic stability using annual inflation rates. Inflation in Southeast Asia has been very moderate by world standards. In Singapore, Malaysia and Thailand, average inflation rates in the last 40 years have been below 6 percent. Most other regions, especially Eastern Europe and Central Asia, Latin America and Caribbean, and Middle East and North Africa, have recorded average inflation at two- or three-digit rates.

As noted earlier, there is dissatisfaction with most openness measures used in prior empirical studies. Rather than rely on Sachs–Warner, we instead use the Freedom to Trade Internationally index, a component of the annual survey Economic Freedom of the World. This index is continuous from 0 to 10 and is based on five main variables: taxes on international trade, regulatory trade barriers, actual size of the trade sector relative to expected, black-market exchange rates, and international capital controls. Besides taxes on trade, policies in the other four areas also play a crucial role in promoting international trade. Hence, this is a relatively comprehensive index of openness, and arguably less vulnerable to the criticisms leveled at Sachs–Warner.[20]

It should be noted that the data panel is unbalanced. Some data, especially on the trade openness measure, are missing in early periods for many poor countries. Thus the results using this variable might overstate the actual values of this index in many developing countries. In general, South Asian economies have the lowest openness scores. Southeast Asia has been relatively open, with an average index of 6.38 compared with the highest value of 7.11 in high-income economies. Within Southeast Asia, Laos and Cambodia are the least open.[21] Singapore and Malaysia are most open; in fact Singapore ranked first worldwide in 2009, with a score close to 10. All economies other than Singapore and Malaysia have greatly increased their openness by this measure since the late 1990s (Figure 4.3).

Estimation results and discussion

Table 4.4 shows estimates of unconditional spillover effects from global growth and East Asian booms. Models I–III in this table use spatially weighted GDP values to measure spillovers, and models IV–VI use spatially weighted GDP growth rates. In each case the first model accounts only for initial GDP and spillovers. The second models bring in measures of Japanese and Chinese

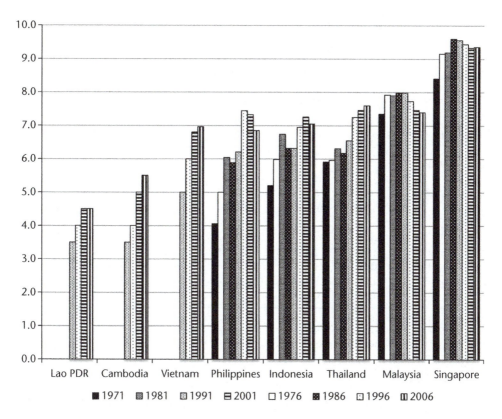

Figure 4.3 Openness indexes for Southeast Asia (averages for half-decade periods beginning with date shown)
Source: see text.

growth booms. The third models add in the openness measure. All are estimated with country fixed effects. With the exception of the Japan effect in model II, all estimates are significant at conventional levels and of expected sign.

The growth effects of global growth spillovers are highly significant. In model III, the openness measure also has a powerful effect on growth. Growth booms in East Asian countries have significant impacts on average GDP growth rates.

Table 4.5 reports conditional results, when we control for the standard inputs to the aggregate production function plus inflation. Once again, all estimates are of expected sign, and significance levels are high: p-values are 0.05 or lower except for the working-age population variable. We estimate four models, varying both the definition of the spillover effect as before, and also the specification of the growth boom effects, by interacting the growth measures for Japan and China with country openness. The test is that more open economies experience a greater impact from the East Asian booms than do less open ones, and that this effect is transmitted through more than one channel. Once again, all openness and the spillover measures are all highly significant. The variables for Japan's growth in the early period and for China's growth in the later period are significant even after controlling for world GDP or growth.

We next ask whether Southeast Asian growth parameters differ from the rest of the world. As already noted, the global growth literature typically finds distinct intercept shift effects for world regions, but rarely tests for different slope effects. If growth experiences differ, then those

Table 4.4 Unconditional spillovers with convergence (dependent variable: growth of per capita GDP)

	I	II	III	IV	V	VI
ln (initial GDP)	−0.06***	−0.062***	−0.065***	−0.049***	−0.052***	−0.057***
	(0.0069)	(0.007)	(0.007)	(0.006)	0.006	(0.006)
W*GDP	0.169***	0.145***	0.082***			
	(0.021)	(0.027)	(0.026)			
W*growth				0.048***	0.048***	0.022***
				(0.006)	(0.008)	(0.008)
JPN gr*1980s		0.154	0.445***		0.370***	0.532***
		(0.12)	(0.123)		(0.133)	(0.132)
CHN gr*90–00s		0.103**	0.181***		0.152***	0.213***
		(0.048)	(0.046)		(0.046)	(0.044)
Openness			0.012***			0.015***
			(0.001)			(0.001)
Constant	1.504***	1.492***	1.461***	1.308***	1.311***	1.357***
	(0.056)	0.0558	(0.054)	(0.046)	(0.049)	(0.047)
Obs/groups	771/137	771/137	706/137	771/137	771/137	706/137
R^2 within	0.124	0.131	0.229	0.123	0.139	0.225

Notes:
*, **, and *** denote significance at 10%, 5%, and 1% respectively.
W*GDP: Spatial weights times GDP of partner countries (Type 3).
W*growth: Spatial weights times GDP growth rate of partner countries.
Country fixed effects included.
Standard errors in parentheses.

differences should appear as significantly different slope coefficients associated with inputs, policies, or the spillover effects from growth or growth booms elsewhere. Table 4.6 shows estimates of the same model as in Table 4.5, only now with separate Southeast Asia interaction terms for each right-hand side variable. Southeast Asia, as a group, differs from the rest of the world in just two respects: schooling has a smaller effect and the East Asian booms a larger one. Of course, since these estimates use OLS we cannot place much weight on the magnitudes of estimates, only on their statistical significance.[22]

To summarize, Southeast Asian economies have grown faster than most other developing regions, but we find that their growth mechanisms do not differ from the rest of the world except in two respects. First, it seems that the influence of schooling on growth is lower in the region than in the world as a whole. Second, East Asian growth booms had a significantly greater impact on growth in Southeast Asia than in other world regions.

Next, in search of quantifiable estimates of spillover effects, we turn to a maximum likelihood estimator. We use the same dataset, only now divided into two subsets, the 1980s–1990s and the 2000s.[23] To save space we report here only the most relevant results, those using the openness-adjusted spatial weights (Type 4 weights). These are shown in Table 4.7, which reports three models. In Model XI we regress the dependent variable, the annual average growth of output per worker only on weighted growth of other countries. The estimate of *rho* (highlighted in bold) is significant and positive, indicating a significant spillover of world growth to the average country in the dataset. In Model XII we fit the standard Mankiw et al. model, including (in logarithmic form) initial income, investment, and the secondary school enrollment rate (a proxy for education) as well as a measure of effective depreciation. All have expected signs and are significant at conventional levels. Following Ertur and Koch, we also include the spatially weighted log of initial world income. In this model, *rho*, the spillover measure, is again positive and significant. In Model XII we

Table 4.5 Growth model with spillovers (dependent variable: growth of per capita GDP)

	VII	VIII
ln(initial GDP)	−7.13***	−6.65***
	0.748	*0.655*
Investmt/GDP	0.052*	0.064**
	0.027	*0.027*
Wking-age pop	0.011	0.011
	0.010	*0.010*
HS enrollmt	0.030*	0.030**
	0.016	*0.015*
Inflation	−0.0009**	−0.0009**
	0.00044	*0.00043*
Openness	0.961***	0.892***
	0.162	*0.165*
JPN gr*1980s	0.460***	0.551***
	0.124	*0.132*
CHN gr*90–00s	0.198***	0.217***
	0.048	*0.046*
W^0*GDP	5.73E–09**	
	2.79E–09	
W^0*growth		2.061**
		0.872
Constant	50.39***	42.28***
	6.012	*5.220*
Obs/groups	629/136	629/136
R^2 within	0.254	0.256

Notes:
*, **, and *** denote significance at 10%, 5%, and 1% respectively.
Country fixed effects included.

further augment the model with the two policy variables, for inflation and openness. Most variables remain of expected sign and significance. The estimate of spillover effects is significant as usual in the early period but marginally outside the 10 percent significance level in the later period.[24]

Focusing on Model XII, we see that openness (here scaled to be between zero and one) is very influential on growth. The estimate, 0.0252, indicates that a doubling of the openness index would directly add 2.5 percentage points to growth. Referring to Figure 4.3 we see that if Laos (openness = 0.35 in 1991–95) were to double its openness index, that would make it almost equal on that measure to Malaysia in the same period. Similarly if the Philippines had been as open as Malaysia, it would have grown at a rate much closer to that enjoyed by Malaysia. In the later period, the estimated effect of openness is twice as large again. Moreover these impacts do not include the gains of greater openness in terms of larger spillover benefits from world economic growth, which are captured separately by the estimate of *rho* multiplied by the openness-adjusted Type 4 spatial weights. Countries that are geographically close to large, fast-growing economies, and which are themselves relatively open to trade and investment flows, benefit disproportionately from growth in the world economy. As the OLS estimates in Table 4.6 already hinted, it is here that Southeast Asian economies can be seen to differ from the vast majority of countries in the world economy.

For each country, *rho* times the sum of its openness-adjusted spatial weights tells us the elasticity of its own growth rate with respect to that in the world economy (as can be seen from

Table 4.6 Growth model with spillovers and SE Asia interactions (dependent variable: growth of per capita income)

	IX		
ln(initial GDP)	−6.97***	SEA*initialGDP	4.25
	0.705		3.24
Investmt/GDP	0.063**	SEA*Inv/GDP	0.081
	0.030		0.092
Wking-age pop	0.011	SEA*Wking age pop	0.032
	0.010		0.066
HS enrollmt	0.037**	SEA*HS enrollmt	−0.197*
	0.016		0.101
Inflation	−0.0009**	SEA*inflation	−0.090
	0.0004		0.063
Openness	0.879***	SEA*openness	−0.316
	0.167		0.948
JPN gr*1980s	0.483***	SEA*JPN gr	1.521**
	0.137		0.597
CHN gr*90–00s	0.183***	SEA*CHN gr	0.420**
	0.047		0.200
W^0*growth	2.012**	SEA*W^0*growth	12.651
	0.882		7.999
Constant		40.897***	
		5.387	
Obs/groups		629/136	
R^2 within		0.281	

Notes:
*, **, and *** denote significance at 10%, 5%, and 1% respectively.
Country fixed effects included.

equation (2)). Likewise, *rho* multiplied by a country's weights for a subset of other countries – such as those in Northeast Asia only – provides a measure of that country's elasticity of growth with respect to an increase in growth in that regional subset. Table 4.8 shows the countries for which this elasticity is significantly larger than for others, as determined by a z-score at 90 percent or higher. Singapore, by virtue of its openness, derives a significantly higher growth "kick" from world growth in both periods. Growth in North America delivers a similar boost only to small economies in Central America and the Caribbean. Growth in Northeast Asia, which was fastest in the world in both periods, and which also gained greater weight over time due to the rapidly increasing GDPs of Japan and then China, also confers the greatest benefits to a small set of countries. The ASEAN-5 countries are among them, and so is Vietnam in the later period.

With this information in hand we can now evaluate the contributions of world and Northeast Asian growth to the overall growth of economies worldwide.[25] Multiplying each country's growth elasticity of spillovers by growth rates in the sources gives us the percentage points of GDP growth attributable to spillovers. These are plotted on the horizontal axes of Figures 4.4–4.7, while observed average growth rates are plotted on the vertical axes. In Figure 4.4, for example, we can see that Malaysia, with average annual growth of output per worker of 3.8 percent, owed 1.75 percentage points (or almost half) of that growth to the effects of growth in the world economy, with the rest coming from growth of domestic resource endowments, investment and openness. Comparing Figure 4.5 (which shows the same data on the vertical axis) we see that just 0.3 percent of that growth, or 16 percent of the total spillover, was directly attributable to

Table 4.7 Maximum likelihood estimates (dependent variable: average annual growth rate of output per worker)

	Early period (1980s–1990s)			Late period (2000s)		
	Estimate	S.e.	estimate/s.e.	Estimate	S.e.	estimate/s.e.
Model X						
Constant	−0.0057	0.003	2.164	0.0080	0.003	2.553
rho	**1.3895**	**0.075**	**18.539**	**0.9510**	**0.139**	**6.857**
sigma2	0.0004	0.000	6.964	0.0005	0.000	8.336
Obs.	97			139		
Model XI						
Constant	−0.2163	0.031	6.999	−0.1050	0.030	3.495
Log initial income	−0.0031	0.002	1.854	−0.0082	0.001	5.788
Log investment	0.0349	0.005	6.593	0.0255	0.006	4.126
Log eff. depctn	−0.0499	0.012	4.225	−0.0271	0.010	2.841
W*log initial inc.	0.0004	0.001	0.272	0.0053	0.002	2.649
rho	**1.1609**	**0.169**	**6.851**	**0.6866**	**0.207**	**3.312**
sigma2	0.0002	0.000	6.892	0.0003	0.000	8.124
Obs	95			132		
Model XII						
Constant	−0.1764	0.046	3.807	−0.1652	0.052	3.186
Log initial income	−0.0062	0.002	2.558	−0.0046	0.002	2.018
Log investment	0.0293	0.007	4.042	0.0124	0.008	1.477
Log eff. depctn	−0.0320	0.015	2.199	−0.0371	0.011	3.418
W*log initial inc.	−0.0011	0.002	0.591	−0.0020	0.004	0.580
Inflation rate	−0.0001	0.000	2.155	0.0012	0.001	2.429
Log openness	0.0252	0.013	1.934	0.0506	0.022	2.320
Log enrollment	0.0002	0.000	1.880	−0.0001	0.000	0.917
rho	**1.2065**	**0.331**	**3.643**	**0.4532**	**0.276**	**1.640**
sigma2	0.0002	0.000	6.041	0.0003	0.000	7.681
Obs	73			118		

Note: Estimate/s.e. ratio greater than 2.00 is significant at 95% or better. Estimate/s.e. greater than 1.66 is significant at 90% or better.

growth in Northeast Asia. Moving to the later period, we see that output per worker in Malaysia grew by 2.8 percent per year, with 1.25 percent due to spillovers from world growth (Figure 4.6), of which almost half was due to growth in Northeast Asia alone. Similarly, in the 1980s and 1990s, Indonesia's output per worker grew at 3.8 percent annually; 1.3 percentage points, almost one-third of total growth, came from global growth spillovers, of which one-fifth (0.3 percentage points) came directly from Northeast Asian growth. By the 2000s, when Indonesia's economy expanded at 5.8 percent per year, it owed almost 1 percent of that to world growth, fully half of which was due to Northeast Asian growth alone. For the majority of countries, as the figures make very clear, spillovers contributed much less to total growth, and those from Northeast Asia less still, in spite of the rapid increase in that region's share of the global economy. Part of the difference is attributable to trade costs (as proxied by distance), but individual country openness also matters greatly, as demonstrated by the extreme case of Singapore, the world's most open economy.

Table 4.8 Countries with significantly high growth elasticity from spillovers

	Source of growth spillovers		
	Entire world	North America	Northeast Asia
1980s–1990s	Canada, Panama, Singapore, Venezuela	Bahamas, Belize, Guatemala, Panama, Venezuela	Fiji, Indonesia, Malaysia, New Zealand, Philippines, Singapore, Thailand
2000s	Belgium, Estonia, Ireland, Luxembourg, Netherlands, Singapore	Bahamas, Belize, Costa Rica, Dom. Rep., El Salvador, Guyana, Haiti, Honduras, Jamaica, Nicaragua, Panama, Trinidad and Tobago	Indonesia, Malaysia, Mongolia, Papua New Guinea, Philippines, Singapore, Thailand, Vietnam

Note: Significance is determined by right-tail z-score of country *i*'s elasticity in a sample of all countries.
North America: USA, Canada, Mexico. Northeast Asia (early): Japan, South Korea; (late): Japan, South Korea, China.
Countries in a region not included in calculations for spillovers from that region.

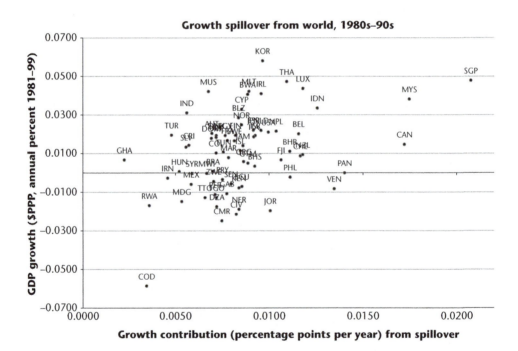

Figure 4.4 GDP growth spillovers from world economic growth, 1980s–1990s

Finally, it should be noted that these spillover estimates are lower bounds in three senses. First, we have separately accounted for the growth effects of openness as one of the explicit regressors; second, we have not accounted for endogenous changes in domestic investment or education driven by trade linkages; and third, for the regional spillovers we have measured only direct effects, excluding third-party influences. Thus the impact on, say, Indonesian growth due to Northeast Asia-driven expansion in Singapore's economy is not counted.

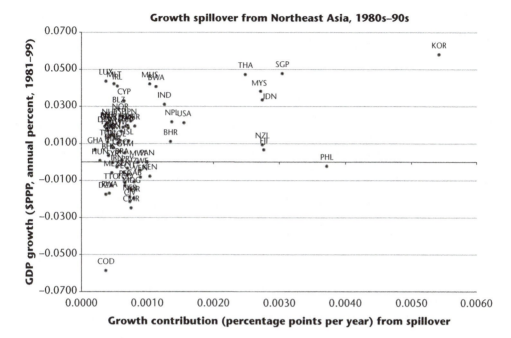

Figure 4.5   GDP growth spillovers from Northeast Asian economic growth, 1980s–1990s

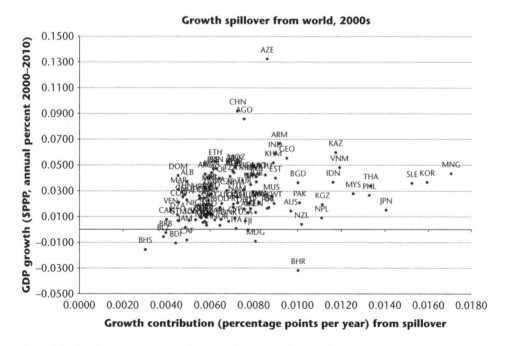

Figure 4.6   GDP growth spillovers from world economic growth, 2000s

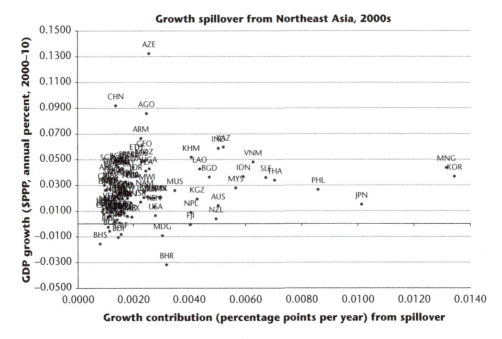

Figure 4.7 GDP growth spillovers from Northeast Asian economic growth, 2000s

Conclusions

Southeast Asia's consistently high economic growth in the last four decades has set this region apart from most of the developing world. Nonetheless most empirical explanations for growth assume the same underlying economic growth dynamics in Southeast Asia as elsewhere. This study advances the discussion by testing for differences in the determinants of growth between Southeast Asia and other countries.

Our estimates reveal that growth spillovers from Northeast Asian booms have significantly larger effects in Southeast Asia than in other world regions. This conforms to historical facts: the post-Plaza Accord East Asian FDI boom continues to benefit the region's development in the long run. These benefits originated from having export-oriented industries with improved labor skills and technology transfers, productivity growth and economic efficiency followed the massive investment inflows from Northeast Asian economies.

Clearly the Southeast Asian countries are fortunate to be located close to Northeast Asia.[26] Still, distance is not the only important variable. Our estimates show that within Southeast Asia, countries that are more receptive to international trade and capital flows benefit even more from growth spillovers. An example is the transition from protecting import-substituting industries to export orientation in Malaysia, Indonesia and Thailand following the Plaza Accord, which resulted in rapid investment inflows and high rates of long-run income growth in these countries. In contrast, the later entrants to the global economy – Philippines, Laos, Vietnam and Cambodia – are still behind their neighbors in the income ladder.

Our research raises some additional unresolved questions. First, how and when will Southeast Asian economies' growth decelerate, as theory and experience indicate it must? This situation may not necessarily happen again as the regional and global contexts have since changed. Unlike many economists who are concerned about the adverse effects of the giant China on Southeast Asia, we provide evidence that China's growth is creating a favorable growth impact on the world economy in general, and to a greater extent than average on its neighbors' development. Southeast Asian economies benefit from being exporters of intermediate goods, raw materials and agricultural products to "the world's factory." In the long run, however, there are different implications and policy lessons within Southeast Asia. The higher-wage economies with greater complementarity with China – Singapore, Malaysia and Thailand – will be better off by promoting freer trade. In contrast, for the less-developed yet resource-rich countries like Indonesia, Laos, Cambodia and Vietnam, the increasing demand for natural resources may reduce incentives for investments in the manufacturing sector and human development, thus diminishing their potential for long-run economic growth and increasing the risk of a "middle-income trap." First and foremost, these countries need better institutions and resource management policies to minimize the potential losses in long-term welfare caused by over-exploitation of their natural resources. Second, given direct competition from a rapidly growing Chinese economy and other low-cost competitors in labor-intensive exports, there is a need to specialize in selected areas that are skill-intensive and highly differentiated (Coxhead and Li 2008). While the rise of fragmentation trade makes it easier to find these niche markets, building capacity in those areas requires intensive investments in human capital and technology transfer. Finally, globalization puts these developing countries at higher risk of growth slowdowns transmitted not only directly from the world economy, but also indirectly through the strength of their links with China.

Acknowledgments

This work has evolved from a thesis project by the first author (Phung 2012). The authors thank participants at seminars at the University of Wisconsin-Madison and the Asian Development Bank Institute, and at the Handbook of Southeast Asian Economics Conference (Bangkok, March 2013) for helpful comments on earlier drafts.

Appendix A: The maximum likelihood model

It can be shown that in Eq. (2), the spatially lagged variable WG is correlated with the error term:

$$Cov\left(WGe'\right) = \sigma^2 W(I - W)^{-1} \neq 0$$

Therefore an OLS estimator will be biased and inconsistent. Following Moreno and Trehan (1997) and Ertur and Koch (2007), such spatial autoregressive model (SAR) can be estimated in a maximum likelihood framework. Given that the error term is normally distributed, the log likelihood function is given by:

$$\ln L(\beta', \rho, \sigma^2) = -\frac{N}{2}\ln(2\pi) - \frac{N}{2}\ln(\sigma^2) + \ln|I - \rho W|$$
$$-\frac{1}{2\sigma^2}[(I - \rho W)G - X\beta]'[(I - \rho W)G - X\beta]$$

The asymptotic covariance matrix of the estimator is:

Asy. Var $(\beta', \rho, \sigma^2) =$

$$\begin{bmatrix} \frac{1}{\sigma^2}X'X & \frac{1}{\sigma^2}(X'W_AX\beta) & 0 \\ \frac{1}{\sigma^2}(X'W_AX\beta)' & tr[(W_A + W'_A)W_A] + \frac{1}{\sigma^2}(W_AX\beta)'(W_AX\beta) & \frac{1}{\sigma^2}tr W_A \\ 0 & \frac{1}{\sigma^2}tr W_A & \frac{N}{2\sigma^4} \end{bmatrix}$$

Appendix B: Countries in the dataset

China

Europe and Central Asia

Albania	Kazakhstan	Montenegro
Armenia	Kyrgyz Republic	Romania
Azerbaijan	Latvia	Russian Federation
Bosnia and Herzegovina	Lithuania	Serbia
Bulgaria	Macedonia, FYR	Turkey
Georgia	Moldova	Ukraine

Latin America and the Caribbean

Argentina	Ecuador	Mexico
Belize	El Salvador	Nicaragua
Bolivia	Guatemala	Panama
Brazil	Guyana	Paraguay
Chile	Haiti	Peru
Colombia	Honduras	Uruguay
Costa Rica	Jamaica	Venezuela, RB
Dominican Republic		

Middle East and North Africa

Algeria	Jordan	Syrian Arab Republic
Egypt, Arab Rep.	Morocco	Tunisia
Iran, Islamic Rep.		

Other Asia and Pacific

Fiji	Mongolia	Papua New Guinea

South Asia

Bangladesh	Nepal	Sri Lanka
India	Pakistan	

Southeast Asia

Cambodia	Malaysia	Thailand
Indonesia	Philippines	Vietnam
Lao PDR	Singapore	

Sub-Saharan Africa

Angola	Gabon	Niger
Benin	Ghana	Nigeria
Botswana	Guinea-Bissau	Rwanda
Burkina Faso	Kenya	Senegal
Burundi	Lesotho	Sierra Leone
Cameroon	Madagascar	South Africa
Central African Republic	Malawi	Tanzania
Chad	Mali	Togo
Congo, Dem. Rep.	Mauritania	Uganda
Congo, Rep.	Mauritius	Zambia
Cote d'Ivoire	Mozambique	Zimbabwe
Ethiopia	Namibia	

High-income economies

Australia	Germany	New Zealand
Austria	Greece	Norway

Bahamas, The	Hong Kong SAR, China	Oman
Bahrain	Hungary	Poland
Barbados	Iceland	Portugal
Belgium	Ireland	Slovak Republic
Canada	Israel	Slovenia
Croatia	Italy	Spain
Cyprus	Japan	Sweden
Czech Republic	Korea, Rep.	Switzerland
Denmark	Kuwait	Trinidad and Tobago
Estonia	Luxembourg	United Kingdom
Finland	Malta	United States
France	Netherlands	

Notes

1 "Economic miracles are a public good: each economist sees in them a vindication of his pet theories" (Bhagwati 2000: 98).

2 Japan, South Korea, Taiwan, Hong Kong, Singapore, Malaysia, Thailand and Indonesia.

3 Radelet et al. 2001 is the only such study in which regional dummy variables are not statistically significant.

4 This index classifies an economy as closed when any of the following criteria holds: (i) its average tariff rate exceeds 40 percent, (ii) its non-tariff barriers cover more than 40 percent of imports, (iii) it has a socialist economic system, (iv) it has a state monopoly of major exports, or (v) its black-market premium exceeds 20 percent during either the decade of the 1970s or the decade of the 1980s. Otherwise, the economy is considered "open."

5 Among papers that we cite here, only Lee and Hong (2010) uses this definition of openness.

6 The most enduring "spillover" narrative in Asia is of course the "flying geese hypothesis," which characterizes spillovers in the form of an international product cycle linked to trade and the cross-border relocation of industries (Akamatsu 1962; Lin 2011).

7 Take as an example the case of imported intermediates. By the Cobb–Douglas assumption, $\sigma Y = P_x X$, where $P_x = (1 + t_x)$ when the world price of intermediates is normalized to unity. Then $X = \sigma Y / P_x$ and thus $\partial X / \partial t_x < 0$. Substituting for X in the Solow production function and solving, we have $\partial Y / \partial t_x$ isomorphic to $-\partial Y / A$. The solution for a lower tariff on capital goods imports is obtained form the dynamic equation for capital growth in equivalent fashion (Estevadeordal and Taylor 2008).

8 These gains do not depend on endogenous growth mechanisms (e.g., Rivera-Batiz and Romer 1991; Grossman and Helpman 1991), empirical support for which remains mixed (Kehoe and Ruhl 2010). The formal derivation of growth gains from lower tariffs on inputs provides a theoretical foundation for many prior assertions of the same phenomenon, e.g., by Radelet et al. 2001: 32–4; Levine and Renelt 1992.

9 The finding that lower tariffs on intermediates raises productivity finds support in a study using firm-level industrial data from Indonesia by Amiti and Konings (2007).

10 Source: World Development Indicators Online.

11 This period includes the major regional recession of 1997–99, but growth rates excluding this episode are also somewhat lower than for the pre-crisis decade.

12 See, for example, World Bank 1993, Radelet et al. 2001, Dowling 1997, Kong 2007.

13 For a good recent review of empirical growth analyses with spillovers see Roberts and Deichmann 2011.

14 With the exception of the Philippines, Southeast Asia's middle-income economies (as well as Singapore, now classed as high income) have a record of good macroeconomic management associated with a strong aversion to inflation. In the five-year period prior to the Plaza Accord these economies were able to maintain the lowest average inflation rate among developing economies. With the exception of South Asia, all other regions recorded two- or three-digit average inflation rates.

15 Compared with weighted average GDP growth in the group of 24 "early entrant" OECD countries plus China, Japan's growth rate lay above the 95 percent confidence interval in nine of the 13 years from 1979 to 1991. Growth rates and shares computed from World Development Indicators Online.

16 See below for additional discussion.

17 In the actual regression analysis the weight matrix may be reduced to a smaller dimension due to variable availability of some countries. In this case, the row sum of this actual weight matrix may not add up to 1.

18 The estimation results are not sensitive to use of weights from adjacent sub-periods.

19 Secondary school enrollment data for Singapore are scaled from enrollment data available at UNICEF's website, http://www.childinfo.org/files/IND_Singapore.pdf

20 Data on disaggregated tariffs by consumption, intermediate and capital goods, as used by Estevadeordal and Taylor, are unavailable for several Southeast Asian economies. Our use of the EFW index is a second-best choice, but superior to the Sachs–Warner index.

21 Values of the EFW openness index data for Cambodia, Laos and Vietnam are missing for many early years. We reconstruct them based on the Penn World Tables openness measure, which is computed as (exports + imports)/GDP.

22 To test for robustness, we run fixed-effects regressions on the same baseline specification but for 10-year sub-periods. Results are in Table 4.7. All independent variables remain significant with expected signs and magnitudes. It could also be that growth spillovers occur through indirect channels rather than through trade. To check for robustness with respect to this possibility, we replicated all the regressions presented in Table 4.7 using a measure of growth spillovers that excludes openness. All major findings remain robust. Similarly, we investigate effects of growth booms in countries other than Japan and China. From Figures 4.1 and 4.2, the obvious (and perhaps only) alternative candidate is the United States, which experienced a sustained growth episode from the second Reagan administration to the end of the Clinton era in 2000. Using the same techniques as for China and Japan, we re-run the growth models already discussed. The US effect is never significant; other coefficient estimates are broadly similar to those already reported.

23 The dependent variable in the maximum likelihood estimation is output per worker in each sub-period.

24 These estimates are robust to a wide range of alternative model specifications. Though we report only the models using Type 4 weights, we also fit the same series of models using weights of Types 1–3. There are 32 models in all. The estimate of *rho* is positive and significant in all but two. The results are also robust with respect to inclusion of "new" countries in the later period of the data. We re-estimated the later data, restricting the sample to only those countries included in the 1980s–1990s period. The main results were unchanged.

25 In the early period, "Northeast Asia" consists only of Japan and Korea, due to data limitations. In the later period this group also includes China.

26 Controlling for shipping distances in growth regressions is a possible direction for future research.

References

Acemoglu, D. and J. Robinson (2012). *Why Nations Fail: The Origins of Power, Prosperity and Poverty.* New York: Crown.

Acemoglu, D., S. Johnson and J. Robinson (2005). "Institutions as a fundamental cause of long-run economic growth." In P. Aghion and S. Durlauf (eds), *Handbook of Economic Growth* Vol. 1. Amsterdam: Elsevier, pp. 385–472.

Akamatsu, K. (1962). "A historical pattern of economic growth in developing countries." *Developing Economies*, supplement issue, 1: 3–25.

Amiti, M. and J. Konings (2007). "Trade liberalization, intermediate inputs and productivity: evidence from Indonesia." *American Economic Review* 97(5): 1611–38.

Athukorala, P-C. and N. Yamashita (2006). "Production fragmentation and trade integration: East Asia in a global context." *North American Journal of Economics and Finance* 17(3): 233–56.

Baldwin, R.E. (2003). "Openness and growth: what's the empirical relationship?" NBER Working Paper No. 9578.

Bergstrand, J.H. (1985). "The gravity equation in international trade: some microeconomic foundations and empirical evidence." *Review of Economics and Statistics* 67(3): 474–81.

Bhagwati, J.N. (2000). *Protectionism.* Cambridge, MA: MIT Press.

Block, S.A. (2001). "Does Africa grow differently?" *Journal of Development Economics* 65: 443–67.

Collins, S.M. and B.P. Bosworth (1996). "Economic growth in East Asia: accumulation versus assimilation." *Brookings Papers on Economic Activity* (2): 135–203.

Conley, T.G. and E. Ligon (2002). "Economic distance and cross-country spillovers." *Journal of Economic Growth* 7: 157–87.

Coxhead, I. (2007). "A new resource curse? Impacts of China's boom on comparative advantage and resource dependence in Southeast Asia." *World Development* 35(7): 1099–119.

Coxhead, I. and M. Li (2008). "Prospects for skills-based exports in resource-rich developing economies: Indonesia in comparative perspective." *Bulletin of Indonesian Economic Studies* 44(2): 199–228.

Deardorff, A. (1998). "Determinants of bilateral trade: does gravity work in a neoclassical world?" In J.A. Frankel (ed.), *The Regionalization of the World Economy*. Cambridge, MA: National Bureau of Economic Research.

Dowling, M. (1997). "Asia's economic miracle: an historical perspective." *Australian Economic Review* 30(1): 113–23.

Easterly, W. and R. Levine (1998). "Troubles with the neighbours: Africa's problem, Africa's opportunity." *Journal of African Economies* 7(1): 120–42.

Eichengreen, B. and Hui Tong (2005). "Fear of China." *Journal of Asian Economics* 17: 226–40.

Ertur, C. and W. Koch (2007). "Growth, technological interdependence and spatial externalities: theory and evidence." *Journal of Applied Econometrics* 22: 1033–62.

Estevadeordal, A. and A.M. Taylor (2008). "Is the Washington Consensus dead? Growth, openness and the Great Liberalization, 1970s–2000s." NBER Working Paper No. 14264.

Frankel, J.A., D. Romer and T. Cyrus (1996). "Trade and growth in East Asian countries: cause and effect?" NBER Working Paper No. 5732.

Grossman, G. and E. Helpman (1991). *Innovation and Growth in the Global Economy*. Cambridge, MA: MIT Press.

Gwartney, J.D., J.C. Hall and R. Lawson (2011). *Economic Freedom of the World: 2010 Annual Report*. Vancouver, BC: The Fraser Institute. www.freetheworld.com.

Horioka, C. and A. Terada-Hagiwara (2011). "The determinants and long-term projections of saving rates in developing Asia." NBER Working Paper No. 17581.

Ianchovichina, E. and T. Walmsley (2003). "Impact of China's WTO accession on East Asia." World Bank Policy Research Working Paper 3109.

Ianchovichina, E., S. Suthiwart-Narueput and M. Zhao (2004). "Regional impact of China's WTO accession." In K.L. Krumm and H.J. Kharas (eds), *East Asia Integrates: A Trade Policy Agenda for Shared Growth*. Washington, DC: World Bank, pp. 57–78.

Kehoe, T.J. and K.J. Ruhl (2010). "Why have economic reforms in Mexico not generated growth?" NBER Working Paper No. 16580.

Kong, T. (2007). "A selective review of recent developments in the economic growth literature." *Asian-Pacific Economic Literature* 21(1): 1–33.

Krugman, P. (1994). "The myth of Asia's miracle." *Foreign Affairs* November–December, 62–78.

Lee, J-W. (1993). "International trade, distortions, and long-run economic growth." *IMF Staff Papers* 40(2): 299–328.

Lee, J-W. and K. Hong (2010). "Economic growth in Asia: determinants and prospects." Manila: Asian Development Bank Economics Working Paper Series No. 220.

Levine, R. and D. Renelt (1992). "A sensitivity analysis of cross-country growth regressions." *American Economic Review* 82(4): 942–63.

Lin, J. (2011). "From flying geese to leading dragons: new opportunities and strategies for structural transformation in developing countries." World Bank Policy Research Working Paper No. 5702.

Mankiw, G.N., D. Romer and D.N. Weil (1992). "A contribution to the empirics of economic growth." *Quarterly Journal of Economics* 107(2): 407–37.

Mátyás, L. (1997). "Proper econometric specification of the gravity model." *World Economy* 20(3): 363–8.

Moreno, R. and B. Trehan (1997). "Location and the growth of nations." *Journal of Economic Growth* 2: 299–418.

Phung, T. (2012). "Does Southeast Asia grow differently?" Master of Science Thesis, Department of Agricultural and Applied Economics, University of Wisconsin-Madison.

Radelet, S., J.D. Sachs and J-W. Lee (2001). "Determinants and prospects of economic growth in Asia." *International Economic Journal* 15(3): 1–29.

Ravenhill, J. (2006). "Is China an economic threat to Southeast Asia?" *Asian Survey* 46(5): 653–74.

Rebelo, S. (1992). "Growth in open economies." *Carnegie–Rochester Conference Series on Public Policy* 36: 5–46.

Rivera-Batiz, L.A. and P.M. Romer (1991). "Economic integration and endogenous growth." *Quarterly Journal of Economics* 106(2): 531–55.

Roberts, M. and U. Deichmann (2011). "International growth spillovers, geography and infrastructure." *World Economy* 34(9): 1507–33.

Rodriguez, F. and D. Rodrik (2001). "Trade policy and economic growth: a skeptic's guide to the cross-national evidence." In Ben Bernanke and Kenneth S. Rogoff (eds), *NBER Macroeconomics Annual 2000*. Cambridge, MA: MIT Press for NBER.

Sachs, J. and A. Warner (1995). "Economic reform and the process of global integration." *Brookings Papers on Economic Activity* (1): 1–118.

Sachs, J. and A. Warner (2001). "The curse of natural resources." *European Economic Review* 45: 827–38.

Thee, Kian Wee (2011). "Indonesia: blessed by strong economic growth and the curse of resources." *East Asia Forum*, 11 January. http://bit.ly/hTG22E

World Bank (1993). *The East Asian Miracle: Economic Growth and Public Policy*. Washington, DC: Oxford University Press for the World Bank.

World Bank (2007). "East Asia and Pacific update April 2007: ten years after the crisis." Washington, DC: World Bank.

Young, A. (1994). "Lessons from the East Asian NICs: a contrarian view." *European Economic Review* 38(3–4): 964–73.

Young, A. (1995). "The tyranny of numbers: confronting the statistical realities of the East Asian growth experience." *Quarterly Journal of Economics* 110(3): 641–80.

Part II

Food, agriculture, and natural resources

5

The dynamics of agricultural development and food security in Southeast Asia

Historical continuity and rapid change

C. Peter Timmer

HARVARD UNIVERSITY *EMERITUS*

Introduction

Food security is not a viable social objective unless it is also a profitable undertaking for input suppliers, farmers and marketers of output. Consumers must then be able to afford to purchase this food, secure in the knowledge that it is safe and nutritious. Achieving food security within these constraints of a complex economic system is a challenge because both poor consumers and small farmers must be effective participants. The standard approaches to food security – involving availability, access and utilization of sufficient food to lead healthy lives for everyone – do not deal with these issues of *who* does *what*.

The purpose of this chapter is to set this challenging task in the context of the long-run dynamic evolution of the rice-based agricultural systems in Southeast Asia. The emphasis is on both "long run" and on "dynamic," because these systems have very deep cultural roots (thus historical continuity and accompanying resistance to change), at the same time that they are changing extremely rapidly, driven by the pace of economic growth and technological innovation. Japan is an early model for Southeast Asia and is quite revealing because of its well-documented early history.[1] Sub-Saharan Africa was held up in the 1960s as the likely success story vis-à-vis Southeast Asia, and this comparative record is also quite revealing (although the African data are reliable only since the 1970s).

In a primitive agrarian economy with little trade, the household-level link between agricultural productivity and food security is quite direct. A century ago many rural households in Southeast Asia would have been heavily dependent on their own food production for subsistence, as Chapter 3 by Booth in this volume suggests. But even then, as Chapter 2 by Williamson indicates, many rural households were already producing commercially for export to urban areas and the world market. The transformation of the Southeast Asian economy from being primarily rural and subsistence-oriented to primarily urban and trade-oriented has been underway for a long time (hence the "long transition" in the title of Coxhead's introductory chapter to this volume), with significant implications for the role of agriculture and the mechanisms for providing food security.

Rapid change in the food systems of Southeast Asia since 1960

The flagship publication of the Food and Agriculture Organization of the United Nations (FAO), *State of Food Insecurity in the World 2012*, provides a sophisticated new methodology for estimating the prevalence of undernutrition and uses it with the latest data to present the best indicators available on the state and dynamics of food security at the country level between 1990–92 and 2010–12 (FAO, WFP and IFAD 2012). Table 5.1 summarizes the key data for Southeast Asia

Table 5.1 Comparative food security indicators

Region/Indicator	Time period (and change from previous time period)				
	1990–92	2000–02	(change)	2010–12	(change)
World					
Prevalence[1]	18.6	14.9	(–3.7)	12.5	(–2.4)
Food supply[2]	114	117	(+3)	121	(+4)
Food deficit[3]	7.2	5.8	(–1.4)	5.1	(–0.7)
Food security gap[4]	6.8	11.2	(+4.4)	15.9	(+4.7)
Sub-Saharan Africa					
Prevalence	32.8	29.7	(–3.1)	26.8	(–2.9)
Food supply	100	104	(+4)	109	(+5)
Food deficit	13.7	12.7	(–1.0)	11.8	(–0.9)
Food security gap	–13.7	–8.7	(+5.0)	–2.8	(+5.9)
South Asia					
Prevalence	26.8	21.3	(–5.3)	17.6	(–3.7)
Food supply	106	104	(–2)	107	(+3)
Food deficit	10.2	8.6	(–1,6)	7.1	(–1.5)
Food security gap	–4.2	–4.6	(–0.4)	–0.1	(+4.5)
Southeast Asia					
Prevalence	29.6	19.2	(–10.4)	10.9	(–8.3)
Food supply	100	107	(+7)	120	(+13)
Food deficit	12.3	7.4	(–4.9)	4.3	(–3.1)
Food security gap	–12.3	–0.4	(+11.9)	15.7	(+16.1)
Developing East Asia					
Prevalence	20.8	14.3	(–6.5)	11.5	(–2.8)
Food supply	107	117	(+10)	124	(+7)
Food deficit	8.2	5.2	(–3.0)	4.0	(–1.2)
Food security gap	–1.2	11.8	(+13.0)	20.0	(+8.2)

Source: FAO, WFP, and IFAD 2012.
Notes:
[1] Prevalence of undernourishment.
[2] Average dietary energy supply adequacy.
[3] Food deficit is the "depth of the food deficit in kcal per capita per day" as a % of MDER (minimum dietary energy requirement).
[4] Food security gap = (Supply – 100) – Food deficit = FSgap. When FSgap = 0, there is exactly enough "surplus" food supply to offset the entire food energy deficit.

along with data for Sub-Saharan Africa, other regions in Asia, and the global total for comparative purposes. For each region, data are shown for 1990–92, 2000–02 and 2010–12, with changes calculated between decades.

Four food security indicators are shown for each region. First is the "prevalence of undernourishment," the "headline" indicator used to measure progress on the Millennium Development Goals (goal 1, target 1.9). It is the proportion of the population at risk of caloric inadequacy and is the traditional FAO measure of hunger. Second is a new measure of average dietary energy supply adequacy. This indicator expresses each country's or region's average supply of food calories available for consumption (including imports) as a percentage of average dietary energy requirements for the population, as calculated by FAO. Third is a measure of the depth of the food deficit facing the undernourished, also as calculated by FAO. It indicates how many calories would be needed to lift the undernourished from their status, normalized by total population, everything else held constant. The measure shown in Table 5.1 uses the "depth of the food deficit in kcal per capita per day" as a percentage of the minimum dietary energy requirement (MDER), so that it is on a similar scale as the food supply measure.

Finally, a "food security gap" is calculated for this chapter to indicate the rough balance between food supplies available and the depth and extent of hunger. This gap is simply the "surplus" food supply available (food supply − 100) minus the food deficit, as calculated and reported in Table 5.1. A negative gap means the food deficit is larger than the food surplus, with the inevitable consequence that people will be hungry even with equitable distribution. Sharply positive levels of the gap mean there is plenty of food for all.[2] Substantial hunger (high "prevalence") in these environments suggests a highly unequal distribution of economic resources. This measure of the food security gap is a particularly sensitive indicator of progress (or lack thereof) in reducing undernourishment, and whether availability or access is the limiting factor.

It is clear from the data in Table 5.1 that Southeast Asia has made substantial progress in reducing food insecurity over the past two decades, compared with global progress. At the global level, prevalence of undernutrition has fallen from 18.6 percent in 1990–92 to 12.5 percent in 2010–12, a decline of 6.1 percentage points (almost a third).

Southeast Asia has done much better during the same two decades, with prevalence dropping by 18.7 percentage points. Most remarkably, the region has moved from negative food security gaps to sharply positive ones – a very large negative gap of −12.3 percent was transformed into a very large positive gap of 15.7 points in just 20 years. Both improved supplies (up 20 percent) and sharply lowered food deficits (down 8 percent) contributed to this amazing performance.

At one level, the relationship between an improving food security gap and reductions in prevalence of malnutrition seems obvious. More food and smaller deficits should translate into less hunger. But as Table 5.2 indicates, there are nuances to the relationship that are worth exploring.

Table 5.2 Relationship between the food security gap and the prevalence of undernutrition

Regression 1: Prevalence of Undernutrition (pou)
pou= −55.8437 − 2.1924 FSgap + 0.0076 FSgap (squared)
(2.40)*   (4.98)**   (3.34)**
R squared = 0.93 N = 231

Sources: Data from FAO, WFP and IFAD 2012, and author's calculations.
Standard errors used to calculate *t*-statistics are robust for country clusters.
* = significance at 5%;
** at 1%

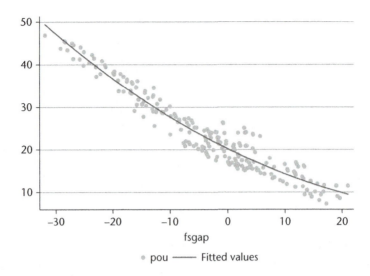

Figure 5.1   Regression 1 fit and residuals (see Table 5.2)

In particular, the relationship is not linear – there are clear diminishing returns to improving the food security gap in terms of lowering the prevalence of undernutrition.[3] The degree of curvature in the relationship between Prevalence of Undernutrition and FSgap is shown in the plot of residuals in Figure 5.1.

The impact of a one percentage point improvement in the food security gap is −2.49 percentage points in the prevalence of undernourishment when evaluated at FSgap = −20, but just −1.89 when FSgap = +20. This 25 percent difference in the marginal response rate points clearly to the need to develop more targeted strategies to reach the remaining poor and hungry as the blunter instruments – increasing food supplies and overall economic growth – lose their impact. Food insecurity becomes less a problem of food availability and general poverty, and more a structural problem of people "left behind." Structural poverty and hunger require a much more sophisticated and targeted approach than the "pro-poor growth with stability" strategy that Asia has tended to use historically (Timmer 2004).

Explaining the stellar performance of Southeast Asia (at least in comparative terms) requires some historical perspective in order to understand how dramatically the food system in Southeast Asia has changed in the past half-century. As a starting point:

1   There was a broad *political mandate* in Southeast Asia to provide food security to both urban and rural populations, a mandate not seen as clearly in much of Africa. Food security was politically important, which led to a strategy of "pro-poor" growth, including major investments in rural infrastructure and agricultural development that included smallholder farms, thus addressing both "availability" and "access" issues of food security (see Tables 5.1 and 5.2).

2   A technological revolution in rice was coupled with (reasonably) good policies on input and output marketing, and public investments in rural infrastructure to make this mandate (largely) possible. Investments in water control – both irrigation and drainage – were critically important in Southeast Asia both for their impact on crop productivity and their stabilizing impact on yields of rice (the next section presents the key dimensions of the agricultural

transformation in Southeast Asia, especially changes in the share of rice, meat, eggs, palm oil and rubber in agricultural GDP, net rice exports relative to wheat imports, and the changing composition of the livestock and poultry sectors as an indicator of commercialization of agriculture).

3   Rapid, inclusive economic growth (resulting largely from 1 and 2) gave (most) households access to the food in their fields and markets, although Cambodia, Laos, Myanmar and East Timor are partial exceptions. Rapid growth and improved access to food in markets stimulated a dietary transformation, which is driven largely by income growth and rural to urban migration. The increasing role of wheat and the declining starchy staple ratio are especially striking, as discussed below.

What's changed, then, is the role of the food and agricultural sector in these societies – the structural transformation itself. This has been driven by these processes and the changing role of rice in the economy. Southeast Asia is now richer, more urban, better connected both within each country and across borders, and it is much better fed than a half-century ago. Those of us who learned about the development process by observing it over these decades in Southeast Asia are astonished at the progress achieved in the face of formidable obstacles at the start. In 1963, Clifford Geertz, in his highly influential *Agricultural Involution*, argued that Javanese peasants were doomed to "shared poverty." In 1968, Gunnar Myrdal wrote in *Asian Drama* that "no economist holds out any hope for Indonesia." Both would no doubt be stunned by the progress in Indonesia specifically and Southeast Asia more broadly.

The three fundamental transformations needed to provide food security

Three transformations drive the link between agricultural development and food security in Southeast Asia and most other parts of the world: structural, agricultural and dietary (Timmer 2009). Especially in Asia, accompanying these three basic transformations have been rapid changes in the entire food marketing system (led by the "supermarket revolution," see Reardon and Timmer 2012), and in the growing importance of urban consumers as drivers of a country's food system. The "endpoint" of the structural transformation – the full integration of factor markets between rural and urban areas – is now within sight in the richest countries of East Asia, but remains a challenge to the middle-income countries in Southeast Asia.

Structural transformation

The structural transformation involves declining shares of agriculture in GDP and employment, almost always accompanied by serious problems closing the gap in labor productivity between agriculture and non-agriculture. The basic *cause and effect* of the structural transformation is rising productivity of agricultural labor. Table 5.3 and Figure 5.2 present the basic long-run data for Japan and Indonesia – from 1880 to 2010 – and shorter time series for the Philippines, Thailand and Vietnam. These four Southeast Asian countries will be used to illustrate the long-run process of structural transformation – they account for 77 percent of rice output and 83 percent of population in the region.[4]

The historical path of structural transformation has been accompanied by falling food prices, leading to a "world without agriculture" (Timmer 2009). But continued financial instability, coupled with the impact of climate change, could lead to a new and uncertain path of rising real

Table 5.3 Structural transformation in Southeast Asia

Country	Indicator Name	1880	1890	1900	1910	1920	1930	1950	1960	1970	1980	1990	2000	2010
JPN	Agriculture, value added (% of GDP)	41.4	36.4	31.6	29.4	23.9	20.0	17.8	13.2	7.7	4.7	3.5	2.3	1.16
JPN	Employment in agriculture (% of total employment)	68.9	64.6	61.0	58.1	54.1	49.7	39.4	30.1	17.3	10.6	7.2	5.1	3.7
JPN	AgshrGAP = AgshrGDP – AgshrEMP	-27.5	-28.2	-29.4	-28.7	-30.2	-29.7	-21.6	-16.9	-9.6	-5.9	-3.7	-2.8	-2.54
JPN	GDP per capita, PPP (constant 2005 international $)	1427	1505	1832	2041	2643	2839	3677	5784	12522	17835	26523	28889	30965
JPN	Logarithm of GDP per capita	7.263	7.317	7.513	7.621	7.880	7.951	8.210	8.663	9.435	9.789	10.186	10.271	10.341
JPN	Agricultural terms of trade									2.74	2.96	2.98	3.16	3.71
JPN	Agriculture value added per worker (constant 2000 US$)										11358	16827	26180	40385
IDN	Agriculture, value added (% of GDP)	44.1	42.5	41.4	40.4	36.7	33.1	35.5	31.0	27.8	21.4	18.5	15.6	13.2
IDN	Employment in agriculture (% of total employment)	76.3	76.3	76.4	76.5	76.8	77.1	72.2	69.9	64.7	56.4	55.9	45.3	38.3
IDN	AgshrGAP = AgshrGDP – AgshrEMP	-32.2	-33.8	-35.0	-36.1	-40.1	-44.0	-36.7	-38.9	-36.9	-35.0	-37.4	-29.7	-25.1
IDN	GDP per capita, PPP (constant 2005 international $)	528	522	583	641	714	864	649	806	978	1508	2032	2623	3789
IDN	Logarithm of GDP per capita	6.269	6.258	6.368	6.463	6.571	6.762	6.475	6.692	6.886	7.319	7.617	7.872	8.240
IDN	Agricultural terms of trade								1.58	1.51	0.93	1	1	1.19
IDN	Agriculture value added per worker (constant 2000 US$)										449.8	492.8	531.5	730.0
PHL	Agriculture, value added (% of GDP)							36	26.9	29.5	25.1	21.9	14.0	12.3
PHL	Employment in agriculture (% of total employment)							76	61	53	51.8	45.2	37.1	35.2
PHL	AgshrGAP = AgshrGDP – AgshrEMP							-40	-34.1	-23.5	-26.7	-23.3	-23.1	-22.9
PHL	GDP per capita, PPP (constant 2005 international $)							1259	1735	2072	2827	2552	2697	3560
PHL	Logarithm of GDP per capita							7.138	7.459	7.636	7.947	7.844	7.900	8.178

(continues in the next page)

Table 5.3 (Continued)

Country	Indicator Name	1880	1890	1900	1910	1920	1930	1950	1960	1970	1980	1990	2000	2010
PHL	Agricultural terms of trade								1.44	1.78	1.76	1.57	1	1.07
PHL	Agriculture value added per worker (constant 2000 US$)										916.5	854.3	912.3	1118.7
THA	Agriculture, value added (% of GDP)							49.0	36.4	25.9	23.2	12.5	9.0	12.4
THA	Employment in agriculture (% of total employment)							85.0	84.0	80.0	70.8	64.0	48.8	41.5
THA	AgshrGAP = AgshrGDP – AgshrEMP							-36.0	-47.6	-54.1	-47.6	-51.5	-39.8	-29.1
THA	GDP per capita, PPP (constant 2005 international $)							704	929	1460	2221.0	3933.0	5497.0	7673.0
THA	Logarithm of GDP per capita							6.557	6.834	7.286	7.706	8.277	8.612	8.945
THA	Agricultural terms of trade								1.1	1.0	1.2	0.9	0.9	1.6
THA	Agriculture value added per worker (constant 2000 US$)										384.2	442.7	551.2	706.0
VNM	Agriculture, value added (% of GDP)											38.7	24.5	20.6
VNM	Employment in agriculture (% of total employment)											70.0	65.0	50.0
VNM	AgshrGAP = AgshrGDP – AgshrEMP											-31.3	-40.5	-29.4
VNM	GDP per capita, PPP (constant 2005 international $)							572	695	639	659	905	1516	2875
VNM	Logarithm of GDP per capita							6.349	6.544	6.460	6.491	6.808	7.324	7.964
VNM	Agricultural terms of trade											1.35	1.07	1.32
VNM	Agriculture value added per worker (constant 2000 US$)											222.3	294.7	367.1

Sources: The primary source for data since 1960 is World Development Indicators from the World Bank. Earlier data for Japan and Indonesia come from Hayami and Yamada (1991) and van der Eng (2010) respectively. Note that there is some controversy over how to compare these two countries over such an extensive time period. Each of the data series used here is based on domestic national accounts, and is merged with the WDI data at an appropriate time period. By contrast, Maddison (1995, 2001) compares these two countries directly with the same methodology and converts their per capita GDP into 1990 Geary–Khamis dollars. Using this technique, the per capita incomes of Japan and Indonesia are much more similar in the starting year than is indicated in the table here: in 1870, for example, Maddison finds that per capita GDP levels are G–K $ 737 in Japan compared with G–K $ 654 in Indonesia (and G–K $ 707 in Thailand). Thus using the country-specific methodologies, the ratio of Japanese to Indonesian per capita GDPs in 1880 is 2.7. Using Maddison's methodology, the similar ratio in 1870 is just 1,1. Using the Maddison methodology would make the respective lines in Figure 5.2 much more similar, but requires a substantially higher growth rate in Japan (or lower growth rate in Indonesia) for the per capita GDP levels to align with WDI data for recent years.

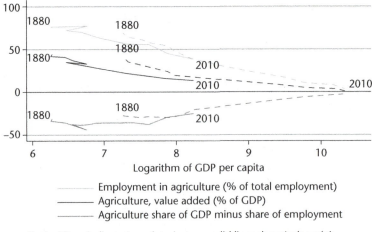

Dashed lines indicate Japan's trajectory; solid lines show Indonesia's.

Figure 5.2   Structural transformation in Japan and Indonesia, 1880–2010

costs for food with a reversal of structural transformation (Timmer and Akkus 2008). Management of food policy, and the outlook for sustained poverty reduction, will be radically different depending on which of these global price regimes plays out, and Southeast Asia has a particularly sharp interest in the outcome.

The structural transformation involves four main features:

1   a falling share of agriculture in economic output and employment,
2   a rising share of urban economic activity in industry and modern services,
3   migration of rural workers to urban settings, and
4   a demographic transition in birth and death rates that always leads to a spurt in population growth before a new equilibrium is reached.

These four dimensions of the historical pathway of structural transformation are experienced by all successful developing economies; diversity appears in the various approaches governments have tried to cope with the political pressures generated along that pathway. Finding efficient policy mechanisms that will keep the poor from falling off the pathway altogether has occupied the development profession for decades. There are three key lessons.

First, the structural transformation has been the main pathway out of poverty for all societies, and it depends on rising productivity in *both* the agricultural and non-agricultural sectors (and the two are connected). The stress on productivity growth in both sectors is important, as agricultural labor can be pushed off of farms into even lower productivity informal service sector jobs, a perverse form of structural transformation that has generated large pockets of urban poverty, especially in Sub-Saharan Africa and India.[5]

Second, in the early stages, the process of structural transformation *widens* the gap between labor productivity in the agricultural and non-agricultural sectors – a process seen especially clearly in Figure 5.2 for Japan and Indonesia, but also happening in the rest of Southeast Asia, as seen in Table 5.3. This widening puts enormous pressure on rural societies to adjust and modernize. These pressures are then translated into visible and significant policy responses that alter agricultural prices. The agricultural surpluses generated in rich countries because of artificially high prices then cause artificially low prices in world markets and a consequent undervaluation of agriculture in poor countries. This undervaluation over the past several decades, and its attendant reduction in agricultural investments, is a significant factor explaining the world food crisis in 2007/08 and continuing high food prices.

Third, despite the decline in relative importance of the agricultural sector, leading to the "world without agriculture" in rich societies, the process of economic growth and structural transformation requires major investments in the agricultural sector itself. This seeming paradox has complicated (and obfuscated) planning in developing countries as well as donor agencies seeking to speed economic growth and connect the poor to it. Indonesia, Malaysia, Thailand and (more recently) Vietnam have escaped much of this paradox, but the Philippines, Cambodia, Laos and Myanmar have not.

For poverty-reducing initiatives to be feasible over long periods of time – to be "sustainable," in current development jargon – the indispensable necessity is a growing economy that success-fully integrates factor markets in the rural with urban sectors, and stimulates higher productivity in both. That is, *the long-run success of poverty reduction hinges directly on a successful structural transformation.* The historical record is very clear on this path.

Managing the ingredients of rapid transformation and coping with its distributional conse-quences has turned out to be a major challenge for policymakers. "Getting agriculture moving" in poor countries is a complicated, long-run process that requires close, but changing, relationships between the public and private sectors. Donor agencies are not good at this. More problematic, the process of agricultural development requires good economic governance in the countries themselves if it is to work rapidly and efficiently. Aid donors cannot hope to contribute good governance themselves – and may well impede it.

The strong historical tendency toward a widening of income differences between rural and urban economies during the initial stages of the structural transformation is now extending much further into the development process. Consequently, with little prospect of reaching quickly the turning point, where farm and non-farm productivity and incomes begin to converge, many poor countries are turning to agricultural protection and farm subsidies sooner rather than later in their development process. The tendency of these actions to hurt the poor is then compounded, because there are so many more rural poor in these early stages. Protection for rice farmers in Indonesia, the Philippines and Thailand illustrates the point clearly.

Agricultural transformation

Although the structural transformation is a general equilibrium process that is not easily visible from inside the agricultural sector, the changing demand and productivity patterns induce significant change within the sector itself (Timmer 1988). This agricultural transformation is driven by changing domestic demand, opportunities for international trade, commercialization of decision making, and technical change that is both commodity specific – e.g., "green revolu-tion" varieties of wheat and rice – and sector-wide, with better inputs, improved knowledge, communications, infrastructure and financial intermediation. Non-staple commodities, such as palm oil, and non-food commodities, such as rubber, play larger roles in certain circumstances. The potential for commodities to be grown as raw materials for bio-fuel production – especially palm oil and cassava – might be a future driver of the agricultural transformation (with highly uncertain consequences for food security).

No single measure of the pace and extent of agricultural transformation captures the complexity and heterogeneity of the process – much is country- and time-specific. The most

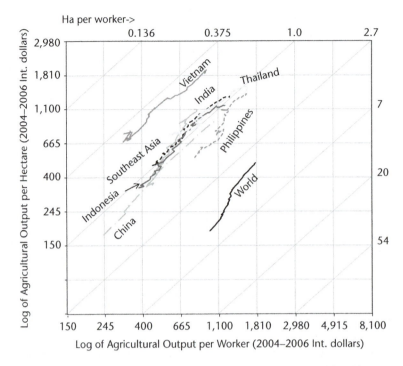

Figure 5.3 Agricultural productivity change in Southeast Asia, 1961–2010, with comparisons
Source: Courtesy of Professor Phil Pardey, University of Minnesota.
Notes: All data are from FAOStat. Land is the sum of pasture and harvested area; Agricultural workers are economically active population in agriculture; Southeast Asia includes: Brunei Darussalam, Myanmar, Indonesia, Cambodia, Lao People's Democratic Republic, Malaysia, Philippines, Timor-Leste, Singapore, Thailand and Vietnam.

graphic and general representation of the process of agricultural transformation is the "Ruttan-a-gram," which measures productivity per hectare on the vertical axis and productivity per worker on the horizontal axis (see Figure 5.3). This two-dimensional perspective on agricultural development was developed in Hayami and Ruttan (1985), where it was used as a powerful tool to demonstrate the multiple paths to successful agricultural transformation. The "Asian Path" relied heavily on new biological and chemical technologies to raise yields in land-scarce, labor-surplus environments, whereas mechanical technologies were used to raise labor productivity in land-abundant, labor-scarce environments. Japan characterized the former approach to raising agricultural productivity; the United States, Canada and Australia/New Zealand characterized the latter. Western Europe was, appropriately, in between these two more extreme approaches.

Figure 5.3 shows the pathways of productivity change in the agricultural sectors of key countries in Southeast Asia from 1961 to 2010. Also shown are pathways for China and India, as well as the world total. Two things are striking. The first is the rapid pace of gain in most countries (indicated by the overall length of the line for each country or region because both axes are measured in logarithms). Indonesia and Thailand have both seen major gains in labor and land productivity over the past half-century; the Philippines and Vietnam have lagged a bit, although Vietnam is clearly catching up rapidly.

The second striking feature is that land consolidation has barely begun in the region. Virtually all of the growth for the region and the key countries in it has been along a constant "iso-area" line, indeed, close to just 1.0 hectare per worker. Uncertain landownership and tenancy laws throughout the region may account for some of this "stickiness" in reported farm size. Outmoded statistical definitions may also be a factor: workers may be counted in the agricultural labor force even if most of their income is derived from off-farm sources.

Thailand is a characteristic example:

> Though the average paddy farm size in Thai Central Plains has begun to increase in the last 10 years, the change is very small. But as the heads of farm families are rapidly aging and their children are not farming, there must be some major changes in the future. Mechanization, especially the use of hired planting machine services, has begun to spread rapidly in some Central Plains provinces. On the other hand, the sons and daughters of old farmers have rented out their farmland to their friends and cousins. They are not willing to rent their land to other people mainly because of the constraints in the farm tenant law. But sooner or later they will sell their land, particularly when there are bubbles. I think it is likely that the paddy farm size will easily reach 200–500 ha in the next ten years because the technology is there for a farm entrepreneur to manage such farm size. We are now observing very large farm size for sugar cane (more than 160 farms with at least 160 ha), rubber (more than 200 farms with at least 160 ha) and more than 11 oil palm farms with at least 3,200 ha.
>
> The number of full-time farmers is not difficult to measure. According to the Labor Force Survey in 2010, the farmers who work more than 40 hours per week in agriculture account for 27 % of total work force, while farmers who earn at least 50 % of their household income from farm are only 13.6% of all workforce (or 31.5 % of all farmers). These numbers are at least better than the [officially] reported 40% agricultural workforce.
>
> (*Nipon Poapangsakorn, personal communication, March 26, 2013*)

Details of the agricultural transformation for the region are shown in Table 5.4, which shows production of important commodities by decade and their share in agricultural value added. Again, two things stand out. First, total agricultural production has risen rapidly over the past half-century, by 3.44 percent per year. This rate is substantially faster than population growth (and faster than growth in the agricultural labor force), so agricultural output per capita has also risen rapidly. It should be obvious that agriculture plays a very dynamic role in the overall structural transformation. Although its share of output falls quite rapidly, agricultural production continues to increase in both total and per capita terms.

Second, although rice production has also risen substantially, other commodities such as meat, eggs and palm oil have increased much more rapidly. The diversification of agricultural production in Southeast Asia has been underway for some time. Going forward, increased focus on higher valued commodities such as animal products and oil palm, and reduced attention to rice, will be the main drivers of the agricultural transformation. Indeed, consumer expenditures on fruits and vegetables now exceed expenditures on rice in several countries in Southeast Asia.

An important challenge in these countries is whether domestic farmers will be able to produce competitively for their own markets. Indonesia and Thailand present an interesting contrast. According to FAO Food Balance Sheet data, Indonesia imported just 1.0 percent of its fruit and vegetable consumption in 1990, and this grew to 5.3 percent by 2009. Thailand exported 13 percent of its fruit and vegetable production in 1990, and this grew to 24.7 percent in 2009. In both countries there was a near doubling of consumption of fruits and vegetables, but much of the growth in Indonesia was provisioned by imports. The role of imported fruits and vegetables is especially critical in supplying supermarkets in Indonesia. Procurement officers for major

Table 5.4 Agricultural transformation in Southeast Asia

	1961	1970	1980	1990	2000	2010	Avg % change/year
Value of production, in 000 International $							
Total agricultural production	32746	43521	62955	87322	121315	176416	3.44%
Rice, paddy production	12133	16829	22470	29487	39874	52481	3.03%
Meat	2584	3844	5239	8888	13723	23388	4.60%
Pig	1272	1868	2231	4282	6407	10926	4.49%
Cattle, excluding buffalo	876	1208	1564	1841	2116	3449	2.80%
Chicken	436	768	1444	2765	5200	9013	6.38%
Eggs	1058	1293	1891	2540	3301	4971	3.21%
Hen eggs	198	331	660	1191	1768	2731	5.50%
"Other" bird eggs, in shell	860	962	1231	1349	1533	2240	1.97%
Ratio of hen eggs to "other"	0.230	0.344	0.536	0.883	1.153	1.219	
Palm oil	105	282	1447	3819	8038	16590	10.88%
Rubber	2068	2776	3546	4748	5879	8544	2.94%
Changing structure of commodity production							
Share of commodity in total production:							
Rice, paddy	0.371	0.387	0.357	0.338	0.329	0.297	
Meat	0.079	0.088	0.083	0.102	0.113	0.133	
Eggs	0.032	0.030	0.030	0.029	0.027	0.028	
Palm oil	0.003	0.006	0.023	0.044	0.066	0.094	
Rubber	0.063	0.064	0.056	0.054	0.048	0.048	
"Other"	0.452	0.425	0.451	0.433	0.416	0.399	
Changing role of rice and wheat						2009	
Net rice exports from SE Asia (mmt)	1.869	−0.801	1.247	4.876	7.293	12.779	
Wheat imports to SE Asia (mmt)	0.969	2.387	4.055	4.848	9.855	13.077	
Net rice exports as % of rice consumption	7.75%	−2.36%	2.77%	9.03%	11.02%	17.02%	

Source: FAOStat.

supermarket chains have had a difficult time establishing reliable domestic suppliers able to meet the quality and safety standards demanded by these chains. The problems and opportunities presented by modern food supply chains are discussed in the final section.

Dietary transformation

The basic drivers of changed dietary patterns are Engel's Law (the share of food in budget expenditures falls with higher incomes, thus providing a buffer against the welfare impact of sudden changes in food prices) and Bennett's Law (the share of starchy staples in the diet falls with higher incomes, as a deep, perhaps "hard-wired," desire for diversity in the diet can be expressed), but long-run changes in relative prices, changing demographics, as well as exposure to "foreign" eating patterns also seem to have an impact.

As with the agricultural transformation, no single measure captures the complexity of dietary changes. Table 5.5 presents several important dimensions of the dietary transformation that is underway in Southeast Asia. Figure 5.4 presents the patterns visually, with the area of each

Table 5.5 Dietary transformation in Southeast Asia

	1961	1970	1980	1990	2000	2009	Avg % change/year
Food supply, (kcal/cap/day)–Total	1814	1955	2153	2164	2417	2657	0.80%
Cereals (ex. Beer)	1173	1320	1429	1370	1482	1549	0.58%
Rice	1057	1176	1246	1187	1234	1256	0.36%
Rice kcal as % of total kcal	58.3	60.2	57.9	54.9	51.1	47.3	
Starchy roots	183	131	143	102	91	101	–1.23%
Wheat	30	61	81	67	119	145	8.00%
Starchy Staple Ratio (SSR)	74.8	74.2	73.0	68.0	65.1	62.1	
Food supply, gm/cap/day							
Animal protein	8.3	10.0	10.6	13.3	17.1	22.8	2.13%
Fat	27	28.6	32.8	39.9	46.3	58.8	1.63%
Wheat as % of rice	2.84	5.19	6.5	5.64	9.64	11.54	

Source: FAO Food Balance Sheets.

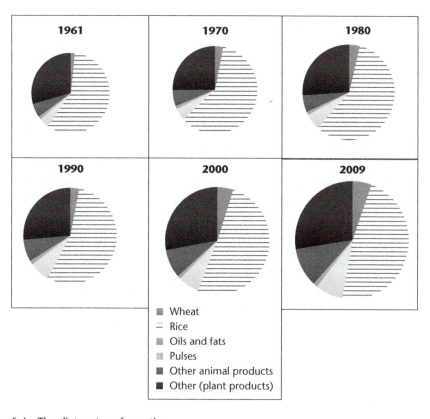

Figure 5.4 The dietary transformation

pie chart proportional to average energy intake per capita for each of the six years depicted. Four things are striking. First, total caloric intake has risen steadily over the past half-century, by 0.8 percent per year. In 1961, average food availability per capita, as measured by FAO Food Balance Sheet data, was just 1814 calories per day. Most citizens of Southeast Asia would have been chronically hungry then. By 2009, the most recent year for which data are available, food available per capita per day reached 2657 calories. At that level, hunger will not be common and obesity will be a rising problem.

Second, the starchy staple ratio – the share of calories coming from cereals and starchy roots – fell from 74.8 percent to 62.1 percent. Intake of animal protein nearly tripled. The quality of the diet in nutritional terms has improved markedly, although the doubling of fat in the diet is a worrisome sign.

Third, rising consumption of animal products will require a modern feed industry to supply domestic producers of poultry, livestock and aquaculture products, unless imports of final goods increase drastically. Domestic farmers have a rapidly growing market for feedstuffs, but at the moment a very large proportion of Southeast Asia's feed ingredients, especially maize and soy meal, is imported.

Finally, wheat calories are increasing 8 percent per year and wheat consumption is now more than a tenth of rice consumption. Southeast Asia imports all of its wheat – Indonesia surpassed Egypt in 2013 as the world's largest importer of wheat. A volatile world market for wheat will increasingly be seen as a threat to food security in Southeast Asia, but national agricultural development strategies cannot be used to cope with that threat. With rice becoming less important to food security in the region, and wheat and feedgrains becoming more important, management of food security will increasingly be a trade and macroeconomic issue rather than an agricultural issue.

The changing role of rice in Southeast Asia's food security: consumption and production

Aggregate time series data show that rice has been an inferior good at the global level since the mid-1990s. This aggregate trend is revealing, but it conceals the wide heterogeneity of rice consumption among individual households (Timmer et al. 2010, from which much of this section is drawn). The heterogeneity is driven by household incomes, by whether the household lives in urban or rural areas, and by many other factors, including cultural heritage and tastes.

A unique set of data – rice consumption by income (or expenditure) quintile, usually for rural and urban households separately, often for several time periods, for a total of 11 countries was assembled by Timmer et al. (2010). China, India and Indonesia alone account for 60 percent of world rice consumption, so having disaggregated data for these countries is crucial to under-standing the underlying dynamics of rice consumption. The Philippines and Vietnam are also large rice consumers – the Philippines is often the world's largest importer and Vietnam is the second largest exporter. Bangladesh is a major rice producer and consumer, with 70 percent of its daily caloric intake still coming from rice.

Six patterns stand out from these household-level data. First, there is overwhelming diversity of rice consumption levels across countries and regions within a country, corresponding to diversity in climate, custom and incomes.

Second, there can be sharp differences in rice consumption by income class for a given country or region at one point in time, especially if they are quite poor. In rural Java–Madura in 1963–64, rice consumption by the top income quintile was 2.552 kg per capita per week, more than three

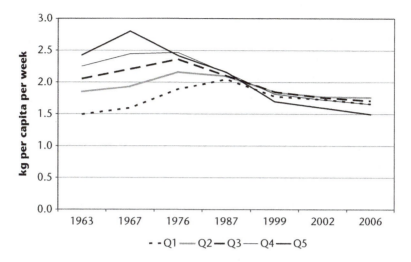

Figure 5.5 Per capita rice consumption by quintile over time, Indonesia, urban areas

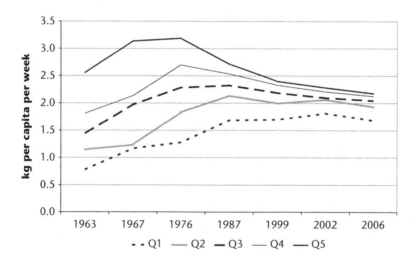

Figure 5.6 Per capita rice consumption by quintile over time, Indonesia, rural areas

times the level of the bottom quintile (see Figures 5.5 and 5.6). At that time, of course, rural Java was desperately poor. The ratio for rural India in 1983 was 2.2, and 1.7 for rural Anhui province in China in 2005.

Third, large differences between rural and urban rice consumption are common, but the differences change substantially over time and by income classes.[6] For example, in 1963–64 Java–Madura, rural rice consumption in the bottom income quintile was only about half that of the same urban quintile, but in the top income quintile rural rice consumption was slightly larger. In most important rice consuming areas, rural rice consumption is significantly higher than urban

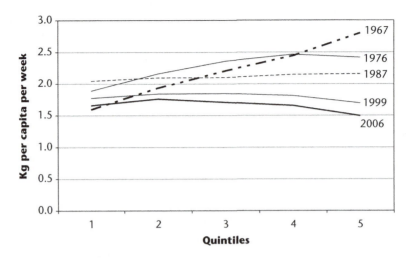

Figure 5.7 Engel curves over time for urban Indonesia
Note: Data for 1967 refer to Java and Madura.

rice consumption. These patterns have sharp implications for future levels of rice consumption when a larger share of the population works in urban areas.

Fourth, the income elasticity of demand for rice from these cross-section data depends on whether the household lives in a rural or urban area. Most income elasticities for urban households are now zero or negative (for example, see the rotation of Engel curves that has taken place over time in urban Indonesia, shown in Figure 5.7). This figure is particularly revealing of the dynamics of rice consumption in Asia – not only are the Engel curves flattening out during progressive time periods, they are also falling in absolute terms.

Income elasticities are more positive in rural areas, no doubt because incomes in these locations are lower on average. There is still at least a modest increase in rice consumption across income quintiles in all countries and most provinces of China. Still, even this effect is dropping sharply over time. In Indonesia, for example, the ratio of rural rice consumption in the top income quintile to that in the bottom quintile dropped from 3.29 in 1963–64 (for Java–Madura) to 2.50 in 1976 (all Indonesia) and to just 1.30 in 2006 (see Figure 5.6). In India, the same ratio dropped from 2.21 in 1983 to 1.07 in 2004–05. Further income growth in rural Asia is likely to drop the response of rice consumption to higher income levels even further.

Fifth, there is a very dramatic convergence of rice consumption patterns across income classes in those countries where we have multiple observations – Indonesia, India and Bangladesh (see Figure 5.8). This convergence is partly a result of flattening Engel curves across income classes as overall income levels rise, but it is also possible that tastes are changing in ways that make food consumption patterns more uniform across households, whatever their income levels and place of residence.

Finally, tastes seem to be changing to become more homogeneous, especially in urban areas. Tastes are hard to measure, but Figure 5.9 shows an example of how age structure affects the demand for wheat and rice in rural and urban Malaysia. The growing role of wheat in Southeast Asia's diets, documented in Tables 5.4 and 5.5, is also striking.

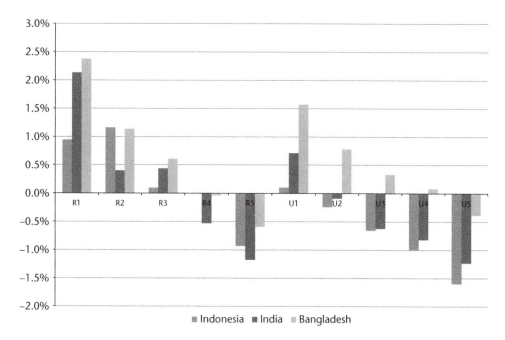

Figure 5.8 Annualized percentage change in rice consumption by quintile and location, Indonesia, India and Bangladesh

Notes: R refers to rural quintiles, U to urban quintiles. Period over which changes are calculated are 1967–2006 for Indonesia, 1983–2005 for India and 1983–2005 for Bangladesh.

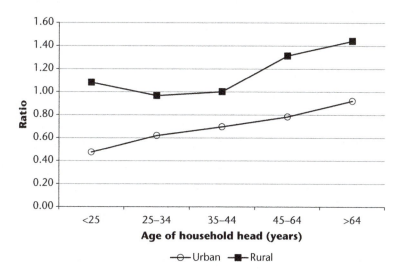

Figure 5.9 Ratio of rice to wheat consumption in Malaysia by age of household head, 1998/99

Source: Raw data: Department of Statistics, Malaysia (1999).

These results from analyzing the disaggregated data on rice consumption strongly support basic econometric findings from time series analysis of rice consumption (Timmer et al. 2010). Except marginally in rural areas, income growth is no longer an important driver of higher rice consumption. In most areas, the move from rural to urban jobs will mean lower rice consumption, perhaps sharply lower. In several important rice consuming countries in Asia, there has been a steady drift downward over time in the whole Engel function, after peaking a decade or two ago.

Each of these trends supports projections of declining rice consumption, starting sooner rather than later, throughout Southeast Asia. Underlying the dynamics of these declines is one more manifestation of Bennett's Law (Bennett 1954), which posits an inherent desire for dietary diversity as incomes rise. Thus, the desire of most Asian consumers to have a more balanced diet than what has traditionally been available to them, especially in rural areas, is not unusual. It is common for rural Asian consumers to get 70 percent of their daily calories from rice – it was the only food staple that could be grown intensively in their monsoon-driven, agro-climatic environment. Furthermore, Asia is the only region in the world where a single food so dominates consumption patterns. As rising incomes, more open trade and global communications present the opportunity to diversify their diets, we should not be surprised that they respond.

The implications of falling rice consumption and a negative income elasticity of demand for rice are powerful for understanding food security in Southeast Asia (Warr 2011). Rice is increasingly the food of the poor, and they do not grow it themselves in quantities sufficient to feed their families. A much broader concept of food security than the ready availability of sufficient rice at stable prices is now needed in the region, one that recognizes the changing nature of food consumption, and of the food marketing system that delivers it (Reardon and Timmer 2012).

Because rice is increasingly the food of the poor, countries that use "high" rice prices as a mechanism to guarantee "macro" food security (often equated with stable rice prices in key urban markets) and a high level of self-sufficiency in rice, are raising their poverty rates. A high price strategy puts "macro" food security at odds with "micro" food security, in contrast to a productivity strategy, where both work together (Dawe 2010).

On average, Southeast Asia obtained about 60 percent of calories from rice in the early 1970s, at the peak impact of the Green Revolution, and that share is now well below 50 percent and falling, as seen in Table 5.5.[7] In Indonesia, the share of total budget expenditures spent on food fell from 60 percent to 40 percent between 1990 and 2010. The budget share spent on rice is falling even faster (see Table 5.A1). Now only 10 percent of the food budget goes to rice (on average – it is higher for the poor), so 90 percent of the food budget is spent on other commodities and value added from processing and convenience.

Following the changing patterns of rice consumption, the share of rice in agricultural output and in the overall economy is also falling rapidly, as was seen in Table 5.4, with data on the agricultural transformation in Southeast Asia. This increasingly diversified, market-driven food economy is more reflective of supply chain dynamics and consumer demand than in the past, and understanding other factors shaping consumer demand for food such as advertising, age structure, urbanization and globalization of tastes, will be necessary for effective planning all the way back the chain to input supply. Some of this planning will need to be done in the public sector to insure that appropriate infrastructure investments are in place, but most of the planning will be in the private sector. Vertically integrated supply chains require remarkably sophisticated logistical planning if they are to be efficient (and competitive).

Linking agricultural development to food security: the dynamics of modern food supply chains in Asia

Modern analyses of food security list five essential components: *availability* of food on farms and in markets, *access* to that food by all households, effective *utilization* of the food within the household (a function of food safety, nutritional status and health), the *sustainability* of the food system that delivers these components, and its *stability* (Timmer 2012). All of these components engage the food marketing system, which transforms commodities in a farmer's field in time, place and form, into food on the table. The food marketing system is changing rapidly, especially as modern supply chains evolve to provision supermarkets (see Figure 5.10), and as concerns for food safety and origin are reflected in the purchasing decisions of increasingly affluent consumers.

Southeast Asia's food marketing system is being transformed before our eyes, as modern supply chains and supermarkets change the nature of farm–market–consumer interactions (Reardon 2010). The spread of modern supply chains has the potential to be a real problem for food security.

Increasingly, modern supply chains are transmitting demand signals from consumers who are shopping in supermarkets, back up the food system, level by level, to processors, farmers and input suppliers. Traditionally, each cell in the food system depicted in Figure 5.10 was connected locally by small traders operating with minimal capital and primitive technology (Reardon and Timmer 2007, 2012). Modern supply chains are far more integrated into the farm-level procurement systems of supermarkets and are coordinated by these firms as they seek to "drive costs out of the system."

	Rice economy (starchy staples)	Non-rice commodities (Fruits and vegetables, meat/dairy, processed foods, wheat)
Farm inputs/ supplies	Smaller area possible Higher yields, stress tolerance Consumer quality	More value/hectare, but what role for small farmers (what "assets" do they need to stay in?)
Farm production (management and knowledge)	Very knowledge-intensive for good management practices Access to inputs by farm size	Knowledge intensive; can there be effective extension for new technologies? Role of farm assets
Procurement/ logistics and wholesalers	Less rural consumption as workers leave; more transportation and storage; greater production instability with climate change	High transaction costs of dealing with small farmers; issues of quality control and product traceability
Processing and value added	Milling technology How to add value; branding?	Large share of consumer food expenditure is spent in this box
Retail/consumer welfare and health dimensions	Supermarkets as suppliers of rice? Increased price stability through private actions? Problems of access by the poor?	Modern supply chains are funneling consumer demand back up the system. The food system is less supply driven

Figure 5.10 Modernizing food supply chains in Southeast Asia: the "10-wheeler" model

Four important trends emerge from the "10-wheeler" perspective in Figure 5.10, when it is overlaid with changing food consumption patterns in Southeast Asia. First, the vertical boxes are increasingly connected by market *and* non-market forces. One key conclusion for suppliers of technology in the private sector is that there can be no effective demand for inputs unless farmers are able to sell surpluses into the market. This market is increasingly controlled by procurement officers for supermarket chains, and their tendency to *consolidate* suppliers may counter the effort by governments seeking to include small farmers. On the other hand, successful efforts to reduce the transactions costs of incorporating small farmers into modern supply chains may simultaneously pay dividends by making these same farmers more accessible to modern input suppliers.

Second, there is a clear and rapid shift from the left side column of Figure 5.10 to the right side – from the rice sector to the non-rice sector. This shift reflects again Bennett's Law. This dietary diversification tends to improve the nutritional quality of the diet, although more processed foods and highly industrialized meat production raise nutritional, environmental and food safety concerns.

Third, this increasingly diversified, market-driven food economy is more reflective of supply chain dynamics and consumer demand than in the past, which makes it more sensitive to rapid income growth and somewhat less sensitive to population growth. Especially in Southeast Asia, where population growth is slowing quickly and income growth continues at a rapid pace, understanding the "Engel elasticities" of the various items in the food shoppers' baskets (i.e., how demand for individual items responds to income growth), as well as other factors shaping consumer demand for food (such as advertising, age structure, urbanization and globalization of tastes) will be necessary for effective planning all the way back the chain to input supply. Many of these broad consumer changes are being driven by changing demand for (and supply of) rice, and these changes too are being felt and seen in supermarkets.

Fourth, as consumers increasingly use supermarkets as the source of their purchased rice, some surprising implications arise for food security. Traditionally, rice has been purchased in small retail shops with multiple grades and varieties available. Prices fluctuated according to local supply and demand conditions and often changed daily during periods of instability. The concentration of purchasing power into a handful of supermarket chains raises the possibility that rice procurement officers will encourage (force) their suppliers to maintain large enough stocks so that supplies will be reliable and that prices can be kept reasonably stable. Indeed, it is easy to imagine supermarkets in Southeast Asia beginning to compete for customers with a promise of "safe, reliable rice supplies, at a stable, fair price." Rice price stability could become a private good rather than the public good it has been historically (Timmer 1989, 2010). The whole debate over how to provide food security in Southeast Asia will be transformed when most rice is purchased in supermarkets. We are still a long way from that situation, but supermarkets are increasingly important as a supplier of even this basic food stable.

Food security in Southeast Asia: the challenges going forward

Southeast Asia has been remarkably successful over the past half-century in using its food and agricultural resources as a base for pro-poor growth and the rapid emergence from hunger and poverty for most of the households in the region. That rapid emergence from poverty also presents a set of challenges, many of which are dealt with elsewhere in this volume in the context of a middle-income trap – Malaysia, Thailand, Indonesia and the Philippines all seem stuck with the problem of building innovation into their educational systems and industrial structures. Within the context of the food and agricultural system, however, five challenges are apparent.

Volatility of the food system and flexibility in food policy

In the short run – over the next 5–10 years – the global food system seems likely to be highly volatile, even if average prices return to the levels considered "normal" before 2007 (Galtier 2013). Managing food price volatility, especially spikes in rice prices, has been a challenge historically to countries in the region and there is no evidence to suggest it will be any easier in the future.[8] An especially worrisome trend has been the recent retreat into autarchy by the Philippines and Indonesia, thus significantly reducing the policy flexibility to cope with production shocks. These shocks seem likely to be more frequent and more severe as climate change accelerates, thus more flexible food policy will be needed, especially with respect to trade. The ASEAN+3 Rice Reserve Scheme, a regional agreement to supply rice in emergencies that is backed by the Association of Southeast Asian Nations (ASEAN) countries plus Japan, South Korea and China, is intended to provide greater stability to rice prices in the region, and thus to increase confidence in more open borders for rice trade. At the moment, however, it is far too small and too hamstrung by bureaucratic procedures to have much impact. Still, the process of discussing the ASEAN+3 food security initiative has encouraged governments in the region to consider the appropriate levels of their own stocks and to restrain from border restrictions that exacerbate price volatility. It is no accident that the price of rice did not follow the prices of wheat and maize in spiking in 2010/11. Countries in Asia learned their lesson in 2007/08 and did not repeat those mistakes.

Growing importance of structural poverty and vulnerability of the near-poor

Southeast Asia has relied heavily on rapid, pro-poor growth, in combination with stable food prices (around a gradually falling trend), to lift millions of households out of poverty. The poverty that remains seems not as well connected to the kind of growth that is happening now – in cities, highly skill-intensive, and using more capital than labor (see Chapter 13 on migration by Sugiyarto in this volume). To eliminate the remaining poverty in these countries, and to protect the large numbers of households that remain "near-poor," a new approach to poverty reduction will need to be developed. More focus on rural education and on connecting remote, poor regions to more dynamic growth centers will be needed. As Chapter 14 by Warr in this volume emphasizes, much of the remaining poverty in the region is in rural areas, but traditional agricultural development programs are unlikely to be their fastest route out of poverty.

Growing net rice exports and the threat from rice surpluses

Rice exports from Southeast Asia have risen rapidly in the past two decades, both absolutely and as a share of rice production. Total rice consumption in the region is falling and continued efforts to expand rice production will need to find export markets if the increased output is to remain profitable in private and social terms. As export markets within Asia dry up – driven especially by self-sufficiency campaigns by rice importers – attention naturally turns to other areas where rice consumption is expanding rapidly: Africa, the Middle East and parts of Latin America. The difficulty is that in all of these markets except the Middle East, countries have ambitious plans to expand their own rice production and become less dependent on Asian imports. Expanding rice surpluses in Southeast Asia, with limited market prospects outside the region, will mean intense competition for the export markets that remain, and this will mean downward pressure (perhaps significant downward pressure) on rice prices. Because so many of the rice intensification programs in Southeast Asia depend on high prices to farmers, the prospect is for huge budget losses or a collapse in farm prices. Either outcome would spell serious political trouble because rice farmers are such a critical political constituency throughout Southeast Asia.

The increasing role of non-staple agriculture: oil palm; rubber, bio-fuels

Although this chapter has focused primarily on the links between agricultural development and food security, and has thus concentrated on the development of food crops, Southeast Asia is also an important supplier of non-food agricultural commodities. The region has long been the dominant supplier of rubber, mostly from plantations, but with a large smallholder rubber economy in Indonesia. In the past 40 years Southeast Asia has replaced Africa as the main supplier of palm oil, and Latin America as the main supplier of coffee. A recent development has been the rapidly expanding role of cassava as the raw material for a regional bio-fuel industry (see Table 5.A2). Cassava has traditionally been the "fall-back" food of the poor – low in protein and micro nutrients, but providing abundant calories very cheaply. The new role for cassava as the base for a regional (and increasingly, in China) bio-fuel industry threatens to convert this "food of the poor" into a "fuel for the rich." Similar concerns have arisen over the use of palm oil to produce bio-diesel, but the European pull-back from importing palm oil for this purpose has more to do with the environmental concerns over deforestation as the main way to expand oil palm plantations than with any perceived conflict between rich fuel consumers and poor vegetable oil consumers.

Climate change and threats to agricultural productivity

The wildcard in all of these discussions about future challenges is the very uncertain impact of climate change on the agricultural sectors in these countries. There is no question that Southeast Asia is highly vulnerable to what is already reasonably certain about climate change – rising sea levels will threaten many coastal activities, including extensive rice-producing areas. Hotter temperatures will reduce productivity of many crops (and even animals). More variable weather will create wider droughts and deeper floods, often in the same growing season.

How can the region respond to these threats? It is already too late to mitigate most of them through global collective action to reduce emissions of greenhouse gases – the action going forward will be agricultural adaptation. Fortunately, most of the countries in the region now accept this fact and have started planning for a more flexible agricultural system. Unfortunately, nearly all of this planning is devoted to technical agricultural factors, with very little attention to better policy design and implementation. The real challenge in coping with climate change will be in the realm of food policy, not agricultural science (Timmer 2013).

Acknowledgments

This chapter has benefited significantly from comments at the authors' workshop in Bangkok, March 22–23, 2013. Although the focus is on Southeast Asia, especially during discussion of agricultural development, it is necessary to broaden the discussion to the rest of Asia when the focus is food security.

Appendix

Table 5.A1 The changing role of rice in Indonesian food consumption

	1990	1993	1996	1999	2002	2005	2008	2009	2010
Susenas: Total energy intake in kcal/capita/day	1901	1879	2020	1849	1986	1997	2038	1928	1926
Susenas: Rice consumption in kg/capita/week	2.272	2.238	2.144	1.995	1.937	1.649	1.804	1.761	1.740
Rice consumption converted to kcal/capita/day	1151	1133	1086	1010	981	835	914	892	881
Susenas: Rice consumption as % of total energy intake	60.5	60.3	53.8	54.6	49.4	41.8	44.8	46.3	45.8
Susenas: Share of food expenditures in total expenditures	60.4	56.9	55.3	62.9	58.5	51.1	45.0	50.6	51.4
Food balance sheet data for total energy intake (kcal/cap/day)	2266	2361	2483	2450	2434	2483	2609	2646	
Food Balance Sheet data for rice consumption (kcal/cap/day)	1187	1268	1291	1325	1237	1221	1251	1256	
FBS: Rice consumption as % of total energy intake	52.4	53.7	52.0	54.1	50.8	49.2	47.9	47.5	
Susenas rice consumption as a % of FBS rice consumption	96.9	89.4	84.1	76.3	79.3	68.4	73.0	71.0	
Susenas total energy intake as a % of FBS total energy intake	83.9	79.6	81.4	75.5	81.6	80.4	78.1	72.9	

Source: Indonesian Socio-Economic Surveys, various years.

Table 5.A2 Transforming the food of the poor to the fuel of the rich

Cassava: Transforming the food of the poor to the fuel of the rich	1961	1970	1980	1990	2000	2009
Statistics for Southeast Asia from FAO Food Balance Sheets						
Cassava Production, 000mt	14574	15653	36112	41283	39633	67213
Net exports	1300	4921	15236	26714	12084	18669
Feed use, domestic	1132	1059	3225	2527	3663	8138
"Other" domestic utilization	1785	1714	2817	3330	10682	25185
Food use	9670	8074	12331	10811	12201	15168
Western European imports of cassava	1416	4305	15768	21209	7451	224
Western European imports as a % of SEAsia net exports	108.9	87.5	103.5	79.4	61.7	1.2
Implicit use of cassava for bio-fuel conversion						
Net exports not to Western Europe for feed, 1990 and after				5505	4633	18445
"Other" utilization above 1990 levels				0	7352	21855
Total for bio-fuel conversion				5505	11985	40300
Approximate land area devoted to cassava production for bio-fuel (in 000 hectares, assuming an average yield of 19.33 mt/ha)				285	620	2085

Source: FAO Food Balance Sheets.

Notes

1 Chapter 4 by Phung, Coxhead and Lian in this volume also emphasizes the important spillover effects from growth and structural change in the Japanese economy on the economies of Southeast Asia.
2 Note that the "supply" variable makes no allowance for the state of nutrition of the population. The "population normalized" food deficit measure indicates how much food energy would be needed *per capita* to bring the undernourished population up to the *minimum* energy requirement. Both indicators need to be examined together to gain an understanding of the relative importance of food availability and food access in driving the extent of undernutrition. The "food security gap" measure does this in a simple (if crude) way.
3 These statistical results are based on annual data for individual countries in each of the regions.
4 Other countries are important for particular commodities – Myanmar and Cambodia for rice; Malaysia for palm oil and rubber. Two other countries considered to be part of Southeast Asia – Laos and East Timor – are largely producers of agricultural commodities but are quite small in economic terms. The last two countries in the region, Singapore and Brunei, are not significant producers of agricultural commodities and do not have concerns about food security except via their dependence on imported food.
5 Both of these cases have been documented in the Stanford Symposium Series on Global Food Policy and Food Security in the 21st Century (Badiane 2011; Binswanger-Mkhize 2012).
6 Typically, expenditure surveys are reported by income class separately for rural and urban households, so average incomes can be quite different for the same quintile of rural and urban households.
7 Table 5.5 actually *understates* the declining role of rice in Southeast Asian diets. In countries with good time series data from household budget surveys, rice consumption seems to be lower than in food balance sheet data, and is declining faster. The clearest evidence is for Indonesia (also the largest rice consumer in Southeast Asia), as can be seen in Table 5.A1. The most likely explanation for the disparity in rice consumption levels between the two sources is a systematic overstatement of the level of and growth in rice production (Rosner and McCulloch 2008). Food balance sheet data are based on domestic production levels, whereas household budget surveys collect data on consumption directly.
8 This is a political statement, not an economic one. With rice rapidly declining in importance in both consumption and production, and the structural transformation reducing the overall role of agriculture in the economy, it "should be" easier to manage food price volatility.

References

Badiane, Ousmane. 2011. "Agriculture and structural transformation in Africa." Stanford Symposium Series on Global Food Policy and Food Security in the 21st Century, Center on Food Security and the Environment (April 7), Stanford, CA.
Bennett, Merrill K. 1954. *The World's Food*, New York: Harper.
Binswanger-Mkhize, Hans. 2012. "India 1960–2010: structural change, the rural non-farm sector, and the prospects for agriculture." Stanford Symposium Series on Global Food Policy and Food Security in the 21st Century, Center on Food Security and the Environment (May 10), Stanford, CA.
Dawe, David (ed.). 2010. *The Rice Crisis: Markets, Policies and Food Security*. London: Earthscan Press with the FAO.
FAO, WFP and IFAD. 2012. *The State of Food Insecurity in the World 2012: Economic Growth Is Necessary but Not Sufficient to Accelerate Reduction of Hunger and Malnutrition*. Rome: FAO.
Galtier, Franck, with collaboration of Bruno Vindel. 2013. *Managing Food Price Instability in Developing Countries: A Critical Analysis of Strategies and Instruments*. CIRAD and AFC. STIN: France. Available at: www.afd.fr/A-Savoir
Geertz, Clifford. 1963. *Agricultural Involution: The Processes of Ecological Change in Indonesia*. Berkeley: University of California Press.
Hayami, Yujiro, and Vernon Ruttan. 1985. *Agricultural Development: An International Perspective*. Revised and expanded edition. Baltimore, MD: Johns Hopkins University Press.
Hayami, Yujiro, and Saburo Yamada. 1991. *The Agricultural Development of Japan: A Century's Perspective*. Tokyo: University of Tokyo Press.
Maddison, Angus. 1995. *Monitoring the World Economy: 1820–1992*. Paris: Development Centre, OECD.
Maddison, Angus. 2001. *The World Economy: A Millennial Perspective*. Paris: Development Centre, OECD.

Myrdal, Gunnar. 1968. *Asian Drama: An Inquiry into the Poverty of Nations.* Harmondsworth: Penguin.

Reardon, Tom. 2010. "Linking food market transformation to improved food security in Asia." Presentation at the ASEAN Food Security Conference, Singapore, June 17. Organized by Nathan Associates, Arlington, VA with support from USAID.

Reardon, Tom and C. Peter Timmer. 2007. "Transformation of markets for agricultural output in developing countries since 1950: How has thinking changed?" In R.E. Evenson and P. Pingali (eds), *Handbook of Agricultural Economics, Vol. 3: Agricultural Development: Farmers, Farm Production, and Farm Markets.* Amsterdam: Elsevier, pp. 2807–55.

Reardon, Tom and C. Peter Timmer. 2012. "The economics of the food system revolution." *Annual Review of Resource Economics* 4 (September): 14.1–14.40.

Rosner, L. Peter, and Neil McCulloch. 2008. "A note on rice production, consumption and import data in Indonesia." *Bulletin of Indonesian Economic Studies* 44(1): 81–92.

Timmer, C. Peter. 1988. "The agricultural transformation." In Hollis Chenery and T.N. Srinivasan (eds), *Handbook of Development Economics*, vol. 1. Amsterdam: North-Holland, pp. 275–331.

Timmer, C. Peter. 1989. "Food price policy: the rationale for government intervention." *Food Policy* 14(1): 17–27.

Timmer, C. Peter. 2004. "The road to pro-poor growth: Indonesia's experience in regional perspective." *Bulletin of Indonesian Economic Studies* 40(2): 177–207.

Timmer, C. Peter. 2009. "A world without agriculture: the structural transformation in historical perspective." Henry Wendt Lecture, Washington, DC: American Enterprise Institute.

Timmer, C. Peter. 2010. "Reflections on food crises past." *Food Policy* 35(1): 1–11.

Timmer, C. Peter. 2012. "Behavioral dimensions of food security." *Proceedings of the National Academy of Sciences (PNAS), Agricultural Development and Nutrition Security Special Feature, PNAS* 109(31): 12315–20.

Timmer, C. Peter. 2013. "Coping with climate change: a food policy approach." Prepared for the Australian Agricultural and Resource Economics Society (AARES) meeting in Sydney, February 7.

Timmer, C. Peter, and Selvin Akkus. 2008. *The Structural Transformation as a Pathway Out of Poverty: Analytics, Empirics, and Politics.* Center for Global Development Working Paper 150, July.

Timmer, C. Peter, Steven Block, and David Dawe. 2010. "Long-run dynamics of rice consumption, 1960–2050." In Sushil Pandey, Derek Byerlee, David Dawe, Achim Dobermann, Samarendu Mohanty, Scott Rozelle, and Bill Hardy (eds), *Rice in the Global Economy: Strategic Research and Policy Issues for Food Security.* Los Banos (Philippines): International Rice Research Institute, pp.139–74.

van der Eng, Pierre. 2010. "The sources of long-term economic growth in Indonesia, 1880–2008." *Explorations in Economic History* 47: 294–309.

Warr, Peter. 2011. "Poverty, food prices and economic growth in Southeast Asian perspective." In Chris Manning and Sudarno Sumarto (eds), *Employment, Living Standards and Poverty in Contemporary Indonesia.* Singapore: Institute of Southeast Asian Studies, pp. 47–67.

6

Natural resources, the environment and economic development in Southeast Asia

Gerald Shively and Tim Smith

Introduction

Growth for the outward-looking economies of Southeast Asia was extremely rapid during the past four decades, driven by expanding world trade and a seemingly insatiable appetite for primary commodities in the industrialized world. The countries of Southeast Asia played a key role in worldwide economic growth throughout the postwar period as suppliers of raw materials.[1] For example, by 1974 ASEAN members accounted for 83 percent of the world's supply of natural rubber, 80 percent of palm oil, 68 percent of tin and 67 percent of coconut products (Sien and MacAndrews 1979). During this period and well into the 1970s and 1980s, concern for the environment was secondary to the goal of economic growth, which was pursued primarily through natural resource extraction (Howard 1993).

With only a few exceptions, the countries of Southeast Asia grew rapidly. Taken as a group, their growth in the 1960s and 1970s exceeded that of any comparison group in the developing world. In many countries this growth was driven by diversification and changes in export structure (Gelb 2011). However, rapid economic growth was rarely accompanied by rapid evolution in laws, regulations and institutions to protect the environment. As internal and external economic forces precipitated economic diversification and early stage industrialization, unplanned manufacturing growth created deleterious environmental spillovers, especially where industrial development was pursued in rapidly urbanizing areas. The inability of the industrial sector to absorb an influx of unskilled rural migrants also gave rise to numerous urban squatter settlements characterized by low quality of life and a range of environmental health risks. By the mid-1990s, many countries of Southeast Asia found themselves confronted by the double burden of resource depletion in the countryside and pollution in urban areas.

The continuing challenge of sustainable development in Southeast Asia stems from two stylized facts. First, the countries of the region are both *producers* and *consumers* of environmental problems. In many cases, environmental problems fall within a country's borders. But in a growing number of cases, problems extend across space, placing cause and effect on different sides of political borders, and complicating economic and environmental policy making. Second, many of the region's environmental problems cannot be easily disentangled from economic growth, demographic change and regional and global integration. For example, land and water degradation result from growth and trade, both of which are influenced by a country's domestic policies and those of its neighbors and trading partners. Moreover, regional economic and environmental cooperation is at times frustrated by the increasing importance of China as a driver of regional and global economic activity and resource use. Going forward, trade, regional and global integration, and the interplay of economic and environmental policy will combine to determine the size and shape of Southeast Asia's environmental footprint.

At the same time, rising incomes are both increasing pressures and creating opportunities for enhanced environmental quality, a pattern broadly consistent with the Environmental Kuznets Curve hypothesis. A stylized U-shaped relationship in which environmental quality declines, and then rises with per capita income can be driven by structural changes in an economy (Panayotou 1993), by policy changes invoked by citizens' preferences (Selden and Song 1995), or by adjustments in trade and endowments resulting from economic transformation (Jaeger and Kolpin 2000). One key driver of environmental change in Southeast Asia is the evolving structure of manufacturing. Generally speaking, as countries develop, the range of products in which they have comparative advantage in trade shifts. This generates three forces that have the potential to affect levels and patterns of industrial pollution (Lucas et al. 1992). First, development can lead to changes in comparative advantage. Second, the location of "dirty" production can shift in response to environmental regulations (the pollution haven hypothesis). And third, policy changes in the domestic economy or among trading partners can affect capital- and pollution-intensive sectors of the economy. Empirical evidence suggests that pollution intensity has tended to grow fastest in countries that are relatively closed, compared with those that are more open to trade. In Southeast Asia, growth driven by openness has often brought environmental harm, but an inward focus has ensured neither environmental protection nor growth.

An additional positive force for environmental improvement in Southeast Asia is an increasingly well-informed citizenry. Local grassroots efforts to improve environmental quality and preserve remaining natural resources continue to expand, and many governments have shown a willingness to place environmental concerns on the policy agenda. Nevertheless, questions regarding how to balance growth and environmental concerns, and how best to implement policies to protect the environment, remain difficult and unanswered in most places. Today, close observers recognize the possibility that Southeast Asia's standing as a center of economic growth could become overshadowed by its reputation as a host to environmental problems.

Rising populations are undoubtedly a proximate, if not ultimate, cause of environmental degradation (Shaw 1989), although population growth is now near, at or below replacement rates in all major Southeast Asian countries except the Philippines (see Jones, Chapter 10 in this volume). As Table 6.1 indicates, overall population in Southeast Asia more than doubled in the 30 years leading up to 2000. And while annual population growth rates have fallen sharply from their peaks of nearly 3 percent in the 1970s, urban population growth rates remain very high, ranging from 1.5 percent in Thailand to 5.0 percent in Lao PDR. Urbanization plays an important role in both expanding the set of environmental challenges and shifting the public's environmental focus. Indeed, many of Southeast Asia's environmental problems directly or indirectly result from rapid urban growth. For example, hydroelectric dams provide electricity for cities and manufacturing, but they simultaneously threaten remaining forests and downstream aquatic ecosystems. Overfishing results from a race to capture valuable export markets, and also from growing affluence and rising domestic demand. And reductions in urban air quality reflect, in part, the rapid rise of Asia's urban middle class and their transportation choices. In short, much of Asia's environmental future will be shaped by continued urban growth and rising consumerism (JEC 2000).

Table 6.1 Population and urbanization in Southeast Asia, 1970–2010

| | Population | | | | | | Population growth (annual average rate) | | | | | |
| | Total (millions) | | | Percent urban | | | Total | | | Urban | | |
Country	1970	2000	2010	1970	2000	2010	1970	2000	2010	1970	2000	2010
Cambodia	6.9	12.4	14.1	16.0	18.6	19.8	1.8	1.8	1.1	8.5	3.2	1.8
Indonesia	118.4	213.4	239.9	17.1	42.0	49.9	2.6	1.3	1.0	4.1	4.4	2.6
Lao PDR	2.7	5.3	6.2	9.6	22.0	33.1	2.5	1.8	1.4	5.2	6.1	5.0
Malaysia	10.9	23.4	28.4	33.5	62.0	72.0	2.5	2.4	1.6	4.6	4.4	2.8
Myanmar	26.2	45.0	48.0	22.8	27.2	32.1	2.4	1.0	0.8	4.0	2.2	2.5
Philippines	35.5	77.3	93.3	33.0	48.0	48.6	2.9	2.1	1.7	3.7	2.0	1.9
Thailand	36.9	63.2	69.1	20.9	31.1	33.7	2.9	1.2	0.6	3.6	1.7	1.5
Vietnam	42.7	77.6	86.9	18.3	24.4	30.4	2.3	1.3	1.0	4.3	3.2	3.1

Source: World Bank: World Development Indicators.

Although this chapter is meant to provide a survey of the economy–environment nexus in Southeast Asia, our space is limited, and we do not attempt to cover all topics of concern in detail.[2] Instead, we focus on several major themes. After reviewing evidence on these topics, we turn our attention to addressing within the context of Southeast Asia one of the major debates regarding economic growth and the environment, namely the extent to which natural resource wealth fosters or retards economic growth.

Evidence regarding natural resources and the environment in Southeast Asia

Forestry and biodiversity

Since World War II, Southeast Asia's forest cover has declined rapidly. Conventional wisdom holds that in heavily agrarian, resource-dependent economies with high rates of population growth, this is to be expected: as populations increase, demand for timber, land and agricultural products increase, and during periods in which agriculture is extensive, rather than intensive, some degree of forest destruction is inevitable. However, while this narrative is accurate in a very broad sense, the specific social, political, demographic and economic causes of deforestation are complex (Hurst 1990). Patterns differ greatly between regions and countries, and often within a single country (Geist and Lambin 2002; Lambin et al. 2001). In Southeast Asia, forest clearing in many cases has resulted less from population growth than from a historical legacy of colonial and post-colonial decisions.[3]

Country-specific forest area trends since the 1980s are summarized in Table 6.2. These are somewhat more nuanced than the longer-term regional trend, with Thailand, Vietnam and Lao PDR all showing net gains in forest area. We note, however, that both Thailand and Vietnam lost the majority of their forest cover between the 1960s and 1990s, so it would be somewhat naive to see this trend as evidence of effective forest protection efforts (Hirsch 1993). Similarly, these data do not show that Thailand became an importer of the wood produced by many of its neighbors, including Lao PDR, in the 1990s, which drove deforestation elsewhere even as Thailand

Table 6.2 Forest cover and deforestation in Southeast Asia, 1980–2010

Country	Forest area (1,000 ha)				Change (annual average rate)		
	1980	1990	2000	2010	1980–90	1990–2000	2000–10
Cambodia	13,484	12,944	11,546	10,094	–0.4	–1.1	–1.3
Indonesia	124,476	118,545	99,409	94,432	–0.5	–1.6	–0.5
Lao PDR	14,470	17,314	16,532	15,751	2.0	–0.5	–0.5
Malaysia	21,564	22,376	21,591	20,456	0.4	–0.4	–0.5
Myanmar	32,901	39,218	34,868	31,773	1.9	–1.1	–0.9
Philippines	11,194	6,570	7,117	7,665	–4.1	0.8	0.8
Thailand	18,123	19,549	19,004	18,972	0.8	–0.3	0.0
Vietnam	10,663	9,363	11,725	13,797	–1.2	2.5	1.8

Source: FAO *Forest Resources Assessment 2010*.

itself began to reforest (Hirsch 1993). Like in Vietnam and Thailand, earlier deforestation in the Philippines was very rapid, largely due to the widespread distribution of forest concessions with very limited constraints on their use. Following the removal of the Marcos regime in 1986, deforestation not only dropped, but reversed slightly (Rola and Coxhead 2005).

To explore the agriculture–forest relationship, Figure 6.1 plots for each country three points, each corresponding to a 10-year average change in cultivated area and a corresponding 10-year average change in forest cover. These data support the conventional narrative of agriculture-led

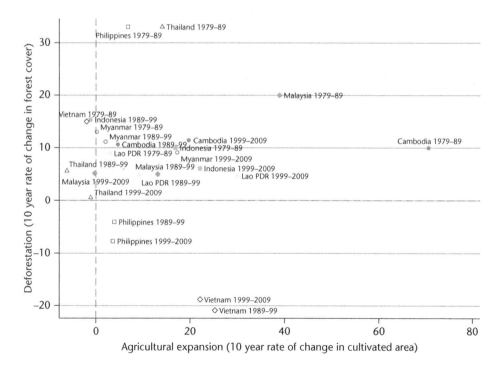

Figure 6.1 Agricultural expansion vs. deforestation in Southeast Asia, 1980–2010
Source: FAO: FAOSTAT Resource Database.

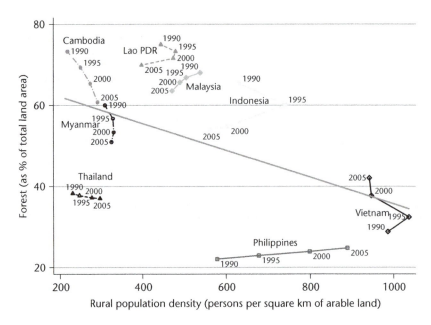

Figure 6.2 Forest area vs. population density in Southeast Asia, 1990–2005
Source: FAO: FAOSTAT Resource Database; World Bank: World Development Indicators.

deforestation: most countries fall inside the northeast quadrant, where positive rates of deforestation coincide with agricultural expansion. As Figure 6.2 shows, however, deforestation has continued in many countries along with very slow, or even negative, rates of change in rural population density. This underscores the importance of structural rather than demographic features as drivers of deforestation.

Perhaps the most important underlying determinant of deforestation has been governance, as a large part of Southeast Asian deforestation has been driven by state-sanctioned timber extraction and transmigration, as opposed to agricultural expansion and change or technological progress (Geist and Lambin 2001). Southeast Asian nations have, historically, been home to some of the largest endowments of forest resources in the world. The highly centralized, often authoritarian governments which ruled most of the region throughout the twentieth century used these endowments to consolidate power through the sale of large forest concessions to large-scale logging interests and the extraction of rents from the subsequent profits (Rola and Coxhead 2005; Lambin et al. 2001).[4] Many governments promoted extraction at unsustainable rates.

Economically, the problem with twentieth century deforestation in Southeast Asia is that resource rents have not always and not everywhere been channeled into other, more sustainable sectors (Barbier 2005). Thailand and Malaysia stand as exceptions, as both nations entered the postwar period poor and resource dependent, like their neighbors, and yet today have diverse economies and relatively low rates of resource extraction, including deforestation (see Table 6.2). A policy focus on promoting export-oriented, labor-intensive manufacturing was a critical component of Thailand's strategy (Coxhead and Jayasuriya 2003). Looking at data from 1979 to 1982, it appears that the Malaysian government was dramatically more effective at holding on to rents from forest concessions than its neighbors, capturing 81 percent of the estimated rents from log harvests, compared with 37 percent and 16 percent for Indonesia and the Philippines (Repetto 1990; Repetto and Gillis 1988; Barbier 1993).

Table 6.3 Biodiversity and species under threat in Southeast Asia, 2012

Country	Native species	Threatened native species	Percentage of native species threatened	Terrestrial protected area in 2010 (%)
Cambodia	974	39	4.0	25.8
Indonesia	2,142	137	6.4	14.2
Lao PDR	1,243	60	4.8	16.6
Malaysia	1,211	63	5.2	18.1
Myanmar	1,396	59	4.2	6.3
Philippines	831	84	10.1	10.9
Thailand	1,833	96	5.2	20.1
Vietnam	1,651	92	5.6	6.2

Source: IUCN *Redbook*, World Bank: World Development Indicators.

Deforestation has driven much of the observed biodiversity loss across Southeast Asia. For example, deforestation in Cambodia resulted in the loss of three-fourths of its wildlife habitat (Howard 1993). While the overall proportions of threatened species shown in Table 6.3 may seem low, and protected areas comprise a relatively large percentage of land area, the number of threatened native species is high and ecologists predict that many species may be lost in the future due to habitat fragmentation started in the nineteenth and twentieth centuries (Sodhi et al. 2004). This dimension of deforestation complicates calculations of economic tradeoffs, as extinctions have unknown costs and species and ecosystems provide benefits that are often uncertain and hard to quantify (Rausser 2000). As in the case of deforestation more generally, there is no simple remedy for the biodiversity loss associated with forest clearing. In most instances payments from bioprospecting are unlikely to be sufficient to provide an adequate incentive for protection; and the institutional and property rights reforms necessary to provide local incentives for conservation are difficult to achieve.

Land resources and the rural environment

Although a comprehensive review of agricultural resources and rural development in Southeast Asia is beyond the scope of this chapter (for a complete discussion of agriculture in the region, see Timmer, Chapter 5 in this volume), it is worth noting here that agriculture continues to exert substantial pressure on the rural land base in Southeast Asia. Table 6.4 reports agricultural land area

Table 6.4 Cultivated area in Southeast Asia, 1979 and 2009

Country	Agricultural land 1979 (1,000s ha)	Agricultural land 2009 (1,000s ha)	Change (%)
Cambodia	2,600	5,555	113.7
Indonesia	38,000	53,600	41.1
Lao PDR	1,605	2,346	46.2
Malaysia	5,022	7,870	56.7
Myanmar	10,377	12,441	19.9
Philippines	10,394	11,950	15.0
Thailand	18,702	19,795	5.8
Vietnam	6,850	10,272	50.0

Source: FAO: FAOSTAT Resource Database.

in 1979 and 2009 for eight countries. As these data illustrate, all countries have registered positive growth in agricultural area over the 30-year period, with the most substantial growth (an annual average rate of nearly 4 percent) occurring in Cambodia, and rates of growth in excess of 1 percent per annum in four countries (Vietnam, Malaysia, Lao PDR and Indonesia). In some cases, such as the growth of coffee cultivation in Vietnam's central highlands, state-sponsorship has been a driver (Doutriaux et al. 2008; Ha and Shively 2008). But in many cases, area expansion represents a more spontaneous rural phenomenon. Regardless of the cause, one natural consequence of agricultural expansion, especially into fragile and upland environments, has been soil erosion and overall land degradation. These have been recognized as problems in the region for several decades (Blaikie 1985; Blaikie and Brookfield 1987). Without compensating investments in protection of soils or soil nutrients, yields decline as a result of continuous cultivation (Cassman and Pingali 1995). Although amenable in some situations to solutions ranging from agroforestry and contour farming to greater use of external and purchased inputs, low farm incomes and high degrees of intra- and inter-year consumption risk often discourage investments in new technologies, even when farmers are made aware of improved farming systems (Shively 2001a).

Unfortunately, many highly degraded formerly forested areas in Southeast Asia have become nearly useless *imperata* grasslands, rehabilitation of which continues to constitute a vexing ecological and policy problem (Garrity et al. 1997, Kosonen et al. 1997). In 1997, Garrity et al. estimated that these grasslands covered approximately 4 percent of Indonesian, Thai and Laotian land area, 3 percent of Myanmar's, 9 percent of Vietnam's, and 17 percent of the Philippines' (Garritty et al. 1997). Reclaiming these grasslands is difficult because *imperata* grasses do not contribute to soil quality, and in fact often serve to further degrade the soil via frequent burning. In the past, high export taxes also undermined replacements for *imperata* in several countries (Tomich et al. 1997). Disincentives are now fewer, and in some cases potential economic returns to *imperata* conversion can be high (Kosonen et al. 1997).

The importance of road networks to environmental outcomes and processes has been highlighted by a number of researchers, beginning with the studies that examined the link between road construction and deforestation in Brazil (Pfaff 1997), Mexico (Deininger and Minten 1999) and Belize (Chomitz and Gray 1996). Over the decade beginning in 2000, heterogeneity in network density between the countries of Southeast Asia was much greater than any variation within countries. Road density remains very low in Myanmar, Lao PDR, Indonesia and Cambodia, and rapid growth in road density has recently occurred only in Vietnam. From a qualitative point of view, the importance of road establishment for forest loss and land clearing is well recognized, since roads facilitate access to forests (for clearing) and facilitate access to markets, which raises the agricultural value of cleared land. In a study of roads in Thailand, Cropper et al. (1999) found that the existence of protected areas (e.g. national parks and wildlife sanctuaries) did not reduce the likelihood of forest clearing, but that road construction promoted clearing, especially near the forest fringe.

For several decades, researchers have been interested in the links between poverty and natural resource use, especially the role of poverty in fostering smallholder-led deforestation (see Shively 2004). Although findings from that literature are mixed, one might reasonably ask whether the situation of the rural poor has improved substantially, and whether income gains have increased or reduced environmental degradation in rural areas. One difficulty in answering this question, of course, resides in developing a plausible counterfactual scenario for rural Southeast Asia. Worsening land degradation and stagnant (and in some cases declining) upland yields have undoubtedly made things more difficult for many rural residents. But several decades of intensification of lowland agriculture and substantial out-migration have also relieved population pressures that undoubtedly would have been more acute (Shively 2001b; Shively and Pagiola

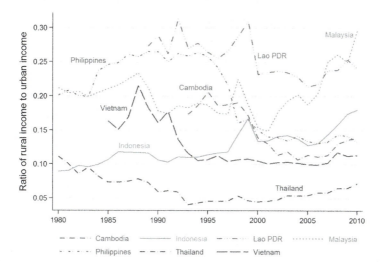

Figure 6.3 Ratio of rural to urban incomes for Southeast Asia, 1980–2010
Source: Computed as ((agricultural GDP share x GDP)/rural population)/((service and industrial GDP share x GDP)/urban population) using constant 2005 PPP GDP figures reported in the World Bank: World Development Indicators.

2004). One economy-wide result may be an incipient structural shift toward a stabilization of rural and farm incomes. Figure 6.3 plots the ratio of rural to urban (PPP) incomes over time, by country, and suggests that in most Southeast Asian countries average rural income has stopped falling vis-à-vis urban income, with the share stabilizing at a relatively constant fraction of 10–30 percent of urban income. For Indonesia, Malaysia and Thailand, data suggest that the urban–rural gap has been closing: rural incomes have actually been increasing compared with urban incomes in these countries since 2000.

Urban environment

According to UN estimates, by 2025 more than 60 percent of the world's population will live in cities. In Southeast Asia, the rising dominance of large cities is reflected in the rising proportion of the urban population living in cities of one million or more, which grew from 13 percent in 1950, to 30 percent in 1975, and 50 percent in 2000. The main environmental issues of importance in urban areas are traffic congestion, deteriorating air and water quality, and increased challenges related to disposal of hazardous and other waste. Domestic sewage disposal is a major cause of water pollution in the region. With the exception of Singapore, most major cities have no comprehensive central sewerage system (Sani 1993). Some key indicators of urban environmental quality are reported in Table 6.5. Although access to sanitation and safe water has improved markedly from earlier periods, it remains highly uneven.

Table 6.5 also reports 2005 data on automobiles per million persons. For many years the fastest growth in car sales in Southeast Asia was observed in Thailand, but recently Indonesia has overtaken Thailand as the Southeast Asian country with the fastest growth in car ownership (Soedarjo 2010). One obvious byproduct of increased motor vehicle ownership is deterioration in air quality. The final column of Table 6.5 reports country-average (urban) indicators of exposure to PM_{10} – particulate matter less than 10 microns in diameter. These particles originate from a wide variety of sources such as motor vehicles, power plants and biomass burning. They can be emitted directly or formed in the atmosphere, for example when sulfur dioxide and NOx react

Table 6.5 Urban environmental quality in Southeast Asia, 1980–2010

Country	Urban population					
	(%)		with access to sanitation (%)	with access to improved water (%)	Automobiles (per million pop.)	PM_{10}[†]
	1980	2010	2010	2010	2005	2009
Cambodia	9.0	19.8	73	87	18,000	37.0
Indonesia	22.1	49.9	73	92	25,000	68.1
Lao PDR	12.4	33.1	89	77	–	44.6
Malaysia	42.0	72.0	96	100	256,000	18.6
Myanmar	24.0	32.1	83	93	4,000	41.2
Philippines	37.5	48.7	79	93	9,000	17.1
Thailand	26.8	33.7	95	97	61,000	52.6
Vietnam	19.3	30.4	94	99	–	50.4

Source: World Bank: World Development Indicators.
Note: [†]PM_{10} reported as country-wide data.

to form fine particles. Major human health effects from exposure to PM_{10} relate to respiratory systems, lung damage, cancer and premature death. Nearly all countries in Southeast Asia exhibit PM_{10} levels that approach or exceed the annual mean air quality standard for PM_{10} of 50 $\mu g/m^3$ established by the United States Environmental Protection Agency (US EPA). Of even greater concern to public health officials are the much smaller $PM_{2.5}$ particles (Schwartz et al. 2002). These tend to have even more pernicious health effects than their larger counterparts but are currently incompletely monitored in the region. A study of air quality in Bangkok and several other Asian cities found evidence that a high ratio of $PM_{2.5}$ to PM_{10} may play an important role in explaining excess mortality risk in urban environments (Wong et al. 2008). Kim Onah et al. (2006) report results from an air-quality monitoring program implemented in six Asian cities over the period 2001–04. In all cities levels of PM_{10} and $PM_{2.5}$ frequently exceeded the corresponding 24-hour US EPA standards. Variations across time and space were found to be associated with both environmental and anthropogenic factors, with samples from heavily trafficked sites showing the highest levels.

Carbon emissions, climate change, impacts and mitigation

Carbon emissions, climate change and potential impacts and mitigation strategies are key emerging issues for the economies of Southeast Asia. Anthropogenic climate change is inextricably linked to the production and consumption of fossil fuels. Data on fossil fuel production is fairly complete for the region. These data show the large and increasing importance of fossil fuel resources and development to the economies of Southeast Asia. High rates of growth in production of coal and petroleum production have been registered for several countries. Only in the case of Indonesia (and for petroleum, Malaysia) has growth in production slowed substantially or reversed.

Table 6.6 reports available data on per capita fossil fuel consumption for the countries of the region at decade intervals from 1980 to 2010, along with the aggregate growth rate in total and per capita energy use. Total energy use increased substantially in all countries over the 40-year period covered by the data. Annual rates of increase in fossil fuel consumption ranged from 1.5 percent

Table 6.6 Fossil fuel consumption in Southeast Asia, 1980–2010

Country	Total energy use (kt of oil equiv.)					Energy use per capita(kg of oil equiv.)				
	1980	1990	2000	2010	% change	1980	1990	2000	2010	% change
Cambodia	–	–	3,412	5,024	47	–	–	279	350	25
Indonesia	55,712	98,623	155,128	207,849	273	383	552	743	864	126
Malaysia	11,902	21,549	47,110	72,645	510	860	1,183	2,012	2,569	199
Myanmar	9,422	10,679	12,841	13,997	49	273	254	265	270	−1.4
Philippines	22,406	28,616	39,872	40,477	81	473	462	514	433	−8.4
Thailand	22,002	41,944	72,284	117,429	434	465	741	1,160	1,768	281
Vietnam	14,392	17,866	28,736	59,230	312	268	271	370	681	154

Source: International Energy Agency (IEA Statistics from OECD/IEA, http://www.iea.org/stats/index.asp) as reported by World Bank: World Development Indicators.
Note: Lao PDR omitted due to lack of data.

(Myanmar) to 12.8 percent (Malaysia). The per capita increase in fossil fuel was greatest in Thailand, where per capita consumption grew at an annualized rate of 7 percent.

Fossil fuel consumption is, of course, a primary contributor to the buildup of greenhouse gasses in the earth's atmosphere, and Southeast Asia's share of total global greenhouse gas emissions is estimated to have been 7.7 percent in 2010 (UNEP 2012).[5] The potential effects of this buildup of greenhouse gasses and the potential impact of induced climate change on the economies and people of Southeast Asia have generated widespread concern. Effects on agriculture and livestock due to temperature and drought stress can be expected. Rayanakorn (2011) underscores that competition for water is among the most important issues surrounding climate change in the Mekong region, where widespread drought in 2010 was accompanied by record low levels for many reaches of the Mekong River. Human health effects due to heatwaves and altered transmission of infectious diseases are also key concerns. According to Patz et al. (2005), the countries of Southeast Asia could experience greater human health risks if the strength or variability of the El Niño/Southern Oscillation (ENSO) intensifies. Sea level rise is an additional risk.

Parry et al. (1992) review findings from three comprehensive regional assessments of climate change conducted by the United Nations Environment Programme (UNEP) in the early 1990s. The studies included Indonesia, Malaysia, Thailand and Vietnam. The UNEP case studies underscore a number of concerns. For example, if sea levels were to rise by 10–30cm by 2030 (the "best" estimate reported by the UNEP), extensive damage to fish and prawn industries throughout Southeast Asia would likely occur. The UNEP studies combined crop modeling with climate forecasts to gauge the likely impacts of climate change on agricultural production. For Indonesia, estimates suggest yield reductions of 4 percent for rice and 25–65 percent for maize. Additional agricultural losses in Indonesia were projected to occur due to sea level rise. Although higher levels of rainfall could increase potential irrigation (by up to 130 percent), the UNEP studies projected that increased rainfall-induced erosion and nutrient leaching would tend to offset these gains.

More recent estimates predict alarming outcomes by 2100 if no action is taken on climate change. Indonesia, the Philippines, Vietnam and Thailand could face annual GDP losses of up to 6.7 percent, when accounting for market, health and environmental costs, as well as the risks of catastrophic weather events (ADB 2009). This estimate is more than double the global average. Recommendations focus on scaling up resource management arrangements, implementing new localized management schemes (particularly for mangrove conservation), and improving the dissemination of climate-related information and technology (such as early warning systems for flood mitigation and heat- and drought-resistant crop varieties). The study also identifies the importance of power development and forest conservation to reducing carbon emissions, due to the substantial share of regional emissions generated from these sources, and the region's relatively large share of total emissions in these categories (ADB 2009).

Ward and Shively (2013) provide a somewhat different perspective on vulnerability to natural disasters by examining past vulnerability to natural events (including floods, drought and storms) in a large cross-section of countries. Figure 6.4 plots a score of vulnerability against GDP per capita. Each dot in the figure represents a country. Among the Southeast Asian countries available in their sample, Laos appears as the most vulnerable and Singapore as the least vulnerable. These findings suggest a strong negative correlation between vulnerability and a country's level of economic development: other things equal, countries reduce their vulnerability to natural disasters through improvements in overall economic wellbeing. This makes sense, since economic performance provides opportunity for protection at the level of individual households, and also increases the capacity of a society and government to provide infrastructure to prevent disasters and respond when they occur. They find that Lao PDR and Singapore have higher than expected vulnerability for a given level of GDP per capita, and Vietnam, Indonesia, the Philippines and Thailand have lower than expected vulnerability compared with countries with comparable levels of GDP per capita. They further argue that for most Southeast Asian countries both the likelihood of natural disaster and the likelihood of impacts are high. Four countries – the Philippines, Thailand, Lao PDR and Vietnam – exhibit probabilities of impact that are above average for their predicted level of natural disaster. This suggests that these countries are both more likely than average to be affected by natural disasters and less well prepared to deal with them than countries at similar levels of development and underlying climate risk.

While recognizing that the threats and risks of climate change in the region remain unclear, some attempts to develop mitigation and adaptation plans have been undertaken (Haque 2003; Stromberg 2007). In recent years, countries with higher levels of government capacity have begun

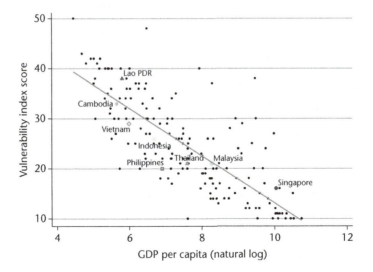

Figure 6.4 Vulnerability and GDP per capita
Source: Based on Ward and Shively 2013.

to move away from an ad hoc approach, working to understand how the state can change behaviors and institutions ex ante to mitigate the impact of disasters, rather than only addressing them after the fact (Haque 2003; Stromberg 2007). Kaosa-ard et al. (2011) argue that well-developed surveillance systems are needed in the region to monitor not only changes in climate, but also the incidence, spread and relevant ranges of infectious diseases and agricultural pests. Such systems are still in early stages of development.

Data on overall, per capita and per GDP carbon emissions in Southeast Asia over the period 2008–12 are provided in Table 6.7. Indonesia is clearly the largest CO_2 producer in the region. Malaysia is currently the most intensive emitter of CO_2, in reflection of its high level of industrial development and relative affluence. Efficiency of emissions remains low in most cases. To consider Southeast Asia's role in reducing global warming, we include in the final column of Table 6.7 indicators for country-level participation in REDD+, an emerging international climate policy mechanism designed to provide developing countries with payments in exchange for voluntary reductions in greenhouse gas emissions. Under REDD+, national governments receive payments, while regional, provincial and local agents are responsible for undertaking land use changes to achieve targets. Several levels of commitment are indicated in Table 6.7, ranging from no approved REDD+ affiliation (Thailand) to initial, planning stage "Partner Country" status (Lao PDR, Malaysia and Myanmar) to fully approved "National Program" status (Cambodia, Indonesia, Philippines and Vietnam). The complexity of articulating REDD+ programs is substantial. For example, in an analysis of how Indonesia's program would have performed, had it been in place during the period 2000–05, Busch et al. (2012) estimate that, controlling for other factors, for every 1,000 USD increase in the per hectare net present value of potential agricultural revenue, deforestation was estimated to increase by 1.4 percent at low-forest cover sites and by 7.3 percent at high-forest cover sites. These estimates suggest that the magnitude of payments required to reduce land clearing are substantial.[6] The poor performance of voluntary incentives in their model stems largely from adverse selection and leakage. They conclude that the ability to maintain REDD+ programs is likely to be frustrated by the inability to verify actions at district levels or to provide a reasonable counterfactual "business as usual" scenario. Such difficulties continue to stand in the way of rapid roll-out of REDD+ programs, although some efforts to launch initiatives are underway.

Table 6.7 Carbon emissions and abatement programs in Southeast Asia, 2008–12

Country	MT (millions)	Carbon emissions in 2008		REDD+ affiliation, 2012
		MT per capita	Kg/GDP (PPP $)	
Cambodia	47.1	0.33	0.16	National Program
Indonesia	1098.4	1.73	0.45	National Program
Lao PDR	40.9	0.25	0.11	Partner Country
Malaysia	335.9	7.57	0.54	Partner Country
Myanmar	219.8	0.27	–	Partner Country
Philippines	123.1	0.92	0.25	National Program
Thailand	336.4	4.19	0.52	None
Vietnam	190.4	1.50	0.53	National Program

Source: Data on total emissions from World Resources Institute Climate Analysis Indicators Tool (CAIT); all other data from World Bank, World Development Indicators; REDD+ affiliation from the UN REDD Program. Millions MT are of CO_2 equivalent, and include land use change and forestry contributions.
Note: The reported per capita and aggregate numbers may be inconsistent, because CAIT uses CO_2-equivalent measures and the World Bank uses CO_2.

Transboundary issues

Aside from continued depletion of open-access fisheries and disagreement over rights of access to fisheries, two other important transboundary environmental issues confront the countries of Southeast Asia. The first is related to the management and use of the Mekong River and its watershed. The second is related to air quality and the recurrent problem of haze that affects a number of countries.[7]

The Mekong River originates in China and flows 4,350 km through China, Myanmar, Lao PDR, Thailand, Cambodia and Vietnam. Its watershed covers 795,000 km^2. One of the few longstanding sub-regional Southeast Asian institutions directed at cooperation on environmental matters is the Mekong River Commission (MRC). It was established in 1957, bringing together Thailand, Laos, Cambodia and South Vietnam, with a focus on coordinating electricity production, irrigation and flood control. However, as Jokinen (2001) indicates, throughout much of its early history, the MRC made little progress on major issues, in part due to conflicts among and within member countries, in part due to the activities and pursuits of non-member countries (such as China and Myanmar), and in part due to conflicts arising from pressures exerted by the outside donor community. A renewed and expanded agreement in 1995 was met with enthusiasm but produced little in the way of tangible results, in part due to conflict among Thailand, Vietnam and Cambodia over establishment of standards for water quality. Given the continued absence of China from the MRC, progress in reconciling differences in upstream and downstream costs and benefits has been slow. China's dam construction has provided, on the one hand, better flood control and increased dry-season flow, but these perceived downstream benefits must be weighed against likely damages to fishing and aquaculture in the lower reaches of the Mekong Basin. A recent review of various modeling studies of the Mekong is provided by Johnston and Kummu (2012). The authors explore a range of issues and note that if all of the dam development projects planned by the six Greater Mekong Subregion countries are actually completed, the Mekong Basin's reservoir capacity would multiply many times over, from 5 km^3 to between 80 and 100 km^3. This is likely to generate a massive change in water flow and quality, creating many new conflicts.

The second major transboundary environmental challenge facing Southeast Asia is worsening air quality, which originates from three main sources: mobile sources (automobiles and other forms of transport), stationary sources (e.g. factories and power generation facilities) and open burning sources, such as forest fires. Afroz et al. (2003), in a study for Malaysia, place the relative overall importance at approximately 70–75 percent for mobile sources, 20–25 percent for stationary sources, and 3–5 percent for open burning and forest fires. Undoubtedly, various sources contribute different amounts and types of pollution in different locations at different points of time, making it difficult to draw broad conclusions about the nature of regional air quality problems. In 2006, for example, motor vehicles produced 98 percent of carbon monoxide emissions in Malaysia and 70 percent of nitrogen oxide emissions, but only 8 percent of particulate matter emissions and 9 percent of sulfur dioxide emissions (Department of Environment 2006). In contrast, power stations produced 50 percent and 44 percent of sulfur dioxide and particulate matter emissions, respectively. Countries in the region have only recently begun to set standards for ambient air quality. Monitoring and enforcement is even less prevalent.

Figure 6.5 plots available country-level data on PM_{10}, the most commonly monitored indicator of air quality worldwide, and in many locations a serious transboundary pollutant.[8] Data reported in the figure are for available years and countries. The data are urban-population weighted PM_{10} levels for residential areas of cities with more than 100,000 residents. According to the World Bank sources, the estimates represent what should be considered the average annual exposure level for the average urban resident being exposed to outdoor particulate matter. For the

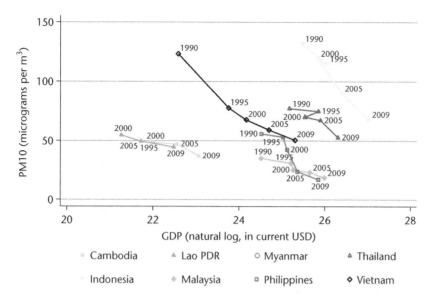

Figure 6.5 PM₁₀ vs. GDP
Source: World Bank: World Development Indicators.

Southeast Asian countries the figure plots PM_{10} exposure levels against GDP per capita. Two features of the graph are worth highlighting. First, generally speaking, PM_{10} levels tend to be positively correlated with the absolute size of an economy, since the size of the economy (in GDP terms) reflects overall production, including industrial production and energy consumption. Second, for all countries, the general trend in PM_{10} levels has been downward over time, which is an encouraging sign and reflects the growing importance of improvements in air quality among citizens and policy makers, and the rapid improvements in air quality that can accompany improvements in technology. This perspective is supported by Figure 6.6, which plots PM_{10}

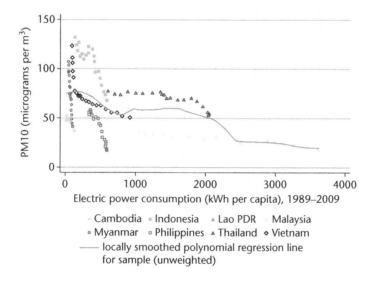

Figure 6.6 Electric power consumption and PM_{10} in Southeast Asia, 1989–2009
Source: World Bank: World Development Indicators.

against electric power consumption for each country. The data indicate a negative correlation between PM_{10} levels and electricity production/consumption. Since electricity consumption is highly correlated with income growth, such a pattern suggests that declines in PM_{10} exposure – in some cases quite rapid declines – are being driven by overall economic growth, and the rapid shift from biomass burning to relatively cleaner sources of energy.

Beyond systematic monitoring of PM_{10}, there have been few country-specific studies on air pollution. Most have been in response to the 1997 incident in which substantial parts of Malaysia, Indonesia and Singapore experienced widespread haze. The seasonal haze problem affects many countries of the region, especially during years in which ENSO-induced droughts occur. Up until 2013, the 1997 event had been widely regarded as the worst in recent experience, and initially brought haze and related transboundary issues to prominence in the region. Quah (2002) identifies forest fires in Indonesia as the primary source, and Singapore, Malaysia, Brunei and Southern Thailand as those most severely affected. Studies of the 1997 haze event by Glover and Jessup (1999) estimated that the cost of the 1997 haze to Singapore alone reached 164 to 286 million USD, though these figures may underestimate the true costs, since not all damages were accounted for (Quah 2002).[9] Although detailed analysis of the June 2013 haze event has not yet been published, preliminary data and popular media accounts suggest that this event was more severe than the 1997 event (SNEA 2013; O'Callaghan 2013).

Resource endowments and economic growth

Several connections can be drawn between natural resources and economic development. The most important, from our perspective, are that low- and middle-income countries are highly dependent on primary product exports, and that this resource dependency tends to be associated with poor economic performance. Improved development prospects often hinge on the protection and sustainable management of natural resources: wise management and reinvestment supports long-run economic development, whilst poor management and low rates of reinvestment undermine development.

Evidence to date suggests that over-reliance on natural resources can reduce savings, investment and growth, thereby lowering the long-term level of consumption and per capita output (Gylfason and Zoega 2006; Sachs and Warner 2001).[10] For example, in a cross-section of 125 countries covering the period 1960–92, Gylfason et al. (1999) find a statistically strong inverse relationship between the size of a country's primary sector and economic growth. This "curse" of natural resources is well accepted, though not unchallenged.[11] The World Bank's Genuine Domestic Savings (GDS) indicator seeks to measure this, and correct for the neglect of resource depletion in the calculation of national statistics. Evaluating Southeast Asian economies using this measure creates some room for optimism. Figure 6.7 plots the available data for the period 1980–2009. The figure indicates that Indonesia, Thailand, the Philippines and Malaysia have maintained positive levels since the early 1980s. Although Laos and Cambodia have seen negative genuine savings for many years, both nations have, along with Vietnam, experienced an uptick in GDS in recent years.

Historically, the "resource curse" has been attributed to Dutch Disease, in which the boom produced by a low-skill primary sector leads to appreciation of the real exchange rate in such a way that it reduces the competitiveness of the export sector, thereby undermining growth of a high-skill secondary sector (Gelb 1988). This is the primary argument put forth by Sachs and Warner (2001), who argue that there is virtually no overlap in the set of countries with large resource endowments and the set with high levels of GDP, and that the stylized pattern is invariant to the inclusion or exclusion of agriculture. Sachs and Warner's data (updated through 1995) are

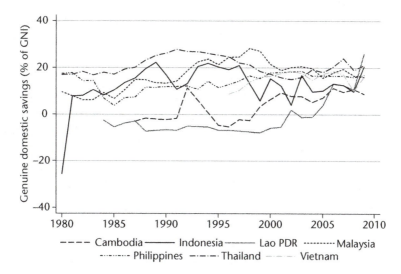

Figure 6.7 Genuine domestic savings as % of gross national income in Southeast Asia, 1980–2009
Source: World Bank: World Development Indicators.

reproduced here in the form of Figure 6.8, where each dot represents a country. The x-axis measures the country's primary export share in 1970, constructed from primary agricultural and forest products and output from minerals and fuel. This serves as an indicator of resource dependence. The y-axis shows real GDP per capita growth registered in the subsequent 25-year period. The first conclusion to be drawn from the plot is that relatively few of the Southeast Asian countries should be regarded as resource dependent as of 1970. The two possible exceptions are Indonesia and Malaysia, the latter of which had a primary export share approaching 0.40 in 1970.[12]

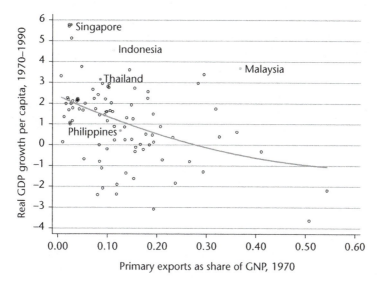

Figure 6.8 Primary export share and per capita growth, 1970–95
Source: Reconstructed by the authors based on data reported by Sachs and Warner.

129

The second conclusion to be drawn is that four of the five Southeast Asian countries included in this analysis (Singapore, Thailand, Indonesia and Malaysia) performed far better than expected for their given level of primary exports. This conclusion is consistent with the findings of Gylfason and Zoega (2006) who regard Indonesia, Malaysia and Thailand as countries with rapid growth but relatively low resource dependence. Even the Philippines, often regarded as the prime example of a country trapped for decades under a system of "crony capitalism" in which natural resource rents served private rather than public ends, performed not much worse than average for its level of natural endowment. Overall, therefore, one lesson that can be drawn from this literature is that the outward-looking countries of Southeast Asia provide a lesson for other countries, namely that, controlling for initial resource dependence, high-growth countries tend to become that way as a result of gradual diversification coupled with high rates of saving and investment (28 percent, on average, compared with 14 percent for the slow-growth countries).[13] Going a step further, Gylfason et al. (1999) argue that the key to this growth has been investment in *human* capital.

Table 6.8 presents the primary export shares for Southeast Asia at five points over the period 1965 to 2011. These data extend the figures and analysis of Barbier (2005). Several features of the series are noteworthy. First, all countries in the region had extremely high primary export shares in 1965 – on the order of 94–99 percent for those countries for which data are available. As Barbier indicates, however, for most of the countries on our list, reliance on a small number of commodities has not been too great, and the top export product has generally not exceeded 30–40 percent of the total value of exports over this time period, compared with 80–90 percent for the top export in many of the slowest growing low-income countries. Diversification, even of primary exports during periods in which primary export shares were high, has been a key feature of the Southeast Asian economies. A second important feature is the steady decline in reliance on primary exports in most Southeast Asian countries. Between 1965 and 1995 (the period in which reliable data exist for all countries of concern here), Lao PDR's primary export share fell by 49 percent, Myanmar's fell by 54 percent, Indonesia's fell by 60 percent, Malaysia's fell by 84 percent, Thailand's fell by 91 percent, and the Philippines's fell by 92 percent. The decline in resource dependency has been a key contributing factor to economic growth in the region. Asia is one of the only regions in which resource dependency has fallen by so much, and so quickly. However, it is worth noting that for most countries in the region, remaining resource dependency rests within the agricultural sector. Finally, while the primary export share has trended downward for most Southeast Asian countries,

Table 6.8 Primary export shares for Southeast Asia, 1965–2011

	1965	*1980*	*1990*	*1995*	*2005*	*2011*
Cambodia	–	–	–	75	5	9
Indonesia	96	96	54	38	42	50
Lao PDR	94	100	90	48	56	80
Malaysia	94	80	33	15	17	24
Myanmar	99	81	89	46	57	71
Philippines	95	49	20	8	5	11
Thailand	95	68	30	9	11	18
Vietnam	–	–	24	22	30	23

Source: Data for 1965, 1980/81, 1990/99 from UNCTAD and various World Bank sources, as reported by Barbier (2005, table 1.1); data for 1995, 2005 and 2011 from UNCTAD *Handbook of Statistics* (2012, table 3.1). Table entries represent primary exports (raw agricultural products, fuel and minerals) as a share of total exports.

data for the first decade of this century suggest some growth in primary export shares. Some of this uptick in the value shares of primary exports reflects strong performance of primary commodity prices throughout much of the decade.[14]

Conclusions: resources, growth and sustainable development

During the 1970s and 1980s most environmental focus in Southeast Asia was oriented toward local and national-level environmental issues such as soil and water conservation and forest conservation. In past decades, as many of the countries of the region have grown, prospered, urbanized and integrated with other economies, attention has begun to shift toward issues related to the environmental effects of trade, aid and investment, and making economic development more environmentally sustainable.

Long-seen as a source for raw materials to fuel economic growth elsewhere, during the past two decades the countries of Southeast Asia have increasingly diversified away from primary exports and begun to leverage their natural resource wealth for domestic purposes. They also have begun to recognize the potential payoffs from greater regional economic integration. A number of free trade agreements and economic partnership agreements have been forged in the region, and economic integration will undoubtedly continue. In coming decades, new regional economic opportunities will combine with income growth to intensify pressures on the Southeast Asian environment and the natural resource base. But future growth is likely to be sustainable only if economies continue to be restructured away from dependence on natural resource-based exports and traditional resource extraction and processing activities. Strengthening national and regional institutions, and reorienting development strategies and expenditures, also will be necessary to accelerate environmental protection and enforcement, especially in the areas of air and water quality. One of the most prominent current examples is fuel subsidies, which are pervasive, highly distortionary, and environmentally problematic. Where possible, access to resources should reflect the true economic and social cost of the extracted resources, with revenues and resource rents reinvested in environmental protection, the development of human capital and the regeneration of natural capital.

Acknowledgments

We acknowledge the helpful comments of Anne Booth, Ian Coxhead, Corbett Grainger, Mingsarn Kaosa-ard, Patrick Ward and Peter Warr.

Notes

1 Historical and sector-specific reviews for Southeast Asia include Poffenberger (1990), Brookfield and Byron (1993), Bryant and Parnwell (1996) and Grove et al. (1998).
2 In particular, we omit any discussion of fisheries and marine resources, which are extremely important to the region but beyond our current scope.
3 Apart from Thailand, all of the countries of Southeast Asia experienced periods of colonial administration. In many cases, independence replaced colonial power with legal frameworks that concentrated power over natural resources in the hands of central governments. In practice, other entities often came to control natural resource extraction and/or marketing, though like central governments, these entities themselves were often controlled by elites (Rola and Coxhead 2005).
4 It has long been recognized that state policies in Southeast Asia have been fundamental to providing and shaping the economic incentives that led to widespread logging in the region (e.g. Barbier 1993; Repetto and Gillis 1988). Hurst (1990) further argued that the debt crisis of the 1980s also encouraged the industry to work at maximum speed using highly destructive extraction methods.

5 The Southeast Asian shares are dominated by Indonesia (3.9), followed by Thailand (0.82), Myanmar (0.72), Malaysia (0.66), Vietnam (0.61), Cambodia (0.38), the Philippines (0.32), Lao PDR (0.20) and Singapore (0.10).

6 The estimates are consistent with figures reported by Zelek and Shively (2003) for the Philippines.

7 *Haze* is a general term that is most frequently used to describe an aggregation of atmospheric dust, smoke and/or vapor that reduces visibility and creates fog-like or cloudy conditions. In the case of the 1997 Southeast Asian haze episode discussed in this section, as many as 20 different contributing elements have been implicated (see Murdiyarso and Abdullah 1998).

8 PM_{10} refers to particulate matter with a diameter < 10 μm. Updrafts of PM_{10} can be transported and redeposited by horizontal and vertical airflows. See, for example, Lee et al. (2013).

9 Some observers have questioned how much the fires in southern Sumatra and Kalimantan contribute to the problem. One competing hypothesis is that the haze might reflect seasonal atmospheric conditions and a periodic buildup from vehicular and stationary sources. This conjecture has been largely ruled out by studies that used lead as a marker for non-forest sources (Afroz et al. 2003).

10 For Southeast Asia specifically, see Phung et al., Chapter 4 of this volume.

11 Brunnschweiler (2008) finds a significant positive association between economic growth and resource abundance.

12 Sachs and Warner's approach and conclusions have been criticized by some observers in part because the data used to construct the x-axis in their figure (and, by extension, ours) tends to conflate resource dependence and trade openness. For example, throughout this period Indonesia had a small export share in GDP but was highly dependent on resource exports.

13 Coxhead (2007) examined the growth trajectories of countries with high initial endowments of natural resources. Of the five countries with robust long-term growth, three (Indonesia, Malaysia and Thailand) are in Southeast Asia.

14 The substantial rise in primary export shares in Laos largely reflects the growth of mining, which provided 45 percent of exports and generated 12 percent of government revenues in 2008 (ICMM 2011). The increase in Myanmar reflects natural gas development and export. Production expanded from 61 billion cubic feet (Bcf) in 1999 to 420 Bcf in 2011 (US EIA 2013).

References

Afroz, R., M.N. Hassan, and N.A. Ibrahim. 2003. "Review of air pollution and health impacts in Malaysia." *Environmental Research* 92: 71–7.

Asian Development Bank (ADB). 2009. *The Economics of Climate Change in Southeast Asia: A Regional Review.* Manila, Philippines: Asian Development Bank.

Barbier, E.B. 1993. "Economic aspects of tropical deforestation in Southeast Asia." *Global Ecology and Biogeography Letters* 3(4–6): 215–34.

Barbier, E.B. 2005. *Natural Resources and Economic Development.* Cambridge: Cambridge University Press.

Blaikie, P. 1985. *The Political Economy of Soil Erosion in Developing Countries.* London: Longman.

Blaikie, P. and H. Brookfield. 1987. *Land Degradation and Society.* London: Routledge.

Brookfield, H. and Y. Byron. (eds). 1993. *South-East Asia's Environmental Future: The Search for Sustainability.* Kuala Lumpur: Oxford University Press and United Nations University Press.

Brunnschweiler, C.N. 2008. "Cursing the blessings? Natural resource abundance, institutions, and economic growth." *World Development* 36(3): 399–419.

Bryant, R.L. and M.J.G. Parnwell. 1996. "Introduction: politics, sustainable development and environmental change in South-East Asia." In Raymond L. Bryant and Michael J.G. Parnwell (eds), *Environmental Change in South-East Asia: People Politics and Sustainable Development.* London: Routledge, pp. 1–20.

Busch, J., R.N. Lubowski, et al. 2012. "Structuring economic incentives to reduce emissions from deforestation within Indonesia." *PNAS* 109(4): 1062–7.

Cassman, K.G. and P.L. Pingali. 1995. "Intensification of irrigated rice systems: learning from the past to meet future challenges." *GeoJournal* 35(3): 299–305.

Chomitz, K.M. and Gray, D.A. 1996. "Roads, land use and deforestation: a spatial model applied to Belize." *World Bank Economic Review* 10(3): 487–512.

Coxhead, I. 2005. "International trade and the natural resource 'curse' in Southeast Asia: does China's growth threaten regional development?" In B. Resosudarmo (ed.), *The Politics and Economics of Indonesia's Natural Resources.* Canberra: Australian National University, pp. 71–91.

Coxhead, I. 2007. "A new resource curse? Impacts of China's boom on comparative advantage and resource dependence in Southeast Asia." *World Development* 35(7): 1099–119.

Coxhead, I. and S. Jayasuriya. 2003. *The Open Economy and the Environment: Development, Trade and Resources in Asia*. Northampton, MA: Edward Elgar.

Cropper, M., C. Griffiths, and M. Mani. 1999. "Roads, population pressures, and deforestation in Thailand, 1976–1989." *Land Economics* 75(1): 58–73.

Deininger, K. and B. Minten. 1999. "Poverty, policies, and deforestation: the case of Mexico." *Economic Development and Cultural Change* 47(2): 313–44.

Department of Environment. 2006. "Environmental Quality Report 2006." Kuala Lumpur: Ministry of Natural Resources and Environment, Malaysia.

Department of Environment. 2013. *Official Air Pollutant Index*. Kuala Lumpur: Ministry of Natural Resources and Environment, Malaysia. http://apims.doe.gov.my/apims/calender.php.

Doutriaux, S., C. Geisler, and G. Shively. 2008. "Competing for coffee space: development induced displacement in the Central Highlands of Vietnam." *Rural Sociology* 73(4): 528–54.

Energy Information Agency (US) 2013. International Energy Statistics database. US Department of Energy, Washington, DC. http://www.eia.gov/cfapps/ipdbproject/IEDIndex3.cfm.

FAOSTAT. Data accessed August 16, 2013 at: http://faostat.fao.org/. Rome: Food and Agriculture Organization of the United Nations.

Garrity, D.P., M. Soekardi, M. van Noordwijk, R. de la Cruz, P.S. Pathak, H.P.M. Gunasena, N. Van So, G. Huijun, and N.M. Majid. 1997. "The *Imperata* grasslands of tropical Asia: area, distribution, and typology." *Agroforestry Systems* 36: 3–29.

Geist, H. and E. Lambin. 2001. "What drives tropical deforestation? A meta-analysis of proximate and underlying causes of deforestation based on subnational case study evidence." LUCC Report Series, Number 4, Land-Cover Change (LUCC) Project, University of Louvain, Department of Geography, Brussels.

Geist, H. and E. Lambin. 2002. "Proximate causes and underlying driving forces of tropical deforestation." *BioScience* 52:143–50.

Gelb, A. 1988. *Windfall Gains: Blessing or Curse?* New York: Oxford University Press.

Gelb, A. 2011. "Economic diversification in resource-rich countries." In R. Arezki, T. Gylfason, and A. Sy (eds), *Beyond the Curse: Policies to Harness the Power of Natural Resources*. Washington, DC: International Monetary Fund.

Glover, D. and T. Jessup. 1999. "Indonesia's fires and haze: the cost of catastrophe." Singapore: Institute of Southeast Asian Studies.

Grove, R., V. Damodaran, and S. Sangwan (eds). 1998. *Nature and the Orient: The Environmental History of South and South-East Asia*. New Delhi: Oxford University Press.

Gylfason, T. and G. Zoega. 2006. "Natural resources and economic growth: the role of investment." *World Economy* 29(8): 1091–115.

Gylfason, T., T.T. Hervertsson, and G. Zoega. 1999. "A mixed blessing: natural resources and economics growth." *Macroeconomic Dynamics*. 3: 204–25.

Ha, D.T. and G.E. Shively. 2008. "Coffee boom, coffee bust, and smallholder response in Vietnam's Central Highlands." *Review of Development Economics* 12(2): 312–26.

Haque, E.C. 2003. "Perspectives of natural disasters in East and South Asia, and the Pacific Island States: socio-economic correlates and needs assessment." *Natural Hazards* 29: 465–83.

Hirsch, P. 1993. *Political Economy of Environment in Thailand*. Manila: Journal of Contemporary Asia Publishers.

Howard, M.C. (ed.). 1993. *Asia's Environmental Crisis*. Boulder, CO: Westview Press.

Hurst, P. 1990. *Rainforest Politics: Ecological Destruction in South-East Asia*. London: Zed Books.

International Council on Mining & Metals (ICMM). 2011. *Utilizing Mining and Mineral Resources to Foster the Sustainable Development of the Lao PDR*. London: ICMM.

Jaeger, W.K. and V. Kolpin. 2000. "Economic growth and environmental resource allocation." Mimeo.

Japan Environmental Council (JEC). 2000. *The State of the Environment in Asia 1999/2000*. Tokyo: Springer.

Johnston, R. and M. Kummu. 2012. "Water resource models in the Mekong Basin: a review." *Water Resource Management* 26: 429–55.

Jokinen, J. 2001. "Reconstructing the Mekong River Commission." In Andrea Straub (ed.), *Institutions, Livelihoods and the Environment. Change and Response in Mainland Southeast Asia*. Copenhagen: Nordic Institute of Asian Studies, pp. 211–42.

Kaosa-ard, M., K. Rayanakorn and A. Adam. 2011. "Climate change: Thailand's new challenge." In K. Rayanakorn (ed.), *Climate Change Challenges in the Mekong Region*. Chiang Mai, Thailand: Chiang Mai University Press.

Kim Onah, N.T. et al. 2006. "Particulate air pollution in six Asian cities: spatial and temporal distributions, and associated sources." *Atmospheric Environment* 40: 3367–80.

Kosonen, M., A. Otsamo, and J. Kuusipalo. 1997. "Financial, economic and environmental profitability of reforestation of *Imperata* grasslands in Indonesia." *Forest Ecology and Management* 99: 237–59.

Lambin, E., B. Turner, H. Geist, S. Agbola, A. Angelsen, J. Bruce et al. 2001. "The causes of land-use and land-cover change: moving beyond the myths." *Global Environmental Change* 11: 261–9.

Lee, S., C.-H. Ho, Y.G. Lee, H.-J. Choi, and C.-K. Song. 2013. "Influence of transboundary air pollutants from China on the high-PM10 episode in Seoul, Korea for the period October 16–20, 2008." *Atmospheric Environment* 77: 430–9.

Lucas, R.E.B., D. Wheeler, and H. Hettige. 1992. "Economic development, environmental regulation and the international migration of toxic industrial pollution: 1960–88." In Patrick Low (ed.), *International Trade and the Environment*. World Bank Discussion Papers No. 159. Washington, DC: World Bank.

Murdiyarso, D. and R. Abdullah. 1998. "The impacts of transboundary haze pollution of the 1997/98 fires episode on health." Satellite Workshop Summary Report. Kuala Lumpur: University Putra and Global Change Impacts Centre for Southeast Asia. 27 October. Accessed August 16, 2013 at: http://www.fire.uni-freiburg.de/course/coursere/my_coure1.htm.

O'Callaghan, J. 2013. "Singapore, Malaysia face economic hit from prolonged smog." *Reuters*, 24 June.

Panayotou, N. 1993. "Empirical tests and policy analysis of environmental degradation at different stages of economic development." Working Paper WP238. Technology and Employment Program. Geneva: International Labour Office.

Parnwell, M.J.G. and R.L. Bryant. 1996. "Conclusion: towards sustainable development in South-East Asia?" In Raymond L. Bryant and Michael J.G. Parnwell (eds), *Environmental Change in South-East Asia: People Politics and Sustainable Development*. London: Routledge, pp. 330–43.

Parry, M.L., A.R. Magalhaes, and N.H. Nih. 1992. *The Potential Socio-economic Effects of Climate Change: A Summary of Three Regional Assessments*. Nairobi, Kenya: United Nations Environment Programme (UNEP).

Patz, J.A., D. Campbell-Lendrum, T. Holloway, and J.A. Foley. 2005. "Impact of regional climate change on human health." *Nature* 438: 310–17.

Pfaff, A. 1997. "What drives deforestation in the Brazilian Amazon? Evidence from satellite and socio-economic data." Policy Research Working Paper Series, Environment, Infrastructure, and Agriculture Division, Washington, DC, World Bank.

Poffenberger, M. (ed.). 1990. *Keepers of the Forest: Land Management Alternatives in Southeast Asia*. West Hartford, CT: Kumarian Press.

Quah, E. 2002. "Transboundary pollution in Southeast Asia: the Indonesian fires." *World Development* 30(3): 429–41.

Rausser, G. 2000. "Valuing research leads: bioprospecting and the conservation of genetic resources." Working Paper, Berkeley Program in Law and Economics, University of California, Berkeley.

Rayanakorn, K. 2011. *Climate Change Challenges in the Mekong Region*. Chiang Mai, Thailand: Chiang Mai University Press.

Repetto, R. 1990. "Macroeconomic policies and deforestation." Prepared for UNU/WIDER project, The Environment and Emerging Development Issues.

Repetto, R. and M. Gillis (eds). 1988. *Public Policies and the Misuse of Forest Resources*. Cambridge: Cambridge University Press.

Rola, A.C. and I. Coxhead. 2005. "Agricultural development and institutional transitions." In I. Coxhead and G. Shively (eds), *Land Use Changes in Tropical Watersheds: Evidence, Causes, and Remedies*. Boston, MA: CAB International, pp. 19–36.

Sachs, J.D. and A.M. Warner. 2001. "The curse of natural resources." *European Economic Review* 45: 827–38.

Sani, S. 1993. "Urban Environment in ASEAN." In M. Seda (ed.), *Environmental Management in ASEAN. Perspectives on Critical Regional Issues*. Singapore: Institute of Southeast Asian Studies, pp. 111–40.

Schwartz, J., F. Laden, and A. Zanobetti. 2002. "The concentration-response relation between PM2.5 and daily deaths." *Environmental Health Perspectives* 110: 1025–9.

Seda, M. 1993. "Global environmental concerns and priorities: implications for ASEAN." In M. Seda (ed.), *Environmental Management in ASEAN. Perspectives on Critical Regional Issues*. Singapore: Institute of Southeast Asian Studies, pp. 1–54.

Selden, T.M. and D. Song. 1995. "Neoclassical growth, the J curve for abatement, and the inverted U curve for pollution." *Journal of Environmental Economics and Management* 29: 162–8.

Shaw, R.P. 1989. "Rapid population growth and environmental degradation: ultimate *versus* proximate factors." *Environmental Conservation* 16(3): 199–208.

Shively, G. 2001a. "Poverty, consumption risk, and soil conservation." *Journal of Development Economics* 65(2): 267–90.

Shively, G. 2001b. "Agricultural change, rural labor markets, and forest clearing: an illustrative case from the Philippines." *Land Economics* 77(2): 268–84.

Shively, G. 2004. "Introduction to the special issue on poverty and forest degradation."*Environment and Development Economics* 9(2):131–4.

Shively, G. and S. Pagiola. 2004. "Agricultural intensification, local labor markets, and deforestation in the Philippines." *Environment and Development Economics* 9(2): 241–66.

Sien, C.L. and C. MacAndrews. 1979. "Environment problems and development in Southeast Asia." In C. MacAndrews and C.L. Sien (eds), *Developing Economies and the Environment: The Southeast Asian Experience.* Singapore: McGraw-Hill International, pp. 3–14.

Singapore National Environmental Agency (SNEA). 2013. *Historical PSI Reading.* Singapore: Government of Singapore. http://www.haze.gov.sg/haze-update/historical-psi-reading/year/2013/month/6/day/20.aspx.

Sodhi, N.S., L.P. Koh, B.W. Brook, and P. Ng. 2004. "Southeast Asian biodiversity: an impending disaster." *Trends in Ecology and Evolution* 12: 654–60.

Soedarjo, A.D. 2010. "Indonesia overtakes Thailand in car sales." *Jarkarta Globe*, 29 July.

Stromberg, D. 2007. "Natural disasters, economic development, and humanitarian aid." *Journal of Economic Perspectives* 21: 199–222.

Tomich, T.P., J. Kuusipalo, K. Menz, and N. Byron. 1997. "*Imperata* economics and policy." *Agroforestry Systems* 36: 233–61.

United Nations Conference on Trade and Development (UNCTAD). 2012. *UNCTAD Handbook of Statistics 2012.* New York: United Nations.

United Nations Environment Programme (UNEP). 2012. *The Emissions Gap Report 2012 – Current and Projected Greenhouse Gas Emissions.* Nairobi: United Nations Environment Programme.

Ward, P. and G. Shively. 2011. "Vulnerability, income growth and climate change." *World Development* 40 (5): 916–27.

Ward, P. and G. Shively. 2013. "Disaster risk, social vulnerability and economic development." Photocopy. Department of Agricultural Economics. West Lafayette, IN: Purdue University.

Wong, C.M., V.V. Nuntavam, H. Kan, Z. Qian, and the PAPA Project Teams. 2008. "Public Health and Air Pollution in Asia (PAPA): a multicity study of short-term effects of air pollution on mortality." *Environmental Health Perspectives* 116: 1195–202.

Zelek, C.A. and G.E. Shively. 2003. "Measuring the opportunity cost of carbon sequestration in tropical agriculture." *Land Economics* 79(3): 342–54.

Part III
Trade, investment, and industrialization

Global production sharing, trade patterns, and industrialization in Southeast Asia

Prema-chandra Athukorala

AUSTRALIAN NATIONAL UNIVERSITY

Archanun Kohpaiboon

THAMMASAT UNIVERSITY

Introduction

Global production sharing (GPS) – the dispersion of separate stages (tasks) of an integrated production process across national boundaries – has been a major factor in the economic dynamism of the Southeast Asian economies. Led by Singapore and Malaysia, the Southeast Asian economies have been major and successful participants in global production networks. "Network products" (parts and components, and final assembly traded within production networks) constitute almost two-thirds of the merchandise exports of Singapore, Malaysia, and the Philippines, almost half those of Thailand, and a smaller but still significant share for Indonesia. From a small and recent base, they are growing quickly in Vietnam, while beginning in 2012 Cambodia has begun to participate in global production networks on a modest scale.

The purpose of this chapter is to document, analyze, and explain Southeast Asia's engagement in global production sharing and to examine its implications for the process of industrial transformation in these countries. The chapter has two main objectives: to broaden our understanding of economic performance and structural changes in the Southeast Asian economies in the era of economic globalization, and to contribute to the wider literature on the role of global production sharing as a prime mover of global economic integration by developing countries.

The remainder of the chapter has four sections. The next section provides a historical overview of Southeast Asia's engagement in global production sharing. This is followed by an examination of trends and patterns of trade based on global production sharing ("network trade") in Southeast Asia from a comparative regional and global perspective. Then the next section probes the implications of global production sharing for growth and structural changes in domestic manufacturing, with a focus on the ongoing debate on industrial upgrading ("graduation from the middle"). The concluding section summarizes key findings and draws some policy inferences.

A brief history

Southeast Asia's engagement in global production sharing dates back to 1968 when two US companies, National Semiconductors and Texas Instruments, began assembling semiconductor devices in Singapore (Lee 2000). By the beginning of the 1970s Singapore had the lion's share of offshore assembly activities of the US and European semiconductor industries. As early as 1972 some multinational enterprises (MNEs) with production facilities in Singapore began to relocate some low-end assembly activities to neighboring countries, particularly Malaysia, Thailand, and the Philippines, in response to Singapore's rapidly rising wages and rental costs. Subsequently, many new MNEs also set up production bases in these countries, bypassing Singapore. By the late 1980s this process had created a new regional division of labor based on differences in relative wage and skill requirements in different stages of the production process. At the time when production bases began to spread to neighboring countries, there was a widespread concern in policy circles in Singapore that the regional spread of MNE operations in the electronics industry could be at their country's expense. However, subsequent developments vividly demonstrated that "the larger the scale and scope of electronic industry, which produces a wide range of heterogeneous end-products, each of which needs a large number of equally heterogeneous components in its manufacture ... the greater the economies of scale and more the opportunities for specialization for all participating countries" (Goh 1990).

The US semiconductor producers set up assembly plants in Hong Kong, South Korea, and Taiwan in the early 1960s, well before their entry into Singapore (Grunwald and Flamm 1985).[1] Yet, by the early 1970s Singapore had become the largest source country for imports of semiconductor devices to the USA, accounting for nearly 25 percent of total imports. By the early 1980s, Southeast Asia accounted for over 70 percent of US total semiconductor devices imports; the combined share of Hong Kong, Taiwan, and Korea had dropped to 17 percent (Table 7.1).

Southeast Asia's dominance in the global semiconductor industry within developing Asia is in sharp contrast to the three East Asian countries' far superior performance in manufactured exports

Table 7.1 Shares of principal Asian exporters in total US imports of semiconductor devices,[a] 1969–83

	1969–70*	*1974–75**	*1979–80**	*1982–83**
Asia[b]	56	73	88	87
East Asia	43	33	19	18
Hong Kong	28	11	4	2
Korea	9	15	11	12
Taiwan	7	8	4	4
Southeast Asia	8	40	67	69
Singapore	8	18	21	14
Malaysia	–	19	30	32
Thailand	–	–	3	4
Indonesia	–	–	2	2
Philippines	–	3	12	18

Source: Compiled from Grunwald and Flamm 1985, table 3.7.
Notes:
[a] aImports belonging to the US tariff items 806.30 and 807.00.
[b] Developing Asia (Asia excluding Japan).
*Two-year averages.
– Less than 0.5 percent.

in general during this period. What explains this difference? The "guided" industrial development policies followed in Taiwan and Korea could have played a role. These countries (Korea in particular) followed the Japanese pattern by relying on non-equity arrangements rather than FDI to access technology and other MNE-controlled assets (Amsden and Chu 2003; Wade 1990). However, following Goh Keng Swee (1993), the architect of modern Singapore's spectacular economic development, one can argue that this difference largely emanated from the nature of the East Asian investment environment at the time. At this time, China's Cultural Revolution was reaching its height, and political stability was a key factor governing the location decisions of assembly operations by electronics MNEs. To quote Goh:

> It is a matter for speculation whether in the absence of the upheaval caused by the Cultural Revolution in the mid- and late 1960s, the large American multinationals – among them National Semiconductor and Texas Instruments – would have sited their offshore factories in countries more familiar to them, such as South Korea, Taiwan and Hong Kong. These had resources and skills superior to Singapore. My own judgment remains that these three areas were too close to the scene of trouble, the nature of which could not but cause alarm to multinational investors.
>
> (Goh 1993: 253)

This argument receives further support from the fact that US semiconductor firms favored Singapore (and subsequently Malaysia, Thailand, and the Philippines) not only over Korea and Taiwan, but also over Hong Kong, a country that followed almost laissez-faire economic policy throughout. By the early 1980s, when political risk had waned and industrial policy had become receptive to FDI, wage levels in these countries had already increased to levels that made them less attractive as labor-intensive assembly locations compared to the Southeast Asian countries other than Singapore.

By the mid-1980s, the hard disk drive assemblers entered Singapore, further boosting the country's role as a global assembly center. During the next five years there was a notable change in the composition of the island's electronics industry with computer peripherals, especially hard disk drives, becoming relatively more important compared to semiconductor assembly. By the late 1980s, most major global players in this industry, including Seagate, Maxtor, Hitachi Metals, Control Data, Applied Magnetic, and Conner Peripherals, had set up assembly plants in Penang, and Singapore had become the world's largest exporter of hard disk drives, accounting for almost half of world production (McKendrick et al. 2000). As had previously happened with the semiconductor industry, a regional production network encompassing Malaysia, Thailand, and the Philippines and centered in Singapore developed by the early 1990s.

Until about the early 1990s, Southeast Asian countries' engagement in global production sharing was predominantly a two-way exchange with the home countries of MNEs: parts and components were brought to these countries for assembly, and the assembled parts and components were then re-exported to the home country to be incorporated in final products. As supply networks of parts and components became firmly established, producers in advanced countries began to move the final assembly of an increasingly broad range of electronics and electrical goods (such as computers, cameras, TV sets, and motor cars) to Southeast Asian locations. This process intensified following the rapid appreciation of the yen after the Plaza Accord in 1985, which propelled Japanese MNEs in electronics and electrical goods industries to relocate assembly plants in Southeast Asia so as to maintain their international competitiveness.

Over the years, Singapore's role in regional production networks has gradually shifted from low-skill component assembly and testing to component design and fabrication, and to providing headquarter services for production units located in neighboring countries. Singapore's attractiveness as the regional center for cross-border production networks has been continuously enhanced by the policy emphasis of the government on infrastructure development, expanding the human capital base, maintaining labor relations in a manner highly conducive for international production, and sound macroeconomic management (McKendrick et al. 2000).

In recent years, the East Asian production networks have begun to spread to Vietnam and Cambodia. Following those countries' adoption of market-oriented policy reforms starting in the late 1980s, a number of Korean, Taiwanese, and Japanese firms set up assembly plants in Vietnam. However, these early ventures were predominantly of the conventional import-substitution variety, with few links to the global production networks of the parent companies. From about the late 1990s firms from Japan, Korea and Taiwan began to enter Vietnamese manufacturing to assemble parts and components for exporting within regional production networks. Initially this was done mostly by small- and medium-scale firms from these countries; the only notable global player was Hitachi from Japan. A major breakthrough occurred with the decision in February 2006 by Intel Corporation, the world's largest semiconductor producer, to set up a $300 million testing and assembly plant (subsequently revised to $1 billion) in Ho Chi Minh City. The Intel plant started commercial operations in early 2011 and is expected eventually to employ over 3,000 workers. The early experience in Singapore, Malaysia, Thailand, and the Philippines indicates that there is something of a herd mentality in the site selection process of MNEs in the global electronics industry, particularly if the first entrant is a major player in the industry.

It seems that, following Intel's entry, this process has already begun to replay in Vietnam (Athukorala and Tran 2012). Following in Intel's footsteps a number of other major players in the electronics industry have already come to Vietnam. These include the Taiwanese-based Hon Hai Precision Industry and Compact Electronics (the world's largest and second-largest electronics contract manufacturers) and Nidec Corporation, a Japanese manufacturer of hard disk drive motors and electrical and optical components. In 2009, Samsung Electronics set up a large plant in Hanoi to assemble handheld products (HHPs) such as smartphones and tablets. Over the past four years, Samsung has been gradually shifting HHP assembly from its plant in China to its Vietnam plant as part of a diversification strategy in response to increasing wages and rental costs in China. In 2009, 65 percent of Samsung's global HHP supply came from China, with Vietnam contributing a mere 3 percent; by the end of 2012 these figures had changed to 45 percent and 33 percent, respectively. In 2012, Samsung Vietnam's production capacity reached 150 million units, and its total exports (about US$11 billion) amounted to 11 percent of Vietnam's total merchandise export earnings.[2]

There are also early signs of regional production networks expanding to Cambodia. In 2011, Minebea, a large Japanese MNE which produces a wide range of parts and components for the automotive and electronics industries, set up a plant (Minebea Cambodia) in the Phnom Penh Special Economic Zone to assemble parts for cellular phones using components imported from its factories in Thailand, Malaysia, and China. Minebea Cambodia currently employs 1,300 workers and has plans to expand to a total workforce of 5,000 within two years. Other MNEs that have set up assembly plant in Cambodia include Sumitomo Corporation, Japan (wiring harnesses for cars); Denso, Japan (motorcycle ignition components); Pactics, Belgium (sleeves for sunglasses made by premier eyewear companies); and Tiffany & Company, USA (diamond polishing). As of 2013 there are signs that a number of other Japanese companies which have production based in China and Thailand are planning to relocate some segments of their production processes to Cambodia. Rising wages and rental costs in China and production disruption caused by floods in Thailand in 2011 are considered the drivers working to Cambodia's advantage (*Business Day* 2013).

Despite obvious advantages in terms of its location and relative wages, Indonesia has remained a small player in regional production networks. Its engagement has so far been limited only to some low-end assembly activities undertaken mostly by Singaporean subcontracting companies in the Batam free trade zone (BFTZ).[3] In the early 1970s two major electronics MNEs, which had already established production bases in Singapore, did set up assembly plants in Indonesia (Fairchild and National Semiconductor, established in 1973 and 1974 respectively), but both plants were closed down in 1986. At that time there was a worldwide slump in semiconductor business. However, it is not clear whether external demand factors played an important role in their departure from Indonesia. Both MNEs continued operation in both Singapore and Malaysia with some restructuring and labor shedding in response to demand contraction. Rather, in Indonesia it seems that an unfavorable business environment, in particular labor market rigidities that hinder restructuring operations in line with global changes in the semiconductor industry, are the major reasons. According to contemporary press accounts, in 1985 Fairchild announced a plan to introduce new technology that would have involved some reduction in their workforce, but the Indonesian Ministry of Manpower opposed any retrenchment resulting from automation (Thee and Pangestu 1998).

The issue of why Indonesia is left behind in global production networks was again brought into sharp relief in September 2011 when the Canadian firm, Research in Motion (RIM), the producer of BlackBerry HHDs, decided to set up an assembly plant in Penang, Malaysia, bypassing Indonesia (Manning and Purnagunawan 2011). Indonesia is the major market for BlackBerry devices in Southeast Asia, accounting for some 75 percent of total annual sales in the region, and almost ten times annual sales in Malaysia. Therefore, when RIM announced its plan to set up a production base in Southeast Asia, there were high hopes in Indonesian policy circles that Indonesia would be the preferred location. Indonesian authorities were perplexed by RIM's decision to go to Penang and the industry minister even threatened to introduce punitive import tariffs on BlackBerrys. However, it is not hard to understand the reason behind RIM's decision. Penang has been a world center of electronics production for nearly three decades (Athukorala 2014), whereas, as discussed, Indonesia has had a chequered record in attracting multinational enterprises involved in global production sharing. Compared to the situation in the 1980s when Fairchild and National Semiconductor closed down their operations, there has not been any notable improvement in the country's investment climate. While the proposed punitive tariff was never implemented, it vividly reflected the ever-present tension in Indonesia between the declared official commitment to an open economy and the continuing protectionist leanings.

Trade patterns

The combined share of Southeast Asia in total world non-oil exports increased from 3.1 percent in the early 1970s to nearly 6 percent by 2009–10.[4] Rapid export growth has been underpinned by a profound shift in export structure away from primary commodities and toward manufactures. The share of manufacturing in total non-oil exports from Southeast Asia stood at 72 percent by 2009–10, up from a mere 11 percent four decades earlier. Among individual countries, the manufacturing share is still significantly lower than the regional average in Indonesia (54 percent), Vietnam (67 percent) and smaller Indochina economies (58 percent), reflecting both the relative wealth of their resource endowments and their later adoption of export-oriented industrialization strategies. But a rapid increase in the share of manufacturing is a common phenomenon observable across all countries in the region.

The past two decades have seen a palpable shift in global production sharing away from mature industrial economies toward developing countries, and in particular countries in East Asia (Table 7.2).

Table 7.2 Geographic profile of world manufacturing trade: total trade and network trade (%)

| | Total manufacturing | | Network products | | | | | |
| | | | Parts and components | | Final assembly | | Total | |
	1992–93	2009–10	1992–93	2009–10	1992–93	2009–10	1992–93	2009–10
(a) Exports								
East Asia	28.3	35.1	29.6	43.2	34.1	39.1	32.2	42.5
Japan	12.3	7.2	15.2	8.3	20.8	8.2	18.4	9.2
Developing East Asia (DEA)	16.0	27.9	14.4	34.9	13.3	30.9	13.8	33.3
China	4.5	14.7	1.7	14.4	2.4	18.9	2.1	17.3
Hong Kong, China	1.8	0.6	1.5	0.6	1.2	0.5	1.3	0.7
Taiwan	2.9	2.6	3.7	4.1	2.0	2.2	2.7	3.2
South Korea	2.3	3.6	2.2	5.8	2.0	3.7	2.1	4.1
Southeast Asia	4.5	6.3	5.2	9.8	5.8	3.3	5.6	7.6
Indonesia	0.6	0.5	0.1	0.5	0.1	0.3	0.1	0.5
Malaysia	1.2	1.8	1.7	3.7	1.9	0.5	1.8	2.5
The Philippines	0.3	0.5	0.5	1.6	0.2	0.3	0.4	1.2
Singapore	1.5	1.3	2.3	2.5	2.6	0.7	2.5	1.9
Thailand	0.8	1.4	0.6	1.6	0.9	1.5	0.8	1.6
Vietnam	0.0	0.3	0.0	0.2	0.0	0.1	0.0	0.1
South Asia	0.9	1.4	0.1	0.5	0.1	0.2	0.1	0.3
Developed countries	72.4	55.5	76.7	51.9	78.6	56.1	77.8	52.4
Developing countries	27.6	44.5	20.8	48.1	22.9	44.4	22.0	47.6
World	100	100	100	100	100	100	100	100

(b) Imports

East Asia	21.7	25.7	30.1	38.9	14.3	18.4	21.0	29.8
Japan	4.1	3.5	4.0	3.9	3.0	3.3	3.4	3.5
Developing East Asia (DEA)	17.6	22.3	26.1	35.0	11.2	15.2	17.6	26.0
China	2.9	9.1	3.0	13.8	1.5	6.3	2.2	10.7
Hong Kong, China	4.4	3.6	5.4	6.3	2.8	2.1	3.9	4.4
Taiwan	2.1	1.6	3.1	2.3	1.4	1.2	2.1	1.8
South Korea	2.0	2.2	3.1	2.5	1.1	1.6	1.9	2.1
Southeast Asia	6.2	5.7	11.5	10.3	4.4	4.2	7.4	7.5
Indonesia	0.8	0.4	1.1	0.3	0.3	0.3	0.6	0.3
Malaysia	1.4	1.4	3.0	2.5	1.1	1.2	1.9	1.8
The Philippines	0.4	0.5	0.6	1.2	0.2	0.5	0.4	0.8
Singapore	2.3	2.0	4.8	4.3	2.0	1.5	3.2	3.3
Thailand	1.3	1.2	2.0	1.5	0.8	0.7	1.3	1.0
Vietnam	0.0	0.4	0.0	0.3	0.0	0.2	0.0	0.2
South Asia	0.9	1.3	0.7	1.1	0.4	0.9	0.6	1.0
India	0.5	1.1	0.4	0.9	0.2	0.8	0.3	0.8
Developed countries	71.4	59.1	82.7	51.0	68.8	66.5	74.7	57.3
Developing countries	28.6	30.9	17.3	49.0	31.2	33.5	25.3	42.7
World	100	100	100	100	100	100	100	100

Source: Data compiled from UN Comtrade database.

The share of developing countries in total world network trade (parts and components, and final assembly) increased from 22.0 percent to 47.6 percent between 1992–93 and 2009–10, with the share of developing East Asia (DEA)[5] increasing even faster, from 13.8 percent to 33.3 percent. Within East Asia, Southeast Asia's share in world network trade increased from 5.6 percent to 7.6 percent during this period. At the individual country level, all major Southeast Asian countries, with the exception of Singapore, have shown an increase in their export market shares. The mild decline in Singapore's share reflects a marked shift in its role in global production networks for high-tech industries away from the standard assembly and testing activities to oversight functions, product design, and capital and technology-intensive tasks in the production process. Some, if not most, of these new activities are in the form of services and are, therefore, not captured in merchandise trade data (Wong 2007).

The share of network trade in total manufacturing trade is much higher in East Asia compared to other major regions (Table 7.3). In East Asia, Southeast Asian countries in particular stand out for their heavy dependence on global production sharing for their export expansion. In 2009–10, network exports accounted for nearly 70 percent of total manufacturing exports in Southeast Asia, up from 57 percent in the early 1990s. Malaysia, Singapore, and the Philippines figure prominently for their heavy dependence on network trade compared to the other countries in the region. The patterns observed on the export and import sides are broadly similar, reflecting growing cross-border trade within production networks.

When total network trade is disaggregated into parts and components (henceforth referred to as components for brevity) and final assembly, countries in Southeast Asia stand out from the rest of East Asia for their heavy reliance on the former, and the increase over time in the degree of component intensity of their trade flows within global production networks. Components accounted for 85 percent of total network exports of Southeast Asia in 2009–10, up from 40 percent in 1992–93. The comparable figures for DEA for 1992–93 and 2009–10 were 39 percent and 59 percent respectively. This comparison clearly points to the growing importance of Southeast Asian countries as suppliers of components to final assembly activities within China-dominated regional production networks. Disaggregated data (not reported here owing to space limitations) show that in 2009–10, over 20 percent of component exports to China originated in Southeast Asia, up from 12 percent in 1992–93. The share of components in total non-oil exports to China from Southeast Asia increased from 38 percent to 63 percent between 1992–93 and 2009–10.[6]

The commodity composition of network exports from Southeast Asia is compared with global patterns in Table 7.4. The data clearly point to the heavy concentration of network exports from Southeast Asia in electronics and electrical goods (SITC 75, 76, and 77), in particular, semiconductor devices compared to total world network exports. Automobiles and other transport equipment account for only 9 percent of Southeast Asian exports, compared to a global average of 30 percent. At the individual country level, the composition of network exports from Thailand is much more diversified compared to the other countries. Thailand's commodity composition is also much more in line with overall global patterns, with automobiles accounting for a much larger share compared to electronics. The striking difference between Thailand and Malaysia relating to the relative importance of automobiles within global production networks is particularly noteworthy. It clearly reflects the contrasting policies of the two countries relating to the domestic automobile industry.

At the early stage of Southeast Asia's engagement in global production sharing, when it was a two-way exchange with the home countries of MNEs involved, there was a clear developed-country bias in the geographic profile of regional manufacturing trade (Table 7.5). However, over the years the geographic profile has shifted towards East Asia as regional production networks have

Table 7.3 Share of network products in manufacturing trade, 1992–93 and 2009–10 (%)

	Parts and components		Final assembly		Total network products		Share of parts and components in network trade	
	1992–93	2009–10	1992–93	2009–10	1992–93	2009–10	1992–93	2009–10
(a) Exports								
East Asia	20.2	36.4	31.6	25.3	51.8	61.7	39.0	59.0
Japan	23.9	36.2	44.5	29.1	68.4	65.3	34.9	55.4
Developing East Asia (DEA)	17.3	38.5	21.8	24.7	39.1	63.2	44.2	60.9
China	7.4	20.5	13.7	36.8	21.1	57.3	35.1	35.8
Taiwan	24.7	44.7	17.6	20.9	42.3	65.6	58.4	68.1
Republic of Korea	18.1	43.2	22.2	25.5	40.3	68.7	44.9	62.9
ASEAN	22.7	59.2	34.1	10.1	56.8	69.2	40.0	85.5
Indonesia	3.8	19.5	5.6	18.0	9.3	37.5	40.9	52.0
Malaysia	27.7	65.5	40.7	13.2	68.4	78.7	40.5	83.2
The Philippines	32.9	71.2	20.5	16.3	53.4	87.5	61.6	81.4
Singapore	29.0	49.5	45.9	18.0	74.9	67.5	38.7	73.3
Thailand	14.1	44.5	29.0	21.4	43.1	65.9	32.7	67.5
Vietnam	–	12.03	–	7.5	–	19.5	–	61.7
South Asia	2.3	8.1	2.9	4.2	5.1	12.3	45.1	65.9
India	3.0	10.4	3.4	3.7	6.4	14.1	46.9	73.8
Developed countries	20.4	25.2	28.5	23.6	48.9	48.8	41.7	51.6
Developing countries	14.6	35.2	21.8	18.4	36.4	53.6	40.1	65.7
World	19.3	28.2	26.3	23.0	45.5	51.2	42.4	55.1

(continues in the next page)

Table 7.3 (Continued)

	Parts and components		Final assembly		Total network products		Share of parts and components in network trade	
	1992–93	2009–10	1992–93	2009–10	1992–93	2009–10	1992–93	2009–10
(b) Imports								
East Asia	27.2	42.0	17.2	19.8	44.4	61.8	61.3	68.0
Japan	19.3	22.2	19.3	39.9	38.6	62.1	50.0	35.7
Developing East Asia	29.0	44.4	16.7	17.3	45.8	61.7	63.3	72.0
China	20.4	42.0	14.0	21.7	34.4	63.7	59.3	65.9
Taiwan	29.5	36.7	18.0	19.0	47.5	55.7	62.1	65.9
Republic of Korea	30.1	35.3	14.6	14.0	44.7	49.3	67.3	71.6
ASEAN	36.0	47.8	18.4	16.2	54.4	64.0	66.2	74.7
Indonesia	27.0	22.8	9.2	34.8	36.1	57.6	74.8	39.6
Malaysia	40.5	55.0	20.2	17.0	60.7	72.0	66.7	76.4
The Philippines	32.6	62.3	15.0	16.3	47.6	78.6	68.5	79.3
Singapore	39.9	51.0	21.9	26.7	61.8	77.7	64.6	65.6
Thailand	30.6	41.0	15.6	7.2	46.2	48.2	66.2	85.1
Vietnam	–	19.1	–	9.6	–	28.7	–	66.6
South Asia	16.6	23.8	12.9	16.5	29.5	40.3	56.3	59.1
India	17.5	22.9	10.6	17.0	28.1	39.9	62.3	57.4
Developed countries	22.6	23.4	25.2	27.8	47.8	51.2	47.3	45.7
Developing countries	11.9	33.6	28.6	19.8	40.4	53.4	29.5	62.9
World	19.6	27.3	26.2	24.4	45.7	51.7	42.9	52.8

Source: Compiled from UN Comtrade database.
Note: – data not available.

Table 7.4 Composition of network products exported from Southeast Asia, 2007–08 (%)

Commodity group*	Indonesia	Malaysia	Philippines	Singapore	Thailand	Vietnam	Southeast Asia	World
Automatic data processing machines (75)	11.4	33.7	27.5	18.2	24.4	22.3	23.1	11.0
Telecommunication & sound recording equipment (76)	18.8	15.8	2.9	9.3	9.3	12.6	10.5	11.9
Electrical machinery excl. semiconductors (77–776)	24.2	11.6	10.9	8.4	14.5	28.5	11.4	12.8
Semiconductors (776)	5.2	25.1	47.5	40.0	12.4	3.4	30.5	8.0
Road vehicles (78)	15.8	1.9	5.7	2.1	20.8	8.6	6.5	23.3
Other transport equipment (79)	5.7	1.5	1.0	2.8	2.7	4.2	2.5	6.6
Professional and scientific equipment (87)	1.2	4.0	0.6	3.0	1.6	1.9	2.7	5.6
Photographic apparatus & optical goods, watches and clocks (88)	1.2	1.4	2.6	1.4	2.9	3.1	1.8	2.0
Other	16.5	5.1	1.3	14.7	11.4	15.4	11.0	18.9
Total	100	100	100.0	100.0	100.0	100.0	100.0	100.0
US$ billion	15.7	78.0	35.0	178.7	70.2	6.9	384.4	5,054.5

Source: Compiled from UN Comtrade database.
Note: *Standard International Trade Classification (SITC) codes given in brackets.

Table 7.5 Direction of Southeast Asian manufacturing trade, 1996–2010[*] (%)

	Asia						North America	Europe	Other
	Total	Korea & Taiwan	Japan	China	Southern Asia	Southeast Asia			
(a) Exports									
1996–97	51.2	4.5	10.7	8.5	1.8	25.7	22.9	15.4	10.6
1999–00	49.0	5.4	10.6	8.3	2.0	22.8	23.4	17.6	10.0
2004–05	57.6	5.9	9.6	14.1	2.7	25.3	18.2	15.1	9.1
2009–10	63.5	7.2	8.3	19.0	3.9	25.1	12.8	12.7	11.1
(b) Imports									
1996–97	59.0	9.9	25.2	6.1	0.8	17.0	17.4	16.2	7.4
1999–00	64.0	11.3	22.9	7.8	0.9	21.1	17.1	13.0	5.8
2004–05	67.6	11.3	18.6	14.2	1.4	22.2	13.2	12.6	6.5
2009–10	70.4	12.9	15.8	18.3	1.7	21.7	11.6	12.6	5.4

Source: Compiled from UN Comtrade database.
Note: * Two-year averages.

expanded to encompass an increasing number of countries, and, in particular, the emergence of China as the premier assembly center within global production networks. Between 1996–97 and 2009–10 the share of Southeast Asian manufacturing exports destined for Asian markets (including Southeast Asia) increased from 51.2 percent to 63.5 percent, accompanied by a decline in the share accounted for by the traditional North American and European markets, from 38.3 percent to 25.5 percent. The share of exports to China in total exports soared from 8.5 percent to 19.0 percent. However, caution is required when treating these figures as indicators of change over time in the relative importance of regional (East Asian) and extra-regional markets for the growth dynamism of Southeast Asian countries. As can be seen in Table 7.6, the increase in exports to

Table 7.6 South Asia: share of parts and components in manufacturing trade flows, 1996–2010[*] (%)

	Asia						North America	Europe	Other
	Asia	Korea & Taiwan	Japan	China	Southern Asia	Southeast Asia			
(a) Exports									
1996–97	50.8	42.5	31.0	41.6	32.4	46.8	47.8	46.6	42.9
1999–00	62.8	56.4	50.2	55.2	36.9	63.1	56.5	53.7	55.1
2004–05	65.3	67.2	53.9	67.5	38.3	59.6	48.6	50.9	54.6
2009–10	66.1	67.4	48.5	68.1	37.6	60.8	42.8	47.4	49.8
(b) Imports									
1996–97	54.0	31.3	32.4	30.1	16.0	51.1	40.2	30.4	35.2
1999–00	65.1	44.8	49.9	45.6	20.5	63.7	57.4	44.8	51.3
2004–05	68.1	52.7	50.5	52.1	10.7	60.5	64.7	45.5	53.1
2009–10	41.3	45.8	45.9	44.2	21.0	51.6	57.3	41.4	47.2

Source: Compiled from UN Comtrade database.
Note: * Two-year averages.

China and the other East Asian countries has largely been the direct outcome of rapid integration of these countries as components suppliers within the rapidly expanding China-centered regional production networks. Components account for over two-thirds of Southeast Asia's intra-East Asian trade. The expansion of component trade depends inexorably on demand for final goods, and extra-regional markets still account for the bulk of final goods exported from these countries. This was vividly illustrated by the behavior of trade flows following the onset of the global financial crisis (GFC). All major economies in Southeast and East Asia, including China, experienced a precipitous trade contraction for over six quarters from about the last quarter of 2008 (Athukorala and Kohpaiboon 2012: table 4).

Southeast Asia and China in production networks

When China began to emerge as a major trading nation in the late 1980s, there was a growing concern in policy circles in Southeast Asia, and in other Asian countries, that competition from China could crowd out their export opportunities. Initially, the "China fear" in the region was mainly related to export competition in standard light manufactures (clothing, footwear, sporting goods, etc.), but soon it turned out to be pervasive as China began to rapidly integrate into global production networks in electrical and electronics products through an unprecedented increase in foreign direct investment in these industries. The rapid increase in China's world market share in these product lines, coupled with some anecdotal evidence of MNEs operating in Southeast Asian countries relocating to China, led to serious concern about possible erosion of the role of Southeast Asian countries in global production networks. These concerns gained added impetus from China's subsequent accession to the World Trade Organization (WTO), which not only provided China with most-favored nation (MFN) status in major markets but also enhanced China's attractiveness to export-oriented investment by reducing the country risk of investment (Athukorala 2009).

As we have noted, there has been a significant contraction in final assembly of consumer electronics and electrical goods exported from Southeast Asia as an outcome of competitive pressures from China.[7] However, this structural shift has not resulted in a "hollowing out" of production bases in Southeast Asia. On the contrary, the past two decades have seen a close complementarity between China and Southeast Asian countries within global production networks, for three reasons.

First, expansion in final assembly in China has created new demand for parts and components assembled in Southeast Asia. Benefiting from this, electronics firms involved in component design, assembly, and testing in Southeast Asian countries restructured their operations by moving into high-value tasks in the value chain. This process was greatly aided by the deep-rooted nature of their production bases and the pool of skilled workers developed over the past three decades.

Second, a number of large electronics MNEs have shifted regional/global headquarter functions to Singapore and Penang. Manufacturing is only part of their operations. Their activities now encompass corporate and financial planning, research and development (R&D), product design and tooling, sales and marketing. Some MNEs which have shifted final assembly of consumer electronics and electrical goods to China, nevertheless perform global headquarter functions relating to their operations in China from Singapore and the state of Penang in Malaysia. Some MNEs now use their affiliated firms in Singapore and Penang as focal points for their global training and skill enhancement programs (Athukorala 2014).

Third, while the electronics industry is still the main engine of manufacturing growth in the region, in recent years the production base has begun to diversify into a number of electronics-related dynamic product lines, in particular in Singapore, Malaysia, and Thailand. These include medical services and equipment, light-emitting diodes (LEDs), and photovoltaic design and development. In the early twenty-first century, Singapore has become a global production hub for medical devices (MIT 2012).

Determinants

A number of factors seem to have underpinned the continued attractiveness of Southeast Asia as a location for assembly activities within global production networks. First, despite rapid growth, manufacturing wages in all Southeast Asian countries except Singapore remain lower than or comparable to those in countries in the European periphery and Latin America. At the same time, there are significant differences in wages among the countries within the region, permitting rapid expansion of intra-regional product sharing systems (Table 7.7).

Second, the relative factor cost advantage of Southeast Asian countries has been supplemented by relatively more favorable trade and investment policy regimes, trade-related infrastructure and communication systems (Athukorala and Hill 2011). This has facilitated cross-border production sharing among these countries by reducing the cost of maintaining "services links" (Jones and Kierzkowski 2001) within production networks. Efficient and speedy services links are vital for the smooth functioning of production networks and are a key determinant of scale economies in global production sharing.

Table 7.7 Average annual compensation per production worker ($US per year)

	1988	1995	2000	2005
Portugal	10,407	19,572	16,795	29,948
Spain	25,267	38,742	32,695	45,766
Ireland	22,578	30,974	32,391	52,875
Poland	–	–	10,487	12,643
Czech Republic	–	–	7,454	12,371
Hungary	–	–	9,342	15,645
Turkey	8,333	16,606	21,493	28,854
Argentina	10,050	29,898	32,700	18,234
Brazil	11,296	23,116	19,142	17,278
Mexico	5,400	8,809	11,527	13,971
Costa Rica	–	–	11,377	14,178
China	–	–	7,180	8,356
Hong Kong	8,009	10,315	14,282	9,374
South Korea	8,153	25,484	28,347	37,585
Taiwan	9,793	22,908	25,313	27,027
Indonesia	6,727	5,876	3,893	4,166
Malaysia	4,971	6,677	7,957	11,685
Philippines	3,955	6,814	7,716	6,827
Singapore	10,200	18,647	24,477	27,516
Thailand	5,000	6,045	6,081	7,324
India	3,762	4,579	6,813	8,835

Source: Compiled from the US Bureau of Economic Analysis (BEA) online database of the *Survey of U.S. Direct Investment Abroad* (http://www.bea.gov/scb/accountarticles/international/iidguide.htm#link123b).
Notes: The data relate to majority-owned manufacturing subsidiaries of US multinational enterprises in each country. Annual compensation included salary/wage plus other remuneration.

Third, as first-comers in this area of international specialization, Southeast Asian countries, in particular Malaysia, Singapore, and Thailand, seem to offer considerable agglomeration advantages for companies already located there. Site selection decisions of MNEs operating in assembly activities are strongly influenced by the presence of other key market players in a given country or neighboring countries. Against the backdrop of a long period of successful operation in the region, many MNEs, particularly the US-based ones, have significantly upgraded the technical activities of their regional production networks in Southeast Asia. As noted, many have assigned global production responsibilities to affiliates located in Singapore, and more recently also to those located in Malaysia and Thailand. All in all, the ASEAN experience seems to support the view that MNE affiliates have a tendency to become increasingly embedded in host countries the longer they are present there and the more conducive the overall investment climate of the host country becomes over time (Rangan and Lawrence 1999). At the formative stage of MNE entry into regional production, there was a general perception that these firms would soon prove to be "fly-by-night" operators. However, the data on firms in operation clearly indicate that most MNEs have established deep roots in the region. For instance, the expansion of the Penang export hub began during 1972–75 with the setting up of assembly plants by eight MNEs – National Semiconductors, Intel, Advanced Micro Devices, Osrum, Hewlett Packard, Bosch, Hitachi, and Clarion (the latter a Japanese auto part producer) – together known locally as the "Eight Samurai." After almost half a century, Penang still remains a vital link in the global production networks of these companies. For some of these firms, the Penang facility is the focal point of their operations in the Asian region (Athukorala 2014).

Global production sharing and manufacturing performance

This section examines the role of global production sharing in the manufacturing performance of Southeast Asia countries. The available production-side data (based on manufacturing surveys) do not permit directly linking network trade with manufacturing performance. The second-best approach, followed here, is to delineate industries in which global production sharing is heavily concentrated, as revealed by the analysis of trade patterns in the previous section, and compare their performance with non-GPS industries. The data are compiled from the INDSTAT database of the United Nations Industrial Development Organization (UNIDO), which brings together data from annual surveys of manufacturing conducted in individual countries in a uniform format at the four-digit level of the International Standard Industrial Classification (ISIC). The list of GPS industries used in data compilation is given in the Appendix at the end of this chapter. We examine the contribution of GPS to the process of industrialization in terms of five performance indicators: share in total manufacturing output (value added), employment, and value added share in gross output, real wages, and labor productivity. These indicators for the five major Southeast Asian countries are summarized in Table 7.8.[8]

The relative importance of GPS industries in domestic manufacturing sectors varies significantly among the five countries.[9] Singapore and Thailand stand out for the continuous increase in the share of GPS industries in total manufacturing during the period 2000–08: from 60.1 percent to 71.6 percent in Singapore, and from 41.2 percent to 46.8 percent in Thailand.[10] In both these countries the increase was accompanied by a notable diversification of the GPS product mix. In Singapore, while the "traditional" electronics industry recorded a modest increase (from 42.4 to 46.8 percent), the "other GPS" category which encompasses new product lines such as medical, surgical and orthopedic equipment, and optical and photographic equipment jumped from 13.4 percent to 21.8 percent. In Thailand, there has been a notable shift in the product mix away from electronics and towards electrical goods and, more importantly, towards automobiles. The output

Table 7.8 Key indicators of manufacturing performance in Southeast Asian countries, 2000–01 and 2007–08

	Composition output (value added)[2] %		Composition of employment (%)		Share of value added in gross output[2] (%)		Real wage (US$)[3]	
	(1) 2000–01	(2) 2007–08	(3) 2000–01	(4) 2007–08	(5) 2000–01	(6) 2007–08	(7) 2000–01	(8) 2007–08
Indonesia								
GPS industries[1]	32.6	27.0	9.7	11.3	41.9	41.7	1,339	1,219
Electronics	6.7	3.3	1.1	1.4	41.3	35.1	1,331	1,212
Electrical appliances	4.4	2.9	1.8	1.2	29.0	29.2	1,296	1,166
Automotive	10.5	13.1	1.8	3.0	51.8	41.9	1,750	1,498
Other	11	7.7	5.0	5.7	38.4	51.6	1,231	1,086
Other manufacturing	67.4	73	80.6	77.4	34.8	32.2	1,198	932
Total	100	100	100	100	35.3	36.9	1,226	1,363
Malaysia								
GPS products	54.8	46.5	47.7	42	19.8	17.8	5,606	6,078
Electronics	36.1	30.2	29.6	25.1	19.8	16.9	5,753	6,033
Electrical appliances	8.1	5.3	8.8	5.7	14.8	13.1	5,613	5,936
Automotive	4.2	3.9	2.8	3.7	23.7	18.2	6,359	5,719
Other	6.4	6.5	6.5	7.5	28.8	22.6	6,617	6,207
Other manufacturing	45.2	54.0	52.3	58	27.7	28.5	5,412	5,323
Total	100	100	100	100	23.2	22.2	8,740	8,464
Philippines								
GPS products	59.6	49.2	40.5	40.7	31.4	26.5	2,960	3,018
Electronics	44.2	32.6	35	31.7	24.3	21.9	2,590	2,638
Electrical appliances	3.1	3.8	1.6	3.9	31.7	22.5	3,097	2,216
Automotive	4.5	4.6	1.6	2.6	29.2	26	4,006	3,555
Other	7.8	8.2	2.3	2.5	38.2	30.7	3,035	3,287
Other manufacturing	41.4	50.8	59.5	59.3	41.6	36.2	2,616	3,076
Total	100	100	100	100	31.9	22.8	4,505	4,425

Singapore

GPS products	60.1	71.6	52.9	61.2	22.5	21.8	21,764	32,264
Electronics	42.8	46.8	30.7	30.3	20.1	20.2	19,151	31,700
Electrical appliances	3.4	2.0	3.6	2.5	19.9	16.1	24,646	36,746
Automotive	0.5	0.9	0.7	1.5	16.2	13.8	25,401	33,555
Other	13.4	21.8	17.9	26.9	35.7	26.1	22,367	32,095
Other manufacturing	39.9	28.4	47.1	38.8	21.6	21.7	20,928	26,672
Total	100	100	100	100	25.7	23.9	33,589	53,545

Thailand

GPS products	41.2	44.9	29.2	23.3	20.2	20.1	2,418	2,836
Electronics	16.0	9.6	13.0	10.3	13.7	15.1	2,277	2,901
Electrical appliances	8.8	12.0	3.8	3.4	23.1	20.3	2,657	2,719
Automotive	8.4	14.3	5.0	5.1	25.1	24.8	3,090	3,429
Other	8.0	9.0	6.4	11.5	22.6	20.6	2,167	2,669
Other manufacturing	58.8	55.1	70.8	76.7	28.2	26.2	2,106	2,600
Total	100	100	100	100	42.6	47.5	3,266	4,041

Source: Compiled using data extracted from UNIDO INDSTAT database supplemented by World Bank, World Development Indicator Database (for consumer price index and implicit manufacturing deflator), Thailand Manufacturing Census (data on manufacturing wages for Thailand).

Notes:

[1] The industry classification used in separating "global production sharing" (GPS) industries is listed in the Appendix at the end of this chapter.

[2] Calculated using data in current $

[3] Nominal average annual wage of production workers in local currency deflated by the consumer price index (2000 = 100) and converted into US dollars using the exchange rate in 2000.

shares of these industries increased from 8.8 percent to 12.0 percent and 8.4 percent to 14.5 percent, respectively.[11] The data clearly illustrate the "outlier status" of Indonesia in terms of the degree to which domestic manufacturing is integrated within global production networks. The share of GPS products in total in Indonesian manufacturing in 2007–08 was 27.0 percent, down from 32.6 percent in 2000–01.[12]

An in-depth analysis of the underlying causes of inter-country differences in the performances of GPS industries is beyond the scope of this chapter. But as discussed above for the case of Indonesia, there is evidence to suggest that at least part of the explanation lies in the nature of investment climate within which GPS industries operate. Notwithstanding rapid increases in labor and rental cost, Singapore has continued to remain an attractive location within global production networks for high-value, more sophisticated tasks in the value chain because of its excellent overall investment climate, in terms of various global business/investment climate rankings (e.g. World Bank 2010; World Bank 2012). The quality of technical and higher education institutions in Singapore has notably improved over the years, in line with the requirements of industrial upgrading within global production networks. Singapore has also maintained a business-friendly immigration policy, so that employers are free to import skilled manpower at high levels to make up for domestic shortfalls (Athukorala 2006). In Malaysia, impediments to further expansion of GPS industries with diversification into other more sophisticated product lines are deeply rooted in the country's long-standing ethnicity-based economic policy. Of particular importance is the growing scarcity of skilled manpower resulting from deterioration in the quality of higher education and the ever expanding role of the public sector, which provides "easy and more secure jobs for local jobseekers" (Gomas 2011; Henderson and Phillips 2007; NAEC 2010). Political instability and poor infrastructure often figures prominently in evidence on the nature of the investment climate in the Philippines (World Bank 2010, 2012; Calimag 2008).

Both within- and between-country differences in the share of employment in GPS industries mirror patterns of production (Table 7.8, columns 3 and 4). However in all five countries, employment shares of GPS industries are smaller compared to their output shares, suggesting that these industries are generally less labor intensive compared to other industries in general. This pattern is consistent with the view that even though global production sharing essentially involves offshoring relatively low-skill intensive segments of the production process from advanced countries, these tasks are relatively more capital and skill intensive compared to existing low-skill activities in the recipient (host) country (Feenstra and Hansen 2003).

Value added shares in gross output in GPS industries (Table 7.8, columns 5 and 6) do not seem to vary in line with these industries' relative contribution to manufacturing output and employment. For instance, in Singapore the share of value added in gross output in these industries *declined* from 22.5 percent to 21.8 percent between 2000–01 and 2007–08 even though (as already noted) their contributions to output and employment recorded impressive increases. In Thailand the increase in employment and output shares of GPS industries has been accompanied by a remarkable stability (at around 20 percent) of the value-added share in output. In Malaysia and the Philippines too, this share has stabilized at around 20 percent without showing any relationship with employment and output shares.

These observed patterns cast doubt on the relevance of the conventional "domestic value added" criterion in assessing the gains from industrialization through global production sharing. Instead, the input structure of component and final assembly in a given country as part of the global value chain is determined as part of the overall process of international production. Expansion in output and employment resulting from engagement in global sharing in a given country depends predominantly (if not solely) on "the volume factor," the expansion of sales turnover (and hence gross output) facilitated by access to a vast global market. Interestingly, value added shares in gross output are much higher in Indonesia compared to the other four countries (47 percent). This is understandable because these industries in Indonesia are predominantly oriented to the domestic market; in such industries there is much more scope to use locally sourced inputs in the production process. All in all, it seems that in an era of global production sharing, forging domestic linkages (increasing domestic value addition) and achieving rapid growth and employment expansion through engaging in international production are not mutually consistent policy objectives (Athukorala and Santosa 1997).

The pessimistic school of thought on national gains from global production sharing holds that, while this form of international exchange may generate new jobs in host countries, MNEs, which are the main actors in this new form of international exchange, tend to restrain real wage growth in a given production location as part of their strategy to maximize profits in their wider global operations. These MNEs have the flexibility to transfer production facilities from one country to another in response to changing labor market conditions, a sharp contrast to the difficulties of such a move for import-substitution MNEs which are essentially "location-bound." Thus, under given labor supply conditions, workers employed in GPS ventures are likely to experience slower real wage growth compared to their counterparts in domestic-market oriented MNE affiliates and indigenous firms.[13]

The data on real wages reported in Table 7.8 are, however, not consistent with this view. In Singapore real wages in GPS industries increased from US$21,764 to US$32,264 between 2000–01 and 2007–08, compared to an increase of wages in other industries from US$20,928 to US$26,672. Similar patterns can also be observed in trends and patterns of real wages in the Philippines, Malaysia, and Thailand, although the gap between wages in GPS industries and other industries in these countries is not as large as in Singapore.

The wage restraint critique is based on the popular characterization of export-oriented MNEs in general as "footloose ventures" whose locational decisions are based largely on unit labor costs. As seen, this characterization is not consistent with the corporate behavior of MNEs involved in global production sharing. New communication technologies and more competitive international markets are causing MNEs to distribute their activities more aggressively across countries through global assembly and marketing networks, as part of their business strategy. In this endeavor, they have little room to take a short-term view of host-country labor market conditions. Moreover, alternative investment locations are available in abundance: low-wage countries are *not* necessarily good locations for investment. While labor cost is important, other factors such as the presence of strong (or potentially strong) indigenous supply capabilities, good infrastructure, political stability, and favorable government policies usually figure prominently in the international investor's locational decisions. This is the simple reason why, despite globally widespread attempts to entice MNE participation in export-oriented industries, so far only a handful of countries have been able to establish themselves as investment locations favored by MNEs in international production. As we have already noted, there is a general tendency for MNE affiliates operating within the global production network to become increasingly embedded in host countries the longer they are present there, and the more conducive the overall investment climate of the host country becomes over time. They may, therefore, respond sluggishly to relative cost changes.[14]

Conclusions

Global production sharing has become an integral part of the economic landscape in Southeast Asia. Trade within global production networks has been expanding more rapidly than conventional final-good trade. The degree of dependence on this new form of international specialization is proportionately larger among the main Southeast Asian economies than in the countries of East Asia. The rapid integration of China into global production networks as the premier assembly center has not been a zero-sum proposition from the perspective of the Southeast Asian countries. Rather, it seems to have added further dynamism to East Asia's role within global production networks. China has opened up opportunities for producing original, equipment-manufactured goods and back-to-office service operations in these countries.

Global production sharing has certainly played a pivotal role in the continued dynamism of East Asia and its increasing intra-regional economic interdependence. This does not, however, mean that the process has lessened the region's dependence on the global economy. The region's growth based on vertically specialized GPS networks depends inexorably on its extra-regional trade in final goods, and this dependence has increased over the years.

Global production sharing has significantly transformed the overall industrial landscape in Southeast Asia. However there are notable differences among countries in terms of trends and patterns of trade and production relating to their engagement in global production networks, and in the resultant developmental gains. Probing these inter-country differences, while paying attention to differences in policy regimes and the overall business climate, is an important item on the future research agenda for broadening our understanding of the economies of Southeast Asian countries.

Appendix

Global Production Sharing (GPS) industries at the four-digit level of the International Standard Industrial Classification (ISIC)

Electronics

3000	Office, accounting and computing machinery
3110	Electric motors, generators and transformers
3120	Electricity distribution and control apparatus
3130	Insulated wire and cable
3140	Accumulators, primary cells and batteries
3210	Electronic valves, tubes, etc.
3313	Industrial process control equipment

Electrical appliances

2930	Domestic appliances
3150	Lighting equipment and electric lamps
3190	Other electrical equipment
3220	TV/radio transmitters and line communication apparatus
3230	TV and radio receivers and associated goods
2925	Food/beverage/tobacco processing machinery

Automotive

3410	Motor vehicles
3420	Automobile bodies, trailers and semi-trailers
3430	Parts/accessories for automobiles
3591	Motorcycles
3599	Other transport equipment

Other GPS

2813	Steam generators
2899	Other fabricated metal products

2911	Engines and turbines (not for transport equip)
2912	Pumps, compressors, taps and valves
2913	Bearings, gears, gearing and driving elements
2914	Ovens, furnaces and furnace burners
2915	Lifting and handling equipment
2919	Other general purpose machinery
2921	Agricultural and forestry machinery
2922	Machine tools
2923	Machinery for metallurgy
2924	Machinery for mining and construction
2926	Machinery for textile, apparel and leather
2929	Other special purpose machinery
3311	Medical, surgical and orthopedic equipment
3312	Measuring/testing/navigating appliances
3320	Optical instruments and photographic equipment
3530	Aircraft and spacecraft parts

Notes

1 The beginning of the international semiconductor industry can be traced from 1961, when the US company Fairchild set up a transistor assembly plant in Hong Kong (Gunwald and Flamm 1985: 69).

2 The discussion here on Samsung's operation in Vietnam is based on a conference presentation made by Seokmin Park, Vice President and Head, Corporate Supply Chain Management of Samsung (Park 2013).

3 Batam, a 715 km² island (almost identical in size to Singapore) located in the Riau Islands Province of Indonesia, was declared a free trade zone in 1989 as part of the Singapore–Johor–Riau (SIJORI) growth triangle (Kumar 1994).

4 The data used in this section for all countries other than Taiwan are compiled from the United Nation's Comtrade database, based on Revision 3 of the Standard International Trade Classification (SITC Rev. 3). Data for Taiwan are obtained from the trade database (based on the same classification system) of the Council for Economic Planning and Development, Taipei. For details on the classification system used in separating network trade (parts and components, and final assembly) from the trade data extracted from these sources, see Athukorala 2011. In order to minimize the effect of possible random shocks and measurement errors, two-year averages are used in inter-temporal comparison throughout this section.

5 As noted, DEA refers to East Asia excluding Japan.

6 Data compiled from the United Nation's Comtrade database. See Note 4.

7 Final assembly is generally more labor intensive than component assembly, production, and testing.

8 We have excluded petroleum refining (ISIC 2320) from total manufacturing in compiling these indicators in order to maintain inter-country comparability.

9 The data on the share of GPS products in total manufacturing reported here (which are based on nominal manufacturing value added) need to be interpreted with care because during this period the prices of these products, in particular electronics and electrical goods, grew at a slower rate compared to those of most other manufactured products. For instance, according to the data for Thailand, the only country in Southeast Asia for which manufacturing sector data at the four-digit ISIC level are available both in current and constant prices, during 2001–08 the implicit price deflator of GPS products sector and other manufactured goods increased at annual rates of 2.8 percent and 5.8 percent respectively (calculated from the National Economics and Social Development Board (NESDB), Thailand database).

10 In Table 7.8, we have reported data only for the two end points of the period under study for want of space, but the time patterns of the data for the interim years are consistent with inference made in this section.

11 For details on the diversification of Thai GPS production base, in particular on the emergence of Thailand as the hub of automobile assembly (the so-called "Detroit of Asia") see Athukorala and Kohpaiboon 2010; Kohpaiboon and Jongwanich 2012; and Kohpaiboon et al. 2010.

12 A notable exception is the expansion of the share of automobiles. In recent years Indonesia has emerged as a regional hub for assembly of multipurpose vehicles by Toyota (Innova and Avanza models) and Honda (Stream and Freed models).

13 For useful syntheses of the contending view on the employment implications of the involvement of MNEs in DC manufacturing see Caves (2007: 110–23).

14 Relative labor cost is presumably an important determinant of export performance in the traditional labor-intensive products such as clothing, footwear, and toys. In these industries MNEs are rarely directly involved in the production process. International trade in these products largely takes places within "buyer-driven" production networks, in which the "lead firms" (mostly retail chains and specialty stores in developed countries) have ample room for changing procurement sources based on cost competitiveness (Gereffi 1999).

References

Amsden, Alice H. and Wa-wen Chu (2003). *Beyond Late Development: Taiwan's Upgrading Policies.* Cambridge, MA: MIT Press.

Athukorala, P. (2006). "International labour migration in East Asia: trends, patterns and policy issues." *Asian-Pacific Economic Literature* 20(1), 18–39.

Athukorala, P. (2009). "The rise of China and East Asian export performance: is the crowding-out fear warranted?" *World Economy* 32(2), 234–66.

Athukorala P. (2011). "Production networks and trade patterns in East Asia: regionalization or globalization?" *Asian Economic Papers* 10(1), 65–95.

Athukorala, P. (2014). "Growing with global production sharing: the tale of Penang export hub." *Competition & Change* 18(3), 221–45.

Athukorala, P. and B.H. Santosa (1997). "Gains from Indonesian export growth: do linkages matter?" *Bulletin of Indonesian Economic Studies* 33(2), 73–95.

Athukorala, P. and H. Hill (2011). "Asian trade: long-term patterns and policy issues." *Asian-Pacific Economic Literature* 24(2), 52–82.

Athukorala, P. and A. Kohpaiboon (2010). *Detroit of the East: Thailand in Global; Automobile Networks.* Geneva: International Trade Centre.

Athukorala, P. and A. Kohpaiboon (2012). "Intra-regional trade in East Asia: the decoupling fallacy, crisis and policy challenges." In M. Kawai, B.M. Lamberte, and Y.C. Park (eds) *The Global Financial Crisis and Asia: Implications and Challenges.* New York: Oxford University Press, pp. 262–91.

Athukorala, P. and Tien Q. Tran (2012). "Foreign direct investment in industrial transition in Vietnam." *Journal of the Asia-Pacific Economy* 17(3), 446–63.

Business Day (2013). "Manufacturers jump ship from China to Cambodia." 10 April. http://www.business-day.com.au/business/world-business/manufacturers-jump-ship-from-china-to-cambodia-20130410-2hk3u.html.

Calimag, Melvin G. (2008). "Intel prepares to close Philippine plant." *Bloomberg Businessweek*, 7 April. http://www.businessweek.com/stories/2008-04-07/intel-prepares-to-close-philippine-plantbusiness-week-business-news-stock-market-and-financial-advice.

Caves, R.E. (2007). *Multinational Enterprise and Economic Analysis*, 3rd edn. Cambridge: Cambridge University Press.

Feenstra, R. and G. Hanson (2003). "Global production sharing and rising inequality: a survey of trade and wages." In E.K. Choi and J. Harrigan (eds), *Handbook of International Trade*. Malden, MA: Blackwell, pp. 146–85.

Gereffi, G. (1999). "International trade and industrial upgrading in the apparel commodity chain." *Journal of International Economics* 48(1), 37–70.

Goh, K.S. (1990). "Singapore and the development issues of the 1990s." Paper presented to the Walter & Phyllis Shorenstein Symposium on Economic Challenges in the Pacific Region, University of California, Berkeley; reproduced in L. Low (ed.), *Wealth of East Asian Nation, Speeches and Writings by Goh Keng Swee*, 1995, pp. 331–68. Singapore: Federation Publication.

Goh, K.S. (1993). "What causes fast economic growth?" Forth K. T. Li Lecture, Harvard University; reproduced in L. Low (ed.), *Wealth of East Asian Nation, Speeches and Writings by Goh Keng Swee*, 1995, pp. 243–58. Singapore: Federation Publication.

Gomas, Edmand T. (2011). "The politics and policies of corporate development: race, rents and redistribution in Malaysia." In H. Hill, Tham Siew Yean, and Ragayah Haji M. Zin (eds), *Graduating from The Middle: Malaysia's Development Challenges*. London: Routledge.

Grunwald, Joseph and Kenneth Flamm (1985). *The Global Factory: Foreign Assembly in International Trade.* Washington, DC: Brookings Institution Press.

Henderson, Jeffrey and Richard Phillips (2007). "Unintended consequences: social policy, state institutions and 'stalling' of the Malaysian industrialization process." *Economy and Society* 36(1), 78–102.

Jones, R. W and H. Kierzkowski (2001). "Globalization and the consequences of international fragmentation." In R. Dornbusch, G. Calvo, and M. Obstfeld (eds), *Money, Factor Mobility and Trade: The Festschrift in Honor of Robert A. Mundell*, pp. 365–81. Cambridge, MA: MIT Press.

Kohpaiboon, A. and J. Jongwanich (2012). "International production network, clusters, and industrial upgrading: evidence from automotive and hard disk drive industries." *Review of Policy Research* 32(2), 211–38.

Kohpaiboon, A., P. Kulthanavit, P. Vijinoparat, and N. Soonthornchawakan (2010). "Global recession, labor market adjustment and international production networks: evidence from the Thai automotive industry." *ASEAN Economic Bulletin Special Issue* 27(1).

Kumar, S. (1994). "Johor–Singapore–Riau growth triangle: a model of sub-regional cooperation." In M. Thant, M. Tang, and H. Kakazu (eds), *Growth Triangles in Asia: A New Approach to Regional Economic Cooperation.* Singapore: Oxford University Press, pp. 175–217.

Lee, K. Y. (2000). *From Third World to First: The Singapore Story: 1965–2000. Memoirs of Lee Kuan Yew*, Vol. 2. Singapore: Singapore Press Holding.

McKendrick, D.G., R.F. Doner, and S. Haggard (2000). *From Silicon Valley to Singapore: Location and Competitive Advantage in the Hard Disk Drive Industry.* Stanford, CA: Stanford University Press.

Manning, C. and R.M. Purnagunawan (2011). "Survey of recent developments." *Bulletin of Indonesian Economic Studies* 47(3), 303–32.

MIT (Ministry of Trade, Singapore) (2012). *Singapore Economic Survey*, First Quarter. Singapore: MIT.

National Economic Advisory Council (NAEC), Malaysia (2010). *New Economic Model for Malaysia*, Parts 1 and 2. Kuala Lumpur: NEAC.

Park, Seokmin (2013). "Samsung Electronics 2013." PowerPoint presentation at the conference on Plugging into Global Value Chain: A Strategy for Growth, Seoul National University, June.

Rangan, S. and R. Lawrence (1999). *A Prism on Globalization.* Washington, DC: Brookings Institution Press.

Thee, K.W. and M. Pangestu (1998). "Technological capabilities and Indonesia's manufactured exports." In D. Ernst, T. Ganiatsos, and L. Mytelka (eds), *Technological Capabilities and Export Success in Asia.* London: Routledge, pp. 211–65.

Wade, R. (1990). *Governing the Market: Economic Theory and the Role of Government in East Asian Industrialization.* Princeton, NJ: Princeton University Press.

Wong, H.K. (2007). "The remaking of Singapore's high-tech enterprise system." In Henry S. Rowen, Marguerite G. Hancock, and Lilliam F. Miller (eds), *Making IT: The Rise of Asian in High Tech.* Stanford, CA: Stanford University Press, pp. 123–74.

World Bank (2010). *Investing across Borders: Indicators of Foreign Direct Regulations in 87 Economies.* Washington, DC: World Bank.

World Bank (2012). *Doing Business 2013.* Washington, DC: World Bank.

8

Foreign direct investment in Southeast Asia

Fredrik Sjöholm

LUND UNIVERSITY AND RESEARCH INSTITUTE OF INDUSTRIAL ECONOMICS

Introduction

Foreign direct investment (FDI) is an important aspect of global economic integration: multinational enterprises (MNEs) account for about 10 percent of world output and 30 percent of world export (UNCTAD 2007). Moreover, around three-quarters of total sales to foreign customers are done through FDI and one-quarter through export (Antrás and Yeaple 2013). FDI is generally perceived as bringing various economic benefits to the host country. It will for instance substitute for domestic savings and thereby allow for greater consumption for a given level of investment. Moreover, MNEs control most of the world's advanced technology which will benefit a host country in terms of higher productivity and incomes. Finally, MNEs have superior access to foreign markets, which increases the host country's exports and, again, output, and incomes.

The source of FDI remains concentrated in high-income countries, although from a handful of developing countries FDI is increasing rapidly. The destinations of FDI, however, have changed over the last decades with an increasing share going to developing countries. More specifically, the share of global FDI to developing countries has increased from about 29 percent in 1970 to 47 percent in 2011 (UNCTAD 2013).

Southeast Asia has been part of this development. Some countries in the region were the prime choices for MNEs that wanted to outsource labor-intensive parts of the production process as early as in the 1960s. The region remains a large recipient of FDI, with MNEs being attracted by a growing market, natural resources, and a competitive base for export-oriented production.

However, attitudes and policies towards FDI differ both between countries and over time within countries. For instance, the centrally planned economies nationalized existing foreign firms and closed their economies to the entry of new ones for many years. At the other extreme, Singapore has at times spent very large sums of public money to attract foreign MNEs (Te Velde 2001). Another example is Indonesia, which has typically liberalized its FDI regime when the economy is doing poorly, and introduced more regulations when raw material prices are increasing and the economy is booming.

The differences in policies toward, and in actual inflows of, FDI makes Southeast Asia an interesting testing ground for examining the determinants of FDI policies and the effects of FDI inflows, which is the aim of this chapter. More precisely, this chapter aims at examining the size of FDI in Southeast Asia and the trends in it. The main determinants of FDI in Southeast Asia as well as their effect on the host countries are also discussed and examined.

FDI in Southeast Asia

Figure 8.1 shows that inflows of FDI to Southeast Asia did not take off until the late 1980s but then increased rapidly. More precisely, annual FDI inflows increased between 1986 and 1997 by more than 1,100 percent in current prices. The Asian crisis in the late 1990s and the crisis in the information and technology industry in the early 2000s (the so-called "dotcom bust") led to a temporary decline in FDI inflows before they started to increase again in 2003. The global financial crisis led to a new fall in FDI inflows in 2008 and 2009 but subsequent years saw a strong recovery: the inflow of close to 120 billion US dollars in 2011 was five times the inflows in 2000. Southeast Asia accounts today for roughly 8 percent of total world FDI inflows (up from 3 percent in 1970). This is equivalent to around 2 percent of total world GDP.

The distribution of FDI to Southeast Asia is seen in Table 8.1. Indonesia received more than one-third of total FDI inflows in the 1970s, but its share declined substantially in later decades. Malaysia and Singapore have received relatively large shares, although the share for the former country has declined in the last decade. Singapore is, by far, the largest recipient of FDI; 58 percent of regional FDI in the 2000s went to Singapore. However, Singapore is a regional hub for both international trade and FDI, and much of the FDI to Singapore ends up in other countries. In other words, FDI flows to Singapore might not contribute to production in Singapore but instead in other countries, often in other Southeast Asian countries.[1] To complicate matters further, some of the FDI inflows to Singapore are "roundtripping," meaning that they flow back to the country of origin.

Thailand has been the second largest receiver of FDI in the 2000s whereas FDI flows to the Philippines have been relatively small throughout the period. Vietnam, Cambodia, and Laos all liberalized their economies in the late 1980s and early 1990s but only Vietnam has any substantial inflows of FDI.

The relative importance of FDI also depends on country size. An alternative measure of the role of inward FDI is the ratio of the inward stock of FDI to GDP, shown for selected Southeast

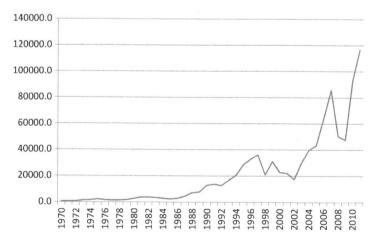

Figure 8.1 FDI inflows to Southeast Asia (1970–2011, millions US dollars)
Source: UNCTAD.

Table 8.1 Shares of total FDI inflows to Southeast Asia, 1970–2011 (%)

	1970–79	*1980–89*	*1990–99*	*2000–11*
Brunei	1	0	1	2
Cambodia	0	0	0	1
Indonesia	36	8	10	6
Laos	0	0	0	0
Malaysia	25	26	23	11
Myanmar	0	0	2	1
Philippines	6	7	6	4
Singapore	24	48	38	58
Thailand	7	11	15	17
Timor-Leste	–	–	–	0
Vietnam	0	0	6	9

Source: UNCTAD.

Asian countries in Table 8.2.[2] It is seen that Asia became a major destination for FDI well before other developing regions did. The inward stock of FDI in 1980, for example, was about 42 percent of GDP in Northeast Asia and 9 percent in Southeast Asia, but only 8 percent in Africa and 7 percent in Latin America. By 1995, Southeast Asia had surpassed Northeast Asia, and the ratios to GDP were 22 percent in Southeast Asia, 21 percent in Northeast Asia, 16 percent in Africa, and 9 percent in Latin America. The relative importance of FDI in Southeast Asia has continued to increase and the share of GDP was 46 percent in 2011, substantially higher than in the other regions where shares varied between 25 and 30 percent.

Table 8.2 The stock of inward FDI as percent of GDP

		1980	*1985*	*1990*	*1995*	*2000*	*2005*	*2011*
Brunei		0.33	0.54	0.94	13.46	63.47	96.76	76.15
Cambodia		5.30	3.58	2.22	10.76	43.09	39.27	53.35
Indonesia		5.73	5.98	6.95	9.32	15.20	14.41	20.45
Laos		0.68	0.09	1.45	12.47	35.58	24.85	32.23
Malaysia		20.33	22.80	22.57	31.15	56.24	32.23	41.11
Myanmar		0.09	0.08	5.44	15.60	44.14	39.52	16.87
Philippines		2.82	5.98	10.22	13.69	23.92	15.16	12.26
Singapore	gross	45.66	60.03	82.57	78.21	119.26	160.87	203.78
	net	39.07	53.97	61.41	36.45	58.04	60.51	70.54
Thailand		3.03	5.14	9.66	10.53	24.38	34.25	40.43
Timor-Leste		–	–	–	–	–	5.50	16.20
Vietnam[a]		59.10	30.25	25.49	34.48	66.07	58.84	60.31
Southeast Asia		9.39	12.51	18.09	22.47	44.48	44.74	46.30
Northeast Asia		41.60	38.59	25.59	20.69	31.80	25.63	25.45
Africa		9.57	10.23	12.12	16.89	25.90	27.71	29.75
Latin America[b]		5.01	8.71	9.11	10.05	20.88	26.62	28.29

Source: UNCTAD STAT online database: http://www.unctad.org/Templates/Page.asp?intItemID=1584&lang=1
Notes: Net is inward FDI stock minus outward FDI stock. GDP is as used in UNCTAD calculations.
[a] 1950–2000 stock estimated by UNCTAD by cumulating inflows from 1970.
[b] Central America and South America.

Looking at individual countries, the highest ratio is to Singapore. For Singapore we show not only total inward stocks, as for the other countries, but also net inward FDI stocks, which might come closer to representing the FDI remaining in the country.[3] Even the net measure suggests that Singapore, together with Brunei, has the largest relative presence of FDI. The high FDI stock in Brunei is surprising in view of the very low level of FDI as late as 1990. Among the other countries we note that the relative stocks of FDI are low in Myanmar, the Philippines, and Timor-Leste, and suspiciously high in Vietnam.[4]

The main source of FDI in Southeast Asia is from within the region. More specifically, about 18 percent of FDI flows are intra-region flows, as seen in Table 8.3. FDI from the European Union is a close second with around 17 percent of total inflows, followed by Japan with 12 percent and the USA with 10 percent.

Balance of payments data on FDI are problematic since the flows often do not originate in the countries to which they are attributed, do not enter the countries that are their supposed destinations, and, if they do enter the declared destinations, do not remain in those destinations. They often represent bookkeeping entries in corporate accounts, but are not necessarily associated with economic activity such as the employment of labor, the production of goods and services, or the installation of capital assets (Lipsey and Sjöholm 2011a).

Another problem is that FDI flows and stocks, as defined by the International Monetary Fund (IMF), include FDI by sovereign wealth funds (SWFs), mainly based in developing countries. SWFs have increased rapidly in importance over the last years and there are currently more than 50 of them originating from more than 40 countries (UNCTAD 2009: 29). They are always state-controlled and typically invest capital received from large current account surpluses, often but not always from exports of oil and gas. The Government of Singapore Investment Corporation and Temasek Holdings (also from Singapore) are two important SWFs from Southeast Asia. While purchases of ownership shares of 10 percent or more meet the IMF definition of FDI in terms of the extent of ownership (10 percent), the activities of SWFs are more akin to portfolio investment than to private FDI with respect to the characteristics ascribed to FDI in the literature. These

Table 8.3 The main sources of FDI in Southeast Asia

Country/region	Value 2009–11	Share of total inflows 2009–11
ASEAN	46,894	18.5
European Union (EU)	43,316	17.1
Japan	29,561	11.7
USA	24,258	9.6
China	10,672	4.2
Hong Kong	10,107	4.0
Cayman Islands	9,429	3.7
Republic of Korea	7,696	3.0
Taiwan	3,938	1.6
United Arab Emirates	1,882	0.7
Total top ten sources	187,754	74.1
Others	65,532	25.9
Total FDI inflow to ASEAN	253,286	100

Source: ASEAN Foreign Direct Investment Statistics Database.
Note: Values in million US dollars and share in percent.

include the parent firm's exploitation of its firm-specific advantages, acquired by experience in the industry, by production in the home country, and by R&D or advertising. The SWFs typically have no firm-specific advantages other than large amounts of capital; they do not generally seek control of firms they invest in; and may move in and out of industries in pursuit of higher returns (or smaller losses), much as private equity firms do.

Finally, the reliance on balance of payments measures makes the role of financial centers important in measurements, since they are important in financial flows despite their lack of connection to productive activity. As was pointed out by UNCTAD (2006), the top recipients of FDI from Singapore included the British Virgin Islands and Bermuda. These flows would almost completely disappear from any measure based on the amount of economic activity involved. Accordingly, a large amount of FDI to Southeast Asia comes from tax havens, which makes it difficult to know the country of origin. For instance, the Cayman Islands is the seventh largest source of FDI to Southeast Asia, as seen in Table 8.3.

Hence, the figures in Tables 8.1–8.3 have to be treated cautiously. An alternative approach is to look instead at the share of production accounted for by multinational firms in various Southeast Asian countries. Such figures are presumably better at capturing the real presence of FDI. One major drawback, however, is that they are only available for some countries and only for the manufacturing sector. Eric Ramstetter has in a large number of studies analyzed FDI using firm-level information. Some of his findings are summarized in Ramstetter (2009) which provides FDI shares in Indonesia, Malaysia, Thailand, Vietnam, and Singapore. The foreign share of employment and output, based on Ramstetter's work, is seen in Figure 8.2.

The figures are not directly comparable across countries since the coverage of surveys and censuses differ. A few conclusions can still be drawn from Figure 8.2. First, the foreign share of output is always higher than the share of employees, which is a reflection that foreign firms tend to be relatively large, capital intensive, and with high productivity.

Second, the foreign share of output is around 40 percent in four out of five countries. It should be noted, however, that the trends in FDI shares differ between the countries (not shown): the shares have increased from previous years in Indonesia and Vietnam, been relatively stable in Malaysia, and declined in Thailand (see Ramstetter 2009).

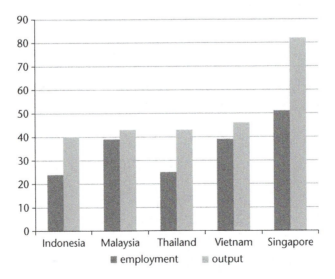

Figure 8.2 The share of foreign MNEs in Southeast Asian manufacturing (%, 2006)

Output is defined differently in the included countries, so foreign shares of employment might be a better measure of the relative importance of FDI. The foreign share of employment is around 25 percent in Indonesia and Thailand and almost 40 percent in Malaysia and Vietnam. Finally, the foreign share in Singapore is substantially larger than in other countries, despite a downward trend (not shown): the foreign share is about 50 percent of employment and more than 80 percent of output.

It would be of great interest to compare the share of FDI in Southeast Asia with the corresponding shares in other countries. Unfortunately, this information is not available for many developing countries, and when it is available it is often based on different types of censuses and surveys, which makes comparisons difficult. For instance, Sjöholm and Lundin (2013) report that the foreign share of Chinese manufacturing in 2004 amounted to 34 percent of employment, 40 percent of value added, and 76 percent of exports. However, these figures are based on surveys including firms with more than 300 employees, which presumably biases the Chinese numbers upward in comparison with the figures in Figure 8.2.

A reasonably good comparison can be made with six European countries, as seen in Appendix Table 8.A1. The foreign share of industrial activities varies substantially between European countries, just as it varies between Southeast Asian countries. For instance, the foreign share in Ireland is 48 percent of employment and 81 percent of sales, and this compares quite closely with the situation in Singapore. At the other end, the foreign share of employment and sales is only around 17 percent in Finland, which is lower than in any Southeast Asian country. Overall, it seems that the share of FDI in Southeast Asia is slightly higher but not very different from what we see in other countries.

Determinants of FDI in Southeast Asia

The previous section showed that the stock of FDI is relatively high in Southeast Asia. It also showed that FDI flows to Southeast Asia have increased over time. The increase rests on two necessary developments. The first is technological changes that have made increased global economic integration possible. The second is an ideological shift among governments and policy-makers with a more positive attitude towards globalization and multinational enterprises. This change in ideology has in turn triggered various institutional changes that tend to increase inflows of FDI.

Technological change

FDI requires complicated operations over long distances. Parts, components, and services need to be shipped between different branches of the multinational firm. Coordination and supervision requires visits by staff and a steady flow of information. Declining transport costs and improvements in communication technologies during the last decades have made all these exchanges easier.

All transport costs have declined. For instance, the World Bank (2009) reports that total freight costs have about halved since the mid-1970s but that different types of transport costs have declined at different rates. Sea freight costs fell dramatically in the first half of the twentieth century, the main reason being the development of greater vessel capacity and standardized containers, which has substantially reduced the cost of unloading and reloading (World Bank 2009: 176–7). The cost of air freight has been falling even more sharply: dramatically with the introduction of the jet engine but also, albeit at a slower rate, after 1970. For instance, Held et al.

(1999: 170) report that average air transport revenue per passenger mile declined from 16 to 11 US cents in fixed prices between 1970 and 1990.

Again, falling trade costs have enabled multinational firms to engage in so-called vertical integration, that is the division of the production chain between affiliates in different countries. Production of different parts and components is located where it is most efficient and then shipped to another country for assembly and re-export. This development of vertically integrated production lines seems to be particularly important in East Asia, as discussed by Athukorala and Kohpaiboon (Chapter 7 in this volume).

Vertically integrated product chains place larger demands on communication compared to production that is kept within the home country. Technological progress in communication technologies has therefore been instrumental in enabling MNEs to operate and expand their foreign affiliates. The World Bank (2009) reports that a three-minute phone call from New York to London fell in fixed prices from about 293 US dollars in 1931 to about 1 dollar in 2001. The development and expansion of the Internet and emails have further advanced the ability to communicate over long distances. Other technological advances have also been important in the ability to establish vertically integrated production chains. The World Bank (2009) argues that:

> The ability to coordinate and control production processes in real time by computerized systems has been central to the vertical disintegration of production processes in the high-income countries and the outsourcing to medium-income countries.

Institutional change

Technological changes have enabled countries and firms to engage in the international economy to an unprecedented extent. However, it might be argued that most of the technological progress that we have witnessed over the last decades has benefited the whole world. Therefore, while it might explain why FDI has increased, it does not necessarily explain why a large share of FDI goes to Southeast Asia. An equally important factor, and one that is crucial in understanding Southeast Asia's role as a host of FDI, is changing regional views on MNEs and the institutional and policy changes that have followed.

A fundamental criterion for attracting FDI is that the host country welcomes such investments. This has not always been the case in East Asia. Developing countries tended for a long time to use import substitution to encourage growth of domestic firms. A natural part of this strategy was to restrict access by foreign multinational firms to the domestic market. The most extreme result of this view was the nationalization of foreign MNEs. Such nationalizations were not restricted to the centrally planned economies in the region but also took place at some points in time in, for instance, Indonesia, Malaysia, and the Philippines.

If nationalization was an exception in most of Southeast Asia, a less extreme version of import substitution was more common, including high tariffs on imports and large restrictions on FDI. One prime reason for the popularity of this development approach was that Japan used this strategy successfully, and that country's success had a strong impact on development strategies across Southeast Asia in the 1960s and 1970s.

Some Southeast Asian countries eventually experimented with a different development strategy, including a stronger reliance on foreign multinational firms. Singapore started this development, and its economic success inspired other countries in Southeast Asia to liberalize their trade regimes and to encourage entry by foreign multinational firms. The timing of this change in development strategy differs across the region with, for instance, Malaysia making changes already in the 1970s, Indonesia in the late 1980s and early 1990s, and the (formerly) centrally planned countries even later. FDI regimes still differ substantially among Southeast Asian countries, with some being more open than others, but all countries have become more open to FDI compared to the situation a few decades ago (Brooks and Hill 2004).

It is interesting that the main reasons for a change in FDI regime in the two countries that pioneered regional reliance on FDI, Singapore and Malaysia, arose from domestic politics. It was domestic political struggles between different groups that made both countries look outward for capital and industrial know-how.

When Singapore was expelled from Malaya in 1965 it lost most of its previous domestic market on the Malay peninsula. The problem was aggravated by loss of exports caused by the conflict with Indonesia under President Sukarno (*konfrontasi*) and by the small size of its own domestic market.

The lack of a sizable domestic market, together with the asset of being the prime location for trade in the region, convinced Singaporean policymakers to abandon an initial attempt at import substituting industrialization (Huff 1994). Instead, Singapore became one of the very first developing countries to attempt the path of export orientation, aiming to overcome the constraint of a small domestic market and to supply the world with labor-intensive manufactures. The question was, who were the industrialists that should provide the exports? The years around independence had witnessed a struggle for power, between the People's Action Party (PAP) under Lee Kuan Yew on the one hand, and leftist and Chinese nationalist groups on the other. Lee Kuan Yew and the PAP managed to secure power by a combination of repression against political opponents and measures to win over substantial parts of the Chinese community.[5] However, a large part of the local Chinese business community opposed the PAP, partly because PAP was dominated by a strong British-educated elite. After it had secured power, therefore, the PAP was reluctant to rely on the domestic business community. Instead, it launched a deliberate effort to attract FDI (Huff 1994). One additional advantage with FDI was the perceived notion that the impact on growth and employment would be faster if foreign firms led the increases in production, since these firms were already connected to the world market. It would arguably have taken a longer time for domestic entrepreneurs to gain access to foreign markets (Sjöholm 2003).

The strategy to rely on foreign MNEs was fortunate in its timing, since it coincided with an increased interest among electronics firms to locate labor-intensive parts of their production outside their home countries. As described by Athukorala and Kohpaiboon (Chapter 7 in this volume), two of the first firms to outsource production to Singapore were Texas Instruments and National Semiconductors, which entered the Singaporean economy in the 1960s. Their choice was determined by several factors. There was uncertainty about locating in Taiwan, Hong Kong, or Korea, which were thought to be too close to an unstable China. There were also large subsidies offered to foreign firms that located in Singapore. The entrance of Texas Instruments and National Semiconductors was soon followed by a large inflow of other MNEs, many in the electronics sector, and this developed into the most important part of Singaporean manufacturing.

The reasons for relying on FDI were different in Malaysia, because the domestic political struggle was of a different nature. In Malaysia, the conflict was mainly between ethnic Malays (*Bumiputeras*) and ethnic Chinese. The latter group dominated the Malaysian economy in the years after independence. Widespread concern about economic marginalization among the ethnic Malays, who as the largest ethnic group had the greatest political influence, led to the launch of the New Economic Policy (NEP) in 1970. NEP introduced special treatment of ethnic Malays in, for instance, access to higher education and public employment. Though the first phase of the NEP was only peripherally concerned with the industrial sector, this changed with the introduction of the Industrial Coordination Act (ICA) in 1975. ICA focused on increasing the low ownership share of ethnic Malays in the industrial sector. Ethnic Malay ownership and employment quotas became mandatory in all firms with more than 25 workers (Drabble 2000).

An unsurprising result of the ICA was reluctance among ethnic Chinese to make fixed investments in industry, since it was widely perceived that such investment might later be captured by ethnic Malays. As a result, the ethnic Chinese share of equity declined from about 70 percent in 1970 to below 30 percent by the late 1970s (Jesudason 1989: tables 5.1 and 5.2).

The decline in ethnic Chinese investment was followed by a slump in industrial production and economic growth. Dr. Mahathir Mohamed, who became prime minister in 1981 and served until 2003, looked for ways to improve the situation and in particular to increase investment and hasten industrialization. To encourage investments from the ethnic Chinese population was viewed as politically difficult, so the government made a deliberate attempt to encourage inflows of FDI. This policy was pursued both during the import substitution phase of 1980–85 and during the later export-oriented policy. Japanese firms were particularly encouraged to invest, partly as a result of Prime Minister Mahathir's "Look East" policy, which tried to imitate Japanese industrial policies and practices.

Policies to encourage inflows of FDI included a decline in the share of equity that foreign firms were required to reserve for Malaysian actors. Such ownership sharing requirements were totally abandoned in export-oriented activities. Hitachi, Intel, and Motorola were some of the firms that took advantage of this change in policy, and set up factories in Malaysia that were heavily focused on exports, either of parts and components to other factories in the region, or of finished goods to markets in Japan, Europe, and North America.

Hence, this discussion points at something important: the deregulation of FDI regimes in key countries of Southeast Asia began as a reaction to domestic political conflicts. It is highly uncertain whether the major FDI recipients in Southeast Asia would have adopted similar policies on FDI in the absence of these domestic conflicts. This is in particular true for the two countries that pioneered the approach of deliberately attracting FDI – Singapore and Malaysia. But it is presumably also true for other countries in the region that were inspired by the experience of the pioneering countries.

Locational advantages

Over time, FDI regimes have been liberalized in most of Southeast Asia. However, merely allowing foreign MNEs to enter is no guarantee that they will actually choose to do so. Hence, to understand FDI inflows, we need also to understand the main reasons why MNEs were attracted to Southeast Asia. As a first step, it is useful to distinguish different motivations for FDI. FDI is pursued for three main reasons: to serve the host country market with products produced locally; to get access to raw materials; and to produce for export.[6]

The domestic market access reason for FDI is typically the most important one. Market access FDI might be a substitute for exports to a country, to minimize transport costs, or a way to avoid other trade costs such as tariffs and non-tariff barriers.[7] The market access reason for FDI is presumably also gaining importance in Southeast Asia because the region's share of total world GDP has doubled since 1960 (World Bank 2009). The attraction of Southeast Asia has increased with rapid growth and development and with the subsequent increase in local demand.

However, the rise of China and India might affect the ability of Southeast Asia to attract market-seeking FDI. Multinational firms are sometimes constrained by internal capacity and can only expand in a limited number of countries. It is possible that India and China, with their large domestic markets, will then be preferred over Southeast Asian countries. It is in this respect of some importance that there has been considerable progress in ASEAN regional integration, in order to make Southeast Asia more of an integrated market. Regional integration is progressing in Southeast Asia, as discussed by Hill and Menon (Chapter 17 in this volume), but the region is still a relatively fragmented market compared to markets in individual countries such as China and India.

A second major motivation for FDI in some Southeast Asian countries is access to raw materials. Indonesia is a prime example of this: a substantial share of FDI in that country is directed towards mining, and a relatively small share to manufacturing (Lipsey and Sjöholm 2011b). The growth of East Asian economies has increased their demand for raw materials and so increased resource-seeking FDI worldwide. Some of this has been directed to Southeast Asia. The home countries of firms engaged in resource-seeking FDI differ slightly from other types of FDI, and a relatively large share of this form of investment comes from European countries. In addition, Chinese FDI to Southeast Asia has increased rapidly in recent years. A large share of Chinese investment in the region is fueled by growing Chinese demand for raw materials (Frost 2005). Chinese investment in Myanmar is a prime example: Chinese state-owned oil companies have made large investments, including construction of a pipeline intended to supply China with 10 billion cubic meters of natural gas annually.

The most interesting type of FDI is when foreign firms can choose between different locations. This is in particular the case when it comes to production for export. Southeast Asia has attracted a large volume of export-oriented FDI. This raises the question of what features or policies in the region cause it to be viewed more favorably as a destination for export-oriented FDI than most other parts of the developing world.

A good general business environment is crucial for attracting export-oriented FDI. Various surveys of business environments in different parts of the world suggest that the business environment in Southeast Asia is good, but perhaps not exceptionally so. One example is the ranking of countries by ease of doing business, published annually by the World Bank. Rankings of the five main developing regions and of individual Southeast Asian countries are shown for the years 2005 and 2012 in Table 8.4. There are 175 countries included in the 2005 survey, and 185 countries in 2012. A low rank represents a favorable business environment, and a high rank indicates difficult conditions. Northeast Asia is by a large margin regarded as the most favorable region for doing business, both in 2005 and 2012. In fact, even the lowest ranked country in Northeast Asia in 2012, China, is still ranked ahead of six Southeast Asian countries. Southeast Asia has the second best ranking among the developing regions, followed by Latin America and Africa.

Looking at the individual Southeast Asian countries, there is great variety in the ease of doing business. The region contains the world's top-ranked country, Singapore, and one of the lowest ranked, Timor-Leste. Three Southeast Asian countries, Singapore, Malaysia, and Thailand, are ranked among the top 10 percent in the world in 2012, and two others, Laos and Timor-Leste, are among the lowest 10 percent. Vietnam, Indonesia, Cambodia, and the Philippines are ranked below the average. The rankings in 2005 and 2012 are relatively stable for most Southeast Asian countries, with the exception of a large improvement in Malaysia and a deterioration in the Philippines.

Other determinants of FDI inflows

The figures in Table 8.4 suggest that there is in Southeast Asia a reasonably good business environment, but not as good as in Northeast Asia and not much better than in Latin America. Moreover, the business environment in Southeast Asia certainly did not stand out as exceptionally good when FDI inflows started to take off a few decades ago. On the contrary, many of the host country indicators regarded as important for foreign multinational firms were relatively weak in Southeast Asia. One example would be the high levels of corruption. Another weakness of the

Table 8.4 The ranking of business climate in Southeast Asia and other regions (2005 and 2012)

	2005	2012
Singapore	2	1
Malaysia	25	12
Thailand	19	18
Brunei	n/a	80
Vietnam	98	99
Indonesia	131	128
Cambodia	142	133
Philippines	121	138
Laos	163	163
Timor-Leste	174	169
Southeast Asia	97	94
Northeast Asia	38	36
Africa	128	139
Latin America	100	102

Source: World Bank. http://www.doingbusiness.org/rankings#
Note: The ranking is based on 175 countries in 2005 and 185 countries in 2012. The criteria behind the ranking have changed over the years making rankings in 2005 and 2012 not directly comparable.

region, historically as well as presently, is the poor overall level of education, as described by Phan and Coxhead (Chapter 12 in this volume).[8]

The main reasons for FDI inflows therefore have to be found elsewhere. Two factors are arguably of large importance, stability and geography.

Political and macroeconomic stability

Macroeconomic stability is a key factor when MNEs choose where to locate their affiliates. Firms seek to avoid macroeconomic turbulence, both because it hurts domestic demand from households and firms, and because economic volatility increases uncertainty. Macroeconomic turbulence will also affect the exchange rate and thereby the landed cost of imports and the value of exports. It is therefore not surprising that several empirical studies find exchange rate volatility to be a negative indicator of FDI inflows to developing countries (e.g. Abbott et al. 2012).

Political stability is also of considerable importance to MNEs. This is so partly because it creates uncertainty about the stability of the policy and regulatory framework, but also because economic turbulence might follow from political turbulence. Political instability therefore discourages fixed investments.[9]

All four major FDI hosts in Southeast Asia – Malaysia, Singapore, Thailand, and Indonesia – have historically demonstrated considerable political and macroeconomic stability in comparison to most other developing parts of the world. For instance, it has already been mentioned that in the 1960s Singapore was viewed by many MNEs as a better choice than Northeast Asian countries because of the latter region's potential political conflicts. Singapore's stability was not only a result of the authoritarian regime's strong grip on power, but was enhanced by a strong policy emphasis on macroeconomic stability.

Malaysia, Thailand, and Indonesia (since 1967) have also had relatively stable macroeconomic policies, in comparison with most other developing countries, For instance, and as noted by

Phung et al. (Chapter 4 in this volume), inflation rates have been lower in Southeast Asia than in most other parts of the world.

Moreover, exchange rate regimes have by and large been managed floats. There have been periods of both fixed and fully floating exchange rates in different countries, but the larger Southeast Asian countries have tended to return to a system of a crawling peg to the US dollar. This has certainly been the case since the end of the Asian Financial Crisis (AFC). The stability of exchange rates has, as discussed above, been a positive factor for FDI inflows (Dutta and Roy 2011).

This is not to say that there have been no major political, financial, and macroeconomic crises. The AFC in the late 1990s was a period of extreme instability that clearly bears witness to the contrary. However, regional crises are relatively infrequent and the recoveries relatively quick. Even Indonesia, which faced a very large decline in GDP and a sharp increase in political turmoil in the late 1990s, managed to restore macroeconomic and political stability in a surprisingly short time. Moreover, some Southeast Asian countries have seen continuous macroeconomic and political turbulence. The Philippines is one such country and also a country that has received lower inflows of FDI than would have been expected from some other country characteristics.

The role of geography

Phung et al. (Chapter 4 in this volume) argued that Southeast Asia has benefited from having strong and fast-growing neighbors in Northeast Asia. Some of this positive growth effect emerges through FDI flows. Southeast Asia has received large amounts of FDI from its Northeast Asian neighbors, from Japan in particular but also FDI from Hong Kong, South Korea, and Taiwan has constituted a large share of FDI since the 1970s (Thee 2011). Some of this FDI came to Southeast Asia in order to gain access to domestic markets. However, a large amount of Northeast Asian FDI to the region has been export oriented.

In the 1970s, Japanese firms favored sending FDI to Hong Kong, Singapore, and Taiwan. However, the appreciation of the Japanese yen, and of other currencies in the Northeast Asian "tiger" economies, resulted in much larger inflows over time to Indonesia, Malaysia, and Thailand. This was particularly the case after the Plaza Accord in 1985, which led to a 60 percent appreciation of the yen against the US dollar. In the wake of this major global currency realignment, Japanese firms producing at home struggled to retain their competitiveness. Many responded by shifting the more labor-intensive parts of their production to Southeast Asia, while keeping more skill-intensive production in Japan. This division of production activities took advantage of Southeast Asia's low-cost, low-skill labor force while retaining the domestic cost advantages of the more skill-abundant, infrastructure-rich Japanese economy for high-tech production.

The Japanese government supported these FDI outflows as a means for Japanese firms to retain competitiveness in the post-Plaza Accord era. Government support took the form of direct subsidies on low-interest loans as well as provision of information about new production locations, and assistance with relocation through the Japan External Trade Organization (JETRO).

The textile industry was one of the first to experience this type of FDI. The search for lower production costs was an important determinant but not the only one. Part of the motivation to outsource textile production was to circumvent quotas on textile exports to the US and European markets that had been introduced in the Multifibre Agreement (MFA), up until the time of its abolition in 2005. Textiles were soon followed by FDI in many other industries, such as footwear, electronics, and auto parts.

Japanese FDI began to decline after the Japanese economic crisis and slowdown from the late 1980s. The Asian crisis in the late 1990s led to a further reduction in Japanese FDI. As was seen in

Table 8.3, FDI inflows from Japan are now less than within-region FDI, and less than inflows from the European Union. However, the production networks and the industrial base established during the era of Japanese FDI to Southeast Asia have remained an important determinant of new FDI from other countries. In other words, Japanese firms have remained in the region, and as a result foreign investors from other countries can rely on a labor force that is experienced in manufacturing, a bureaucracy accustomed to dealing with foreign firms, and a well-developed network of domestic suppliers.

The emergence of China as a major destination for FDI does not seem to have had a negative impact on FDI to Southeast Asia. While a large share of final assembly activities now takes place in China, production of parts and components has not left Southeast Asia.

Effects of FDI in Southeast Asia

Industrialization, growth, and trade

Changing attitudes towards FDI in Southeast Asia and other developing regions arise from the notion that foreign multinational firms might contribute to economic growth and development. This is a reasonable belief. Some Southeast Asian countries would presumably have developed at a reasonable pace even without FDI inflows, but it is difficult to imagine that their progress would have been as impressive as we have seen over the last decades.

Empirical studies confirm that FDI has contributed to the rapid economic growth of Southeast Asia (e.g. Urata et al. 2006). That has been the case for most countries in the region, even though the impact of FDI is hard to disentangle from the effects of other forms of liberalization or other contributors to development, such as investment in human capital (Carkovic and Levine 2005; Lipsey and Sjöholm 2011b).

Some of the growth effect seems to come from a reallocation of market shares and the exit of weak local firms following the entry of foreign MNEs (e.g. Okamoto and Sjöholm 2005). However, there are in particular two other growth-enhancing aspects of MNEs that make them attractive to host countries: their access to foreign markets and to new technologies.

MNE's access to foreign markets is of considerable importance to countries that want to increase production by producing for export markets. Export is difficult: it requires detailed knowledge about foreign institutions, regulations, distribution networks, and preferences. MNEs are in a good position to enter foreign markets because of their experience of operation in many countries. It is therefore not surprising that foreign firms are always more export intensive than domestic firms. This is also the case in Southeast Asia, as seen in Figure 8.3, which is based on calculations by Ramstetter (2009). Figure 8.3 shows foreign shares of manufacturing exports for four countries. All have high export shares, ranging from 50 percent in Indonesia to 89 percent in Singapore. Moreover, all four countries have foreign export shares that are higher than the foreign shares of employment or output (Figure 8.2), which shows the relatively high export intensities of foreign MNEs.

The figures on exports from foreign multinational firms can be compared to data for European countries in Table 8.A1. The FDI share of exports varies between 17.5 percent in Finland and 92.3 percent in Ireland. Just as in the earlier comparison of output and employment, there is considerable variation in the FDI share of exports both in Southeast Asia and in Europe.

The positive impact of FDI on exports means that the Southeast Asian countries have been able to overcome the constraints imposed by small domestic markets on scale of production. The exact contribution that these export opportunities have had on development is difficult to estimate but it is likely to be rather high.

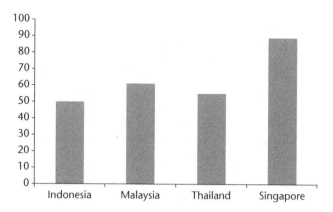

Figure 8.3   Foreign share of manufacturing export (2006)

The second main contribution of foreign FDI has been in providing greater access to technology. Much of the industrial innovation in the world, whether in product or process technologies, is developed in MNEs. Some large MNEs have R&D budgets that are large even in comparison to the total R&D expenditures in the smaller developing Southeast Asian countries. FDI is therefore a way to get access to new technologies, and these in turn increase productivity and economic growth.

There is ample evidence that foreign MNEs in Southeast Asia have superior technologies. One indication is the figures on output and employment in Figure 8.2, which suggest that productivity should be higher in foreign than in domestic firms. This has been confirmed in firm-level studies on Thailand (Ramstetter 2006), Vietnam (Tran 2007), Indonesia (Arnold and Javorcik 2009), and Malaysia (Ramstetter and Ahmad 2009).[10]

The relatively high productivity of foreign firms has benefited broad segments of their host country populations. For instance, it is well established that foreign MNEs pay higher wages than domestic firms (e.g. Lipsey and Sjöholm 2004a, 2006; Movshuk and Matsuoka-Movshuk 2006; Ramstetter and Ahmad 2009) and that the presence of FDI also increases wages in local firms (Lipsey and Sjöholm 2004b).

High wages for employees is important, but equally important is how many workers are employed in MNEs. To create job opportunities in the modern sector and thereby be able to move people out of agriculture and informal services is a key challenge for any country trying to improve incomes and welfare (Lewis 1954). As discussed previously, MNEs, with their knowledge of markets, technologies, and distribution channels, could play an important role in such employment creation. It is therefore no surprise that MNEs are always larger than local firms, irrespective of which country one is examining. Equally important but less closely examined, MNEs are not only relatively large, but the growth in their employment has historically been relatively high. More specifically, Lipsey et al. (2013) examine employment growth in MNEs and local firms in Indonesia. Their results show a positive effect of FDI on employment. Employment growth is about 5.5 percentage points faster in MNEs than in local plants, and local plants acquired by MNEs grew about 11 percentage points faster than their pre-acquisition rates. Considering that foreign plants are on average considerably larger than domestic plants, the difference in the number of jobs created was large. Finally, the positive effect on employment depends on the trade regime: unlike FDI during export-oriented policy regimes, FDI during import-substitution periods did not generate high employment growth.

Spillovers

The impact of FDI on indigenous firms is an issue much discussed by academics and policymakers alike. It is not obvious that the existence of externalities, often referred to as spillovers, deserves such attention. Inflows of FDI will, as already described, increase access to foreign markets and new technologies with positive effects on the host economy irrespective of the existence of externalities. In fact, the most FDI-intensive country in Southeast Asia, Singapore, has relatively few indigenous firms that can benefit from spillovers, but it is also economically the most successful country in the region. The focus on spillover effects on indigenous firms is partly for political reasons: many countries in the region have been promoting indigenous firms and are reluctant to see an economy dominated by foreign MNEs.

Whereas it seems clear that FDI benefits the host economies, it is less certain how they affect indigenous firms. On the one hand, foreign MNEs increase factor costs and product market competition for local firms, and so might force them to operate at a lower scale of production or might even force them out of the market. On the other hand, foreign MNEs might benefit indigenous firms in upstream and downstream industries through increased market activity for suppliers and customers. There might also be positive within-industry effects on indigenous firms, if they manage to learn about new technologies or foreign markets from the MNEs. One such mechanism for learning could be the recruitment of personnel from the MNEs, but the same result could also be obtained merely through demonstration effects.

The academic literature on externalities from FDI tends to find positive effects. The effects might differ depending on the context, in particular on absorptive capacity, which in turn depends on the skill level of the indigenous firms. Moreover, it seems from the literature that between-industry spillovers are more common than within-industry spillovers (Görg and Greenaway 2004).

Most studies on spillovers in Southeast Asia focus on productivity effects, but there are also studies on wage spillovers. Almost all studies find evidence of positive spillovers: local firms benefit from the presence of foreign firms.[11] For productivity, the positive effect is likely to come from technology spillovers, new technologies and knowledge that are made available to domestic firms, and from increased competition, a pressure to improve to secure market shares and survival. For wages, the positive effect of FDI is likely to be the result both of increased productivity through the discussed spillovers, and through increased demand for labor. Since the foreign plants also have higher productivity and pay higher wages than local firms, the two factors together imply that a higher foreign presence raises both general productivity and wage levels.

Concluding remarks

The last decades of economic development in Southeast Asia have been impressive. The region's success in economic growth is partly explained by the region's ability to integrate into the global economy through trade and FDI. Multinational firms are key actors in the global economy and Southeast Asia has been relatively successful in attracting FDI inflows. Aggregate figures on FDI show a larger regional share of global FDI inflows than of global incomes. Also, more reliable data on actual production in MNEs and in indigenous firms in a selection of Southeast Asian countries suggest that the share of FDI is relatively large. More precisely, several countries have FDI shares of manufacturing output around 40 percent, and in Singapore it is over 80 percent.

One main reason for the inward FDI can be traced to domestic political developments in Singapore and Malaysia. In both countries, at important stages in their development governments have chosen not to depend on the indigenous business community, and instead encouraged inward FDI by foreign MNEs. The strong economic performance of Singapore and Malaysia arguably encouraged other countries in the region to liberalize their own FDI regimes.

It is one thing to permit foreign MNEs to establish themselves in a country, but another to convince them actually to do so. The business environment in Southeast Asia is relatively good, which is of course important. However, it is difficult to argue that the business environment is exceptionally good by developing country standards, or that it was so at the time when FDI started to flow into the region on a large scale. Hence, other factors have presumably also been important. Two such factors that seem important are stability and geography. Stability – whether political or macroeconomic – is certainly not something that has characterized all countries in the region at all times, but it has been high in the main FDI host countries in comparison to most other developing parts of the world.

Moreover, Southeast Asia has benefited by its fortunate geographic location. When Japanese and other Northeast Asian countries' MNEs started to outsource labor-intensive parts of their production, Southeast Asia was ideally located. With time, networks of producers of parts and components have developed in the region, and this in turn has attracted new firms. These networks are not footloose but have remained relatively intact over the last decades, despite large changes taking place within Southeast Asia itself as well as in other parts of the world.

It is safe to say that Southeast Asia has benefited from inflows of FDI. In particular, foreign firms have increased growth by expanding production and by introducing new technologies. They have also benefited broad segments of the populations by providing modern sector employment and relatively high wages.

To make predictions of future development is difficult. In the second decade of the twenty-first century, there are some signs of more restrictive FDI policies in an important neighboring country, China, and these could spill over to FDI regimes in the region (Sjöholm and Lundin 2013). Moreover, the FDI regime in Indonesia, the largest economy in Southeast Asia, is once again becoming more restrictive (Lipsey and Sjöholm 2011b). However, it is also clear that there are many other developments that suggest that FDI inflows will remain large in the region. For instance, the ASEAN economic integration continues, with lower barriers to intra-regional trade, investment, and labor mobility making the region more attractive to MNEs. Most recently, Myanmar has begun to liberalize its economy. The lifting of international sanctions on that country following political reforms in 2012 is likely to greatly increase FDI inflows. Also, other formerly centrally planned economies in the region have the potential to attract more FDI. Hence, there are reasons to believe that FDI will remain an important aspect of Southeast Asian economic development well into the future.

Appendix

Table 8.A1 The share of foreign firms in a selection of countries (%)

	Finland	France	Ireland	Holland	Poland	Sweden
Employment	17.2	26.2	48.0	25.1	28.1	32.4
Sales	16.2	31.8	81.1	41.1	45.2	39.9
Exports	17.5	39.5	92.3	60.0	69.1	45.8

Source: OECD, AMNE Database.

Notes

1 For a description of the entrepôt role of Singapore, see Low et al. (1998).
2 See also Lipsey and Sjöholm (2011a).
3 Net stock of FDI is defined as gross inward stock minus outward stock.

4 One reason for high Vietnamese FDI stocks could be that Vietnam is not following international standards in defining FDI. They use, for instance, approved rather than realized FDI. For a further discussion see Ramstetter (2011: 24).

5 Lee Kuan Yew served as prime minister of Singapore from 1959 to 1990, and the PAP has remained the party of government throughout Singapore's post-colonial history.

6 In practice, most FDI involves more than one motive. Foreign subsidiaries might for instance produce for both the local market and export.

7 The latter type of FDI, tariff-jumping FDI, is sometimes distinguished from other types of market access reasons for FDI. The relative importance of tariff-jumping FDI has presumably declined as trade barriers have come down in recent decades.

8 See also Booth (1999a; 1999b) and Sjöholm (2005) on the poor quality of education in Southeast Asia.

9 It is here important to note that stability can be achieved both in authoritarian and in democratic countries.

10 The result for Thailand is less clear than the results for the other countries: foreign MNEs tend to have relatively high labor productivity but it is uncertain if they have relatively high total factor productivity.

11 Many of these studies are conducted on Indonesia because of the availability of good data. See Lipsey and Sjöholm (2011b) for an overview of spillover studies on Indonesia. See also e.g. Ministry of Trade and Industry (2012) for Singapore, Pham (2009) for Vietnam, Aldaba and Aldaba (2012) for the Philippines, and Kohpaiboon (2006) for Thailand. All of these studies find positive spillovers from FDI.

References

Abbott, Andrew, David O. Cushman, and Glauco De Vita (2012). "Exchange rate regimes and foreign direct investment flows to developing countries." *Review of International Economics* 20(1), 95–107.

Aldaba, R.M. and F.T Aldaba (2012). "Do FDI inflows have positive spillover effects? The case of the Philippine manufacturing industry." Philippine Institute for Development Studies, Policy Notes, No. 2012-01.

Arnold, J.M. and S. Beata Javorcik (2009). "Gifted kids or pushy parents? Foreign acquisitions and plant performance in Indonesia." *Journal of International Economics* 79, 42–53.

Antrás, Pol, and Stephen R. Yeaple (2013). "Multinational firms and the structure of international trade." NBER Working Paper no. 18775.

Booth, A. (1999a). "Education and economic development in Southeast Asia: myths and realities." *ASEAN Economic Bulletin* 16(3), 290–306.

Booth, A. (1999b). "Initial conditions and miraculous growth: Why is South East Asia different from Taiwan and South Korea?" *World Development* 27(2), 301–22.

Brooks, D.H. and H. Hill (2004). "Divergent Asian views on foreign direct investment and its governance." *Asian Development Review* 21(1), 1–36.

Carkovic, M. and R. Levine (2005). "Does foreign direct investment accelerate economic growth?" In T.H. Moran, E.M. Graham, and M. Blomström (eds), *Does Foreign Direct Investment Promote Development?* Institute for International Economics, Center for Global Development, Washington, DC.

Drabble, John H. (2000). *An Economic History of Malaysia, c. 1800–1990: The Transition to Modern Economic Growth*. Basingstoke: Macmillan.

Dutta, Nabamita, and Sanjukta Roy (2011). "Foreign direct investment, financial development and political risks." *Journal of Developing Areas* 44(2), 303–27.

Frost, Stephen (2005). "Chinese outward direct investment in Southeast Asia: How big are the flows and what does it mean for the region?" *Pacific Review* 17(3), 323–40.

Görg, Holger, and David Greenaway (2004). "Much ado about nothing? Do domestic firms really benefit from foreign direct investment?" *World Bank Research Observer* 19(2), 171–97.

Held, David, Anthony G. McGrew, David Goldblatt, and Jonathan Perraton (1999). *Global Transformations: Politics, Economics and Culture*. Stanford, CA: Stanford University Press.

Huff, W.G. (1994). *The Economic Growth in Singapore: Trade and Development in the Twentieth Century*. Cambridge: Cambridge University Press.

Jesudason, J.V. (1989). *Ethnicity and the Economy: The State, Chinese Business and Multinationals in Malaysia*. Singapore: Oxford University Press.

Kohpaiboon, Archanun (2006). "Foreign direct investment and technology spillover: a cross-industry analysis of Thai manufacturing." *World Development* 34(3), 541–56.

Lewis, W. Arthur (1954). "Economic development with unlimited supplies of labour." *Manchester School of Economic and Social Studies* 22(2), 139–91.

Lipsey, R.E. and F. Sjöholm (2004a). "Foreign direct investment, education, and wages in Indonesian manufacturing." *Journal of Development Economics* 73, 415–22.

Lipsey, R.E. and F. Sjöholm (2004b). "FDI and wage spillovers in Indonesian manufacturing." *Review of World Economics* 140(2), 321–32.

Lipsey, R.E. and F. Sjöholm (2006). "Foreign firms and Indonesian manufacturing wages: an analysis with panel data." *Economic Development and Cultural Change* 55(1), 201–21.

Lipsey, R.E. and F. Sjöholm (2011a). "South–South FDI and development in East Asia." *Asian Development Review* 28(2), 11–31.

Lipsey, R.E. and F. Sjöholm (2011b). "FDI and growth in East Asia: lessons for Indonesia." *Bulletin of Indonesian Economic Studies* 47(1), 35–63.

Lipsey, R.E., F. Sjöholm, and Jing Sun (2013). "Foreign ownership and employment growth in a developing country." *Journal of Development Studies* 49(8), 1133–47.

Low, L., E.D. Ramstetter, and H.W.C. Yeung (1998). "Accounting for outward direct investment from Hong Kong and Singapore: Who controls what?" In Robert E. Baldwin, Robert E. Lipsey, and J. David Richardson (eds), *Geography and Ownership as Bases for Economic Accounting*, Studies in Income and Wealth 69. Chicago, IL: University of Chicago Press.

Ministry of Trade and Industry (2012). *Productivity Spillovers to Local Manufacturing Firms from Foreign Direct Investment*. Report. Singapore: Ministry of Trade and Industry.

Movshuk, Oleksandr, and Atsuko Matsuoka-Movshuk (2006). "Multinational corporations and wages in Thai manufacturing." In E.D. Ramstetter and F. Sjöholm (eds), *Multinational Corporations in Indonesia and Thailand*. Basingstoke: Palgrave-Macmillan.

OECD (2013). AMNE Database – Activity of Multinational Enterprises.

Okamoto, Y. and F. Sjöholm (2005). "FDI and the dynamics of productivity in Indonesian manufacturing." *Journal of Development Studies* 41(1), 160–82.

Pham, T.H. (2009). "Assessment of FDI spillover effects for the case of Vietnam: a survey of micro-data analyses." In J. Corbett and S. Umezaki (eds), *Deepening East Asian Economic Integration*. ERIA Research Project Report 2008-1, pp. 473–95. Jakarta: ERIA.

Ramstetter, Eric D. (2006). "Are productivity differentials important in Thai manufacturing?" In E.D. Ramstetter and F. Sjöholm (eds), *Multinational Corporations in Indonesia and Thailand*. Basingstoke: Palgrave-Macmillan.

Ramstetter, Eric D. (2009). "Firm- and plant-level analysis of multinationals in Southeast Asia: the perils of pooling industries and balancing panels." ICSEAD Working Paper no. 2009-22.

Ramstetter, Eric D. (2011). "Recent downturns in inward direct investment in Asia's large economies." ICSEAD Working Paper no. 2009-22.

Ramstetter, Eric D. and Ahmad, Shahrazat B.H. (2009). "Foreign multinationals in Malaysian manufacturing after the crisis." ICSEAD Working Paper no. 2009–13.

Sjöholm, F. (2003). "Industrial upgrading in a globalized economy: the case of Singapore." In Mats Lundahl (ed.), *Globalization and its Enemies*. Stockholm: EFI.

Sjöholm, F. (2005). "Educational reforms and challenges in Southeast Asia." In F. Sjöholm and J. Tongzon (eds), *Institutional Change in Southeast Asia*. London: Routledge.

Sjöholm, F. and Nannan Lundin (2013). "Foreign firms and indigenous technology development in China." *Asian Development Review* 30(2), 49–75.

Te Velde, D.W. (2001). *Policies Towards Foreign Direct Investment in Developing Countries: Emerging Best-Practices and Outstanding Issues*. London: Overseas Development Institute.

Thee, Kian Wie (2011). "Foreign direct investment from Northeast Asia to Southeast Asia." *Indonesian Quarterly* 38(2), 188–212.

Tran, Tien Q. (2007). "Foreign direct investment in industrial transition: a case study of Vietnam." PhD Thesis, Australia National University.

UNCTAD (United Nations Congress on Trade and Development) (2006). *World Investment Report, 2006: FDI from Developing and Transition Economies: Implications for Development*. New York: United Nations.

UNCTAD (2007). *World Investment Report*. New York: United Nations.

UNCTAD (2009). *World Investment Report*. New York: United Nations.

UNCTAD (2010). *World Investment Report, 2010: Investing in a Low-Carbon Economy*. New York: United Nations.

UNCTAD (2013). Inward and outward foreign direct investment flows, UNCTADStat. Available at: http://unctadstat.unctad.org/TableViewer/tableView.aspx?ReportId=88

Urata, S., S. Y. Chia and F. Kimura (eds) (2006). *Multinationals and Economic Growth in East Asia: Foreign Direct Investment*. London: Routledge.

World Bank (2009). *World Development Report 2009: Reshaping Economic Geography*. Washington, DC: World Bank.

9

Regional trade agreements and enterprises in Southeast Asia

Ganeshan Wignaraja

ASIAN DEVELOPMENT BANK INSTITUTE

Introduction

Trade has played an important role in the economic development of Southeast Asia over past decades. In this volume, in Chapter 7 Athukorala and Kohpaiboon analyze Southeast Asia's engagement in global production networks and implications for industrialization. They conclude that global production sharing – particularly trade in parts and components – has become a fundamental part of Southeast Asia's trade pattern and facilitated the process of industrialization. Interestingly, Athukorala and Kohpaiboon conclude by suggesting that the relationship between global production networks and trade policy is a topic for future research. In Chapter 17, Hill and Menon describe Southeast Asia's outward-oriented commercial policy. They argue that Southeast Asian economies have generally adopted more liberal economic policies with increasingly decisive unilateral liberalization. Alongside such reforms, they mention that Southeast Asia created the Association of Southeast Asian Nations (ASEAN) but that the organization has a mixed record on promoting regional economic integration. One of the negative aspects highlighted by Hill and Menon is the emergence of a complex web of regional trade agreements (RTAs) and trade rules centered on ASEAN.

Dissecting the ASEAN-centered RTA web is interesting (see Das 2012; Kawai and Wignaraja 2013; WTO 2011). Following a somewhat hesitant start, the 1992 ASEAN Free Trade Area (AFTA) has become the basis for the ASEAN Economic Community (AEC), which is scheduled to begin in late 2015. Since 2005, ASEAN has also effected five ASEAN+1 RTAs (including the People's Republic of China [PRC], Korea, Japan, India, and Australia/New Zealand) to foster integration with large neighbors. Southeast Asia also has several bilateral RTAs, and negotiations are underway for two mega-regional RTAs – the Regional Comprehensive Economic Partnership (RCEP) and the Transpacific Partnership (TPP).

However, there is little research on how the web of ASEAN RTAs affects Southeast Asian economies at the micro-level. The very few micro-level studies on Southeast Asia include Kumar (1992), Hiratsuka et al. (2009), Wignaraja (2010), and Kawai and Wignaraja (2011).[1] This chapter uses recent data from manufacturing firms in three Southeast Asian economies (Indonesia, Malaysia, and the Philippines) to examine the impacts of key ASEAN RTAs (such as AFTA, the ASEAN–China RTA, and the ASEAN–Korea RTA) on enterprises. It seeks to improve our understanding of the impacts of RTAs in Southeast Asia and to enrich the literature on firm-level impacts of RTAs. The next section briefly reviews the literature on RTAs. This is followed by discussion of the enterprise dataset and then a description of the use of ASEAN RTA preferences and reasons for non-use, before an econometric analysis on the determinants of firm-level RTA use. The final section concludes with policy implications.

Literature on RTAs

Since Viner (1950) coined the terms "trade diversion" and "trade creation," economists and policymakers have been ambivalent about the welfare implications of customs unions and RTAs. The worldwide growth of RTAs over recent decades has intensified the international debate on the effects of RTAs on economies and firms between those who see net benefits of agreements and those who view them as harmful (WTO 2011). Ambivalence about RTAs is also visible in Southeast Asia (for overviews of the RTA debate in Asia see Dent 2006, and Das 2012). Early academic interest focused on assessing the economic consequences for Southeast Asian economies of establishing AFTA (see the papers in Imada and Naya 1992; and World Bank 2007) and the creation of an ASEAN–China RTA (see Chirathivat 2002; Tongzon 2005).

Academic work on RTAs on Southeast Asia falls into two camps. One camp uses sophisticated computable general equilibrium (CGE) models to simulate the welfare effects of RTAs, particularly ASEAN+1 RTAs, on Southeast Asian economies. Such studies show potential gains from elimination of import tariffs on trade in goods and liberalizing cross-border trade in services. While the underlying model assumptions and RTA scenarios vary, CGE studies typically suggest that full implementation of various ASEAN+1 RTAs bring gains to members of these agreements and limited losses to non-members.[2] These studies conclude that the magnitude of gains for ASEAN differs between RTAs. Large projected gains for ASEAN arise from RTAs with large economies like China and Japan. But even larger gains for ASEAN can occur from large region-wide RTAs like RCEP and TPP. One problem is that Cambodia, Laos, and Myanmar are not covered separately in CGE studies due to the lack of data for these countries (Tongzon 2005). Another is that CGE models do not incorporate rules of origin and non-tariff measures, which may afford more protection for domestic industries than tariffs.

Another camp questions whether potential gains from RTAs from CGE models can be translated into actual gains for Southeast Asian economies and firms within them.[3] Informed by Bhagwati's (1995, 2008) famous insight on the "spaghetti bowl"[4] – known in Asia as the "noodle bowl" – this research pays attention to utilization of tariff preferences, rules of origin (ROOs), and the discriminatory effects of RTAs in Southeast Asia. The key conclusions from this research are that the AFTA CEPT utilization rates (based on the shares of export values enjoying preferences) are extremely low and that AFTA is not particularly effective (see McKinsey and Company 2003; Baldwin 2006; Avila and Manzano 2007; and Hill and Menon, Chapter 17 in this volume).[5] Low margins of preference and cumbersome bureaucracy related to satisfying the 40 percent regional value content rule are cited as the main problems with AFTA use (Manchin and Pelkmans-Balaoing 2007; World Bank 2007). This evidence has fed suggestions that AFTA and other ASEAN FTAs are discriminatory and a drain on the scarce trade negotiation capacity of ASEAN members. Typically, however, this research was based on data from the 1990s and early 2000s, which does not capture the impact of the recent spurt in RTAs involving Southeast Asian economies.

A major challenge facing research on the impact of RTAs in Southeast Asia is the lack of published information on trade flows enjoying preferences. Transaction records on exports and imports for preferential tariff purposes are filed with origin authorities like national customs authorities or trade ministries but not published. Thailand is an exception; it publishes annual information on RTA preference use but in the Thai language. Using Thai data, Chirathivat (2008) shows that the overall actual utilization rate for Thailand's RTA partners has been rising, nearly doubling from 16 percent to 27 percent between 2005 and 2008.[6] The 2008 utilization rates of Thailand's partners vary by market, with 72 percent for the Thailand–Australia RTA and 28 percent for AFTA. Using data from Thai secondary sources, Kawai and Wignaraja (2013) show that the overall actual utilization rate for Thailand's RTA partners rose further to around 61 percent in 2011. Meanwhile the RTA utilization figure for the Thailand–Australia RTA increased to 91 percent and AFTA to 52 percent.

In the absence of published data on preference utilization, micro-level data from interviews with firms or large-scale enterprise surveys can be useful. In an early study, Kumar (1992) interviewed 15 trading companies and manufacturers in Kuala Lumpur, Singapore, and Jakarta to identify possible impediments to successful implementation of AFTA in the future. Kumar reported that the main bottlenecks were likely to be non-tariff barriers (standards, testing procedures, and customs procedures), a lack of information about the CEPT scheme, domestic investment regulations, and subsidy schemes. In spite of obvious gaps in methodology (such as a very small sample of firms from several countries), this early study provided clues to reasons for not using AFTA which are discussed in the descriptive analysis section using more recent enterprise survey data.

To provide micro-level evidence on the Asian noodle bowl, the Asian Development Bank (ADB) and the Asian Development Bank Institute (ADBI), conducted comprehensive enterprise surveys on the business impact of RTAs in several Asian countries (see Kawai and Wignaraja 2011). Japan, the People's Republic of China (PRC), Korea, and three Southeast Asian economies (Singapore, Thailand, and the Philippines) were included in the first round of surveys. In the total sample of 841 Asian firms from the six economies, 28 percent said they used RTA preferences. Interestingly, average RTA use in the three Southeast Asian economies was reported to be somewhat lower than in manufacturing giants like Japan and PRC. Furthermore, only 20 percent of the sample firms said that multiple ROOs significantly added to business costs. Weighing up the firm-level evidence, the study concluded that concerns about the Asian FTA noodle bowl effect on business may be overstated at the time of the surveys. Nonetheless, the study also noted the risk of an Asian noodle problem in the future with the growing RTA numbers in the region.

Two studies have explored the determinants of RTA use at firm level using econometric analysis. Using a sample of Japanese firms, Takahashi and Urata (2008) examined the influence of several enterprise characteristics (e.g. firm size, trading relations with RTA partners, the ratio of overseas sales in total sales, overseas business bases, and manufacturing membership) on RTA use. Firm size and trading relations with RTA partners were positive and significant. Takahashi and Urata concluded that large firms were more likely to use RTAs, reflecting the costs of such practices and that trading experience in RTA markets also influenced the likelihood of RTA use.

In their study of Japanese multinational companies (MNCs) including those in Southeast Asia, Hiratsuka et al. (2009) tested the relationship between firm size and RTA use with some enterprise characteristics (e.g. the share of local inputs in total inputs, the share of imports with zero tariffs, and sector and country dummy variables). A key finding is that large firm size (proxied by employment) was positively related to RTA use. Another is that firms that are actively engaged in international fragmentation are likely to use RTAs for exports.

These two studies provide useful insights on the determinants of firm-level RTA use. Nonetheless, they focus on firms from Japan, a developed industrial economy with relatively well-functioning markets and institutions. It is difficult to draw conclusions from this study for newly industrializing Southeast Asian economies with imperfect markets and institutions.

Furthermore, there may be methodological gaps in these studies. In Takahashi and Urata (2008), the exclusive use of dummy variables as regressors resulted in a model with weak explanatory power. Meanwhile, Hiratsuka et al. (2009) employ sophisticated panel data analysis for a large sample of Japanese MNCs but only a few explanatory variables were explored which may contribute to omitted variable bias in the results. Thus, there is a need for research on firm-level RTA use in Southeast Asian economies using a comprehensive set of determinants in econometric analysis.

Enterprise dataset

This chapter uses a cross-section dataset of 595 manufacturing firms in Southeast Asia located as follows: Indonesia (206 firms), Malaysia (234 firms), and the Philippines (155 firms). All three Southeast Asian economies are founder members of ASEAN and have been closely involved in negotiating and implementing AFTA and ASEAN+1 RTAs. Thus, invaluable insights on the business impact of RTAs can be gained from their experience. The survey data are of good quality due to methodical data entry and extensive data checking, which provides for reliable cross-country/cross-firm comparisons. Additionally, the data are relatively recent and of current policy interest.

The dataset used here comes from the ADB/ADBI enterprise survey dataset which focused on the critical question posed by the spread of RTAs – How do they affect business? A questionnaire designed by the ADB and ADBI (with inputs from partners) was used to collect information from firms on issues such as characteristics of firms, RTA preference use, impediments to RTA use, and sources of institutional support for firms. Firms were selected from a sample frame of manufacturing exporters using random sampling. The questionnaires were administered in person or through telephone interviews, which provides for more reliable information than mailed questionnaire surveys. The first round of enterprise surveys in six Asian economies was conducted in 2007–08 (including a Philippines survey conducted in 2008) and the findings were published in Kawai and Wignaraja (2011).[7] Using a revised questionnaire and a similar survey methodology, a second round of enterprise surveys was conducted in Indonesia in early 2011 and in Malaysia in late 2011/early 2012.

Some attributes of the Southeast Asian firms are shown in Table 9.1. Large and giant firms make up the majority of firms in Indonesia (77 percent) and the Philippines (59 percent) while SMEs dominate the Malaysian sample. A breakdown of the sample by industry suggests that

Table 9.1 Characteristics of firms

Country and survey year	Indonesia (2011)		Malaysia (2012)		Philippines (2008)	
	Firm Count	%	Firm Count	%	Firm Count	%
Number of respondents	206	100.0	234	100.0	155	100.0
By size(a)						
SME	48	23.3	207	88.5	64	41.3
Large	113	54.9	20	8.5	81	52.3
Giant	45	21.8	7	3.0	10	6.5
By manufacturing sector						
AUTO	22	10.7	47	20.1	36	23.2
Other manufacturing sectors	184	89.3	187	79.9	119	76.8

Source: Author's calculations based on Asian Development Bank (ADB)/Asian Development Bank Institute (ADBI) survey data.
Notes: SME = small or medium-sized enterprise.
SMEs have 100 or fewer employees, large firms have 101 to 1,000 employees, and giant firms have over 1,000 employees.

automotive firms account for 23 percent of firms in the Philippines, 20 percent in Malaysia, and 11 percent in Indonesia. Other manufacturing industries (such as electronics and clothing) account for the rest.

Descriptive analysis of RTA use

The findings from the enterprise surveys in Southeast Asia on the use of tariff preferences in major RTAs (like AFTA, the ASEAN–China RTA, and the ASEAN–Korea RTA) are described here. AFTA seeks to increase ASEAN's competitive edge as a production base in the world market through the elimination, within ASEAN, of tariff and non-tariff barriers. AFTA envisaged achieving a low tariff rate of 0 to 5 percent for goods originating within ASEAN (in the normal track of the inclusion list) with differential adjustment for ASEAN-6 countries and CLMV countries.[8] By 2010, the ASEAN-6 countries had impressively eliminated 99 percent of all tariffs for products in the inclusion list but high tariffs remained for sensitive products. However, tariff elimination in the CLMV countries has proceeded at a slower pace than in the ASEAN-6 and tariff levels remain relatively high and variable across industries. The ASEAN–China and ASEAN–Korea RTAs extend the notion of preferential tariffs among members (with differential adjustment for CLMV countries) to create a huge trade bloc encompassing China and another large bloc with Korea.

One might assume therefore that firms would make significant use of concessions under such RTA schemes once they are in effect. Nonetheless, as discussed in the previous section, early studies seem to indicate that AFTA CEPT utilization rates (based on shares of export value enjoying preferences) are extremely low. This evidence has fed suggestions in some quarters that AFTA and other ASEAN+1 RTAs are discriminatory and a drain on the scarce trade negotiation capacity of ASEAN members. A virtual absence of published data on the use of AFTA and ASEAN+1 RTAs from official sources makes it difficult to verify these early findings. Useful insights on the use of ASEAN RTAs, however, are available from firm-level data.

Patterns of RTA use

Table 9.2 shows data from the ADB/ADBI firm surveys on Southeast Asia on tariff preference use and future plans in ASEAN RTAs.[9] The data suggest greater use of preferences from AFTA in

Table 9.2 Firms using and planning to use ASEAN RTAs (Number of firms (percentage of total respondents))

	Indonesia						Malaysia						Philippines	
	AFTA		ASEAN–China RTA		ASEAN–Korea RTA		AFTA		ASEAN–China RTA		ASEAN–Korea RTA		AFTA	
	No. of firms	%	No. of firms	%	No. of firms	%	No. of firms	%	No. of firms	%	No. of firms	%	No. of firms	%
Users	64	31.1	45	21.8	32	15.5	49	20.9	47	20.1	17	7.3	31	20.0
Future users	25	12.1	27	13.1	16	7.8	73	31.2	71	30.3	41	17.5	63[a]	40.7
Users and future users	89	43.2	72	35.0	48	23.3	122	52.1	118	50.4	58	24.8	31	60.7
Number of respondents	206	100	206	100	206	100	234	100	234	100	234	100	155	100

Source: Author's calculations based on Asian Development Bank (ADB)/Asian Development Bank Institute (ADBI) survey data.
Note: [a] Refers to firms that plan to use AFTA or recently implemented RTAs.

2008 and the two ASEAN+1 RTAs (the ASEAN–China RTA and the ASEAN–Korea RTA) in 2011–12 than conventionally believed. AFTA preferences are used by about 31 percent of the responding Indonesian firms, 21 percent of Malaysian firms, and 20 percent of Philippines firms. Based on firms' future plans to use AFTA, these figures are likely to rise to 43 percent for Indonesian firms, 52 percent for Malaysian firms, and 61 percent for Philippines firms. It is possible that the present use of AFTA by Southeast Asian firms may be partly linked to low margins of preferences. Increased business use of AFTA in the future may be related to the creation of an ASEAN Economic Community by 2015. A larger regional market is expected to offer increased business opportunities to firms within ASEAN as well as heightened competition such that even low margins of preference offer a competitive advantage.

ASEAN–China preferences are used by 22 percent of Indonesian firms and 20 percent of Malaysian firms. Incorporating firms' future plans on the ASEAN–China RTA suggests that preference use may rise to 35 percent in Indonesian firms and 50 percent in Indonesian firms. Margins of preference are relatively high in the case of the ASEAN–China RTA, which means firms have an incentive to use the agreement. The present preference use of the ASEAN–China RTA is related to the relatively recent implementation of the agreement. The ASEAN–China RTA was in effect through an early harvest scheme since 2005 and tariff elimination on most products for ASEAN-6 countries and China occurred as recently as 2010.

There seems less business interest in the ASEAN–Korea RTA compared to other ASEAN RTAs. About 16 percent of Indonesian firms and 7 percent of Malaysian firms use the ASEAN–Korea RTA. Factoring in firms' future plans increases use of the ASEAN–Korea RTA to 25 percent for Malaysian firms and 23 percent for Indonesian firms. Less business interest in the ASEAN–Korea RTA may be caused by the fact that Korea is a smaller market than PRC, offering somewhat less business opportunities, and less central to the global production networks.

Benefits and costs of RTAs

Preferential tariffs are usually cited as the main benefit of ASEAN FTAs and increased documentation relating to RTA use as the main cost. It may be the case, however, that other benefits (e.g. increased FDI) and costs (e.g. increased competition from imports) may arise from ASEAN RTAs and it is fascinating to investigate this issue further using firm-level data. A related point is whether firms perceive the benefits of ASEAN RTAs as exceeding costs, or vice versa. Greater than expected use of AFTA and the more recent ASEAN–China and ASEAN–Korea agreements at firm level are indicative of net benefits from these RTAs for enterprises.

Table 9.3 provides data from the ADB/ADBI surveys on perceptions by firms of a variety of benefits and costs of ASEAN RTAs. For each of the benefits and costs, the table provides the number of respondents and percentage of total respondents. In the case of AFTA, Southeast Asian enterprises typically report greater benefits than costs. As expected, the most important benefit from AFTA is preferential tariffs, which encourages imports of intermediate inputs (74 percent of firms in Malaysia, 71 percent in the Philippines, and 42 percent in Indonesia). A second benefit is wider market access, which results in higher export sales (58 percent of firms in the Philippines, 44 percent in Malaysia, and 36 percent in Indonesia). The main cost from AFTA is increased competition from the entry of imports and foreign direct investment (51 percent of firms in Malaysia, 36 percent in Indonesia, and 36 percent in the Philippines). Documentation costs associated with AFTA are considered somewhat less important (33 percent of firms in Indonesia, 31 percent in Malaysia, and 26 percent in the Philippines).

Southeast Asian firms suggest that net benefits also arise from the ASEAN–China and ASEAN–Korea RTAs. The ASEAN–Korea RTA shows a similar ranking of benefits and costs to that of

Table 9.3 Benefits and costs of ASEAN RTAs (Number of firms (percentage of firms that use the FTAs))

| | Indonesia | | | | | | Malaysia[a] | | | | | | Philippines | |
| | AFTA | | ASEAN–China RTA | | ASEAN–Korea RTA | | AFTA | | ASEAN–China RTA | | ASEAN–Korea RTA | | AFTA | |
	No. of firms	%	No. of firms	%	No. of firms	%	No. of firms	%	No. of firms	%	No. of firms	%	No. of firms	%
Benefits														
Preferential tariffs	27	42.2	26	57.8	10	31.3	90	73.8	79	66.9	19	32.8	22	71.0
Market access	23	35.9	11	24.4	11	34.4	54	44.3	36	30.5	16	27.6	18	58.1
New business opportunities	8	12.5	6	13.3	9	28.1	44	36.1	43	36.4	5	8.6	11	35.5
Concentration of production	17	26.6	11	24.4	8	25.0	41	33.6	51	43.2	10	17.2	11	35.5
Costs														
Increased competition	23	35.9	17	37.8	7	21.9	62	50.8	52	44.1	10	17.2	11	35.5
Documentation costs	21	32.8	13	28.9	7	21.9	38	31.1	39	33.1	10	17.2	8	25.8
Competitive disadvantage	11	17.2	3	6.7	4	12.5	32	26.2	21	17.8	5	8.6	5	16.1
Relocation of production	3	4.7	3	6.7	4	12.5	32	26.2	44	37.3	10	17.2	8	25.8
Number of respondents	64	100	45	100	32	100	122	100	118	100	58	100	31	100

Source: Author's calculations based on Asian Development Bank (ADB)/Asian Development Bank Institute (ADBI) survey data.
Notes: [a] Results are for firms that use and plan to use FTA.
Multiple responses were allowed.

AFTA but the ASEAN–China RTA produces a somewhat different ranking. Preferential tariffs are the main benefit from the ASEAN–China RTA for Malaysian and Indonesian firms. However, the second benefit for Malaysian firms is new business opportunities, while Indonesian firms see equal benefit from market access and concentration of production. Meanwhile, Indonesian firms perceive increased competition and documentation costs to be the top costs from the ASEAN–China RTA. Malaysian firms also see competition as the main cost from the ASEAN–China RTA, closely followed by costs of relocating production.

Reasons for not using RTAs

The discussion above indicated a somewhat higher use of preferences from AFTA and the ASEAN–China RTA than conventionally thought and pointed to increased use in the future. But present levels of use of these two ASEAN RTAs may be suboptimal in relation to potential use. Furthermore, the majority of the sampled Southeast Asian firms are not currently using ASEAN RTAs. To investigate this key issue, the ADB/ADBI surveys asked non-users of ASEAN RTAs about the main reasons for not using these RTAs. Table 9.4 provides findings for total respondents and as a percentage of total respondents.

By far the main reason for not using ASEAN RTAs is a lack of information. Most firms said that they had heard about AFTA and other ASEAN RTAs. However, about 84 percent of responding firms in Indonesia, 79 percent in the Philippines, and 72 percent in Malaysia said that they do not use ASEAN RTAs because they do not know the detailed tariff preferences and other provisions of ASEAN RTAs or how to use them. Thus, our findings confirm the early prediction of Kumar (1992) who suggested that a lack of information (along with non-tariff barriers and domestic investment regulations) was likely to be an impediment to implementation of AFTA.

Table 9.4 Impediments to using RTAs

	Indonesia		Malaysia		Philippines	
	No. of Firms	%	No. of Firms	%	No. of Firms	%
Lack of information about RTAs	82	83.7	119	71.7	86	78.9
Use of EPZ schemes/ITA	30	30.6	35	21.1	31	28.4
Delays and administration costs in acquiring certificates of origin	24	24.5	49	29.5	34	31.2
Small margin of preference in RTAs	8	8.2	61	36.7	9	8.3
Too many exclusions in RTAs					14	12.8
Arbitrary classification of product origin ("rent seeking")	22	22.4	54	32.5	20	18.3
NTMs in RTA partners	8	8.2	8	4.8	6	5.5
Confidentiality of information required for rules of origin					11	10.1
Not interested in trading with RTA partners	20	20.4	71	42.8	42	38.5
Respondents	98	100	166	100	109	100

Source: Author's calculations based on Asian Development Bank (ADB)/Asian Development Bank Institute (ADBI) survey data.
Notes: Responses were collected for firms that currently don't use FTAs. RTA = Regional trade agreement, EPZ = Export processing zone, NTM = Non-tariff measures. Multiple responses were allowed.

This seems surprising as AFTA is Asia's best-known agreement and its preference scheme has been in effect for over two decades. The ASEAN–China RTA is also nearly a decade old, as its "early harvest" scheme of tariff liberalization took effect in 2005. In addition, over the years, Southeast Asian governments have attempted to disseminate information to business on how to use preferences in ASEAN RTAs through many outreach efforts, including printed leaflets, websites, and occasional short seminars. Part of the answer may be that ASEAN RTAs are complex legal texts (often running into hundreds of pages) drafted by ASEAN officials with experience of international trade law. Businesses, particularly SMEs, lack in-house international trade law skills to interpret provisions in ASEAN RTAs and the incentive (or the ability) to pay for specialist consultancy services. Furthermore, business outreach services provided by Southeast Asian governments may be ineffective for several reasons. For instance, the quantity of available outreach services could be woefully insufficient to support the needs of a large population of SMEs, and the quality of outreach services may be poor due to gaps in skills and funding in public support institutions.

A second reason is that ASEAN RTA partners (i.e. Southeast Asian economies, PRC, and Korea) may not necessarily be the main trading partners of the responding firms. About 43 percent of Malaysian firms, 39 percent of Philippine firms, and 20 percent of Indonesian firms said that they were not interested in trading with existing RTA partners. Instead, the key trading countries of such firms were likely to be the USA or EU, with which RTAs do not exist for the three Southeast Asian countries.

A third reason is delays and administrative costs related to rules of origin. Delays and administrative costs involved in claiming origin were mentioned by 31 percent of Philippines firms, 30 percent of Malaysian firms, and 25 percent of Indonesian firms. Part of the explanation seems to lie with cumbersome domestic procedures for applying for preferential certificates of origin. The sole issuers of certificates of origin in the three Southeast Asian economies – notably, the Bureau of Customs in the Philippines, the Ministry of Trade in Indonesia, and the Ministry of International Trade and Industry in Malaysia – are said to be less efficient than private institutions.[10]

About 10 percent of Philippines firms mentioned an additional issue concerning rules of origin: the confidentiality of information required in certificate of origin applications. This low figure indicates that the design of the regional value content (RVC) rule in the ASEAN FTAs generally seems acceptable to firms and that firms are willing to provide accounting information as a part of the process of meeting the origin criteria. It may additionally reflect the fact that the option rule was formally adopted by ASEAN in August 2008 whereby firms are able to choose between using an RVC rule or a change in tariff classification (CTC) rule to prove origin. Even before formal adoption, the option rule had started to be phased in for priority integration sectors in AFTA.

A fourth reason for not using ASEAN RTAs is the existence of other incentive schemes for export promotion – such as export processing zones (EPZs) and the Information Technology Agreement (ITA) for electronics. The availability of these alternative export promotion schemes meant that some firms had little incentive to use ASEAN RTAs and deal with their administrative procedures. About 31 percent of Indonesian firms, 28 percent of Philippines firms, and 21 percent of Malaysian firms mentioned this issue.

Other reasons for not using ASEAN RTAs include: small margins of preference (highlighted particularly by 37 percent of Malaysian firms), arbitrary classification of product origin (also known as "rent seeking"), non-tariff measures (NTMs) in RTA partners, and too many exclusions in ASEAN RTAs. NTMs, mentioned by less than 10 percent of firms in each of the three Southeast Asian economies, are not presently a serious barrier for using ASEAN RTAs. However, the continuing fragility of the world economy and risks to growth in Southeast Asian economies may induce an increase in protectionist pressures including the use of murky NTMs (e.g. government procurement, export incentives, and technical barriers to trade) to protect domestic industries.

Econometric investigation of RTA use

In this section we use data from the three country surveys to evaluate reasons for adoption or non-adoption of RTAs by firms. In simple linear probability terms, the model may be described as follows:

$$Y = \beta X + \varepsilon \tag{1}$$

The dependent variable in this model, Y, is a binary variable that takes the value of 1 if a firm decides to use an RTA, and zero otherwise. X is a matrix of explanatory variables related to firm and industry characteristics, β is the vector of coefficients, and ε is the vector of error terms.

Since the dependent variable is binary, we use a probit model. The data are cross-sectional observations at firm level. The hypotheses and explanatory variables are as follows.

Firm size is expected to have a positive effect on the probability of using RTAs, because large firms have relatively better access to resources (such as skills, finance, and information) which puts them in a better position to use RTAs than small firms. Size is represented by total employment.[11]

A *firm's geographical location* and *membership of the automotive industry* are expected to be positively associated with RTA use. Firms concentrated in major industrial centers are more likely than geographically isolated firms to use RTAs, for two reasons. First, geographical clusters of networked firms are characterized by information spillovers and exchanges (including know-how on tariff preferences, rules of origin, and origin administration). Second, public and private sector RTA support institutions are more likely to provide technical assistance to firms in major industrial centers. As tariffs on automotive vehicles and parts are relatively high in Asia, firms in the automotive industry have an incentive to use RTAs. Geographical location and automotive industry membership are represented by two dummy variables: LOCATION which takes on a value of 1 if the firm is located in a major industrial area and 0 otherwise; and AUTO which takes on a value of 1 if the firm is an automotive manufacturer or parts supplier and 0 otherwise.

Export experience in multiple markets is expected to be positively associated with RTA use. Firms with experience of several export markets may be more likely to develop knowledge of international markets and trade regulations (including import tariffs, RTA preferences, rules of origin, and custom procedures). Given this, export experience of multiple markets is considered to be positively associated with the probability of using RTAs. This is proxied by a dummy variable which takes a value of 1 if a firm exports to more than one market and 0 otherwise.

Building technological capabilities at firm level leading to greater cost efficiency is expected to have a positive influence on the probability of using RTAs. Acquiring the requisite technical competence requires conscious investments in creating new skills and information to operate imported technologies efficiently. Typically, this involves a range of engineering activities as well as research and development. Simple learning by doing – i.e. passively undertaking production tasks repetitively over time – can also contribute to building technological competence. Efficient, technologically capable firms are more likely to trade internationally and use RTAs than less technologically capable firms. We use two variables to represent technological capabilities at firm level. First, we use the ratio of R&D expenditures to sales (R&D) to represent active technological efforts. This variable was included in the estimation for Indonesia and Malaysia only, as R&D data for the Philippines were not available from the ADB/ADBI firm surveys. Second, we use the number of years a firm has been in commercial operation (AGE) as a proxy for learning by doing.

Acquiring knowledge about RTAs at firm level is expected to have a positive influence on the probability of using RTAs. RTA texts are complex, lengthy legal documents requiring significant investment in specialist skills (e.g. trade law, customs procedures, and business strategy) to derive the benefits of RTAs. Firms that have acquired relevant in-house RTA expertise, or those that actively build linkages with RTA support institutions, are more likely to use RTAs than other firms. Two dummy variables are used here. One (RTA KNOWLEDGE) takes a value of 1 if the firm has some or a thorough knowledge of RTA provisions, or 0 otherwise. The other (RTA SUPPORT) is 1 if the firm engages with public or private support institutions and 0 otherwise.

Probit coefficients and the results for the individual country regressions are shown in Table 9.5. A baseline specification (equation i) is provided for all three Southeast Asian countries, together with an alternative specification (equation ii) with the ratio of R&D to sales for Indonesia and Malaysia. The pseudo R^2 in equation (i) and (ii) suggest that the regressions explain about 20 percent of the

Table 9.5 Probit regressions of factors affecting the use of RTAs

	Indonesia		Malaysia		Philippines	Pooled probit	
	(i)	(ii)	(i)	(ii)	(i)	(i)[a]	(ii)[b]
SIZE	0.0000	0.0000	0.0001	0.0001	0.0001	0.0000	0.0000
	0.75	0.83	1.34	1.25	0.31	1.06	1.02
AUTO	1.233	1.3274	0.4653	0.4441	0.665	0.7842	1.1805
	2.64***	2.8***	2**	1.89*	2.15**	3.46***	2.67***
LOCATION	0.5469	0.6103	0.4559	0.4444	−0.3067	0.2842	0.4936
	2.32**	2.55**	2.2**	2.12**	−1.01	2.22**	3.23***
MULTIPLE MARKET	0.0456	−0.0056	1.0714	1.0028	−0.0831	0.591	0.6624
	0.15	−0.02	5.19***	4.77***	−0.21	3.93***	3.93***
AGE	0.0285	0.0319	0.0089	0.0102	0.044	0.0219	0.0179
	2.45**	2.65***	0.99	1.11	2.49**	3.52***	2.64***
R&D		0.0199		0.0094			0.012
		1.97**		2.15**			3.02***
RTA KNOWLEDGE	1.1727	1.1768	0.4515	0.4821	0.6838	0.8577	0.8285
	4.8***	4.77***	2.12	2.21**	1.73*	6.13***	5.31***
RTA SUPPORT	0.418	0.443	−0.2705	−0.3387	0.7653	0.5046	0.3676
	1.70*	1.78*	−0.37	−0.46	2.74***	2.94***	1.59
MALAYSIA DUMMY						0.3915	
						1.81*	
INDONESIA DUMMY						0.7547	0.4215
						4.07***	2.39**
Constant	−1.354	−1.5002	−1.3038	−1.3505	−1.8847	−2.3672	−2.0424
	−3.83***	−4.11***	−1.76*	−1.80*	−3.71***	−10.31***	−7.25***
n	199	199	234	234	155	588	433
Wald Chi2	70.53***	74.33***	51.18***	55.63***	37.56	183.01***	147.82***
Pseudo R2	0.26	0.27	0.19	0.20	0.24	0.24	0.25

Source: Author's calculations based on Asian Development Bank (ADB)/Asian Development Bank Institute (ADBI) survey data.
Notes:
[a] Includes all three economies, i.e. Indonesia, Malaysia, and the Philippines.
[b] Indonesia and Malaysia only.
Dependent binary variable: 1 = firm uses FTAs.
Coefficients are estimated using robust standard errors; z-value in parenthesis: *** is significant at the 1% level, ** is significant at the 5% level and * is significant at the 10% level.

variation in the data. Key explanatory variables are mostly significant (some at the 1 percent level) and have the expected signs.

The findings highlight the important links between learning – via building technological capabilities as well as acquiring knowledge about RTAs – and the probability of RTA use. R&D is a significant predictor of RTA use (significant at 5 percent level in both Indonesia and Malaysia) with firms that spend more on R&D and engineering activities more likely to be users. This shows the critical link between actively investing in technical competence, engaging in international trade, and the likelihood of a firm using an RTA. Examination of marginal effects (see Table 9.6) suggests that a firm which invests 0.5 percent of total sale on R&D has a 52 percent probability of using RTA in Indonesia and 24 percent in Malaysia.

AGE also matters in predicting RTA use (statistically significant at the 1 percent level in Indonesia and 5 percent level in the Philippines) with older firms more likely to be users. This indicates that learning by doing fosters trading and using RTAs. On average, the likelihood of a five-year-old firm using an RTA is 42 percent in Indonesia, 25 percent in Malaysia, and 12 percent in the Philippines.

We now turn to the proxies for acquiring knowledge about RTAs. Strikingly, RTA KNOWLEDGE plays a significant role in the likelihood of RTA use in all three Southeast Asian countries. It is significant at the 1 percent level in Indonesia, 5 percent level in Malaysia, and 10 percent level in the Philippines. This shows that firms that have acquired relevant in-house RTA expertise are more likely to use RTAs than other firms. On average, firms that have some or thorough understanding of RTAs have a 33 percent higher probability of using an RTA in Indonesia, 14 percent in the Philippines, and 12 percent in Malaysia.

Similarly, FTA SUPPORT is a significant predictor of RTA use (1 percent level in the Philippines and 10 percent level in Indonesia). Accordingly, firms that actively build linkages with RTA support institutions are more likely to use RTAs than other firms.

Table 9.6 Marginal effects of factors affecting the use of RTAs[c]

	Indonesia		Malaysia		Philippines	Pooled data	
	(i)	*(ii)*	*(i)*	*(ii)*	*(i)*	*(i)*[a]	*(ii)*[b]
SIZE	0.0000	0.0000	0.0000	0.0000	0.0000	0.0000	0.0000
AUTO	0.3559	0.3756	0.1222	0.1140	0.1392	0.2147	0.3314
LOCATION	0.1579	0.1727	0.1197	0.1141	–0.0642	0.0778	0.1386
MULTIPLE MARKET	0.0132	–0.0016	0.2813	0.2575	–0.0174	0.1618	0.1860
AGE when AGE = 5	0.4353	0.4249	0.2483	0.2467	0.1199	0.2833	0.3422
R&D when R&D = 0.5%		0.5207		0.2355			0.3681
RTA KNOWLEDGE	0.3385	0.333	0.1185	0.1238	0.1431	0.2349	0.2326
RTA SUPPORT	0.1207	0.1254	–0.0710	–0.0870	0.1602	0.1382	0.1032
INDONESIA DUMMY						0.1072	0.1183
MALAYSIA DUMMY						0.2066	

Source: Author's calculations based on Asian Development Bank (ADB)/Asian Development Bank Institute (ADBI) survey data.

Notes

[a] Includes all three economies, i.e. Indonesia, Malaysia, and the Philippines.

[b] Indonesia and Philippines only.

[c] Marginal effects provide a good approximation to the amount of change in Y that will be produced by a 1-unit change in X. For binary dependent variables – they give you a single number that expresses the effect of a variable on $P(Y = 1)$. Marginal effects for continuous variables measure the instantaneous rate of change.

Meanwhile, the proxies for geographical location (LOCATION) and automotive industry membership (AUTO) are also significant and positive for all three Southeast Asian countries. Firms concentrated in major industrial centers or which are members of the automotive industry are more likely to use RTAs than other firms. The proxy for export experience in multiple markets (MULTIPLE MARKET) is positive in sign and significant only for Malaysia. This provides support for the association between export experience of more than one market and RTA use in Malaysia.

SIZE is not significant in any of the three Southeast Asian countries. This is a puzzle given the findings of Takahashi and Urata (2008) and Hiratsuka et al. (2009) for Japanese firms that large rather than small firms use RTAs. This result may be due to the size of the sample or the proxy for firm size used here. Further investigation is needed on the effect of firm size on RTA use with larger enterprise datasets and alternative proxies for firm size (e.g. capital employed or generated).

For robustness, pooled probit regressions models were also estimated for total sample of Southeast Asian firms using country dummies. Concatenating across the whole sample of Southeast Asian firms increases the number of observations, yielding greater degrees of freedom. Table 9.6 provides two different pooled regression models. Equation (i) is the pooled baseline model for firms from all three Southeast Asian countries, while equation (ii) is a pooled model with the R&D to sales ratio for firms from Malaysia and Indonesia only.

The pooled results confirm the findings from the individual regressions. Most of the key explanatory variables are significant in equations (i) and (ii) with positive signs. FTA KNOWLEDGE shows significance at the 1 percent level in both equations while FTA SUPPORT is significant at the 1 percent level in equation (i). Furthermore, AGE is significant (1 percent level) in both equations while R&D is significant (1 percent level) in equation (ii). AUTO, LOCATION, and MULTIPLE MARKETS are also significant. However, firm size is not significant in either equation. The country dummies are also significant in both equations indicating some differences between countries.

Conclusion and implications

This chapter has examined patterns and determinants of RTA use in three Southeast Asian countries, with the aim of enhancing our understanding of the impacts of AFTA and ASEAN+1 RTAs from the perspective of enterprises. Gathering original firm-level data in Southeast Asia is a very difficult exercise in many respects. Firm surveys are expensive and time-consuming to accomplish. Handling firm-level data requires specialist data processing and interpretation skills. Both the resources and the skills are in short supply in Southeast Asia. Nonetheless, as published information is very limited, original firm-level data provides invaluable micro-level evidence on what is actually happening in trade and industrialization in Southeast Asia.

Several important findings emerge from the research. First, use of ASEAN RTAs is somewhat higher than conventionally thought and seems set to rise in the future when firms' future plans on RTA use are factored in. More business interest is visible in some ASEAN RTAs (e.g. AFTA and the ASEAN–China RTA) than others (e.g. the ASEAN–Korea RTA). This seems to be related to enterprise perceptions of the greater benefits of such agreements (e.g. preferential tariffs and market access) relative to their costs (e.g. increased competition from the entry of imports and foreign investment, documentation costs, and costs of relocating production). Accordingly, it seems that the potential gains from ASEAN RTAs are gradually being translated into actual gains for business.

Second, different reasons for not using ASEAN RTAs are suggested than conventionally emphasized reasons like low margins of preference and documentation costs associated with rules of origin. Instead, by far the main reason for non-use of ASEAN RTAs is a lack of information – firms do not know the detailed tariff preferences and other provisions of ASEAN RTAs or how to use them. Another important reason for non-use is that ASEAN RTA partners are not necessarily the main trading partners of the responding firms.

Third, a more comprehensive set of factors influencing RTA use at firm level was explored in the context of Southeast Asian economies than in the two studies of Japanese firms (by Takahashi and Urata 2008 and Hiratsuka et al. 2009) and the findings are different. The likelihood of RTA use in the Southeast Asian economies is particularly influenced by learning at firm level via building technological capabilities as well as acquiring knowledge about RTAs. The age of the firm also matters in predicting RTA use with older firms more likely to be users. Finally, firms concentrated in major industrial centers or members of the automotive industry are more likely to use RTAs than other firms.

These findings from firm-level data add additional insights that complement the more macro-level analyses of global production networks and trade policy (Athukorala and Kohpaiboon, Chapter 7 in this volume) and commercial policy (Hill and Menon, Chapter 17 in this volume). The micro-level evidence of business impacts of RTAs in this chapter can help advance the international and regional policy debate on RTAs in Southeast Asia.

Trade policy in Southeast Asia is in a state of flux, characterized by the slow progress in the 13 years of talks on the World Trade Organization (WTO) Doha Round, the spread of ASEAN+1 RTAs and bilateral RTAs, and ongoing negotiations for mega-regional agreements (like RCEP and TPP). The trade facilitation agreement reached in December 2013 at the WTO Ministerial in Bali was an achievement for the WTO, but the outlook for concluding the Doha Round remains unclear. Against a backdrop of protectionist tendencies, it is uncertain whether Southeast Asian countries have the appetite for further unilateral trade liberalization. Residual trade barriers to services and investment remain key issues in Southeast Asia and there is a risk of protectionist tendencies (particularly murky non-tariff measures) amid a fragile world economy (for a detailed account see Kartika and Atje 2013; Nikomborirak and Jitdumrong 2013). As governments view RTAs as a means to reduce trade barriers and insure against protectionist tendencies, they will remain an integral part of regional trade policy for the foreseeable future.

The micro-level evidence from the three Southeast Asian economies indicates that enterprises typically view AFTA and the two ASEAN+1 RTAs (the ASEAN–China RTA and the ASEAN–Korea RTA) as being more beneficial than costly to business activity. This suggests that the early literature on AFTA was overly pessimistic about its harmful business impacts. The broader development implications of ASEAN RTAs (in the sense of whether they matter for output, employment, and productivity) in Southeast Asian economies is an important area for future research. The business impacts of RTAs on services sector and services firms is another fruitful area for future research.

Two key policy implications follow from the research for Southeast Asian economies. One is the need to significantly improve business support services on RTAs, particularly for SMEs. This means the provision of integrated information services for firms to learn about RTAs, comprehensive technical advisory services for firms to use RTAs, university courses on RTAs and business, and greater participation of business associations in RTA negotiations and providing RTA training programs. The other is the need for a systematic effort in Southeast Asian economies and in the ASEAN Secretariat to develop an online database of official information on utilization of preferences of individual RTAs. Until this is established, firm-level analysis provides a fruitful avenue for further study of RTAs in Southeast Asian economies.

Acknowledgments

Thanks are due to Ian Coxhead and a reviewer for comments and to Menaka Arudchelvan for research assistance. The views expressed in this chapter are solely mine and do not reflect the views of the Asian Development Bank (ADB), its Institute (ADBI), its Board of Directors, or the governments they represent.

Notes

1 See next section for a review of these studies and other work on Southeast Asia.
2 For a recent selection of CGE studies, see Francois and Wignaraja (2008); Kawai and Wignaraja (2009); Kitwiwattanachai et al. (2010); Petri et al. (2011); and Estrada et al. (2012).
3 Athukorala and Kohpaiboon (2011), for instance, examine the impact of the Australia–Thailand RTA on bilateral trade between the two countries, looking particularly at the implications of ROOs and use of tariff preferences. They argue that the use of officially announced preference rates in trade flow modeling is likely to exaggerate trade flow effects of RTAs.
4 Bhagwati (1995, 2008) argued that discriminatory trade liberalization occurs under multiple, overlapping RTAs and that this is a serious problem because the same commodity can be subject to different tariffs, tariff reduction trajectories, and ROOs for obtaining preferences. With a growing number of RTAs, the international trading system is likely to become chaotic. Bhagwati also suggested that coping with multiple tariffs and ROOs in RTAs can raise transaction costs for enterprises, particularly small and medium enterprises (SMEs).
5 McKinsey and Company (2003) reported that less than 5 percent of intra-ASEAN trade in 2000 made use of AFTA preferences. Baldwin (2006) provides evidence suggesting that overall AFTA utilization rates were under 3 percent in the late 1990s but had risen somewhat to 4 percent in Malaysia and 11 percent in Thailand by 2002. Similarly, Avila and Manzano (2007) report an overall AFTA utilization rate of 15 percent in the Philippines for the early 2000s. In this volume, in Chapter 17 Hill and Menon say that "less than 10 percent of intra-ASEAN trade avails of AFTA concessions" but they do not provide a source or a date for this figure.
6 The Thai case of RTA use seems different to the widely cited Australian experience. An influential study by Pomfret et al. (2010) shows a notable fall in the share of Australian imports claiming preferential treatment over time and this is attributed to the increasing number of zero-rated MFN tariff lines. Meanwhile, Chirathivat (2008) and Kawai and Wignaraja (2013) show a rise in RTA use in Thailand over time which may be linked to formerly excluded items being brought within AFTA and relatively high MFN tariffs within Asia.
7. For more details of the firm survey methodology used in the ADB/ADBI studies see Appendix 2A.1 in Kawai and Wignaraja (2011).
8 The ASEAN-6 countries are Brunei, Thailand, Malaysia, Indonesia, the Philippines, and Singapore. The CLMV countries are Cambodia, Laos PDR, Myanmar, and Vietnam.
9 As it is difficult to collect information from firms on the proportion of exports or imports under preferences, these surveys use a simpler measure of RTA use – the number of firms using RTAs for exports as a share of sample firms. While such a proxy is not ideal, we expect it to be reasonably accurate; in Thailand, the utilization rate of RTAs based on certificates of origin matches with the utilization rate found in the Thai firm survey (see Kawai and Wignaraja 2011).
10 A recent study reported lower levels of business complaints in PRC where certificates of origin for the ASEAN–China RTA are being issued by chambers of commerce rather than public institutions (Wignaraja 2010).
11 Data on capital employed or generated was not available from the ADB/ADBI firm surveys.

References

Asian Development Bank (ADB) (2013), Asian Regional Integration Center Database. Accessed June 2013. www.aric.adb.org

Athukorala, P. and A. Kohpaiboon (2011), "Australia–Thailand Trade: Has the FTA Made a Difference?" *Working Papers in Trade and Development* No. 2011/12. Canberra: Arndt-Corden Department of Economics, Crawford School of Economics and Government, Australian National University.

Avila, J. and G. Manzano (2007), "Philippines." In *Trade Issues in East Asia: Preferential Rules of Origin. Policy Research Report. East Asia and Pacific Region, Poverty Reduction and Economic Management.* Washington, DC: World Bank.

Baldwin, R. (2006), "Multilateralizing Regionalism: Spaghetti Bowls as Building Blocks on the Path to Global Free Trade." *World Economy*, 29, 1451–518.

Bhagwati, J.N. (1995), "US Trade Policy: The Infatuation with FTAs." *Columbia University Discussion Paper Series* 726. New York: Columbia University.

Bhagwati, J.N. (2008), *Termites in the Trading System: How Preferential Agreements Undermine Free Trade.* Oxford: Oxford University Press.

Chirathivat, S. (2002), "ASEAN–China Free Trade Area: Background, Implications and Future Development." *Journal of Asian Economics*, 13, 671–86.

Chirathivat, S. (2008), "Thailand's Strategy Towards FTAs in the New Context of East Asian Economic Integration." Paper prepared for ADB, ADBI, and ERIA Joint Conference on the Asian Noodle Bowl, Asian Development Bank Institute, Tokyo, 17–18 July.

Das, D. (2012), "Idiosyncratic Features of Contemporary Regional Economic Architecture in Asia." *Journal of East Asian Economic Integration*, 16(2), 117–37.

Dent, C. (2006), *New Free Trade Agreements in the Asia-Pacific.* Basingstoke: Palgrave Macmillan.

Estrada, G., D. Park, I. Park, and S. Park (2012), "China's Free Trade Agreement with ASEAN, Japan and Korea: A Comparative Analysis." *China and World Economy*, 20(4), 108–26.

Francois, J.F. and G. Wignaraja (2008), "Economic Implications of Asian Regionalism." *Global Economy Journal*, 6(3), 1–46.

Hiratsuka, D., K. Hayakawa, K. Shino, and S. Sukegawa (2009), "Maximising the Benefits from FTAs in ASEAN." In J. Corbett and S. Umezaki (eds), *Deepening East Asian Integration*, ERIA Research Report 2008–1. Jakarta: Economic Research Institute for ASEAN and East Asia.

Imada, P. and S. Naya (eds) (1992), *AFTA: The Way Ahead.* Singapore: Institute of Southeast Asian Studies.

Kartika, P. and R. Atje (2013), "Toward AEC 2015: Free Flow of Goods within ASEAN." In S. Das Basu (ed.), *ASEAN Economic Community Scorecard: Performance and Perception.* Singapore: Institute of Southeast Asian Studies.

Kawai, M. and G. Wignaraja (2009), "Multilateralizing Regional Trade Agreements in Asia." In R. Baldwin and P. Low (eds), *Multilateralizing Regionalism: Challenges for the Global Trading System.* Cambridge: Cambridge University Press.

Kawai, M. and G. Wignaraja (eds) (2011), *Asia's Free Trade Agreements: How Is Business Responding?* Cheltenham: Edward Elgar.

Kawai, M. and G. Wignaraja (2013), "Patterns of Free Trade Areas in Asia." *Policy Studies* No. 65. Honolulu: East West Center.

Kitwiwattanachai, A., D. Nelson, and G. Reed (2010), "Quantitative Impacts of Alternative East Asia Free Trade Areas: A Computable General Equilibrium (CGE) Assessment." *Journal of Policy Modeling*, 32, 286–301.

Kumar, S. (1992), "Policy Issues and the Formation of the ASEAN Free Trade Area." In P. Imada and S. Naya (eds), *AFTA: The Way Ahead.* Singapore: Institute of Southeast Asian Studies.

McKinsey and Company (2003), *ASEAN Competitiveness Study,* Final Report, McKinsey & Company.

Manchin, M. and A.O. Pelkmans-Balaoing (2007), "Rules of Origin and the Web of East Asian Free Trade Agreements." *World Bank Policy Research Working Papers* 4273. Washington, DC: World Bank.

Nikomborirak, D. and S. Jitdumrong (2013), "An Assessment of Services Sector Liberalization in ASEAN." In S. Das Basu (ed.), *ASEAN Economic Community Scorecard: Performance and Perception.* Singapore: Institute of Southeast Asian Studies.

Petri, P., M. Plummer, and F. Zhai, (2011), "The Trans-Pacific Partnership and Asia-Pacific Integration: A Quantitative Assessment." *East–West Center Working Papers*, Economic Series 119 (October). Honolulu: East–West Center.

Pomfret, R., U. Kaufmann, and C. Findlay (2010), "Use of FTAs in Australia." *RIETI Discussion Paper Series* 10-E-042. Tokyo: Research Institute of Economy, Trade and Industry.

Takahashi, K. and S. Urata (2008), "On the Use of FTAs by Japanese Firms." *RIETI Discussion Paper Series* 08-E-002. Tokyo: Research Institute of Economy, Trade and Industry.

Tongzon, J.L. (2005), "ASEAN–China Free Trade Area: A Bane or Boon for ASEAN Countries." *World Economy*, 28(2), 191–210.

Viner, J. (1950), *The Customs Union Issue.* New York: Carnegie Endowment for International Peace.

Wignaraja, G. (2010), "Are ASEAN FTAs Used for Exporting?" In P. Gugler and J. Chaisse (eds), *Competitiveness of ASEAN Countries: Corporate and Regulatory Drivers*. Cheltenham: Edward Elgar.

World Bank (2007), *Trade Issues in East Asia: Preferential Rules of Origin. Policy Research Report. East Asia and Pacific Region, Poverty Reduction and Economic Management*. Washington, DC: World Bank.

World Trade Organization (WTO) (2011), *The WTO and Preferential Trade Agreements: From Co-existence to Coherence*. Geneva: World Trade Organization.

Part IV
Population, labor, and human capital

10

The population of Southeast Asia

Gavin W. Jones

NATIONAL UNIVERSITY OF SINGAPORE

Introduction

The total population of Southeast Asia in 2010 was 593 million, give or take as many as 10 million.[1] The population had doubled in the 38 years since 1972, and had increased by 48 per cent over the quarter-century since 1985. This chapter will first touch briefly on the longer historical context of this growth, and proceed to examine the components of recent population growth, assess some explanations for what has happened and look into the future to see how the population is likely to evolve over the coming decades. All nations of Southeast Asia except Timor-Leste are now members of ASEAN. Therefore 99.8 per cent of Southeast Asia's population lives in ASEAN countries, and in dealing with the population of Southeast Asia, the chapter will be dealing as well with the population of ASEAN.

A rapid decline in mortality beginning in the late 1940s and, in some countries, a rise in fertility, led to an acceleration in population growth in the 1950s and 1960s. It is not surprising, therefore, that in the 1960s concern about rapid rates of population growth was building up throughout the region, and that by 1970 all of the then-members of ASEAN (except Brunei) had adopted policies to reduce these rates. The introduction of these policies coincided with the beginnings of a downturn in the rates of population growth, occasioned by a fertility decline which resulted in birth rates declining faster than death rates. The extent to which the policies and associated programmes were responsible for this fertility decline will be discussed later.

Table 10.1 shows the basic facts of population size and growth rates in ASEAN countries. The density figures reveal little without studying regional variation at a more disaggregated level. For example, Indonesia's figure of 126 per sq. km encompasses provincial figures of 1,217 for West Java and 9 for Papua. It is important to note that, though by world standards overall population densities are not high in Southeast Asian countries, they are very high in important areas of the three largest countries: Java–Bali in Indonesia, the Red River delta in Vietnam and the Visayan region of the Philippines. Indeed, 59 per cent of Indonesia's population lives in provinces where population density exceeds 650 per sq. km. In Indonesia, Vietnam and the Philippines, the high population density in the regions concerned has influenced population policy and in particular policy toward migration.

Table 10.1 Southeast Asian countries: population size, growth rates and population density

Country	Population (thousands)				Population growth rates (average annual)				Population density (persons per sq. km)
	1980	*1990*	*2000*	*2010*	*1975–80*	*1985–90*	*1995–2000*	*2005–10*	*2010*
Brunei	189	252	327	401	3.66	2.83	2.35	1.71	69
Cambodia	6,506	9,532	12,447	14,365	–2.41	3.05	2.53	1.46	79
Indonesia	150,820	184,346	213,395	240,676	2.37	1.90	1.47	1.39	126
Lao PDR	3,235	4,192	5,317	6,396	1.30	2.87	2.02	1.99	27
Malaysia	13,833	18,209	23,415	28,276	2.33	2.89	2.45	1.80	86
Myanmar	32,865	39,268	44,958	51,931	2.36	1.78	1.33	0.69	77
Philippines	47,064	61,629	77,310	93,444	2.76	2.63	2.19	1.70	311
Singapore	2,415	3,017	3,919	5,079	1.30	2.15	2.36	2.44	8,218
Thailand	47,483	57,072	63,155	66,402	2.25	1.68	1.11	0.26	129
Timor-Leste	581	743	830	1,079	–2.65	2.60	–0.31	1.62	73
Vietnam	54,023	67,102	78,758	89,047	2.20	2.22	1.24	0.94	268
Southeast Asia	*359,012*	*445,361*	*523,831*	*597,097*	*2.25*	*2.08*	*1.56*	*1.22*	*133*

Source: United Nations Population Division, 2012.

The population situation in historical context

Southeast Asia is one of the most sparsely settled regions of the Asian continent. Two centuries ago, it was a region of forests, swamps and jungles, broken only here and there by significant concentrations of human settlement. The nineteenth and twentieth centuries saw an extraordinary multiplication of the population: from little more than 30 million in 1800 to 80 million in 1900 and 524 million in 2000.[2] At the beginning of the twentieth century, much of Central and East Java had population densities comparable to the very populous rural areas of China and India. Other densely settled areas in Southeast Asia, all of them based on wet rice cultivation, included the Red River delta, parts of Luzon and the Visayas, and the Chao Phaya and Irrawaddy deltas. But even the recent decades of rapid population increase have left overall population densities in Southeast Asia well below those of countries such as Japan, Korea, Bangladesh and India.[3]

The demographic history of these countries over the last two centuries has been one of frontier expansion into previously empty or sparsely populated regions, some of it officially planned but most of it spontaneous. In the Philippines the main movement was to Mindanao; in Thailand to sparsely settled *changwats* towards the Burmese, Laos and Cambodian borders; in Vietnam towards the mountain rim in the north and to the central highlands; in Peninsular Malaysia to the state of Pahang, and in Indonesia to Sumatra and, more recently, to Kalimantan, Sulawesi and Papua. The Philippine land frontier had ceased to exist by the late 1960s and the Thai frontier by the late 1970s. Though parts of Indonesia, Myanmar and, particularly, Laos have a continuing "frontier" character, the possibility of moving to new land is closed to the vast majority of Southeast Asia's agricultural population. Further increases in agricultural production will therefore depend on intensification of cultivation in already settled areas.

Table 10.2 Urbanization levels in Southeast Asian countries, 1950–2030

Country	1950	1975	2000	2010	2020 (projected)	2030 (projected)
Brunei	26.8	62.0	71.2	75.5	78.6	80.7
Cambodia	10.2	4.4	18.6	19.8	22.0	25.6
Indonesia	12.4	19.3	42.0	49.9	57.2	63.0
Lao PDR	7.2	11.1	22.0	33.3	43.5	50.9
Malaysia	20.4	37.7	62.0	70.9	77.7	81.9
Myanmar	16.2	23.9	27.0	31.4	36.9	42.8
Philippines	27.1	35.6	48.0	45.3	44.3	46.3
Singapore	100	100	100	100	100	100
Thailand	16.5	23.8	31.4	44.1	55.8	63.9
Vietnam	11.6	18.8	24.3	30.4	36.8	43.0
Southeast Asia	*15.5*	*23.3*	*38.1*	*44.5*	*50.6*	*55.8*

Source: United Nations Population Division, 2014.

Economic development in Southeast Asia is discussed elsewhere in this volume. The region as a whole has done well economically in recent decades. It comprises some of the most developed countries of Asia, as well as some that are much further behind.

Although Southeast Asia's level of urbanization is fairly low by world standards, it has been gradually rising. In 2010, roughly 44 per cent of Southeast Asia's population lived in urban areas, twice the proportion in 1970 (see Table 10.2). Singapore and Malaysia are highly urbanized, while almost exactly half of Indonesia's population and close to half in the Philippines and Thailand, live in urban areas. Elsewhere, urban proportions are much lower. Conditions of life for the rural population have been changing dramatically, in ways that blur the formerly sharp distinction between urban and rural areas. Secondary and tertiary industries provide an increasing share of jobs in rural areas. Isolation has been broken down by developments in transport and communication. This both makes travel to towns easier than in the past, and means that villagers who in the past may have had very infrequent access to news of or influence from the outside world are now watching the same TV programmes as urbanites, and are able to keep in regular touch with absent family members by cell phone.

Southeast Asia boasts some of the world's largest cities in Jakarta, Manila and Bangkok. The 2010 censuses recorded populations of 9.6 million and 11.9 million in the metropolitan areas of DKI Jakarta and Metro Manila, respectively, but even a decade earlier, there were approximately 17 million in their built-up extended metropolitan regions (Jones and Douglass, 2008: 49) and more than 20 million, or roughly the population of Australia, living within about 60 kilometres of the downtown area. High levels of urban primacy characterize Thailand, Cambodia and the Philippines in particular, though primacy in Thailand is declining somewhat as regional cities are growing more rapidly than the Bangkok agglomeration, and in the Philippines Davao City and Cebu are now substantial cities. Indonesia and Malaysia have a more balanced hierarchy of cities, but even here the populations of the main urban agglomerations – the Jabodetabek metropolis focusing on Jakarta and the Klang Valley metropolis focusing on Kuala Lumpur – are multiples of the population of the second largest city in each country. Vietnam shows a bi-polar urban pattern, reflecting its elongated shape and its political history, with Hanoi and Ho Chi Minh City providing the foci for the northern and southern regions respectively.

National boundaries were never coterminous with the domains of different ethnic groups in Southeast Asia. For example, in Thailand, there is a Vietnamese population in the northeast, hilltribe groups in the north that straddle the border with Myanmar and Laos, and a Malay population in the far south. In Indonesia, where there are more than 1,000 ethnic and sub-ethnic groups (though only 15 with more than 1 million population in 2000: Suryadinata et al., 2003: 6–9), large groups such as the Batak, Miningkabau and Buginese, all of which have a tradition for travelling widely throughout the country, are widely represented outside their heartlands of North Sumatra, West Sumatra and South Sulawesi, respectively. But the ethnic mix was significantly complicated, in the cases of Malaysia, Singapore and Indonesia, in particular, by the policies of colonial overlords, and then later in Indonesia and Vietnam by resettlement programmes conducted by post-colonial governments. In the case of Indonesia, these programmes served to spread large Javanese, Madurese and Balinese populations to many parts of the archipelago.

Trends in vital rates and population growth

Table 10.1 (cols 6 to 8) shows the slowing of population growth rates in ASEAN countries. These growth rates reflect their passage through the demographic transition – the movement from high levels of mortality and fertility toward low levels, and the establishment of a new balance of slow population growth at these lower levels. However, the movement towards this new balance differs considerably between countries. In the mortality transition, Singapore, Malaysia and Thailand have been in the vanguard, followed by Vietnam and the Philippines. In terms of fertility transition, again Singapore and Thailand are in the vanguard, followed by Vietnam, while Malaysia and Myanmar have recently reached replacement level. The outcome of these trends is that in terms of rates of natural increase, Singapore is lowest, followed by Thailand and then Myanmar (on account of its relatively high death rate). But these rates of natural increase are not mirrored in every case by rates of population growth; in both Singapore and Malaysia, net migration has added considerably to population growth.

The trends in mortality and fertility need to be examined in a little more detail. The early stages of demographic transition in the region were ushered in by a downturn in mortality shortly after the end of the Second World War, due to the application of modern science and technology to problems of disease control and historically unprecedented improvements in levels of living. The introduction of penicillin and other antibiotics in the later 1940s and 1950s, and the spread of massive public health campaigns (including programmes of DDT spraying to reduce the incidence of malaria, and inoculation campaigns against the major endemic diseases of childhood) were major factors behind the plummeting death rates. Whereas shortly after the end of the Second World War, close to one in five babies born in ASEAN countries would fail to live to the age of 5, by 1985 the chances of death at these ages had been cut by two-thirds.

As shown in Table 10.3, in the more favoured countries, progress in lowering mortality has been remarkable. Singapore's infant mortality rate of 2 per thousand live births is one of the lowest in the world; even Malaysia's rate of 5 is below that of the USA. However, there is scope for further substantial declines in the other countries, especially in Myanmar, Lao PDR, Cambodia and Timor-Leste, as a result of their low levels of development, poorly developed health services and many isolated regions. In these four countries, infant mortality rates are estimated to be around 50, and maternal mortality ratios remain high.

There is considerable uncertainty about maternal mortality ratios, as evidenced by the wide differences between lower and upper bounds in the estimates in Table 10.4. They remained shockingly high in many countries of the region in 1990, but have been lowered by 63 per cent in

Table 10.3 Infant mortality rates and expectation of life at birth, Southeast Asian countries, 1965–70 to 2005–10

Country	Infant mortality rate		% decline in IMR	Expectation of life at birth	
	1965–70	*2005–10*		*1965–70*	*2005–10*
Brunei	39	5	–87	66.0	77.5
Cambodia	130	51	–61	45.4	69.5
Indonesia	117	29	–75	50.2	69.6
Lao PDR	147	47	–68	45.6	65.8
Malaysia	51	5	–91	62.9	74.0
Myanmar	131	53	–60	48.2	64.2
Philippines	68	23	–66	60.1	67.8
Singapore	24	2	–91	67.2	81.2
Thailand	76	12	–84	58.7	73.3
Timor-Leste	201	51	–75	37.5	64.5
Vietnam	118	16	–87	47.9	75.1
Southeast Asia	*106*	*27*	*–75*	*52.1*	*70.3*

Source: United Nations Population Division, 2012.

Table 10.4 Maternal mortality ratios, Southeast Asian countries, 2010 (maternal deaths per 100,000 live births)

Country	MMR	Range of uncertainty	
		Lower estimate	*Upper estimate*
Lao PDR	470	260	840
Cambodia	250	160	390
Indonesia	220	130	350
Myanmar	200	120	330
Philippines	99	66	140
Vietnam	59	29	130
Thailand	48	33	70
Malaysia	29	12	64
Brunei	24	15	40
Singapore	3	2	7
Southeast Asia	*150*	*100*	*220*

Source: UNFPA, UNICEF, WHO, World Bank, 2012.

the region as a whole since then (from 410 to 150), well ahead of the worldwide reduction of 47 per cent over this period (UNFPA et al., 2012). Southeast Asia has lower MMRs than South Asia, but still double those of Latin America and quadruple those of East Asia. Much improvement is still needed, notably in Indonesia, where on the basis of development indicators MMRs below those in the Philippines and Vietnam might have been expected, rather than well above them. Part of Indonesia's problem lies in the difficulty of providing quality maternal care services in an archipelagic nation with poor transport and communications in many areas, but this is a problem equally shared by the Philippines.

Consistent with demographic transition theory, which posits that a decline in infant mortality is an important precondition for significant declines in fertility, there was a delay between the beginnings of a sharp decline in mortality rates and the beginnings of fertility decline. Fertility first began to decline in Singapore in 1957, followed by Malaysia and Thailand in the mid-1960s, the Philippines and Indonesia in the late 1960s and in the early 1970s by Myanmar and Vietnam (see Figure 10.1 and Table 10.5). The decline accelerated markedly over the 1970s and into the early

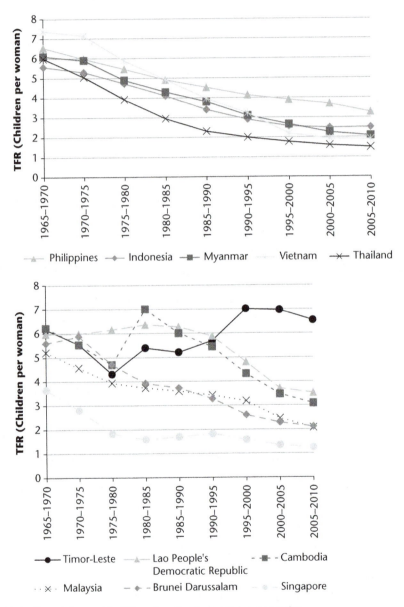

Figure 10.1 Trends in total fertility rates, Southeast Asian countries

Source: United Nations Population Division, 2012.

Note: The total fertility rate shows the number of children that would be born to a woman if she experienced, throughout her reproductive age span, the age-specific fertility rates recorded in the particular year.

Table 10.5 Total fertility rates, percentage changes in rates, and percentage decline towards the replacement level, Southeast Asian countries, 1965–70 to 2005–10

Country	TFR 1965–70	TFR 2005–10	% change in TFR	% decline towards replacement level
Brunei	5.59	2.11	–62.3	100
Cambodia	6.22	3.08	–50.5	76
Indonesia	5.57	2.50	–55.1	88
Lao PDR	5.98	3.52	–41.1	63
Malaysia	5.21	2.07	–60.3	100
Myanmar	6.10	2.07	–66.1	100
Philippines	6.54	3.27	–50.0	74
Singapore	3.65	1.26	–65.5	*100
Thailand	5.99	1.49	–75.1	*100
Timor-Leste	6.16	6.53	6.0	–9
Vietnam	7.38	1.89	–74.4	100
Southeast Asia	*6.06*	*2.35*	*–61.2*	*94*
South Asia	*5.92*	*2.72*	*–54.1*	*84*
East Asia	*5.28*	*1.61*	*–69.5*	*100*

Source: Calculated from data in United Nations Population Division, 2012.
Note: * The replacement level of TFR is approximately 2.1. Singapore and Thailand have fertility rates far below this.

1980s, and soon led to declines in rates of population growth. Indeed, the fertility declines in Singapore, among the Chinese and Indians in Malaysia, and in Thailand were among the most rapid ever experienced in world history.[4] During the 20 year period between 1965–70 and 1985–90, Southeast Asian fertility overall fell by 41 per cent, with even sharper declines in Thailand, Singapore and Vietnam. It is noteworthy that Thailand and Vietnam were predominantly rural populations at the time their fertility was declining most rapidly. Smaller countries of Southeast Asia had a much more chequered fertility history over this period. Lao PDR had no decline at all, Cambodia's fertility was deeply affected by the trauma of the Khmer Rouge period in power, and Timor-Leste showed little decline.

The 20-year period between 1985–90 and 2005–10 was marked by continuing fertility declines throughout Southeast Asia. Singapore's fertility fell to ultra-low levels, and in Thailand it also went well below replacement level. Fertility in Southeast Asia as a whole fell almost to replacement level. Of the countries where fertility remained relatively high in the late 1980s, Cambodia and Lao PDR experienced quite rapid declines, but the Philippines failed to lower its fertility very much over this period, endowing the age structure with an enormous potential for further population growth. Indonesia's fertility decline stalled over the past decade and, contrary to earlier expectations, remained about 14 per cent above replacement level in 2010. As shown in the last column of Table 10.5, between 1965–70 and 2005–10, Southeast Asia as a whole had gone 94 per cent of the way to reaching replacement level fertility, and most individual countries had either achieved replacement level or closely approached it.

What factors have been responsible for the timing of the onset, and the speed, of the observed fertility decline in the region? The theory of demographic transition argues that aside from the steady declines in infant and child mortality levels, which reduces the number of children parents need to produce in order to ensure that a given number survive to maturity, other forces in developing economies subvert the largely corporate, family-based way of life in traditional societies and replace it with individualism and growing personal aspirations. With a changing perception of the costs and benefits of children, closely related to increased education and growing work opportunities for women in urban settings, the cultural and familial "props" sustaining high fertility – religious doctrines, moral codes, laws, community customs, marriage conventions and family organization – gradually weaken. The "bottom line" in demographic transition theory's explanation of fertility change is economic determinism, though ideational factors are also present in the theory.

Socio-economic explanations are relevant in a very broad brush way in explaining Southeast Asian fertility transition. On the whole, the better-off countries have the lowest fertility and the less developed countries the highest: compare Singapore and Thailand with Lao PDR and Cambodia. But explanations based on socio-economic indicators do not adequately explain many aspects of fertility trends in the region: why fertility declined substantially in many areas that were predominantly rural, with low scores on a range of development indicators (e.g. Northern Vietnam in the 1960s and 1970s (Bryant, 2007: 103); Myanmar[5]; some of the provinces of Indonesia). Nor can they explain why the Philippines, which ranked high amongst the countries of the region in socio-economic indicators in the 1960s, failed to lead the way in fertility transition, or why the Malays, though benefiting from positive discrimination under the New Economic Policy in Malaysia, had a period of increased fertility and then very sluggish decline in the 1980s and 1990s, while fertility of the other ethnic groups was declining rapidly (Jones, 1990). A broader understanding of fertility trends in the region requires a recognition that institutional factors, including governance, are important in understanding the broad setting of fertility decline (McNicoll, 2006), and that opportunity structures rewarding increased investment in a smaller number of children may emerge among poor populations as well as those that are experiencing rapid economic development.

An important – and sometimes overlooked – element in Southeast Asian fertility trends is trends in marriage patterns. In Southeast Asian societies, there is little childbearing outside marriages recognized as such by the community. Therefore the two factors determining fertility are the amount of a woman's reproductive period she spends within marriage, and the level of marital fertility. The marriage element is a very important determinant of fertility; for example, the fertility decline for Malays in Malaysia over the 1960s was almost entirely due to rising age at marriage (Jones, 1990: 513), and more than one-third of the decline in total fertility rates (TFR) in Myanmar from 4.7 in 1983 to 2.4 in 2001 was attributable to the nuptiality effect (Jones, 2007: 21). There has been a tendency for female age at marriage to rise throughout the region and more recently for a substantial proportion of women in the cities to reach their mid-forties without marrying (around 15 per cent in Bangkok and 14 per cent in Singapore). This helps to account for the below-replacement fertility evident in the major cities of the region. Those women who do marry, many of them not until their late twenties or thirties, are not producing enough children to make up for those who do not marry.

The rapid pace of fertility decline that characterized countries such as Thailand and Indonesia can certainly be related to the rapid pace of economic and social development in these countries, including the transport and communications revolutions; and government family planning efforts. The gradual development of all-weather road systems (very rapid in Thailand during the 1960s and 1970s, and in Indonesia since the 1970s), ended the isolation of large numbers of villages; and development of public transport facilities, such as the up-country buses of Thailand and the "Bis Malam" and colts in Indonesia, gave even poor villagers more ready access to large cities. Perhaps even more important was the spread of radio and television into the villages, and more recently the remarkable spread of the cell phone. The perceptions and aspirations of rural dwellers, even those in isolated areas, were undoubtedly profoundly affected by the urban-dominated images they receive via the media and the greater ease of communication. At the same time, educational opportunities were expanding, thus providing the incentive for rural and urban parents alike to focus on having fewer children and educating them in the hope of achieving upward economic and social mobility.

An important factor entirely absent in the European demographic transition was organized family planning programmes (mostly beginning around the late 1960s) to foster smaller family size norms and to make contraception readily available. The history of these programmes in a number of Southeast Asian countries is documented and analysed in Robinson and Ross (2007). There is debate over where such organized provision of family planning services fitted into the explanatory picture, and the answers clearly differ greatly by country. Pritchett (1994) argued that the impact of these programmes has been greatly exaggerated, but Bongaarts (1997), while accepting some of Pritchett's arguments, nevertheless demonstrated the impact to have been substantial. Phillips and Ross (1992) argued that the effect of these programmes is stronger when they operate in a context of rapid social and economic development.

Sharp declines in fertility in many settings (not only in Southeast Asia) where real income and other development indicators do not appear to be rising significantly indicate clearly that high levels of modernization on the Western model are not a necessary condition of fertility decline. "Modernization" insofar as it affects fertility must be viewed broadly. The factors identified in demographic transition theory are important – education, industrialization, urbanization and changes in the family. But in some contexts (including perhaps Myanmar) thwarted hopes and economic stagnation can lead to delayed marriage and caution in family building.

Considering the Southeast Asian populations with fertility now below replacement level (Singapore, Thailand, Chinese Malaysians, Vietnam), fertility has been influenced, first, by the decreasing proportion married and, second, by some factors that have influenced marital fertility:

- The costs of childbearing are increasing, both the direct financial costs and the opportunity costs of women's interrupted career development, the latter particularly important for the growing proportion of women reaching higher levels of education.
- There is increasing pressure, especially in the cities, to engage in "intensive parenting", arranging tutoring outside of school hours, etc., to ensure that the child is "successful". Women bear the brunt of fulfilling social expectations about intensive parenting.
- Related to these two factors, "work–life balance" issues place pressure on parents, particularly mothers, who contemplate combining a career and childrearing in the relatively family-unfriendly workplaces of the region.

Migration – internal and international

Internal and international migration are often dealt with separately in regional population studies. There are two main reasons. First, internal migration, unlike international migration, does not directly affect national population growth rates. Second, it does not raise the same legal issues in relation to citizenship and other matters. A case can be made, however, for considering both kinds of migration together, because the motivation to migrate is on the whole similar. International migration in recent decades has raised rates of population growth in Malaysia and Singapore far above what would have resulted from natural increase alone. In other countries, it has had less effect, though refugee migration has been important in particular periods in lowering population growth rates in Vietnam, Cambodia, Lao PDR and Myanmar. A tradition of working overseas has resulted in much permanent outmigration from the Philippines and the residence overseas of about 10 per cent of the Philippine workforce at any given time. About 6 million Indonesians are currently working overseas as contract labour migrants and about 3 million Myanmarese are living outside Myanmar, mainly in Thailand (Hugo, 2012: table 2). In recent decades, organized marriage migration involving women from poorer countries, particularly the Philippines and Vietnam, moving to wealthier Asian countries such as Japan, South Korea, Taiwan and Singapore, has assumed greater prominence (Jones, 2012). Although much smaller in number than labour migration flows, the impact on the population of the source and destination countries is more permanent.

The volume of internal migration in the region has been far larger than that of international migration. There has been a shift over time from dominance of the "frontier" migration movements mentioned earlier to largely rural–urban movements and, more recently, as the percentage living in urban areas has increased, to a greater share of urban–urban movements. Some of the recent internal migration has led to significant regional population shifts as well, as areas less favoured economically have lost population to more prosperous regions. Thus in Malaysia, Perak's share of the national population fell from 17.8 per cent in 1980 to 11.0 per cent in 2000, following the collapse of the tin mining sector, and in Indonesia, Central Java's share of national population fell from 19 per cent in 1961 to 15 per cent in 2000.

Three countries of the region – Indonesia, Malaysia and Vietnam – conducted long-term programmes of officially sponsored resettlement of population. In the case of Indonesia, the transmigration programme reached its peak in terms of numbers resettled in the 1970s and early 1980s. But controversy built up over whether the programme represented merely a "transfer of poverty", over environmental impacts, land alienation and the impact on local populations in major destination areas such as Papua and parts of Kalimantan (Hardjono, 1989). Little new settlement actually occurred after budgetary difficulties in funding the programme emerged in the mid-1980s, though ethnic violence in some regions between settlers and the local population in the 1990s and 2000s was a continuing negative legacy of the programme. In Vietnam, ambitious targets to resettle population in New Economic Zones were adopted in 1976, after reunification. The results were disastrous and the goals had to be greatly scaled down (Desbarats, 1987). In Malaysia, resettlement programmes which were much more expensive per settler family than those in Indonesia or Vietnam did succeed in creating prosperous conditions in most settlement areas.

Far more important in more recent times have been the spontaneous flows of migration arising from people seeking better education and job prospects in other regions. Such flows have long served – though imperfectly – as an equilibrating mechanism between areas of greater and lesser economic potential (as in the case of net outflows from the Visayas to both Luzon and Mindanao). Though significant problems are recognized to be associated with the movement of particular ethnic groups to other areas and the movement of poor rural dwellers to the cities, no country in the region has moved seriously to restrict such movement, with the exception of a brief period when Jakarta attempted to prevent movement to the city and a controversial decision by Vietnam in late 2012 to prevent movement into the capital, Hanoi.

Demographic momentum

High fertility populations have a broad-based age pyramid, with about 45 per cent of the population aged below 15. Rapid declines in fertility undercut this age pyramid, and lead to very substantial changes in age structure. These changes can be illustrated with reference to Thailand, whose changing age pyramids are shown in Figure 10.2. In 1970 (not shown), Thailand's population had a typical developing country structure, with the broad-based age pyramid reflecting the ever-increasing cohorts of babies being born. A steady fertility decline after 1970 led to an undercutting of the base of this pyramid by 1990, whereas the large "baby

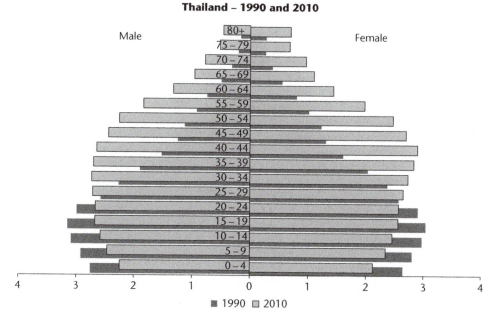

Thailand – 1990 and 2010

Male

Female

■ 1990 □ 2010

Figure 10.2 Thailand's age structure, 1990 and 2010 (Numbers in millions)

boom" cohorts were by this time moving into the reproductive ages. By 2010, the base of the pyramid had assumed the more rectangular form typical of low fertility countries, and the high fertility "bulge" had moved to the middle working ages. Projections for Thailand show further changes in the age pyramid by 2030, with the pot-shaped bulge moving up into the elderly age groups, and all age groups below 40–44 being progressively smaller.

The age pyramids for the Philippines (Figure 10.3) show a very different picture. Here, delayed fertility decline has led to a marked broadening of the base of the population pyramid. Whereas in Thailand, the number of small children declined from over 6 million in 1970 to not much over 4 million in 2010, the number of small children in the Philippines grew from the same base of over 6 million in 1970 to well over 11 million in 2010. The potential for future population growth is immense.

In cases where fertility sinks to replacement level and then does not deviate from this level, the age structure gradually changes and eventually reaches a point at which annual births and deaths are equal. But it takes considerable time for the age structure to adapt, and in the meantime substantial population increase can take place. This is generally referred to as demographic momentum – the influence on population growth of high-growth-potential age structures inherited from the past. In Thailand, fertility reached replacement level in about 1990 and then sank lower. Yet according to the UN low projection, population will keep increasing for 30 years from that point, and population will level off only after growing by a further 23 per cent or so.[6]

Such changes in age structure are occurring in most Southeast Asian countries. For the region as a whole, fertility is projected by the United Nations to reach replacement level in 2015, and fall further thereafter, but the population is projected to increase for a further 40 years, by 22 per cent, before it begins to decline.

As absolute numbers of reproductive-age women have been increasing very rapidly, in many cases the annual number of births were increasing despite quite rapidly declining fertility. The

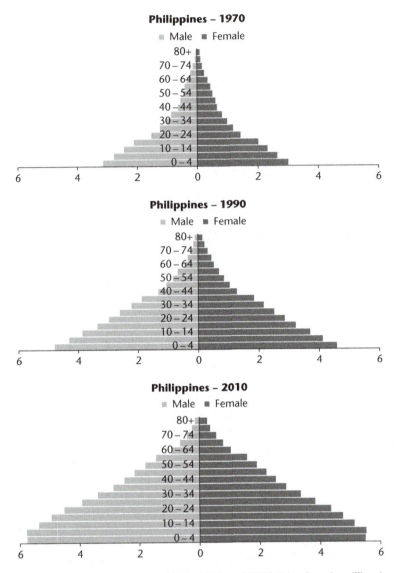

Figure 10.3 Philippines's age structure, 1970, 1990 and 2010 (Numbers in millions)

trends in fertility rates and birth numbers in Figure 10.4 are revealing. In Southeast Asia as a whole, the fertility decline has been sharp enough to cause annual birth numbers to level off by the late 1980s and then begin falling. This pattern is shown to a more marked extent in Thailand. In the Philippines, however, though fertility has been declining gradually, the annual number of births has been increasing steadily. Malaysia shows an interesting pattern in which sharp fertility declines appeared to be presaging a decline in births from the late 1970s but stalling of the fertility decline generated steadily increasing annual numbers of births through the 1980s and early 1990s. But into the 2000s, fertility decline was strong enough to reduce annual birth numbers. In Indonesia, the decline in fertility was enough to lower annual births somewhat from the late 1980s, but the stalling of fertility decline led annual births to rise again in the 2000s.

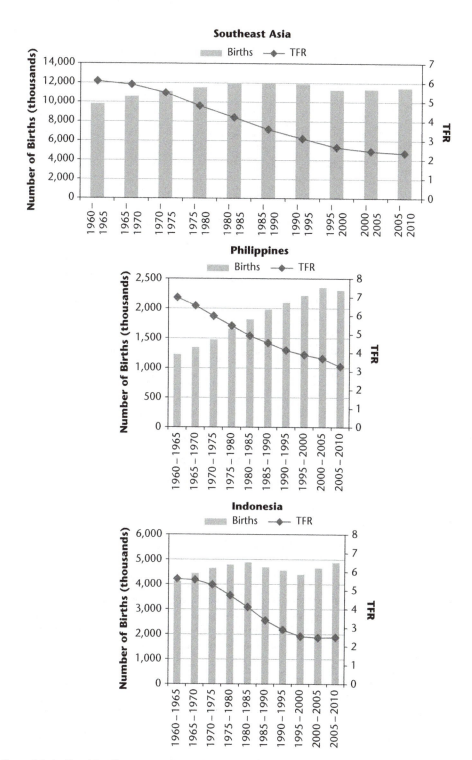

Figure 10.4 Total fertility rate and number of births (in thousands) in various Southeast Asian countries, 1960–2010

Source: United Nations Population Division, 2012.

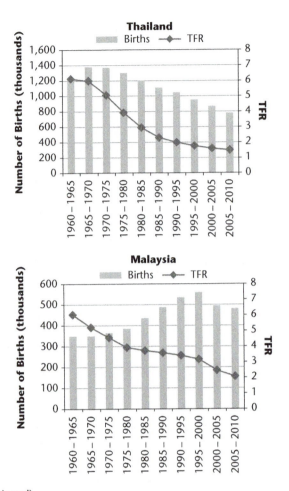

Figure 10.4 (continued)

Prospects for future population growth

Southeast Asia's population growth rate was very rapid in the 1960s and 1970s, but has fallen steadily since then (see Figure 10.5). The growth rate is currently about 1.2 per cent, enough, if continued, to double Southeast Asia's population in the next 58 years. But, of course, such a doubling will not take place, because the growth rate is trending downwards – and will reach 0.75 per cent per annum in the 2025–30 period, and lower thereafter, if the UN medium projection is followed.

Figure 10.6 presents the results of the United Nations "medium" population projections as they relate to Southeast Asian countries.[7] It portrays three key facts for each country: the total population size in 2010, represented by the width of the base line; the rate of growth projected to 2030, represented by the height of the column; and the projected absolute population increase, represented by the area of the column.

Although the greatest absolute increase in population is expected to be recorded in Indonesia, the greatest relative increase will be in Lao PDR, followed by the Philippines, Cambodia and

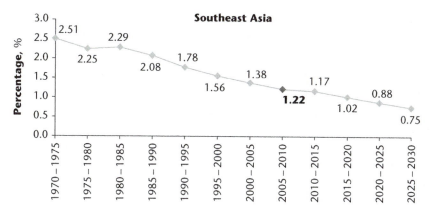

Figure 10.5   Population growth rates in Southeast Asia, 1970–75 to 2025–30
Source: United Nations Population Division, 2012, Medium Projection.

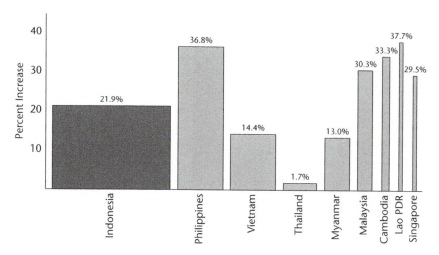

Figure 10.6   Southeast Asian countries: projected population growth, 2010–30

Malaysia. The Philippines will add 34 million to its population over this period, two-thirds as many as Indonesia will add, despite starting from a much smaller population base. Four decades ago, the Philippines and Thailand, with comparable populations, were increasing at much the same rate. The sharp divergence in both population size and prospects for future growth caused by divergent fertility trends in the two countries, already shown in Figures 10.2 and 10.3, is clearly evident in Figure 10.6.

In the context of Asia as a whole, Southeast Asia's projected population growth (126 million or 21 per cent over the 20-year period 2010–30) occupies an intermediate position. East Asia's population, dominated by China, is expected to barely increase (by 6 per cent) over the same period. But South Asia's population is projected to increase by 24 per cent, somewhat more than the projected growth in Southeast Asia. Interestingly, however, more than half the Southeast Asian countries (Lao PDR, Philippines, Malaysia, Cambodia and Timor-Leste) are expected to have faster population growth than India.

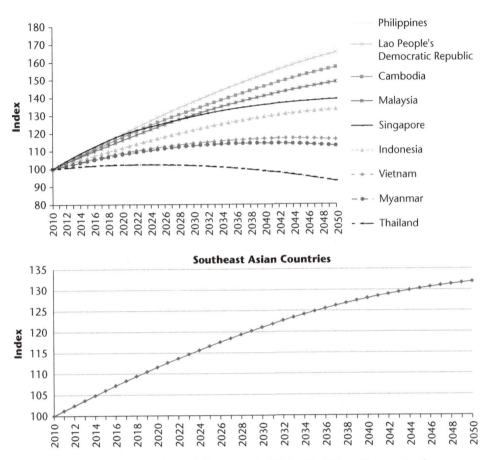

Figure 10.7 Index of projected population growth, 2010–50 – UN medium projection
Source: United Nations Population Division, 2012, Medium Projection.

Population projections are subject to considerable uncertainty, particularly beyond a 20-year time span (Scherbov et al., 2011). In the absence of unexpected wars or natural disasters, the greatest uncertainty relates to fertility trends and migration patterns. While the UN medium projection is often used as the "most likely" scenario, this is by no means certain. In the previous set of United Nations projections, even the low projection was too high in the case of Thailand (Jones and Im-Em, 2011: 4–7). In order to illustrate this uncertainty, Figures 10.7 and 10.8 show the index of population growth projected for the ASEAN countries over the 40-year period beyond 2010. Both the medium and low projections indicate a trend toward cessation of population growth in Southeast Asia towards the middle of the twenty-first century. The medium projection shows an increase of only 9 per cent between 2030 and 2050, and the low projection no increase at all. The projections show the beginning of population decline in the region by 2040 in the case of the low projection, a decline delayed until 2063 in the case of the medium projection.

For individual countries as well, there are substantial differences between the medium and low projections in the growth of population projected over the 40 years following 2010. For example, in Vietnam, the medium projection shows population growth continuing until 2044, with a total

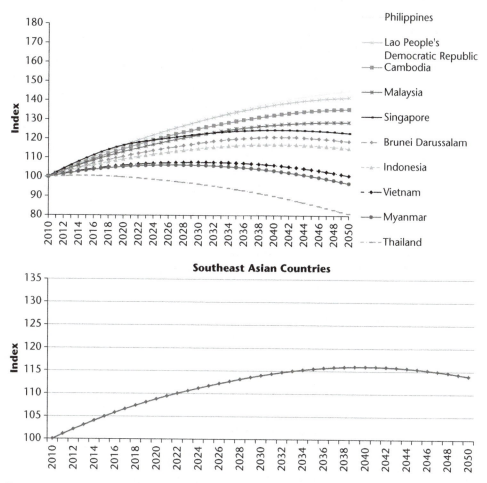

Figure 10.8 Index of projected population growth, 2010–50 – UN low projection
Source: United Nations Population Division, 2012, Low Projection.

increase of 17 per cent, after which population decline sets in. The low projection, on the other hand, shows a growth of only 8 per cent by 2031, after which population begins to decline. In the Philippines, both medium and low projections show substantial growth – an extraordinary 68 per cent in the medium projection and still growing after 2050; 45 per cent in the low projection, and on the verge of levelling off at that point.

Changing age structure and its implications

The effect of changing age structure on population growth through demographic momentum has already been discussed. In this section the changing size of different age groups within the population, and some of its implications, will be discussed. Sharp changes in fertility have led to divergent growth of different age groups as smaller cohorts move up through the age structure. Two aspects of changing age structures are much discussed, namely the ageing of the population and the "demographic dividend" (Bloom et al., 2003). But they are not the only aspects. Changes in population structure at younger ages have major implications for educational planning and manpower planning.

ASEAN has benefited greatly from the demographic dividend in recent decades. This dividend results from the steady decline in fertility rates, leading to rising proportions of the population in productive age groups. This means that output per effective consumer grows more rapidly than output per worker. Aside from Lao PDR and Cambodia, this trend has been in evidence in all ASEAN countries ever since 1970. The dependency ratio is made up of two components: the youth dependency ratio and the old age dependency ratio. These are notionally considered to be measured by the ratio of the population aged 0–14 to 15–64, and of the population aged 65+ to 15–64, respectively. Of course, these are very crude indicators, because many people continue to work beyond the age of 65, and many in the 15–64 age group are not in the workforce. What happens over the course of demographic transition is that the youth dependency ratio continuously declines as a result of fertility decline, and there is a considerable delay before the elderly dependency ratio rises very much; during this interval of 50 or so years, the total dependency ratio is falling, and this is what is referred to as the demographic dividend.

Figure 10.9 shows trends in the dependency ratio and its two components in Southeast Asia as a whole, as well as in Indonesia, Philippines, Thailand, Singapore and Vietnam. These examples cover the range of situations found in Southeast Asia. For Southeast Asia as a whole, right up to 2030, there will continue to be high proportions in the working age groups. But whereas for the Philippines, the total dependency ratio declines steadily but slowly throughout the entire period shown, in Thailand, the decline was much more rapid over the 1980s and 1990s, and the ratio is expected to start increasing after about 2015. In Singapore, the population ageing process will be very rapid, resulting in a sharper rise in the overall dependency ratio after about 2015.

As estimated by Mason and Kinugasa (2008: 394), the cumulative effect of the demographic dividend was to raise output per effective consumer between 1960 and 2000 by about 30 per cent in Thailand and 36 per cent in Singapore. Expressed differently, the demographic dividend accounted for 13.6 per cent of Singapore's GDP growth and 15.5 per cent of Thailand's GDP growth.

The population ageing process in the region is inevitable, even in the poorest countries (see Figure 10.10). Singapore and Thailand are well ahead of the other Southeast Asian countries in the population ageing process, followed by Vietnam and Indonesia. Trends in ageing in the region to date appear modest when compared with the upsurge in the proportion of elderly population that will occur from 2015 onwards. At present, no Southeast Asian country is anywhere near the levels of ageing already reached in Japan (23 per cent aged 65 and over), but Singapore will be closely approaching this level by 2030, and Thailand will be only slightly behind. Vietnam is expected to experience particularly rapid ageing in the 15 years following 2015.

Population trends in the region have been closely related to educational developments, in an interactive process. Declining fertility has facilitated increases in educational enrolment ratios; rising educational levels, in turn, have contributed to the decline in both fertility and mortality levels (Lutz, 2009; Hannum and Buchmann, 2005). The achievement of universal primary school education in Thailand, Malaysia and Indonesia was greatly assisted by the decline in fertility, and the (lagged) deceleration in growth of the school-age population. Indeed, in Thailand, the numbers entering the primary school age groups began to decline around 1980. During the 1980s they also began to decline in some Indonesian provinces, notably East Java, Bali and North Sulawesi, and in the country as a whole by the late 1980s. By contrast, the numbers entering the primary school age groups in the Philippines and Malaysia continued to rise, and although they have now more or less levelled off in Malaysia, they will rise further over the next two decades in the Philippines. Happily, in the two countries of the region with low school enrolment ratios,

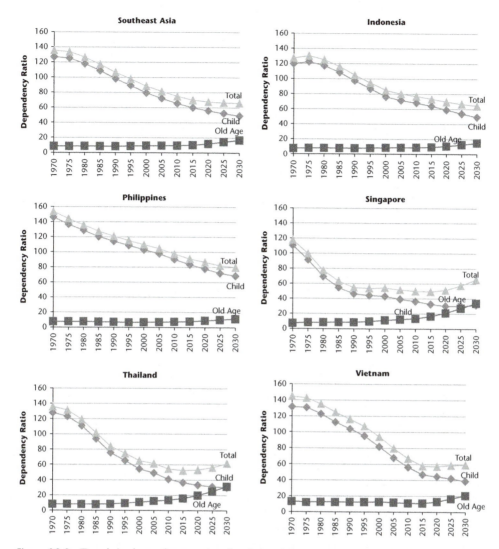

Figure 10.9 Trends in dependency ratios, Southeast Asian countries, 1970–2040
Source: United Nations Population Division, 2012, Medium Projection.

Cambodia and Lao PDR, the numbers of primary school-age children have already ceased to increase, thus easing the task of raising enrolment ratios.

There was a further lag before the numbers in the secondary school ages levelled off or decreased. This decrease began in Thailand around 1985, and in Indonesia by the early 1990s. Success in achieving universal primary school education (though the "universality" was actually only in terms of all children spending at least some time in primary school, because not all of them were completing primary school) led to an increased emphasis on raising the proportion of children being retained into junior high school and senior high school education. Figure 10.11 shows that over the past two decades, all the large countries of Southeast Asia have made substantial gains in raising the gross secondary school enrolment ratio to levels around the 80 per cent already achieved somewhat earlier by the Philippines. Such increases should in time assist

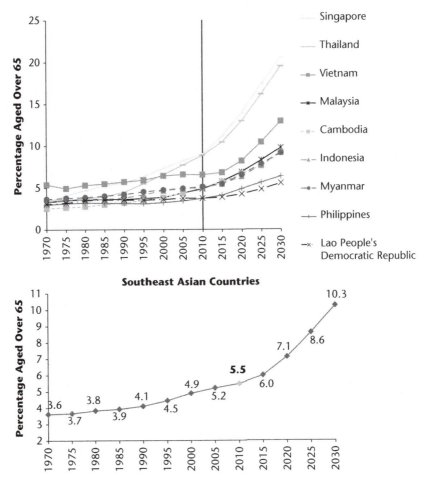

Figure 10.10 Percentage of population aged over 65, 1970–2030
Source: United Nations Population Division, 2012, Medium Projection.

in raising labour productivity. However, all countries of the region face issues of employability of their educated young people, and of quality issues in their education systems (see Suryadarma and Jones, 2013, for a comprehensive study on Indonesian education issues).

Demographic trends ensure that the working-age population in ASEAN countries will continue to grow rapidly for some time. Already, in the countries where the fertility transition has been completed, or nearly so (Singapore, Thailand, Vietnam, Malaysia, Myanmar), the high fertility "bulge" has already pushed into the middle and later working ages, where numbers are growing rapidly, though numbers in the late teenage to early thirties are already roughly constant or declining (see Figure 10.12). In the other Southeast Asian countries, too, the key functional group experiencing rapid growth over the 20-year period following 2010 will be the population in the middle to older working ages. Thus throughout the region, the working-age population is ageing, and its growth rate is slowing.

Of course, the growth of the workforce, as distinct from that of the working-age population, can be influenced by changing activity rates, especially for females. However, there appears to have been little change in female activity rates for the population aged 15–64 over the past 20 years

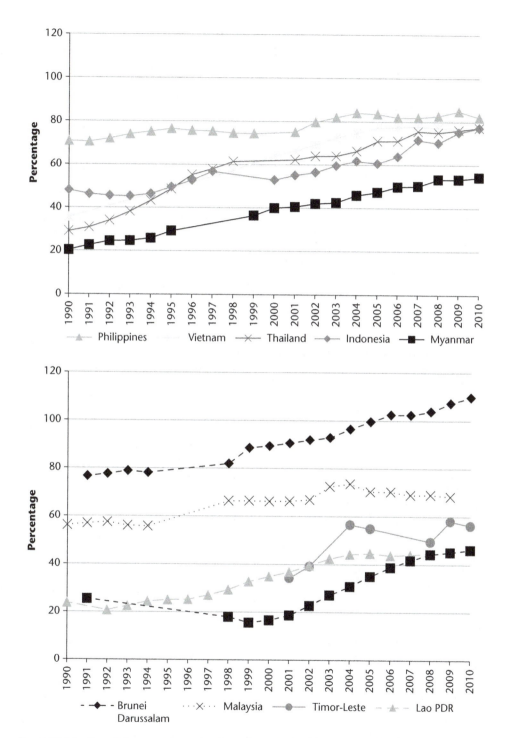

Figure 10.11 Trends in secondary school enrolment ratio (% gross), Southeast Asian countries
Source: World databank.

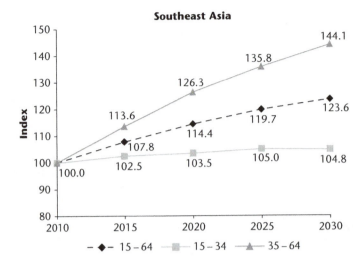

Figure 10.12 Index of projected population growth in different working age groups, 2010–30 – UN medium projection
Source: United Nations Population Division, 2012, Medium Projection.

Table 10.6 Female labour force participation rates, 1990 and 2010

Country	All ages 15–64		Ages 15–24		Ages 25–34		Ages 35–64	
	1990	*2010*	*1990*	*2010*	*1990*	*2010*	*1990*	*2010*
Indonesia	52	53	42	41	55	54	58	60
Malaysia	45	46	42	32	50	65	44	45
Myanmar	76	79	56	58	90	90	84	85
Philippines	49	51	40	36	53	55	56	60
Thailand	80	70	75	40	85	81	80	76
Vietnam	81	78	75	59	90	89	81	84

Source: ILO, Key Indicators of the Labour Market (http://www.ilo.org/empelm/what/WCMS_114240/lang-en/index.htm)

in any of the large countries of the region, except for some decline in Thailand (see Table 10.6). Declines have occurred for some countries at ages 15–24, presumably because of extended schooling. While there is little to note by way of trends, throughout the two decades Thailand, Vietnam and Myanmar have had much higher rates than Indonesia, the Philippines and Malaysia, indicating that there must be potential for the latter three countries to be making more effective use of their rapidly growing numbers of well-educated women.

Some policy issues

During the 1970s and 1980s, fertility reduction remained a key policy aim of three of the largest countries of Southeast Asia – Indonesia, Thailand and Vietnam. Malaysia moved to a pro-natalist stance in 1982 under the leadership of Mahathir Mohammad, a pro-natalism that was quietly shelved subsequently, and Philippines policy waxed and waned depending on the willingness of different administrations to take on the Catholic hierarchy over its implacable opposition to modern contraception. The two smaller Indo-Chinese countries – Cambodia and Lao PDR – took a very different stance from that of Vietnam. Although relatively high fertility rates were sources of economic and human resource development problems in both countries, the trauma of the suffering and the major population declines of the Khmer Rouge years in Cambodia, and the small population size and large land resources in Lao PDR delayed the introduction of anti-natalist policies in both countries.

The 1990s saw continuing declines in fertility rates and population growth rates, not only in Southeast Asia but across the globe, a disapproval for the setting of targets for population growth and fertility that surfaced at the International Conference on Population and Development in Cairo in 1994, and lessened international attention to issues of dealing with rapid population growth. All of these factors influenced policy in Southeast Asian countries, though planners in both Thailand and Vietnam took time to adjust to the need to modify the long-established goal of fertility reduction as fertility sank below replacement level.

Although ASEAN's fertility rate, hovering barely above replacement level, is quite satisfactory, the current level is a composite of countries with high, medium and low fertility, and fertility is less than ideal in some of the countries. From a policy point of view, countries in the region can be grouped as follows:

- Fertility too low – Singapore, Thailand
- Fertility about right – Malaysia, Myanmar, Vietnam, Brunei
- Fertility too high – Philippines, Indonesia, Cambodia, Lao PDR, Timor-Leste.

Longer-term population planning must take into account the need for fertility to settle at around replacement level, or ideally somewhat below replacement, given the continued population growth expected in Southeast Asia as a result of population momentum, and environmental and other concerns. Fertility much higher or much lower than this level over the longer run is not sustainable, unless substantial migration balances (either in- or out-) are entertained; these are likely to bring their own problems. Though both the socio-economic and cultural situation is different in ASEAN from that among the economically advanced East Asian countries, Singapore and Thailand are already in danger of entering the low-level fertility trap situation (Lutz et al., 2006; Lutz, 2008) with the problems of redressing over-low fertility. The key need is to devise policies that will support the aspirations of women to combine careers and childbearing. Educational levels of women have risen rapidly, and throughout the region, educated women are bearing the brunt of family-unfriendly policies and workplaces, requiring them to make difficult decisions about their key aspirations in life. It is noteworthy that European countries with high levels of female labour force participation are among the highest-fertility countries in Europe, because they have developed a socio-economic-familial system that facilitates the raising of children while both partners are working.

While Singapore and Thailand are increasingly worried about low fertility, the Philippines has reason to be concerned about its continuing relatively high fertility. Recent relatively rapid fertility declines in both Cambodia and Lao PDR might leave the Philippines as the highest-fertility country in the region, except for the minnow of Timor-Leste. The Philippines has high population density, serious land tenure issues, relatively high unemployment rates, high levels of poverty and inequality, and a history of sluggish economic growth. It remains a basically well-educated population, providing the human resource base for development if only economic and social policy can be appropriately reformed. Happily, the past few years have seen an encouraging improvement in economic growth rates. In order to set the scene for continued economic growth, a policy to reduce fertility rates, based on widespread provision, on a voluntary basis, of a range of effective family planning methods, would seem to be an essential component of the economic and social policy "mix". Yet it was only at the end of 2012 that the "Responsible Parenthood and Reproductive Health Act" was enacted after first being filed in Congress 13 years earlier. The role of the Catholic hierarchy in blocking this for so long places the Philippines in a unique position compared with the Catholic countries of Europe and Latin America, where the Church's influence on government policy and the contraceptive practice of the population appears to have been much more limited. Even so, as Hull (2012: 46–8) and McNicoll (2006: 19) remind us, it would be inappropriate to attribute the delayed fertility decline in the Philippines solely to the influence of the Catholic church.

Since the Cairo Conference, the reproductive health approach has drawn attention more to the individual needs of people than to demographic targets. However, effective reproductive health programmes, an important component of which is to meet unmet need for contraception, will certainly impact fertility. Women with unmet need for family planning are defined as sexually active women of reproductive age who desire to avoid or postpone childbearing but are not using any method of contraception. For South and Southeast Asia as a whole, unmet need has fallen from 18 per cent in 1990–95 to 11 per cent in 2000–05. This is encouraging, but the evidence that rates of induced abortion are quite high in Southeast Asia (and not only as a result of pregnancies to unmarried women) underlines the further gains in welfare that can be made by meeting unmet need for contraception. About 28 per cent of pregnancies in Southeast Asia end in abortion (Singh et al., 2009), and a substantial proportion of these are unsafe abortions. A further controversial issue in almost all ASEAN countries concerns the provision of contraceptive services and advice to the unmarried. With increasingly delayed marriage, large numbers of single women are in need of family planning services, and not only the teenagers who tend to be the focus of controversy.

The projected trends in ageing in the region will need continuing attention from planners. The decline in ageing support ratios (population 20–64/population 65+) will be particularly sharp over the decade from 2010 to 2020 in Singapore, and in the decade of the 2020s in Thailand. In the 20 years between 2010 and 2030, the ageing support ratio will halve in Malaysia. At sub-regional level, migration patterns may be creating pockets – particularly in rural areas – where the proportion of elderly is much higher. Such trends will require major adjustments of policies with regard to income support programmes, reorientation of health services, and labour market policy, including retirement ages. It will also require a rethinking of the underlying foundation for policies throughout the region, the belief that families can and should play the key role in supporting their elderly members.

Family support for the elderly can notionally be divided into three categories: financial assistance, emotional support and physical support. The first two of these do not require co-residence, particularly in the age of the cell phone. However, for three reasons, there will be less possibility of the family providing intensive care for disabled or frail elderly. These reasons are the lowered proportion of children per elderly person, the increased labour force participation of women (the traditional carers) and the movement of children to other localities. These trends have major implications for policy on elder care. Despite the tradition in Asian families of caring for family members in various kinds of need, this traditional reliance on family will be subjected to intense pressures. Governments will almost inevitably be forced to step in.

The care needs of the elderly should not be exaggerated. The great majority of the elderly do not need care; for example, in Thailand, more than 80 per cent of those in their seventies and even 65 per cent of those aged over 80, say that they can care for themselves (Knodel and Chayovan 2011: table 1). The positive contributions made by the elderly in society and family, for example through taking care of grandchildren and through serving as mentors and confidants of their grandchildren as they enter adolescence, need to be recognized and supported. Moreover, ageing does not pose the same urgency that it does in East Asian countries. There is still time to develop effective social security systems, community programmes and adaptations at the household level.

Given the rising proportion of the elderly, there is a need to develop appropriate income maintenance systems (Park, 2011; Asher, 2012). The key problem is that until average income in a country reaches a certain level, and until most workers are in formal sector employment, it is difficult to put in place comprehensive income support schemes. The coverage of pension schemes in the region is skewed towards urban areas and the formal sector, especially the government sector – or, in other words, the better-off sections of the population – and except in Singapore and Malaysia (the only countries in the region approaching universal coverage), the schemes are mainly pay-as-you-go schemes. Thus a major section of the labour force is not covered at all (coverage is less that 30 per cent in the Philippines and Thailand; less than 20 per cent in Indonesia and Vietnam (Park and Estrada, 2012: figure 1.11), and those covered cannot always be sure that the pension system will be able to honour its promises. With a rising proportion of elderly in the population, all countries are looking to improve their income support schemes, but progress to date has been modest.

One brighter aspect of ageing in the region in the context of rising individual incomes is the possible benefit to be derived from the "second demographic dividend". As noted by Mason and Kinugasa (2008), there are many ways in which changes in mortality and life expectancy could influence savings rates. They conclude (p. 398) that

> The widespread presumption that population ageing is bad for economic growth is unwarranted. … (For) countries that encourage capital accumulation as a means of meeting retirement needs, aging can serve as a fundamental force for creating a wealthier and more prosperous society.

In the interest of deriving maximum benefit from the demographic dividend, the ASEAN countries need to be devoting more resources to the education and health sectors. In competition with the giants of Asia – China and India – ASEAN has to raise the quality of its human capital, and attention is needed at all levels of the education system. In the health sector, too, levels of infant and maternal mortality are still high in some ASEAN member states. There are two issues here: first, whether a sufficient share of budgetary resources is being devoted to education and health, and second, whether ways can be found to make more effective use of these resources.

There are many problematic aspects of international migration in the region, and an urgent need for a regional agreement dealing with such issues. With regard to labour migration, there are underlying push and pull factors that policy must take into account. The wealthier Southeast Asian countries will inevitably be magnets, as will countries outside the region – Japan, South Korea and Taiwan, not to mention the Gulf States, Europe and the USA. The middle-income countries of the region – Malaysia and Thailand – are experiencing in and out movements, but the net effect of migration patterns in both countries is to lower their average level of human capital.[8] Malaysia has introduced policies to attract back skilled emigrants, but the variety of reasons for their emigration in the first place, in many cases related as much to dissatisfaction with ethnic policies in Malaysia as to purely economic considerations, does not bode well for such policies. Malaysia and Thailand face important issues regarding the provision of education for the children of undocumented migrants. All Southeast Asian countries need policies to prevent abuse of domestic workers, many of whom are international migrants.

Greater labour mobility in the region, guided by appropriate laws and regulations, could be of benefit to all countries (Chia, 2008). Remittances are very important for the economies of the major migrant-sending counties, especially the Philippines but also Indonesia, Myanmar,

Cambodia and Laos. Policies to facilitate the utilization of remittances for productive purposes need to be prioritized.

With regard to the continuing urbanization of Southeast Asia, and the appropriate stance to adopt toward the growth of mega-urban regions, urban planners in the region will need to ponder a World Bank study (World Bank, 2009) which makes the case for a positive view of urban agglomeration, arguing that spatial concentration of economic activity rises with development, and that governments should not resist it by seeking to target investment and policy attention to the lagging areas of their countries. Instead they should adopt a neutral stance on the location of development activities, but make judicious investments in transport and communications which will enable disadvantaged areas to become connected to the centres of growth. "The challenge for government is to allow – even encourage – 'unbalanced' economic growth, and yet to ensure inclusive development" (p. 20) through a "well-calibrated blend of institutions, infrastructure and interventions" (p. 6).

Intermediate cities are now tending to grow more rapidly than the largest cities. This conclusion holds, except in the case of Manila, even when appropriate urban agglomeration populations are used for these large cities (see Jones and Douglass, 2008: 56); but planning for intermediate cities certainly receives less attention. In both Indonesia and the Philippines, regional autonomy means that the planning mechanism for intermediate cities needs to integrate national-level planning, dealing with the overall planning design for the nation's urban areas, with local-level planning that takes into account particular circumstances and the resources available at the local level. As for the mega-urban regions (Jakarta and Manila in particular), there is an urgent need for planning mechanisms that enable the interests of a range of administrations (national, provincial, district and sub-district) to be balanced in planning for these highly populous regions that cut across different administrative jurisdictions.

Conclusion

The changing population of Southeast Asia is both fascinating, because of the diversity of situations, and challenging, because population dynamics will influence the well-being of the populations concerned. The diversity is well illustrated by the fertility rate. Although about half of the ASEAN countries share ASEAN's overall ideal fertility level, some do not – most notably the Philippines and Singapore. When we broaden the discussion from fertility policy to reproductive health policy, none of the ASEAN countries can be fully satisfied with their situation, because none of them can claim that their populations have access to a varied mix of contraceptive services, adequate counselling (especially for adolescents and the unmarried), and adequate reproductive health services. And while the region has made great gains in lowering mortality rates, both infant and maternal mortality remain a serious concern in some countries.

The concern of a few decades ago – rapid population growth – has been replaced by a sanguine attitude to population trends, based on the evidence that fertility has fallen everywhere in the region and is likely to fall further. Nevertheless, we cannot be certain how low fertility is likely to go in countries such as Vietnam and Malaysia, and in the largest country of the region – Indonesia – fertility has fallen only marginally over the past decade and remains above replacement level. Nevertheless, the odds are on further fertility declines, and a decade from now, other countries may be joining Singapore and Thailand in searching for policies to raise fertility rates.

In a world of low population growth in Southeast Asia, greater attention is likely to be given to migration, both internal and international. Internal migration will continue to redistribute population from rural to urban areas, and from regions of lesser to greater economic opportunity. International migration, likewise, will be directed towards the more favoured countries of the region, be it in the form of temporary labour migration (skilled or unskilled), undocumented movements or marriage migration. Ethnic heterogeneity of countries or sub-national areas is likely to be increased by such migratory movements.

Finally, the conventional wisdom in many quarters is that the emerging giants of the twenty-first century are China and India. Southeast Asia lacks a "giant", and even if ASEAN succeeds in giving these countries some demographic ballast in the geo-political sphere, it will still remain subsidiary to the main game. In terms of the demographic bonus, though, Southeast Asia is in a strong position relative to both China (which faces a declining labour force and rapid ageing) and India (where continuing labour force growth cannot be fully utilized for development because of deficiencies in its education system and hence failure to build its human capital base). If Southeast Asia can capitalize on its advantages, it can well play an important role in the "Asian century".

Acknowledgement

The author acknowledges the valuable research assistance of Cynthia Lai Uin Rue.

Notes

1 The uncertainty is overlooked in most discussions of population in the region. It stems from incomplete census counts, as revealed by post-enumeration surveys, and the difficulty of enumerating the substantial number of undocumented international migrants in countries such as Malaysia and Thailand.
2 Some of the best treatments of this historical growth can be found in Zelinsky, 1950; Nitisastro, 1970; Peper, 1970; Reid, 1987; Hugo et al., 1987; Owen, 1987; Doeppers and Xenos, 1998; Van Landingham and Hirschman, 2001; Henley, 2005; Hirschman and Bonaparte, 2012.
3 Population density of Southeast Asia is nearly identical to that of China. But if the western and north-western provinces of Tibet, Xinjiang, Qinghai and Inner Mongolia are excluded, population density in China rises sharply.
4 Declines in total fertility rates (TFR) from 5.5 to 2.2 took only 15 years in Singapore (1960–75), and 20 years in Thailand (1970–90). The only declines in the world to match these in speed were in Iran (15 years, 1986–2001) and China (21 years, 1969–90).
5 The government of Myanmar did not declare any official population policy and formerly restricted access to contraceptives, though many were smuggled in from neighbouring Thailand and Bangladesh. In the late 1990s, it did begin a birth spacing programme, the reach of which was limited both geographically and in availability of particular methods (Ministry of Health and UNFPA, 1999: 35). Myanmar also remained poorer than many of its neighbours. Nevertheless, the pace of fertility decline in Myanmar matched that of the much-heralded decline in Indonesia, and fertility rates continued to decline to levels well below those in the Philippines and Malaysia (see Figure 10.1).
6 The UN projections actually understate the speed of fertility decline in the most recent period; therefore population growth can be expected to cease earlier than the UN projected, even in its low projection, and after a smaller increase. See Jones and Im-Em (2011: 4).
7 Note that in Figure 10.6, Brunei Darussalam and Timor-Leste have been omitted. Their populations are too tiny (totalling 0.3 per cent of Southeast Asia's population) to show up in the figure. In some later figures as well, Timor-Leste has been omitted. This is because its trends are so different from other countries that including it in the figures requires use of a scale that obscures differences between the larger countries.
8 For example, while comprehensive data are not available, the average educational level of emigrants from Malaysia is very high (see Hugo, 2012), while most of those moving in permanently – for example, from Indonesia and the Philippines to Sabah – have much lower educational levels.

Bibliography

Asher, M.K., 2012, "Social pensions for the elderly in Asia: fiscal costs and financing methods", in S.W. Handayani and B. Babajanian (eds), *Social Protection for Older Persons: Social Pensions in Asia*, Manila: Asian Development Bank.

Bloom, David E., David Canning and Jaypee Sevilla, 2003, *The Demographic Dividend: A New Perspective on the Economic Consequences of Change*, Santa Monica, CA: RAND Corporation.

Bongaarts, John, 1997, "The role of family planning programmes in contemporary fertility transitions", in Gavin W. Jones et al. (eds), *The Continuing Demographic Transition*, Oxford: Clarendon Press.

Bryant, John, 2007, "Theories of fertility decline and the evidence from development indicators", *Population and Development Review*, 33(1): 101–27.

Chia Siow Yue, 2008, "Demographic change and international labour mobility in Southeast Asia: issues, policies and implications for cooperation", in Graeme Hugo and Soogil Young (eds), *Labour Mobility in the Asia-Pacific Region: Dynamics, Issues and a New APEC Agenda*, Singapore: Institute of Southeast Asian Studies.

Desbarats, Jacqueline, 1987, "Population redistribution in the Socialist Republic of Vietnam", *Population and Development Review*, 13(1): 43–76.

Doeppers, Daniel F. and Peter Xenos (eds), 1998, *Population and History: The Demographic Origins of the Modern Philippines*, Monograph No. 16, Center for Southeast Asian Studies, University of Wisconsin.

Hannum, Emily and Claudia Buchmann, 2005, "Global educational expansion and socio-economic development: an assessment of findings from the social sciences", *World Development*, 33(3): 333–54.

Hardjono, J., 1989, "The Indonesian transmigration program in historical perspective", *International Migration*, 26: 427–39.

Henley, David, 2005, "Population and the means of subsistence: explaining the historical demography of island Southeast Asia, with particular reference to Sulawesi", *Journal of Southeast Asian Studies*, 36: 337–72.

Hirschman, Charles and Yih-Jin Young, 2000, "Social context and fertility decline in Southeast Asia: 1968–70 to 1988–90", in C.Y. Cyrus Chu and Ronald Lee (eds), *Population and Economic Change in East Asia, supplement to Population and Development Review*, Vol. 26.

Hirschman, Charles and Sabrina Bonaparte, 2012, "Population and society in Southeast Asia: a historical perspective", in Lindy Williams and Michael Philip Guest (eds), *Demographic Change in Southeast Asia: Recent Histories and Future Directions*, Ithaca, NY: Cornell Southeast Asia Program Publications.

Hugo, Graeme, 2012, "Changing patterns of population mobility in Southeast Asia", in Lindy Williams and Michael Philip Guest (eds), *Demographic Change in Southeast Asia: Recent Histories and Future Directions*, Ithaca, NY: Cornell Southeast Asia Program Publications.

Hugo, Graeme, Terence Hull, Valerie Hull and Gavin Jones, 1987, *The Demographic Dimension in Indonesian Development*, Kuala Lumpur: Oxford University Press.

Hull, Terence H., 2012, "Fertility in Southeast Asia", in Lindy Williams and Michael Philip Guest (eds), *Demographic Change in Southeast Asia: Recent Histories and Future Directions*, Ithaca, NY: Cornell Southeast Asia Program Publications.

Hull, Terence H. and Valerie J. Hull, 1997, "Politics, culture and fertility transitions in Indonesia", in Gavin W. Jones, Robert Douglas, John C. Caldwell and Rennie D'Souza (eds), *The Continuing Demographic Transition*, Oxford: Clarendon Press.

Jones, Gavin W., 1990, "Fertility transitions among Malay populations of Southeast Asia: puzzles of interpretation", *Population and Development Review*, 16(3): 507–37.

Jones, Gavin W., 1997, "The thoroughgoing urbanization of East and Southeast Asia", *Asia Pacific Viewpoint*, 38(3): 237–49.

Jones, Gavin W., 2007, "Fertility decline in Asia: the role of marriage change", *Asia-Pacific Population Journal*, 22(2): 13–32.

Jones, Gavin W., 2012, "International marriage in Asia: What do we know, and what do we need to know?" in Doo-Sub Kim (ed.), *Cross-Border Marriage: Global Trends and Diversity*, Seoul: KIHASA.

Jones, Gavin W. and Mike Douglass, 2008, *Mega Urban Regions in Pacific Asia: Urban Dynamics in a Global Era*, Singapore: NUS Press.

Jones, Gavin W. and Wassana Im-Em (eds), 2011, *Impact of Demographic Change in Thailand*, Bangkok: NESDB and UNFPA.

Knodel, John and Chanpen Saengtienchai, 2007, "Rural parents with urban children: social and economic implications of migration on the rural elderly in Thailand", *Population, Space and Place*, 13(3): 193–210.

Knodel, John and Napaporn Chayovan, 2011, "Intergenerational family care for and by older people in Thailand", paper presented to the Conference on Shifting Boundaries of Care Provision in Asia: Policy and Practice Changes, Asia Research Institute, National University of Singapore, 14–15 March.

Knodel, John, Apichat Chamratrithirong and Nibhon Debavalya, 1987, *Thailand's Reproductive Revolution: Rapid Fertility Decline in a Third World Setting*, Madison: University of Wisconsin Press.

Lutz, Wolfgang, 2008, "Has Korea's fertility reached the bottom? The hypothesis of a 'low fertility trap' in parts of Europe and East Asia", *Asian Population Studies*, 4(1): 1–4.

Lutz, Wolfgang, 2009. "*Sola schola et sanitate*: human capital as the root cause and priority for international development?" *Philosophical Transactions of the Royal Society B*, 364: 3031–47.

Lutz, Wolfgang, V. Skirbekk and M.R. Testa, 2006, "The low fertility trap hypothesis: forces that may lead to further postponement and fewer births in Europe", in D. Philipov, A.C. Liefbroer and F.C. Billari (eds), *Vienna Yearbook of Population Research*, Vienna: Vienna Institute of Demography.

McGee, T.G., 1967, *The Southeast Asian City: A Social Geography of the Primate Cities of Southeast Asia*, London: Bell.

McNicoll, Geoffrey, 2006, "Policy lessons of the East Asian demographic transition", *Population and Development Review*, 32(1): 1–25.

Mason, Andrew and Tomoko Kinugasa, 2008, "East Asian economic development: two demographic dividends", *Journal of Asian Economics*, 19: 389–99.

Ministry of Health, Union of Myanmar, and UNFPA, 1999, *A Reproductive Health Needs Assessment in Myanmar*, Yangon.

Nitisastro, Widjojo, 1970, *Population Trends in Indonesia*, Ithaca, NY: Cornell University Press.

Owen, Norman, 1987, "The paradox of nineteenth-century population growth in Southeast Asia: evidence from Java and the Philippines", *Journal of Southeast Asian Studies*, 18: 45–57.

Park, Donghyun (ed.), 2011, *Pension System and Old Age Income Support in East and Southeast Asia*, London: Routledge.

Park, Donghyun and Gemma B. Estrada, 2012, "Developing Asia's pension systems and old-age income support", ADBI Working Paper Series No. 358, Tokyo: Asian Development Bank Institute.

Peper, Bram, 1970, "Population growth in Java in the nineteenth century", *Population Studies*, 24: 71–84.

Phillips, James F. and John A. Ross, 1992, *Family Planning Programmes and Fertility*, Oxford: Oxford University Press.

Pritchett, L.H., 1994, "Desired fertility and the impact of population policies", *Population and Development Review*, 20(1): 1–55.

Reid, Anthony, 1987,"Low population growth and its causes in pre-colonial Southeast Asia", in Norman G. Owen (ed.), *Death and Disease in Southeast Asia: Explorations in Social, Medical, and Demographic History*, Singapore: Oxford University Press.

Robinson, Warren C. and John A. Ross (eds), 2007, *The Global Family Planning Revolution: Three Decades of Population Policies and Programs*, Washington, DC: World Bank.

Scherbov, S., W. Lutz and W.C. Sanderson, 2011, "The uncertain timing of reaching 8 billion, peak world population and other demographic milestones", *Population and Development Review*, 37(3): 571–8.

Singh, Susheela, Deirdre Wulf, Rubina Hussain, Akinrinola Bankole and Gilda Sedgh, 2009, *Abortion Worldwide: A Decade of Uneven Progress*, New York: Guttmacher Institute.

Suryadarma, Daniel and Gavin Jones (eds), 2013, *Education in Indonesia*, Singapore: Institute of Southeast Asian Studies.

Suryadinata, Leo, Evi Nurvidya Arifin and Aris Ananta, 2003, *Indonesia's Population: Ethnicity and Religion in a Changing Political Landscape*, Singapore: Institute of Southeast Asian Studies.

United Nations Population Division, 2010, *World Population Prospects: The 2010 Revision*, New York: United Nations.

United Nations Population Division, 2012, *World Population Prospects: The 2012 Revision*, New York: United Nations.

United Nations Population Division, 2014, *World Urbanization Prospects: The 2014 Revision*, New York: United Nations.

UNFPA, UNICEF, WHO, World Bank, 2012, *Trends in Maternal Mortality 1990 to 2010*, New York: United Nations.

Van Landingham, Mark and Charles Hirschman, 2001, "Population pressure and fertility in pre-transition Thailand", *Population Studies*, 55: 233–48.

Williams, Lindy and Michael Philip Guest (eds), 2012, *Demographic Change in Southeast Asia: Recent Histories and Future Directions*, Ithaca, NY: Cornell Southeast Asia Studies Program.

World Bank, 2009, *World Development Report 2009: Reshaping Economic Geography*, Washington, DC: World Bank.

Zelinsky, Wilbur, 1950, "The Indochinese Peninsula: a demographic anomaly", *Far Eastern Quarterly*, 9: 115–45.

11

The determinants and long-term projections of saving rates in Southeast Asia

Charles Yuji Horioka

ASIAN GROWTH RESEARCH INSTITUTE; OSAKA UNIVERSITY; AND NATIONAL BUREAU OF ECONOMIC RESEARCH

Akiko Terada-Hagiwara

ASIAN DEVELOPMENT BANK

Introduction

Southeast Asia has, in general, been characterized by high domestic and national savings rates almost across the board in recent years, and these high saving rates have made possible high levels of domestic investment but have also led to large capital outflows (current account surpluses) (see, for example, the data presented in Park and Shin 2009). To put it another way, Southeast Asia has oversaved and underinvested, leading to large current account imbalances (surpluses), as asserted by Bernanke (2005) and others.

The purpose of this chapter is to present data on trends over time in domestic saving rates in 12 economies in developing Asia during the period 1966–2007 and to analyze the determinants of those trends. We then use our estimation results to explain past trends in domestic saving rates in Southeast Asia and to project future trends up to 2030. The six Southeast Asian economies included in our analysis are Indonesia, Malaysia, the Philippines, Singapore, Thailand, and Vietnam. Six other Asian economies included in the analysis are the People's Republic of China (hereafter PRC); Hong Kong, China; India; Republic of Korea (hereafter Korea); Pakistan; and Taipei, China, which together with the six Southeast Asian economies comprise 95 percent of the GDP of developing Asia.

We use the domestic saving rate (which comprises household saving, corporate saving, and government saving) as the dependent variable in our analysis, in part because it is the total saving of the economy as a whole that matters for many purposes (such as for external imbalances) and in part because data on domestic saving are much more readily available than data on the saving of each sector.

This chapter contributes to the literature in several respects. First, it presents and compares data on both nominal and real domestic saving rates, even though few past studies have looked at real rates despite their importance. Second, it examines the nonlinear impact of financial sector development on the saving rate, which is particularly relevant for our sample of countries. Finally, it generates long-term projections based on the estimation results.

This chapter is organized as follows: in the next section, we present our estimation model of the determinants of domestic saving rates. We then discuss past trends in domestic saving rates and in the determinants thereof in developing Asia, followed by the empirical results concerning the determinants of domestic saving rates in developing Asia. We then discuss our future projections of domestic saving rates in developing Asia before concluding.

To summarize the main findings of this chapter, we find that domestic saving rates in developing Asia have, in general, been high and rising but that there have been substantial differences from economy to economy, that the main determinants of the domestic saving rate in developing Asia during the 1960–2007 period appear to have been the age structure of the population (especially the aged dependency ratio), income levels, and the level of financial sector development, that the direction of impact of each factor has been more or less as expected, and that the impacts of income levels and the level of financial sector development are nonlinear (convex and concave, respectively).

We also find that the domestic saving rate in Southeast Asia will decline over the next two decades because the negative impact of population aging thereon will more than offset the positive impact of higher income levels but that there will be substantial variation from economy to economy, with the rapidly aging economies showing a sharp decline in their domestic saving rates from the start and Vietnam showing an increase in its domestic saving rate until 2020 because the positive impact of higher income levels will more than offset the negative impact of population aging.

Estimation model of the determinants of domestic saving rates

In this section, we discuss the estimation model we will use in our econometric analysis of the determinants of domestic saving rates in developing Asia. There have been many previous empirical analyses of the determinants of saving rates using cross–section or panel cross–country data or time series data for individual countries, among them Modigliani (1970), Feldstein (1977, 1980), Modigliani and Sterling (1983), Horioka (1989), Edwards (1996), Dayal–Ghulati and Thimann (1997), Bailliu and Reisen (1998), Higgins (1998), Loayza, et al. (2000), Chinn and Prasad (2003), Luhrman (2003), International Monetary Fund (2005), Bosworth and Chodorow–Reich (2007), Kim and Lee (2008), Park and Shin (2009), and Hung and Qian (2010), and a smaller number of studies that conduct similar analyses of the determinants of current account balances, among them Chinn and Ito (2007, 2008) and Ito and Chinn (2009). The present study is based most closely on Higgins (1998), Bosworth and Chodorow–Reich (2007), and Park and Shin (2009).

These studies suggest an important role for demographic variables based on the life cycle model. Looking first at the impact of the age structure of the population, since the aged typically finance their living expenses by drawing down their previously accumulated savings, the aged dependency ratio (the ratio of the aged population to the working–age population) should have a negative impact on the saving rate, and similarly, since children typically consume without earning income, the youth dependency ratio (the ratio of children to the working–age population) should also have a negative impact on the saving rate. Moreover, a higher youth dependency ratio means more children to provide care and financial assistance during old age and thus less need to save on one's own for old age, and hence the youth dependency ratio could have a negative impact on the saving rate for this reason as well. Park and Shin (2009) and most other studies find that the aged dependency ratio and the youth dependency ratio both decrease the saving rate, as expected.

One would expect the age structure of the population to influence primarily the household saving rate, but we use the real domestic saving rate as the dependent variable in our analysis for the reasons noted earlier. Note, however, that household saving comprises a sizable share of domestic saving and that, even though corporate saving has exceeded household saving in most economies in recent years, corporate saving can be regarded as part of household saving if households are assumed to see through the corporate veil (see Matsubayashi and Fujii (2012) for evidence that corporate saving is at least partly a substitute for household saving and Horioka and Terada–Hagiwara (2014) for an analysis of corporate saving in Asia). For all of these reasons, the domestic saving rate is a good proxy for the household saving rate.

A high growth rate of real GDP is another important factor, creating a virtuous cycle in which rapid income growth makes it easy to save, and high saving feeds back through capital accumulation to promote further growth. Bosworth and Chodorow–Reich (2007) as well as Park and Shin (2009) find that both contemporaneous and lagged real per capita GDP growth rates increase the saving rate. Moreover, Park and Shin (2009) also find that the level of per capita income has a significant nonlinear or more precisely convex relationship with the saving rate in Asia, but Bosworth and Chodorow-Reich (2007) do not find a significant effect.

Aside from demographic and GDP–related variables, financial sector development is also considered to be a crucial determinant of saving rates, but the direction of its impact is both theoretically and empirically ambiguous. Wang et al.'s (2011) theoretical analysis of the impact of financial sector development on the saving rate finds that, if both households and firms are subject to financial friction and if financial sector development occurs first in the corporate sector and then spreads to the household sector (a likely scenario), then financial sector development will have a hump–shaped impact on the saving rate, initially increasing the saving rate by increasing firms' ability to borrow and invest but then reducing the saving rate by weakening the precautionary saving incentives of households. Turning to empirical studies, Loayza, et al. (2000) find that financial sector development has a negative impact on the saving rate, Park and Shin (2009) find that its impact is insignificant, and Wang et al. (2011) find a hump–shaped relationship. By contrast, anecdotal evidence suggests that relaxing financial constraints by increasing the availability of saving instruments and accessibility to banks may promote *higher* saving, as argued by Chinn and Prasad (2003) and Jha et al. (2009). Thus, both the theoretical and empirical literature suggests the possibility of a nonlinear relationship between financial sector development and the saving rate, and this chapter investigates this possibility.

Finally, the real interest rate should, in theory, have an impact on the saving rate although the direction of its impact is theoretically ambiguous.

Thus, the reduced form estimating equation we will estimate is as follows:

$$SR_{i,t} = \beta_{0,i} + \beta_1 * AGE_{i,t} + \beta_2 * DEP_{i,t} + \beta_3 * LNGDP_{i,t} + \beta_4 * LNGDPSQ_{i,t}$$
$$+ \beta_5 * CREDIT_{i,t} + \beta_6 * CREDITSQ_{i,t} + \beta_7 * X_{i,t} + u_{i,t}$$

where i = 1, … 12 (1 = PRC, 2 = Hong Kong, China, 3 = Indonesia, 4 = India, 5 = Korea, 6 = Malaysia, 7 = Pakistan, 8 = Philippines, 9 = Singapore, 10 = Thailand, 11 = Taipei, China, and 12 = Vietnam); and t = 1, … 8 (1 = 1966–70, 2 = 1971–75, 3 = 1976–80, 4 = 1981–85, 5 = 1986–90, 6 = 1991–95, 7 = 1996–2000, and 8 = 2001–07).

$SR_{i,t}$ represents the real domestic saving rate in country i at time t; $AGE_{i,t}$ is the aged dependency ratio (the ratio of the population aged 65 or older to the population aged 15–64); $DEP_{i,t}$ is a youth dependency ratio (the ratio of the population aged 14 or younger to the population aged 15–64); $LNGDP_{i,t}$ is the log of per capita real GDP; $LNGDPSQ_{i,t}$ is the square of $LNGDP_{i,t}$, $CREDIT_{i,t}$ is the ratio of private credit from deposit money banks and other financial institutions to GDP; $CREDITSQ_{i,t}$ is the square of $CREDIT_{i,t}$, and $X_{i,t}$ is a vector of the other explanatory variables included in the estimation model. $\beta_{0,i}$ is a constant plus country fixed effects when a fixed effects model is estimated. In addition, in some variants, we include $CHGDP_{i,t}$, the growth rate of real per capita GDP, and/or $RINT_{i,t}$, the real interest rate.

In addition, we also try using one–period lags of variables relating to $LNGDP_{i,t}$, $CREDIT_{i,t}$, and $CHGDP_{i,t}$ in lieu of contemporaneous values because these variables are endogenous and thus using lagged values would alleviate simultaneity bias.

Refer to Appendix Table 11.A1 for the variable definitions and data sources and to Table 11. A2 for descriptive statistics.

Past trends in domestic saving rates in developing Asia

In this section, we discuss past trends in the domestic saving rate and in the determinants thereof in the 12 developing Asian economies in our sample. First, in Figure 11.1 and Table 11.1, we present data on past trends in both the nominal as well as real domestic saving rates for each of the 12 developing Asian economies in our sample for each five–year subperiod during the 1966–2001 period and for the most recent period, which includes the years from 2001 to 2007.

Nominal domestic saving rates are computed as the ratio of gross domestic saving to gross domestic product (both measured in current local currency units) and are taken from the *World*

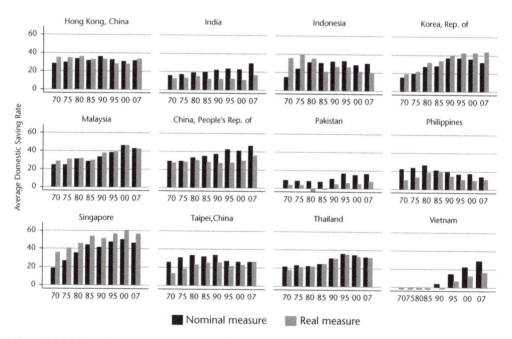

Figure 11.1 Trends over time in domestic saving rates in developing Asia, 1966–2007

Sources: Data on gross domestic saving rates were taken from World Development Indicators of the World Bank, and data on net domestic saving rates were taken from Penn World Tables (PWT), version 6.3.

Notes: Gross domestic saving rates were computed as gross domestic savings (current LCU) divided by GDP (current LCU), while net domestic saving rates were computed as 100 – kc – kg, where "kc" is the consumption share of real GDP per capita and "kg" is the government share of real GDP per capita. "70" denotes the average for 1966–70, "75" the average for 1971–75, "80" the average for 1976–80, "85" the average for 1981–85, "90" the average for 1986–90, "95" the average for 1991–95, "00" the average for 1996–2000, and "07" the average for 2001–07.

Table 11.1 Trends over time in gross domestic saving rates in developing Asia

Nominal measure

	1966–70	1971–75	1976–80	1981–85	1986–90	1991–95	1996–2000	2001–07	Average
PRC	28.9	29.1	33.0	34.8	37.0	41.9	40.7	46.2	37.8
Hong Kong, China	28.2	29.4	33.5	31.6	36.0	32.6	30.4	31.5	31.6
Indonesia	14.3	23.9	30.8	30.1	31.9	32.4	28.1	29.9	27.8
India	15.5	16.7	18.7	19.4	21.9	23.0	22.4	29.0	22.2
Korea, Rep. of	15.2	19.0	27.0	27.8	36.5	36.4	35.6	31.8	28.8
Malaysia	24.3	24.2	31.1	28.1	33.3	37.8	45.8	42.6	33.4
Pakistan	8.9	8.0	7.9	7.2	10.3	16.4	14.9	16.1	11.2
Philippines	21.9	23.6	26.2	21.0	19.0	16.3	17.1	13.8	19.1
Singapore	18.4	26.3	34.9	43.8	41.0	47.3	49.9	46.3	39.8
Thailand	21.2	22.8	22.1	24.3	30.8	35.8	34.3	32.2	27.9
Taipei, China	25.3	30.4	33.0	31.6	33.4	27.2	26.0	26.0	28.7
Vietnam					3.9	14.6	22.2	29.0	17.4
Average 1/	19.8	22.0	25.7	26.6	30.0	33.2	32.9	37.5	

Data source: World Bank, World Development Indicators
Note: Computed as Gross domestic savings (current LCU) / GDP (current LCU)
1/ weighted by average real GDP of each period

Table 11.1 (Continued)

Real measure

	1966–70	1971–75	1976–80	1981–85	1986–90	1991–95	1996–2000	2001–07	Average
PRC	27.3	28.3	30.1	28.1	27.0	27.7	29.4	35.6	29.2
Hong Kong, China	35.0	34.6	35.7	33.0	33.1	28.2	27.9	33.7	32.6
Indonesia	35.7	39.3	35.2	20.7	26.0	25.8	21.0	19.4	27.9
India	12.2	13.1	14.5	12.0	12.1	12.4	10.9	16.4	13.0
Korea, Rep. of	18.8	21.9	31.8	33.4	39.3	42.2	42.4	43.7	34.2
Malaysia	28.5	31.0	31.5	29.7	37.5	39.0	46.0	42.5	35.7
Pakistan	3.8	3.4	-3.8	-0.8	4.8	5.9	5.2	7.7	3.3
Philippines	10.2	13.2	18.1	18.9	14.2	10.6	9.7	10.8	13.2
Singapore	35.8	40.4	45.4	53.7	51.3	56.2	60.2	56.4	49.9
Thailand	17.9	21.0	21.7	24.8	30.4	35.2	32.8	31.7	26.9
Taipei,China	13.4	18.4	23.1	25.1	25.5	21.7	22.6	26.4	22.0
Vietnam	-2.4	-2.4	-2.4	-2.4	-1.7	6.9	12.6	16.8	3.1
Average 1/	18.8	21.0	23.0	21.2	22.8	24.3	24.8	29.4	

Data source: Penn World Tables (PWT), version 6.3
Note: Computed as 100 – kc – kg, where "kc" is the consumption share of real GDP per capita and "kg" is the government share of real GDP per capita.
1/ weighted by average real GDP of each period

Development Indicators of the World Bank. Real domestic saving rates are computed by subtracting the consumption and government shares of real GDP from 1 and are taken from the Penn World Table, version 6.3 (Heston et al. 2009). The nominal and real measures can show divergent trends if trends in GDP and capital goods deflators differ significantly.

The last column of Table 11.1 shows the average domestic saving rates for the 1966–2007 period as a whole, computed from the 5–year averages by weighting each figure by the average real GDP for the corresponding time period. As can be seen from this table, there is enormous variation in domestic saving rates among the Southeast Asian economies in the sample with the nominal domestic saving rate ranging from a whopping 39.8 percent in Singapore to 33.4 percent in Malaysia, 27.9 percent in Thailand, 27.8 percent in Indonesia, 19.1 percent in the Philippines, and 17.4 percent in Vietnam. Nonetheless, domestic saving rates were relatively high in Southeast Asia as a whole relative to the rest of the world throughout the 1966–2007 period.

Moreover, the real domestic saving rate showed even more variation among the Southeast Asian economies in the sample, ranging from a whopping 49.9 percent in Singapore to 35.7 percent in Malaysia, 27.9 percent in Indonesia, 26.9 percent in Thailand, 13.2 percent in the Philippines, and 3.1 percent in Vietnam during the 1966–2007 period as a whole. In fact, Vietnam showed negative real domestic saving rates until it transitioned to a market economy in the 1990s. Thus, the rank ordering of the six Southeast Asian economies is virtually identical regardless of whether we look at nominal or real domestic saving rates.

Moreover, the nominal and real domestic saving rates of most individual Southeast Asian economies also showed upward trends during most or all of the 1966–2007 period, with the primary exceptions being that the nominal and real domestic saving rates of Thailand, the real domestic saving rate of the Philippines, and the nominal domestic saving rate of Indonesia have started declining in recent years and that the nominal domestic saving rate of the Philippines and the real domestic saving rate of Indonesia has been declining throughout the 1966–2007 period.

Given that the rank orderings of countries and trends over time are broadly similar regardless of whether we use nominal or real domestic saving rates, given that using a real measure is preferable from a theoretical point of view, and given that a number of authors (such as Aghion et al. 2009 and Shioji and Vu 2012) have used a real measure of saving, we decided to use the real domestic saving rate as our dependent variable throughout our regression analysis. Note, however, that we also tried using the nominal domestic saving rate and that the results were qualitatively very similar. The main difference between these models is that the coefficient of the AGE variable (to be defined later) is higher in absolute magnitude when the nominal domestic saving rate is used than when the real domestic saving rate is used.

Various factors affected the trends in domestic saving rates described above. First of all, many of the economies in our sample experienced rapid demographic transition. The aged dependency rate also increased (from 6.5 percent to 10.2 percent on average) during the same period. Population aging has been particularly significant in East Asia, i.e. Hong Kong, China; Korea; and Taipei, China, but also in Singapore from Southeast Asia. Meanwhile, the aged dependency rate has been declining somewhat in Pakistan and Vietnam. The youth dependency rate shows a uniform picture, declining in all of the economies in our sample, though to a lesser extent in Pakistan.

Financial sector development played an especially significant role in developing Asia. James et al. (1989) discuss the role played by financial incentives, such as raising interest rates on time and saving deposits, in increasing the domestic saving rate when the financial system was still shallow in the 1970s (in Korea and Singapore, for example). Financial deepening accelerated in many Asian economies after the mid-1980s, driven by financial liberalization, which relaxed financial constraints and eased access to credit. However, these earlier forms of financial deepening tend to be more relevant for the corporate sector, as often discussed in the context of the financial development and growth nexus (see King and Levine, 1993, for example), and thus they presumably had a positive impact on the saving rate as firms' investments became more profitable and the increasing demand for credit pushed up interest rates. By contrast, improved access to credit by households and the resultant decline in precautionary saving tend to occur at a later stage of development, and thus the negative impact of financial sector development on saving rates will presumably tend to come later. The developing Asian economies in our sample recorded deepening of their credit markets to more than 100 percent of GDP by the 2000s except in India, Indonesia, Pakistan, the Philippines, and Vietnam, and thus further financial deepening can be expected to contribute toward reducing their saving rates, unlike in the case of earlier financial incentives and/or the relaxation of financial constraints.

Moreover, these demographic and financial developments were accompanied by the continuing but uneven increase in per capita GDP and its growth rate.

Estimation results: determinants of domestic saving rates in developing Asia

In this section, we present our estimation results concerning the determinants of domestic saving rates in the 12 developing Asian economies in our sample during the 1966–2007 period (see Horioka and Terada-Hagiwara (2012) for the full set of results).

The country fixed effects results for the basic specification are as follows (figures in parentheses are t–statistics):

$$SR_{i,t} = 182.03 + I_i - 0.95 * AGE_{i,t} - 0.03 * DEP_{i,t} - 43.13 * LNGDP_{i,t}$$
$$\phantom{SR_{i,t} =} (5.99) \quad\quad (-2.71) \quad\quad\quad (-0.23) \quad\quad\quad (-8.73)$$
$$+ 2.92 * LNGDPSQ_{i,t} + 14.48 * CREDIT_{i,t} - 6.46 * CREDITSQ_{i,t} + u_{i,t}$$
$$(9.24) \quad\quad\quad\quad (2.94) \quad\quad\quad\quad (-3.99)$$

Number of observations: 78
R–squared: within = 0.76, between = 0.61, and overall = 0.70

where

$I_i = \{12.75, -11.82, 2.43, -4.87, 5.32, 7.60, -12.91, -7.23, 11.62, 4.16, -5.97, -2.79\}$
for i = 1, 2, 3, … 12.

As expected, both *AGE* and *DEP* have a negative impact on the domestic saving rate, but only the coefficient of *AGE* is statistically significant. *LNGDP* has a nonlinear (convex) impact on the domestic saving rate, with its impact being negative at low-income levels and positive at higher-income levels. Conversely, *CREDIT* has a nonlinear (concave) impact on the domestic saving rate, with its impact being positive at low levels of *CREDIT* and negative at high levels of *CREDIT*.

As for the impact of the other explanatory variables, the coefficient of *CHGDP* was positive in all cases but was statistically significant only in the random effects model, and the coefficient of *RINT* was not statistically significant in any case. Thus, the results for the variants with *RINT* and *CHGDP* are not shown.

The results discussed thus far are based on contemporaneous values for all of the explanatory variables, but the variables relating to *LNGDP*, *CREDIT*, and *CHGDP* are endogenous. Thus using lagged values for these variables would alleviate the endogeneity problem. Using lagged values for *LNGDP*, *LNGDPSQ*, *CREDIT*, and *CREDITSQ* yields the following country fixed effects results for the basic specification (the figures in parentheses are t–statistics):

$$SR_{i,t} = 102.49 + I_i - 1.34 * AGE_{i,t} - 0.02 * DEP_{i,t} - 24.63 * LNGDP_{i,t}(-1)$$
$$\quad\quad (2.00) \quad\quad (-3.33) \quad\quad (-0.09) \quad\quad (-2.93)$$
$$\quad\quad + 1.96 * LNGDPSQ_{i,t}(-1) + 6.70 * CREDIT_{i,t}(-1) - 3.51 * CREDITSQ_{i,t}(-1) + u_{i,t}$$
$$\quad\quad (4.17) \quad\quad\quad\quad\quad (1.08) \quad\quad\quad\quad\quad (-1.65)$$

Number of observations: 78
R–squared: within = 0.60, between = 0.59, overall = 0.66

where

I_i= {11.05, –7.56, .07, –5.94, 7.26, 6.41, –14.91, –10.43, 13.22, 4.45, –5.56}
for i = 1, 2, 3, … 12.

As can be seen from comparing these estimation results to the estimation results without lags, the results are broadly consistent except that the coefficient of AGE is considerably larger in absolute magnitude and the coefficients of all of the other explanatory variables are smaller in absolute magnitude in the case of the estimation results with lags.

Finally, the results of the fixed effects models show that the country fixed effects are significant for most economies (except for Korea, Malaysia, and Singapore) with a significant negative sign when the PRC is taken as the reference country, indicating a much higher domestic saving rate in the PRC than predicted by the other explanatory variables.

In sum, the main determinants of the domestic saving rate in developing Asia during the 1966–2007 period appear to be the age structure of the population (especially the aged dependency ratio), income levels, and (to a lesser extent) the level of financial sector development, except as noted above, the direction of impact of each factor is more or less as expected, and the impacts of income levels and the level of financial sector development are nonlinear (convex and concave, respectively).

Projections of domestic saving rates in developing Asia for 2011–30

In this section, we discuss our projections of domestic saving rates in the 12 developing Asian economies in our sample up to 2030. Our projections are based on the coefficients in the basic country fixed effects model with lags, the United Nations (UN) projections of the age structure of the population (the aged and youth dependency ratios, median variant), and the GDP projections of Lee and Hong (2012).

Since projections of financial sector development are not available, we assumed that financial deepening progresses according to the level of per capita income. We projected in which World Bank income group each country would belong in 2011–20 and 2021–30 using Lee and Hong's (2010) GDP projections and assigned to each country the 2008 value of the financial sector development variable (private credit to GDP ratio) for the income group to which it is projected to belong in each time period except that, for economies in which the financial sector has already deepened beyond the average value for the income group to which they are projected to belong (Hong Kong, China; the PRC; Taipei, China; and Vietnam in 2011–20, and these same countries minus the PRC in 2021–30), the financial sector development variable was assumed to remain at the same value as in the recent past (the average value for 2000–07). The average 2008 values of the financial sector development variable for each income group were 130 percent for the high income group, 105 percent for the upper middle income group, and 46 percent for the lower middle income group, as shown in Beck et al. (2009). Hong Kong, China; Korea; Malaysia;

Singapore; the PRC; and Taipei, China are projected to belong to the high income group, Thailand to the upper middle income group, and Indonesia, India, Pakistan, the Philippines, and Vietnam to the lower middle income group by 2021–30.

Our projections suggest that all of the developing Asian economies in our sample are projected to post steady growth, which will lead to higher income levels, which in turn will create upward pressure on their domestic saving rates. At the same time, however, population aging will eventually occur in all of the developing Asian economies in our sample, which will create downward pressure on their domestic saving rates. Whether domestic saving rates increase or decrease and how fast they increase or decrease will depend on the relative strengths of these two effects.

We find dramatic differences among these economies in projected future trends in their domestic saving rates, but this is not surprising because there is a 40– to 50–year gap in the timing of population aging, as can be seen from Table 11.2 (see Jones, Chapter 10 in this volume, for more detailed data on the substantial disparities among the economies of Southeast Asia in the timing of population aging and other demographic trends). As a result of these dramatic differences in the timing of the demographic transition in the coming decades, the decline in domestic saving rates arising from population aging will not occur simultaneously in the economies of developing Asia but will rather be spread out over close to a half-century, with the decline in domestic saving rates in some economies being offset by the increase in domestic saving rates in other economies until at least 2030.

As can be seen from Table 11.3, the domestic saving rate is projected to decline in five out of the six Southeast Asian economies in the sample (with the sole exception of Vietnam) in 2011–20 and in all six of the Southeast Asian economies in the sample in 2021–30, but there is enormous variation in the speed of the decline, with economies in which population aging is expected to occur the soonest (such as Singapore and Thailand) being projected to show the sharpest declines in domestic saving rates, and economies in which population aging is expected to occur less rapidly being projected to show slower declines in domestic saving rates (as in the case of Indonesia, Malaysia, and the Philippines) or to show an increase in domestic saving rates early on, followed by a decline (as in the case of Vietnam).

Table 11.2 Population aging in developing Asia

Economy	The Period during which the Population Aged 65 and Older Reaches 14 Percent the Total Population
PRC	2020–25
Hong Kong, China	2010–15
Indonesia	2040–45
India	2050–55
Korea, Rep. of	2015–20
Malaysia	2040–45
Pakistan	After 2055
Philippines	2050–55
Singapore	2015–20
Thailand	2020–25
Taipei,China	2015–20
Vietnam	2030–35
Japan	1990–95

Data Source: The United Nations' (U.N.) projections available at http://esa.un.org/unpp, and the *Statistical Yearbook for Taipei, China*, available at http://www.cepd.gov.tw/encontent/m1.aspx?sNo=0000063

Table 11.3 Future trends in real domestic saving rates in developing Asia

Economy	2001–07	2011–20	2021–30
	Fitted	Projected	Projected
PRC	31.82	30.30	31.88
Hong Kong, China	29.75	24.33	20.02
Indonesia	24.08	21.59	20.80
India	14.54	14.92	15.91
Korea, Rep. of	42.02	35.53	37.36
Malaysia	44.65	43.74	41.97
Pakistan	6.66	7.01	10.05
Philippines	14.90	12.91	11.81
Singapore	58.74	47.02	40.43
Thailand	31.31	28.59	23.53
Taipei, China	25.10	20.68	15.65
Vietnam	16.76	19.19	15.44
Developing Asia	27.38	26.33	27.21

Notes: Authors' calculation. Refer to the main text for explanation.

Summary and conclusions

In this chapter, we presented data on trends over time in domestic saving rates in 12 economies in developing Asia, of which six are in Southeast Asia, during the 1966–2007 period, conducted an econometric analysis of the determinants of those trends, and projected trends in domestic saving rates in these same economies up to 2030 based on our estimation results. We found that domestic saving rates in developing Asia have, in general, been high and rising but that there have been substantial differences from economy to economy, that the main determinants of the domestic saving rate in developing Asia during the 1960–2007 period appear to have been the age structure of the population (especially the aged dependency ratio), income levels, and the level of financial sector development, that the direction of impact of each factor has been more or less as expected, and that the impacts of income levels and the level of financial sector development are nonlinear (convex and concave, respectively).

We also find that the domestic saving rate in Southeast Asia will decline over the next two decades because the negative impact of population aging thereon will more than offset the positive impact of higher income levels thereon but that there will be substantial variation from economy to economy, with economies in which population aging is expected to occur the soonest (such as Singapore and Thailand) being projected to show the sharpest declines in domestic saving rates, and economies in which population aging is expected to occur less rapidly being projected to show slower declines in domestic saving rates (as in the case of Indonesia, Malaysia, and the Philippines) or to show an increase in domestic saving rates early on, followed by a decline (as in the case of Vietnam).

Turning finally to the policy implications of our findings, our finding that the domestic saving rate will decline over the next two decades implies that the current account surpluses of the Southeast Asian economies will decline over time and that the worldwide saving glut that is purported to exist will be reduced over time, even if no action is taken. In fact, there is even the possibility that a saving shortage will eventually emerge in the world economy as a whole as the population aging process spreads to more and more countries.

Acknowledgments

We thank the Japanese Ministry of Education, Culture, Sports, Science, and Technology for Grant–in–Aid for Scientific Research Category B (topic number 22330083) and Category S (topic number 20223004), the Global Center of Excellence (GCOE) Program of the Graduate School of Economics and the Institute of Social and Economic Research of Osaka University, and the Philippine Center for Economic Development (PCED) for their financial support (Horioka). The empirical analysis in sections 2 and 4 and the future projections in section 5 draw heavily from Horioka and Terada–Hagiwara (2012).

Appendix

Table 11.A1 Variable definitions and data sources

Variable	Var. name	Data source	Note
Real domestic saving rate	SR	Computed as 100 – kg – kc. Heston et al., Penn World Table version 6.3 (PWT)[1]	kg is government share of real GDP per capita, and kc is consumption share of real GDP per capita. Both from PWT.
Aged dependency ratio	AGE	"SP.POP.DPND.OL" from *World Development Indicators (WDI)* of the World Bank[2] and the *Statistical Yearbook* for Taipei,China[3]	Ratio of the population aged 65 or older to the population aged 15–64
Youth dependency ratio	DEP	"SP.POP.DPND.YG" from WDI and the *Statistical Yearbook* for Taipei,China	Ratio of the population aged 0–14 to the population aged 15–64
Log of real per capita GDP	LNGDP	"rgdpch" from Penn World Table version 6.3	Real GDP per capita (2005 constant prices: Laspeyres)
Real per capita GDP growth	CHGDP	"grgdpch" from Penn World Table version 6.3	Growth rate of real GDP chain per capita (rgdpch)
Private credit by deposit money banks and other financial institutions (% of GDP)	CREDIT	"pcrdbofgdp" from Beck and Demirgüç-Kunt (2009) and line 32D from *International Financial Statistics (IFS)* of the International Monetary Fund for the PRC	
Nominal interest rate	INT	IFS, and www.cbc.gov.tw (Taipei, China's central bank's website) for Taipei,China.[4]	Used data on the deposit rate (line 60L of IFS) except for India, Pakistan, and the Republic of Korea, for which we used the discount rate (line 60 of IFS)
Inflation rate	INFL	"NY.GDP.DEFL.KD.ZG" from WDI	
Real interest rate	RINT	IFS, WDI, and www.cbc.gov.tw	Computed as $\ln((1+INT/100)/(1+INFL/100))$

Notes

[1] Available at http://pwt.econ.upenn.edu/php_site/pwt_index.php

[2] Available at http://devdata.worldbank.org/dataonline/

[3] Available at http://www.cepd.gov.tw/encontent/m1.aspx?sNo=0000063

[4] Available at http://www.cbc.gov.tw/ct.asp?xItem=30010&CtNode=517&mp=2

Table 11.A2 Descriptive statistics

Variable	No. of Obs.	Mean	Std. Dev.	Minimum	Maximum
SR	78	25.2	14	–3.8	60.2
AGE	78	7.8	2.2	5.7	16.3
DEP	78	56.8	18.6	20.3	87.6
LNGDP	78	8.5	0.9	6.7	10.5
CREDIT	78	0.7	0.5	0.1	2.2
CHGDP	78	4.6	2.8	–2.7	12.3
RINT	70	1.1	3	–7.5	8.7

Note: Refer to Appendix Table 1 for variable definitions and data sources.

Bibliography

Aghion, Philippe, Comin, Diego, Howitt, Peter, and Tecu, Isabel (2009), "When Does Domestic Saving Matter for Economic Growth?" mimeo. Harvard University.

Apergis, Nicholas, and Tsoumas, Chris (2009), "A Survey of the Feldstein–Horioka Puzzle: What Has Been Done and Where We Stand," *Research in Economics*, 63(2), 64–76.

Asian Development Bank (2009), "Rebalancing Asia's Growth," in Asian Development Bank (ed.), *Asian Development Outlook*. Manila: Asian Development Bank.

Bailliu, J., and Reisen, H. (1998), "Do Funded Pensions Contribute to Higher Savings? A Cross-Country Analysis," mimeo. OECD Development Centre, Paris.

Beck, Thortsen, Demirgüç-Kunt, Asli, and Levine, Ross (2009), "Financial Institutions and Markets across Countries and over Time: Data and Analysis," Policy Research Working Paper No. 4943, Washington, DC: World Bank.

Bernanke, Ben (2005), "The Global Saving Glut and the U.S. Current Account Deficit," Remarks made at the Sandridge Lecture, Virginia Association of Economics, Richmond, Virginia. Available at: http://www.federalreserve.gov/boarddocs/speeches/2005/200503102/

Bosworth, Barry, and Chodorow-Reich, Gabriel (2007), "Saving and Demographic Change: The Global Dimension," CRR WP 2007–02, Center for Retirement Research, Boston College, Boston, MA.

CEIC data manager, WEB. New York, NY.

Chinn, Menzie D., and Prasad, Eswar S. (2003), "Medium-term Determinants of Current Account in Industrial and Developing Countries: An Empirical Exploration," *Journal of International Economics*, 59 (1), 47–76.

Chinn, Menzie D., and Ito, Hiro (2007), "Current Account Imbalances, Financial Development and Institutions: Assaying the World 'Saving Glut,'" *Journal of International Money and Finance*, 26(4), 546–69.

Chinn, Menzie D., and Ito, Hiro (2008), "Global Current Account Imbalances: American Fiscal Policy versus East Asian Savings," *Review of International Economics*, 16(3), 479–98.

Dayal-Ghulati, A., and Thimann, C. (1997), "Saving in Southeast Asia and Latin America Compared: Searching for Policy Lessons," IMF Working Paper WP/97/110. Washington, DC: International Monetary Fund.

Edwards, Sebastian (1996), "Why Are Latin America's Savings Rates So Low? An International Comparative Analysis," *Journal of Development Economics*, 51(1), 5–44.

Feldstein, Martin (1977), "Social Security and Private Savings: International Evidence in an Extended Life Cycle Model," in Martin Feldstein and Robert Inman (eds), *The Economics of Public Services* (An International Economic Association Conference Volume).

Feldstein, Martin (1980), "International Differences in Social Security and Saving," *Journal of Public Economics*, 14(2), 225–44.

Feldstein, Martin S., and Horioka, Charles Y. (1980), "Domestic Saving and International Capital Flows," *Economic Journal*, 90(358), 314–29.

Heston, Alan, Summers, Robert, and Aten, Bettina (2009), Penn World Table Version 6.3, Center for International Comparisons of Production, Income and Prices at the University of Pennsylvania, August.

Higgins, M. (1998), "Demography, National Savings, and International Capital Flows," *International Economic Review*, 39(2), 343–69.

Horioka, Charles Yuji (1989), "Why Is Japan's Private Saving Rate So High?" in Ryuzo Sato and Takashi Negishi (eds), *Developments in Japanese Economics*. Tokyo: Academic Press, pp. 145–78.

Horioka, Charles Yuji (1992), "Future Trends in Japan's Saving Rate and the Implications Thereof for Japan's External Imbalance," *Japan and the World Economy*, 3(4), 307–30.

Horioka, Charles Yuji, and Terada-Hagiwara, Akiko (2012), "The Determinants and Long-term Projections of Saving Rates in Developing Asia," *Japan and the World Economy*, 24(2), 128–37.

Horioka, Charles Yuji, and Terada–Hagiwara, Akiko (2014), "Corporate Cash Holding in Asia," *Asian Economic Journal*, 28(3), forthcoming.

Hung, Juann H. and Qian, Rong (2010), "Why Is China's Saving Rate So High? A Comparative Study of Cross-Country Panel Data," Working Paper Series 2010–07. Washington, DC: Congressional Budget Office.

International Monetary Fund (2005), "Global Imbalances: A Saving and Investment Perspective," in International Monetary Fund (ed.), *World Economic Outlook 2005*. Washington, DC: International Monetary Fund.

International Monetary Fund (2009), "Corporate Savings and Rebalancing in Asia," in International Monetary Fund (ed.), *World Economic and Financial Surveys, Regional Economic Outlook, Asia and Pacific*. Washington, DC: International Monetary Fund.

International Monetary Fund. *International Financial Statistics*. Washington, DC: International Monetary Fund. Various issues.

Ito, Hiro, and Chinn, Menzie (2009), "East Asia and Global Imbalances: Saving, Investment, and Financial Development," in Takatoshi Ito and Andrew K. Rose (eds), *Financial Sector Development in the Pacific Rim*. East Asian Seminar on Economics, National Bureau of Economic Research conference volume, vol. 18. Chicago, IL: University of Chicago Press, pp. 117–50.

James, William E., Naya, Seiji, and Meier, Gerald M. (1989), "Domestic Savings and Financial Development," in *Asian Development, Economic Success and Policy Lessons*. Madison: University of Wisconsin Press.

Jha, Shikha, Prasad, Eswar, and Terada-Hagiwara, Akiko (2009), "Saving in Asia: Issues for Rebalancing Growth," ADB Economics Working Paper Series no. 162. Manila: Asian Development Bank.

Kim, Soyoung, and Lee, Jong-Wha (2008), "Demographic Changes, Saving, and Current Account: An Analysis Based on a Panel VAR Model," *Japan and the World Economy*, 20(2), 236–56.

King, Robert, and Levine, Ross (1993), "Finance, Entrepreneurship and Growth: Theory and Evidence," *Journal of Monetary Economics*, 32(3), 513–42.

Lee, Jong-Wha, and Hong, Kiseok (2012), "Economic Growth in Asia: Determinants and Prospects," *The World Economy* 24(2), 114–27.

Loayza, Norman, Schmidt-Hebbel, Klaus, and Serven, Luis (2000), "What Drives Private Saving across the World?" *Review of Economics and Statistics*, 82(2), 165–81.

Luhrman, M. (2003), "Demographic Change, Foresight and International Capital Flows," MEA Discussion Paper Series 03038. Mannheim Institute of the Economics of Aging, University of Mannheim, Germany.

Matsubayashi, Yoichi, and Fujii, Takao (2012), "Substitutability of Savings by Sectors: OECD Experiences," mimeo. Graduate School of Economics, Kobe University, Japan.

Modigliani, Franco (1970), "The Life-cycle Hypothesis and Intercountry Differences in the Saving Ratio," in W. A. Eltis, M. F. G. Scott, and J. N. Wolfe (eds), *Induction, Growth, and Trade: Essays in Honour of Sir Roy Harrod*. Oxford: Oxford University Press, pp. 197–225.

Modigliani, Franco, and Sterling, Arlie (1983), "Determinants of Private Saving with Special Reference to the Role of Social Security: Cross Country Tests," in Franco Modigliani and Richard Hemming (eds), *The Determinants of National Saving and Wealth*. Proceedings of a Conference held by the International Economic Association at Bergamo, Italy. London: Macmillan.

Ogaki, Masao, Ostry, Jonathan D., and Reinhart, Carmen M. (1996), "Saving Behavior in Low- and Middle-Income Developing Countries: A Comparison," *International Monetary Fund Staff Papers*, 43(1), 38–71.

Park, Donghyun, and Shin, Kwanho (2009), "Saving, Investment, and Current Account Surplus in Developing Asia," ADB Economics Working Paper Series no. 158. Manila: Asian Development Bank (April).

Shioji, Etsuro, and Vu, Tuan Khai (2012), "Physical Capital Accumulation in Asia–12: Past Trends and Future Projections," *The World Economy* 24(2), 138–49.

Terada-Hagiwara, Akiko (2011), "Have Filipino Households Become Less Prudent?" *Journal of Development Studies*, 48(5), 673–85.

Wang, Pengfei, Xu, Lifang, and Xu, Zhiwei (2011), "Financial Development and Aggregate Saving Rates: A Hump–Shaped Relationship," mimeo. Hong Kong University of Science and Technology, Hong Kong (October).

Wei, Shang-Jin, and Zhang, Xiaobo (2009), "The Competitive Saving Motive: Evidence from Rising Sex Ratios and Savings Rates in China," NBER Working Paper No. 15093 (September). Cambridge, MA: National Bureau of Economic Research.

World Bank. *World Development Indicators*. Washington, DC: World Bank. Various issues.

12

Education in Southeast Asia

Investments, achievements, and returns

Diep Phan

BELOIT COLLEGE

Ian Coxhead

UNIVERSITY OF WISCONSIN-MADISON

Introduction

Human capital investments have played a crucial role in the early economic success of East Asian economies. In *The East Asian Miracle*, an important early investigation into the sources of the region's rapid economic growth,[1] the World Bank (1993) stated that

> The growth and transformation of systems of education and training ... has been dramatic ... the [High Performing Asian Economies] HPAEs' enrollment rates have tended to be higher than predicted for their level of income ... By 1987, East Asia's superior education systems were evident at the secondary level. (p. 43) ... Primary education is by far the largest single contributor to HPAEs' predicted growth rates ... Physical investment comes second ... followed by secondary school enrollment.
>
> *(p. 52)*

Given Southeast Asia's rapid growth, the claim has often been made that these countries too have benefited from high rates of human capital investment. This claim, however, is less robust for Southeast Asia, and even for the Southeast Asian "Miracle" economies, than for Northeast Asia. In an important region-wide survey, Anne Booth (2003) described the claim that the Southeast Asian economies invested heavily in education at an early stage and in an equitable manner as "gross over-generalisation." Even among the eight "Miracle" economies, she points out significant differences in the timing and extent of human capital investments between those in Northeast Asia (Japan, South Korea, and Taiwan) and those in Southeast Asia (Singapore, Malaysia, Indonesia, and Thailand). In fact, human capital investments in Southeast Asia started late and have generally not achieved as much as in Northeast Asia: educational attainment has been lower while inequality in access to education has been severe (Booth 2003; Khoman 2005).

Taiwan and South Korea are among the world's most successful growth stories. Both countries quickly climbed up the production ladder toward the most technology-intensive production processes and by the late 1990s had achieved high-income status. In both countries, rapid expansion of their human capital helps explain their successful transition from middle to high-income (Eichengreen et al. 2013). Within East Asia, Japan, Hong Kong, Singapore, Taiwan, and South Korea are the technological leaders, with Japan the most advanced. South Korea most closely approximates Japan's manufacturing capacity, followed by Taiwan. Singapore is the only Southeast Asian country that has joined this group, but together with Hong Kong, it is the furthest behind Japan (World Bank 2012: 11).

Thailand, Malaysia, and Indonesia have made impressive progress in economic growth and poverty reduction, but their movement up the production quality ladder slowed after the Asian financial crisis. They still occupy predominantly low-value-added niches of manufacturing such as assembly and processing. They are still some years, or in the case of Indonesia perhaps decades, away from becoming leading industrial nations (World Bank 2012: 11). Eichengreen et al. (2013) have presented evidence that growth slowdown or the middle-income trap is less likely in countries where the population has a relatively high level of secondary and tertiary education and where high-technology products account for a relatively large share of exports. If this is so then it seems clear that for Thailand, Malaysia, and Indonesia the lack of high quality human capital helps to explain their growth slowdowns.

It is against this background that we consider human capital in the growth and development of Southeast Asian economies. Human capital includes both health and education, but due to space limitations we will discuss only education (for more on health see Chapter 16 by Nobles in this volume). The chapter has three primary goals. We first review recent educational data for Southeast Asia. By the early 1990s, most governments in the region had conceded that their human capital investments had fallen short of what is required to sustain a high growth rate. Most emphasized the need to prioritize education (especially higher education), to sustain growth. Did this translate into policy changes, and has Southeast Asia been successful in catching up with Northeast Asia? We also expand the analysis to include the poorer Southeast Asian economies. Some of these, such as the Philippines, were not classified as HPAEs by the authors of the *East Asian Miracle* study. Others, including Vietnam, Laos, and Cambodia, started to grow and integrate with the global economy at least a decade later than their neighbors, in the early 1990s. Their delayed entry to the global economy has had significant implications for their growth strategies and for their efforts to increase the supply of human capital.

Second, we note that conditions in the world economy have changed significantly since the HPAEs underwent their growth accelerations. What are the implications of new global trading arrangements and configurations, including the rise of China as a key player in regional trade, for human capital incentives and policies in Southeast Asia?

Third, with these insights in hand, we examine human capital policies using examples from the Philippines, Vietnam, and Indonesia. A short concluding section brings the chapter to a close.

The supply of education and human capital

In this section, we examine changes in educational achievements in Southeast Asian countries, focusing most closely on developments in the early years of the twenty-first century.

Quantity of education

In aggregate data, the primary school net enrollment rate (NER), which measures the population's basic education level, is one of the most important widely accessible indicators of educational achievement. Increasing primary NER is a general trend observed in most developing countries.

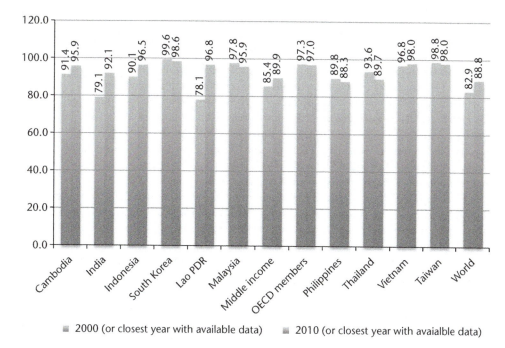

■ 2000 (or closest year with available data)   ■ 2010 (or closest year with avaialble data)

Figure 12.1   Primary school net enrollment rates (%)
Source: Taiwan data are from 2012 Taiwan Education Statistical Indicators; all other countries' data are from World Bank.

By the late 2000s, near universal primary school enrollment has been achieved in most countries of East and Southeast Asia and Latin America, though other regions still lag behind (UNESCO 2010: table 2.2). Except for the Philippines and Laos, most Southeast Asian countries' primary NERs were at least 90 percent by 2008 (see Figure 12.1).

The NER, however, does not tell us whether children actually complete primary school. Nor does it indicate where children are in the cycle, or whether they dropped out and returned. Table 12.1 shows the rate of survival to grade 5. Malaysia and Singapore are the only countries

Table 12.1 Survival rate to grade 5, 2009

Country/region	Survival rate (%)	Female/Male ratio
Cambodia	62	1.08
Indonesia	86	1.07
Japan	100	1
Lao PDR	67	1.02
Malaysia	98	1
Myanmar	75	1.07
Philippines	79	1.09
Republic of Korea	99	1
Singapore	99	1
East Asia and Pacific	87	1.06
Latin America and Caribbean	92	0.98
South and West Asia	66	0.94
Sub-Saharan Africa	69	0.97

Source: UNESCO 2012.

with rates close to 100 percent. Other Southeast Asian countries, including Cambodia, Laos, Myanmar, the Philippines, and to a lesser extent Indonesia, are lagging on this measure. In Laos, less than 70 percent of children reach grade 5. These data suggest that the simple NER overstates the success of Southeast Asian countries in providing basic education. There is much more work to be done to keep children in school and help them complete primary education.

Another widely accessible indicator, the mean years of schooling, tells us a little more about the extent of basic education. Figure 12.2a shows that in the 1950s and 1960s, Southeast Asian countries and Northeast Asian countries started out with similarly low levels of education (about three to four years per person, on average, for most countries in both regions). Twenty years later, average schooling in South Korea and Taiwan had leaped significantly ahead, creating a major gap in educational levels between Northeast Asia and Southeast Asia.

We re-examine data on mean years of schooling in Figure 12.2b, taking into account the fact that in any given year, countries were at different levels of development. Using data on gross national income per capita (constant international prices of 2005), we choose comparable base years for countries. Lao PDR and Cambodia in 1995 were comparable, in per capita incomes, to Vietnam in 1990, Indonesia in 1970, Thailand in 1965, China in 1985, the Philippines in 1960, and Malaysia, Singapore, and South Korea in 1955. Figure 12.2b shows a similar story as in Figure 12.2a. Even after taking into account countries' levels of development, South Korea's human capital development was ahead of that of most Southeast Asian countries. It's interesting to note that within Southeast Asia, only Vietnam's human capital development seems more in line with that of South Korea when this country was at similar stages of development.

During the 1980s and 1990s most Southeast Asian governments made major efforts to broaden and deepen the supply of educational opportunities. In Indonesia and Thailand, for example, governments pledged in the early 1990s to achieve the goal of nine-year education for all.

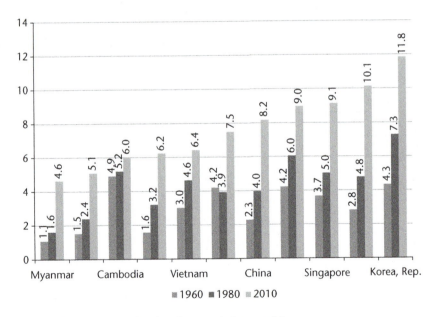

Figure 12.2a Mean years of schooling for population age 15+
Source: Data are from Barro-Lee Educational Attainment Dataset.
Note: USA = 8.4 (1950) and 13.1 (2010).

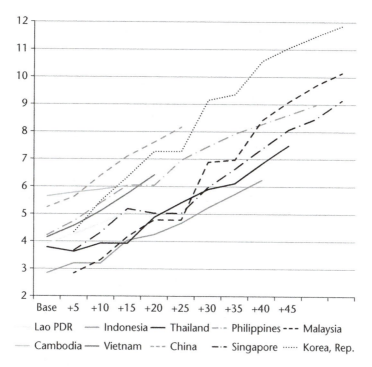

Figure 12.2b   Mean years of schooling for population age 15+ for comparable stage of development (based on GNI per capita)

Source: Data are from Barro-Lee Educational Attainment Dataset.

Notes: Base year for Vietnam was 1990, Lao PDR 1995, Cambodia 1995, Indonesia 1970, Thailand 1965, China 1985, Philippines 1960, Singapore 1955, Malaysia 1955, South Korea 1955.

Region-wide, these efforts led to increased expenditures on teacher training, construction of new classrooms, and upgrading of existing school facilities. The results can be seen in a rapid increase in average years of schooling of almost all countries in the region between 1980 and 2000. Despite such improvements, however, by 2000 average years of schooling in Southeast Asian countries were still well below those attained by South Korea and Taiwan two decades earlier. Korea, for example, attained a secondary net enrollment rate of 60 percent in 1978, but this level was not reached by the Philippines, Thailand, or Indonesia until well into the 2000s, and as of 2010 had yet to be attained in Myanmar, Lao, Cambodia, and Vietnam.[2] Moreover, the growth rate of educational achievements in the decade to 2010 has often been slow or uneven, making it even harder to close the gap with Northeast Asia. In Thailand, for example, public education expenditure as a share of GDP declined from its peak of 5.4 percent in 2000 to 3.8 percent in 2010, inspite of robust GDP growth during most of those years. Similar slippage in educational investment rates has been noted in several regional countries at various points in the past 20 years (Booth 2003).

The lower average schooling rate of Southeast Asian countries is a result of lagging enrollment rates in both secondary schools and tertiary education. As can be seen in Figure 12.3, by 2000 secondary school net enrollment rates in South Korea and Taiwan were approaching 100 percent, significantly higher than Southeast Asia and other middle-income countries and even higher than the average for OECD countries. In Southeast Asia, Singapore is the only country that has attained universal secondary school enrollment.[3]

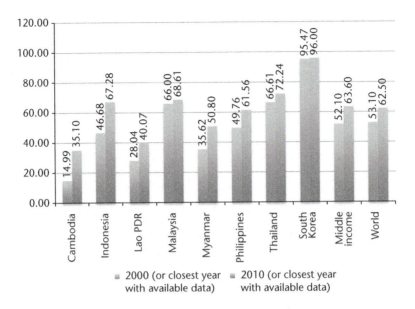

Figure 12.3 Secondary school net enrollment rates (%)
Source: Taiwan data are from 2012 Taiwan Education Statistical Indicators; all other countries' data are from World Bank database.

The importance of higher education cannot be overemphasized. It delivers skills and research for productivity and innovation, both of which are critical for long-run economic growth. The gap in tertiary education between Northeast Asia and Southeast Asia (and China) is even more staggering than the gap in secondary education. Figure 12.4 shows that in 1973, South Korea's

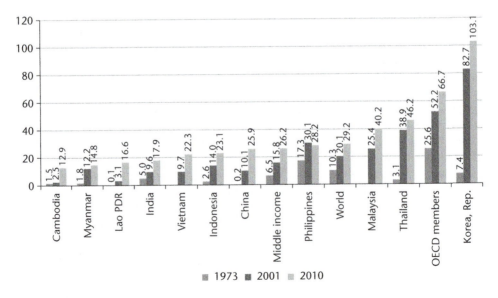

Figure 12.4 Tertiary gross enrollment rates (%)
Source: Taiwan data are from 2012 Taiwan Education Statistical Indicators; all other countries' data are from World Bank database.

gross enrollment rate (GER) in tertiary education was just as low as in Southeast Asia or in a typical middle-income economy. Yet by 2001, this rate had shot up to well over 80 percent, leaving all the Southeast Asian countries behind. Moreover, there was almost no gap in schooling attainment between urban and rural areas: access was relatively equal (Zhang et al. 2012). By 2010, South Korea's tertiary GER reached over 100 percent – one of the highest in the world, surpassing even the other OECD countries. Similarly, Taiwan started out in 1973 with a higher tertiary GER than most other countries in Asia except the Philippines. The rate of increase was slower in Taiwan than in South Korea, so by 2001 and 2010, Taiwan's tertiary GERs were below South Korea's. Even so, the expansion of Taiwan's tertiary education was significantly faster than in most Southeast Asian countries. Even in Singapore where educational achievement is the highest in Southeast Asia, the rate of enrollment in tertiary education is well below that of Taiwan.[4]

While there have been notable recent increases in tertiary GER in Southeast Asia (especially in Malaysia and Singapore), the growth rate has not been high enough to allow for catch-up.

The slow improvement in tertiary education is exacerbating skill shortages in many Southeast Asian countries, although the situation does vary by country. According to a recent World Bank report (2012), there are clear quantity gaps; that is there are simply not enough skilled workers to fill the needs of the labor market, in Vietnam and Cambodia. These quantity gaps are revealed by a number of indicators: high and rapidly increasing education premium across sectors, high tertiary professionalization rate, low unemployment rate, significant time required to fill professional vacancies, low ratios of tertiary educated workers, and low tertiary GER. Hence a supply push is strongly needed in both Vietnam and Cambodia to increase the number of graduates. In Thailand, there is also an overall quantity gap in the skilled labor market but not because of low tertiary GER as in the previous group of countries (and hence the policy recommendation is not a supply push). Rather the problem seems a lack of tertiary education of the current adult population. In Indonesia and the Philippines, there are quantity gaps in specific sectors (manufacturing in Indonesia and services in the Philippines), so there is a need for reallocation of skilled workers across sectors.

Quality of education

Quality of education in most Southeast Asian economies is low. Expansion of education has often been achieved at the cost of quality.

Measures of educational quality are hard to identify, since there are few natural experiments to control for unobservables such as student quality and motivation. Accordingly, most measures are of inputs, in the belief that these are correlated with output. One such measure is public education expenditure per pupil. Figure 12.5 shows that once again, Southeast Asian economies have lagged behind their Northeast Asian counterparts. This is partly because South Korea and Taiwan both have much higher per capita income, which enables them to spend more per student. Figure 12.6 shows public expenditure per pupil as a percentage of GDP per capita. As expected, after controlling for differences in per capita GDP, Southeast Asian countries spend as much per pupil as South Korea. But it is worrying that for a number of Southeast Asian countries (Malaysia, Thailand, the Philippines, and Cambodia), this number declined in the 2000s, a trend that is certainly against the goal of catching up in human capital investment and achievement. There are also concerns in these countries about the quality of educational services per unit of expenditure.

Other measures of educational quality at primary level are pupil/teacher ratio and the proportion of teachers trained. These are shown in Table 12.2. Most Southeast Asian countries have made progress in decreasing the number of pupils per teacher in primary schools to 20 or less

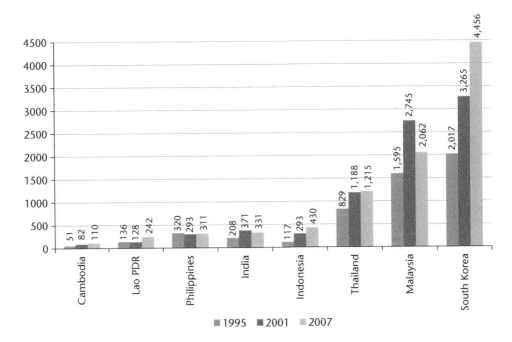

Figure 12.5 Total public education expenditure per pupil (2005 international dollars)
Source: World Bank.
Notes: For 1995 data series: Philippines and Laos data are for year 1996, India 1997, Cambodia 1998. For 2001 data series: India data are for the year 2001. For 2007 data series, India data are for the year 2006.

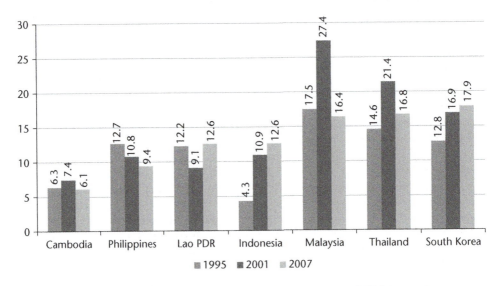

Figure 12.6 Public education expenditure per pupil as percentage of GDP per capita
Source: World Bank.

Table 12.2 Pupil/teacher ratio in primary education

Country or territory	School year ending in		
	1991	*1999*	*2010*
Cambodia	33	53	48
China	22	22	17
Indonesia	23	22	16
Japan	21	21	18
Lao PDR	27	31	29
Malaysia	20	20	13
Myanmar	48	31	28
Philippines	33	35	31
Republic of Korea	36	32	21
Singapore	26	...	17
Thailand	22	21	...
Vietnam	35	30	20
	Weighted average		
World	26	26	24
East Asia and Pacific	23	24	18
Latin America and Caribbean	27	26	22
South and West Asia	39	36	39
Sub-Saharan Africa	37	42	43
Low income countries	42	43	43
Middle income countries	27	27	24
High income countries	17	16	14

Source: UNESCO 2012.

by 2010, which is lower than for most other developing countries. The exceptions are Cambodia, Laos, and the Philippines, where this ratio has remained persistently above 30. Cambodia, where the ratio is as high as 48, faces a crisis of teacher availability.

How well do educational experiences translate into abilities or skills? Among the few internationally comparable measures of realized educational quality are standardized test scores such as the Program for International Student Assessment, or PISA.[5] The most recent 2012 round of PISA evaluations covered 65 countries, including five in Southeast Asia (Indonesia, Thailand, Malaysia, Singapore, and Vietnam). Out of these 65 countries (including many developing countries), Indonesia is almost at the bottom of the list, while Malaysia and Thailand are near the bottom. Singapore was among the very top performers at second rank. Vietnam also ranked remarkably high at seventeenth place, above OECD averages on all three tests including math, reading, and science (PISA 2012).

These indicators of educational quality should be interpreted with considerable caution. While low expenditure per student, high pupil/teacher ratio, low survival rate to grade 5, or poor performance on international standardized tests certainly raise concerns over the quality of education, high performance in these areas does not necessarily imply high quality of education. Reliance on quantitative assessment methods as guides to the design of education policy can lead to a preference for intensive drilling and coaching practices at the expense of pedagogical approaches that promote creative and critical thinking and other essential skills. This problem is well acknowledged in Singapore, a country with stellar performance in most indicators of educational quality, whether expenditure per student, graduation rates, or performance on international standardized tests. This led the Singaporean government in 1997 to adopt a policy initiative named Thinking Schools, Learning Nation. This aimed for desired learning outcomes such as creative, critical, analytical, and flexible thinking, the exercising of initiative, communication skills, problem-solving, cooperative team work, and research skills (Tan 2013: 170). However, it is questionable whether such a program can really promote higher-order thinking skills in an education system where student success is still judged primarily on performance in exams.

Vietnam's surprising performance in the 2012 PISA raised many questions (The Economist 2013). On the one hand, it might reflect the fruit of Vietnam's educational investment. On the other hand, it masks many ongoing problems in the country's educational system. For example, the high score may be a result of Vietnam's low retention rate, so that many weaker students drop out of school and hence were not included in the sample for PISA testing. Many Vietnamese education specialists argue that the score does not reflect the fact that Vietnam's educational system, as in the case of Singapore, emphasizes rote memorization and passing exams over critical and creative thinking.

Of course, one reason for low and slowly rising indicators of educational quality, especially at primary and lower secondary levels, is the rapid expansion of schooling infrastructure and resources in order to raise enrollment rates. This rapid expansion has, it seems, often come at the cost of lower quality overall. Indonesia, for example, took advantage of its oil export windfalls in the 1970s to embark on a massive school construction program. This succeeded in raising primary school enrollment rates and average years of education for primary-school-age students. However, the construction of schools and other physical infrastructure greatly exceeded the rate at which properly qualified teachers could be trained. In the 1990s, the government once again implemented a similar school construction program, this time to increase facilities for lower secondary education. The same successes and mistakes can be observed, as rapid expansion of schools leads to recruitment of under-qualified teachers (Baunto 2011: 59). In recent years, quality of education has remained low in Indonesia. According to some studies, infrastructure is deteriorating and indicators such as teacher qualifications and classroom quality need to be improved (Granado et al. 2007).

If educational quality is poor at the lower schooling levels, it is not surprising that low educational quality is also widespread at tertiary level. Universities in Southeast Asian countries have low international rankings. Only two regional universities, both located in Singapore, appear in the top 500 global rankings compiled by Shanghai Jiao Tong University.[6] Functionally, institutions of higher education in low- and middle-income East Asia (Southeast Asia included) are widely judged to have failed in their mandates to deliver skills to match labor market needs and produce research for innovation (World Bank 2012).

Access to education

Equality in access to education matters, because it is a social injustice that disadvantaged groups in the population have fewer opportunities. It also matters because no country can afford to waste talent. Countries must be able to draw from wide talent pools to supply their labor markets with the most skilled and productive workers and to promote innovation and technological development. This is a matter of survival as the global economy becomes increasingly knowledge-intensive.

To measure contemporary equity in access to education, we compare mean years of schooling for populations aged 17–22 across different groups. Table 12.3 shows that by the early 2000s, many Southeast Asian economies had closed the educational gap between males and females.

Table 12.3 Mean years of schooling for population aged 17–22 by gender

	Cambodia 2000	Indonesia 2002	Laos 2000	Myanmar 2000	Philippines 1998	Thailand 2000	Vietnam 2002
Female	4.03	8.97	4.61	5.97	9.57	n/a	8.26
Male	5.50	8.88	6.28	6.06	8.88	n/a	8.33
Female/male	0.73	1.01	0.73	0.98	1.08	n/a	0.99
	Cambodia 2010	Indonesia 2007	Laos 2006	Myanmar 2010	Philippines 2008	Thailand 2005	Vietnam 2010
Female	6.83	3.28	5.20	n/a	9.98	12.17	9.08
Male	7.09	3.21	6.29	n/a	8.98	11.53	8.88
Female/male	0.96	1.02	0.83	n/a	1.11	1.06	1.02

Source: World Inequality Database on Education (http:www.education-inequalities.org).

Female to male ratios of mean years of schooling were around one in Indonesia, Myanmar, the Philippines, Thailand, and Vietnam. Cambodia and Laos were the only two countries with significantly lower ratios (0.74 for Cambodia and 0.73 for Laos in 2000). By the latter half of the decade, educational inequality by gender improved in both countries, as the ratio increased to 0.97 in Cambodia in 2010 and 0.92 in Laos in 2006.

While most Southeast Asian countries have made respectable progress in eliminating gender inequality in schooling, improvements in other dimensions of educational inequality have been slower. In particular, rural areas are severely underserved with schools and teachers relative to cities and towns. Although there was a declining trend in the rural–urban gap in educational achievement in many Southeast Asian countries during the 2000s (see Table 12.4), the gap nonetheless remained high. The situation in Laos is especially severe. Mean years of schooling of the rural population were less than half of that of the urban population in 2000. The situation improved by 2006 but mean years of schooling of rural population remained well below that of the urban population. In the Philippines, the rural–urban ratio of mean years of schooling did not improve. And there remains stark regional disparity: in the best performing region (National Capital Region), 84 percent of the population has reached (although not necessarily finished) secondary education, whereas in the lowest performing region (Autonomous Region of Muslim Mindanao) it is just 45 percent (Mesa 2007). Of course, positively selected internal migration accounts for

Table 12.4 Mean years of schooling for population aged 17–22 by rural/urban

	Cambodia 2000	Indonesia 2002	Laos 2000	Myanmar 2000	Philippines 1998	Thailand 2000	Vietnam 2002
Rural	4.33	7.93	3.79	5.42	8.34	n/a	7.95
Urban	6.95	9.90	8.78	7.80	9.89	n/a	9.73
Rural/urban	0.62	0.80	0.43	0.69	0.84	n/a	0.82
	Cambodia 2010	Indonesia 2007	Laos 2006	Myanmar 2010	Philippines 2008	Thailand 2005	Vietnam 2010
Rural	6.56	3.21	4.56	n/a	8.62	11.10	8.81
Urban	8.58	3.02	8.33	n/a	10.17	13.31	9.50
Rural/urban	0.76	1.06	0.55	n/a	0.85	0.83	0.93

Source: World Inequality Database on Education (http:www.education-inequalities.org).

some of the regional gap. But this merely begs the question why more educated workers should need to move in order to realize a return on their skills.

In Indonesia, rural–urban disparity has declined, but only slightly, and still persists within provinces and between districts, particularly at the primary level. The disparity in enrollment rates among provinces decreased from 54 percent in 1997 to 30 percent in 2002, and disparity within provinces increased from 46 percent to 69.5 percent. The problem is more pronounced at junior high and senior high school levels. Among subnational jurisdictions, richer districts spend much more on average per student, partly due to their wealth and partly due to the greater support for tertiary enrollment among these demographics. On the other hand, poorer districts tend to exert a greater fiscal effort as they allocate a higher proportion of their budget to education (Granado et al. 2007).

In Thailand, the distribution of public education expenditure is skewed. Public spending per pupil on education in poor provinces is lower than in rich ones, and certainly lower than in the capital city, Bangkok. The consequence is that education accessibility differs starkly across regions in all levels, with Bangkok and the adjacent eastern region being more privileged than the northeast part of the country. Students in Northeastern Thailand get the lowest education subsidy per head at most education levels, except pre-school and primary school. As a result, perhaps, this region has the smallest number of students that graduate with "good level" in the O-NET test (Ordinary National Education Test) for lower secondary school and the A-NET test (Advanced National Education Test) for upper secondary school, credentials that are very important in determining a student's qualification for further education. Meanwhile, among all regions of the kingdom, the northeast region also produces the greatest variation in test scores among its schools (Laovakul 2009). This and other regional discrepancies in development-oriented public spending provides a key to understanding the deep political divisions in Thai society, which erupted into violence and extreme political instability in the mid-2000s and show no sign of abating.

Table 12.5 shows that there was not one common trend in educational inequality by income groups among Southeast Asian countries. In Vietnam, inequality in years of education among different income groups clearly declined between 2002 and 2010. In Indonesia and the

Table 12.5 Relative mean years of schooling for population aged 17–22 by income quintile (base = quintile 1)

	Cambodia 2000	Indonesia 2002	Laos 2000	Myanmar 2000	Philippines 1998	Thailand 2000	Vietnam 2002
Poorest 20%	1.00	1.00	1.00	1.00	1.00	n/a	1.00
Poor	0.84	1.19	1.84	1.19	1.26	n/a	1.48
Middle	1.11	1.33	2.42	1.33	1.49	n/a	1.64
Rich	1.54	1.46	2.49	1.60	1.65	n/a	1.78
Richest 20%	2.26	1.65	2.43	1.90	1.71	n/a	1.98
	Cambodia 2010	Indonesia 2007	Laos 2006	Myanmar 2010	Philippines 2008	Thailand 2005	Vietnam 2010
Poorest 20%	1.00	1.00	1.00	n/a	1.00	1.00	1.00
Poor	1.21	1.18	1.55	n/a	1.34	1.22	1.12
Middle	1.42	1.35	2.18	n/a	1.51	1.27	1.22
Rich	1.66	1.50	2.82	n/a	1.65	1.37	1.26
Richest 20%	1.95	1.61	3.79	n/a	1.76	1.55	1.35

Source: World Inequality Database on Education (http:www.education-inequalities.org).

Philippines, inequality by this measure was unchanged. However, according to Granado et al. (2007), in Indonesia inequalities remain at the junior and senior secondary levels, but have diminished at primary level. Despite lack of access to lower level of education by the poor, public education expenditures are skewed toward tertiary level, accounting for a higher percentage of government spending than in most other countries. In Cambodia, the trend in educational achievement across income group is unclear, as the gap in mean schooling years widened between the three middle quintiles and the lowest quintile, but narrowed between the richest and the poorest quintiles. It is clear from Table 12.5 that of all Southeast Asian countries for which we have data, Laos has the highest inequality in educational achievements by income level. During the 2000s, this inequality became much worse.

Finally, it is important also to note that access to education is differentially affected by major economic shocks. During the Asian crisis years, wealthier households were better able to smooth consumption, by borrowing and drawing down savings, than were poorer households. Studies from Indonesia clearly show poorer households responding to lower real earnings by increasing household labor supply and reducing discretionary spending. As a result, while all but the richest quintile of households reported reduced lower enrollments and educational spending for school-age children, declines were largest among the poorest households (Thomas et al. 2004). Income-elastic spending on education by poor households leaves their children vulnerable to macroeconomic shocks in ways that are qualitatively dissimilar to wealthy households, and which are likely to have lasting effects on their labor market mobility and earnings as adults.

Summary

In the most rapidly growing Southeast Asian economies, the onset of the Asian crisis in 1997 was at least partly a consequence of underinvestment in education that impeded the transition from labor-intensive to more skill-intensive activities as real labor costs began to rise. Since recovering from the crisis, Southeast Asian countries have continued to make progress in expanding overall access to education and raising average educational levels, following trends established in the pre-crisis era. By the end of the 2000s, most countries in the region had achieved universal or near universal primary school enrollment. However, much work remains to raise primary school retention and completion rates. Secondary and tertiary school enrollments have also increased steadily and, as a result, average years of education among the population aged 15 and older continue to rise. Despite such progress, the gap in educational levels between Southeast Asian countries and their counterparts in Northeast Asia, in particular South Korea and Taiwan, remains high.

Progress on quantity measures, however, tends to mask a more serious problem: the quality of education in Southeast Asian countries remains low at all levels, and there has not been much improvement in the past 10 years. Low-income countries, including Laos, Cambodia, Myanmar, and to a lesser extent Vietnam, lag far behind the others in both overall access to education and in quality of education. They are on par with (or in the case of Vietnam, only slightly above) averages for low and lower middle income countries. But they are well below levels reached by Taiwan and South Korea at comparable stages of those countries' development.

With regard to education inequality, most Southeast Asian countries have made respectable progress in eliminating the gender gap in education, but disparities in other dimensions persist. Inequity in access to education is especially bad in Laos, where indicators of education inequality are the highest in the Southeast Asian region, and some indicators even worsened during the 2000s. School enrollments and expenditures among poor households remain vulnerable to negative shocks from the macroeconomy or labor markets. An implication is that greater volatility from the global market may in the long run produce greater separation in educational outcomes between rich and poor households.

Growth, globalization and the demand for skills

The global economy has changed significantly since the 1960s. It has become more closely interknit, thanks to lower trade barriers and transport costs and the increasing influence of large developing economies like China and the other BRICs in international trade and capital markets. Recent global growth has had more than one relevant feature. It includes ongoing commodity price booms, intensified competition in global markets for labor-intensive manufactures, increased international demand for skill-intensive intermediate goods, and the unbundling of production processes across international platforms. How does this new global context affect human capital development in Southeast Asian economies, especially the latecomers to globalization?

The emergence of China and India as major economic powers is a sea-change in international economic organization. The resulting changes in global factor endowments and trade patterns have already influenced Asian trade and investment patterns. These changes have introduced new complementarities as well as competition among economies. When China first began to attract large-scale foreign investment and expand its export-oriented labor-intensive manufacturing industries, there was widespread concern that it would become a major threat to the continuing economic growth of developing Asian economies. It is now clear, however, that for many Asian economies China's growth boom has generated a new dynamic, reflected in a pronounced acceleration in intra-Asian trade and regional economic integration (Eichengreen and Tong 2006; Athukorala and Kohpaiboon, Chapter 7 in this volume). India's increased growth and trade since the 1990s may hold the promise of an impending second round. Indeed, in the global recession of 2008–10, the resilience and growth of these two giant Asian economies acquired even more prominence as a positive influence.

All Southeast Asian economies have been drawn into the China-centered international production network, resulting in some cases in major changes in production structure and the volume and direction of their international trade (Lall and Albaladejo 2004; Coxhead 2007). This reorientation toward China has had three big types of sectoral impact. First, the producers of labor-intensive manufactures have encountered intense competitive pressures – just as in rich countries. Second, natural resource exporters have enjoyed a sustained commodity price boom, global market fluctuations notwithstanding. Third, manufacturers of more skill-intensive goods such as parts and components for computers, mobile phones, and other electronic devices have found opportunities to expand through participation in so-called "fragmentation trade" (i.e. trade in parts and components for assembly into finished goods elsewhere) with China (see Athukorala and Kohpaiboon, Chapter 7 in this volume).

These changes affect each economy differently. The first of these impacts, that of intensified competition in low-end manufacturing and assembly, is obvious. The clearest feature of China's transition from near autarky to integration with the global economy from the 1980s to the 2000s was the addition of several hundreds of millions of workers to the global supply of low-skilled labor. As may be expected, this enormous shift raised the relative scarcity, and thus returns to, global stocks of all other productive factors – capital and human capital in particular. Two decades of historically unprecedented corporate profits worldwide, prior to the 2008 global financial crisis, speak to the extent of this effect. For labor-abundant countries, however, this change has of course been less positive. Global competition in the markets for labor-intensive products has never been more intense, nor profit margins in these industries thinner.

These conditions are fundamentally different to those faced by the earlier Asian globalizers, even as recently as the early 1990s. The implication is clear: whereas Taiwan, South Korea, and more advanced Southeast Asian economies such as Malaysia and Thailand enjoyed over a decade of dominance in world markets in garments, footwear, and the assembly of simple electronics, the transitional contribution of exports based on such activities to economic growth in poorer Southeast Asian economies like Vietnam, Laos, Cambodia may be very brief indeed. The duration of their reign as key global producers of labor-intensive products will depend largely on exogenous factors, including global economic conditions, economic and policy innovations in other low-income countries, and in some cases the preferential trade policies of importing countries. This places a very high premium on efforts to ensure that the economy is prepared to move smoothly away from dependence on labor-intensive assembly as labor costs increase. Investments in human capital are without doubt at the top of this preparation list, since skills shortages constrain the transition from labor-intensive to skill-intensive processes. The combination of low skills and rising real wages was partly responsible for the sudden decline experienced by many of Thailand's key export-oriented manufacturing industries in the mid-1990s, a factor contributing to that country's economic crisis in 1997–98 (Warr 1999).

The second impact, the China-driven boom in global markets for natural resource products, is also quite clear, but the numbers are big enough to merit review. China is now the world's largest consumer of most of the main metals (accounting for a quarter or more of world imports), and a major consumer of energy. It is the largest world consumer of many agricultural products (including wheat, rice, palm oil, cotton, and rubber), and the second largest in others (soybeans, soybean oil, tea). Between 1990 and 2003, Chinese demand for major metals grew at an average yearly rate of 14.7 percent; from 1999 to the late 2000s it grew at over 17 percent and absorbed around two-thirds of incremental global output. For any country that is specialized in primary commodity production, China is a major export destination and the primary driver of a sustained export boom. Most Southeast Asian economies are abundant in natural resources, especially relative to China, and regional resource exports to China have indeed risen greatly. This resource boom, however, can impose a penalty on profitability in other tradable sectors, for which real exchange rate appreciations and the spending effects of a resource export boom make it harder to compete in domestic factor markets and the global product market. These effects are widespread, but were most noticeable in Indonesia during the 2000s (Thee 2011). Other than mining, which accounts for only a small fraction of employment, agriculture and natural resource sectors are not skill-intensive relative to manufacturing processes, nor do earnings in those industries reward skills as highly (Di Gropello et al. 2011: figure 2.6).[7] The relative decline of growth in manufacturing has also slowed growth of demand for skills, other things equal, and with it the premium on higher education and specialized training. In addition, the spending effect of the resource export booms has driven up prices and employment in many low-skill non-traded industries, particularly construction and personal services, which offer exceptionally low returns to skills (ibid.).

The third impact of China's growth and globalization on Southeast Asia's human capital markets is more subtle. As global trade barriers and transport costs have fallen, firms have been quick to abandon the vertically integrated manufacturing model, in which all (or nearly all) stages of production take place within the borders of a single country. Increasingly, parts and components, especially of electrical and electronic products and machinery, are manufactured in specialized plants located wherever economic logic or business expediency dictates, then shipped to China or another low labor cost location for final assembly and packaging. The wealthy Northeast Asian economies (Korea, Japan, and Taiwan) and Singapore are leaders in this trade, and upper middle-income Southeast Asian economies such as Malaysia and Thailand have developed significant exports of skill-intensive electronics parts and components to assembly plants in China. The more China's factories grow, the more they draw in imports from locations such as these. So long as China's economy continues to expand, and so long as it maintains its preeminent position as the preferred location for labor-intensive assembly operations, countries that can occupy specialized, skill-intensive niches in the parts and components trade will be beneficiaries.

Human capital policy

Policies to develop human capital can be approached from both supply and demand sides. From the former, since human capital is the scarce factor of production in low and middle-income economies, solving supply constraints and increasing access have typically been the primary concerns of most studies of education and education policy. In the next subsection, we discuss the efforts of Southeast Asian countries in addressing such concerns.

But resolving supply constraints only is insufficient, because strong incentives to invest in skills and education are needed to stimulate the demand for schooling. These incentives are largely determined by the returns to skills or education. The literature on the returns to education is large, and there is generally much heterogeneity in estimated returns depending on the dataset used, the country studied, and the empirical strategy employed. For lack of space we do not summarize estimates of returns to education in Southeast Asia here. Instead, we focus on discussing whether and why the returns are optimal or distorted, and their implications. We present three country examples: the Philippines, Vietnam, and Indonesia. In all three, there exist macroeconomic and development policies that are not related directly to education but can nevertheless exert a significant impact on returns to schooling. As a result, these policies influence the accumulation of human capital and pose challenges to long-run economic growth.

Educational investments in Southeast Asia

The perception of high social gains to educational investments motivates separate study of public investment in this sector. When educational investments are measured by public expenditures on education (the most widely available metric), Southeast Asia does not stand out from other developing regions (Orazem and King 2008). In the 2000s most Southeast Asian countries other than Malaysia had below-average public spending on education as a percentage of GDP when compared with other developing countries (Table 12.6). In Thailand and the Philippines, public educational spending as a percentage of GDP even declined from 1999 to 2010. For Indonesia, Thailand, and the Philippines, average real annual growth rates from 1999 to 2010 were disappointingly low – especially so for the Philippines. Per capita public spending on education in Indonesia and the Philippines were also lower than the average of lower middle-income countries, while Thailand's level is lower than the average of upper middle-income countries.

Malaysia is an exception to the above trend. That country has maintained a high level of public educational expenditure, usually at least 5 percent of GNP, for several decades. As a result, its per capita education spending is also higher than the average for middle-income countries. This is partly because education is not just an economic policy in Malaysia, but also a social policy, as the government seeks to "unify various racial groups in national building through education" (Loke and Hoon 2011: 95). But there is concern over the cost-effectiveness of this high level of government spending on education (Booth 2003: 188).

Cambodia and Laos significantly increased their human capital investments during the 2000s. In 1999, both countries had very low per capita spending on education. By 2010, both had caught

Table 12.6 Public spending on education

	Income group (as of 2010)	Public education spending (% of GNP)		Average real annual growth rate in public education spending (%)	Public education spending per capita (current US$)	
		1999	*2010*	*1999–2010*	*1999*	*2010*
Cambodia	Low income	1.0	2.7	38.22	3	20
Indonesia	Lower middle income	2.8	3.1	3.09	16	78
Laos	Low income	1.0	3.3	10.05	3	33
Malaysia	Upper middle income	6.1	5.9	7.03	204	477
Philippines	Lower middle income	3.3	2.7	0.82	34	56
Thailand	Upper middle income	5.1	3.9	3.04	99	162
Singapore	High income	3.0	3.3	9.68	738	1,301
Vietnam	Lower middle income	3.5	5.5	n/a	n/a	64
Low income countries		3.1	4.6	7.2	15	22
Lower middle income countries		4.3	4.8	3.1	83	105
Upper middle income countries		4.6	4.7	5.3	250	332
High income countries		5.0	5.4	2.3	1,489	1,792
World		4.5	4.9	2.7	528	644

Source: Expenditure data from UNESCO (2012); GDP deflator from World Bank.

up to the average level for low-income countries. This improvement was thanks to the increase of public education spending from 1 percent of GDP in 1999 to about 3 percent in 2010, coupled with rapid economic growth during this period. The end result was very high growth rates in public education spending during 1999–2000. Since the two countries started from very low levels of educational spending, however, there is still a large gap between them and the rest of Southeast Asia, as we will see below. Vietnam is another country whose government significantly stepped up its budget on education during the 2000s, from 3.5 percent of GDP in 1999 to 5.5 percent in 2010. As a proportion of total state budget, spending increased almost every year during the 2000s, from 15.5 in 2001 to 20 percent in 2009 (Vu 2012: 48).

Indonesia is another country to undergo an exceptional rate of increase in educational spending. A constitutional amendment in 2002 required that government at all levels devote no less than 20 percent of spending to education. Given the very low initial level, this goal, which has taken a decade since to reach, has in effect elevated public educational spending in Indonesia into the lower mid-range of comparable countries. Even after this massive shift in the allocation of public spending, however, Indonesia spends less per student (as a share of GDP) at both primary and secondary levels than do most regional economies (Al-Samarrai and Cerdan-Infantes 2013).

Singapore's public educational spending stayed at around 3 percent of GDP during the 2000s. But because of a high GDP growth rate, the absolute level of educational spending by the Singaporean government has risen faster than the world average. As a result, there was a substantial increase in per capita spending on education, from US$738/person in 1999 to US$1,301 in 2010. This city-state has rapidly closed the gap with other high-income countries in per capita educational spending.

In summary, during the 2000s, Southeast Asia's record in educational investments was not particularly impressive because their public spending on education as a percentage of GDP was below the average of all developing countries. However, within the decade, many countries in

Southeast Asia, including Laos, Cambodia, Vietnam, Indonesia, and Singapore, significantly increased their public educational expenditure, which probably explained these countries' increase in access to education especially at lower levels. But as seen at the beginning of this chapter, increased access often came at the cost of quality of education. Furthermore, educational achievements in Southeast Asian countries continued to lag behind their neighbors in Northeast Asia, even when comparing at comparable years of development.

Even if Southeast Asian countries succeeded in pushing up the supply of their educated workers in both quantity and quality, there remain other barriers to successful human capital development. We next present examples from the Philippines, Vietnam, and Indonesia to examine economic and development policies that may not directly relate to human capital but can still have strong influence on its outcome.

The Philippines: returns to skills and brain drain

The Philippines experience makes it sadly clear that increases in the supply of educated workers are not a panacea for growth if they do not have opportunities to put their skills to work at home. We have already seen that the Philippines, one of the region's poorest performers in long-term growth, has also had very high indicators of educational achievement. Until the 1990s, it was the regional leader in tertiary enrollment rates. In the 1970s, the Philippine tertiary gross enrollment rate (GER) averaged 18.5 percent while in other countries it remained in the low single digits. Only in the 1990s did tertiary GERs in Singapore, Malaysia, and Thailand begin to surpass those in the Philippines.[8] Thus the Philippines, as with some South Asian countries, has experienced a brain drain – that is, it has become a net exporter of skilled labor in spite of its lower-middle income status.

The proximate causes of this discrepancy are not hard to identify. Several decades of persistent and severe macroeconomic and policy instability in the Philippines discouraged fixed investment, and the resulting lack of installed capital effectively compelled skilled workers to seek higher returns through emigration. From the 1970s through the 2000s, gross fixed capital formation (GCFC) in the Philippines was appreciably lower as a fraction of GDP than in any of the large Southeast Asian economies, averaging 21.7 percent as compared with 24.2 percent in Indonesia, 27.9 percent in Malaysia, 28.4 percent in Thailand, and 33.3 percent in Singapore.[9] Over the decades, high rates of educational achievement, initially perhaps due to strong cultural predispositions, have come to reflect the recognition that productive employment requires emigration, and that schooling – and preferably a tertiary or vocational credential – is the key to winning a well-paying job abroad. As a result, about 10 percent of the Philippine population lives abroad, and remittances from overseas Filipinos, at about 13 percent of GDP, were until very recently the country's largest single source of foreign exchange earnings, and exceeded FDI inflows by many multiples. Moreover the ratio of skilled to less-skilled workers among Philippine workers abroad has risen over time, by the 2000s exceeding one-third of all emigrants (Burgess and Haksar 2005).

The problem of brain drain has been extensively researched and is reasonably well understood. Less has been written on determinants of growth in the demand for education, especially at post-primary levels where most Southeast Asian countries fall below predicted enrollment and completion rates. In rapidly growing economies the opportunity cost of staying in school can be very high, and the returns to additional years of education may be low when most employment growth is concentrated in farming, resource sectors, and light manufacturing. Moreover those economies in which the burden of distortionary development policies is relatively great face larger challenges. Vietnam and Indonesia embody both types of challenge; hence their cases merit closer attention.

Vietnam: factor market distortions and the demand for training

Earlier in the chapter we presented evidence that although Vietnam's educational investments and achievements have exceeded those of other developing countries at comparable income levels, the country still lags far behind other Southeast Asian economies, and its human capital base is still weaker than required to escape the middle-income trap. A straightforward policy recommendation is that Vietnam must increase its investment in human capital, or its government must spend more on education. However, such a policy can only deal with supply-side constraints. In the case of Vietnam, there are further problems with the demand side, or the incentives to invest in education.

Since *doi moi* (or renovation) in 1987, the Vietnamese government has liberalized a number of markets and removed trade restrictions, contributing to the country's rapid economic growth and poverty reduction in the past two and a half decades. But while the government liberalized output markets, it retains substantially greater control over factor markets, i.e. those for land, labor, and capital. Interventions in these critical markets have negative consequences for long-run economic growth and income distribution, including the incentives to invest in education. The connections (as we shall argue) are indirect, but nonetheless unambiguous.

Despite liberalization and privatization efforts, the state sector (that is, public administration as well as state-owned firms) continues to dominate the Vietnamese economy, and government policies continue to strongly favor state firms at the expense of private enterprise and the overall economy. State firms receive cheap credit from Vietnam's state banking system and, as in China and other well-known cases, this causes them to become excessively capital-intensive in their choice of technique relative to the economy's overall factor endowments. Moreover, because capital and skills are complementary inputs, state firms therefore also employ more skill-intensive technologies. However, their hiring of skilled workers is limited. Few of these firms produce for the world market, so their growth is constrained by domestic demand, which has increased less quickly than exports. As in China, this combination results in the rationing of high-paying jobs in state-sector companies. This rationing in turn generates rents that add to the incomes of white-collar workers in state-sector enterprises. Anecdotal evidence suggests that the price of entry to a state-sector job can be as high as one or two years of salary, implying that such jobs are capable of generating substantial rents. Meanwhile, the capital-starved private sector, which has generated most new employment during Vietnam's transition, seeks mainly workers with lower-secondary school education and offers much lower rewards to higher levels of educational attainment. This system has several implications for the demand for high school and tertiary education.

First, returns to schooling at upper-secondary and tertiary levels are contingent on expectations of state employment. For wage earners, the state-sector jobs return 5–9 percent higher earnings per year of education, compared with 3–4 percent per year in non-state employment (Phan and Coxhead 2013). Family connections are strong predictors of employment in state firms, so for the majority of students who lack such connections, the benefit–cost ratio of an additional year of schooling after middle school and into university is much lower. Schooling costs are a major financial burden on families, so policy-induced segmentation of the skilled labor market raises the dropout rate among students who do not expect to have access to state-sector jobs. This results in a lower overall rate of human capital accumulation.

Second, families with connections to state-sector employment invest much more heavily in their children's education (Coxhead and Phan 2013). As long as the dichotomous labor market persists, conditions in Vietnam are ideal for a deepening inequality of income and opportunity between those who have the right family connections and those who lack them.

Third, the requirement of a university degree for most skilled state-sector jobs appears to have sparked a race for higher education credentials, rather than for skills as such. On the positive side, diplomas are among the few tangible benefits that most students can expect from Vietnam's largely unreformed higher education system (Chirot and Wilkinson 2010). But Vietnam's own Ministry of Education has estimated that only 30 percent of those receiving university degrees are adequately trained for the jobs they seek.[10]

An additional implication of this two-track market for skills is that investments in Vietnam's educational infrastructure may be less productive than the government, and the international donor community that supports it, may expect. With only a limited number of high-paying jobs for skilled workers, high school retention rates and university enrollment rates may be constrained as much by low demand as they are by lack of buildings, teachers, and learning materials.

What are the prospects for change? In 2012 Vietnam's government announced plans for reforms, which, if implemented, would reduce the privileges and influence of state-sector companies. But prospects for real progress in reform are clearly constrained by the complex and opaque politics of the one-party state. More positively, the capacity of private-sector firms to mobilize capital from non-state financial markets and from the world market has increased somewhat in recent years, and because greater access to capital also means higher demand for skilled workers, this trend should also help undermine the salary gap that so clearly drives differential returns to secondary and post-secondary education. However, the private sector is still very much on the losing end of Vietnam's financial policies, gaining little from credit expansions and suffering greatly when monetary policies are tightened to fight inflation.

The presence of wholly foreign-owned firms continues to grow (albeit from a very low base when measured by employment shares), and in time their expansion will also help create new demand for workers with applicable skills. Here, the constraint is of a chicken-and-egg type, in which greenfield investments by medium and high-tech companies are discouraged by lack of a suitably skilled workforce. Foreign firms have addressed the skills shortage by training their own workers abroad,[11] and foreign institutions of higher education are also expanding in-country vocational training, but these are very costly ways to compensate for the failings of the country's own system of education.

Finally, there are a few signs that some domestic higher education institutions are finally beginning to acquire enough independence to design and offer meaningful curricula, often in partnership with foreign institutions, but their programs are also quite costly for most Vietnamese students. Vietnam's long-run development prospects are greatest if the problem of market segmentation leading to low educational incentives and diminished employment opportunities for skilled workers is addressed at its source.

Indonesia: resource booms and returns to skills

Southeast Asian countries are relatively resource-rich but have evolved manufacturing sectors that are advanced by the standards of the developing world. Among these economies, however, Indonesia has lagged in terms of investments associated with productivity growth and progress up the technological ladder (Thee 2005; Frankema and Lindblad 2006; Timmer 1999).

In 1970–96 Indonesia was one of only a few resource-rich developing economies worldwide clearly to escape the "curse" of natural resource wealth. A relatively large share of their OPEC-era oil export revenue windfall was used for productivity-enhancing investments in other tradable sectors, notably agriculture and manufacturing (Pinto 1987; Coxhead 2007) and in other development activities, including a huge program of primary school construction begun in 1974, which had a small but statistically significant effect on human capital accumulation, as measured by earnings (Duflo 2001). Gains from these investments were consolidated in the 1980s, during a remarkable period of economic opening and internal reform that offset the negative effects of a huge fall in global oil prices. This momentum, however, has not been maintained in the post-Asian crisis era in spite of a healthy rate of overall economic growth.

Indonesia's productivity growth rate, never high by regional standards, has diminished in the 2000s and now accounts for a negligible fraction of GDP growth (IMF 2011). Growth has instead been fueled by capital accumulation and resource exploitation. Industries whose growth has large effects on the demand for skills have languished. The principal reasons for Indonesia's low performance in skills-based industries have been identified by Bird and Hill (2006) as a relatively low policy weight applied to skills upgrading relative to other policies; lack of adequate educational and training infrastructure for production of skilled workers; and the "fundamental discontinuity" of the crisis itself and of the subsequent political upheavals and transition to democracy. To these three reasons we may add two more: the impact of China's expansion on Indonesia's tradable manufacturing sectors in general, and on labor-intensive and skill-intensive industries in particular (Coxhead 2007; Eichengreen et al. 2004), and the intersectoral effect of commodity market booms that have driven prices of some of Indonesia's key natural resources, agricultural and horticultural exports to all-time highs (World Bank 2007). As previously discussed, the effects of these sustained shocks are likely to have been substantial. At the same time, and by contrast with Thailand and Malaysia, Indonesia has been very slow to develop capacity to exploit opportunities in skill-intensive parts and components trade (Coxhead and Li 2008).

In a highly competitive East Asian regional economy, investments in vertically unbundled skill-intensive industries are highly sensitive to capacity, cost, and efficiency. On investments in human and physical capital, Indonesia continues to lag behind its neighbors. As of 2000, only 5 percent of Indonesians over the age of 25 were recorded as having completed *any* kind of post-secondary education, compared with 7.5 percent in Malaysia and 11.3 percent in Thailand. FDI as a percentage of GDP was 2.7 percent in 2000, equivalent to Thailand and the Philippines, but far behind Malaysia and even Vietnam. Indonesia's rankings on measures of logistics costs are unimpressive (Coxhead and Li 2008). Added to this, Indonesia's foreign investment rules have been notoriously unstable by regional standards. Foreign investors at the skill-intensive margin have stayed away, for the most part, leaving Indonesia on the sidelines of the parts-and-components revolution.

Sluggish investment growth in manufacturing, and the associated loss of opportunities for productivity and efficiency gains through learning by doing (van Wijnbergen 1984), exporting (Sjöholm 1999; Blalock and Gertler 2004), and the hosting of foreign direct investment (Suyanto and Bloch 2009) also depresses returns to investments in human capital (Purnastuti et al. 2013; Coxhead 2014). As noted earlier, the sectors of Indonesian industry that have grown most quickly since the Asian crisis and with the rise of China are those in which skill premia are relatively low. Meanwhile educational costs remain high, and quality low.[12] So, in addition to its difficulties in improving the (quality-adjusted) *supply* of education, Indonesia also faces a paradoxical shortage of *demand* for schooling. Both are important in determining whether the country succeeds in its efforts to decisively reduce poverty and transition to upper middle-income.

One very important reason to intervene in favor of a more skill-intensive pattern of growth has to do with dimming prospects for future natural resource-based growth (see Shively and Smith, Chapter 6 in this volume). The country's oil and gas reserves are nearing exhaustion, and its old-growth forests and fisheries are being rapidly depleted (Resosudarmo 2005). According to the World Development Indicators, Indonesia's "genuine" savings rate, taking account of these and related environmental trends as well as net additions to the stock of human capital, is far below its measured savings rate based on the conventional System of National Accounts.

Though Indonesia is currently a marginal player in global high-tech markets, these markets are expanding very rapidly. There is scope to develop comparative advantage in niche markets in this area, if steps are taken to ensure that the economic and institutional conditions for productive investments are in place. The goal of sustaining and increasing output in skill-intensive sectors, as a means to avoid the middle-income trap, creates a mandate for interventions that promote FDI and encourage young Indonesians to stay in school. But whether this strategy can succeed depends on many factors – not least, the "inertia" built into attempts to change the educational profile of the labor force (Suryadarma and Jones 2013).

Conclusions

The global economy has changed significantly with profound implications for the role of human capital in economic growth and development. Our discussion has made it clear that Southeast Asian economies, no matter at what stage of development, cannot afford to be slow in developing their human capital base. Singapore, the most advanced regional economy, needs to continue its efforts in human capital development to compete with other Asian technological leaders including Japan, Taiwan, South Korea, and Hong Kong. The two upper-middle income Southeast Asian economies, Malaysia and Thailand, must aggressively invest in human capital and upgrade technologies to take advantage of the fact that their production is complementary to China's, so that they can move up the production ladder and become leaders in some advanced industrial processes and avoid the middle-income trap. For low and lower-middle income regional economies that were latecomers to globalization (Vietnam, Laos, Cambodia, Myanmar, and to a lesser extent Indonesia), the threat of a middle-income trap is even more severe. The global mobility of production platforms in labor-intensive industries means that they can no longer rely on their abundance of unskilled labor to maintain the momentum of industrialization. They have to either find niches for their own products (to avoid direct competition with China and other low-cost producers), or find ways to make their products complementary to China's (to become players in the East Asian regional production system). At the same time, skills upgrading is now more important than ever, because one way to gain from regional integration is to quickly move into specialized intermediate goods. For this to happen, they must solve the skill supply constraint to avoid the new resource curse, in which they specialize in resource exports and forgo the chance to industrialize.

Recognizing the importance of a skilled labor force, many countries in Southeast Asia have stepped up their efforts in human capital development, expanding educational access, especially for primary and lower secondary school levels, and raising average years of schooling. However, they have performed much less well in raising educational quality and reducing inequality in access. And in every measure, they still lag far behind the achievements of their Northeast Asian neighbors at comparable stages of development. It seems they also lag behind what is required to overcome the middle-income trap.

Moving forward, what recommendations can one make for Southeast Asian countries regarding human capital policy? Clearly, much stronger commitment to human capital development from governments, in the form of increased public spending on education expenditure, is a step in the right direction. However, to develop human capital requires much beyond spending more money to reduce supply constraints, since there must also be sufficient demand for skills and of the right kind. In some countries, the recommendation is to create policies that promote skill-intensive sectors and generate skilled jobs. In other countries, what are needed are less new policies than the removal of existing distortions that reduce the incentives to acquire higher education.

Acknowledgments

The authors thank Zhilong Ge at Beloit College for his excellent research assistance, and Anne Booth and other seminar participants for helpful comments on earlier drafts.

Notes

1 The "Miracle" economies were identified as Japan, Hong Kong, South Korea, Singapore, Taiwan, Indonesia, Malaysia, and Thailand.
2 Source of data: World Development Indicators Online (accessed 10 July 2013).
3 Data on Singapore's secondary school enrollment rate are seldom available in international datasets, but according to that country's Ministry of Education, Singapore has achieved near universal education at primary and secondary levels (http://www.moe.gov.sg/initiatives/compulsory-education/ (accessed 19 March 2013)).
4 According to International Labour Organization (ILO) data, it was 34 percent in 2002. http://www.ilo. org/public/english/region/asro/bangkok/skills-ap/skills/singapore_tertiary_education.htm
5 For more information on PISA methodology visit: http://www.oecd.org/pisa
6 http://www.arwu.org/ARWU2010.jsp (accessed 16 July 2013).
7 A large global literature finds similar results elsewhere, notably that education has little or no impact on productivity or wages for on-farm work, though it does have an impact in non-farm employment (Fafchamps and Quisumbing 1999; Yang 1997).
8 Source: World Development Indicators Online (accessed 22 July 2013).
9 Source: World Development Indicators Online (accessed 22 July 2013).
10 http://www.reuters.com/article/2009/05/13/vietnam-education-idUSPEK46232520090513 (accessed 13 May 2013).
11 http://blog.oregonlive.com/higher-education/2012/08/portland_state_university_welc.html (accessed 13 May 2013).
12 "The weight of evidence indicates that the quality of education in Indonesia is very poor. The catalogue of qualitative defects in Indonesian primary schools is long, and includes poorly trained teachers, high rates of teacher absenteeism, an emphasis on rote learning, insufficient textbooks, poor quality buildings and a lack of toilets and running water. The effect of such factors on the cognitive abilities of students is very important" (Suryadarma and Jones 2013: 5).

References

Al-Samarrai, S., and P. Cerdan-Infantes, 2013. "Where did all the money go? Financing basic education in Indonesia." In D. Suryadarma and G. Jones (eds), *Education in Indonesia*. Singapore: ISEAS, pp. 109–38.
Baunto, A.L., 2011. "Education reforms in Indonesia." In C. Brock and L.P. Symaco (eds), *Education in Southeast Asia*. Oxford: Symposium Books.
Bird, K., and H. Hill, 2006. "Indonesian industrial policies: before and after the crisis." In Yun-Peng Chu and H. Hill (eds), *The East Asian High-Tech Drive*. Cheltenham: Edward Elgar, pp. 335–76.
Blalock, G., and P. Gertler, 2004. "Learning from exporting revisited in a less developed setting." *Journal of Development Economics* 75: 397–412.
Booth, A. 2003. "Education and economic development in Southeast Asia: myths and realities." In K.S. Jomo (ed.), *Southeast Asian Paper Tigers? From Miracle to Debacle and Beyond*. London: Routledge.
Burgess, R., and V. Haksar, 2005. "Migration and foreign remittances in the Philippines." IMF Working Paper No. WP/05/111.
Chirot, L., and B. Wilkinson, 2010. "The intangibles of excellence: governance and the quest to build a Vietnamese apex research university." http://www.ash.harvard.edu/extension/ash/docs/Apex.pdf (accessed 15 May 2013).
Coxhead, I. 2007. "International trade and the natural resource 'curse' in Southeast Asia: does China's growth threaten regional development?" *World Development* 35(7): 1099–119.

Coxhead, I. 2014. "Did Indonesia's boom leave its poor behind? Adverse labor market trends in the post-crisis era." Manuscript, University of Wisconsin-Madison.

Coxhead, I., and M. Li. 2008. "Prospects for skills-based export growth in a labour-abundant, resource-rich developing economy." *Bulletin of Indonesian Economic Studies* 44(2): 199–228.

Coxhead, I., and D. Phan. 2013. "Princelings and paupers? State employment and the distribution of human capital investments among Vietnamese households." *Asian Development Review* 30(2): 26–48.

Di Gropello, E., with A, Kruse and P. Tandon. 2011. *Skills for the Labor Market in Indonesia: Trends in Demand, Gaps, and Supply.* Washington, DC: World Bank.

Duflo, E. 2001. "Schooling and labor market consequences of school construction in Indonesia: evidence from an unusual policy experiment". *American Economic Review* 91: 795–813.

The Economist. 2013. "Education in Vietnam: very good on paper." http://www.economist.com/blogs/banyan/2013/12/education-vietnam (accessed 2 May 2014).

Eichengreen, B., and H. Tong. 2006. "Fear of China." *Journal of Asian Economics* 17(2): 226–40.

Eichengreen, B., Y. Rhee, and H. Tong. 2004. "The impacts of China on the exports of other Asian countries." NBER Working Paper No. 10768.

Eichengreen, B., D. Park, and K. Shin. 2013. "Growth slowdown redux: new evidence on the middle income trap." NBER Working Paper Series No. 18673. http://www.nber.org/papers/w18673 (accessed 8 May 2014).

Fafchamps, M., and A. Quisumbing. 1999. "Human capital, labor allocation and productivity in rural Pakistan." *Journal of Human Resources* 34: 369–406.

Frankema, E., and J. T. Lindblad. 2006. "Technological development and economic growth in Indonesia and Thailand since 1950." *ASEAN Economic Bulletin* 23(3): 303–24.

Granado, F.J.A. del, W. Fengler, A. Ragatz, and E. Yavus. 2007. "Investing in Indonesia's education: allocation, equity, and efficiency of public expenditures." Policy Research Working Paper 4329. Washington, DC: World Bank.

International Monetary Fund (IMF). 2011. "Indonesia: selected issues." IMF Country Report No. 11/310. Washington, DC: IMF.

Khoman, S. 2005. "Education." In Peter Warr (ed.), *Thailand after the Crisis*. London: Routledge.

Laovakul, D. 2009. "Regional disparity in Thailand." Online ppt presentation, Faculty of Economics, Thammasat University (accessed 20 March 2013).

Lall, S., and M. Albaladejo. 2004. "China's competitive performance: a threat to East Asian manufactured exports." *World Development* 32(9): 1441–6.

Loke, S.H., and C.L. Hoon. 2011. "Education in Malaysia: development and transformations." In C. Brock and L.P. Symaco (eds), *Education in South-East Asia*. Oxford: Symposium Books, pp. 95–119.

Mesa, E.P. 2007. "Measuring education inequality in the Philippines." *Philippine Review of Economics* 44(2): 33–70.

Orazem, P.F., and E.M. King. 2008. "Schooling in developing countries: the roles of supply, demand and government policy." In T.P. Schulz and J. Strauss (eds), *Handbook of Development Economics*, Vol. 4. Amsterdam: North-Holland, pp. 3475–559.

Phan, D., and I. Coxhead. 2013. "Long-run costs of piecemeal reform: wage inequality and returns to education in Vietnam." *Journal of Comparative Economics* 41(4): 1106–22.

Pinto, B. 1987. "Nigeria during and after the oil boom: a policy comparison with Indonesia." *World Bank Economic Review* 1(3): 419–45.

PISA (Programme for International Student Assessment). 2012. *PISA 2012 Results in Focus*. www.oecd.org/pisa (accessed 2 May 2014).

Purnastuti, L., P.W. Miller, and R. Salim. 2013. "Declining rates of returns to education: evidence for Indonesia." *Bulletin of Indonesian Economic Studies* 49(2): 213–36.

Resosudarmo, B. (ed.). 2005. *The Politics and Economics of Indonesia's Natural Resources*. Singapore: ISEAS.

Sjöholm, F. 1999. "Exports, imports and productivity: results from Indonesian establishment data." *World Development* 27(4): 705–15.

Suryadarma, D., and G. Jones (eds). 2013. "Meeting the education challenge." In D. Suryadarma and G. Jones (eds), *Education in Indonesia*. Singapore: Institute for Southeast Asian Studies, pp. 1–15.

Suyanto, R.A.S., and H. Bloch. 2009. "Does foreign direct investment lead to productivity spillovers? Firm level evidence from Indonesia." *World Development* 37(12): 1861–76.

Tan, J. 2013 "Singapore: the Malay ethnic minority – playing perennial catch-up in education?" In Lorraine Pe Symaco (ed.) *Education in South-East Asia*. London: Bloomsbury Academic.

Thee, K.W. 2005. "The major channels of international technology transfer to Indonesia: an assessment." *Journal of the Asia-Pacific Economy* 10(2): 214–36.

Thee, K.W. 2011. "Indonesia: blessed by strong economic growth and the curse of resources." www.eastasiaforum.org

Thomas, D., K. Beegle, E. Frankenberg, B. Sikoki, J. Strauss, and G. Teruel. 2004. "Education in a crisis." *Journal of Development Economics* 74: 53–85.

Timmer, M.P. 1999. "Indonesia's ascent on the technology ladder: capital stock and total factor productivity in Indonesian manufacturing, 1975–95." *Bulletin of Indonesian Economic Studies* 35(1): 75–97.

UNESCO. 2010. *Reaching the Marginalized*. EFA Global Monitoring Report. Paris: UNESCO.

UNESCO. 2012. *Youth and Skills: Putting Education to Work*. EFA Global Monitoring Report. Paris: UNESCO.

van Wijnbergen, S. 1984. "The Dutch disease: a disease after all?" *Economic Journal* 94: 41–55.

Vu, L.H. 2012. "An overview of access to and inequality in the Education System of Vietnam." *Asia-Pacific Development Journal*, 19(1): 37–62.

Warr, P.G. 1999. "What happened to Thailand?" *World Economy* 22(5): 631–50.

World Bank. 1993. *The East Asian Miracle: Economic Growth and Public Policy*. Oxford: Oxford University Press.

World Bank. 2007. "East Asia and Pacific update April 2007: ten years after the crisis." http://go.worldbank.org/JEQO45CMX0 (accessed 28 November 2007).

World Bank. 2012. *Putting Higher Education to Work: Skill and Research for Growth in East Asia*. World Bank East Asia and Pacific Regional Report. Washington, DC: World Bank.

Yang, D. 1997. "Education and off-farm work." *Economic Development and Cultural Change* 45: 613–32.

Zhang, L., H. Yi, R. Lo, C. Liu, and S. Rozelle. 2013. "The human capital roots of the middle income trap: the case of China." *Agricultural Economics* 44(s1): 151–62.

13

Internal and international migration in Southeast Asia

Guntur Sugiyarto[1]

ASIAN DEVELOPMENT BANK

Introduction

The Southeast Asia region[2] consists of 10 countries: Brunei Darussalam, Cambodia, Indonesia, Lao PDR, Malaysia, Myanmar, the Philippines, Singapore, Thailand, and Vietnam. These countries are members of the Association of Southeast Asian Nations (ASEAN). In terms of population size and land area, the countries in the region vary considerably. The region is home to 619 million people, of whom about 418 million are of working age (15–64 years old), and has a labor force (the economically active population having and/or looking for a job) of about 290 million. The number of workers in the labor force across countries varies considerably, since labor force participation rates are similar across the countries in the region. Therefore, the number of jobs needed across the countries also varies in line with the size of the labor force. Given their different levels of development, the types of job needed will also vary. Population age structures across countries also show significant variation, with some countries already completing the demographic transition (Singapore and Thailand), while others still have relatively young populations (Lao PDR, Philippines, Cambodia, and Indonesia; see Jones, Chapter 10 in this volume). Their different levels of development are also reflected in key demographic indicators, such as the Total Fertility Rate (TFR), Infant Mortality Rate (IMR), Maternal Mortality Ratio (MMR), and Age Dependency Ratio (ADR), as shown in Table 13.1. More developed countries have lower TFR, IMR, MMR, and ADR. These variations in population and demographic factors are in large measure reflections of progress in their economies. Singapore, for instance, has achieved the status of a high-income country, and the earnings of the average Singaporean are many multiples of those of the majority of the Southeast Asian population.

Economically, the region is one of the most dynamic in the world (see Phung et al., Chapter 4 in this volume), and in the twenty-first century, the countries of ASEAN, which account for virtually all of Southeast Asia, have become much more closely integrated in terms of intra-regional trade and investment. Intra-ASEAN trade now accounts for about 25 percent of total regional trade, and intra-ASEAN FDI is about 23 percent of total inward FDI, and both these figures are increasing[3] (for details and trends see Hill and Menon, Chapter 17 in this volume). Therefore, the countries in the region are economically close, and becoming even more interconnected as development proceeds and as ASEAN institutions become more effective at lowering internal barriers. The intertwining of regional economies can only increase further in the

Table 13.1 Basic key indicators of countries in Southeast Asia

Countries	Land Total Surface ('000 km²)	Population Total (million) 2013	Population Average Annual Growth Rate (%) 2008–2013	Density (persons per km² of total surface area) 2013	Total Fertility Rate (births per woman) 2012	Age Dependency Ratio (Number of persons aged < 15 and > 65 to Number of persons aged 15–64 years, %) 2012	Infant Mortality Rate (deaths per 1,000 live births) 2012	Maternal Mortality Ratio (per 100,000 live births) 2010	Per Capita GNI, Atlas Methiod (US$) 2012
Brunei Darussalam	5.77	0.41	1.6	70	2.0	42	7	24	31,590
Cambodia	181.04	14.68	1.5	81	2.9	57	34	250	880
Indonesia	1,904.57	248.82	1.5	131	2.4	52	26	220	3,420
Lao PDR	236.80	6.66	2.2	28	3.1	65	54	470	1,270
Malaysia	330.80	29.95	1.7	91	2.0	47	7	29	9,820
Myanmar	676.59	61.65	1.1	91	2.0	44	41	200	...
Philippines	300.00	97.40	1.5	325	3.1	62	24	99	2,500
Singapore	0.72	5.40	2.2	7,540	1.3	36	2	3	47,210
Thailand	513.12	64.62	0.4	126	1.4	39	11	48	5,210
Vietnam	330.96	89.71	1.1	271	1.8	42	18	59	1,550

Source: ADB Basic Statistics, 2013.

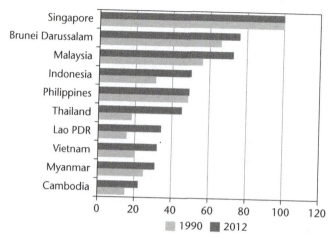

Figure 13.1 Urbanization rates in Southeast Asia region, 1990 and 2012 (%)
Source: ADB Key Indicators 2013.

future given ASEAN's commitment to a regional economic union by 2020 (i.e. the ASEAN Vision 2020), which will, among other factors, be achieved through the establishment of the ASEAN Economic Community (AEC) from 2015 onwards (ASEAN Secretariat 2011). Progress in economic growth and in regional integration is also reflected in regional labor markets. In line with the increasing level of development, urbanization and international migration in the region have increased significantly.

In terms of urbanization, more than half (51 percent) of the region's population now live in urban areas, up from 44 percent in 2000. Singapore tops the list, of course, with an urbanization rate of 100 percent (Figure 13.1). Other countries with high urbanization rates are Brunei and Malaysia, each with more than 70 percent. On the other hand, urbanization rates in the transitional economies of Cambodia, Lao PDR, Myanmar, and Vietnam (CLMV) are still very low, averaging less than 40 percent. However, urbanization rates in these economies, as in the middle-income countries of Thailand, Indonesia, and Malaysia, have all increased tremendously in the past two decades, as Figure 13.1 reveals. Only the Philippines has not shown a significant increase in urbanization over this period.[4]

Urbanization is driven by industrialization and the associated growth of service sectors such as construction, local trade and transportation, and finance. Urbanization accounts for the majority of internal migration in Southeast Asia. Except in areas of rapid plantation growth, there has been limited expansion of employment in agriculture or in the rural economy.

On the international front, the region is one of the main sources of migrants worldwide. It contributes more than 13 million or 6 percent of the total global migrant stock, which is estimated at 216 million (World Bank 2011). With this number, if all migrants were combined as a single country it would be the fifth most populous one in the world.

In line with the expansion of intra-ASEAN trade and FDI, the number of intra-ASEAN migrants is also significant. In 2010, the stock of migrants internal to the region was estimated at 3.9 million, or 30 percent of total international migrants from Southeast Asia. This is the official figure, but the actual number including the undocumented migrants could be much bigger.[5] Therefore, about one-third of international migrants from the region stay in the region, while the rest spread all over the world. More recent estimates both of total migrants and of the intra-ASEAN share are even larger: 14 million migrants, almost 6 million of whom are intra-ASEAN.

About 90 percent are hosted by just three countries, Thailand, Malaysia, and Singapore (Baruah 2012). The Philippines contributes the most number of intra-regional migrants (about 34 percent) despite the fact that the region is not the main destination for Filipino migrants. The second main contributor is Indonesia with a 20 percent share.[6]

For migration to the rest of the world, the main destinations of international migrants from Southeast Asia are the Middle East, North America, Europe, and East Asia. Some ASEAN countries also have historical links with other countries that generate bilateral migration, such as between Vietnam and Russia, France and the USA; the Philippines and the USA, and Indonesia and the Netherlands. However, migrants go to many destinations; Filipino migrants are the most widespread, working in more than 200 countries worldwide.[7] Vietnam, for reasons that are linked to its history, is another country that has migrants spread across many countries around the world.

International migration within and beyond the region is increasing for a variety of reasons. The main causes are:

(i) Global economic and demographic imbalances across countries and regions in the world. Some countries and regions have become centers of economic growth, and in so doing attract migrant workers from other countries. This is further strengthened by aging populations in many parts of the world (i.e. the more developed countries), which stimulates demand for foreign workers to replace the aging workforce and/or to take care of the aged.

(ii) Increasing globalization and global production networks bring along migrant workers from different parts of the world as part of the production process. Foreign trade liberalization and investment facilitation (also as part of FDI) frequently involves allowances for foreign workers to work in the destination country.[8]

(iii) Adverse effects of climate changes that have forced some people to move across countries and regions. Climate change is responsible for rising sea levels, more frequent and greater flooding, and other natural disasters such as tropical storms, giving rise to a new phenomenon of climate-induced migration.[9] Migrants moving away from weather-affected regions can sometimes be classified as refugees, but many have also become economic migrants.

(iv) "Labor exporting" policies of developing countries to reduce domestic unemployment and increase productivity of labor in the short term. International migration has now become an integral part of development strategy in many countries, including some in Southeast Asia, to overcome excess supply of labor and low labor productivity.

International migration brings benefits to sending countries by generating remittances that support consumption expenditures of migrants' families, the country's balance of payments position, and financial sector development. In addition, migration can also generate social and other gains in the form of knowledge and skills acquired abroad that could be useful if and when applied in the home country.[10] However, international migration also brings economic and social costs to the household, community, and country.

In general, international migration is relatively more difficult and costly than internal movement. This is why internal migration is usually much more significant than international migration in terms of the number of migrants involved and the total amounts of remittances generated. Moreover, given the proximity and lower cultural barriers, internal migration directly involves many more poor people from poorer regions than does international migration, which is widely found to be positively selected on skills and abilities.

At a global scale, international migrants mainly come from the middle income groups in source countries. There is thus an inverse U-shape relationship between GDP per capita and the frequency of outmigration. This can be seen both within countries, but also across countries:

there are relatively fewer outmigrants from the poorest and richest countries (Adams and Page 2003). The smaller numbers of international migrants from poor countries are mainly due to the relatively greater costs of international migration and the fact that many poor workers lack the requisite skills, abilities, and of course network connections to go abroad. On the other hand, internal migrants typically also have more friends, families, and relatives in the city to help them migrate and to reduce the overall costs of migration. Therefore, internal migration in general has been claimed to have greater potential than international migration to reduce poverty and contribute to economic growth in developing countries (Deshingkar 2006). On the other hand, international migrants often take advantage of much greater earnings differentials than are available to those who only move internally.

The remainder of this chapter examines current trends and dynamics of urbanization and international migration in Southeast Asia, highlighting key features. The next section discusses conceptual issues important to the understanding of migration, especially in the context of increasing connectivity within the region and globalization worldwide. This discussion provides a foundation for the rest of the chapter. The coverage is by no means exhaustive, but covers key points for understanding migration in the Southeast Asian context. The following section discusses internal migration, and is essentially about urbanization as discussed above. It is followed by a discussion of international migration, which is divided into two parts: international migration within the region (intra-ASEAN migration) and international migration from the region to the rest of the word. This breakdown is necessary, because the two types of migration have very different institutional challenges and policy implications. The final section highlights key challenges and policy implications with particular attention to the so-called ASEAN Vision 2020, which articulates the regional aspiration to create an economic union, including greater openness in labor markets, by 2020.

Understanding migration

Migration is a fundamental economic behavior; people move from place to place in an effort to raise their earnings power. In this context, orderly internal or international migration can have positive impacts on the communities of origin and destination. Economic migration also has the potential of facilitating transfers of knowledge and skills, and of contributing to cultural enrichment.

Conceptually, migration is a spatial issue involving movements of people from their residential place to a new destination by crossing administrative borders for a certain period of time. Based on the coverage area, migration can be classified into internal (domestic) and international, and based on the time span, it can be categorized into life-time migration, current migration, and frequent (or circular) migration. Life-time migrants are those born in a different place than their current place of residence. Current migrants are those who migrated to a different place in the last five years or similar period, and frequent or circular migrants are those who move many times over a certain period of time. Moreover, based on the intention to stay, migration can also be grouped into temporary and permanent migration. These different time spans and intents are not strictly or uniformly imposed in the categorization of migration in this chapter, as official data are typically very unclear about definitions and criteria. This lack of clarity is unfortunate, since the economic and policy implications for each type and motivations for migration are very different. More interestingly, analyses or concerns on migration from the host country perspective often perceive migration as permanent, and as such to be a source of problems (in addition to potential benefits).[11] On the other hand, from the home or sending country perspective migration is often seen as temporary, incorporating the expectation that migrants will return home, bringing with them "social, political and other remittances" (i.e. better knowledge, skills, wider exposure, more experience, etc.) in addition to financial flows remitted during the migration period.

Remittances are integral to migration. Economic migrants see themselves as part of a larger decision-making unit, and their move to a new labor market is typically driven by the interests of that larger unit.[12] Migrants usually try to maintain links and relationships with family and relatives in their place of origin. Remittances also sustain migrants' social support system, which is common in the Asian context. In many main sending countries in Asia, such as Indonesia and the Philippines, migrants are even considered as "modern-day heroes" because of the home country's expectation of remittances to help not only the migrant families but also the domestic economy in general.[13]

For labor migration, workers tend to move if there is a significant wage difference between the origin and destination, but the decision to move is based more on significant difference in expected income rather than just wage difference (Harris and Todaro 1970). This implies that migrants are economically rational looking for higher income in the destination. This view is in line with opportunity theory referring to migration as a result of perceived opportunities in the destination compared to origin (Stouffer 1940). Furthermore, there are "intervening obstacles" between the origin and destination and the perceived opportunities are seen differently by migrants of different backgrounds or personal characteristics, including gender (Lee 1966). Meantime, Zipf's inverse distance law and gravity model emphasize the role of distance and population density (economic opportunity) which have a negative and positive relationship, respectively. Longer distance will result in fewer migrants and similarly for the less number of opportunities.

The new economics of labor migration consider migration as part of a household or family strategy to deal with limitations at the home place and to improve living standards. It is no longer an individual issue and the factors affecting migration decisions are also no longer only economic aspects, but also non-economic issues such as information, insurance, and social capital that make migration networks important (Stark and Bloom 1985). In terms of stages, migration can take place in one stage or in multiple stages. Those who migrate further tend to go to bigger cities and most migrants are adult. Men are the majority of migrants but women have increasingly become more significant. More and more women have migrated currently so that the latest UN data show migrant stock worldwide has already gender-balanced as women migrants contribute to half of the stock (see Dumont et al. 2007). Internal and international migrations have become common as more and more people migrate in search for a better life. The decision to migrate is part of economic strategy directly associated to benefits and costs of migration showing that migrants are rational and consider the costs and benefits of migration (Pienkos 2006).

In a macro or global context, migration involves releasing excess labor from less productive areas to more productive ones, making migration desirable for it can potentially improve overall growth and productivity in the origin and destination. Therefore, if managed properly, migrations can be translated into increasing overall income and reducing poverty.

The importance of internal migration in comparison to international migration can be seen in that internal migrants outnumber international migrants by an order of magnitude, i.e. about 3.5 times at the global level (IOM 2010). The role of internal migration and remittance in the economy has also increased significantly. Internal migration and remittances can be more important for poverty reduction compared to international migration and remittance. It is important to note that internal and international migrations and their remittances are not the same, but they have some linkages (Skeldon 2008). It is important to look at both internal and international migrations and remittances as migration has become such an important factor in development, especially in the context of increasing gaps in wages, productivities, and living standards, as well as other factors.[14] And the role of women should be taken into account in understanding migration and considering policy actions.[15]

Urbanization in Southeast Asia

Urbanization is commonly defined as a process of the increasing number and share of urban population in the total population. This is as a result of a combination between natural growth of population in urban areas, and movement of people from rural to urban areas. The former also includes the reclassification of rural areas as urban. Statistically speaking, more and more rural areas have become urban due to increasing population density, a higher share of workers with non-agriculture as their main income source, and greater access to or availability of "urban facilities" like schools, hospitals, and markets.[16] Accordingly, in an extreme case, urbanization can still increase although there is no natural population growth in an urban area and no actual movement of people from rural to urban. In this case the urbanization is purely because of rural development into urban. This point is very important in understanding urbanization rates and/or trends as their number can be much higher than the growth of urban population.[17]

Rural–urban migration constitutes the major part of internal migration. Other internal migrations such as from urban to rural and rural to rural areas are usually negligible. There is also government-sponsored migration that is quite different with other normal internal migration. Examples from populating Highland in Vietnam and transmigration programs from Java to outer Java in Indonesia give valuable lessons that spreading population in a country for various seemingly good reasons can be problematic if we ignore the human rights and characteristics of the indigenous people.

Urbanization in Southeast Asia started at a very low base, lower than Africa, but has increased at a scale and speed seldom seen. From 1950 to 2010, Asia's urban population has increased by more than 1.4 billion, and from 2000 to 2020 the number is expected to increase by 822 million people. By 2050, Asia will be transformed as its urban population will double from 1.6 to 3.1 billion with an urbanization rate of 63 percent. This is an increase of 20.4 percentage points from 2010 or about 0.5 percentage points annually (Table 13.2). The numbers for Southeast Asia are even more staggering (Table 13.3). The urbanization rate in this region will be 66 percent by 2050, about 3 percentage points higher than the Asian average. Moreover, five of the 10 countries in the region are expected to have more than 20 percentage point increases in urbanization rates (the Asian benchmark): Lao PDR (31.5), Vietnam (25.5), Myanmar (24.7), Indonesia (22.2), and Thailand (22.0). This is in addition to Singapore and Malaysia, which are already highly urbanized.

Table 13.2 Level of urbanization and its percentage change across different regions

Region	Level of Urbanization (%)			Percentage Point Change (%)	
	2000	2010	2050	2000–2010	2010–2050
Europe	70.8	72.7	82.2	1.9	9.5
Latin America and the Caribbean	75.5	78.8	86.6	3.4	7.8
Northern America	79.1	82.0	88.6	2.9	6.6
Africa	35.6	39.2	57.7	3.6	18.5
Asia	35.5	42.5	62.9	7.0	20.4
China, People's Rep. of	35.9	49.2	77.3	13.3	28.1
India	27.7	30.9	51.7	3.3	20.8

Source: ADB estimates based on UN (2012).

Table 13.3 Level of urbanization and its percentage change across different countries in Southeast Asia

Region	Urbanization Rates (%)			Percentage Point Change (%)	
	2000	2010	2050	2000–2010	2010–2050
Southeast Asia	38.2	44.1	66.0	5.9	21.9
Brunei Darussalam	71.2	75.6	85.9	4.4	10.3
Cambodia	18.6	19.8	37.6	1.2	17.8
Indonesia	42.0	49.9	72.1	7.9	22.2
Lao PDR	22.0	33.1	64.6	11.1	31.5
Malaysia	62.0	72.0	86.0	10.0	14.0
Myanmar	27.2	32.1	56.8	4.9	24.7
Philippines	48.0	48.6	65.6	0.7	17.0
Singapore	100.0	100.0	100.0	0.0	0.0
Thailand	31.1	33.7	55.7	2.6	22.0
Vietnam	24.4	30.4	55.9	6.0	25.5

Source: ADB Estimates.

Urbanization in Asia is also characterized by very high population density, as reflected in the growing number of megacities (cities with more than 10 million inhabitants). Asia now is a home to 12 out of 23 megacities in the world. Three are in Southeast Asia: Manila, Bangkok, and Jakarta.[18] By 2025, the number of megacities in Asia is expected to increase to 21, out of 37 megacities in the world, and by 2050, the urbanization rate in Asia is to reach 63 percent, still below but closer to the global urbanization rate of 67 percent.

The speed of this process is also noteworthy. On current estimates, it would only take 95 years for Asia to raise its urbanization rate from 10 percent to 50 percent, while for other world regions the times were much longer: 210 years for Latin America and the Caribbean, 150 years for Europe, and 105 years for North America.

It is important to put in perspective, however, that despite the very strong urbanization trends, the Asian urbanization level has still a long way to go as in 2010 the urban share of Asia's population was still only 43 percent, lower than the global urbanization rate of 52 percent (Figure 13.2). The urbanization rate in Southeast Asia is higher, i.e. already 44 percent in 2010 and would increase to 66 percent in 2050.

There are positive and negative impacts of urbanization. On the positive side, the massive urbanization has accompanied the rise of the middle class and the decline of poverty. The middle class (defined as having expenditure of $2–$20 per person per day, in purchasing power-adjusted currency units) in Asia has risen significantly, i.e. from 21 percent in 1990 to 56 percent in 2008, while poverty (defined as <$2 per capita per day) has declined considerably from 79 percent in 1998 to 43 percent in 2008 (ADB 2010).[19] Cities have become the centers of growth, and their rise has also in general improved delivery of services such as education, health, and sanitation. However, urbanization also brings serious challenges of resource allocation and environmental degradation. Urban growth has outstripped urban development, placing stress on resources such as water supply and waste disposal as well as provision of urban services such as schools and policing.

International migration

As mentioned above, global economic and demographic imbalances, increasing globalization, and the effects of climate change all encourage or force people to move. In 2010, there were almost

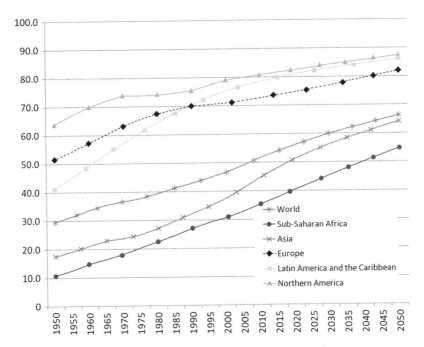

Figure 13.2 Urbanization rates in Asia compared with other regions (%)
Source: Derived from the World Urbanization Prospects: The 2014 Revision, UN DESA.
Notes: Level of urbanization is based on country definition of urban.

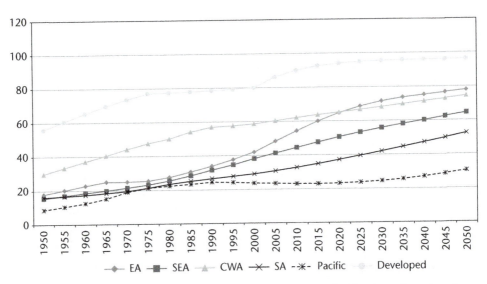

Figure 13.3 Urbanization rates in Southeast Asia region compared with other sub-regions (over 5-year interval, %)
Source: Derived from the World Urbanization Prospects: The 2014 Revision, UN DESA.
Notes: Level of urbanization is based on country definition of urban. Regional grouping is based on ADB Key Indicators.

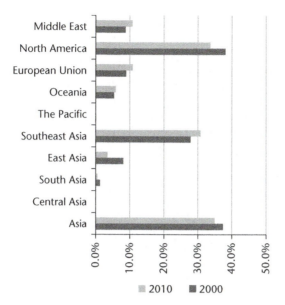

Figure 13.4   Main destinations of international migrants from Southeast Asia based on migrant stock, 2000–10 (%)
Source: Calculated from the Migrant Stock (see Appendix).

one billion migrants (internal and international) worldwide – roughly one in seven of the world's population. The total number of international migrants was 214 million people[20] and the total number of internal migrants was 740 million (IOM 2010). Remittances sent home by international migrants came to $414 billion in 2009, of which $316 billion was sent to developing countries alone.[21] Remittances have become the second most important source of external funding in developing countries. This poses challenges to create efficient and equitable migration systems that benefit labor migrants and their families while contributing to long-term economic growth and development.

Southeast Asia has become a major net exporter of labor, receiving a significant amount of global remittances. Where Asia contributes about 31 percent of the global migrant stock, Southeast Asia's contribution is around 6 percent, equivalent to 2 percent of population. This is still lower than the global share of 3 percent. It should be noted, however, that much intra-ASEAN migration is illegal and is not reflected in the official statistics.

It is important to note some key trends of international migration in the region:

(i)   It is expected that the total number of international migrants will increase in the future. This is for the various reasons described in previous sections. The opening of Myanmar's economy, higher minimum wages in labor importers such as Thailand, and freer labor mobility under the proposed AEC from 2015 and beyond, will further increase international migration, especially intra-ASEAN migration.

(ii) There have been some shifts in the main destinations of migrants. For instance, the oil boom in the Middle East in 1973 and its economic expansion afterwards attracted many migrants from Southeast Asia who worked as construction labor, household help, and in other low-skilled jobs. The Middle East remains dependent on imported labor and continues to attract workers. Meanwhile, rapid growth in the industrializing economies of East Asia has also shifted migrant destinations to these countries.

(iii) There are an increasing number of temporary migrant workers on fixed and short-term contracts. Permanent migration is limited to countries such as Australia, Canada, and New Zealand, where permanent residency can be obtained after the fixed contract ends.

(iv) Most migrants are semi- and unskilled workers in casual jobs such as in construction, manufacturing, service, and domestic work.

(v) There is a significant number of illegal migrants very vulnerable to abuse and exploitation.

(vi) There is an increasing number of women, as more and more of them migrate within the region and to the rest of the world, mostly for low wage occupations.[22]

(vii) There is an increasing commercialization: recruitment agencies have come to occupy a critical space, often acting both as employer and as recruiter. Strong push factors and limited public employment opportunities have made the role of private intermediaries dominant, and this has given rise to numerous problems. The widespread practice of "fly now, pay later" schemes among low skilled workers attests to the special vulnerability of migrants, since these arrangements can easily turn into debt bondage to recruiting agencies or their employers.

At the global level, remittance flows to developing countries have been significant. Remittance inflows to developing countries were estimated to be $414 billion in 2013, much bigger that those of Overseas Development Assistance (ODA) and other private flows. More importantly remittance inflows have been the most stable of all, steadily increasing despite economic shocks in the destination and home countries (Figure 13.5). Considering that developing economies have been up and down, the stable and increasing flows of remittances show their countercyclical nature which is very good for the economies. This is in contrast with other financial inflows, such as FDI and other private flows, that tend to decline when the countries are in crisis and increase during

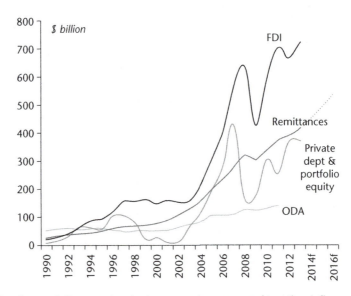

Figure 13.5 Remittance inflows to developing countries compared to other inflows
Source: Ratha 2014.

booms. The amount of remittance flows to Southeast Asia has been very significant. For example, remittance inflows to the Philippines have been around 10 percent of the country's GDP in recent years, while the flows to Indonesia and Vietnam are also significant at around 7–8 percent of GDP. These figures refer only to official remittances, while the unofficial remittances are also significant (ADB 2012b).

International migration within the region

Intra-ASEAN migration is very significant, amounting to 3.9 million migrants compared with about 12.9 millions going to the rest of the world.[23] Therefore, about 31 percent of the international migration in the region is intra-ASEAN migration. On the other hand, there are about 6.7 million migrants from the rest of the world in Southeast Asia, making the region a net exporter of migrants (Note: the figures are for 2010 to correspond to the population data).

The main destinations of migrants from Southeast Asia are North America (34 percent), within the region (31 percent), the Middle East (11 percent), and the European Union (11 percent). These destinations change following the dynamic developments in the destination countries. On the other hand, the intra-ASEAN migration has two main patterns. The first is centered around the Mekong river, with Thailand as the hub and the four neighboring countries of Cambodia, Lao PDR, Myanmar, and Vietnam as the suppliers,[24] and the second is around Malaysia with Singapore, Brunei Darussalam, and Malaysia as the main destinations for migrant workers from Indonesia and the Philippines. Most of these migrants are unskilled or semi-skilled labor for construction, agriculture, and domestic work (Manning and Bhatnagar 2004; Kaur 2010; UN Women 2013; Orbeta and Gonzales 2013).

Intra-ASEAN migration has a long historical background (see Ananta and Arifin 2004). Countries of the region share some similarities in tradition, and even (in some cases) language. This reduces the barriers to crossing borders, even for those with low education or skills.[25] Of course, present-day borders also reflect colonial-era boundaries, which were drawn up with little consideration for the socio-cultural aspects of indigenous populations. As a result, there are some ethnic groups separated by national boundaries into different countries,[26] and this too encourages seemingly "natural" migration from the migrant's perspective. These historical anomalies further complicate problems related to the governance and management of migration. Finally, as mentioned before, the increasing globalization, global production networks, and regional integration, as well as the adverse impacts of climate change further drive migrations within and outside the region. Therefore, the management of international migration in the region is increasingly complex, requiring not only national but regional and global policy actions.

Key driving factors

The countries of Southeast Asia vary considerably in geographic area, resources, population and labor force, economic size and development levels. Their differences are in many cases very significant, creating geographic, demographic, and economic imbalances that induce migration. For example, Indonesia is the biggest country in terms of area, population, and labor force. It is also the biggest economy based on GDP. Yet per capita income in Indonesia is considerably lower than in its faster-growing neighbors, Malaysia and Singapore, and this has induced substantial migration from Indonesia to its neighbors. The situation is similar between the Philippines and Malaysia/Singapore, and between Cambodia[27], Lao PDR, Myanmar, and Vietnam and Thailand.

Therefore, Singapore, Malaysia, and Thailand have become the magnets for migrant workers from their surrounding countries.

The dynamics of population growth also contribute to inter-country differentials. Population growth rates in 2010 ranged from 0.2 percent (Thailand) to 2.7 percent (Indonesia), implying very different rates of labor force growth both now and for some time into the future. Second, there is a rising rate of age dependency in the slower-growing populations resulting from declining fertility and mortality rates and increasing life expectancy. In both Singapore and Thailand, the shares of population aged 65+ is nearly 10 percent, while shares in other countries still range from 3.8 percent to 6.5 percent. A higher age dependency ratio in some countries will also affect migration flows.

Demographic and economic imbalances create disparities that make people want to move within or across countries inside or outside the region. They move in search of a better living standard either now or in the future. They look for better income opportunities, education, and health services, and other amenities. Moreover, countries in the region will face increasingly free labor mobility as part of the ASEAN commitments to make the region an economic community with freer mobility of skilled workers from January 2015 (ASEAN Secretariat 2009). This was supported by a declaration on the Protection and Promotion of the Rights of Migrant Workers (12th ASEAN Summit, 2007) covering all migrants of different skills.[28] This was followed by establishment of the ASEAN Committee on the Implementation of the Declaration (ACMW) in September 2008. The ACMW reports to the Senior Labor Officials Meeting (SLOM), which is also conducted regularly. There is also a regular ASEAN Forum on Migrant Labor (AFML) that produce a series of recommendations to improve the overall governance of migration and the welfare of migrant workers. The AFML is an annual event of the ACMW attended by member states, workers' organizations, employers, and representatives of civil society. These organizational innovations reflect increasing policy concerns around the role of international labor migration within the region.

Dynamics and trends

To some extent, the dynamics of international migration in the region can be analyzed from its two economic growth centers: Thailand (attracting migrant workers from its neighboring countries along the Mekong river of Cambodia, Lao PDR, Myanmar, and Vietnam); and Singapore and Malaysia – and Brunei some extent (absorbing migrant workers from Indonesia and the Philippines).[29] Accordingly, based on the estimates of international migration stock, the 10 countries in Southeast Asia can be classified as net importer or net exporter of international migrants. Brunei Darussalam, Malaysia, Singapore, and Thailand are now commonly considered as the net importers, while the other six countries Cambodia, Indonesia, Lao PDR, Myanmar, the Philippines, and Vietnam are the net exporters (Table 13.4). Compared to their number of labor force, small countries like Brunei and Singapore import relatively more migrants while the bigger countries such as Malaysia and Thailand import relatively less. Migrants coming to Brunei and Singapore already account for about 73 percent and 75 percent of their labor force, respectively, while the ratios in Malaysia and Thailand are only 19 percent and 3 percent.

The nature of migration shows some general features. In Thailand, there are many illegal migrant workers from neighboring countries, attracted by higher wages. They work in services and also in agriculture and fisheries. Malaysia and Brunei are dependent on migrant workers,[30] mostly from Indonesia (many are illegal) for plantation and construction labor, while Singapore and Malaysia are dependent on domestic workers from Indonesia and the Philippines. The

Table 13.4 International labor migration within ASEAN, 2010

	Population ('000)	Labor Force ('000)	Outward Migration ('000)	Inward Migration ('000)	Net Migration Flow ('000)	
Singapore	5,184	2,632	297	1,967	1,670	Net Import
Malaysia	23,251	12,250	1,431	2,358	876	
Thailand	63,878	38,977	811	1,157	346	
Brunei Darussalam	414	202	24	148	124	
Cambodia	14,953	8,050	350	336	(15)	Net Export
Lao PDR	6,437	3,179	367	19	(348)	
Myanmar	61,187	27,337	515	98	(417)	
Indonesia	237,641	117,578	2,504	397	(2,107)	
Vietnam	88,257	47,936	2,226	69	(2,157)	
Philippines	94,010	39,639	4,276	435	(3,840)	
ASEAN	**600,212**	**297,780**	**10,626**	**6,915**	**(3,710)**	

Source: World Bank data on Bilateral Estimates of Migrant Stocks in 2010.

Philippines is the major labor exporter in the region, contributing the most, but it hosts only a small number of ASEAN migrants. Southeast Asia is however not the main destination of Filipino migrant workers; their share in intra-ASEAN migrants is only about 8 percent (Pasadilla 2011). Filipinos go in much larger numbers to the USA, Canada, Australia, and the Middle East. In the region, the Philippines exports the largest number of migrants to the world, followed by Vietnam and Indonesia. In 2010, the Philippines sent about 3.8 million international migrants to the world, while Vietnam and Indonesia sent about 2.1 million each.

It should be noted, however, that in the context of sending or receiving international migrants, the overall situation of countries in the region is very dynamic. As a result, their status as a net exporter or net importer can change following the dynamics of economic growth and demographic changes. Table 13.5 shows the dynamics of net international migration across countries in the region. It shows that for some countries not only have

Table 13.5 Dynamics of net international migration rate across countries and time periods, 1990–2015 (per 1,000 population)

Southeast Asia	1990–1995	1995–2000	2000–2005	2005–2010	2010–2015
Brunei Darussalam	2.2	3.1	3.5	2.0	1.8
Cambodia	3.4	3.0	1.6	−1.8	−3.7
Indonesia	−0.3	−0.8	−0.8	−1.1	−1.1
Lao PDR	0.0	−1.3	−3.5	−4.2	−2.5
Malaysia	5.4	3.3	3.8	3.2	0.6
Myanmar	−0.7	−0.6	0.0	−4.4	−2.1
Philippines	−1.0	−2.1	−2.1	−2.8	−2.8
Singapore	8.5	14.3	13.7	11.36	30.9
Thailand	1.8	−3.8	1.9	3.4	1.5
Vietnam	−1.0	−0.9	−0.8	−1.1	−1.0

Source: ADB Key Indicator Data Base.

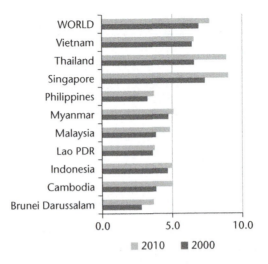

Figure 13.6 Aging in Southeast Asia countries as reflected in the shares of population aged 65+,
2000–10

Source: ADB Key Indicators 2013.

the rates gone up and down but they can also switch from positive to negative, implying a move from net importer to net exporter, and vice versa. Brunei and Singapore are continuously net importers while Indonesia, Myanmar, the Philippines, and Vietnam are consistently net exporters. Cambodia and Thailand change their status as net exporter or net importer in some periods.

One demographic condition that is key to migration is aging, as reflected in the share of people aged 65 and more. Figure 13.6 shows that aging in Singapore and Thailand, for instance, has been increasing very fast over 2000–10, such that they are now above the world average level. This is going to influence immigration, as aging populations need migrants from other countries to replace their position in the labor force and/or to provide care for them. The aging situation in the net importing countries such as Brunei and Malaysia, however, is still relatively very low, contributing little to immigration demand.

International migration from the region to the rest of the world

Key driving factors

The main driving factor of international migration from Southeast Asia to the rest of the world is the massive difference in average wage rates in origin and destination countries. In some cases, the difference is more than 12 times, suggesting that working for only one month in the destination country is equivalent to working for more than one year in the origin country (Figure 13.7). Worse still, the average wage rate of a lower profession in the destination countries is still a way higher than that of higher professions in the origin country. An example of this is that medical doctors in the Philippines are often found to be willing to work abroad as a nurse or paramedic than to stay home and work as a medical doctor. Typical salaries of medical doctors in the Philippines are much lower than those of lower-skilled medical personnel in the destination countries.

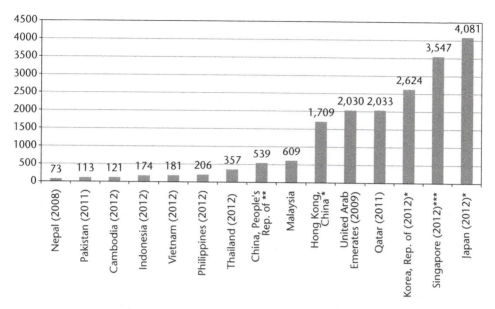

Figure 13.7 Wages disparities across selected countries: average monthly wage in US$ (2012 or latest available)

Source: ILO, *Global Wage Database* as quoted in Baruah 2014.

Notes:

*Based on an establishment survey with broad coverage. HongKong (China) and Japan refer only to full-time employees;

**Based on an establishment survey, calculated as employment-weighted average of urban units and private enterprises;

***Based on administrative records from the Central Provident Fund Board.

Main patterns and trends

The destinations of labor migrants from Southeast Asia to the rest of the world vary considerably. They have expanded to include both developed and other developing countries in Asia and the rest of the world. The three main regional labor exporters, for instance, have very different traditional destinations reflecting historical links. Migrants from the Philippines go in disproportionate numbers to the USA, Canada, and Australia, while Indonesian migrants go mostly to the Middle East (more than 50 percent) and Malaysia (about 20 percent). Vietnamese migrants are distributed between the USA (about 51 percent) and different places such as France (9 percent), Australia, Canada, P.R. China, and Germany (7 percent each). Most migrants from Thailand go to Taipei, China (28 percent).

Moreover, in addition to the private sector driven migration, there is also a systematic migration arranged by government-to-government programs. Under these types of arrangements, the governments of Japan, South Korea, and Taipei, China import relatively young workers from Indonesia, the Philippines, and Thailand to work under the internship or employment permit systems (EPS) or their equivalent system for a fixed duration, such as 2–5 years. The workers must pass a special test including the foreign language test of the destination countries. Thousands of workers have been recruited through these programs, which continue up to now.[31]

Key challenges and policy implications

The discussion above shows the dynamics and complexity of urbanization and international migration in the region. Managing migration flows and migrant issues calls for coordinated policy actions from local to global levels. This is important since uncoordinated and inconsistent policies can further create and/or worsen the existing imbalances that further exacerbate migration problems. For example, policies on minimum wages and other social protections as well as on other governance of labor migration can only be effective if they are implemented consistently across countries.

The massive and rapid urbanization across countries in the region, with associated spillover effects across sectors and borders, has created formidable challenges for policymakers. This includes meeting the demands of the urban populations for facilities, resources, and services. Over-urbanization is evident in many cities, where provision of basic infrastructure is inadequate to meet demand. This is made worse by the fact that agriculture, which still continues as a source of livelihood of many and provides food staples for most of the population in the region, is not performing well to say the least. The urbanization problem is also made much more complex with the cross-border movements of people across the countries in the region. The available indicators show strong asymmetrical flows of migrant workers to the centers of agglomeration such as in Malaysia, Singapore, and Thailand that put a burden on the destination countries and strain diplomatic relationships. Better urban planning and development to make cities greener and more sustainable are really needed. The previous approach of "build now and clean up later" is no longer applicable as cities in Asia, including in Southeast Asia, are now already among the dirtiest cities in the world – that is, among other factors they are characterized by polluted air, water, and land at alarming levels.

With regard to the migration of people, if the region is really to move to one economic community with free mobility of products and services, including workers, there should be put in place better governance of migration both for internal and international migration including the management of migrant workers. The signings of MOUs and bilateral agreements on migration issues among participating countries, the mutual recognition agreements (MRAs) among ASEAN leaders on some occupations associated with skilled workers, the developments of national qualification frameworks and their associated ASEAN qualification reference framework, are examples of key steps in the right direction towards a freer mobility of skill and talent as a key factor in an economic community. All of them, however, need to be implemented in a systematic and orderly manner in line with the ASEAN economic community aspiration and the needs of migrant workers. The latter are clearly evident so that nationalist approaches and over-protected borders will drive migrants underground promoting illegal migration. In the meantime, an introduction of guest worker programs in the context of circular migration can be a good option to temporarily meet the skill needs and labor market gap. Along this line, continuously improving the quality of human resources is a must and in fact badly needed as the region is still dominated by a low educated and unskilled labor force, especially in the main sending countries. It is also important to make sure that the education and training provided by the education sector is in line with the skills demand to reduce the skill mismatch, which is also a growing concern in the region.

The key challenges facing policymakers include dealing with the problem of aging and its consequences, managing the demand for labor, addressing illegal or undocumented migration, and how to make migration not a necessity but a choice. The ASEAN community has recognized the importance of labor migration in the region as reflected in the countries' development strategies as well as in the ASEAN vision and mission. On the ASEAN level, it is already included in two of the three ASEAN Blueprints, i.e. the Economic Community Blueprint and the Social-Cultural Community Blueprint. The economic blueprint calls for the free flow of skilled labor while the socio-cultural blueprint provides for the protection and promotion of the rights of migrant workers.

International migration has been well established as a structural feature of the region although some nations still dismiss it as a temporary, passing phenomenon. Many countries in the region have developed international migration policies as part of their development strategy but this has not been informed by high quality research relating to the causes and effects of migration (Hugo 2005).

The complexities of the issues and their driving factors, however, indicate that there will be no "one-fit-for-all" solution that can overcome the problems. In fact, the policies should be developed in the context of "win–win–win solutions", i.e. must be beneficial to the sending and receiving areas or countries, as well as the migrants and their families. One thing for sure is that the region should aim to obtain the benefits of freer labor mobility as was envisioned in the ASEAN leaders' agreements as part of making the region one economic community. Within this context, governments and other key stakeholders in the region need to

(i) facilitate labor migration in order to fill the gap and maximize resources as well as accommodate the choice of workers to work wherever they like;
(ii) protect the rights of migrants including by mainstreaming gender policies in the governance of migration and remittances;[32]
(iii) lower transaction costs of remitting to attract more remittances and reduce the use of informal channels;
(iv) facilitate investments or productive use of remittances to stimulate long-term growth and reduce countries' dependency on migration;
(v) adopt the Migration for Development Framework in which migration is seen as a circular and temporary solution of gaps created by economic and socio-demographic imbalances within and across countries in the region and with the rest of the world.

Moreover, there should be consistent and relevant policy throughout the region as the migrant workers from many Asian sending countries are predominantly unskilled while the established agreement, policy discussion, and overall plan are more for skilled workers. From the sending country perspective, this calls for increasing the quality of migrants by investing more on their education and training as a more educated and skilled labor force can be expected to be able to create employment to also reduce the demand or pressure for migrating abroad. ASEAN is moving towards having *One Vision, One Identity*, and *One Community* that requires freer mobility of people and workers across countries. The former has been achieved with the free visa arrangements for a short visit but more is needed to facilitate labor mobility of different skills. The countries in the region have agreed to "create a single market and production base that is stable, prosperous, highly competitive and economically integrated with an effective facilitation for trade and investment in which there are free flow of goods, services and investment, as well as freer movement of skilled labor" (ASEAN 2012). The Mutual Recognition Arrangements (MRAs) have been signed for eight types of occupations: Engineer, Nursing, Architect, Surveyor, Accountant, Medical Practitioners, Dental Practitioners, and Tourism Professionals, but all these need to be put in practice since progress in the overall implementation so far is still slow and uneven. The complexity of the regulation and institutional arrangements at the country and regional levels contributes further to the challenges that strengthen the call for consistent and coordinated actions.

Appendix

Table 13.A1 Migrant stock matrix, 2000 and 2010 ('000)

To / From	Asia	Central Asia	South Asia	East Asia	Southeast Asia	The Pacific	Oceania	European Union[1]	North America[2]	Middle East[3]	World
2000											
Asia	**20,871**	1,462	10,774	4,424	4,174	37	1,303	3,717	9,754	7,238	51,267
Central Asia	1,527	**1,445**	3	64	16	0	3	269	196	737	10,140
South Asia	11,223	3	**10,637**	133	443	6	212	1,793	1,981	5,624	21,058
South Asia (excl. India)	6,461	3	**6,202**	60	195	1	97	988	626	3,276	11,541
East Asia	4,428	12	6	**3,432**	973	4	370	775	3,719	22	9,885
Southeast Asia	**3,667**	1	126	794	**2,730**	16	525	874	3,738	855	9,798
The Pacific	26	0	2	1	13	**11**	193	6	120	0	385
Oceania	97	0	5	53	21	17	**407**	278	131	16	964
European Union[1]	312	89	29	76	110	8	2,156	**14,005**	6,928	1,737	30,282
North America[2]	228	2	21	128	73	4	103	748	**10,989**	165	12,989
Middle East[3]	176	54	44	22	56	1	221	6,339	1,490	**6,025**	16,207
World	26,998	5,929	10,938	5,542	4,517	72	4,713	36,097	40,868	17,625	**167,067**
2010											
Asia	**19,102**	1,312	7,641	4,299	5,817	33	2,078	5,545	12,024	12,686	62,645
Central Asia	1,263	**1,250**	2	10	0	0	5	371	173	375	10,710
South Asia	8,297	59	**7,528**	85	618	6	422	2,590	3,108	10,846	26,654
South Asia (excl. India)	5,678	59	**5,270**	62	287	1	165	1,598	936	5,920	15,293
East Asia[4]	5,035	2	39	**3,754**	1,238	2	642	1,173	4,289	85	11,945

Southeast Asia										
The Pacific	4,492	0	72	450	3,955	16	752	1,397	4,324	1,380	12,852
Oceania	15	0	0	1	6	9	256	15	129	0	484
European Union[1]	72	0	4	19	25	25	556	259	130	6	1,067
North America[2]	402	228	10	54	105	5	2,557	16,800	6,015	1,684	31,712
Middle East[3]	193	2	5	109	75	3	156	872	13,345	79	15,468
World	129	82	21	12	14	0	330	9,383	1,869	7,546	21,671
	27,648	2,558	12,170	6,134	6,700	87	6,448	46,820	50,105	29,341	203,135

Source: ADB calculations using data from *Global Bilateral Migration Database* (Global matrixes of bilateral migrations covering 1960–2000), World Bank, http://econ.worldbank.org (accessed 10 May 2012).

Note: 2010 inbound data for Afghanistan, Algeria, the People's Republic of China, Lebanon, Republic of the Maldives, Morocco, Pakistan, Tuvalu, and Vietnam are totals. Bilateral data for these countries are unavailable.

[1] Refers to 27 members: Austria, Belgium, Bulgaria, Cyprus, Czech Republic, Denmark, Estonia, Finland, France, Germany, Greece Hungary, Ireland, Italy, Latvia, Lithuania, Luxembourg, Malta, the Netherlands, Poland, Portugal, Romania, Slovakia, Slovenia, Spain, Sweden, and the United Kingdom.

[2] Refers to Canada, Mexico, and the United States

[3] Includes 21 countries: Algeria, Bahrain, Egypt, Iran, Iraq, Israel, Jordan, Kuwait, Lebanon, Libya, Morocco, Oman, Palestine, Qatar, Saudi Arabia, Sudan, Syria, Tunisia, Turkey, United Arab Emirates, and Yemen. No data for Palestine. No outbound data for Saudi Ara

[4] Data for Taipei,China unavailable.

Table 13.A2 Migrant to population ratio, 2000 and 2010 (%)

To / From	Asia	Central Asia	South Asia	East Asia	Southeast Asia	The Pacific	Oceania	European Union[1]	North America[2]	Middle East[3]	World
2000											
Asia	**0.61**	0.04	0.31	0.13	0.12	0.00	0.04	0.11	0.28	0.21	1.49
Central Asia	2.12	**2.01**	0.00	0.09	0.02	0.00	0.00	0.37	0.27	1.03	14.11
South Asia	0.83	0.00	**0.79**	0.01	0.03	0.00	0.02	0.13	0.15	0.42	1.56
South Asia (excl. India)	2.01	0.00	**1.93**	0.02	0.06	0.00	0.03	0.31	0.19	1.02	3.58
East Asia	0.30	0.00	0.00	**0.23**	0.07	0.00	0.03	0.05	0.25	0.00	0.67
Southeast Asia	**0.67**	**0.00**	0.02	**0.15**	**0.50**	**0.00**	**0.10**	**0.16**	**0.69**	**0.16**	**1.80**
The Pacific	0.34	0.00	0.02	0.01	0.16	**0.14**	2.50	0.07	1.55	0.00	4.99
Oceania	0.42	0.00	0.02	0.23	0.09	0.08	**1.76**	1.20	0.57	0.07	4.17
European Union[1]	0.07	0.02	0.01	0.02	0.02	0.00	0.45	**2.95**	1.46	0.37	6.37
North America[2]	0.06	0.00	0.01	0.03	0.02	0.00	0.02	0.18	**2.67**	0.04	3.16
Middle East[3]	0.05	0.01	0.01	0.01	0.01	0.00	0.06	1.70	0.40	**1.61**	4.33
World	0.45	0.10	0.18	0.09	0.08	0.00	0.08	0.60	0.68	0.30	**2.80**
2010											
Asia	**0.51**	0.04	0.21	0.12	0.16	0.00	0.06	0.15	0.32	0.34	1.69
Central Asia	1.57	**1.56**	0.00	0.01	0.00	0.00	0.01	0.46	0.22	0.47	13.33
South Asia	0.52	0.00	**0.47**	0.01	0.04	0.00	0.03	0.16	0.19	0.68	1.66
South Asia (excl. India)	1.37	0.01	**1.27**	0.01	0.07	0.00	0.04	0.38	0.23	1.42	3.68
East Asia[4]	0.35	0.00	0.00	**0.26**	0.09	0.00	0.05	0.08	0.30	0.01	0.84

Southeast Asia	**0.75**	**0.00**	**0.01**	**0.07**	**0.66**	**0.00**	**0.13**	**0.23**	**0.72**	**0.23**	**2.14**
The Pacific	0.16	0.00	0.00	0.01	0.06	**0.09**	2.66	0.15	1.34	0.00	5.03
Oceania	0.27	0.00	0.01	0.07	0.09	0.09	**2.07**	0.97	0.48	0.02	3.98
European Union[1]	0.08	0.05	0.00	0.01	0.02	0.00	0.51	**3.36**	1.20	0.34	6.35
North America[2]	0.04	0.00	0.00	0.02	0.02	0.00	0.03	0.19	**2.93**	0.02	3.39
Middle East[3]	0.03	0.02	0.00	0.00	0.00	0.00	0.07	1.92	0.38	**1.55**	4.45
World	0.41	0.04	0.18	0.09	0.10	0.00	0.09	0.69	0.74	0.43	**2.98**

Source: ADB calculations using data from *Global Bilateral Migration Database* (Global matrixes of bilateral migrations covering 1960–2000), World Bank, http://econ.worldbank.org (accessed 10 May 2012). Population data (for countries with available data) from *World Economic Outlook Database April 2012*, International Monetary Fund.

Note: 2010 inbound data for Afghanistan, Algeria, the People's Republic of China, Lebanon, Republic of the Maldives, Morocco, Pakistan, Tuvalu, and Vietnam are totals. Bilateral data for these countries are unavailable.

[1] Refers to 27 members: Austria, Belgium, Bulgaria, Cyprus, Czech Republic, Denmark, Estonia, Finland, France, Germany, Greece, Hungary, Ireland, Italy, Latvia, Lithuania, Luxembourg, Malta, the Netherlands, Poland, Portugal, Romania, Slovakia, Slovenia, Spain, Sweden, and the United Kingdom.

[2] Refers to Canada, Mexico, and the United States.

[3] Includes 21 countries: Algeria, Bahrain, Egypt, Iran, Iraq, Israel, Jordan, Kuwait, Lebanon, Libya, Morocco, Oman, Palestine, Qatar, Saudi Arabia, Sudan, Syria, Tunisia, Turkey, United Arab Emirates, and Yemen. No data for Palestine. No outbound data for Saudi Arabia

[4] Data for Taipei,China unavailable.

Table 13.A3 Regional share of migrant destination (% of total)

To	Asia	Central Asia	South	East	Southeast	The Pacific	Oceania	European Union[1]	North America[2]	Middle East[3]	World (Total in '000s)
From											
2000											
Asia	**40.71**	2.85	21.02	8.63	8.14	0.07	2.54	7.25	19.03	14.12	51,267
Central Asia	15.06	**14.25**	0.03	0.63	0.15	0.00	0.03	2.65	1.94	7.27	10,140
South Asia	53.30	0.02	**50.51**	0.63	2.10	0.03	1.01	8.51	9.41	26.71	21,058
South Asia (excl. India)	55.98	0.03	**53.74**	0.52	1.69	0.01	0.84	8.56	5.42	28.38	11,541
East Asia	44.79	0.13	0.06	**34.72**	9.84	0.04	3.75	7.84	37.62	0.22	9,885
Southeast Asia	**37.43**	**0.01**	1.29	**8.11**	**27.86**	**0.16**	**5.36**	**8.92**	**38.15**	**8.73**	9,798
The Pacific	6.80	0.03	0.48	0.20	3.29	**2.80**	50.10	1.46	31.11	0.04	385
Oceania	10.02	0.00	0.57	5.47	2.17	1.81	**42.21**	28.81	13.57	1.65	964
European Union[1]	1.03	0.29	0.10	0.25	0.36	0.03	7.12	**46.25**	22.88	5.74	30,282
North America[2]	1.75	0.02	0.17	0.98	0.56	0.03	0.79	5.76	**84.60**	1.27	12,989
Middle East[3]	1.09	0.33	0.27	0.14	0.34	0.00	1.36	39.11	9.19	**37.18**	16,207
World	16.16	3.55	6.55	3.32	2.70	0.04	2.82	21.61	24.46	10.55	**167,067**
2010											
Asia	**30.49**	2.09	12.20	6.86	9.29	0.05	3.32	8.85	19.19	20.25	62,645
Central Asia	11.79	**11.67**	0.02	0.10	0.00	0.00	0.04	3.46	1.62	3.50	10,710
South Asia	31.13	0.22	**28.24**	0.32	2.32	0.02	1.58	9.72	11.66	40.69	26,654
South Asia (excl. India)	37.13	0.38	**34.46**	0.40	1.88	0.01	1.08	10.45	6.12	38.71	15,293
East Asia[4]	42.15	0.02	0.32	**31.43**	10.36	0.02	5.38	9.82	35.91	0.71	11,945

Southeast Asia	**34.95**	**0.00**	**0.56**	**3.50**	**30.77**	**0.12**	**5.85**	**10.87**	**33.65**	**10.74**	**12,852**
The Pacific	3.20	0.00	0.04	0.12	1.26	1.79	52.93	3.00	26.70	0.01	484
Oceania	6.73	0.00	0.34	1.74	2.32	2.34	52.06	24.28	12.15	0.56	1,067
European Union[1]	1.27	0.72	0.03	0.17	0.33	0.02	8.06	52.98	18.97	5.31	31,712
North America[2]	1.25	0.01	0.03	0.70	0.48	0.02	1.01	5.64	86.28	0.51	15,468
Middle East[3]	0.59	0.38	0.10	0.05	0.06	0.00	1.52	43.30	8.62	34.82	21,671
World	13.61	1.26	5.99	3.02	3.30	0.04	3.17	23.05	24.67	14.44	**203,135**

Source: ADB calculations using data from *Global Bilateral Migration Database* (Global matrixes of bilateral migrations covering 1960–2000), World Bank, http://econ.worldbank.org (accessed 10 May 2012).

Note: 2010 inbound data for Afghanistan, Algeria, the People's Republic of China, Lebanon, Republic of the Maldives, Morocco, Pakistan, Tuvalu, and Vietnam are totals. Bilateral data for these countries are unavailable.

[1] Refers to 27 members: Austria, Belgium, Bulgaria, Cyprus, Czech Republic, Denmark, Estonia, Finland, France, Germany, Greece, Hungary, Ireland, Italy, Latvia, Lithuania, Luxembourg, Malta, the Netherlands, Poland, Portugal, Romania, Slovakia, Slovenia, Spain, Sweden, and the United Kingdom.

[2] Refers to Canada, Mexico, and the United States.

[3] Includes 21 countries: Algeria, Bahrain, Egypt, Iran, Iraq, Israel, Jordan, Kuwait, Lebanon, Libya, Morocco, Oman, Palestine, Qatar, Saudi Arabia, Sudan, Syria, Tunisia, Turkey, United Arab Emirates, and Yemen. No data for Palestine. No outbound data for Saudi Arabia.

[4] Data for Taipei,China unavailable.

Notes

1 Senior Economist, Asian Development Bank. The views expressed here are personal.

2 Geographically, other countries such as Timor Leste and Papua New Guinea can also be included in the South East Asia region or South East Asia and Pacific Region, but this chapter considers only the ASEAN member countries.

3 ASEAN Statistics Leaflet at: http://www.asean.org/resources/publications/asean-publications/item/asean-statistics-leaflet-2012

4 There is a need for some caution when discussing "raw" urbanization rates. In addition to movement of people from rural to urban areas, the increasing share of urban population is also attributable to the changes in the definition and designation of urban areas.

5 In certain periods during the amnesty program and other assessment exercises, the number of irregular migrants is much bigger than the official number, especially in Malaysia and Thailand. Some authors even argue that the two countries have been dependent on illegal workers for it is cheaper and faster to recruit them, as well as more profitable. Strong push factors and bureaucratic processes and corruption in both sending and receiving countries contribute to this situation (see Ananta and Arifin 2004)

6 Source: Bilateral migrant stock in 2011 and http://www.asean.org/resources/2012-02-10-08-47-55

7 http://publications.iom.int/bookstore/index.php?main_page=product_info&cPath=41_7&products_id=971

8 This links to trade in services negotiations of the WTO trade liberalization under Mode 4 (see Manning and Bhatnagar 2004 for an example of discussion on this issue).

9 Climate change triggers population movements within and across countries due to increasing intensity of extreme weather events such as a rise in sea level and acceleration of environmental degradation. Climate change has adverse effects on livelihoods, public health, food and water security that in turn will affect human mobility, increasing migration and displacement. There are no reliable estimates on the number of climate-change induced migration but the forecasts vary from 25 million to 1 billion by 2050. In 2010, more than 30 million people in Asia and the Pacific were displaced by environmental disasters (http://www.adb.org/news/events/researchers-workshop-climate-change-and-migration-asia- and-pacific).

10 Migration is also associated with political remittance in which the migrant diaspora influences positively the policy-making process and political changes in the home country.

11 Recall the complaint of Max Frisch "We asked for workers but human beings came" that sums up the concept and resentment that migrant workers will stay in the host country with their family and have different values and way of life that might not necessarily be compatible with those in the host country.

12 In some cases, the decision to send out a migrant is made without the consent of the person moving, a frequent manifestation of human trafficking in very poor areas or during times of unusually great economic hardship.

13 One can observe that there are "special treatments" such as special terminals, lines for immigration and customs, connecting transport, and even trolleys (with a special marked sign for them) for the international migrants in the main airports in Indonesia and the Philippines to facilitate their migration process, as well as their return. This seems very protecting and facilitating but the reality on the ground can be very different. In short, migrants are very vulnerable at each point of their journey and they can easily become victims of abuse and extortion.

14 In addition to gaps in economic and demographic (aging and young population) factors, immigration policies, improving connectivity, and commercialization of migration are commonly cited as the driving factors of migration. The commercialization of migration has currently become significant and it has become very dominant for some types of occupation. Migration has become a lucrative business and many recruiters act as employer in the outsourcing type business arrangement. They recruit and hire migrants, pay all their placement and other initial fees that would be reimbursed directly from salary deductions. In many cases, the total costs can be translated into more than six months of salary. Overcharging of recruitment and placement fees and "other costs" imposed by recruiters are the main source of abuse and malpractice in the migration market. This is made more complicated as the role of the recruiters as the middle man can sometimes go beyond the normal limit for they also host or provide accommodation for migrants during the slack or temporary period. This is the area in which the role of the government is very critical, especially in getting the right balance between facilitating migration and protecting migrants. Too restrictive regulation can drive the market underground putting migrants in a more risky situation.

15 There is also a view linking migration with a country's welfare system that argues migrants are attracted to a country with generous welfare systems (see Giulietti and Wahba 2012 for an example).

16 Statistically, the categorization of an area (i.e. a village or other administrative level) into rural or urban is usually based on a scoring system derived from the combination of three variables: (i) population density, (ii) share of non-agricultural income, and (iii) number of urban facilities. The higher the number the more urban is the area. This could then be combined with some special treatment by classifying the area as a city or the capital city of a district and/or province, special economic zone, etc. The applications of this approach across countries are very different which means the classification of urban or rural across countries is not consistent. Some countries, for instance, just use population density, while others use population density and share of non-agriculture income.

17 Various estimates show about 40 percent of the increase in the urban population in developing countries comes from migration or reclassification of rural to urban. In the People's Republic of China and Indonesia, however, rural–urban migration and reclassification of rural and urban are estimated to account for more than 70 percent of urban growth in the 1980s and about 80 percent in the 1990s (ADB 2012a).

18 In addition, the three most densely populated big cities in the world now are in Asia, i.e. Mumbai, Kolkata, and Karachi, and 8 of the 10 most densely populated cities in the world are also in Asia.

19 The prosperity of nations is intimately linked to the prosperity of their cities. No country has ever achieved sustained economic growth or rapid social development without urbanizing. (Sources: UN Habitat State of the World's Cities 2010/2011 – Cities for All: Bridging the Urban Divide).

20 The latest estimate of the total number of international migrants worldwide is about 216 million people.

21 World Bank estimate.

22 For example, in Indonesia, women constituted 83 percent of outgoing migrants in 2009, and in Lao People's Democratic Republic, they represent 70 percent of the migrant workforce (ILO 2013).

23 Compared to the ASEAN population this is about 2 percent of the total population, which is still lower than the global rate of around 3 percent.

24 Migrant workers in Thailand are estimated about 5 percent of total Thai labor force. They work mainly in agriculture, construction, fishing and seafood processing, manufacturing and domestic work. Between 2010 and 2012, 1,331,637 migrants completed the nationality verification process, of whom about 88.6 percent were workers from Myanmar, 8.8 percent and 2.6 percent were Cambodia and Lao PDR, respectively.

25 Existing artifacts scattered across the countries in the region show that some countries in the region were previously part of bigger old kingdoms, so they share some similarities in their culture including their languages. This helps in reducing cultural shock and in easing the overall migration process. Between Indonesia and Malaysia, and the Philippines and Malaysia, there used to be no border controls allowing workers to move freely. Moreover, the historical facts indicate that Java island, for instance, has been a source of migrants for centuries while on the other hand Malaysia has been one of the major labor importers. For some centuries back, some countries in the region have been labor-surplus while others have been labor-scarce, so that labor crossing countries' borders is an old phenomenon. Another interesting point from the historical perspective is that the government position and attitude toward migration is never consistent (see Kaur 2009 for an introduction on the issue).

26 In Thailand, for instance, there is a significant number of Vietnamese in the northeast and Malay in the southern part. This population mix-up can also be found in other countries in the region.

27 Despite the fact that Cambodia is one of the main migrant sending countries in the region, the latest evidence shows that it has experienced skills shortages that hinder its development. The share of firms reporting skills as a major constraint to growth increased from 6.5 percent in 2003 to 15.5 percent in 2007 (ADB 2012b).

28 The declaration promotes the full potential and dignity of migrant workers in a condition of freedom, equity, and stability in accordance with the laws, regulations, and policies of respective ASEAN member states. The declaration also defines the obligations of the sending and receiving states and the commitments of the entire ASEAN community to protect and promote the rights of migrant workers (ILO 2013).

29 From the supply side, the flows of migrant workers from the migrant exporting countries are partly as a result of inabilities of the sending countries' economies to create more jobs to cater for the increasing numbers in the labor force, which in most cases are growing faster than their population growths.

30 The illegal aspect of the foreign workers is not necessarily something to do with breaking immigration law on the migrant workers' side but it can be driven by economic factors, such as a strong demand for foreign workers, expensive costs of hiring foreign workers legally, and the increasing role of the informal

sector. The lack of natural borders (such as between Thailand and its neighboring countries) and the cheap "costs" of crossing the borders are also conducive for illegal migrants. Increasing global competition can also make companies work in tight margins, encouraging them to use cheap illegal foreign workers. This phenomenon happens not only in developing countries but also in the developed ones.

31 For details and statistics about these programs in Korea see: http://www.moel.go.kr/english/statistics/ major_statistics.jsp ; Japan: at Japan International Training Cooperation Organization: http://www.jitco.or. jp/about/statistics.html ; and Taipei, China: *Foreign Workers Statistics*, Council of Labor Affairs, Taipei, China. See also: http://www.adbi.org/files/2012.01.19.cpp.day2.sess3.4.won.migrant.workers.eps.pdf (for EPS), http://www.adbi.org/conf-seminar-papers/2012/02/06/4888.foreign.born.healthcare.work-ers.japan/ and http://www.adbi.org/conf-seminar-papers/2012/02/06/4876.labour.migration.asia.2010. 2011/ (for Japan).

32 Along with this social protection policy, it is important for ASEAN countries to establish social security portability that can facilitate a more orderly labor movement within the region, foment greater social cohesion and more "buy-in" for the integration efforts (Pasadilla 2011).

Bibliography

Adams, R. Jr. and Page, J. 2003. "International Migration, Remittance and Poverty in Developing Countries." World Bank Policy Research Working Paper 3179, December.

ADB 2008. *Asian Development Outlook 2008: Workers in Asia.* Manila: ADB.

ADB 2012a. *Key Indicators for Asia and the Pacific 2012.* Manila: ADB.

ADB 2012b. *Asian Development Outlook 2012: Confronting Inequality in Asia.* Manila: ADB.

ADB 2012c. *Global Crisis, Remittances and Poverty in Asia.* Manila: ADB.

ADB 2013. *Key Indicators for Asia and the Pacific 2013.* Manila: ADB.

ADBI 2012. *ASEAN 2030 Toward a Borderless Economic Community: Draft Highlights.* Tokyo: ADBI.

Ananta, A. and Arifin, E. N. (eds) (2004). *International Migration in South East Asia.* Institute of Southeast Asian Studies. Singapore.

Arunanondchai, J. and Fink, C. 2007. "Trade in Health Services in the ASEAN Region." World Bank Policy Research Working Paper 4147, March.

ASEAN 2012. ASEAN Statistics Leaflet: Selected Key Indicators.

ASEAN Secretariat 2009. *ASEAN Annual Report 2008–2009.* Jakarta: ASEAN.

ASEAN Secretariat 2011. *ASEAN Economic Community Chartbook 2011.* Jakarta: ASEAN.

ASEAN Secretariat 2012. *Repository Matrix of Legislations and Policies on Migrant Workers of ASEAN Member States.* Jakarta: ASEAN.

Baruah, N. 2012. "Reflection and Sharing on Implementation of the Hanoi and Bali Recommendations." The 5th ASEAN Forum on Migrant Labour, Siem Reap, Cambodia.

Baruah, N. 2013. "Trends and Outlook for Labour Migration in Asia." The 3rd ADBI–OECD–ILO Roundtable on Labour Migration in Asia: Assessing Labour Market Requirements for Foreign Workers and Developing Policies for Regional Skills Mobility. Bangkok, Thailand.

Baruah, N. 2014. "Labour Migration Landscape in Asia: Recent Trends in Migration and Policies." ADBI, OECD and ILO Roundtable on Labour Migration in Asia, Tokyo. Bangkok: ILO.

BNP2TKI 2011. *A History of Indonesian Labour Migrant Placement.* Badan National Penempatan dan Perlindungan Tenaga Kerja Indonesia, Jakarta.

Capannelli, G. 2013. "Key Issues of Labor Mobility in ASEAN." Presentation at the 3rd ADBI–OECD–ILO Roundtable on Labour Migration in Asia: Assessing Labour Market Requirements for Foreign Workers and Developing Policies for Regional Skills Mobility. Bangkok, Thailand.

Capannelli, G. 2014. "Managing Labor Migration under the ASEAN Economic Community: Key Issues." The 4th ADBI–OECD–ILO Roundtable on Labor Migration in Asia. Tokyo, 27–28 January.

Chiaki, I. 2006. *International Labor Migration and its Effects on Poverty Reduction: Critical Review on the Current Literature.* Tokyo: JICA.

Deshingkar, P. 2006. "Internal Migration, Poverty and Development in Asia." Paper for Session 3: Realising the Potential for Poverty Reduction. Parallel Group 3A: Topic Paper 2. The Asia 2015 Conference: Promoting Growth, Ending Poverty, London, United Kingdom. http://www.odi.org/ sites/odi.org.uk/files/odi-assets/publications-opinion-files/5669.pdf

Deshingkar, P. and Grimm, S. 2005. "Internal Migration and Development: A Global Perspective." Overseas Development Institute. No. 19. International Organization for Migration. Geneva Switzerland. http:// www.prb.org/Source/mrs_19_2005.pdf

Dumont, J.C. 2013. "Assessing Labour Market Requirements for Foreign Workers and Developing Policies for Regional Skills Mobility." The 3rd ADBI–OECD–ILO Roundtable on Labour Migration in Asia. Bangkok, Thailand.

Dumont, J.C., Martin, J.P., and Spielvogel, G. 2007. "Women on the Move: The Neglected Gender Dimension of the Brain Drain." Institute for the Study of Labor IZA Discussion Paper No. 2920. OECD.

Franck, A.K. and Spehar, A. 2010. "Women's Labour Migration in the Context of Globalization." WIDE, Brussels, Belgium.

Giulietti, C. and Wahba, J. 2012. "Welfare Migration." Centre for Population Change Working Paper Number 18.

Global Commission on International Migration 2005. "Migration in an Interconnected World: New Directions for Action." Report of the Global Commission on International Migration.

Harris, J.R. and Todaro, M.P. 1970. "Migration, Unemployment and Development: A Two-Sector Analysis." *American Economic Review* 60(1): 126–42.

Hatton, T.J. and Williamson, J.G. 2004. "International Migration in the Long-Run: Positive Selection, Negative Selection and Policy." Working Paper 10529. Cambridge, MA: National Bureau of Economic Research. http://www.nber.org/papers/w10529

Hear, N.V., Bakewell, O. and Long, K. 2012. "Drivers of Migration. Migrating out of Poverty." Research Programme Consortium Working Paper 1. University of Sussex, UK.

House of Commons International Development Committee 2004. "Migration and Development: How to Make Migration Work for Poverty Reduction." Sixth Report of Session 2003–04.

Hugo, G. 1998. "The Demographic Underpinnings of Current and Future International Migration in Asia." *Asian and Pacific Migration Journal*, 7(1): 1–26.

Hugo, G. 2002. "Effects of International Migration on the Family in Indonesia." *Asian and Pacific Migration Journal*, 11(1): 13–46.

Hugo, G. 2003. "Information, Exploitation and Empowerment: The Case of Indonesian Overseas Workers." *Asian and Pacific Migration Journal*, 12(4): 439–466.

Hugo, G. 2005. "Migration in the Asia-Pacific Region." A paper prepared for the Policy Analysis and Research Programme of the Global Commission on International Migration.

International Centre for Migration Policy Development 2012. "Advancing Regional Cooperation on International Migration among Southeast Asian Countries." Report of the Conference on Migration and Development: Taking Stock of the Situation in Southeast Asian Countries. Manila, Philippines.

International Labour Organization (ILO) 2013. "Background Paper: Progress on the Implementation of the Recommendations Adopted at the 3rd and 4th ASEAN Forum on Migrant Labour." Bangkok, Thailand.

IOM 2002. "Gender and Migration." Fact sheet. Geneva, Switzerland.

IOM 2009. "Rural Women and Migration." Fact sheet. Geneva, Switzerland. http://www.iom.int/jahia/webdav/shared/shared/mainsite/published_docs/brochures_and_info_sheets/Rural-Women-and-Migration-Fact-Sheet-2012.pdf

IOM, 2010. "Migration and Development in Indonesia." Fact sheet. International Organization for Migration in Indonesia. http://www.iom.or.id

International Organization for Migration, Economic and Social Commission for Asia and the Pacific, International Labour Organization, Joint United Nations Programme on HIV/AIDS, United Nations Development Programme, United Nations Population Fund, United Nations Children's Fund, United Nations Development Fund for Women 2008. "Situation Report on International Migration in East and South-East Asia. Regional Thematic Working Group on International Migration including Human Trafficking." Bangkok: IOM.

Jones, G.W. 2013. "The Population of Southeast Asian Countries." Asia Research Institute Working Paper Series 196. Singapore.

Katseli, L.T. et al. 2006. "Policies for Migration and Development: A European Perspective." Development Centre. Policy Brief No. 30. OECD.

Kaur, A. 2004. "Mobility, Labour Mobilisation and Border Controls: Indonesian Labour Migration to Malaysia since 1990." The 15th Biennial Conference of the Asian Studies Association of Australia, Canberra, 29 June–2 July.

Kaur, A. 2009. "Labor Crossing in Southeast Asia: Linking Historical and Contemporary Labor Migration." *New Zealand Journal of Asian Studies* 11(1): 276–303.

Kaur, A. 2010. "Labour Migration in Southeast Asia: Migration Policies, Labour Exploitation and Regulation." *Journal of the Asia Pacific Economy*, 15(1): 6–19.

Kundu, A. 2009. "Urbanisation and Migration: An Analysis of Trends, Patterns and Policies in Asia." United Nations Development Programme. Human Development Reports. Research Paper 2009/16.

Larsen, J.J. 2010. "Migration and People Trafficking in Southeast Asia." *Trends & Issues in Crime and Criminal Justice* No. 401. Australian Government. Australia Institute of Criminology.

Lee, E. 1966. "A Theory of Migration." *Demography*, 3: 47–57.

Manning, C. and Bhatnagar, P. 2004. "The Movement of Natural Persons in South East Asia: How Natural." Australian National University Working Paper.

Manning, C. and Sidorenko, A. 2006. "The Regulation of Professional Migration in ASEAN: Insight from the Health and IT Sectors." Australian National University Working Paper.

Martin, S.F. 2003. "Women and Migration." United Nations Division for the Advancement of Women (DAW) Consultative Meeting on Migration and Mobility and How This Movement Affects Women. Malmö, Sweden, 2–4 December.

OECD and ASEAN Secretariat 2013. *Southeast Asian Economic Outlook 2013: With Perspectives on China and India.* Jakarta, Indonesia.

Orbeta, A. Jr. and Gonzales, K. 2013. "Managing International Labor Migration in ASEAN: Themes from a Six-Country Study." Discussion Paper Series No. 2013–26. Philippine Institute for Development Studies. Manila.

Paitoonpong, S. and Chalamwong, Y. 2012. "Managing International Labor Migration in ASEAN: A Case of Thailand." Thailand Development Research Institute (TDRI). Bangkok.

Pasadilla, G.O. 2011. "Social Security and Labor Migration in ASEAN." ADB Institute Research Policy Brief 34. Tokyo, Japan.

Pienkos, A. 2006. "Caribbean Labour Migration: Minimizing Losses and Optimizing Benefits Port of Spain." International Labour Office.

Ratha, D. 2014. "Trends and Outlook for Migration and Remittances Worldwide." The 4th ADBI–OECD–ILO Roundtable on Labour Migration in Asia. ADBI, Tokyo, Japan.

Resosudarmo, Budy P., Chikako Yamauchi, and Tadjuddin Effendi, 2009. "Rural–Urban Migration in Indonesia: Survey Design and Implementation." RUMICI Project. Australian National University, Canberra.

Sheng, Y.K. 2011. "Urban Challenges in South-East Asia." Paper presented at the 5th Asia-Pacific Urban Forum organized by the UN Economic and Social Commission for Asia and the Pacific (UN ESCAP). Bangkok, Thailand.

Sirkeci, I., Cohen, J.H., and Ratha, D. (eds) 2012. *Migration and Remittances during the Global Financial Crisis and Beyond.* Washington, DC: World Bank.

Skeldon, R. 2000. "Trafficking: A Perspective from Asia." *International Migration Review* 38(3). Special Issue.

Skeldon, R. 2003. "Migration and Poverty." Paper presented at the conference on African Migration and Urbanization in Comparative Perspective, Johannesburg, South Africa, June 4–7.

Skeldon, R. 2008. "International Migration as a Tool in Development Policy: A Passing Phase?" *Population and Development Review*, 34(1): 1–18.

Stark, O. and Bloom, D.E. 1985. "The New Economics of Labour Migration." Department of Economics and Population Sciences, Harvard University, Cambridge, MA and Department of Economics, Bar-Ilan University.

Stouffer, S.A. 1940. "Intervening Opportunities: A Theory Relating to Mobility and Distance." *American Sociological Review*, 5(6): 845–67.

Suhariyanto, K., Sugiyarto, G., and Avenzora, A. 2010. "The Impact of Global Crisis on Remittances and Poverty: Country Case Studies Indonesia." *Global Crisis, Remittances, and Poverty in Asia*, Chapter 4. Asian Development Bank.

UN Women 2008. *Gender Dimensions of Remittances: A Study of Indonesian Domestic Workers in East and South-East Asia.* Bangkok. Available from: http://www.migrationunifem-apas.org/Publications/Gender_Dimensions_of_Remittances.html

UN Women 2013. "Managing Labour Migration in ASEAN: Concerns for Women Migrant Workers." Thailand.

UN Women Issue Briefs on Women's Human Rights in the ASEAN Region Labor Migration and Women Migrant Workers (Undated).

UN Women–UNDP 2010. *Migration, Remittances and Gender-Responsive Local Development: Case Study of the Philippines.* New York. Available from: http://www.un-instraw.org/view-document-details/747-migration-remittances-and-genderresponsive-local-development-the-case-of-the-philippines.html

United Nations 2002. *International Migration Report 2002.* New York.

United Nations 2005. *2004 World Survey on the Role of Women in Development: Women and International Migration.* New York.

United Nations Entity for Gender Equality and the Empowerment of Women (UN Women) 2007. "Labour Migration and Women Migrant Workers." Bangkok.

World Bank 2011. *Migration and Remittances Factbook 2011.*

World Bank and International Monetary Fund 2013. *Rural–Urban Dynamics and the Millennium Development Goals.* Washington, DC.

Part V
Poverty and political economy

14

The drivers of poverty reduction

Peter Warr

AUSTRALIAN NATIONAL UNIVERSITY

Introduction

Does economic growth benefit the poor and does the answer depend on the nature of the growth? These questions are hotly debated throughout the world and the answers are important for policy formulation. One form the debate has taken asks whether the poverty-reducing propensity of economic growth depends on its sectoral composition – whether the growth occurs in the agricultural, industrial or services sectors of the economy. The countries of Southeast Asia illustrate these issues very well. Over recent decades these countries have each experienced wide fluctuations in both growth rates (aggregate and sectoral) and poverty reduction outcomes. In all these countries, whether economic growth does or does not deliver sustained reductions in poverty incidence, and what kinds of growth reduce poverty the most, are questions of ongoing policy debate.

A related policy debate concerns the effect that changes in relative prices have on poverty, particularly the real price of food. Some Southeast Asian governments have protected their agricultural sectors, thereby raising the real price of food, ostensibly because higher food prices benefit poor farmers. Indonesia, the Philippines and, more recently, Thailand, are examples. But changes in relative prices produce both gainers and losers and both groups will include some poor people. Poor farmers who are net sellers of food will indeed benefit if real food prices increase. But poor consumers will lose and this group includes not only the urban poor but many rural poor people as well, especially landless agricultural workers, who sell labor and buy food. Small farmers who are net buyers of food will also be harmed. The net effect of these two opposing sets of forces – producing gainers and losers – is not obvious.

Several of the countries of Southeast Asia enjoyed economic booms from the late 1980s until 1996 and in all the countries that experienced this rapid growth considerable progress was made in reducing poverty. But in the late 1990s most of these same countries were affected by the Asian financial crisis and were experiencing deep recessions. Economic hardship was felt at all levels of the income distribution, but the implications for the poorest people were of particular concern. Macroeconomic recovery has subsequently occurred in all of these countries, but at varying rates and with varying outcomes for poverty incidence. Attention has thus been re-focused on the variables that drive changes in poverty incidence.

In the post-crisis environment, restoration of economic growth is a policy priority in all Southeast Asian countries, but not just *any* growth (Bourguignon 2001). Reflection on the boom period, the crisis that followed it and the subsequent recovery has convinced many policy makers and independent observers that the quality of growth is important and not just the rate. But what is 'quality' growth? One criterion for determining the quality of growth, though certainly not the only one, is its effects on the poor (Fields 1980). What kinds of growth are most (and least) beneficial for the poor? Much of the development economics literature has dealt with the manner in which the distribution of income is affected by the rate and composition of economic growth. This chapter explores some of these issues in the context of Southeast Asia. In particular, it asks how absolute poverty incidence changes with economic growth and how these effects depend on the characteristics of the growth, such as its sectoral composition, and changes in the relative price of food.

The analysis focuses on the eight poorest countries of Southeast Asia, all of which were affected by the 1997–99 financial and economic crisis. The four most affected by the crisis were Thailand, the first to succumb; Indonesia, the most severely affected; Malaysia, where the crisis produced the most radical macroeconomic policy responses; and the Philippines, where the pre-crisis boom was least pronounced but where the crisis itself was nevertheless significant. The four less affected, but very poor countries, were Cambodia, Laos, Myanmar and Vietnam.[1] The two richest ASEAN countries, Brunei and Singapore, are not covered in this study because their recorded levels of poverty incidence are very low. Myanmar is necessarily excluded from the quantitative analysis because its national accounts data over recent decades are considered unreliable. Finally, Cambodia was also excluded from the quantitative analysis because the number of data points available is only two, meaning only one data point on the change in poverty incidence.

The six remaining ASEAN countries listed above were chosen for the quantitative analysis of this study because for all six poverty incidence is a serious policy concern and because data on poverty incidence and economic growth are available, covering a significant time period. Nevertheless, the intervals between available data points vary and are often several years long. This means that the total number of data points on changes in poverty incidence over time that are available for any one of these countries is small and statistical analysis of the relationship between poverty incidence and economic growth is highly problematic for any one of them, taken individually. But analysis of this kind becomes feasible when the data are appropriately pooled across countries.

There are reasons for thinking that pooling data for this particular group of six countries is reasonable. First, these countries have roughly similar economic structures. All are market-oriented economies with large agricultural sectors consisting primarily of small farming units. Agriculture dominates total employment, but not national output. In all of these countries, industrial production has combined export-oriented production with protected production for domestic markets. All have large services sectors providing residual employment opportunities for those not employed in agriculture or industry. The rural populations dominate the total numbers of poor people, but rural to urban migration has been a prominent feature of the long-term development process. These facts suggest that the underlying relationship between sectoral growth and poverty reduction might be similar among these six countries, whereas this may not apply among countries whose structural features differ widely.

Second, despite their structural similarities these countries have different economic histories. As noted above, all except the Philippines experienced growth rates above their long-term historical norms during the boom decade from the mid-1980s to the mid-1990s. Aggregate poverty incidence, both rural and urban, declined significantly. This was followed by recessions of varying depth from 1997 onwards, during which poverty incidence typically increased. But aside from this similarity their detailed experiences have been quite different. The rates at which agriculture has contracted as a share of GDP during the process of long-term economic growth have differed, along with rates of industrialization. The above facts suggest that these countries provide six different sets of empirical experience around a similar underlying structure, the circumstances in which pooling data is most likely to be appropriate. The diversity of their experience offers a natural experiment that may have useful lessons to offer.

The next section discusses some measurement issues affecting poverty measurement. This is followed by a summary of available data on poverty incidence in the eight countries of Southeast Asia with significant levels of poverty incidence (all of ASEAN except Brunei and Singapore) and data on economic growth in all eight countries except Myanmar. Then the analytical framework used to analyze the determinants of poverty reduction in the six ASEAN countries mentioned above, for which statistical analysis is possible, is set out before a description of the statistical method and the results, followed by the conclusion.

Measuring poverty

Before we can analyze the determinants of poverty or the causes of changes in it, we must first quantify it. By *poverty incidence*, we mean here the headcount index – the proportion of the population whose expenditures or incomes fall below a fixed threshold, the poverty line, the monetary value of which is adjusted over time to maintain a constant real purchasing power. Before turning to the more technical aspects of poverty measurement, five observations regarding the broader dimensions of poverty measurement will be discussed.

First, although poverty entails more than just a low level of income or expenditure, the various dimensions of poverty do tend to be highly correlated. People who are poor by one measure tend, generally speaking, to be poor by another. This means that accuracy in measuring poverty by a narrow measure like real incomes or real expenditures may be useful even though it does not capture all of the elements of poverty that may reasonably be considered relevant.

Second, it is important for users of poverty measures to be able to compare poverty incidence over time. This means that when changes are made in the way poverty is measured by government statistical agencies, these changes should take the form of *adding* to the set of measures already in place, rather than *replacing* them. That is, poverty incidence using 'old' measures should continue to be published on an ongoing basis even when new and possibly superior measures are introduced.

Third, objective quantification is important. As far as possible, poverty measures need to avoid personal opinion affecting the measures, because such opinions differ among individuals and can change over time. Subjectivity can enter at the level of primary data collection or at the level of analysis.

Fourth, poverty estimates are controversial and can have political consequences. The statistical organizations responsible for compiling household survey data, and the subsequent analysis of those data to produce estimates of poverty incidence, are nearly always government agencies. In some countries the politicization of poverty measures has caused the informed public to lose confidence in the integrity of the government statistical agencies responsible for the poverty estimates.[2] The continued openness of this process is the means by which public confidence in the reliability of the estimates can be maintained.

Fifth, measures of poverty have hitherto concentrated on households' capacity to purchase essential goods and services in the marketplace, using their own money. These goods are valued at the prices paid. Those goods and services provided by the government or local community at no charge (or at nominal charges) are ignored (or largely ignored). Although the provision of these goods and services affects welfare and changes in their level of provision is clearly relevant for poverty, correctly measured, this issue has not yet been properly addressed by statistical agencies.

Six kinds of technical issues are involved in measuring poverty incidence over time.

1. Are we discussing *absolute or relative poverty*? Measures of 'absolute poverty' relate to that part of the population whose incomes (or expenditures) fall below a given level (the poverty line) whose value is held fixed in real purchasing power over time and across social groups. 'Relative poverty' means *inequality*, and to avoid confusion it is probably better to use that term. It compares the incomes (or expenditures) of the poor with those of the rich, or some other reference group. The two concepts are different because the overall size of the economic pie may change at the same time as its distribution is changing. Not surprisingly, when the overall size of the economic pie is changing significantly, measures of absolute poverty and inequality do not necessarily move together and may not even change in the same direction. This chapter is concerned with absolute poverty incidence.

2. What *variable* is used for the calculations of poverty incidence? In Thailand, Malaysia and the Philippines the basis has been *household incomes* per household member, adjusted for gender and age distribution of the household. Thailand has recently begun reporting separate poverty estimates based on household expenditures and household incomes, respectively, but using the same numerical poverty lines for both. Indonesia and the newer ASEAN countries – Vietnam, Cambodia and Laos – use household expenditures. In Myanmar, household expenditures were used as the basis for the poverty estimates reported by the United Nations Development Programme (UNDP) in 2005 and 2010, but earlier government estimates based on household incomes were also published. The latter are not reported in this study because it is not clear how the poverty lines were adjusted over time in response to changing consumer prices.

    The use of household expenditures for poverty measurement is more consistent with economic theory, in that expenditures are more directly related to household welfare than incomes. In addition, the measurement of income is problematic in rural areas where much of the return to labor is in-kind and not easily converted to monetary values – a particular problem in subsistence agriculture. The distinction between income-based and expenditure-based measures of poverty is especially important when we are considering the impact on poverty of a short-term change in incomes. For example, poverty measures based on expenditure should not rise as much in response to a negative income shock as measures based on expenditures because households smooth essential expenditures over time by borrowing, selling assets and deferring non-essential expenditures.

3. What is the *poverty measure*? Most studies of poverty focus on the *headcount measure of absolute poverty incidence*, which means the proportion of the population whose incomes fall below a given threshold, held constant in real terms over time and across regions. At a conceptual level, this measure has the disadvantage that changes in it are due mainly to changes in the living conditions of members of the population with incomes or expenditures close to the poverty line. Other measures of absolute poverty incidence lacking this disadvantage have been calculated from time to time, such as the poverty gap and poverty gap squared measures, but these measures are normally highly correlated with the headcount measure.

4. What *data source* is used for the calculations? Household level survey data are essential, but the statistical design and frequency of these surveys varies between countries. For example, in Thailand the periodic Socio-Economic Surveys (SES) conducted by the Thai government's National Statistical Office (NSO) provide virtually the sole source of reliable information at the household level that can be compared over time (Krongkaew 1993; Warr 2005). In the Philippines the corresponding survey is the Family Income and Expenditure Survey, conducted every three years by the National Statistical Coordination Board (Balisacan 2001). In Indonesia, the SUSENAS survey conducted by the Central Bureau of Statistics plays a similar role. It is conducted annually, but the specialized 'consumption module', which provides the

most reliable basis for poverty estimation based on expenditures, is conducted only every three years. In Laos, the government's Lao Expenditure and Consumption Survey (LECS), conducted by the Bureau of Statistics, is the sole reliable basis for poverty estimates but these surveys have been undertaken only every five years since 1992/93.

5. How is the *base level of the poverty line* determined? Some concept of the minimum level of income or expenditure per person must be established for a household to be classified as non-poor. Although studies of poverty measurement often give great attention to this matter, drawing upon studies of minimum nutritional requirements (Ravallion 1992), the level of this poverty line necessarily involves a large element of arbitrariness.

6. What is the *poverty line deflator*? This involves the way the poverty line is adjusted over time to keep its real purchasing power constant. Although this may seem a minor technical matter, it is a central issue for poverty measurement over time and across regions where consumer prices vary. Empirical studies of poverty incidence differ in their handling of this issue. The ideal deflator uses the actual expenditure pattern of the poor to weight price changes at the commodity level. This deflator may, at times, behave differently from the overall consumer price index (CPI), which reflects 'average' expenditure patterns. In particular, when the prices of food items move relative to other consumer goods prices the two series may diverge significantly because the share of food in the poverty line basket is higher than its share in the CPI basket.

Data on poverty incidence

Figure 14.1 and the upper half of Table 14.1 summarize World Bank data on annual rates of poverty reduction in developing countries within six major regions of the world: Southeast Asia; China (listed here as a 'region' because of its size); Europe and Central Asia; Latin America and the

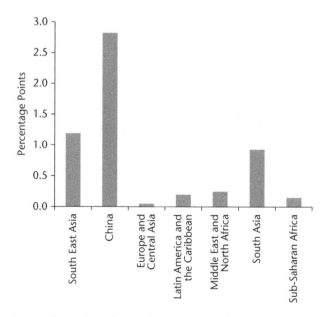

Figure 14.1 Annual rates of poverty reduction (percentage points per year)
Source: Author's calculations.

Table 14.1 Developing regions and countries: annual rates of poverty reduction, 1981 to 2008

Country/region	Start value	End value	Start year	End year	Difference	Difference per year
China[a]	84.02	16.25	1981	2005	67.77	2.82
Europe and Central Asia[a]	1.91	0.47	1981	2008	1.44	0.05
Latin America/Caribbean[a]	11.89	6.47	1981	2008	5.42	0.20
Middle East/North Africa[a]	9.56	2.7	1981	2008	6.86	0.25
South Asia[a]	61.14	35.97	1981	2008	25.17	0.93
Sub-Saharan Africa[a]	51.45	47.51	1981	2008	3.94	0.15
South East Asia[a]	45.04	12.81	1981	2008	32.23	1.19
Cambodia[b]	34.7	25.9	2004	2009	8.8	1.35
Indonesia[b]	63.3	12.5	1976	2011	50.8	1.45
Laos[b]	46.0	27.6	1992	2007	18.4	1.23
Malaysia[b]	52.4	3.8	1970	2009	48.6	1.25
Philippines[b]	51.4	24.2	1961	2009	27.2	0.57
Thailand[b]	61.1	8.1	1969	2009	53.0	1.38
Vietnam[b]	58.1	12.6	1993	2011	45.5	2.53

Sources:
[a]World Bank, Povcal database. Poverty line: US$ 1.25 per day at 2005 purchasing power parity (PPP).
[b]Individual country national data sources using national poverty lines.
Note: Start values and end values of poverty incidence are expressed in percent of population.

Caribbean; the Middle East and North Africa; South Asia; and Sub-Saharan Africa. The periods covered are 1981 to 2008 for most regions. The extraordinary rate of poverty reduction in China dominates all others, but Southeast Asia is second, followed by South Asia. In historical terms, the 1.2 per cent annual rate of poverty reduction achieved in Southeast Asia is truly remarkable, an achievement only overshadowed by the even more rapid rate (2.8 per cent per annum) achieved in China.

What could explain the huge variation among regions in the rate of poverty reduction? Figure 14.2 compares the data in Figure 14.1 with data on real GDP growth per person over the same periods. The correlation is unmistakable. Correlation does not necessarily mean causation, and it would be absurd to suggest that economic growth was the sole determinant of poverty reduction, but these data suggest that it is an important one.

Among the individual countries of Southeast Asia the World Bank 'povcal' data set is less useful than the data available from individual country governments because in the former the number of data points is smaller and its decomposition into its rural and urban components is also less complete. Accordingly, all subsequent poverty data presented in this chapter for Southeast Asia will be based on national poverty lines, using poverty incidence estimates obtained from the statistical agencies of the individual countries.

Available data on the headcount measure of poverty incidence in the Southeast Asian countries listed above are summarized in the lower half of Table 14.1 and in Figure 14.3. Poverty reduction was most rapid in Vietnam, followed by Cambodia,[3] Indonesia, Thailand, Laos, Malaysia and the Philippines. There is again considerable variation. Vietnam's annual rate of poverty reduction was 4.4 times that of the Philippines. Why? One reason is presumably that national income per person grew 7.7 times as rapidly. The correlation between annual rates of poverty reduction and annual rates of GDP growth per person is shown in Figure 14.4. Again, correlation does not necessarily mean causation, though it could mean that, even though other factors must surely have been important as well.

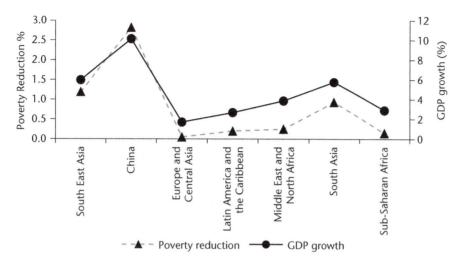

Figure 14.2 Annual rate of poverty reduction and economic growth (percentage points per year)

Source: Author's calculations.

Notes: 'Poverty Reduction' means the annual rate of poverty reduction based on the World Bank poverty line of US$ 1.25 per day at 2005 purchasing power parity from 1981 to 2008 (2005 in the case of China). 'GDP growth' means the average annual rate of growth of real GDP per capita over the same period as above.

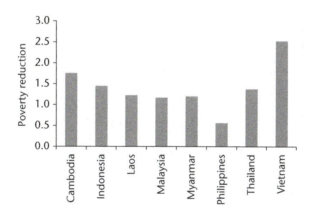

Figure 14.3 Southeast Asia: annual rates of poverty reduction (percentage points per year)

Source: Author's calculations.

Figures 14.5 to 14.12 summarize the available data on national poverty, rural poverty and urban poverty. For most countries of Southeast Asia, the absolute magnitudes of the reductions in poverty incidence, at all three levels, are stunning. The relationship between these three measures is as follows. We shall write N, N^R and N^U for the total, rural and urban populations, respectively, where $N = N^R + N^U$. Let $\alpha^R = N^R / N$ and $\alpha^U = N^U / N$ for the rural and urban shares of the total population, respectively, where $\alpha^R + \alpha^U = 1$. The total number of poor people is given by $N^P = N_P^R + N_P^U$, where N_P^R and N_P^U denote the number in poverty in rural and urban areas, respectively. Aggregate poverty incidence is given by

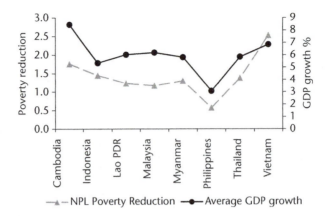

Figure 14.4 Southeast Asia: annual rate of poverty reduction and economic growth (percentage points per year)

Source: Author's calculations.

Notes: 'NPL Poverty Reduction' means the average annual rate of poverty reduction based on national poverty lines over the periods indicated in Table 14.1 and using the data summarized there. 'GDP growth' means the average annual rate of growth of real GDP per capita over the same periods as above.

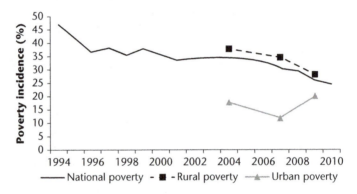

Figure 14.5 Cambodia: poverty incidence, 1994 to 2010
Source: Author's calculations.

$$P = N_P/N = (N_P^R + N_P^U)/N = \alpha^R P^R + \alpha^U P^U, \tag{1}$$

where $P^R = N_P^R + N^R$ denotes the proportion of the rural population that is in poverty and $P^U = N_P^U/N^U$ the corresponding incidence of poverty in urban areas.

Now, differentiating (1) totally, we obtain a key relationship,

$$dP = \alpha^R dP^R + \alpha^U dP^U + (P^R - P^U)d\alpha^R. \tag{2}$$

From (2), the change in poverty incidence may be decomposed into three parts: (i) the change in rural poverty incidence, weighted by the rural population share, (ii) the change in urban poverty incidence weighted by the urban population share, and (iii) the movement of populations from rural to urban areas weighted by the difference in poverty incidence between these two areas.

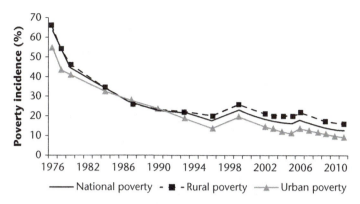

Figure 14.6   Indonesia: poverty incidence, 1976 to 2010
Source: Author's calculations.

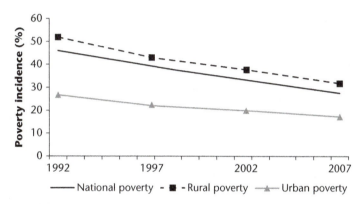

Figure 14.7   Laos: poverty incidence, 1992 to 2007
Source: Author's calculations.

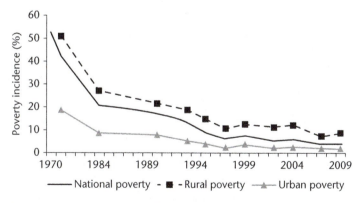

Figure 14.8   Malaysia: poverty incidence, 1976 to 2009
Source: Author's calculations.

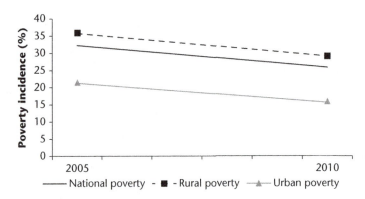

Figure 14.9 Myanmar: poverty incidence, 2005 to 2010
Source: Author's calculations.

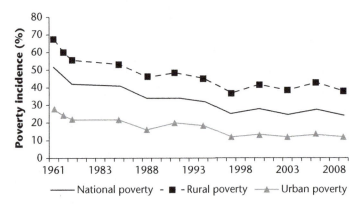

Figure 14.10 The Philippines: poverty incidence, 1976 to 2008
Source: Author's calculations.

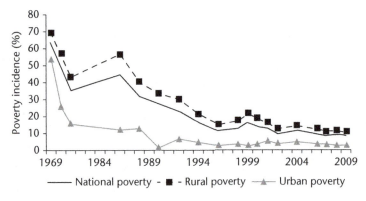

Figure 14.11 Thailand: poverty incidence, 1969 to 2009
Source: Author's calculations.

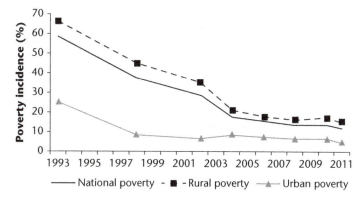

Figure 14.12 Vietnam: poverty incidence, 1993 to 2011
Source: Author's calculations.

The last of these terms is described by Anand and Kanbur (1985) and by Ravallion and Datt (1996) as the 'Kuznets effect'. As the population moves from rural to urban areas, a change in aggregate poverty incidence will occur even at constant levels of rural and urban poverty incidence, provided that the levels of poverty incidence in these two sectors is different. In growing economies, we expect to find that the rural population share is falling ($d\alpha^R < 0$). Furthermore, the incidence of poverty in rural areas typically exceeds that in urban areas (($P^R - P^U) > 0$). Thus, the expected sign of ($P^R - P^U)d\alpha^R$ is negative. How important the Kuznets effect is as a determinant of overall poverty reduction is, of course, an empirical matter.

Table 14.2 summarizes the data presented in Figures 14.5 to 14.12 by taking the mean rate of change of total poverty incidence and decomposing it as in equation (2). For example, the mean annual change in the aggregate level of poverty incidence for Indonesia was −1.28 percentage

Table 14.2 Data decomposition: mean annual changes in poverty incidence

	Actual							
	Indonesia	*Laos*	*Malaysia*	*Myanmar*	*Philippines*	*Cambodia*	*Thailand*	*Vietnam*
National[a]	−1.281	−1.227	−0.932	−1.300	−0.695	−1.760	−1.301	−2.174
Urban[b]	−0.313	−0.129	−0.150	−0.305	−0.177	0.131	−0.191	−0.188
Rural[c]	−0.911	−1.051	−0.524	−0.973	−0.401	−1.357	−1.107	−1.887
Migration[d]	−0.057	−0.046	−0.259	−0.022	−0.117	−0.534	−0.003	−0.099
	Normalized (National = 100)							
National[a]	100	100	100	100	100	100	100	100
Urban[b]	24.43	10.54	16.05	23.44	25.41	−7.47	14.67	8.65
Rural[c]	71.10	85.70	56.22	74.86	57.72	77.11	85.11	86.80
Migration[d]	4.46	3.77	27.73	1.69	16.87	30.36	0.22	4.55

Sources: Author's calculations, using data sources as in Table 14.1. The decomposition of the change in aggregate poverty incidence follows equation (2).
Notes: National = Urban + Rural + Migration.
[a] Mean annual value of dP, the y-o-y change in national poverty incidence.
[b] Mean annual value of $\alpha^U dP^U$, the y-o-y population share-weighted change in urban poverty.
[c] Mean annual value of $\alpha^R dP^R$, the y-o-y population share-weighted change in rural poverty.
[d] Mean annual value of ($P^R - P^U) d\alpha^R$, the y-o-y migration-induced change in national poverty.

points per year (i.e. an annual reduction, on average, in the nation-wide headcount incidence of poverty from numbers like 20 per cent to numbers like 18.72 per cent of the total population). Equation (2) is an identity and must apply at all points in the data set. It must therefore apply at the means of the data. The equation shows that this mean aggregate change in poverty incidence can be decomposed into three components: average poverty reduction in urban areas, average poverty reduction in rural areas, and the average movement of population between these two areas. In understanding the table it is important that the rows 'Urban' and 'Rural' do not mean the average rate of poverty reduction in urban and rural areas, but these rates multiplied by their population shares, as indicated on the right-hand side of equation (2).

The second half of the table normalizes the decomposition by dividing all values by the mean change in aggregate poverty (−1.28 for Indonesia, for example) and multiplying by 100. In Indonesia, for example, reductions in rural poverty accounted for 71 per cent of the overall reduction in poverty, reduced urban poverty for 24 per cent and rural to urban migration for about 5 per cent of the overall reduction in poverty at the national level. In all eight countries, reductions in rural poverty account for more than half of the total reduction in poverty and in all except Malaysia and Cambodia reductions in urban poverty were more important than migration effects.

The above calculations are, of course, merely descriptions of the data. We now turn to the question of what caused these observed changes in poverty incidence. It is hypothesized in this chapter that poverty reduction is driven by economic growth, possibly influenced by its sectoral composition, and by the relative price of food, meaning the price of food as a component of the consumer price index relative to the overall consumer price index. The average data on these variables and the correlations between them at an individual country level are summarized in Table 14.3. We now turn to a regression model intended to sort out the causal relationships among these variables.

The growth–poverty nexus

Conceptual background

Poverty incidence and its change over time depend on many factors, of which economic variables are at most only part of the story. Among the economic variables, many issues are relevant aside from simply the overall growth rate of output. Changes in commodity prices play a role, along with tax and public expenditure policies. But policy discussion in almost all countries is heavily concerned with economic growth and its sectoral composition. Policy makers rightly wish to know the extent to which this growth is inclusive. In particular, they wish to know whether concern with growth is consistent with the goal of reducing poverty. Does economic growth cause poverty reduction and, if so, to what extent? Does the sectoral composition of that growth matter for its poverty-reducing effects? Do relative prices, especially the relative price of food, matter for poverty reduction?

Three methodological approaches can be found in the literature for addressing these questions empirically. Each is problematic, but in different ways. General equilibrium modeling (GEM) has the advantage of permitting controlled experiments with the models, changing only one exogenous variable at a time and finding the effects on all endogenous variables of interest. This approach permits detailed analysis of the economic mechanisms through which output growth operates on poverty incidence (Fane and Warr 2003). Since the distinction between the exogenous and endogenous variables within the models is unambiguous, by construction, there are clear *causal* relationships between changes in the exogenous variables and their effects on the

Table 14.3 Average rates of poverty reduction, economic growth and variable correlations

	Indonesia	Laos	Malaysia	Philippines	Thailand	Vietnam
Poverty reduction per year						
Total	−1.28	−1.23	−0.93	−0.76	−1.30	−2.17
Urban	−1.12	−0.61	−0.37	−0.45	−0.65	−0.78
Rural	−1.25	−1.34	−0.91	−0.76	−1.55	−2.46
Growth rate per capita per year						
GDP	4.53	4.35	4.57	0.74	3.51	5.68
Agriculture	0.38	2.27	0.04	0.13	0.29	0.59
Industry	1.79	1.36	2.41	−0.03	1.81	2.88
Services	2.49	1.23	2.46	0.72	1.54	2.26
Annual food CPI/general CPI	*0.92*	*1.03*	*0.96*	*1.04*	*1.00*	*1.09*
Correlation between total poverty reduction per year and independent variables						
GDP	−0.56	0.12	−0.53	−0.26	−0.52	0.04
Agriculture	−0.71	−0.86	−0.12	−0.18	−0.51	−0.34
Industry	−0.34	0.96	−0.51	−0.24	−0.37	−0.23
Services	−0.25	0.54	−0.23	−0.17	−0.58	0.44
Food CPI/general CPI	0.45	−0.87	0.67	−0.52	0.37	0.63
Correlation between rural poverty reduction per year and independent variables						
GDP	−0.52	0.12	−0.56	−0.32	−0.51	−0.10
Agriculture	−0.69	−0.86	0.20	−0.23	−0.49	−0.33
Industry	−0.29	0.96	−0.47	−0.27	−0.36	−0.34
Services	−0.24	0.54	−0.43	−0.25	−0.57	0.30
Food CPI/general CPI	0.39	−0.87	0.66	−0.42	0.35	0.60
Correlation between urban poverty reduction per year and independent variables						
GDP	−0.60	0.38	−0.32	−0.61	−0.19	0.80
Agriculture	−0.41	−0.70	0.23	−0.25	0.25	0.10
Industry	−0.13	1.00	−0.26	−0.58	−0.21	0.59
Services	−0.50	0.74	−0.28	−0.49	−0.25	0.80
Food CPI/general CPI	0.51	−0.71	0.58	−0.31	0.16	0.19
Years covered	*1976–2011*	*1992–2007*	*1970–2009*	*1961–2009*	*1969–2009*	*1998–2011*
Observations	*18*	*3*	*11*	*10*	*18*	*7*

Source: Author's calculations.

Notes: All growth rates are in real, per capita terms. 'Agriculture' means the per capita growth rate of real value-added in agriculture, and similarly for 'Industry' and 'Services'. Consequently, the sectoral GDP share-weighted sum of the per capita growth rates of the three sectors is equal to the per capita growth rate of GDP.

For each country, the number of observations appearing in the final row of the table is the number of observations of poverty reduction, equal to the number of observations of poverty incidence minus one.

endogenous variables. These models are nevertheless subject to the objection that these causal relationships are predetermined in that they are built into the structure of the models themselves. For example, the qualitative result that economic growth reduces poverty is a direct consequence of the structural assumptions of the models. Moreover, the quantitative results are a function of the chosen values of the large numbers of behavioral parameters necessarily used within the models. Although the key parameters can be varied to show their implications for the relationships of interest, the fact remains that the true values of these parameters are largely unknown.

A second approach relies solely on household survey data to construct the distribution of real expenditures across households and to analyze the relationships among variables calculated from this distribution. For example, this approach computes the relationship between changes in the mean of the expenditure data and changes in the level of poverty incidence, calculated from the same distribution. Changes in the mean of real household expenditures is taken to be a measure of (or proxy for) economic growth. These analyses have the advantage of working with internally consistent data and can provide a description of relationships among various features of the expenditure distribution. The problem is that these relationships lack a *causal* basis. It is no more true to say that changes in the mean of the distribution of household expenditures causes changes in poverty incidence than to say the reverse. But policy application requires knowledge of causal relationships. Statistical descriptions of relationships among variables constructed from the distribution of household expenditures do not provide that. In any case, the rate of change of mean household expenditures is not the same thing as economic growth, meaning the expansion of economic output. The link between output growth and poverty incidence is the causal relationship we wish to study. Beyond this, we wish to ask how the sectoral composition of economic growth might influence the rate at which poverty incidence declines and this is clearly impossible with this second approach.

A third approach assembles statistical data on changes in poverty incidence and data on output growth and its composition. It then regresses the former on the latter. The fact that separate data sets are involved – the national accounts for economic growth and household survey data for poverty incidence – has both advantages and disadvantages. Suppose it is found that economic growth leads to reductions in poverty incidence. It could not be said that this finding was a mere statistical artifact arising from the use of the same flawed data set to measure both variables, because quite different data sets are used to measure the two sets of variables. But this also creates problems. The frequency of the data may not be the same. National accounts data are available at least annually, but this is seldom true of poverty incidence data, which are usually available only at intervals of two to three years at least. The advantage of this approach is that it focuses directly on a causal relationship of strong policy interest (Ravallion and Datt 1996). Despite its limitations, this is the approach used in the present study.

The economic development literature has emphasized the sectoral composition of growth in relation to its implications for poverty reduction, but this emphasis has been based primarily on a priori theorizing, rather than evidence. The obvious argument is that in most poor countries a majority of the poor lives in rural areas and is employed in agriculture. From this it has seemed probable that growth of agriculture is more important for poverty reduction than growth of industry or services. But this conclusion does not necessarily follow. Sectoral growth rates may not be independent. Expansion of capacity in one sector – say, food processing – may stimulate output growth elsewhere – say, fruit production. More importantly, people are potentially mobile; given sufficient time, even poor people can presumably move to whichever sector is generating the growth. Rural poverty may therefore be reduced by urban-based growth, drawing the poor away from rural areas (Fields 1980). When sectoral interdependence and intersectoral factor mobility are taken into account, it is not obvious whether the sectoral composition of growth is important for poverty reduction or not.

Even if labor were fully and instantaneously mobile, poverty incidence could still be affected by the sectoral composition of growth. To a first order of approximation, the level of absolute poverty presumably depends on the demand for the factors of production owned by the poor, especially unskilled labor and, to a lesser extent, agricultural land. Growth in different sectors has differential effects on the demands for these factors, depending on these sectors' factor intensities, and may have different effects on poverty, inequality, or both. Finally, the distinction rural/urban is not synonymous with the distinction agriculture/non-agriculture. Much agricultural production may occur in full- or part-time farming on the fringes of urban areas and much industrial and services activity may occur in rural areas.

Only careful quantitative analysis can resolve questions of this kind, but the limited availability of data that can support statistical analysis has been an impediment to the systematic study of poverty incidence and its determinants. Some recent studies have attempted to explore the relationships involved by analyzing cross-sectional data sets across countries, or across regions or households for individual countries, while others have attempted to assemble long-term time-series data sets on poverty incidence for individual countries. The time-series approach is generally preferable, in that it makes possible a direct study of the determinants of changes in poverty at an aggregate level.

Unfortunately, in most developing countries, the consumer expenditure surveys on which studies of poverty incidence must be based are conducted only intermittently. Data are thus available at most only with intervals of several years between observations. This is true of all the Southeast Asian countries. The data are most extensive for Indonesia and Thailand, but even when all national time-series observations on poverty incidence are assembled for them, the number of observations of poverty incidence for each country is only 19, giving 18 observations of changes in poverty incidence. For Malaysia the corresponding numbers are only 12 and 11, for the Philippines 11 and 10 and fewer for others. These numbers are insufficient to sustain formal statistical analysis for any one of these countries, but when all Southeast Asian countries are pooled, the total number of observations of changes in poverty incidence is 67, adequate for the purposes of the present study.

In each country the value of the national poverty line is held constant over time, but since the meaning of the poverty lines is different in each of the countries, we should not assume that the same quantitative relationship between poverty incidence and aggregate growth will necessarily exist in all Southeast Asian countries. In the present study, intercept dummy variables were used for five of the remaining six countries. It must be recognized that the use of dummy variables is an imperfect way of capturing the possible effects of different national poverty lines. The strong assumption being made is that the underlying relationship between changes in poverty incidence (the dependent variable) and the rate of growth (the independent variable) is linear and with the same slope in all countries, differing only in the intercept terms.

Each interval between the data points for poverty incidence is used to construct the values of the dependent variables described below, with the calculated value divided by the number of years corresponding to that time interval. This gives an annual rate of change for the variable concerned. These annualized rates of change then become the variables used in the regression analysis described below.

Poverty and aggregate growth

We now turn to the manner in which poverty incidence is affected by economic growth. For simplicity, we hypothesize initially the simplest possible relationship between these variables, where the total number of households in poverty, N_P, depends on the aggregate level of real income per unit of population, Y, and the relative price of food, R^F. Thus, poverty incidence is given by

$$P = N_P/N = \varphi(Y, R^F). \tag{3}$$

Totally differentiating this equation,

$$dP = \varphi_Y Yy + \varphi_R dR^F, \tag{4}$$

where dP represents the change in poverty incidence, dR^F represents the change in the real price of food and lower case Roman letters represent the proportional changes of variables represented in levels by upper case Roman letters. Thus $y = dY/Y$ is the growth rates of aggregate real income per person. In this case, we estimate relationships of the kind

$$dP = a + by + cdR^F, \qquad (5)$$

and test whether the coefficients b and c are significantly different from zero.

Poverty and sectoral growth

Whether the sectoral composition of economic growth is significant for poverty reduction can be investigated as follows. The level of real GDP per person is given by

$$Y = Y_a + Y_i + Y_s, \qquad (6)$$

where Y_a, Y_i, and Y_s denote value-added (contribution to GDP) per person in the total population, measured at constant prices, in agriculture, industry, and services, respectively. The overall real rate of growth per person can be decomposed into its sectoral components from

$$y = H_a y_a + H_i y_i + H_s y_s, \qquad (7)$$

where $H_k = Y_k / Y$, $k = (a,i,s)$, denotes the share of sector k in GDP. By estimating the equation

$$dP = a + b_a H_a y_a + b_i H_i y_i + b_s H_s y_s + cdR^F \qquad (8)$$

and testing whether $b_a = b_i = b_s$, we may test directly whether the sectoral composition of growth affects the rate of poverty reduction. By testing whether $c = 0$ we can test whether the price of food plays a significant role in determining changes in poverty incidence and, if so, in what direction.

Estimation results

Poverty and aggregate growth

Equation (5) was estimated as described above and the results are summarized in Table 14.4. Because the dependent variable is the change in poverty incidence (a negative value indicating a reduction in poverty) a negative estimated coefficient means that an increase in the variable is associated with a reduction in poverty. A positive sign indicates the opposite. In regression (1) dummy variables were estimated for all countries except Indonesia (the base country). All country dummy variables were insignificant except Vietnam. The coefficient on aggregate GDP growth was negative as expected and highly significant (99 percent confidence level). Higher rates of GDP growth per capita induce larger reductions in poverty. The coefficient on food price was positive and significant at the 90 percent level, indicating that a higher relative price of food reduces the rate at which poverty declines. To test whether endogeneity of the food price variable is important the equation was re-estimated in regression (2) without this variable. If GDP growth was affecting poverty via the price of food dropping this variable (not controlling for the price of food) should increase the estimated coefficient on GDP growth. The coefficient does increase, but not greatly.

In regression (3) the insignificant variables (except the constant term) were all dropped, in line with the general-to-specific approach of Hendry (1995), and the equation was re-estimated. The estimated coefficient on aggregate growth remains significant. The estimated relationship is highly significant and the Ramsey RESET test suggests that it has no omitted variables, although with low degrees of freedom, this test is relatively weak. The Breusch–Pagan/Cook Weisberg test for

Table 14.4 National poverty and aggregate growth

	(1)	(2)	(3)
	Dependent variable: Change in national poverty		
Independent variables:			
GDP growth p.c.	–0.182***	–0.219***	–0.229***
	(0.066)	(0.060)	(0.057)
Real price of food	4.541*		
	(2.694)		
Laos	–0.666	–0.243	
	(0.962)	(0.911)	
Malaysia	–0.155	–0.024	
	(0.592)	(0.588)	
Philippines	–0.702	–0.413	
	(0.681)	(0.649)	
Thailand	–0.814	–0.543	
	(0.549)	(0.512)	
Vietnam	–2.284**	–1.638**	–1.673**
	(0.893)	(0.749)	(0.721)
Constant	–3.291	0.094	–0.242
	(2.634)	(0.452)	(0.292)
N	58	58	58
R^2	0.324	0.301	0.223
adj.R^2	0.229	0.219	0.209
F-statistic	3.42	3.66	16.05
p-value	0.0046	0.0043	0.0002

Source: Author's calculations.
Notes: 'p.c.' means per capita. Standard errors in parentheses.
* denotes significantly different from zero at 90 percent confidence level.
** denotes significantly different from zero at 95 percent confidence level.
*** denotes significantly different from zero at 99 percent confidence level.

heteroskedasticity indicates the absence of heteroskedasticity. The results indicate that more rapid growth of real GDP per capita and reductions in the real price of food are both significant sources of poverty reduction.

Poverty and sectoral growth

Is the sectoral composition of the growth important? Equation (8) was now estimated to capture the behavior of the dependent variable when the sectoral composition of growth appears on the right-hand side of the equation. The results are shown in Table 14.5 and they follow the pattern of presentation used in Table 14.4. The findings support the notion that growth of agriculture and the real price of food are significant determinants of the rate of poverty reduction. Other components of GDP had the expected signs, but were statistically insignificant. All country intercept dummy variables except Vietnam were highly insignificant and were dropped.

An F-test of the hypothesis that the coefficients on share-weighted sectoral growth rates per capita were all equal ($b_a = b_i = b_s$) was rejected at the 5 percent level of significance. In short, the data indicate that the growth of agriculture is more important for poverty reduction than the growth of either industry or services. The data also confirm that the real price of food is an

Table 14.5 National poverty and sectoral growth

	(4)	(5)	(6)
	Dependent variable: Change in national poverty		
Independent variables			
Agricultural growth p.c.	−1.232**	−1.107**	−0.739**
	(0.523)	(0.526)	(0.344)
Industrial growth p.c.	−0.096	−0.147	
	(0.124)	(0.122)	
Services growth p.c.	−0.206	−0.258*	
	(0.135)	(0.133)	
Real price of food	4.436		6.211***
	(2.735)		(2.256)
Laos	0.939	1.200	
	(1.230)	(1.240)	
Malaysia	−0.776	−0.515	
	(0.659)	(0.649)	
Philippines	−1.002	−0.617	
	(0.685)	(0.653)	
Thailand	−1.019*	−0.668	
	(0.560)	(0.525)	
Vietnam	−2.205**	−1.447*	−2.420***
	(0.898)	(0.780)	(0.753)
Constant	−3.889	0.364	−6.656***
	(2.664)	(0.481)	(2.175)
N	58	58	58
R^2	0.377	0.343	0.261
adj. R^2 R^2	0.260	0.235	0.206
F-statistic	3.22	3.19	4.69
p-value	0.0049	0.0054	0.0026

Source: Author's calculations.
Notes: 'p.c.' means per capita. Standard errors in parentheses.
* denotes significantly different from zero at 90 percent confidence level.
** denotes significantly different from zero at 95 percent confidence level.
*** denotes significantly different from zero at 99 percent confidence level.

important determinant of poverty reduction – lower real food prices are associated with higher rates of poverty reduction.

A similar exercise was now conducted with changes in rural poverty as the dependent variable (Table 14.6) and changes in urban poverty (Table 14.7). In the case of rural poverty, the results are qualitatively similar to those obtained for national poverty in Table 14.5, but stronger. Agricultural and services growth contribute to poverty reduction, but the effect of industrial growth is statistically insignificant. Higher real prices of food are strongly associated with increases in poverty incidence. In the case of urban poverty (Table 14.7) the attempted explanation was unsuccessful. Only the real price of food was significant, in the same direction as above.

Because rural poverty dominates total poverty the findings on rural poverty largely explain the total poverty results. Growth of agriculture, and to a lesser extent growth of services, are associated with poverty reduction, along with lower levels of the real price of food. Agriculture and services are both labor-intensive sectors. Growth of output in these sectors increases the demand for unskilled labor, the principal income source for most poor people. An increase in agricultural

Table 14.6 Rural poverty and sectoral growth

	(7)	(8)	(9)
	Dependent variable: Change in rural poverty		
Independent variables			
Agricultural growth p.c.	−1.716**	−1.585**	−0.982**
	(0.672)	(0.670)	(0.446)
Industrial growth p.c.	−0.105	−0.159	
	(0.160)	(0.156)	
Services growth p.c.	−0.291*	−0.346**	−0.362**
	(0.173)	(0.169)	(0.158)
Real price of food	4.646		7.105**
	(3.513)		(2.922)
Laos	1.458	1.732	
	(1.581)	(1.579)	
Malaysia	−1.139	−0.865	
	(0.846)	(0.826)	
Philippines	−1.255	−0.852	
	(0.880)	(0.831)	
Thailand	−1.489**	−1.121	−0.987*
	(0.720)	(0.669)	(0.566)
Vietnam	−2.614**	−1.821*	−2.920***
	(1.154)	(0.993)	(0.975)
Constant	−3.649	0.805	−7.443**
	(3.422)	(0.612)	(2.817)
N	58	58	58
R^2	0.374	0.351	0.246
adj. R^2 R^2	0.257	0.246	0.189
F-statistic	3.19	3.32	4.32
p-value	0.0042	0.0041	0.0042

Source: Author's calculations.
Notes: 'p.c.' means per capita. Standard errors in parentheses.
* denotes significantly different from zero at 90 percent confidence level.
** denotes significantly different from zero at 95 percent confidence level.
*** denotes significantly different from zero at 99 percent confidence level.

output simultaneously raises the return to land and a surprisingly large number of poor rural people also own land. Finally, part of the effect of an increase in agricultural output operates through a reduction in food prices, also strongly associated with poverty reduction.

Counterfactual projections

To what extent is poverty reduction sensitive to variations in the overall rate of economic growth, on the one hand, and to variations in its sectoral composition, on the other? These questions are explored in Figures 14.13 to 14.18. The analysis concentrates on rural poverty because the econometric results summarized above were most significant in this case. Each figure shows, first, the actual data on rural poverty ('Actual'), reproduced from Figures 14.7 to 14.12, and the level projected from the econometric model reported in Table 14.6 using the actual data on the independent variables for that particular country, as used in the econometric estimation

Table 14.7 Urban poverty and sectoral growth

Independent variables	(10)	(11)	(12)
	Dependent variable: Change in urban poverty		
Agricultural growth p.c.	0.642	0.683	
	(0.461)	(0.453)	
Industrial growth p.c.	–0.082	–0.099	
	(0.110)	(0.105)	
Services growth p.c.	–0.143	–0.160	
	(0.118)	(0.114)	
Real price of food	1.460	3.691*	
	(2.407)	(1.928)	
Laos	–1.078	–0.991	
	(1.083)	(1.067)	
Malaysia	0.807	0.894	
	(0.580)	(0.558)	
Philippines	0.133	0.260	
	(0.603)	(0.562)	
Thailand	0.246	0.361	
	(0.493)	(0.452)	
Vietnam	–0.321	–0.071	
	(0.791)	(0.671)	
Constant	–1.881	–0.482	–4.164**
	(2.344)	(0.414)	(1.859)
N	58	58	58
R^2	0.173	0.167	0.076
adj. R^2	0.018	0.031	0.006
F-statistic	1.12	1.23	1.09
p-value	0.368	0.303	0.372

Source: Author's calculations.
Notes: 'p.c.' means per capita. Standard errors in parentheses.
* denotes significantly different from zero at 90 percent confidence level.
** denotes significantly different from zero at 95 percent confidence level.

('Predicted'). The difference between these two series indicates the magnitude of model prediction error, or the absence of 'goodness of fit'.

The next two series use this econometric model to simulate alternative counterfactual time paths of rural poverty incidence when the independent variables differ from the data in the following ways. The first ('Simulated') is the projected time path of rural poverty incidence when the rate of growth per capita is half its observed value but its sectoral composition is the same as observed in the data. That is, at each time period each sectoral growth rate per capita is half its observed value. The final series ('Simulated_GDP') is the projected time of rural poverty incidence when each sector grows at the GDP growth rate. That is, the overall growth rate is the same as the observed rate, but all sectoral growth rates are the same.

In all countries, halving the growth rate of each sector reduces the rate of rural poverty reduction considerably. But for some countries, the implication of equal growth rates is even more dramatic. These are the countries – Malaysia, the Philippines and Thailand – where the data

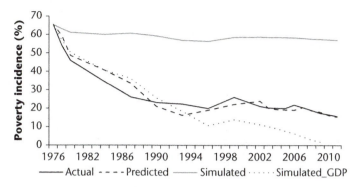

Figure 14.13 Indonesia: rural poverty reduction – data and counterfactual projections
Source: Author's calculations.

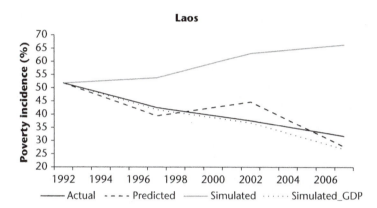

Figure 14.14 Laos: rural poverty reduction – data and counterfactual projections
Source: Author's calculations.

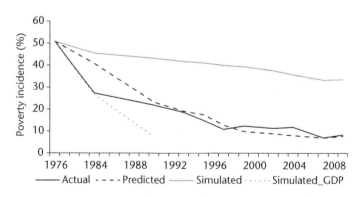

Figure 14.15 Malaysia: rural poverty reduction – data and counterfactual projections
Source: Author's calculations.

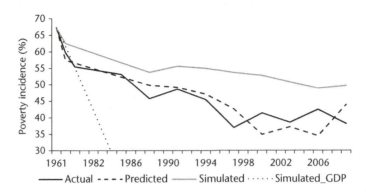

Figure 14.16 Philippines: rural poverty reduction – data and counterfactual projections
Source: Author's calculations.

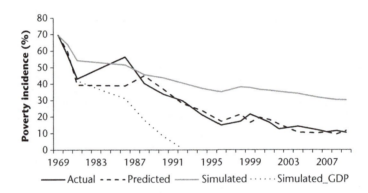

Figure 14.17 Thailand: rural poverty reduction – data and counterfactual projections
Source: Author's calculations.

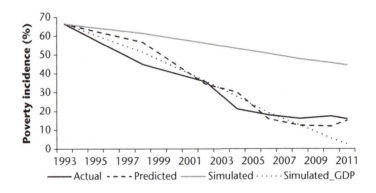

Figure 14.18 Vietnam: rural poverty reduction – data and counterfactual projections
Source: Author's calculations.

indicate the slowest growth of agriculture relative to GDP. Equivalently, these are the countries where agriculture's share of GDP has declined the most rapidly. The point here is not that equal sectoral growth rates would be a sensible objective of policy. Structural transformation is a necessary feature of economic development. Rather, the point is to illustrate the finding from the econometric results that the rate of poverty reduction depends not only on the overall rate of economic growth but also on its sectoral composition.

Conclusions

The nations of Southeast Asia have achieved significant reductions in poverty incidence in recent decades. The achievement of poverty reduction was overwhelmingly attributable to the high rate of growth of GDP per person, but changes in the sectoral composition of the growth also had an impact. The results confirm that the poverty reduction outcome was strongly related to growth of agriculture and services, but *not* to the growth of industry. The results also indicate that reductions in the real price of food contribute significantly to poverty reduction. Increases in the real price of food do the opposite.

The importance of agricultural development for poverty reduction is widely understood but the contribution of the services sector is larger and its role has been much less widely appreciated. More surprisingly, the results indicate that the growth of industry has not contributed to poverty reduction in Southeast Asia. Similar results have been obtained using data for India (Ravallion and Datt 1996), except that in the case of India the negative effects of industrial growth were stronger. On the other hand, earlier results for Taiwan (Warr and Wang 1999) showed that the growth of industry was strongly associated with poverty reduction.

These differences may be due to the role of industry policy. Taiwan's more outward-oriented trade policy apparently induced a form of industrial development that was labor-intensive, small-scale and with a large rural component. This pattern of industrialization was conducive to a massive reduction of poverty incidence, occurring in both rural and urban areas. In India, heavy protection of industry led to a capital-intensive, large-scale and urban-based pattern of industrial development which did not serve the interests of the poorest groups. The countries of Southeast Asia studied here are intermediate between these two extreme cases in so far as industry policy is concerned and the estimated results on the impact of industrial growth are intermediate as well.

The principal income source of poor people is their own labor – largely unskilled. Agricultural land is also an important asset, but much less so. Development that increases the demand for these two resources raises the incomes of poor people and consequently reduces poverty incidence. This presumably explains the differences in the poverty-reducing power of growth in different sectors of the economy which have been analyzed in this chapter. In the Southeast Asian countries studied here, considered as a group, growth of the agricultural and services sectors have each reduced poverty considerably. Growth of the industrial sector has not. The results support the hypothesis that an import-substitution based industry policy promotes a pattern of industrialization that does not advance the welfare of poor people because it contributes insufficiently to expanding the demand for the principal resource that they own – unskilled labor.

Acknowledgments

Excellent research assistance from Dung Doan and Ramesh Paudel is gratefully acknowledged. The author is responsible for all defects.

Notes

1 They were less affected than the first four countries because pre-crisis levels of short-term capital inflows had been much smaller and they were therefore less vulnerable to a sudden capital outflow (Warr 2003).
2 For example, in Indonesia in 2007, demonstrators outside the Central Bureau of Statistics offices in Jakarta claimed that the poverty data had been 'manipulated' and did not relate to the true situation of poor people. See, for example: http://www.asia-pacific-action.org/node/142 [accessed 21 December 2010].
3 It should be noted that for Cambodia the period of observation is only four years.

References

Anand, Sudhir and S. M. R. Kanbur, 1985. 'Poverty Under the Kuznets Process', *Economic Journal*, 95, 42–50.

Balisacan, Arsenio M., 2001. 'Poverty in the Philippines: An Update and Reexamination', *Philippine Review of Economics and Business*, 38, 16–51.

Bourguignon, Francois, 2001. 'The Growth Elasticity of Poverty Reduction: Explaining Heterogeneity across Countries and Time Periods', unpublished manuscript.

Fane, George and Peter Warr, 2003. 'How Economic Growth Reduces Poverty: A General Equilibrium Analysis for Indonesia', in A. Shorrocks and R. Van der Hoeven (eds), *Perspectives on Growth and Poverty*, Tokyo: United Nations University Press, pp. 217–34.

Fields, Gary S., 1980. *Poverty, Inequality and Development*, Cambridge: Cambridge University Press.

Hendry, David F., 1995. *Dynamic Econometrics*, Oxford: Oxford University Press.

Krongkaew, Medhi, 1993. 'Poverty and Income Distribution', in Peter Warr (ed.), *The Thai Economy in Transition*, Cambridge: Cambridge University Press, pp. 401–37.

Ravallion, Martin, 1992. *Poverty Comparisons*, London: Routledge.

Ravallion, Martin, 1997. 'Can High-inequality Developing Countries Escape Absolute Poverty?', *Economics Letters*, 56, 51–7.

Ravallion, Martin, and Gaurav Datt, 1996. 'How Important to India's Poor Is the Sectoral Composition of Economic Growth?', *World Bank Economic Review*, 10, 1–25.

Warr, Peter, 2003. 'What Caused the Asian Crisis', in Dilip K. Das (ed.), *An International Finance Reader*, London: Routledge, pp. 381–400.

Warr, Peter, 2005. 'Boom, Bust and Beyond', in Peter Warr (ed.), *Thailand Beyond the Crisis*, London: Routledge, pp. 1–65.

Warr, Peter and Wang Wen-thuen, 1999. 'Poverty, Inequality and Economic Growth in Taiwan', in Gustav Ranis and Hu Sheng-cheng (eds), *The Political Economy of Development in Taiwan: Essays in Memory of John C. H. Fei*, London: Edward Elgar, pp. 133–65.

15

The political economy of policy reform

Insights from Southeast Asia

Hal Hill

AUSTRALIAN NATIONAL UNIVERSITY

Introduction

Although it may not seem obvious to non-economists, economists broadly agree on many key economic policy issues. But economics as a discipline has provided much less guidance on why and how economic policy reform occurs, and how to develop institutional mechanisms that enable governments to adopt 'good' economic policy. Political scientists are adept at identifying coalitions, constituencies, institutions and interest groups, but they less commonly examine the implications for economic policy. Thus, work at the intersection between economics and politics, of why and how policy reform takes place, remains relatively unexplored territory. There is no generally accepted template, much less a 'rule book', for how to engineer successful policy reform. This is especially so in developing countries: political processes are more personalistic, institutions are often less well established, outcomes are more fluid, and the detailed case study literature on economic policy making is in its infancy. We therefore need more case study evidence, of both success and failure, to understand why and how successful reform occurs.

Southeast Asia offers a fascinating opportunity for social science researchers interested in these issues. The economic performance of most of the major economies for most of the period since 1970 has been significantly better than the developing world average. But there is much diversity in the record of growth and reform. The reform experience ranges across the major policy U-turns and the incremental reforms, successes and failures, the macroeconomy and the sectors, and with both international and domestic factors playing a role. This diversity of the region, reflected also in levels of development and political/institutional structures, both cautions against generalization but also adds to the richness of the subject matter.

This chapter offers an analytical survey of the evidence on economic policy reform in Southeast Asia. To narrow down the topic to manageable, paper-length proportions, we focus primarily on macroeconomic and trade policy reform in three of the lower-middle economies, Indonesia, the Philippines and Vietnam. The next section introduces the issues and provides some country and institutional context. This is followed by a dissection of a series of reform episodes in these countries. The final section then draws some broader lessons and implications.

Issues and context

Some definitions

I define 'reform' for these purposes as a durable and significant policy change that improves aggregate socio-economic welfare, consistent also with an objective function that recognizes distributional and environmental considerations. The underlying rationale is concern for general welfare, the public interest, rather than particular vested interests. Economists have typically defined reform as measures that increase productivity and growth rates, but these goals could obviously be redefined to encompass a broader set of non-economic objectives. In addition to particular measures, reforms can also be about policy-making processes, for example greater transparency in policy making, such as that firms claiming special assistance have to submit to a process of public scrutiny and justification.

Obviously, not all policy changes would meet this definition of reform. For example, a redistribution program would not, unless it could be shown that this program resulted in increased productivity, or met more widely accepted social objectives (e.g. social stability). Similarly, programs that are essentially window-dressing exercises, such as anti-corruption campaigns introduced by a deeply corrupt regime, or 'one-stop-service' investment programs without significant bureaucratic reform, would not meet this definition. It is important to emphasize durability, in the sense that the reforms can be implemented and will not be quickly overturned by a successor administration.

Reforms come in many forms, from the so-called 'big bang' to the incremental. The literature focuses on the former, which constitute a major change in policy direction and which, if they are durable, are sometimes referred to as 'turning points' that lead to accelerated growth and improved living standards. Asian examples include China in 1978, India in 1991, Indonesia in 1966, and Vietnam (and its two Indo China neighbors) in the late 1980s. For some countries it is not possible to discern such turning points, in the sense that the general policy orientation has been broadly consistent, and policy reforms consist of incremental progress. In Southeast Asia, Malaysia, Singapore and Thailand best fit this characterization. The experience of other countries might be best described as 'zig zag reform', with progress followed by regress.[1]

The nature of reforms and their bureaucratic complexity also differs. Some measures are straightforward, stroke-of-the pen deregulations, which range across the big bang/incremental spectrum. Examples include the decision to introduce a floating exchange rate, to replace non-tariff barriers with tariffs, to remove certain regulatory requirements, to open an industry up to competition, and to render redundant a particularly corrupt agency. These decisions of course require careful prior evaluation, and a judgment that the parties that previously benefited from the reforms will not be able to sabotage them. But once this 'due diligence' has been undertaken, implementation of the reforms themselves is relatively straightforward.

By contrast, other reforms require a bureaucracy to implement them, and therefore administrative feasibility is a key consideration. For example, a prerequisite of successful tax reform is a competent and honest tax administration. This may be an interactive process, in the sense that the reforms are designed to lessen the scope for discretionary interventions (e.g. a value added tax that builds in an incentive for compliance, simpler tax rates and regulations, etc.). Some measures may go hand in hand, entailing a different mix of interventions, more of some and less of others. For example, financial liberalization entails relaxed barriers to entry and less bureaucratic intervention in the operations of financial institutions. However, a market-based financial system also requires careful and credible prudential supervision.

Drivers of reform

The literature typically identifies the key drivers of reform as a mixture of factors, including necessity, the triumph of ideas, and the conjunction of reform-oriented political leadership aided by technocratic advisors. Typically several of these factors are present in the case of successful reforms. An understanding of the drivers of reform in turn requires identification of the key policy actors. We summarize here some salient points in the literature.

First, the 'crisis hypothesis' as a reform driver was a key conclusion of the comparative study of Lal and Myint (1996, p. 288), who concluded that 'Turning points [in economic policy] are invariably associated with macroeconomic crises.' Or it could be some other major event, such as a military defeat (or threat), the cessation of external support, or a natural disaster. The underlying hypothesis is that reform is a difficult process, and societies have a natural ('Olsonian') tendency to become sclerotic. A crisis may be helpful in persuading the community that the current order is unacceptable and requires change. Political leadership may be emboldened, and willing to tackle difficult issues. For example, Bardhan (1998) draws attention to India's 1991 balance of payments crisis as a trigger for reform, which enabled the government to push aside the formidable vested interests that had built up around the post-independence dirigiste regimes, both financial and ideological.

Obviously, however, not all crises trigger major reforms. Instead they may result in failed states, or at least an inability to seize the opportunity to reform. That is, the hypothesis only works in certain circumstances. For example, the collapse of the communist regimes in the former Soviet Union and Eastern Europe led to a deep economic contraction and several countries did not regain pre-crisis living standards for over a decade or two (Pomfret, 2002). Moreover, deep crises may result in a political and institutional vacuum, and an incapacity to undertake effective reform. In the transition to a new, perhaps democratic, environment, power is generally diffused, structures are established to deliberately weaken the state, and policy lacks credibility. Indonesia in 1998 and the Philippines in 1986 are relatively mild examples of these twin crises, although in the former case, economic recovery occurred surprisingly swiftly given the depth of the crisis (Aswicahyono et al., 2009).

Second, effective reform requires a coherent intellectual agenda, an analysis of what needs to be done, how, and in what sequence. Thus, ideas are a central prerequisite (Krueger, 2007). These ideas spring from a variety of sources, but are most commonly associated with think tanks and economics faculties of leading universities. A common characterization is that a key group of technocrats had received training in leading universities abroad – Chile's 'Chicago Boys' and Indonesia's 'Berkeley Mafia' are oft-cited examples – but the channels of influence are in reality much broader.[2] In some cases, the reform agenda is formulated and driven by observing success abroad, most commonly in the neighborhood. The bureaucracy may also become a driver where there is a realization that the system they are administering is increasingly dysfunctional.

Technocrats are generally politically powerless. To translate their ideas into policy, they need to convince political leaders of the case for reform, and to work with them in implementing reform. That leader does not need to be a technical economist – in fact such cases are rare – but at least a person open to persuasion and able to grasp intuitively if not technically the case for reform. Obviously, there has to be a close working relationship and a sense of trust between these leaders and their technocrats. In centralized, authoritarian regimes, the key is the technocrats having access to the president or ruling party. Here the technocrats may engage in what Hadi Soesastro (1989) termed 'low politics' in the Indonesian case. That is, the technocrats seized the opportunity created by the sudden decline in international oil prices in the early 1980s to persuade President Soeharto to implement far-reaching reforms, but without having to engage in large-scale, high-profile public or parliamentary persuasion.

However, approaches to reform change, sometimes radically, in democratic regimes. Politicians have to persuade an electorate, the technocrats have to engage in the public discourse, to persuade political and opinion leaders, and also to ameliorate or buy off potential opposition (and losers). There is a higher potential for policy change in regimes with a low dispersal of power, in the words of MacIntyre (2003). That is, policy reform is likely to be more difficult where power is more diffused, and there are more 'veto players' present. It might be argued that, while reform is slower under a democratic regime, it is likely to be more durable, since the reform process will be consensus-driven and pay attention to potential losers. Nevertheless, in presidential regimes, where both the executive and senior echelons of the bureaucracy turn over, elections may result in significant policy change. Two examples since the mid-1990s where reformists were followed by democratically elected reform-skeptics are Colombia and the Philippines. In both cases, the growth momentum decelerated.[3]

Third, convincing politicians of the case for reform is a key challenge. Political leaders by definition have short-term horizons, and a political predisposition to favor a particular constituency. Arguing the case for reform when the benefits may be uncertain and long term in nature, and the short-term costs potentially high, is perhaps the most important challenge in the policy reform agenda. The reforms need to produce a dividend as quickly as possible. Where painful decisions are needed, external support may occasionally be useful. Technocrats themselves may attempt to 'pick a political winner', and lend their credibility to a particular candidate. There may also be scope for institutionally embedding reform momentum. Bates (1994, p. 30) for example argues for 'creating institutions that possess the power to commit [politicians] to collectively rational strategies'. Examples include measures that impose fiscal discipline on a government, or create 'agencies of restraint', staffed by professionals and with public reporting responsibilities (e.g. a productivity or competition commission).

Fourth, as noted, the bureaucracy is a key actor. It may range from being a passive bystander to an active player in a negative or positive sense. The literature generally makes two presumptions concerning their role. The first is a division between the key economic policy agencies such as finance ministries and central banks, which are more likely to be staffed by economists and to favor 'orthodox' policies, alongside line and sectoral ministries, which are more likely to favor, and be captured by, sectoral interests. The second is the notion that much of the bureaucracy, especially the latter groups, will be reluctant reformers, since most but not all reforms will reduce their discretionary authority and hence the scope for rent-seeking. Reform outcomes will therefore depend on the relative strength of these contending groups. More generally, outcomes will be shaped by the relative power of the executive, legislature and bureaucracy, and the scope of the reformers to variously persuade, co-opt or bypass bureaucratic resistance.

Fifth, there are various conjectures concerning the impact of external actors and factors. Two have already been identified: crises, some of which are exogenous (in the form of negative external shocks) and which have unpredictable effects; and ideas, many of which originate from abroad. Other foreign influences may also shape the process. There is the demonstration effect of successful reforming economies, especially if they are located nearby. This is the 'competitive liberalization' thesis referred to by Indonesia's Minister for Tourism and Creative Economy, Mari Pangestu (2012), and others. The intellectual ascendancy of openness as an engine of economic progress is highlighted in several country studies of trade liberalization (Rajapatirana, 2001). Foreign investors have become more interested in global economic integration, and therefore their earlier interest in establishing 'tariff factories' behind high protective barriers in developing countries has waned (Bhagwati, 2002).

The evidence on donor (particularly IMF and World Bank) conditionality is mixed. Jeffrey Sachs (1994, p. 504) has opined that 'Countries cannot be transformed without the generous and farsighted involvement of the international community.' A large literature of course argues the contrary case (see for example Easterly, 2006), that aid encourages the recipient countries to postpone difficult policy reforms. International agencies can play an effective role if there is a domestic interest in, and will for, reform (Krueger and Rajapatirana, 1999). However, in the absence of these factors, externally mandated reform attracts domestic opprobrium, implementation is likely to be spasmodic, and the reforms are therefore generally not durable. These arguments are also consistent with the cross-country econometric evidence that finds aid contributes to growth only when 'good policies' are present (Burnside and Dollar, 2000).

Sixth, the more successful reforms are invariably comprehensive. Political constraints may in reality result in piecemeal reform. But the danger is that significant gaps in the reform agenda may undermine the entire process. The literature on the interaction between macroeconomic and trade policy illustrates this issue, and also provides an intellectual rationale for the sequencing of reforms. As Rajapatirana (2001) and other analysts of successful trade liberalization point out, a willingness to allow a large depreciation boosts the competitiveness of tradable goods industries, and facilitates a lowering of protection. Krueger (1978, p. 231) goes further, arguing that the 'failure to devalue by a sufficient margin will prevent sustained liberalization'; moreover, a 'realistic real exchange rate [is] an essential condition for sustained liberalization'. In a similar vein, Pinera (1994, p. 228) warns against partial reforms on the basis of the Chilean experience: 'It is no use freeing trade and opening up the capital markets if one is going to leave the labor markets untouched.'

Southeast Asian case studies

In this section we summarize four major Southeast Asian policy reform episodes. It needs to be acknowledged immediately that there are two forms of sample selection bias in these case studies. First, their selection is inevitably arbitrary, based on documented research and my own research interests. Moreover, the samples selected focused mainly on success stories, working on the principle that economic policy can fail for any number of reasons, but success is more elusive and therefore needs to be investigated. Second, to the extent that the case studies focus primarily on changes in policy direction, the three more advanced economies in the region, Singapore, Malaysia and Thailand, are under-represented since they have had much more consistent policy regimes since the 1970s, and therefore there has been less need to undertake far-reaching change of policy settings. These three, for example, belong to the tiny handful of countries that have remained 'always open' in the Sachs–Warner sense, and to have avoided serious inflation episodes (though not a major growth slowdown during the Asian economic crisis and the global economic recession).

Vietnam's doi moi, and beyond[4]

Vietnam's major reforms from the mid-1980s are of particular interest since they have been highly successful, yet they were undertaken in very difficult circumstances. The country was verging on being a pariah state: frozen out of relations with the USA, at loggerheads with its neighbors, China to the north and ASEAN to the south and west, about to lose the support of its principal international benefactor, the Soviet Union, and having minimal contact with the international financial institutions (IFIs). There was a weak technocracy with very limited knowledge of how to manage the transition process and run a market economy.

Riedel and Comer (1997) argue that policy makers learnt mainly from their bitter experience with a decade of central planning, including disastrous attempts at agricultural collectivization and nationalizations. In their words:

> The leadership of Viet Nam did not decide to 'go market' because of any kind of ideological conversion from Marxism–Leninism to capitalism; instead it discovered the hard way that the alternative to a market economy does not work.

The Chinese experience, although in its infancy, was closely observed, as this was the country against which it benchmarked its performance. Riedel and Comer (1997) stress that the term chosen at the Sixth Party Congress in December 1986, *doi moi* (renovation), connotes gradualism. However, the hyperinflation of 1986–88 threatened to undo the early reforms, and this resulted in a successful stabilization program in 1989 that was 'pure IMF orthodoxy, albeit without the IMF behind it'. The main elements were raising interest rates, devaluing and unifying the exchange rate, the legalization of gold holdings, and reduced public sector deficits. The latter was achieved by reducing government expenditure to GDP by six percentage points. Subsidies to state-owned enterprises (SOEs) were largely eliminated, half a million soldiers were demobilized, and major state investment programs were cut. In early 1989 it was decided to liberalize prices and eliminate the system of state procurement.

Further reforms followed. The budget constraints of SOEs were hardened, they were weaned off central bank credits, and increasingly forced to buy inputs in the market. Some were closed, others brought under the control of the Ministry of Finance. Several laws were introduced clarifying the rights of enterprises. The liberalization of the FDI regime commenced in 1988. Trade reform involved the freedom to engage in international trade and the establishment of export processing zones. Reform of the import regime proceeded more slowly, as did financial sector reform. The pace of reform slowed in the mid-1990s, a factor compounded by the Asian economic crisis. However, a 'second doi moi' got underway in the late 1990s, involving further reform of the enterprise laws, more liberal trade and investment regulations, and additional SOE reforms. Vietnam then enjoyed strong economic growth for a decade, until 2008 when a combination of domestic policy mis-steps and the global economic recession again slowed growth. This success has bequeathed further problems, including in macroeconomic policy, industry policy and state enterprise reform (Leung, 2010; Pham and Riedel, 2012), but there seems little doubt that moderately high growth is now entrenched.

This appears to be a case of reform initially triggered by necessity, anticipating a large reduction in its external revenues, and disappointment with its central planning experience. It was undertaken by an authoritarian regime intent on national economic development, and anxious to learn from and keep up with its neighbors. Apart from necessarily abrupt macroeconomic stabilization, the reforms were mostly gradual and effective. There was a strong export response to the decision to unify the exchange rate, adjust prices to international levels, and free up the trade regime. The country did not experience the Eastern European economic collapse owing to its effective reforms and the absence of a large and inefficient heavy industry sector. There was also some good fortune, in the discovery of large oil deposits, which effectively substituted for Soviet aid. Two unusual features were the absence of a group of well-trained technocrats, and the country's international isolation. It is difficult to think of a more compelling case of successful reform against formidable odds in recent times.

Trade liberalization: (I) Indonesia in the 1980s

Trade liberalization has been central to policy reform. This is based on the premise that, once macroeconomic stabilization has been achieved and a workable political system has been established, openness is the key policy lever to ensure a competitive economy, and a discipline on both rent-seekers and policy backtracking. That is, the political economy dynamic, not guaranteed but more likely, is that the efficient, internationally oriented sectors of the economy producing tradable goods and services will exert pressure on the unreformed sectors of the economy, and will demand better quality governance and institutions. The struggle for trade liberalization also illustrates up close how and why reform succeeds. In the words of Bhagwati (2002), the literature on the political economy of trade liberalization emphasizes the interplay of 'ideas, interests, and institutions'. We focus here on two major, though quite different, trade liberalizations, in Indonesia and the Philippines.

Indonesia achieved comprehensive reform in the mid-1980s, which elevated growth rates and almost certainly averted a serious debt crisis. This followed an earlier, more significant and highly successful change in policy direction in the period 1966–68. While we focus here mainly on the trade reform, the broader context is also relevant. By way of background, the Indonesian economy grew strongly over the period 1967–82, driven by the return to sensible and credible economic management, and large oil and aid revenues. In the early 1980s, however, the global economy began to slow down, and oil prices fell sharply, from about $30 to less than $10 per barrel. With oil, gas and related commodities generating about three-quarters of merchandise exports and two-thirds of government revenue, the Indonesian economy looked precarious. Growth slowed considerably in the early 1980s, but it remained throughout the decade, and by the end of the period it was growing as fast as it had been in the oil boom period.

The details of the reforms are explained elsewhere (see e.g. Hill, 2000). Fiscal policy remained prudent, with immediate adjustment on the expenditure side (mainly the shelving of an ambitious heavy industry program), and a series of effective tax reform measures that lifted revenue. Donors also responded quickly and generously. In addition, there were two large nominal exchange rate depreciations, in 1983 and 1986. Combined with low inflation, these provided a major boost to competitiveness. Once macroeconomic stabilization was secured, the government turned to microeconomic measures, and implemented a comprehensive reform package. In trade policy, most non-tariff barriers (NTBs) were gradually removed, while tariffs were lowered and unified. Exporters were placed on a free-trade footing through an effective duty exemption and rebate system. A sweeping reform of customs sidelined the deeply corrupt and obstructive import/export procedures. Foreign investment restrictions were relaxed. The financial sector was deregulated and the stock market reactivated. Many regulatory barriers to entry were removed, particularly in sectors formerly dominated by SOEs, such as the strategically important inter-island shipping industry.

What explains the success of these reforms?[5] As most analysts of this episode note, strong opposition to the reforms was to be expected. The dominant ideological predisposition of the influential policy community was suspicious of liberalism. As soon as the macroeconomic stabilization and liberalization of the late 1960s began to bear fruit, the pendulum swung back towards dirigisme and control, reinforced by the huge commodity windfall gains. As an indication of the sensitivities, whenever liberal reforms were introduced, they were always referred to by the neutral term 'deregulation'. Moreover, vested interests had built up around the complex system of controls and intervention, in the business sector, the SOEs and the bureaucracy. There was by contrast a weak export sector and a tiny, marginalized intellectual community calling for reforms.

The key to the success of the reforms was an able, coherent and powerful group of reformers known as the 'technocrats'. This group, the so-called Berkeley Mafia, had occupied all the major economic policy portfolios since the beginning of the Soeharto era. Although lacking any significant political party support, they had strong technical credentials. Most important, they had developed close relations with Soeharto before he came to power, and they had overseen the remarkably successful stabilization and recovery in the second half of the 1960s. This was moreover a political system characterized by Mackie and MacIntyre (1994) as one in which 'Soeharto [was] in supreme control'. In addition, from the margins, external actors were helpful. Relations with Japan were exceptionally close. Japan had become the country's major donor and investor, and it viewed Indonesia as a strategically crucial partner. Throughout this period, it extended its credit lines on highly concessional terms and rolled over most of its debt. This was still the cold war era, and Indonesia's relations with the USA were also very close. The IFIs provided useful policy and analytical advice on a range of issues. However, it should be noted that the reforms were not part of any formal IMF and World Bank conditionality, a factor that made them easier to sell domestically.

There were in addition three facilitating factors that enabled the reforms to be introduced with little opposition and boosted their effectiveness. One was broad-based development, presided over by an authoritarian regime that had nevertheless delivered rapid growth. Second, there was no serious domestic opposition to the reforms that could mobilize popular opposition. The 'economic nationalists' and those in the large SOE sector were either neutralized or pushed aside. The personal, egregious vested interests centered on the Soeharto family were not then significant, unlike a decade later at the time of the Asian financial crisis. Third, the regional (East Asian) climate was conducive. Other countries were liberalizing. The Plaza Accord was opening up trade and investment opportunities with Northeast Asia. And China was not yet then a really serious export competitor.

In his comprehensive assessment of the reforms Soesastro (1989) argues that the process was driven by necessity much more than theory and ideology. The reformers deliberately maintained a strategy of 'low politics', avoiding grand ideological debates that would have been polarizing and may have derailed the reforms. Although there was opposition from within the bureaucracy and vested interests in the protected sectors, the packages were implemented effectively, and there was a steady flow of new initiatives. Basri and Hill (2004) explained these trade policy dynamics with reference to changes in the relative influence of several key policy actors over this period. That is, they identify the key policy actors, their general trade policy preferences, and how influential they were during each major episode of the Soeharto period.

The drift towards increased protection in the 1970s occurred because both the technocrats and foreign influences on policy were on the wane, at least in the realm of microeconomic policy. They were less needed during these 'good times', and there was less imperative to follow their policy orthodoxy. Moreover, neither group was completely united on core trade policy issues. Economic nationalists were becoming increasingly powerful in this decade, and they were able to build opportunistic alliances with various rent-seekers. By contrast, in the mid-1980s, the opposition to trade liberalization was on the wane. The technocrats were united and stronger in their resolve to reform and, at that time of looming crisis, they had the ear of Soeharto. Foreign influences were clearly pro-reform, and they had more weight. Indonesia needed funding from the IFIs to help it adjust to lower oil prices. Foreign investors were becoming more interested in the country as a low-cost export platform or as part of internationally integrated manufacturing operations, rather than as a relatively small and protected domestic market. Neighboring countries, most especially China, were liberalizing and growing rapidly, in the process constituting a powerful demonstration effect. Finally, the idea of coordinated, open, region-wide liberalization, in the form of both APEC and AFTA, was beginning to take root in elite government and business circles.

Summing up, this was a very successful reform in which the core elements were a group of able and credible policy advisors, with access to the key source of power in the country, and not seriously compromised by vested interests. The trigger, which enabled the technocrats to persuade Soeharto of the case for reform, was a developing external crisis. At the margins, various external actors and factors were helpful (technical advice, funds, and other countries reforming). The high quality of both design and implementation produced results, and won over a further constituency. This is one of the best examples of successful reform in an authoritarian growth-oriented state.

Trade liberalization: (II) The Philippines

The Philippine trade liberalizations were eventually just as effective and apparently durable as those of Indonesia. But by contrast they were much slower, spanning about 15 years, a deep crisis, a transition from authoritarian rule to democracy, and three administrations. The case for reform was comprehensively argued in major academic publications from the late 1960s, and by the country's leading university economics department, whose graduates have traditionally dominated the main economic policy institutions of government. The major international agencies were also heavily involved, both in advocacy and conditions-based lending programs. The slow pace of reform, spread over more than 20 years, therefore attests to the strength of the opposition, and especially the role of several key veto players.

Philippine trade and industry policies have been extensively documented and analyzed, probably more than any other developing Asian country.[6] The introduction of 'temporary' import controls in the late 1940s in response to a balance of payments emergency, combined with an ideological predisposition to support 'national firms', resulted in one of the most comprehensive and prolonged periods of import substitution in the developing world. Reform since then has been halting and piecemeal. The peso depreciation of 1970 and the introduction of export incentives provided some relief for export-oriented activities, but had little overall effect on the incentives regime owing to the widespread use of quantitative restrictions (QRs). By the late 1970s, the intellectual battle for liberalization was largely won, and the World Bank provided a major program of structural adjustment assistance. Average tariff rates and their dispersion around the mean began to fall from 1980, and import licensing was relaxed. A major political and foreign exchange crisis from 1983 to 1986 temporarily set back the reforms, as comprehensive controls on foreign exchange and imports were introduced. However, the crisis-driven exchange rate depreciation boosted competitiveness for the tradables sectors, and there was renewed reform momentum from 1987. By the end of the decade the original trade liberalization program was back on track, albeit delayed. The reforms continued through the 1990s, during both the Aquino and Ramos administrations, and with only a brief and temporary halt in the wake of the 1997–98 Asian economic crisis.

Bautista and Tecson (2003) emphasize the key role of the professional economics community, which staffed major economics agencies by the 1980s. Economists at the University of the Philippines were the key actors here, combined with a quasi-independent government agency, the Philippine Institute for Development Studies, which employed many of its graduates. Supporting this intellectual foundation were three additional sets of factors. First, World Bank programs in the late 1970s and early 1980s provided additional financial and human capital resources, particularly during the adjustment phase. Second, there was a realization by the late 1970s that the Philippines was both growing and liberalizing more slowly than its East Asian neighbors, and thus competitive liberalization became a factor of some influence. Third, the reformist Ramos administration (1992–98) inherited the trade liberalization agenda, and implemented it vigorously, not only by completing the schedule of tariff cuts and decontrol but also by a range of other major policy advances, including macroeconomic stabilization, the floating of the currency, and the removal of many regulatory barriers to competition. Perhaps most importantly, the faster economic growth over this period was the most significant reform dividend, for a country where 'growth pessimism' had become widespread owing to decades of poor performance.

This was a case of slow but apparently durable reform in a number of respects. It commenced under the Marcos regime, at a time when the reformers were being increasingly pushed out by the inner circle of 'crony capitalists' (Sicat, 1985). There was a temporary setback during the crisis of

335

1983–87. But the reforms were reinstituted by the Aquino administration, which in other respects was regarded as a rather indecisive and weak regime, attempting to manage economic recovery from a deep crisis and a sudden transition to an unpredictable democracy, and against a backdrop of frequent coup attempts. The reform process was then largely completed under the more effective reforming Ramos administration. Many of the policy implementers remained in the bureaucracy over this period, and academic economists continued to occupy the high ground in the debate.

Consistent with the analysis above, Bernardo and Tang (2008) and De Dios and Hutchcroft (2003, pp. 54–5) identify several sets of drivers. First, the crisis and its aftermath had, with a lag, a galvanizing effect in strengthening the reformers. Second, there was a growing awareness that the Philippines was falling behind in the global trend towards openness, combined with a range of looming regional and multilateral obligations, including WTO, APEC and AFTA. Third, the removal of the US bases in 1992 'had left the country feeling more exposed' (p. 54), and aware of the need to engage more with its neighborhood. De Dios and Hutchcroft also emphasize the importance of leadership, in particular 'the deft and savvy leadership of the president and his key advisors, especially Almonte (who, like Ramos, was a former military officer)' (p. 55). One striking feature, common in such episodes, was the reformers' 'often expressed marked distrust of the Philippine business elite', many of whom were regarded as beneficiaries of the status quo and therefore as obstacles to reform.

One interesting political economy issue is that while protection for manufactures in the Philippines has declined significantly, that for agriculture has risen, and now on average exceeds manufacturing. A similar trend is also observable in Indonesia over the past decade. David (2003) offers three explanations, all of which are applicable to post-crisis Indonesia. First, the sustained intellectual reform effort, and the subsequent policy response, was concentrated where the problem was, that is high and variable levels of manufacturing. Second, agricultural interests are able to exploit loopholes in various international trade agreements, which permit the imposition of various protectionist measures in the guise of other objectives, such as health and quarantine. The slow pace of agricultural trade liberalization in the OECD north has also been seized upon by these local vested interests. Third, democratization has empowered influential rural constituencies, who are able to dress up their demands for protection by playing on sentimental notions of food self-sufficiency (and rural development more generally).

Legislated central bank independence and fiscal rules

Several Southeast Asian economies have adopted explicit policies designed to ensure central bank independence and to impose fiscal policy rules that limit deficit financing. We examine here the central banks of Indonesia and the Philippines, and Indonesia's fiscal policy law of 2003.

The crises in both countries, Indonesia in 1997–98 and the Philippines in 1985–86, triggered a reappraisal of macroeconomic policy. Both had experienced bouts of high inflation, especially Indonesia which had hyperinflation in the mid-1960s, and again briefly in 1998. In both countries, also, the central banks were effectively an arm of government, with little operational autonomy and extensive interference, while the crises had a devastating impact on public debt. So there was a determination to improve macroeconomic management, which attracted broad political support and was consistent with the IMF programs that operated in the wake of the crises. Of the two countries, Indonesia had had the more prudent fiscal policy, after it adopted the so-called 'balanced budget' rule in 1970, which meant that the government could spend no more than the sum of its domestic revenue and overseas development assistance (ODA).

While similar in important respects, the modalities of reform differed. The Philippines embarked on a major overhaul of its central bank in 1993, when a new institution, Bangko Sentral ng Pilipinas (BSP), was established (Gochoco-Bautista and Canlas, 2003). The former practice of the board being dominated by cabinet secretaries, who had an interest in the central bank accommodating fiscal deficits and a bias towards a strong peso, was disbanded, as was the objective of exchange rate targeting. The BSP gradually moved to what is considered monetary policy best practice of inflation targeting and a floating exchange rate regime; the former was formally adopted in 2001.

This was one of the most important and successful reforms in Philippine economic history. The BSP has a highly credible record of monetary policy management, operating as an island of excellence in a system not otherwise known for its high institutional quality. Inflation has remained low throughout the post-reform period, which has been characterized by great volatility, including political turbulence and large exogenous economic shocks. The exchange rate operated as the necessary 'shock absorber' in response to the sorts of events that in the past would have resulted in a significant economic slowdown in the country, and possibly a balance of payments crisis. Moreover, the financial sector has remained intact without any serious bank runs or failures since 1993.

Fiscal policy settings were also notably improved during the Ramos administration, with three successive years of budget surpluses in the mid-1970s, a highly unusual event in the country's economic history (Sicat and Abdula, 2003). However, fiscal policy rules were not institutionally embedded, and for much of the Estrada and Arroyo administrations (1998–2010), the government ran deficits, and for several years the Congress blocked appropriation bills, resulting in 're-enactment' provisions, that is, the previous year's budgetary provisions were employed.

The Indonesian story differs in two respects. First, although the government formally adopted the principle of central bank independence, the path to reform has been rocky and the inflation record less impressive. But, second, fiscal policy has been more prudent, such that public debt fell remarkably fast, from about 100 percent of GDP in 2000 to 24 percent in 2011. The independence of Bank Indonesia (BI) became law in 1999 during the early, chaotic post-Soeharto period. Although BI could no longer purchase government bonds to finance the fiscal deficit, and operational autonomy has been more or less preserved, the BI has been the subject of continuous controversy, with three successive governors ending their terms either in jail or house arrest. With regard to fiscal policy, Law number 17/2003 required that the budget deficit be no greater than 3 percent of GDP and public debt to be less than 60 percent of GDP. Essentially this measure was modeled on the Maastricht Principle and, unlike the EU, Indonesia has kept well within these limits, even during the global economic slowdown of 2008–09.

Why and how were these major reforms introduced? In both cases, there was a constellation of forces at work. First, they were introduced after very deep crises. There was a broad recognition of the costs of bad policy, and a predisposition to reform. Second, the reforms did not confront any immediate and powerful vested interests. They were not controversial, and there was no grand ideological debate over them. In fact, especially in the Indonesian case, they were introduced without much fanfare, almost 'reform by stealth'. Third, they had strong backing inside government, from key technocrats in the central bank and ministry of finance. Fourth, they occurred under the presidency of leaders who were both predisposed to reform (especially Ramos) and inclined to listen to their technocratic advisors.[7] Fifth, on the role of the IFIs: all three measures occurred while the countries were under IMF programs, which is presumptive evidence that the IMF played a role. But in both countries, the IMF's role was then controversial (and still is in Indonesia), and so it is unlikely that the reforms could have been achieved if any of the four factors mentioned above were strongly negative. Moreover, Indonesia's fiscal law was introduced precisely because the government wanted to exit the IMF program a year ahead of schedule, owing to its unpopularity, and this strengthened the hand of President Megawati's advisors, who urged that some institutional restraints on fiscal policy needed to be in place prior to the exit.

Summing up: nine (cautious) conclusions

The political economy of reform is a complex, multidimensional issue, in which there is no well-established body of analytical literature that provides guidance, much less a template. There is therefore a tension in that literature, between the academic desire for analytical parsimony, and the case study literature that (rightly) emphasizes the complex interplay of history, institutions, ideas, leadership, diverse actors, and external influences. This chapter, part of my ongoing research into this topic, has attempted to steer a middle path, drawing on Southeast Asian and other case study material to highlight factors that appear to be consistently, or least substantially, present during significant and durable reform episodes. The caveat of course is that it is difficult to generalize across a highly diverse set of institutional circumstances, development stages, and policy issues. What works in highly disciplined, effective and controlled Singapore may not in freewheeling and unpredictable Philippine politics. But several recurring themes stand out. These are invariably present in some form in most successful reforms. Typically also they are interactive, so that their aggregate impact is greater than the sum of their parts.

First, ideas are needed to drive an intellectual agenda, sometimes well formulated in advance, on other occasions developed in response to specific circumstances. From this 'ideas factory', moreover, there needs to be a group of individuals willing to assume public office, to interact closely with political leaders, and to work together as a united team. However, the link between ideas and policy is an indirect and tenuous one. As the experience of countries as diverse as India and the Philippines demonstrates, there may be long lags between the articulation of ideas and their adoption. These two countries also illustrate that having a strong domestic economics profession is no guarantee that good policies will be adopted.

Second, political leadership is essential, generally featuring a key individual or group of leaders who understand the case for reform and are prepared to actively promote it. Reforms are obviously more likely to be durable the more institutionally embedded they are, and the less they depend on a particular individual. One of the keys to Malaysian success, for example, seems to be the broad ideological consistency of all six of its post-independence prime ministers, notwithstanding personality differences.

Third, major negative exogenous shocks, economic crises, the imminent cessation of external support, and a dawning realization that 'the system is broken' have all played a role. The first (a sharp terms of trade decline) was the trigger for Indonesia's major reforms in the 1980s. The third and fourth were the key factors in Vietnam's doi moi, and they were of some relevance in the Philippine reforms of the 1990s. The second resulted in substantial macro and financial sector reforms in the economies affected by the 1997–98 Asian financial crisis. But crises are at best only a possible precipitating influence, and there is no guarantee of positive impacts. The crisis reportedly slowed reform in Vietnam for several years. The mid-1980s Philippine crisis in effect incapacitated government for some time, and it took that country 20 years for its per capita GDP to recover to early 1980s levels. And the current global economic recession has thus far had little positive reform impact, and may have spurred anti-globalization sentiments in some quarters.

Other external factors evidently have mixed effects. The Southeast Asian experience lends support to the international literature that suggests that, putting aside the special but important case of humanitarian assistance, aid works only if accompanied by good domestic policies. It is not clear that donors can influence the domestic reform agenda. Donors have worked effectively with growth-oriented regimes in East Asia, but there is no decisive evidence that donors triggered the establishment of the regimes.

Conditions-based programs have a very mixed record, and often invite a nationalist backlash. A stronger view (e.g. Easterly, 2006) asserts that aid is a malign influence since it enables recipient governments to postpone hard policy decisions. With the possible exception of the Philippines (and perhaps Cambodia), the latter view receives little support in Southeast Asia, in contrast arguably to the South Pacific and parts of Africa.[8] As the region as a whole progressively moves into the middle-income group, ODA as a share of GDP is anyway declining. Where donors can perhaps be most effective is in supporting domestic 'agents of change', through building up local analytical capacity, training a future generation of policy makers, and (discreetly) supporting reform-oriented think tanks.

An increasingly powerful external factor is the demonstration effect of a successful reforming economy, resulting in a process of 'competitive liberalizations'. This factor seems to be much more important in Asia than either Latin America or Africa, with Singapore and China (and more recently India) the standouts.

Fourth, reforms are durable only if they deliver, and thereby win over a constituency of support. This requires that they be reasonably comprehensive, so they are not sabotaged by 'unreformed' sectors of the economy. This also implies that implementation is critical. However, the evidence on explicit compensation measures to facilitate reform is mixed. Macroeconomic stabilization is invariably the bedrock upon which reforms are built. For example, trade liberalization can be jeopardized by misaligned exchange rates resulting from macroeconomic imbalances.

Fifth, reform is not a linear progression, and thus long time horizons are needed. For example, the lag between the articulation of the case for trade policy reform and its implementation took over 30 years and over 20 years respectively in India and the Philippines. Advocates of reform have to be prepared for setbacks. Most donors do not have the patience or time horizons to stay the course. The sometimes slow pace of reform emphasizes again the importance of having the strong ideas embedded in key domestic institutions, including universities, think tanks, and sections of the bureaucracy, on hand to quickly take advantage of (sometimes unexpected) reform opportunities.

Moreover, governments may experience reform fatigue, and the key reformers may be increasingly bypassed. An example of the former occurred in Indonesia after the appointment of the 1993 cabinet. The role of the technocrats was downgraded. As a result – and this is at best an exploratory counter-factual – they did not have the capacity to follow through on the financial liberalization they had introduced a few years earlier. Examples of the latter include the Marcos regime from the late 1970s (on which see Sicat, 1985) and the increasingly populist Thai economic policy in the Thaksin era and beyond (Ammar, 2011). A key reform strategy is therefore to 'lock in' and institutionalize reforms, to insulate key technocratic institutions, and to render backtracking by a future regime more difficult. Examples, all adopted by some Southeast Asian governments, include independent central banks with a clear inflation objective, legislated restrictions on the extent of fiscal deficits, agencies that require recipients of public subsidies to be subjected to some form of public scrutiny, and broad regional and multilateral trade agreements. Of course, there can never be guarantees against the emergence of a really venal regime, other than through a system of democratic checks and balances.

Sixth, the rules of the game change, sometimes dramatically, in the transition from authoritarian to democratic systems, where voice, accountability and public persuasion become important arbiters of reform success. This is most clearly illustrated in the two Southeast Asian countries that have swung from authoritarian to democratic rule in recent times, Indonesia and the Philippines. The two major changes concern the speed and modalities of reform. Since there are fewer policy actors in authoritarian regimes, once the inner circle is convinced of the need for change, decisions can be taken very quickly. Reformers do not first have to win their case in the courts of public opinion and parliaments, and fewer concessions need to be made to potential losers. Conversely, it might be argued that, while reform in democratic systems is slower, it is more likely to be durable as consultative processes have garnered more widespread community support. Moreover, as Nye (2011) emphasizes in the Philippine context, with effective leadership democratic space may provide scope to mobilize the support of those groups disadvantaged by politically inspired favors (e.g. regulatory restrictive practices) to achieve reform.

Seventh, institutions in some broad sense are critical, but it is not necessary to have high-quality institutions to reform. China, Indonesia and Vietnam began to institute effective reform programs with very weak bureaucracies and at extremely low levels of per capita income. What mattered were a clear reform agenda, political commitment, and then a sequence of tackling the really big issues first, such as macroeconomic stabilization, openness to trade and investment, and major supply-side investments. This experience therefore casts some doubt on the 'institutions rule' hypothesis, commonly associated with Rodrik (2003).

But the expression of institutions, that is bureaucracies, clearly do matter, especially where implementation, as distinct from 'stroke-of-the-pen' reforms, is central, such as tax reform, decentralization and judicial development. The general presumption is that the bureaucracy is a reluctant reformer, to the extent that reform entails a loss of privileges. But this glosses over the heterogeneous nature of most bureaucracies, which typically range from reform-minded segments with analytical strength, such as ministries of finance and central banks, to patronage-based line and infrastructure departments. The relative strengths of the executive and the bureaucracy, and the institutional independence of the latter, also matter. If, as in the Philippines, senior echelons of the bureaucracy turn over with each administration, the executive is generally able to operate with little bureaucratic resistance.[9]

Eighth, the Southeast Asian experience demonstrates that it is easier to implement relatively prudent macroeconomic policies and broadly open commercial policy than it is to undertake microeconomic reform. Two political economy factors are at work here. First, the political consensus in most countries now generally recognizes the costs of macroeconomic instability, and therefore key policy actors are willing to accept that central banks and large fiscal deficits are broadly 'off-limits' to political interference. Trade policy is also governed in substantial measure by ASEAN commitments. Second, these policy settings, especially macroeconomic policy, are easier to sustain also because there are fewer 'veto' players, in contrast to industry policy, state enterprises, government procurements and so on, where political considerations intrude to a far greater extent. In both these policy areas, the role of the three more advanced countries, Singapore, Malaysia and Thailand, as traditionally open, low inflation economies, is crucial in setting regional standards.

It is important not to overstate the macro/micro distinction, however. Trade policy remains contested and politicized in most of the countries, and the foundations of macroeconomic policy are shaky in several of them. Examples of the latter include Vietnam's recent macro-economic instability, the Philippine budget travails for much of the past decade, large and highly distorted subsidies in Indonesia and Malaysia, the recent bout of fiscal populism in Thailand, and much else.

Ninth, there does not seem to be any clear association between the propensity to reform and the level of corruption. Corrupt regimes that are also growth-oriented frequently display a capacity for partial reform, on the presumption that growth offers greater opportunities for both political longevity and rent-seeking. Hun Sen's Cambodia and Soeharto's Indonesia are perhaps the outstanding Southeast Asian examples. In such regimes, of course, the nature of the corrupt activities switches, primarily from tradables (where rent-seeking is more likely to be disciplined by trade openness) to non-tradables. Of course, there is a corruption threshold beyond which regimes begin to lose political legitimacy and the will to reform, and institutions are undermined. Soeharto around the mid-1990s and Marcos in the early 1980s are the clearest Southeast Asian examples of this phenomenon.

Acknowledgments

Reprinted with permission from *Asian Development Review* 30 (1): 108–30. For very helpful comments and discussions, I wish to thank the journal editors, the two discussants, Eric Sidgwick and Myo Thant, two anonymous referees, and the general discussion.

Notes

1 The economic histories of Latin America frequently emphasize this point (Edwards, 2010).
2 The importance of a united team of advisors is stressed in much of the literature. See for example Boediono (2005) in the case of Indonesia and Joan Nelson's (1984) earlier comparative study in which she concludes that 'cases of clear failure all traced collapse in large part to deeply divided economic teams'.
3 See Edwards (2001) and De Dios and Hutchcroft (2003) respectively.
4 There is now an extensive literature on Vietnam's reforms. I have drawn in particular on Leung (2010), Riedel and Comer (1997), and Rama (2011).
5 For political economy explanations by Indonesia's leading economists, see Azis (1994), Soesastro (1989), and the collection of interviews with the key ministerial policy makers of the era in Thee (2003).
6 See for example Power and Sicat (1971), Baldwin (1975), Bautista et al. (1979), Medalla et al. (1995) and Bautista and Tecson (2003).
7 The Indonesian reforms occurred during the administrations of Presidents Habibie (central bank independence) and Megawati (the fiscal law).
8 Nye (2011) draws attention to the problem of donors' short time horizons in grappling with the complex Philippine political economy.
9 See for example De Dios and Hutchcroft (2003) and Fabella (2007).

Bibliography

Ammar Siamwalla (2011), 'Thailand after 1997', *Asian Economic Policy Review*, 6 (1), pp. 68–85.
Aswicahyono, H., K. Bird, and H. Hill (2009), 'Making Economic Policy in Weak, Democratic, Post-crisis States: An Indonesian Case Study', *World Development*, 37 (2), pp. 354–70.
Azis, I. (1994), 'Indonesia', in J. Williamson (ed.), *The Political Economy of Reform*, Institute for International Economics, Washington, DC, pp. 385–416.
Baldwin, R.E. (1975), *Foreign Trade Regimes and Economic Development: The Philippines*, National Bureau for Economic Research, New York.
Balisacan, A.M. and H. Hill (eds) (2003), *The Philippine Economy: Development, Policies and Challenges*, Oxford University Press, New York, and Ateneo de Manila University Press, Manila.
Bardhan, P. (1997), 'Corruption and Development: A Review of the Issues', *Journal of Economic Literature*, 35, pp. 1320–46.
Bardhan, P. (1998), 'Epilogue on the Political Economy of Reform in India', in *The Political Economy of Development in India*, Oxford University Press, Delhi.
Basri, M.C. and P. van der Eng (eds) (2004), *Business in Indonesia: New Challenges, Old Problems*, Institute of Southeast Asian Studies, Singapore.
Basri, M.C. and H. Hill (2004), 'Ideas, Interests and Oil Prices: The Political Economy of Trade Reform during Soeharto's Indonesia', *World Economy*, 27 (5), pp. 633–56.
Basri, M.C. and H. Soesastro (2005), 'The Political Economy of Trade Policy in Indonesia', *ASEAN Economic Bulletin*, 22 (1), pp. 3–18.
Bates, R. (1994), 'Comment', in J. Williamson (ed.), *The Political Economy of Reform*, Institute for International Economics, Washington, DC.

Bautista, R.M. and G. Tecson (2003), 'International Dimensions', in A.M. Balisacan and H. Hill (eds), *The Philippine Economy: Development, Policies and Challenges*, Oxford University Press, New York, and Ateneo de Manila University Press, Manila, pp. 136–71.

Bautista, R.M., J.H. Power and Associates (1979), *Industrial Promotion Policies in the Philippines*, Philippine Institute for Development Studies, Makati.

Bernardo, R.L. and M.G. Tang (2008), 'The Political Economy of Reform during the Ramos Administration (1992–98)', Working Paper No. 39, Commission on Growth and Development, World Bank, Washington, DC.

Bhagwati, J. (2002), 'Introduction: The Unilateral Freeing of Trade *Versus* Reciprocity', in J. Bhagwati (ed.), *Going Alone: The Case for Relaxed Reciprocity in Freeing Trade*, MIT Press, Cambridge, MA.

Boediono (2005), 'Managing the Indonesian Economy: Some Lessons from the Past', *Bulletin of Indonesian Economic Studies*, 41 (3), pp. 309–24.

Burnside, C. and D. Dollar (2000), 'Aid, Policies, and Growth', *American Economic Review*, 90 (4), pp. 847–68.

David, C. (2003), 'Agriculture', in A.M. Balisacan and H. Hill (eds), *The Philippine Economy: Development, Policies and Challenges*, Oxford University Press, New York, and Ateneo de Manila University Press, Manila, pp. 175–218.

De Dios, E.S. and P.D. Hutchcroft (2003), 'Political Economy', in A.M. Balisacan and H. Hill (eds), *The Philippine Economy: Development, Policies and Challenges*, Oxford University Press, New York.

Djiwandono, J.S. (2005), *Bank Indonesia and the Crisis: An Insider's View*, Institute of Southeast Asian Studies, Singapore.

Easterly, W. (2006), *White Man's Burden: Why the West's Efforts to Help the Rest of the World Have Done So Much Ill and So Little Good*, Penguin, New York.

Edwards, S. (2001), *The Economics and Politics of Transition to an Open Market Economy*, Colombia, Development Centre Studies, OECD, Paris.

Edwards, S. (2010), *Left Behind: Latin America and the False Promise of Populism*, University of Chicago Press, Chicago, IL.

Edwards, S. and D. Lederman (2002), 'The Political Economy of Unilateral Trade Liberalization: The Case of Chile', in J. Bhagwati (ed.), *Going Alone: The Case for Relaxed Reciprocity in Freeing Trade*, MIT Press, Cambridge, MA.

Fabella, R. (2007), 'What Happens When Institutions Do Not Work: Jueteng, Crises of Presidential Legitimacy, and Electoral Failures in the Philippines', *Asian Economic Papers*, 5 (3), pp. 104–25.

Gochoco-Bautista, M.S. and D. Canlas (2003), 'Monetary and Exchange Rate Policy', in A.M. Balisacan and H. Hill (eds), *The Philippine Economy: Development, Policies and Challenges*, Oxford University Press, New York, and Ateneo de Manila University Press, Manila, pp. 77–105.

Haggard, S. (2000), *The Political Economy of the Asian Financial Crisis*, Institute for International Economics, Washington, DC.

Hill, H. (2000), *The Indonesian Economy*, Cambridge University Press, Cambridge, second edition.

Hill, H., Tham Siew Yean, and Ragayah Haji Mat Zin (eds) (2012), *Malaysia's Development Challenges: Graduating from the Middle*, Routledge, London.

Krueger, A.O. (1978), *Foreign Trade Regimes and Economic Development: Liberalization Attempts and Consequences*, Ballinger, Cambridge, MA.

Krueger, A.O. (2007), 'Policy Reform and Economic Growth', paper presented to a KDI conference, Seoul, July.

Krueger, A.O. and S. Rajapatirana (1999), 'The World Bank's Policies towards Trade and Trade Policy Reform', *World Economy*, 22 (6), pp. 717–40.

Lal, D. and H. Myint (1996), *The Political Economy of Poverty, Equity and Growth*, Oxford University Press, Oxford.

Leung, S. (2010), 'Vietnam: An Economic Survey', *Asian Pacific Economic Literature*, 24 (2), pp. 83–103.

MacIntyre, A. (2003), *The Power of Institutions: Political Architecture and Governance*, Cornell University Press, Ithaca, NY.

Mackie, J.A.C. and A. MacIntyre (1994), 'Politics', in H. Hill (ed.), *Indonesia's New Order: The Dynamics of Socio-Economic Transformation*, Allen & Unwin, Sydney.

Medalla, E.M., G.R, Tecson., R.M, Bautista., J.H. Power and Associates (1995/96), *Philippine Trade and Industrial Policies: Catching Up With Asia's Tigers*, volumes I and II, Philippine Institute for Development Studies, Makati.

Nelson, J.M. (1984), 'The Political Economy of Stabilization: Commitment, Capacity and Public Response', *World Development*, 12 (10), pp. 983–1006.

Nye, J.V.C. (2011), 'Taking Institutions Seriously: The Political Economy of Development in the Philippines', *Asian Development Review*, 28 (1), pp. 1–21.

Pangestu, M. (1996), *Economic Reform, Deregulation, and Privatization*, Centre for Strategic and International Studies, Jakarta.

Pangestu, M. (2012), 'Globalization and its Discontents: An Indonesian Perspective', *Asian-Pacific Economic Literature*, 26 (1), pp. 1–17.

Pham, T.T.T. and J, Riedel., (2012), 'On the Conduct of Monetary Policy in Vietnam', *Asian Pacific Economic Literature*, 26 (1), pp. 34–45.

Pinera, J. (1994), 'Chile', in J. Williamson (ed.), *The Political Economy of Reform*, Institute for International Economics, Washington, DC, pp. 225–31.

Pomfret, R. (2002), *Constructing a Market Economy: Diverse Paths from Central Planning in Asia and Europe*, Edward Elgar, Cheltenham.

Power, J.H. and G.P. Sicat (1971), *The Philippines: Industrialization and Trade Policies*, Oxford University Press, London.

Rajapatirana, S. (2001), 'Developing-Countries' Trade Policies in the 1990s: Back to the Future', in D. Lal and R. Snape (eds), *Trade, Development and Political Economy: Essays in Honour of Anne O. Krueger*, Palgrave, London.

Rama, M. (2008), 'Making Difficult Choices: Vietnam in Transition', Working Paper No. 40, Commission on Growth and Development, World Bank, Washington, DC.

Riedel, J. and B. Comer (1997), 'Transition to a Market Economy in Vietnam', in W.T, Woo., S, Parker., and J.D. Sachs (eds), *Economies in Transition: Comparing Asia and Eastern Europe*, MIT Press, Cambridge, MA.

Rodrik, D. (ed.) (2003), *In Search of Prosperity: Analytical Narratives on Economic Growth*, Princeton University Press, Princeton, NJ.

Sachs, J. (1994), 'Life in the Economic Emergency Room', in J. Williamson (ed.), *The Political Economy of Policy Reform*, Institute for International Economics, Washington, DC.

Sachs. J. and A. Warner (1995), 'Economic Reform and the Process of Global Integration', *Brookings Papers on Economic Activity*, 1 (1), pp. 1–118.

Sicat, G.P. (1985), 'A Historical and Current Perspective of Philippine Economic Problems', *Philippine Economic Journal*, 24 (1), pp. 24–63.

Sicat, G.P. (2003) *Philippine Economic and Development Issues*, Anvil, Manila.

Sicat, G.P. and R. Abdula (2003), 'Fiscal Policy', in A.M. Balisacan and H. Hill (eds), *The Philippine Economy: Development, Policies and Challenges*, Oxford University Press, New York.

Soesastro, M.H. (1989), 'The Political Economy of Deregulation in Indonesia', *Asian Survey*, 29 (9), pp. 853–69.

Thee, K.W. (ed.) (2003), *Recollections: The Indonesian Economy, 1950s–1990s*, Institute of Southeast Asian Studies, Singapore.

Williamson, J. (ed.) (1994), *The Political Economy of Reform*, Institute for International Economics, Washington, DC.

Part VI
Twenty-first-century challenges

16

Dual-burdens in health and aging

Emerging population challenges in Southeast Asia

Jenna Nobles

UNIVERSITY OF WISCONSIN-MADISON

Five decades, three transitions

The last half-century in Southeast Asia was characterized by rapid population change. Family size is less than half of its 1970 value and the mean age at death has nearly doubled. In Chapter 10 in this volume, Jones characterizes the dramatic shifts in mortality and fertility that brought on these changes.

In this chapter, I argue that the diversity of population trends within countries also presents a set of challenges for continued growth and development. In wealthier regions, fertility has fallen toward or below replacement; the population is aging; and the health profile is converging toward patterns typically associated with "developed" countries. In poorer regions, the fertility transition is incomplete, the population continues to grow, and increased investment in child nutrition and survival is still needed.

These subnational differences are nontrivial. In 2005, infant mortality in Laos ranged from 18 per thousand in Vientiane to 122 per thousand in Sekong (NSC 2005). About 20 percent of young children in Jakarta are overweight or obese while more than a third of children in the Eastern Indonesian islands – and nearly half in Nusa Tenggara Timur – are stunted (UNICEF 2012). One in 25 people in the Central Highlands of Vietnam are elderly; 1 in 10 are elderly in the Red River Delta. Future policymakers will need to navigate the dual-burden of expanding investments in child health and wellbeing in impoverished areas, while simultaneously addressing the emerging needs of growing numbers of the elderly in cities and more developed regions. National policies of food production, pricing, and distribution will need to manage the needs of population segments facing a dearth and a surfeit of calories. Health services will be forced to straddle the coterminous rise in rates of liver, cervical, and breast cancer alongside the emergence of multidrug-resistant tuberculosis.

I describe trends in the within-country divergence of fertility, mortality, and the attendant age structure of nine Southeast Asian countries. I then consider new challenges produced by attendant shifts in epidemiology. I note the emergence of several *dual-burdens* that are specific to countries transitioning in the latter years of the twentieth century – among them, those in Southeast Asia.

The emergence of these challenges likely reflect – and possibly contribute to – high levels of vertical and regional inequality among many Southeast Asian populations (Table 16.1).

Table 16.1 Vertical and regional inequality, Southeast Asian countries

	Gini coefficient		Group coefficient of variation
	1990–95	2008–11	2004
Cambodia	38.5	37.9	n/a
Indonesia	29.2	38.9	0.810
Lao PDR	30.4	36.7	0.337
Malaysia	46.7	46.2	0.397
Philippines	43.8	43.0	0.536
Thailand	45.3	40.0	1.069
Vietnam	35.7	35.6	1.062

Source: Brown and Langer 2009; OECD 2013.
Note: Data unavailable for Myanmar.

Horizontal inequality is particularly acute in Thailand, Vietnam, and Indonesia. And though Laos has one of the lowest levels of horizontal inequality among low-income nations, regional variation in poverty is qualitatively high. Over 75 percent of the South-central highland population lives in poverty, relative to 17 percent of the population in Vientiane (Epprecht et al. 2008).

The emerging population challenges are also a function of the pace at which these countries have moved through the major population transitions. As Jones (Chapter 10 in this volume) describes, the changes to mortality and fertility that took place over 80–120 years in most European countries occurred in less than 40 years in most Southeast Asian countries. As such, within-country variation in the pacing of these transitions produced rapid regional variation in the age structure, growth rate, and attendant state investment needs.

In addition, most Southeast Asian countries experienced the onset and swift movement into two other major population transitions during the demographic transition. These two transitions accompany the demographic transition as stylistic descriptions of population change. The *epidemiologic transition* (Omran 1971) describes the change from a burden of disease dominated by infection to one dominated by chronic illness resulting from the development of chemotherapies, antibiotics, and vaccines that facilitate survival through exposure to infection.

The *nutrition transition* (Popkin 1994, 2006; Popkin et al. 2013) describes the process by which population dietary patterns shift from locally produced staples like lentils, rice, wheat, and sorghum, to animal products and processed foods, the latter typically produced by multinational corporations (see Table 5.5 and Figure 5.4 in Timmer, this volume). Accompanying this latter transition is a marked change in anthropometry, including increases in overweight and obesity – conditions that have exacerbated the burden of chronic ailments such as cardiovascular disease, diabetes, and some forms of cancer.

Of course, recent decades are characterized by three significant reversals of the epidemiologic transition: HIV/AIDS, pandemic flu, and the emergence of drug-resistant forms of infectious illness (Barrett et al. 1998; Coker et al. 2011). Whereas well-resourced populations had largely completed the transition to chronic illness (and seen the major decline in infectious disease) *prior* to these reversals, Southeast Asia is navigating them concurrently. Moreover, the global nutrition transition began in well-resourced countries in the mid-1980s, well after the demographic and epidemiologic transitions were largely complete. By contrast, countries in Southeast Asia experienced the effects of the nutrition transition beginning in the early 1990s, when four of the nine countries referenced in this chapter had fertility above 3.5 births per woman, when infant mortality in the region exceeded 45 per thousand and, most importantly, in the presence of high levels of *under*nutrition in resource-poor areas.

The concurrent nature of these events, alongside considerable subnational spatial inequality, has created a number of complicated policy challenges. Some of these will strain even well-developed, high-functioning state institutions.

Variation in fertility, mortality, and population aging

In comparison with demographic transitions occurring elsewhere in the late nineteenth and early twentieth centuries (Jones, Chapter 10 in this volume; Livi-Bacci 1992), fertility decline happened remarkably quickly in Southeast Asia (Attané and Barbieri 2009). Table 16.2 describes the observed or projected duration of the fertility transition by country.

One artifact of the speed at which these countries moved through the transition is that population aging arises much more quickly than it does in populations undergoing slower fertility transitions. The relative size of the elderly to the working-age population is much larger than in countries where fertility decline spans three or more generations. Moreover, a recognition, acknowledgment, and policy response to these trends – including the reorganization of public transfers and state investments – must be embraced by both the populace and state institutions over the span of a few decades.

A second artifact is that variation in the onset of fertility decline *within* countries can quickly produce stark regional distinctions in the age structure, growth rate, and attendant policy needs, particularly if some regions fall below replacement and the population begins to age while others are still growing.

To assess this process in Southeast Asia, I construct several descriptive statistics capturing variation in fertility decline and implied variation in population growth. Though national-level fertility data are compiled by the United Nations for most countries, subnational fertility trends require data collection with exhaustive regional sampling and are not readily available for the period of fertility transition for most Southeast Asian countries. However it is possible to use IPUMS census data[1] to calculate the mean "children ever born" (CEB) by province for women who have largely completed fertility – specifically, women aged 40–49 at the time of data collection.

The CEB estimate is not directly comparable to the period total fertility rate (TFR), the most commonly used fertility metric, which summarizes age-specific fertility rates in a period. "Children ever born" for 40–49 year-olds captures cohort fertility spanning the 30 years prior to measurement for women who survive to the end of their reproductive period. In contexts with declining fertility, CEB estimates for 40–49 year olds will be substantially larger than period total

Table 16.2 Duration of fertility transition: TFR values above 5 to less than 2.3

Country	Duration (years)	Period
Singapore	15	1960–1975
Vietnam	20	1975–1995
Thailand	20	1970–1990
Myanmar	25	1975–2000
Laos	35	1990–2025
Malaysia	40	1965–2005
Cambodia	45	1990–2035
Indonesia	45	1970–2015
Philippines	65	1975–2040

Source: UN Population Prospects, 2012 Revisions.

fertility in the same year. Insofar as subnational regions are proceeding through a fertility transition at a reasonably similar *pace* (but different timing of onset), the CEB measures will approximate cross-provincial variation in the *level* of fertility.

Table 16.3 presents the highest and lowest provincial CEB values for available census samples. Values are also included for the urban capital regions when these are not the lowest regions

Table 16.3 Children ever born to women age 40–49, by country, province, and period

Cambodia				*1998*	*2008*
Phnom Penh				4.00	2.85
Krong Pailin				4.68	4.50
Otdar Mean Chey				6.32	4.79
Preah Vihear				6.52	5.10
Interdecile range				*1.39*	*1.14*
Indonesia	*1971*	*1980*	*1990*	*2000*	*2010*
East Java	4.35	4.49	3.98	3.02	2.39
East Kalimantan	4.46	5.30	4.67	3.97	3.01
North Sumatra	6.76	6.73	5.85	4.74	3.66
Maluku and North Maluku	6.85	6.36	5.47	4.46	3.72
Interdecile range	*2.17*	*1.83*	*1.51*	*1.58*	*1.34*
Malaysia	*1970*	*1980*			
Kuala Lumpur	5.46	4.81			
Langkawi	3.81	5.14			
Jerantut	3.88	5.51			
Mersing	7.77	5.90			
Jelebu	7.79	5.20			
Port Dickson	8.03	6.42			
Interdecile range	*2.45*	*1.89*			
Philippines			*1990*		
Metro Manila, dist 1			3.59		
Metro Manila, dist 2			3.49		
Catanduanes			5.93		
Camarines Sur			5.94		
Interdecile range			*1.60*		
Thailand	*1970*	*1980*	*1990*	*2000*	
Bangkok	5.27	4.14	2.77	1.98	
Yala	3.94	4.43	3.59	2.90	
Mae Hong Son	4.17	4.87	3.40	3.01	
Nong Khai	7.65	6.24	4.43	2.84	
Phichit	7.79	5.00	2.95	2.04	
Interdecile range	*2.04*	*1.67*	*1.36*	*1.04*	
Vietnam			*1989*	*1999*	*2009*
Ha Noi			3.72	2.37	2.21
Thai Binh			3.56	2.72	2.13
Hai Phong			3.61	2.79	2.20
Son La			6.03	4.43	3.18
Lai Chau			6.10	4.97	3.98
Interdecile range			*1.76*	*1.46*	*1.15*

Note: Author's calculations with IPUMS-International data (Minnesota Population Center 2013).

(e.g. Malaysia in 1970). The interdecile range – that is, the difference between CEB at the 10th and 90th percentile of mean values by province – is also included.

At the earlier stages of the transition, stark differences exist in regional fertility levels. In 1970s Indonesia, two additional children per woman separated the highest and lowest fertility provinces. In Malaysia, the difference exceeded four children. In Cambodia in 1998, women in Preah Vihear produced 2.5 additional births relative to women in Phnom Penh. A similar gap is observed in the 1990s between the highest fertility provinces and the National Capital Region in the Philippines.

Importantly, fertility falls in nearly every region; some regions simply lag others. In most cases, the gaps in children-ever-born narrow as fertility declines. The interdecile ranges trend toward 1 in each of the countries for which data are available. This is, to some degree, expected. Fertility decline typically decelerates as family size reaches and falls below 2 births. However, an important note is warranted about these gaps. Differentials in population *growth* are a function of the *proportionate* difference in fertility (considered more explicitly below); though the absolute gap in children declines, variation in the growth rate may be stable or even increase.

In some cases, the temporal lag separating regions persisted through the transition. For example, fertility observed in the central Java city of Yogyakarta in 1971 was achieved by many of the outer islands only in the 1990s. Papua, one of the poorest provinces, exhibited fertility in 2010 reached by Eastern Java in 1985 and by Yogyakarta in 1980.[2]

Because these CEB differentials measure *completed* fertility – much of which took place two decades before these measures were collected – they do not capture the most recent extension of these trends. More recent estimates can be drawn from the *period* total fertility. For countries in which the fertility decline is still underway, large regional fertility differences persist into the contemporary period. For example, in Cambodia, fertility fell from 4.0 to 3.1 during the last decade. In the provinces of Mondal Kiri and Banteay Meanchey, fertility fell by 2 births per woman, an extraordinarily rapid change. By contrast, in Koh Kong and Prey Veng, fertility declined by only about half a birth per woman. In more remote Strung Treng, fertility remained above 4.0 for the decade (NIS et al. 2011).

Table 16.4 summarizes these contemporary differentials; TFR values are shown for the regions or provinces with the highest and lowest levels of fertility.[3] Laos and the Philippines are the only two countries in which fertility is above replacement across regions; nevertheless the differentials are still large. In the Southern region of Laos, fertility is almost 2 additional births per woman over the Central region. Cambodia, Indonesia, Malaysia, Myanmar, and Vietnam all contain regions with above-replacement and regions with below replacement fertility. Every region in Thailand has below-replacement fertility, though the level in Bangkok (0.88) is much lower than the level in the Northeast region (2.04).

The implication of these gaps for differentials in population growth is larger than may be widely appreciated. To facilitate interpretation, I approximate these regions' net reproduction rates (NRR) and the percentage change in the population size over ten years *implied* by the associated intrinsic growth rates. The NRR is interpreted as the number of girls a cohort of women would produce if they experienced a given schedule of fertility and mortality rates, i.e. the reproduction of a female cohort. A value of 1.00 indicates replacement. Values greater than 1.00 imply population growth and those less than 1.00 imply population decline.[4] For illustrative purposes, the approximated NRR values can be used to generate an estimate of how much fertility and mortality could shift a region's population size if these rates persisted over ten years. In reality, of course, regional population growth rates are also shaped by population momentum, interregional migration, and secular fertility decline. However, such illustrative estimates are useful to capture the regional variation in growth implied by observed fertility and mortality schedules – this is effectively the underlying population "pressure" generated by regional fertility differentials.

Table 16.4 Total fertility rate and associated growth by region, 1995–2011

	Total fertility rate		Approximated NRR[a]		Implied 10-yr growth attributable to fertility and mortality schedules[b]	
Cambodia	*2000*	*2008*	*2000*	*2008*	*2000*	*2008*
Phnom Pehn	2.1	2	1.00	0.95	0%	−2%
Rattanak Kiri	6.3	4.9	2.81	2.18	47%	34%
Indonesia	*2000*	*2010*	*2000*	*2010*	*2000*	*2010*
East Java	1.66	1.51	0.77	0.70	−9%	−12%
Nusa Tenggara Timur	3.29	2.56	1.53	1.19	17%	7%
Laos	*1995–9*	*2005*	*1995–9*	*2005*	*1995–9*	*2005*
Southern Region	5.39	4.84	2.55	2.29	42%	36%
Central Region	4.5	3.07	2.15	1.47	33%	15%
Malaysia	*2000*	*2010*	*2000*	*2010*	*2000*	*2010*
Kelantan	4.5	3.7	2.14	1.76	32%	23%
Kuala Lumpur	2.6	1.5	1.24	0.72	8%	−12%
Myanmar	*1997*	*2007*	*1997*	*2007*	*1997*	*2007*
Yangon	1.76	1.72	0.82	0.80	−7%	−8%
Rakhine	4.47	2.87	2.07	1.33	31%	11%
Philippines	*1998*	*2011*	*1998*	*2008*	*1998*	*2008*
NCR	2.5	2.3	1.18	1.09	6%	3%
MIMAROPA	5.6	4.1	2.61	1.91	43%	27%
Thailand	*1996*	*2006*	*1996*	*2006*	*1996*	*2006*
Bangkok	1.26	0.88	0.57	0.44	−19%	−26%
Northeast Region	2.44	2.04	1.14	0.98	5%	−1%
Southern Region	2.85	1.52	1.19	0.71	7%	−12%
Vietnam	*2005*	*2011*	*2005*	*2011*	*2005*	*2011*
Southeast	1.85	1.59	0.87	0.75	−5%	−10%
Central Highlands	3.07	2.58	1.46	1.23	15%	8%

Source: *TFR data* Cambodia: National Institute of Statistics. Indonesia: Badan Pusat Statistik. Laos: National Statistical Center. Malaysia: Department of Statistics. Myanmar: Fakultat and Than Thwe 2004 (1997 estimates) and UNFPA (2007 estimates). Philippines: Demographic and Health Survey (1998 estimates) and National Statistics Office (2011 estimates). Thailand: National Statistical Office. Vietnam: General Statistics Office.

Notes:

[a] The net reproduction rate captures how many female children a woman would have if she survives to the end of her reproductive period. The NRR is approximated using NRR = TFR*[p(Am)/(1+SRB)]. When lifetable data were not available, survival to the mean age at maternity was estimated from life expectancy in each country.

[b] The intrinsic growth rate is estimated using Coale's (1957) first approximation. As such, the population change expected after 10 years of exponential growth at this rate is estimated as $e^{[(\ln NRR)/27)*10]}$.

The estimates are revealing. In 1998, fertility in the MIMAROPA region of the Philippines (the region comprising the islands of Mindoro, Marinduque, Romblon, and Palawan) was generating population growth seven times greater than that occurring in Manila (the National Capital Region). Though fertility declined in both regions by 2008, the proportionate gap in implied growth was still large. Aside from population momentum, fertility in the Rakhine region of Myanmar was sufficiently high in 1997 to increase its population by over a third if sustained for a decade; by contrast fertility in Yangon would result in population shrinkage. This differential decreased substantially over the following decade as Myanmar continued through the fertility transition. In Malaysia, fertility differentials operate with a force sufficient to grow the region of Kelantan, Malaysia, by a fourth and shrink Kuala Lumpur by a tenth.

Another means of conceptualizing the implications of regional population variation is to consider the period in which regions will no longer need to keep expanding primary education – or, the year in which the number of children in a region stops growing. Incidentally, this is not synonymous with the year in which fertility drops below replacement. After a population reaches replacement-level fertility, population momentum – i.e. the legacy of past fertility trends – results in continued growth in the size of birth cohorts as long as the number of women in their reproductive years continues to increase (e.g. see Figure 10.5 in Jones, this volume). In Indonesia, the child population stopped growing in 2009 in Eastern Java but is not expected to stop growing until after 2030 in Papua (BPS 2005; 2013). In the Philippines, the relevant years are 2015 in Manila, 2030 in Cataduanes, and 2040 in Ifugao province. In the sub-central region of Thailand, the size of new birth cohorts stopped growing in 2000; in the Southern region, this is not expected until after 2020.

Ultimately, the implications of these differences for population welfare depend in large part on (i) whether and how interregional movement redistributes the population across regions and (ii) the economic relationships between migrants and their natal families. Sugiyarto (Chapter 13 in this volume) discusses these issues in greater length. With the possible exception of Malaysia, internal movement in Southeast Asia is smaller in magnitude than that observed in Latin America and Southern Africa (Bell and Muhidin 2009). Nevertheless the flows involve several million young adults, and involve sufficient relocation (with smaller offsetting return flows) to create a similar impact on population redistribution as that observed in other world regions (ibid.). Indeed, the heightened age-selectivity of Southeast Asia migrants will mitigate regional differentials in population aging if the young relocate from higher to lower fertility areas. If working-age adults are the healthiest or the best educated, migration may reduce gaps in the age structure but exacerbate inequality in poverty and the health burden (Zhu et al. 2013).

Existing data suggest that even in the presence of migration, regional differences in population fertility and mortality schedules are sufficiently large to generate marked subnational variation in aging. A common metric for summarizing these patterns is the dependency ratio, which compares the proportion of "dependents" (net consumers) to "workers" (net producers). This metric masks variation in the composition of dependents, which changes from the young (children age 0–14) to the old (adults age 65 and older) in transitioning populations (see Figure 16.1).

To capture variation in regional age-composition, I calculate the percentage of dependents who are elderly[5] across provinces, regions, and over time. The trajectories for subnational

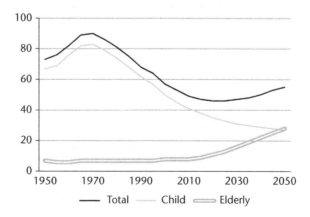

Figure 16.1 Total, child, and elderly dependency ratio, Southeast Asia, 1950–2050
Source: United Nations 2010.

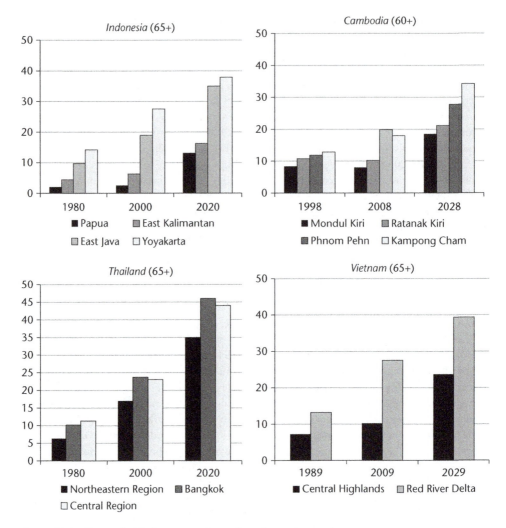

Figure 16.2 Share of elderly among dependents by region and year

Source: Indonesia 1980, 2000 IPUMS, 2020 BPS Projections (2005); Thailand 1980, 2000 IPUMS, 2020 NDEBS Projections (2004); Vietnam 1989, 2009 IPUMS, 2029 GSO Projections (2010); Cambodia Demographics of Population Aging, 2012. National Institute of Statistics.

Notes: Authors' calculations. In Cambodia, projection only available on population size 60 and older.

regions with the highest and lowest values of this measure in the initial period are graphed in Figure 16.2.

In 1998 Cambodia, working-age adults were primarily engaged in the support of children (versus the elderly) across the country. By 2028, the care burden will diverge. One-third of dependents will be elderly in Kampong Cham, versus a fifth in the poorest regions of Mondul Kiri and Ratanak Kiri. In 1980, nearly all dependents were children in the Indonesian province of Papua. By 2020, one-tenth are expected to be elderly. As such, the working-age population will still largely devote resources to the support of children. By contrast, Eastern Java will shift to an arrangement in which 1 in 3 dependents are elderly. The demand for old age care will increase rapidly, whereas the demand for child care is likely to be largely stable, if not declining (remember that the child population in East Java stopped growing before 2010).

Age-specific population projections hinge on predictions about how internal migration will change moving forward. In most cases, these estimates assume similar interregional migration patterns to those observed at present. It may be that migration responds to the acceleration of aging and possible increases in labor demand in low fertility regions. If this happens, subnational disparities in the age *structure* will be lessened.

Notably, the magnitude of the *care* burden captured in these figures is unlikely to be substantially affected by interregional migration. Most countries still rely heavily on the *family* for elderly support (e.g. Frankenberg et al. 2002; Knodel and Saengtienchai 2007). In the absence of a major shift from private to public management, responsibility for care of the growing elderly share will fall on adult children regardless of their location. Internal migration will thus affect patterns of care by structuring whether children are available for physically proximate interaction versus providing care through remittances and technologically supported forms of communication. Data from both Cambodia and Thailand suggest that migrant children provide substantial social and economic support to elderly parents in rural regions (Knodel and Saengtienchai 2007; Zimmer and Knodel 2013).

Of course, the average number of adult children available for this kind of care will decline alongside fertility reduction (Jones 2012). In 2020, elderly support will come from children born in the 1970s and 1980s, when the average number of children had fallen to 3–4 in the wealthier regions. By 2045, the elderly will be relying on children born in the 2000s, when the average number of children per family in wealthier regions was 1–2.

To sum, then, subnational variation in fertility, mortality, and age structure are perhaps best thought of as *engines* of inequality in population pressure. In the near term, additional investment in family planning accessibility and children's schooling is needed in regions that are still growing. In the populations described here, these are (in most cases) regions with higher levels of poverty. Diverting investments toward the new policy challenges associated with aging (public pensions, chronic care management) risks exacerbating regional inequality. In this sense, discussions of generational equity may also take on a decidedly regional frame moving forward.

Longer run, the labor challenges generated by the diversity of age structures within countries may be mitigated by internal migration. This will depend, in part, on efforts to liberalize the movement of circular labor and to shift the economic safety net for the elderly from the family to the state.

As noted at the start of this section, subnational variation in population parameters may both increase, and respond to, spatial economic inequality. This diversity has implications for multiple population phenomena. In the following discussion, I focus in greater depth on emerging variation in the population disease profile. As I will discuss, subnational variation in health conditions is characteristic of transitioning populations. What distinguishes the experience in Southeast Asia is the temporal alignment of these social and spatial lags in population change with (a) major epidemiologic reversals of the trend away from infectious disease, and (b) the introduction of the global nutrition transition.

Population health: changing patterns of disease

Between 1970 and 2010, all Southeast Asian populations experienced marked declines in overall infectious disease mortality (Dans et al. 2011). In fact, the majority of the mortality decline during this period is attributable to a reduction in deaths from tuberculosis, malaria, and diarrheal disease. This has a particularly pronounced effect on infant and child death, which declined to a fourth of its 1970 value by 2010 (IHME 2013). Longer lifespans increased the population at risk of mortality from forms of *chronic* diseases, including cancer and cardiovascular disease. In fact, by 2008, the age-standardized cancer burden in Southeast Asia matched that of North America – approximately 2,450 disability-adjusted life years (DALYs) per 100,000 persons (Soerjomataram et al. 2012).

DALYs capture the total disease burden by summing both life years lost and years lived with disability; these are attributed to specific diseases and disease patterns through population data on cause of death and on reported health conditions. The top panel of Figure 16.3 depicts the temporal change in DALYs between 1990 and 2010 in Southeast Asia. The region has experienced sizable declines in the burden of malaria, measles, and diarrheal disease. Tuberculosis has declined by almost a third but remains high; the illness accounted for 5 percent of the region's

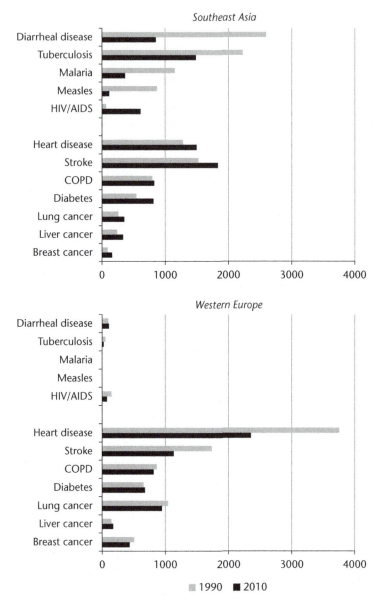

Figure 16.3 Loss of disability–adjusted life years, rate per 100,000 population
Source: Global Health Metrics, 2013.
Notes: Disability–adjusted life years sum years lost to mortality due to cause i and years lived with disability due to cause i. DALYs presented in rates per 100,000 population.

DALYs and 6 percent of the region's deaths in 2010 (IHME 2013). As of 2011, the region had more than 90,000 cases of multi-drug resistant tuberculosis (WHO 2013).

DALYs attributable to most chronic diseases increased during the period. The population diabetes burden increased by 55 percent and the burden of stroke by 20 percent. These changes are particularly concerning because they may be underestimated; adult chronic conditions are more likely to go undetected in the absence of accessible health care. For example, Witoelar et al. (2012) combined biomarker and interview data to demonstrate that only one-third of Indonesian adults with hypertension are diagnosed. Breast, liver, and lung cancer increased, though to a lesser extent. In combination with declines in infectious disease, all three cancers now have a population burden comparable in magnitude to malaria and exceeding that of measles.

Notably, the substitution of chronic for infectious disease did not proceed cleanly along a path predicted by epidemiologic transition theory. In a striking reversal of infectious disease decline, DALYs attributable to HIV/AIDS increased nearly tenfold over the two decades, accounting for 2 percent of deaths in the region by 2010. The burden was disproportionately driven by increases in Thailand, Myanmar, and Malaysia, where the disease now accounts for 4–5 percent of deaths. Of these three, Thailand experienced the fastest increase in AIDS; yearly new infections increased from 0 in 1985 to over 140,000 in 1991 (UNDP 2004). By 2000, the disease accounted for 11 percent of deaths (IHME 2013). The decline (reaching 5 percent of deaths by 2010) is generally regarded as evidence of successful management and distribution of antiretroviral therapy, prevention and education efforts targeted at at-risk populations, and an aggressive coordinated response at the national and local levels (UNDP 2004). Though prevalence continues to increase in neighboring countries like Myanmar, the anticipated enlargement of antiretroviral distribution is expected to generate continued reduction in *new* cases – from 35,000 in the mid-1990s to less than 20,000 in 2015 (National AIDS Programme 2009).

In general, the rise of chronic diseases occurred in a much different context in Southeast Asia than in, for example, wealthy populations, where increases occurred largely outside of a major infectious disease burden. By contrast, populations in Southeast Asia must still navigate both forms of illness. The dual-burden is easily visible when the DALYs for Southeast Asia are compared with those for Western Europe (Figure 16.3). DALYs attributable to stroke, diabetes, chronic obstructive pulmonary disease (COPD), and liver cancer are similar or larger in Southeast Asia than in Western Europe. Yet, the tuberculosis, measles, and malaria burden in Southeast Asia dwarfs that of Western Europe. The HIV/AIDS burden is eight times larger in Southeast Asia.

Moreover, the coexistence of infectious and chronic diseases may have costs that exceed a simple summation of the burden from each. It is now widely believed that the experience of infection and inflammation accompanying communicable disease affects susceptibility to certain chronic conditions (Finch and Crimmins 2004; McDade 2012; Simanek et al. 2011). If future reductions in infectious conditions are achieved, the cohorts experiencing these conditions as children are likely to age with a higher inflammation load and attendant risk of certain forms of heart disease and cancer.[6] Effectively, the "legacy" of these conditions may stay in the population for the decades ahead.

The acceleration of the chronic disease burden has resulted in part from the onset of the *nutrition* transition in Southeast Asian populations. The nutrition transition broadly describes patterns of change in the food supply, the diet, activity trends, and the cumulative effect of these changes on physical health. Like other low- and middle-income countries, Southeast Asian populations have followed closely on the heels of much wealthier nations through the transition. Despite the welcome reduction in food insecurity, the nutrition transition carries a number of new costs. Cheaper calories and food production improvements that support better distribution may provide an important source of basic calorie support in resource-poor areas. However some of these food sources – particularly those built from hydrogenated oils and corn – are actually bereft

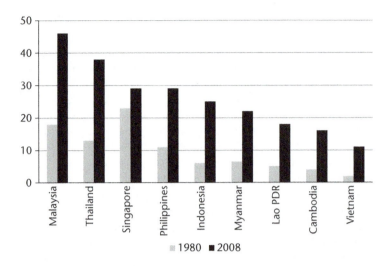

Figure 16.4 Prevalence of overweight and obesity in adult females, 1980–2008
Source: Adapted from Stevens et al. 2012.
Notes: Indicated by body mass index (kg/m^2) > = 25.0

of micronutrients. In regions in which food scarcity is relatively low, the excess, low-nutrient, food supply has resulted in potentially harmful increases in body mass.

The prevalence of both overweight and obesity has increased rapidly since 1980 across Southeast Asia (Figure 16.4). As a comparison, in 2008 the prevalence of overweight and obesity among adult women in the European Union was just short of 50 percent, a figure nearly attained by Malaysia during the period. These changes are typically accompanied by a number of economic costs, including foregone work, greater health care needs, and shorter lifespans (Finkelstein et al. 2005; Usfar et al. 2010). Moreover, many Southeast Asian countries lack the infrastructure to support comprehensive chronic disease management (Kanchanachitra et al. 2011) – particularly for conditions that require vigilant symptom oversight, like diabetes (Dans et al. 2011).

The global nature of this process has several origins. Relaxed trade regulation and the development of global markets supported large food conglomerates' penetration of lower-income nations (Brownell and Warner 2009). Advances in food production technology have significantly reduced the price of producing high-calorie products with stable properties for storage, transport, and global distribution (Popkin 2006). The development of edible oils and high fructose sweeteners has perhaps had the most profound effect on the restructuring of diets, and specifically on the provision of low-nutrient, high calorie foods in low-income nations (Popkin et al. 2013).

Over the last decade, production of edible oils has grown particularly rapidly in Malaysia and Indonesia. The two countries are expected to cover 36 percent of global palm oil production by 2020 (OECD–FAO 2011). Consumption of vegetable oil in these countries is also expected to increase. Whereas the share of vegetable oil consumption for dietary purposes is expected to increase 2 percentage points globally between 2008 and 2020, consumption in Indonesia and Malaysia is expected to increase by 5 and 6 percentage points, respectively. In fact, by 2020 only residents of China, India, and the USA will consume more vegetable oil per person than residents of Indonesia (OECD–FAO 2011).

The effects of these dietary changes on physical health are magnified in the context of increasingly sedentary lifestyles (Usfar et al. 2010) Physical inactivity is now the sixth-leading risk factor for death in Southeast Asia (IHME 2013), accounting for about half a year of life expectancy in the region (Lee et al. 2012). Consistent with data on body mass, the highest attributable risk burden for inactivity (1.35 years of life) is found in Malaysia (ibid.).

What makes these changes so remarkable – and so challenging – is the existence of concurrent unresolved, acute malnutrition in pockets of these populations. For example, the prevalence of acute undernutrition in the United States has been limited to 5 percent (or less) of the child population for the last 50 years (Fryar and Ogden 2012). By contrast, many Southeast Asian populations still battle high levels of food insecurity among the poor (Timmer, Chapter 5 in this volume). In the Eastern islands of Indonesia more than one-third of children are *stunted* (UN 2011). Indicated by a height-for-age value less than two standard deviations below that recommended by the World Health Organization, stunting represents a particularly severe form of malnutrition. Stunting is difficult to ameliorate after the first few years of life (Pinstrup-Andersen et al. 1995) and carries penalties for cognitive functioning, educational attainment and, ultimately, employment and wages (Strauss and Thomas 1998, 2007; Victora et al. 2008). As such, non-governmental organizations in the region consider child malnutrition to be an important hurdle to continued economic development.

The recent, rapid changes in *overnutrition* have surprised academics, policymakers, and health professionals alike. A number of countries now face the dual-burden of navigating simultaneous over- and undernutrition (Doak et al. 2004; Römling and Qaim 2011). Figure 16.5 includes recent estimates of the leading indicators of under- and overnutrition: (a) the proportion of children under age 5 who are stunted (height-for-age z-scores $<= -2.0$) and (b) the proportion of adults over age 20 who are overweight and obese (body mass index, kg/m^2 $>=25.0$).

More than a third of the adult populations in Singapore, Thailand, and Malaysia are overweight or obese. In Indonesia and the Philippines, the combined prevalence of overweight and obesity is one-fifth and one-fourth, respectively.[7] Yet, none of these populations have stunting levels as low as that found in the OECD countries; only Singapore has less than 5 percent of young children who are stunted. Instead, Thailand and Malaysia still have 14 and 16 percent of young children exhibiting stunting. In Indonesia and the Philippines, more than one-third of young children are stunted. Perhaps, unsurprisingly, these differences spatially align with subnational variation in

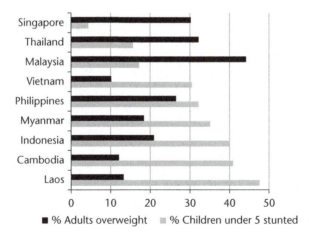

Figure 16.5 Anthropometry in Southeast Asian countries, 2006–11
Source: World Health Organization. Data collected between 2006 and 2011.
Notes: Overweight references adult with values of weight (kg) / height (m)^2 greater than 25. Stunting refers to children with height-for-age values more than 2 standard deviations below the age- and sex-specific median observed in well-nourished populations.

economic development and infrastructure. Child malnourishment is more prevalent in less-resourced, largely agricultural regions, including the Southern Highlands in Laos, the Zamboanga peninsula in the Philippines, and the Kampong Speu province in Cambodia (FAO 2013).

The dual-burden is likely to be persistent. Since 1980, the prevalence of overweight adults in the region has increased at a faster rate than the prevalence of stunting among young children has declined (Stevens et al. 2012a, 2012b; Popkin et al. 2006). Though efforts to improve under-nutrition in Southeast Asian nations have been quite effective (Timmer, Chapter 5 in this volume) and are well regarded by policy organizations (Engesveen et al. 2009), the populations of Indonesia, Cambodia, Lao PDR, and East Timor have some of the highest levels of stunting in the world (WHO 2013).

Moreover, the experience of undernutrition among young children may actually increase the obesity burden moving forward. Specifically, research on the developmental origins of disease indicates that children who are malnourished very early in life – including the gestation period – exhibit multiple physiological traits that improve the body's ability to weather conditions of scarcity (Gluckman et al. 2011). In the presence of improved living conditions, these children may be predisposed to excess weight gain as they age (Popkin et al. 2013; Uauy et al. 2011).

Macroeconomic pricing dynamics also reinforce this dual-burden. The dietary patterns that contribute to overweight status include the rising consumption of animal products. As a result of increased livestock management, more of the population's staple grains are used as feed. Redirecting these calories to livestock will come at a cost if the diminished supply for human consumption is accompanied by price increases. In effect, providing animal-based nutrition for the wealthy may exacerbate food insecurity among the poor. In Southeast Asia, the supply of animal content calories increased in every country between 1980 and 2009; the most striking increases are observable in Cambodia and Vietnam, where the supply increased fivefold (Figure 16.6). As a

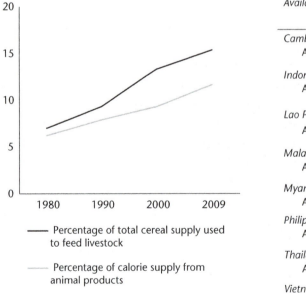

Available Kcals/day per capita		1980	2009
Cambodia	Total	1731	2383
	Animal products	43	230
Indonesia	Total	2157	2646
	Animal products	73	162
Lao PDR	Total	1968	2377
	Animal products	104	220
Malaysia	Total	2765	2902
	Animal products	411	510
Myanmar	Total	2220	2493
	Animal products	108	368
Philippines	Total	2296	2580
	Animal products	246	395
Thailand	Total	2058	2862
	Animal products	194	315
Vietnam	Total	1962	2690
	Animal products	108	545

—— Percentage of total cereal supply used to feed livestock

—— Percentage of calorie supply from animal products

Figure 16.6 Animal products in food supply, Southeast Asia, 1980–2009
Source: UN Food and Agricultural Organization, 2013.

proportion of the total calorie supply, calories from animals increased from 6 percent to 12 percent. This appears to have affected the use patterns of staple cereals. By 2009, more than 15 percent of the region's cereal supply was used to feed livestock.

These trends present a number of challenges. Moving forward, the policies designed to fulfill caloric needs of children in resource-poor homes will need to include strategies to reduce the risk that such programs do not increase body mass among other household members. In both Chile and Mexico, major antipoverty programs have inadvertently contributed to adult obesity (Gorden-Larsen and Jones-Smith 2012). Further these programs will need to focus on the micronutrient content of subsidized foods. In essence, the cheapest foods – in terms of production, storage, and transport – may not be the most effective at improving the health trajectories and minimizing the health costs incurred by poor children as they age.

Conclusions and some policy insights

Population growth has rapidly decelerated alongside rising human capital and family planning support in Southeast Asia. Despite the welcome reprieve from looming resource-depletion and concerns about widespread hunger (e.g. Lam 2011), the speed of this transition has almost certainly generated new challenges for the future. Larger families have historically provided the means of navigating challenges of poverty, health declines, and old-age care (Hirschman and Bonaparte 2012; Sasat and Bowers 2013). Rapid fertility change has halved family size in only a few decades, effectively weakening the primary social safety net in the region. The extent of this challenge is likely as yet unrealized; for most Southeast Asian countries, accelerated population aging still lies ahead.

Moreover, subnational variation within countries involves sizable spatial and social *lags* in population change. These demographic differences risk exacerbating regional wealth inequalities. Moving forward, national policy must navigate challenges typically associated with "developing" societies at the same time as it mitigates problems associated with abundance.

In complement to other topics discussed in this volume, the present chapter investigates aspects of population health as a manifestation of this process. Indeed, the coexistence of under- and overnutrition in countries exemplifies this type of inequality. Changes in the production, sourcing, and distribution of food do not indicate an imminent end to this challenge. Moreover, in many countries, chronic conditions have overtaken infectious disease as the primary source of mortality; nevertheless a number of serious infectious disease threats remain. The coexistence of these conditions may generate more challenges than either would alone.

As discussed earlier and by Wignaraja in Chapter 9 of this volume, subnational variation in economic development – and population pressure – may be leveled by certain forms of internal and international movement, particularly if remittances and social support from migrants are high. Generally, labor policy in the region has become increasingly liberalized, including growing guest-worker programs in Singapore, Malaysia, and Thailand (e.g. Kaur 2010).

Labor policy is also linked directly with several of the population health issues described in this chapter. Both health worker shortages and loss of human capital through health worker migration are still high. In combination, Indonesia, Vietnam, Laos, Cambodia, and Myanmar need 230,000 additional doctors, nurses, and midwives to meet the minimum health worker recommendations set by the WHO. Moreover, existing health workers in Indonesia and Cambodia are dominated by nurses and midwives, who outnumber doctors 7:1 in Indonesia and 5:1 in Cambodia. Human capital loss is particularly acute in the Philippines. Over 13,000 Filipino nurses migrate abroad annually – though not primarily to the Southeast Asian countries experiencing extreme health worker shortages but instead to the USA, UK, and Saudi Arabia (Kanchanachitra et al. 2011).

Other health-related policy may best operate through food distribution, subsidies, and urban planning structured to improve health conditions. In less-resourced areas, greater attention to nutritional supplementation during "the first 1000 days" versus school-based interventions may be critical (Pinstrup-Andersen et al. 1995; WFP n/d). In better-resourced areas, food guidelines and public health efforts will be important to generate ideational change (Usfar et al. 2010): specifically, high body mass may be a new indicator of *mal*nourishment. Successful efforts to prevent dietary health problems of the latter nature are underway in Singapore, one of the few populations in the world exhibiting recent declines in obesity (Toh et al. 2002; Ho 2010). Broadly, the Southeast Asian region may benefit from harnessing a similarly aggressive stance toward large food conglomerates as has been taken (in some cases, quite recently) against large tobacco corporations (Brownell and Warner 2009; Sangthong et al. 2012; Tan and Foong 2013).

Further gains in infectious disease management will depend on both environmental change and infrastructure development. As Shively and Smith (Chapter 6 in this volume) note, more than a quarter of urban residents in Cambodia and Indonesia still lack access to sewage management. In combination with the environmental landscape of Southeast Asia, rapid urbanization and poor living conditions "enable microbes to exploit new ecological niches" (Coker et al. 2011: 599).

A critical resource moving forward will be adequate surveillance of population inequality in the various metrics considered here. Across the scholarship on Southeast Asian population and epidemiologic change, one finds a persistent appeal for better data (Dans et al. 2011; Kaur 2010). Though national averages suggest continued improvement in a number of markers of population development – education, fertility rates, mortality rates, calories per capita, infrastructure for disease management – the spatial lags in these trends appear nontrivial from the limited data available. Future growth in highly diverse countries like Indonesia, Thailand, and Vietnam will depend in part on the continued provision of services and support for those in the least resourced regions, while new programs are developed for the (arguably more visible) populations of urban centers. Motivating distribution decisions will ultimately depend on successfully documenting the severity of spatial inequality in these populations.

Acknowledgments

The author is indebted to Charles Hirschman for his contributions to the arguments in this chapter. The author is also grateful for comments from and conversations with Alberto Palloni and Ian Coxhead.

Notes

1 Integrated Public Use Microdata Series; Minnesota Population Center (2013). www.ipums.org.
2 Importantly, the lag observed in the Demographic and Health Survey data (2007, in particular) relative to the BPS census data may be exacerbated by an under-enumeration of unmarried women. Hull and Hartanto (2009) argue that Indonesia has fertility that is, in fact, quite close to replacement when adjustments for under-enumeration are made.
3 Singapore is excluded because its geographic size is too small to estimate "regional" variation with a comparable interpretation to that observed in the other countries examined here.
4 Arriving at the NRR from the TFR requires the sex-ratio at birth (SRB) and the probability of survival to the mean age at maternity (Am). Human populations display remarkably little variability around an Am of 27, so I use this approximation. I estimate maternal survival to this age, p(Am), using regional data on life expectancy when region-specific lifetables were not available. Because of data limitations, the p(Am) is assumed stable over the period that TFR data are available. In most cases the national SRB is used. For these reasons, the NRR values are approximate.
5 [population age 65+ / (population age 0–14 + population age 65+)]

6 For example, important links have been demonstrated between hepatitis and liver cancer and between rheumatic fever and heart disease (Perz et al. 2006; Guilherme and Kalil 2010).
7 Notably, the prevalence of overweight and obesity is, if anything, underestimated here. Recent scholarship in nutritional science indicates that the harmful cardiometabolic effects of body weight may accrue at lower BMI levels in Asian populations (Usfar et al. 2010). As a result, a cut-off of 23 kg/m^2 has been suggested as an appropriate indicator of overweight (Wen et al. 2009).

References

Attané, Isabelle and Magali Barbieri. 2009. "The demography of East and Southeast Asia from the 1950s to the 2000s." *Population* 64(1): 9–146.

Badan Pusat Statistik (BPS). 2005. *Proyeksi Penduduk Indonesia 2000–2025.* Jakarta.

Barrett, R., C.W. Kuzawa, T. McDade, and G.J. Armelagos. 1998. "Emerging and re-emerging infectious diseases: the third epidemiologic transition." *Annual Review of Anthropology* 27: 247–71.

Bell, Martin and Salut Muhidin. 2009. "Cross national comparisons of internal migration." Human Development Research Paper 2009–30. United Nations Development Programme. New York.

Brown, Graham and Arnim Langer. 2009. "Spatial and ethnic inequalities and development." *UNRISD Flagship Report: Combating Poverty and Inequality.* Geneva: United Nations.

Brownell, K.D. and K.E. Warner. 2009. "The perils of ignoring history: big Tobacco played dirty and millions died. How similar is Big Food?" *Milbank Quarterly* 87: 259–94.

Coker, R.J., B.M. Hunter, J.W. Rudge, M. Liverani, and P. Hanvoravongchai. 2011. "Emerging infectious diseases in Southeast Asia: regional challenges to control." *The Lancet* 377(9765): 599–609.

Dans, Antonio, Nawi Ng, Cherian Varghese, E. Shyong Tai, Rebecca Firestone, and Ruth Bonita. 2011. "The rise of chronic non-communicable diseases in Southeast Asia: time for action." *The Lancet* 377 (9766): 680–9.

Doak, Colleen M., Linda S. Adair, Margaret Bentley, Carlos Monteiro, and Barry M Popkin. 2004. "The dual-burden household and the nutrition transition paradox." *International Journal of Obesity* 29(1): 129–36.

Engesveen, Kaia, Chizuru, Claudine Prudhon, and Roger Shrimpton. 2009. "Assessing countries' commitment to accelerate nutrition action demonstrated in PRSPs, UNDAFs and through nutrition governance." United Nations *Standing Committee on Nutrition News* 37: 10–16.

Epprecht, M., N. Minot, R. Dewina, P. Messerli, and A. Heinimann. 2008. "The geography of poverty and inequality in the Lao PDR." Swiss National Center of Competence in Research (NCCR) North–South, University of Bern, and International Food Policy Research Institute (IFPRI), Bern: Geographica Bernensia.

Finch, C.E. and E.M. Crimmins. 2004. "Inflammatory exposure and historical changes in human life-spans." *Science* 305: 1736–9.

Finkelstein, E., C. Ruhm, and K. Kosa. 2005. "Economic causes and consequences of obesity." *Annual Review of Public Health* 26: 239–57.

Food and Agricultural Organization of the United Nations (FAO). 2013. "Nutrition country profiles." http://www.fao.org/ag/agn/nutrition/profiles_en.stm (accessed June 15, 2013).

Frankenberg, E., A. Chan, and M.B. Ofstedal. 2002. "Stability and change in living arrangements in Indonesia, Singapore, and Taiwan, 1993–1999." *Population Studies* 56: 201–13.

Fryar, Cheryl D. and Cynthia L. Ogden. 2012. "Prevalence of underweight among children and adolescents aged 2–19 years: United States, 1963–1965 through 2007–2010." National Center for Health Statistics.

General Statistics Office (GSO). 2011. *Fertility and Mortality in Vietnam: Trends, Patterns, and Differentials.* Hanoi.

Gluckman, P.D., M.A. Hanson, and F.M. Low. 2011. "The role of developmental plasticity and epigenetics in human health." *Birth Defects Research (Part C)* 93: 12–18.

Gordon-Larsen, P. and J. Jones-Smith. 2012. "Challenges in ameliorating hunger while preventing obesity." *Lancet* 380: 787–9.

Guilherme, L. and J. Kalil. 2010. "Rheumatic fever and rheumatic heart disease: cellular mechanisms leading autoimmune reactivity and disease." *Journal of Clinical Immunology* 30: 17–23.

Hirschman, Charles and Sabrina Bonaparte. 2012. "Population and society in Southeast Asia." In Linda Williams and Philip Guest (eds), *Demography of Southeast Asia.* Ithaca, NY: Southeast Asia Program, Cornell University Press.

Ho, Ting Fei. 2010. "Prevention and management of obesity among children and adolescents – the Singapore experience." In Jennifer A. O'Dea and Michael P. Eriksen (eds), *Childhood Obesity Prevention*. Oxford: Oxford University Press.

Hull, Terence H. and Wendy Hartanto. 2009. "Resolving contradictions in Indonesian fertility estimates." *Bulletin of Indonesian Economic Studies* 45(1): 61–71.

Institute for Health Metrics and Evaluation (IHME). "Global burden of disease." http://www. healthmetricsandevaluation.org/gbd (accessed July 23, 2013). University of Washington.

Jones, G. 2012. "Changing family sizes, structures, and functions in Asia." *Asia-Pacific Population Journal* 27(1): 83–102.

Kanchanachitra, C., M. Lindelow, T. Johnston, P. Hanvoravongchai, F.M. Lorenzo, N.L. Huong, et al. 2011. "Human resources for health in Southeast Asia: shortages, distributional challenges, and international trade in health services." *The Lancet* 377(9767): 769–81.

Kaur, Amarjit. 2010. "Labour migration in Southeast Asia: migration policies, labour exploitation and regulation." *Journal of the Asia Pacific Economy* 15(1): 6–19.

Knodel, J. and C. Saengtienchai. 2007. "Rural parents with urban children: social and economic implications of migration for the rural elderly in Thailand." *Population, Space, and Place* 13: 193–210.

Lam, David. 2011. "How the world survived the population bomb: lessons from 50 years of extraordinary demographic history." *Demography* 48: 1231–62.

Lee, I-M., E.J. Shiroma, F. Lobelo, P. Puska, S.N. Blair, and P.T. Katmarzyk. 2012. "Effect of physical inactivity on major non-communicable diseases worldwide: an analysis of burden of disease and life expectancy." *The Lancet* 380: 219–29.

Livi-Bacci, Massimo. 1992. *A Concise History of the World Population*. Cambridge, MA: Blackwell.

McDade, T.W. 2012. "Early environments and the ecology of inflammation." *Proceedings of the National Academy of Sciences* 109: 17281–8.

Minnesota Population Center. 2013. *Integrated Public Use Microdata Series, International: Version 6.2* [Machine-readable database]. Minneapolis: University of Minnesota.

National AIDS Programme Myanmar. 2009. "HIV estimates and projections, Myanmar 2008–2015."

National Institute of Statistics (NIS), Directorate General for Health, and ICF Macro, 2011. "Cambodia demographic and health survey 2010." Phnom Penh, Cambodia and Calverton, Maryland, USA: National Institute of Statistics, Directorate General for Health, and ICF Macro.

National Statistics Centre of Lao PDR (NSC). 2005. *Population Census 2005*.

OECD. 2013. "Poverty and inequality disparities in Cambodia, Lao PDR, Myanmar and Viet Nam." In *Southeast Asian Economic Outlook 2013: With Perspectives on China and India*. Paris: OECD Publishing.

OECD–FAO. 2011. *Agricultural Outlook 2011–2020*. Rome.

Omran, A.R. 1971. "The epidemiologic transition." *Milbank Memorial Fund Quarterly* 49(4): 509–38.

Perz, Joseph F., Gregory L. Armstrong, Leigh A. Farrington, Yvan J.F. Hutin, and Beth P. Bell. 2006. "The contributions of hepatitis B virus and hepatitis C virus infections to cirrhosis and primary liver cancer worldwide." *Journal of Hepatology* 45(4): 529–38.

Pinstrup-Andersen, P., D. Pelletier, and H. Alderman (eds) 1995. *Child Growth and Nutrition in Developing Countries: Priorities for Action*. Ithaca, NY: Cornell University Press.

Popkin, Barry M. 1994. "The nutrition transition in developing countries: an emerging crisis." *Nutrition Reviews* 52(9): 285–98.

Popkin, Barry M. 2006. "Global nutrition dynamics: the world is shifting rapidly toward a diet linked with noncommunicable diseases." *American Journal of Clinical Nutrition* 84(2): 289–98.

Popkin, Barry, Linda S. Adair, and Shu Wen Ng. 2013. "The global nutrition transition: the pandemic of obesity in developing countries." *Nutrition Review* 70(1): 3–21.

Römling, Cornelia, and Matin Qaim. 2011. "Direct and indirect determinants of obesity: the case of Indonesia." Working Paper. Göttingen: Georg-August-University of Göttingen.

Sangthong, Rassamee, Wit Wichaidit, and Chittawet Ketchoo. 2012. "Current situation and future challenges of tobacco control policy in Thailand." *Tobacco Control* 21: 49–54.

Sasat, Siriphan and Barbara J. Bowers. 2013. "Spotlight Thailand." *The Gerontologist* 53(5): 711–17.

Simanek, A.M., J.B. Dowd, G. Pawelec, D. Melzer, A. Dutta, and A.E. Aiello. 2011. "Seropositivity to cytomegalovirus, inflammation, all-cause and cardiovascular disease-related mortality in the United States." *PLoS ONE* 6(2): e16103.

Soerjomatam, Isabelle, Joannie Lortet-Tieulent, D. Maxwell Parkin, Jacques Ferlay, David Forman, and Freddie Bray. 2012. "Global burden of cancer in 2008: a systematic analysis of disability adjusted life-years in 12 world regions." *The Lancet* 380: 1840–50.

Stevens, G.A., M.M. Finucane, C.J. Paciorek, et al. 2012a. "Trends in mild, moderate, and severe stunting and underweight, and progress towards MDG 1 in 141 developing countries: a systematic analysis of population representative data." *Lancet* 380: 824–834.

Stevens, G.A., G.M. Singh, Y. Lu, G. Danaie, J.K. Lin, M.M. Finucane, et al. 2012b. "National, regional, and global trends in adult overweight and obesity prevalences." *Population Health Metrics* 10(22): 1–16.

Strauss, John and Duncan Thomas. 1998. "Health, nutrition, and economic development." *Journal of Economic Literature* 36: 766–817.

Strauss, John and Duncan Thomas. 2007. "Health over the life course." In T. Paul Schultz and J. Strauss (eds), *Handbook of Development Economics*. Amsterdam: North-Holland.

Tan, Yen Lian and Kin Foong. 2013. "Tobacco industry tangos with descriptor ban in Malaysia." *Tobacco Control*: online first.

Toh, Cheong Mui, Jeffery Cutter, and Suok Kai Chew. 2002. "School-based intervention has reduced obesity in Singapore." *British Medical Journal* 324(7334): 427.

Uauy, Ricardo, Juliana Kain, and Camila Corvalan. 2011. "How can the Developmental Origins of Health and Disease (DOHaD) hypothesis contribute to improving health in developing countries?" *American Journal of Clinical Nutrition* 94(6 Suppl): 1759S–1764S.

United Nations. 2011. *World Population Prospects: The 2010 Revision*. At: data.un.org (accessed 10 June 2013).

United Nations Children's Fund (UNICEF) Indonesia 2012. "Maternal and child nutrition." UNICEF Issue Briefs. October.

United Nations Development Program. 2004. *Thailand's Response to HIV/AIDS: Progress and Challenges*. MDG Report. Bangkok, Thailand.

Usfar, A.A., E. Lebenthal, Atmarita, E. Achadi, Soekirman, and H. Hadi. 2010. "Obesity as a poverty-related emerging nutrition problem: the case of Indonesia." *Obesity Reviews* 11: 924–8.

Victora, Cesar G., Linda Adair, Caroline Fall, Pedro C. Hallal, Reynaldo Martorell, Linda Richter, and Harshpal Singh Sachdev. 2008. "Maternal and child undernutrition: consequences for adult health and human capital." *The Lancet* 371(9609): 340–57.

Wen, Chi Pang, Ting Yuan David Cheng, Shan Pou Tsai, Hui Ting Chan, Hui Ling Hsu, Chih Cheng Hsu, and Michael P. Eriksen. 2009. "Are Asians at greater mortality risks for being overweight than Caucasians? Redefining obesity for Asians." *Public Health Nutrition* 12(4): 497–506.

Witoelar, Firman, John Strauss, and Bondan Sikoki. 2012. "Socioeconomic success and health in later life: evidence from the Indonesia Family Life Survey." In J.P. Smith and M. Majmundar (eds), *Aging in Asia: Findings from New and Emerging Data Initiatives*. Washington, DC: National Academies Press, pp. 309–41.

World Food Programme (WFP) n/d. "First 1000 Days." http://wfpusa.org/what-wfp-does/1000-days

World Health Organization (WHO) 2013. "Tuberculosis control in the South-East Asia Region." Annual TB Report 2013. Regional Office for South-East Asia.

Zhu, Yu, Martin Bell, Sabine Henry, and Michael White. 2013. "Rural–urban linkages and the impact of internal migration in Asian developing countries." *Asian Population Studies* 9(2): 119–23.

Zimmer, Zachary and John Knodel. 2013. "Older-age parents in rural Cambodia and migration of adult children: a case study of two communes in Battambang province." *Asian Population Studies* 9(2): 156–74.

17

Southeast Asian commercial policy
Outward-looking regional integration

Hal Hill

AUSTRALIAN NATIONAL UNIVERSITY

Jayant Menon

ASIAN DEVELOPMENT BANK

Introduction

The ten Southeast Asian economies have had highly diverse experiences with global and regional economic integration. During the colonial era they were more or less connected to the global economy through the metropolitan powers, sometimes on a preferential/discriminatory basis. In the early post-colonial era, only Singapore, Malaysia and Thailand remained "always open", in the sense defined by Sachs–Warner, and also in Myint's (1972) typology of outward-looking economies. Indonesia and Burma deliberately chose to disengage from the global economy, while the Philippines adopted a comprehensive import-substituting industrialization strategy. The three Indochinese economies were increasingly engulfed in conflict, and then isolated from the west and from global markets for more than a decade from 1975.

However, among the six less open economies, there has been in recent decades a generalized transition towards more liberal economic policies, with a series of increasingly decisive unilateral liberalizations, and no significant reversals. Indonesia led the way from the late 1960s, with further consolidations in the 1980s. The Philippines began to reform cautiously in the early 1980s, and more firmly in the 1990s. The three Indochina economies began a major transition from plan to market from the late 1980s, led by Vietnam's *doi moi* reforms. Completing the wave of reforms, it now appears very likely that Myanmar is in the process of making this transition.

Alongside these largely unilateral reforms, Southeast Asia has also established in the Association of Southeast Asian Nations (ASEAN) a regional association that is by far the most durable and effective in the developing world.[1] After the early hesitant steps, it has become an increasingly important tool of regional economic integration, from the 1992 ASEAN Free Trade Area, AFTA, to the ASEAN Economic Community (AEC), scheduled to commence in late 2015. ASEAN is an unusual, and often misunderstood, form of regional integration. The key to its longevity, and the sub-title of our chapter, is its outward-looking regional integration, as emphasized by the Indonesian economist Hadi Soesastro (2006). That is, for political economy reasons – 70 percent of intra-ASEAN trade is through or with free-trade Singapore – it will never become an EU-type arrangement with common external trade barriers, and it is likely to continue to multilateralize most of its regional trade concessions.

Initially focused on trade liberalization, ASEAN's regional integration agenda is increasingly directed to services trade, investment, labor migration and macroeconomic policy. The latter in particular has been driven by the two recent economic shocks that have affected the region, the Asian financial crisis (AFC) of 1997–98 and the global financial crisis (GFC) of 2008 – and particularly the former. These events had their origins in macroeconomic and financial sector policies within and beyond the region, and they exposed the inadequacy of existing financial safety net arrangements, particularly those that did not involve the International Monetary Fund. The events also highlighted the need for the smaller ASEAN economies to engage with the much larger Northeast Asian economies, giving rise to the "ASEAN Plus Three" regional economic architecture centered, among other initiatives, on the Chiang Mai Initiative Multilateralization (CMIM), which is now proposed in some quarters as the region's principal financial safety net.

This chapter is organized as follows: in the next section we trace the evolution of ASEAN and its changing objectives and modalities, before examining the record on merchandise trade, which was the main focus of initiatives for ASEAN's first quarter-century. The broader agenda from the late 1990s is then investigated, including services trade, foreign investment, migration and regional commercial architecture. The following section addresses a major contemporary – and as yet untested – priority, that of a regional financial safety net. We draw out the main conclusions in the final section.

As with postwar moves toward greater European integration, ASEAN cooperation is of course about much more than economics. The drive for closer relations initially grew out of a recognition that these countries had been divided by their colonial experiences, and also by a desire to overcome the regional tensions that were ever-present in the early post-colonial era. In the Cold War geopolitics of the 1960s, and the perceived threat of communism from China and Indochina, ASEAN's founders were also staunchly anti-communist. But closer political relations in turn required tangible initiatives in economics, business, education, culture and many other fields. Any evaluation of ASEAN economic cooperation has to be seen in light of these broader objectives of a more peaceful and harmonious regional neighborhood.

The evolution of ASEAN[2]

ASEAN was formally established in August 1967. In a region that had been plagued by conflict during the preceding quarter of a century, and divided by a diverse colonial past, ASEAN has first and foremost forged diplomatic cohesion among its member countries' population of about 600 million people. Formed initially by leaders of five of the member countries,[3] the Bangkok Declaration – ASEAN's founding document – was broad and general in its objectives. These included: "To accelerate the economic growth, social progress and cultural development in the region ... To promote regional peace and stability ... To promote active collaboration and mutual assistance ... in the economic, social, cultural, technical, and administrative spheres." Subsequently, ASEAN has developed into a close-knit grouping with around 700 meetings each year on economic, political, cultural, educational and security matters. ASEAN has also been able to effectively project itself regionally and internationally through a wide range of initiatives.

There are four more or less distinct phases in the evolution of ASEAN. The *first phase* commenced with its establishment in 1967, in a highly uncertain regional and global environment overshadowed by conflict. This was at the height of the Cold War, the Indochina conflict was at its peak, and China was in the throes of the Cultural Revolution. Indonesia had only recently renounced its intention to "crush" Malaysia; Malaysia and Singapore had separated after a brief union; Malaysia and the Philippines were (and still are, periodically) in dispute over Sabah; and there were (or had recently been) significant leftist insurgencies in most of the region. Thailand was widely regarded in the West as a likely next "domino" to fall to the communist advance. Earlier attempts at establishing a regional association, such as the Association of Southeast Asia (ASA), and a possible three-nation "Malay" grouping, Maphilindo, had not progressed. A major facilitating factor in the 1967 meeting and declaration was regime change in Indonesia in early 1966, with the Soeharto administration signaling its intention to rejoin the international community, to focus on economic development and to seek better relations with its neighbors. Then, as now, ASEAN has been able to progress only as fast as its dominant power.

The vision of ASEAN's first leaders therefore focused primarily on establishing regional harmony. While all were strongly anti-communist in outlook, they explicitly emphasized socio-economic cooperation and development rather than defense and security. In 1969 the ASEAN foreign ministers commissioned a study on ASEAN economic cooperation to be conducted by the United Nations. The Kansu Report (named after its leader, Professor G. Kansu) was completed in 1972. But it was not widely circulated, and was not formally published until 1974 (as UNDESA, 1974). Its recommendations on economic cooperation reflected both popular thinking at the time and the inclination of ASEAN member countries. Specifically, it proposed trade liberalization through selective, or product-by-product, tariff negotiations, package deal arrangements for large industrial projects and financial cooperation.

The *second phase* commenced with the Bali Summit of the five leaders in February 1976. This marked the beginning of a formal set of regional cooperation measures. These comprised the ASEAN Preferential Trading Agreement (APTA), the ASEAN Industrial Projects (AIPs), the ASEAN Industrial Complementation (AIC) and the ASEAN Industrial Joint Ventures (AIJVs). APTA, the most significant of the four, represented the first attempt to promote intra-ASEAN trade through institutional integration and regional trade preferences. The AIPs, on the other hand, were designed to establish in each member country a large-scale, inter-governmental project. The AIC and the AIJVs were aimed at promoting specialization in complementary products and to facilitate the pooling of resources.

These initiatives were broadly consistent with the Kansu and other reports. They reflected the desire on the part of leaders to "put some flesh on the bones" of regional cooperation, at least in a minimal, non-threatening way. A major trigger was the reunification of Vietnam in April 1975 and communist takeovers in Cambodia and Laos. ASEAN meanwhile became a more active organization in international affairs. It began to caucus as a group, for example in the United Nations and on issues of common concern, such as market access for its labor-intensive manufactures and tropical cash crops. Dialogue-partner relationships with a wide array of countries and regions were established, and some of these formed the basis for subsequent regional trade architecture initiatives. ASEAN also began to be active diplomatically, especially in its attempts to isolate Vietnam for its 1978 overthrow of the Khmer Rouge regime in Cambodia.

However, none of the four economic cooperation programs had any significant impact on regional economic relations (Imada and Naya, 1992). Indeed, they were explicitly designed to have minimal effect. The tariff cuts of APTA were on a product-by-product basis rather than across-the-board. Hence its commodity coverage was narrow, the tariff cuts were too small to have any discernible effect on trade, and in addition implementation was half-hearted. Moreover, APTA failed to deal with non-tariff barriers (NTBs), which were generally a more serious impediment to trade than tariffs. The AIP, AIC and AIJVs also had limited success. In the case of the AIJVs, for example, the Philippines and Thailand were in dispute over wanting to produce the same automotive parts. More generally, the failure of these initiatives was symptomatic of the members' unwillingness and unpreparedness to pursue either trade liberalization or regional integration at the time.

There was little further progress during the 1980s. Brunei's accession in 1984 occurred as that country became independent. During 1984–87, the Philippines was engulfed in economic and political crises, and effectively disengaged from ASEAN. The collapse in global commodity prices in the mid-1980s pushed both Indonesia and Malaysia – and by extension Singapore – into recession, in turn prompting swift and effective reforms, but lessening interest in the broader regional agenda.

A *third phase* commenced in 1992 with another leaders' Summit at which the ASEAN Free Trade Area, AFTA, was announced. This marked a clear break with the past. The emphasis was on stronger economic cooperation: for the first time, "free trade" was the regional objective, there was a clear timetable for implementation, and a "negative list" approach was adopted, in that all goods trade was to be included within AFTA unless explicitly excluded. The six leaders agreed to reduce the common effective preferential tariff (CEPT) rates to 0–5 percent by 2008, with an interim target of 20 percent by 1998–2000. This deadline was subsequently advanced to 2005 and then again to 2003. The leaders also agreed that each country would have at least 85 percent of its tariff lines in the "Inclusion List" by 2000, and 90 percent by 2001.

A range of regional and external drivers triggered this more decisive approach. First, there was general recognition that the 1976 measures had been cosmetic and ineffective. Second, there was increased self-confidence in the region. Indonesia in particular had weathered the mid-1980s debt crisis effectively, and had introduced sweeping economic policy reforms. Third, substantive regional associations were coming into vogue elsewhere, especially with the signing in 1991 of the EU Maastricht Accord and the imminent extension of NAFTA to Mexico, a middle-income competitor in the crucial US export market. Fourth, China, having begun to implement its own program of economic reforms from the late 1970s, was now growing very fast and attracting large FDI inflows. The ASEAN leaders felt they had to present the region as a competitive single-market alternative to China. Fifth, other changes in the regional and global commercial architecture were gathering momentum and threatened to overshadow the slow-moving ASEAN. Notable here were the establishment of the multilateral Asia Pacific Economic Cooperation (APEC) process in 1989 and the promulgation of the World Trade Organization's (WTO) Uruguay trade round in 1995.

The ASEAN leaders built on this renewed vigor by seeking to extend the geographic spread and commercial depth of the association. By the early 1990s, Vietnam had clearly signaled its intention to adopt market-oriented reforms and to look outwards. ASEAN's earlier antipathy towards this communist regime gave way to pragmatism, fueled on both sides by a common apprehension towards China. Thus Vietnam joined in 1995, followed by Laos and Myanmar in 1997, and after a delay owing to its domestic political instability, Cambodia in 1999. The addition of the so-called CLMV countries brought ASEAN membership to its present-day level of ten countries.

Over almost two decades since the mid-1990s ASEAN has played a constructive role in its commercial engagement with the three reforming states of mainland Southeast Asia, although Myanmar was until recently one of the world's most isolationist states despite ASEAN's attempts to engage it. Finally, commencing in 2012, in a major policy shift, it too is beginning to reintegrate with the regional and global economy. Membership of ASEAN reinforced the outward orientation of the latecomers, built confidence in their reform momentum, and enabled them to learn from their more advanced neighbors. The four mainland states negotiated phased-in arrangements for accession to AFTA and other agreements. Thus Vietnam was given until 2006 to bring down tariffs on products in its Inclusion List to no more than 5 percent. For Laos and Myanmar it was 2008, while owing to its delayed accession Cambodia had until 2010.

By the mid-1990s, and consistent with the global trend toward preferential trade agreements (PTAs), ASEAN began to cautiously develop arrangements for liberalized regional trade in services and investment, and for harmonization of customs and other measures. The ASEAN Framework Agreement on Services (AFAS) was signed at the Fifth ASEAN Summit meeting in Bangkok in 1995. This was an ambitious agreement with two main objectives: to substantially eliminate all restrictions (both discriminatory and market access measures) to trade in services among member countries, and to liberalize trade in services by expanding the depth and scope of liberalization beyond steps undertaken by member-states under the General Agreement on Trade in Services (GATS). ASEAN was also one of the first regional groupings in the developing world to adopt formal instruments to try to promote and protect cross-border investment among its members. A number of agreements were signed, the most significant of which was the Framework Agreement on the ASEAN Investment Area (AIA) in October 1998, subsequently expanded and consolidated into the ASEAN Comprehensive Investment Agreement (ACIA) in February 2009.

However, just as the original leaders' dream of "one Southeast Asia" was being realized, in mid-1997 the Asian financial crisis suddenly erupted with unexpected ferocity. For ASEAN as an institution, the crisis had two principal effects. First, the region as a whole lost some of its commercial attractiveness, especially as China and India were largely unaffected by the crisis. Moreover, ASEAN was seen by many as an ineffective and feeble institution, unable to respond decisively at a time of crisis. In addition to the AFC, it was unable to play any role in the two other major regional flashpoints of that period. These were the Timor crisis of 1998–99, which led to the creation of a newly independent state, Timor Leste in 2002, and Indonesia's forest fires of 1997–98 that severely disrupted life in neighboring Malaysia and Singapore.[4]

Second, the crisis led to a general rethinking of the future of regional economic cooperation, and the need for some sort of coordinated macroeconomic response capacity to avert such future events. This led to the current *fourth phase* in the evolution of ASEAN, which is dominated by two key features. These are the return to growth, and the struggle to define its rationale and identity, against the backdrop of a fast-changing regional and global environment, including a plethora of initiatives affecting commercial policy architecture.

Four features have dominated the region's commercial policy in the twenty-first century, and all have posed new and difficult challenges for ASEAN. These developments, and their implications for ASEAN, are discussed in more detail below. The first is the spread of PTAs/FTAs. Singapore in particular, frustrated with the slow pace of progress within ASEAN, began to break ranks and embark on a bold strategy of signing FTAs with its global trade partners. Although causing strain within the grouping, this had a domino effect, with other ASEAN countries feeling compelled to follow.

Second, there has been a recognition that ASEAN is too small to address some of the broader, post-crisis macroeconomic coordination issues. For example, ASEAN is too small to seriously contemplate coordinated macroeconomic policy, such as a common currency. In the case of emergency and crisis prevention measures, including currency swaps and fiscal standby agreements, the huge international reserves accumulated in Northeast Asia since the AFC dictate that these economies will be the major players in any regional and international agreements on such issues.

Third, ASEAN has now largely completed the "easy phase" of intra-regional trade liberalization. As of 2010, zero tariffs applied to 99 percent of the tariff lines in the Inclusion List of the ASEAN-6. The average tariff for ASEAN-6 under the CEPT scheme is down to 1.5 percent, from 12.8 percent when the tariff-cutting exercise commenced in 1993. For the CLMV, 49.3 percent of the tariff lines in the Inclusion List are already at 0 percent, bringing the ASEAN average to 80.3 percent (MITI, 2013). What remains are the politically more sensitive areas, heavy industry and food crops in particular. An unstated tenet of ASEAN trade liberalization is that the concessions would be "multilateralized" as long as it was politically acceptable domestically for the signatories to do so. But for more contentious liberalizations, progress has been slower and exemptions, such as rice and iron and steel in many countries, and automobiles in Malaysia, have proliferated.

Fourth, the rise of fragmentation trade has called into question the viability of all forms of PTAs that do not multilateralize their concessions. East Asia has been the dominant player in this fast-growing segment of international trade, which involves the physical relocation of stages of the production process that can be transferred to lower-cost sites (See Athukorala and Kohpaiboon, Chapter 7 in this volume). Parts and components in the electronics and automotive industries have been the major segment of this trade, although it is now spreading rapidly to (poorly measured) services trade through Build Operate Transfer (BOT) facilities. Within East Asia, the ASEAN countries stand out for their heavy dependence on fragmentation trade. In 2009–10, for example, parts and components accounted for 45 percent of ASEAN manufactured exports, up from 29 percent in 1992–93. The shares are higher still for some countries: 73 percent for the Philippines in 2009–10 (up from 24 percent in 1992–93), 55 percent in Malaysia (from 37 percent) and 50 percent in Singapore (from 32 percent) (Athukorala, 2011).

Clearly, the management of global production facilities, sourcing inputs from many countries for assembly in a single location, is fundamentally incompatible with PTAs: some countries may be signatories to various PTAs, and these agreements, each with its own specific rules of origin, are unlikely to be mutually compatible. The response of governments and multinational enterprises (MNEs) in these industries has been to locate such activities in free trade zones, thus placing their operations on a free trade footing. More recently, governments have come to recognize the impracticality of any form of trade barriers – unilateral or preferential – in this segment of manufacturing, through the establishment of the International Technology Agreement (Bhagwati, 2008), to which the major Southeast Asian electronics exporters are signatories.

We now look more closely at these issues, focusing in turn on merchandise trade; trade in services, investment and migration; and the broader integration issues.

The earlier agenda: merchandise trade

Two features dominate ASEAN trade. First, the ASEAN economies trade predominantly with the rest of the world. Since 1970, intra-regional trade has generally constituted between 15 percent and 30 percent of total ASEAN trade (Figure 17.1). Although this share has been trending upwards, it remains low relative to other regions. The fact that the ASEAN economies are only a small share of global trade flows is partly to account, and adjustment for "trade intensity" increases it, significantly for some countries. Intra-regional trade is now also less commodity based, with manufactures playing a larger role, increasingly through Singapore-centered global production networks.

The second feature is that Singapore dominates intra-ASEAN trade flows, as revealed in Table 17.1. The largest single trade flow is between Singapore and Malaysia, as it always has been in the postwar era. Singapore's trade with Indonesia and Thailand is also very large. The largest non-Singapore trade flows involve the region's second most open economy, Malaysia, with the two neighbors with which it shares a land boundary, Indonesia and Thailand. The matrix also shows the small scale of official trade of the poorer mainland states, although Vietnam is rising fast. The countries also differ with respect to the importance of ASEAN within their total trade. ASEAN markets constitute about a third of total trade for Singapore, and nearly a quarter of total trade for Malaysia. The share is much lower for Indonesia, where natural resource exports to

Figure 17.1 Intra-ASEAN trade shares, 1970–2012
Source: UNCTAD, 2009. Handbook of Statistics Online (1970–89 data), ARIC Integration Indicators Database, ADB.

Table 17.1 Major intra-ASEAN trade flows, 2012, % of total intra-ASEAN trade

ASEAN country	Partner					
	Indonesia	Malaysia	Philippines	Singapore	Thailand	Vietnam
Indonesia	–	3.8	0.7	7.1	3.0	0.8
Malaysia	3.1	–	0.8	9.3	3.9	1.5
Philippines	0.6	0.6	–	1.5	1.0	neg
Singapore	10.4	14.9	2.0	–	4.2	2.1
Thailand	3.2	4.2	1.2	3.1	–	1.6
Vietnam	neg	1.3	0.5	1.5	1.4	–

Source: IMF Direction of Trade Statistics, downloaded from the ARIC Integration Indicators Database, ADB.
Notes: Top 10 flows in bold; neg = very small, <0.5%.

extra-regional markets are important, and for the Philippines, whose commercial patterns have always been the least ASEAN-centered of the five original member countries.

Two important implications for the governance of regional economic architecture flow from this analysis. First, it does not make sense for ASEAN to contemplate the formation of a customs union, since the major trade is outside the region. That is, the costs of trade diversion would almost certainly exceed the benefits of trade creation. Second, Singapore's dominance of intra-ASEAN trade flows, and the country's non-negotiable commitment to open borders, means that any attempt to set a common external trade regime at anything other than that defined by Singapore is not feasible, since the latter would be a veto player. This does not necessarily preclude the adoption of free trade within ASEAN alongside differing trade policies for each state. Such an arrangement would imply a two-tier trade policy for all but Singapore, which is technically feasible but would obviously be administratively cumbersome and subject to widespread corruption. In any case, the fact that less than 10 percent of intra-ASEAN trade avails of AFTA concessions suggests that this approach is virtually irrelevant. The margins of preference between the AFTA and most favored nation (MFN) rates are already very low, and the administrative procedures render the AFTA option unattractive. We return to this issue below.

The twenty-first-century agenda: services, FDI and regional economic architecture

As noted, ASEAN has had a deeper regional economic integration objective since the 1990s. In this section we address the issues upon which policy makers have focused beyond the first-round efforts that were mainly directed at merchandise trade. Following AFTA, ASEAN has signed agreements relating to trade in services, intra-regional investment and labor movements. The economies are increasingly integrated in all these respects, but they are all market-driven, with little if any formal implementation of the regional initiatives.

Deepening integration: services trade, FDI, labor

Under the 1995 AFAS agreement, negotiations over the liberalization of services have focused on five sectors, namely financial services, transport, telecommunications, tourism and professional business services. Progress has however been limited, owing to the lack of the political commitment required to open up the services market, weaknesses in negotiation frameworks, legal restrictions and institutional limitations (Rajan and Sen, 2002). These problems have been compounded by the global tendency to liberalize services trade last, whether in the form of a general market liberalization or specifically privatization and FDI liberalization.

Of course, although it is notoriously difficult to measure, intra-ASEAN service trade is intense, driven by proximity (which generally matters more for services than merchandise trade) and complementarity. In the majority of ASEAN countries, tourists from the region are the largest group of visitors. In financial services and telecommunications, Singapore and Malaysia are major investors throughout the region. Intra-regional flows of education and health services are growing rapidly. These are essentially market-driven transactions, which can be facilitated by simplified visa arrangements (such as the current ASEAN-wide visa-free facility) and other harmonization measures that lower transaction costs. However, it would hardly make sense for ASEAN governments to give preferential access to neighboring service providers over the best-practice global alternative.

In the case of FDI, there are a number of sequentially related agreements, starting in 1987 with the ASEAN Agreement for the Promotion and Protection of Investment, commonly known as the ASEAN Investment Guarantee Agreement (IGA). More than a decade later, the Framework Agreement on the ASEAN Investment Area (AIA) was signed in October 1998. The most significant initiative of the AIA was the preferential, or discriminatory, treatment afforded to ASEAN investors in member countries for a fixed period of time. This preferential treatment was to take the form of access to particular industrial sectors available only to ASEAN member countries on a reciprocal basis. However, in 2007, the 39th Meeting of the ASEAN Economic Ministers (AEM) effectively nullified this preferential treatment when the provisions were extended to foreign-owned ASEAN-based investors. In February 2009, the ASEAN Comprehensive Investment Agreement (ACIA) was signed. This was intended to be more comprehensive in that it deals with liberalization, promotion, facilitation and protection, and also adopts a single negative list approach.

Regional investment flows have risen rapidly over this period. But these are predominantly market-driven, and there is no evidence that they have been induced by the special provisions offered under the AIA and ACIA initiatives. That is, although some of ASEAN's investment provisions may represent a medium for regional protectionism or sectoral sheltering rather than liberalization, in practice they appear to have little impact.

Singapore, with its extraordinarily high savings rate and international reserves, and its large government-linked corporate (GLC) sector, has emerged as a major foreign investor, globally and regionally (Hill and Jongwanich, 2014). Its scale is such that in several ASEAN countries it is among the top three foreign investors. Its investments are in a broad range of sectors, including banking, telecoms, hotels and real estate. As the major regional headquarters for MNEs, Singapore is also a base for these companies investing elsewhere in the region. Malaysia too has become a major investor abroad, with a similar set of drivers at work – high savings rates, loss of comparative advantage in labor-intensive activities and an activist GLC sector. For example, in the 2000s both countries emerged as major investors in Indonesia in a diverse range of sectors, including banking, oil palm, hotels and telecommunications. Thailand is now a major investor in the small neighboring Indochinese economies in a wide range of service, manufacturing and resource-based activities.

Table 17.2 provides estimates of realized FDI for each ASEAN economy by source – ASEAN and extra-ASEAN – for the period 2010–2012. These are indicative of longer-term shares. Extra-ASEAN economies dominate these flows, and are typically five to seven times larger than those originating from within ASEAN. This applies to all economies, including the mainland transition economies which, in the early reform phase, received much of their FDI from neighboring ASEAN countries. It also needs to be noted that the intra-ASEAN share in total FDI flows to the region is less than the corresponding share for trade. This is to be expected given that among the ASEAN-10 countries, only Singapore is an outward investor at a global scale.

Regional labor markets are becoming increasingly integrated. Here too ASEAN has signed several formal accords since 2000, including the January 2007 ASEAN Declaration on the Protection and Promotion of the Rights of Migrant Workers. Substantial liberalization in the movement of professional labor is envisaged as part of the forthcoming ASEAN Economic Community. However, intra-ASEAN labor flows mainly occur independently of these arrangements, and they are largely market-driven, dictated by large inter-country wage differentials and open labor markets. Labor flows to, from and within the ASEAN countries are significant. Several lower-income countries are major labor exporters, particularly the Philippines, where remittances are the fourth largest in the developing world. The two richer countries, Singapore and Malaysia, together with tiny Brunei, have always had very open labor markets, with 20 percent or more of their workforces made up of temporary foreign workers. The number of foreign workers in Thailand has been growing very rapidly; these migrants originate mainly in its poorer neighbors, particularly Myanmar. In none of these cases is there a deliberate preference for workers from other ASEAN countries but, in practice, proximity and ethnic/cultural similarities result in the majority of these foreign workers coming from neighboring countries. This is particularly the case with Malaysia, where it is estimated that 75 percent of foreign workers are from Indonesia. Given the former's delicate ethnic mix, it is widely believed that the dominant Malay community tacitly supports these large inflows. The Philippines is Malaysia's second largest source of migrant workers, with particularly large inflows to the East Malaysian states.

The rise of FTAs

As noted, with the exception of ASEAN itself, the countries of Southeast Asia generally eschewed preferential trading arrangements until the late 1990s, preferring a combination of multilateral and unilateral measures. The former had resulted in a global trading environment that generally

Table 17.2 Intra- and extra-regional FDI flows, 2010–12 (data as of October 2013) (value in US$ million; share to total in percent)

Country	2010–12[b] average			Share to total, 2012			Share of intra-ASEAN, 2012		
	Intra-ASEAN	Extra-ASEAN	Total net inflow	Intra-ASEAN	Extra-ASEAN	Total net inflow	Intra-ASEAN	Extra-ASEAN	Total net inflow
Brunei Darussalam	79	838	917	n.a	n.a	n.a	n.a	n.a	n.a
Cambodia	365	712	1,077	2.6	1.1	1.4	33.6	66.4	100.0
Indonesia	7,422	10,200	17,622	39.8	13.1	18.0	40.4	59.6	100.0
Lao PDR	88	222	309	0.4	0.2	0.3	25.0	75.0	100.0
Malaysia	2,001	8,184	10,186	14.0	7.3	8.5	29.9	70.1	100.0
Myanmar	186	1,633	1,819	0.6	1.1	1.0	10.2	89.8	100.0
Philippines	37	1,933	1,970	0.7	2.9	2.5	5.2	94.8	100.0
Singapore	5,749	49,253	55,001	36.1	54.2	50.9	13.0	87.0	100.0
Thailand	571	9,032	9,603	-0.4	12.0	9.7	-0.8	100.8	100.0
Vietnam	1,360	6,602	7,962	6.3	7.9	7.6	15.1	84.9	100.0
Total	17,832	88,330	106,161	100.0	100.0	100.0	18.3	81.7	100.0
ASEAN-5[a]	15,780	78,602	94,382	90.2	89.6	89.7	18.4	81.6	100.0
BCLMV[a]	2,052	9,728	11,779	9.8	10.4	10.3	17.4	82.6	100.0

Source: ASEAN Foreign Direct Investment Statistics Database.

Notes: Details may not add up to totals due to rounding errors.

[a] ASEAN-5 consists of Indonesia, Malaysia, the Philippines, Singapore and Thailand; BCLMV comprises Brunei Darussalam, Cambodia, Lao PDR, Myanmar and Vietnam.

[b] Data for 2012 are preliminary figures; no data available for Brunei Darussalam. Myanmar's and Lao PDR's data on "by source country" are not yet available, intra-/extra-ASEAN breakdowns shown are estimated by the ASEAN Secretariat.

The FDI is on a net basis, and computed as follows: Net FDI = Equity + Net Inter-company Loans + Reinvested Earnings. The net basis concept implies that the following should be deducted from the FDI gross flows: (1) reverse investment (made by a foreign affiliate in a host country to its parent company/direct investor); (2) loans given by a foreign affiliate to its parent company; and (3) repayments of intra-company loan (paid by a foreign affiliate to its parent company). As such, FDI net inflows can be negative.

Table 17.3 FTA status, ASEAN by country, as of July 2013

Country	Proposed	Under negotiation		Signed but not yet in effect	Signed and in effect	Total
		Framework Agreement signed	Negotiations launched			
Brunei Darussalam	6	2	2	0	8	18
Cambodia	4	0	2	0	6	12
Indonesia	6	1	6	2	7	22
Lao PDR	4	0	2	0	8	14
Malaysia	7	1	6	1	12	27
Myanmar	4	1	2	0	6	13
Philippines	7	0	2	0	7	16
Singapore	6	1	10	2	19	38
Thailand	8	3	6	0	12	29
Vietnam	4	1	6	0	8	19

Source: ARIC FTA Database, ADB.
Notes:
Proposed: parties consider a free trade agreement (FTA), with the governments or relevant ministries issuing a joint statement on its desirability or establishment of a joint study group/joint task force for the conduct of feasibility studies.
Framework Agreement signed: the parties initially negotiate the contents of a framework agreement (FA), which serves as a framework for future negotiations.
Negotiations launched: the parties, through the relevant ministries, declare the official launch of negotiations or set the date for such, or start the first round of negotiations.
Signed but not yet in effect: parties sign the agreement after negotiations have been completed. However, the agreement has yet to be implemented.
Signed and in effect: provisions of FTA come into force, after legislative or executive ratification.

supported export expansion with few serious trade barriers, apart from some agricultural and labor-intensive manufactured products. Meanwhile there was a series of significant domestic liberalizations in the 1980s and 1990s, most particularly in the three communist states, but also in Indonesia and the Philippines.

Not unrelated to these developments has been the proliferation of various forms of FTAs. Table 17.3 lists each ASEAN country's participation in FTAs as of July 2013: 98 FTAs have been signed or are under implementation, 54 are under negotiation, and 56 are proposed. These numbers include a variety of agreements, ranging from the comprehensive to the so-called "trade-lite", and thus they are not strictly comparable. Singapore has been the major ASEAN adopter of FTAs, with 21 concluded, and 17 under negotiation or proposed. It accounts for 20 percent of the regional FTAs under implementation.

Three general observations need to be made about these agreements. First, they vary considerably in their scope, depth and coverage. The larger economic powers, notably Japan and the USA, are able to extract specific requirements, for example, the exclusion of sensitive agricultural products in the case of the former, and intellectual property rights in the latter. Where ASEAN rules apply, the agreements are more likely to be multilateralized and have less restrictive rules of origin (ROOs). Some of the agreements are very minor, and have little functional significance. Second, there is considerable variation in the capacity of the ASEAN governments to implement these agreements. Singapore, for example, has high-quality analytical and negotiating capacity, while Laos has practically none of these resources at its disposal and it struggled for years just to satisfy the requirements for WTO membership. FTAs involving the transition countries are a clear distraction from the more important task of general trade and other reforms.

Third, there is the issue of whether these and the broader regional initiatives discussed in the following section will collapse into a plurilateral, pan-Asian agreement. For instance, it is argued that the "ASEAN Plus Six" (APS) Regional Comprehensive Economic Partnership (RCEP) could pave the way for consolidating many ASEAN+1 FTAs under a single regional agreement. However, there are few details of how these FTAs could be folded into a much broader multilateral agreement. It is also perplexing that advocates of this approach often argue that bilateral agreements are able to achieve much deeper integration because only two parties are involved, but then inexplicably expect the same results from a consolidated agreement involving many more parties.

Even if the "consolidation approach" may be able to address the proliferation of often overlapping FTAs, and make the best of the current mess, other options could achieve the same outcome without creating yet another FTA. Two such alternatives include the multilateralization of preferential accords, and the dilution of ROOs. The original members of ASEAN have employed the multilateralization approach with success, and today close to 90 percent of the preferences of their FTAs are available to non-members on an MFN basis. This is a model of how so-called "open regionalism" can work. As a result, overall tariffs have fallen sharply on trade with all countries, because the FTA liberalization program has been more ambitious and rapid than the WTO alone could have delivered. Consequently, utilization rates of remaining preferences have also fallen to negligible levels. Joining a new East Asian FTA would be a step backwards, as it would bring this process of multilateralizing preferences to a halt (Hill and Menon, 2008).

If members of the FTA are not yet ready to give up reciprocal preferences, then liberalizing ROOs could be an interim step in preparing the groundwork for that process. This could be done by harmonization, and expanding the so-called "rules of cumulation" (i.e. the number of countries whose value added qualifies). If rules of cumulation are sufficiently expanded and then harmonized across different agreements, the outcome might no longer require formal multilateralization of tariff accords. Here again, a new and larger FTA is not required, and it would in fact be a less desirable option.

Both these alternatives could be applied to intra- and extra-regional FTAs. The consolidation approach, on the other hand, is only designed for intra-regional FTAs. But most FTAs are extra-regional. For instance, a consolidated agreement like RCEP could potentially neutralize a third of all FTAs. But these figures in turn prompt the question why most FTAs are extra-regional to begin with. A common explanation is that they are designed to restore market access in traditional trading partners that may have joined a regional FTA (see Menon, 2007). If this is true, then RCEP may itself spark a new wave of extra-regional FTAs. With more countries outside the region than inside, an East Asian FTA could actually be counterproductive, leading perversely to an increase in the total number of FTAs. "Consolidation" therefore does not appear to provide a solution, and may actually contribute to the problem, by adding another strand to the "noodle bowl" of FTAs or, worse still, inducing a new wave of extra-regional FTAs.

From ASEAN to the ASEAN Economic Community, Regional Comprehensive Economic Partnership and beyond?

ASEAN has developed an elaborate set of extra-regional agreements, ranging from general statements about the desirability of closer economic relations through to what on paper appear to be firm commitments to economic integration (see for example Plummer and Chia, 2009). Until around 2000, the former prevailed, and involved little more than official dialogues and sporadic business cooperation programs. However, in recent years, ASEAN has made significant commercial policy commitments, initially in the form of "ASEAN Plus Three" (APT), with the three being China, Japan and South Korea, and more recently "ASEAN Plus Six" (APS), which is the APT group together with Australia, New Zealand and India, and the expanded East Asia Summit (EAS) or "ASEAN Plus Eight", bringing in Russia and the USA. While ASEAN's ASEAN Economic Community (AEC) and APS's RCEP focus on economic integration, the EAS has morphed into a politico-security forum. In addition, there are various formal agreements with other economic communities, such as the AFTA–CER, involving ASEAN and Australia–New Zealand, and ASEAN Plus One, where ASEAN may negotiate with a particular country (or bloc) on a specific issue.

ASEAN's regional economic integration efforts are geared towards creating an AEC. The ASEAN leaders had originally intended to create the AEC by 2020, but in early 2007 they advanced the deadline to 2015. The AEC envisions ASEAN as a competitive economic region with a single market and production base. At the 13th ASEAN Summit held in Singapore on 20 November 2007, ASEAN leaders adopted the ASEAN Economic Blueprint – containing 17 "core elements" and 176 priority actions – to serve as a guide for establishing the AEC. Given the diversity within ASEAN, and sensitivities regarding different issues and sectors, it was agreed that liberalization of goods, capital and (skilled) labor flows proceed at different speeds according to member countries' readiness. Thus, despite the blueprint and the various priority actions and schedules, it remains to be seen to what extent concrete liberalization initiatives will be implemented, or whether the blueprint will remain essentially a vision statement.

ASEAN's own assessment records its progress towards the AEC at about 70 percent as of 2013. A lot of this relates to tariff liberalization and other "low hanging fruit" reforms. ASEAN has removed customs duties on most intra-ASEAN trade but, as noted earlier, this has been achieved mainly through AFTA. Assessments of progress towards realizing an AEC involve significant amounts of double counting, whereby reforms undertaken under different initiatives and before the AEC proposal was launched are still being added to the tally. Despite the double counting, there have been other positive developments.

ASEAN member-states have formally adopted a Customs Code of Conduct, the national and regional "Single Window" systems, the ASEAN Harmonized Tariff Nomenclatures, and the WTO's mode of customs valuation. They have concluded "framework" agreements on liberalization of trade in services, investment, goods in transit, multi-modal and inter-state transport, and information and communications technology. They have agreed on mutual recognition agreements (MRAs) or their equivalent for three types of goods and seven professions, and have also concluded a "framework" agreement on MRAs.[5] Although most of these agreements are shot through with loopholes under the general cover of "flexibility", and some of them have not been ratified by all ASEAN states, they do manifest ASEAN's recognition of the desirability of regional economic integration and each member-state's commitment to it (Severino and Menon, 2013). Although it is highly unlikely that ASEAN will meet its self-imposed deadline of 2015, it would have come a long way towards increasing integration.

As recent disputes over property rights in the South China Sea have shown,[6] progress on the economic front cannot be divorced from geo-political challenges facing ASEAN as a group. Indeed, these events have reminded us that ASEAN was born as, and in many ways designed to be, a politico-security pact, and that the economic agenda is a more recent experiment. Given the interdependence between economics and geo-politics, however, the institution will have to weather the challenges that the latter poses on its cohesion if it is to progress on the former.

The ASEAN Framework on the RCEP was formally endorsed at the 19th ASEAN Summit held in November 2011, and negotiations kicked off on 20 November 2012, on the sidelines of the East Asia Summit in Phnom Penh, Cambodia. Although membership in the RCEP is based on open accession, it will start with the ten ASEAN countries and the "Plus Six", all of whom have bilateral FTAs with ASEAN. In recognition of each member country's development needs, the RCEP's Negotiating Principles provide for special and differential treatment, with additional flexibility for the least-developed ASEAN countries. Although negotiations are meant to be completed by 2015, the difficulties noted earlier in folding multiple, disparate agreements into a single regional agreement suggests that this target is an ambitious one. There is also a real risk of a "race to the bottom", in which the lowest common denominator prevails in order to secure consensus. If this happens, then the RCEP will contribute little to reform or the regional trade landscape, merely adding to the existing clutter.

The Trans-Pacific Partnership (TPP) involves some but not all ASEAN members, namely Brunei, Malaysia, Singapore and Vietnam.[7] Brunei and Singapore were part of the original "P4" agreement (with Chile and New Zealand) which preceded the TPP, but why Malaysia and Vietnam have joined while the other six ASEAN countries have not, suggests that motivations are varied, and extend beyond economics into the geo-political sphere. The TPP agenda is wide-ranging and demanding, much more so than most other high quality FTAs, let alone Doha's requirements. It is unclear if many TPP members, especially the developing country ones, will be able to comply with these stringent requirements. The TPP has already missed three deadlines – the latest one being October 2013. There is also concern that the TPP is degenerating into a series of bilateral deals, with a USA–Japan agreement at its core. Given sensitivities across members on different issues, a variety of exemptions are anticipated, and can only be accommodated through bilateral arrangements (see Menon, 2014). Another challenge involves its current limited membership, which excludes China and Korea. A significant increase in Asian membership is needed before it can be a serious alternative to the RCEP. But as with the RCEP, it is too early to tell what form the TPP will take.

ASEAN also participates in a range of broader regional and multilateral initiatives. These include APEC and WTO-based negotiations (e.g. the current Doha Round). Its official position is that it regards these processes as consistent with ASEAN objectives and therefore supports them. However, in practice, ASEAN does not appear to have played an effective catalytic role in recent years. One ASEAN country, Indonesia, is a member of the G20, which appears to be morphing into the principal global forum for addressing key development issues, such as measures to prevent a recurrence of financial crises and to address climate change. It is too early to judge whether Indonesia attempts to represent ASEAN interests at these meetings. Institutionally, ASEAN also has observer status at the G20. In sum, ASEAN is moving cautiously and uncertainly towards being at the center of a potentially large, yet still undefined, economic grouping.

Does East Asia have a workable financial safety net?[8]

In this section, we examine progress in developing a financial safety net for the region in the event of a crisis. When the Asian financial crisis hit, the ASEAN Swap Arrangement (ASA) proved sorely inadequate in providing the liquidity needed by its members, given its small size.[9] There was little choice but to resort to assistance from the International Monetary Fund (IMF). Following disenchantment with the way in which the IMF dealt with the AFC, the region has been working on bolstering its own financial safety net. The first step toward establishing such a scheme came soon after, in May 2000, with the launch of the Chiang Mai Initiative (CMI), as part of the APT process. The CMI resources grew from just $1 billion to $84 billion to 2008, the year in which the global financial crisis erupted.

If the AFC lit the fuse for the need to transform the ASA into the CMI, then the GFC highlighted the continued shortcomings of that transformation. Despite the CMI having grown rapidly in size, it was still too small, and the absence of rapid-response mechanisms forced affected countries to turn to bilateral swaps with the USA, China, Japan and regional agencies. What followed was a radical transformation of the CMI. First, it was multilateralized, so that the CMIM would be a self-managed reserve pooling arrangement, governed by a single contract, reducing costly and wasteful duplication. Second, the size of the pool was increased to $120 billion in May 2009. A decision was also taken to establish an ancillary institution in the form of an independent regional surveillance unit, the ASEAN+3 Macroeconomic Research Office (AMRO), which came into being in May 2011.

Since the GFC, continuing macroeconomic problems in the Eurozone and persistent risks of further deterioration have highlighted the need to strengthen the CMIM's capacity to act as a regional financial safety net (Azis, 2012). To address this need, the 15th Meeting of APT Finance Ministers in May 2012, agreed to (i) double the total size of the CMIM to $240 billion; (ii) increase the IMF de-linked portion to 30 percent in 2012, with a view to increasing it to 40 percent in 2014, subject to review should conditions warrant; and (c) introduce a crisis prevention facility.

These are impressive developments over a relatively short period of time. However, the critical question is whether these reforms are sufficient to provide the region with a working option in the event of a crisis. Is it likely that the CMIM will be called upon when the next crisis strikes? Unfortunately, for a number of reasons the CMIM still appears unusable, either as a co-financing facility in tandem with the IMF or as a stand-alone alternative. Several major reforms are required for it to be a viable financial support mechanism.

First, since it is a reserve-pooling arrangement, there is actually no fund but a series of promises. This may not be a problem per se, but it becomes one when there are no rapid response procedures to handle a fast-developing financial emergency. Unless these procedures are stream-lined, the CMIM is unlikely to be called upon even as a co-financing facility. If the CMIM is to be a real substitute for the IMF and serve its role as a true regional alternative, then the size of the fund, or the portion de-linked from an IMF program, also needs to be increased substantially.[10] Unlike the IMF, the CMIM does not have an *exceptional access* clause, that is, one that allows a country to borrow amounts above their quota in exceptional circumstances (Menon and Ng, 2013). But if there is a full-blown systemic crisis in East Asia that spreads across several members, then this clause will not be of much value either. This is another reason why membership would also need to increase beyond APT, not just to bolster the size of the fund, but also to diversify it. Obvious candidates for an initial expansion would include Australia, India and New Zealand, the other three that make up the APS grouping.

Without these changes, APT is unlikely to turn to the CMIM either as a co-financier or as a substitute for the IMF, which explains why countries continue to take the high-cost mercantilist route of self-insurance through excessive holdings of foreign exchange reserves, and why they continue to pursue bilateral swap arrangements (BSAs) separately, often with other CMIM members. Japan is also looking to strengthen bilateral relations with ASEAN directly, matching China in bypassing the APT process, and is expected to revive bilateral currency swap agreements with Malaysia, Singapore and Thailand and to strengthen existing bilateral arrangements with Indonesia and the Philippines. Some see this as early warning signs of an unraveling of the CMIM, as a result of rising tensions involving territorial disputes, as well as competition amongst the "Plus Three" to gain influence in Southeast Asia.[11] If this process continues or spreads, we could see a return of the "noodle bowl" of bilateral swap agreements that the CMIM's single agreement was designed to rectify. In fact, BSAs are quickly becoming the main instrument in Asia's financial safety net, although they remain somewhat ad hoc. But shifting national reserves to a regional fund that is unlikely to be used could actually be counterproductive, as it weakens a country's first line of defense in the event of a financial crisis.

If AMRO could gain sufficient credibility, then the CMIM's small size and limited membership would be less binding constraints. After all, even the IMF relied upon other partners to fund the bailouts in Asia in 1997/98 and in Europe during and after the GFC. In both of these scenarios, the IMF led the rescue and set the terms, and this is what matters. AMRO needs to be able to fulfill a similar role. Although APT may appear to have a co-financing facility with the IMF in the CMIM, it is not a usable one. If it wants its own regional safety net, then it has far to go. Exactly how far is still unclear, but hopefully it can be made workable before, rather than because of, the next crisis.

Summing up

ASEAN has significant achievements to its credit. It is a durable and effective functioning entity, more so than any other regional organization in the developing world. For a region characterized by great diversity and a history of conflict, and notwithstanding more recent but occasional border skirmishes, Southeast Asia has been comparatively peaceful since the mid-1980s, as the four mainland states progressively re-entered the regional and international mainstream. ASEAN in aggregate has been a region of rapid economic development and rising living standards. One can debate the direction of causality between this outcome and the establishment of the association, but undeniably the determination of the region's leaders to forge more cordial relations has facilitated economic development.

ASEAN has also been diplomatically skillful in playing "balance of power" politics (Acharya, 2009). There is no clear economic and political leadership in East Asia, where the economic giants of the past and the future – Japan and China respectively – are engaged in a battle of constant diplomatic rivalry. Courted by both powers, ASEAN has thus been able to advance its own interests considerably, and become either the arbiter or driver of almost every major initiative on regional commercial and security architecture.

Yet, on the other side of the ledger, ASEAN has not progressed very far in terms of becoming a formal economic entity. This proposition can be illustrated with reference to the standard theory of customs unions (Table 17.4). In over four decades, it has not progressed beyond the first phase, of loosely exchanging trade preferences, while maintaining separate, and still quite variable, trade regimes. As noted, it is very unlikely to progress to the next stage of a customs union with common external tariffs. Deeper integration, affecting factor markets and a common macroeconomic policy regime as in the EU, is even further off.

Table 17.4 Indicators of economic integration

Indicator	ASEAN	EU	NAFTA	CER	Mercosur
Free trade in goods	part	yes	yes	yes	part
Free trade in services	part	yes	part	yes	part
Capital mobility (FDI)	part	yes	part	yes	part
Labor mobility	no	yes	no	yes	no
Competition law converging	no	yes	no	yes	no
Monetary union	no	yes	no	no	no
Unified fiscal policy	no	part	no	no	no

Source: Authors' interpretation.

Moreover, ASEAN runs the risk of being consigned to the status of a diplomatic talk-shop. In the words of a former secretary general, "regional economic integration seems to have become stuck in framework agreements, work programmes and master plans" (Severino, 2006, p. 247). ASEAN has a long history of issuing declarations, action plans and charters, yet with limited capacity – and arguably, in some cases limited intention – for implementation. It has generally prevaricated on whether to become a formal customs union. It has developed a plan for labor market integration, while some of the largest labor movements in the world (relative to the size of the recipient economy) have occurred outside this framework. Even after one of the deepest economic crises in the region's history, ASEAN has been unable to develop a set of emergency support mechanisms, and it remains unclear whether the formally constructed regional financial safety nets will ever be workable. At its root, the "ASEAN Way" is an institutionalized mechanism that renders very unlikely the prospect of a fundamental change in direction. The most likely outcome is that member countries' policy regimes will converge over time, to the point where preferential arrangements become redundant. As the region's commercial hub, Singapore sets the standard in this respect, and one to which the lower-income members of ASEAN might aspire.

It is therefore not surprising that ASEAN's greatest economic achievement has been more to do with what AFTA has indirectly induced rather than what has been mandated. Recognizing that most of the region's trade is extra-regional, in order to minimize the potential costs of trade diversion the original ASEAN members have been reducing their external tariffs in conjunction with falling barriers to intra-ASEAN trade. The ASEAN-6 countries have also undertaken several waves of multilateralizing preferences, where they have voluntarily offered their AFTA concessions to non-members on a non-discriminatory basis. When the preferences are fully multilateralized, the margins of preference are zero, as is the potential for trade diversion. This was the case for more than two-thirds of the tariff lines for the ASEAN-6 countries through to 2002, and the proportion has increased since then: in 2008, the trade-weighted preference margin for intra-ASEAN trade was a mere 2.3 percent (WTO, 2011). Furthermore, because preferential tariff reduction schedules have been ambitious and rapid, AFTA has accelerated the pace of multilateral trade liberalization in the ASEAN-6 countries. As a result, 72.9 percent of trade traveled at a zero MFN rate in 2008 (WTO, 2011). Instead of jeopardizing multilateralism, it has hastened the speed at which these countries have moved towards their goal of free and open trade.

Acknowledgments

This chapter draws heavily on, and updates, the authors' ongoing research on ASEAN economic integration, in particular Hill and Menon (2012a, 2012b). We are most grateful to Anna Cassandra Melendez for excellent research assistance and the participants at the March 2013 Bangkok conference for helpful comments.

Notes

1 For example, for a commentary on the ineffectiveness of the major South American initiative, known as Mercosur, see "Mercosur RIP?", *Economist*, July 14, 2012.
2 The literature on ASEAN and its development is voluminous. In addition to Hill and Menon (2012a), see Chia (2011), and the references cited in both these papers.
3 Indonesia, Malaysia, the Philippines, Singapore, and Thailand.
4 For instance, Soesastro (1999, p. 158–9) observed: "The public has been largely disappointed with ASEAN. Its perception is that of a helpless ASEAN, an ASEAN that cannot move decisively, an ASEAN that is trapped under its organizational and bureaucratic weight, and an ASEAN that fails to respond to real, current problems and challenges."

5 MRAs covering traded goods would avoid duplication in the testing of products at both the exporting and importing ends, while those pertaining to services usually provide for the mutual recognition of professional credentials.

6 See, for instance, "Getting in the Way", *Economist*, 17–23 May 2014.

7 Other current members are Australia, Canada, Chile, Japan, Mexico, New Zealand, Peru and the USA. Like RCEP, it has an open access clause for membership.

8 This section summarizes the key arguments outlined in Hill and Menon (2012b). See the original article for a detailed discussion of the various institutional arrangements, as well as the reforms required to make the CMIM a viable proposition.

9 See Hill and Menon (2012b) for details, including a more comprehensive discussion of the evolution of the arrangements.

10 During the AFC, Thailand received over $17 billion in emergency liquidity from an IMF-led consortium. Yet, Thailand (and the four other original ASEAN members) can access only a fraction of this amount, about $7 billion in 2012 US dollars, from the CMIM without an IMF program. Indonesia received almost six times ($40 billion) the amount of its de-linked portion of the CMIM, or an even greater multiple if converted into today's dollars. Korea was the other crisis-hit country that availed of an IMF-led program and bilateral support that totaled $57 billion, yet today its full quota with the CMIM is about $38 billion (see Hill and Menon 2012b, table 2, for details).

11 See, for instance, Park (2013) and "Japan, ASEAN to launch new Framework for Financial Cooperation in May", *Kyodo News*, 25 April 2013. http://english.kyodonews.jp/news/2013/04/221835.html

References

Acharya, A. (2009), *Whose Ideas Matter? Agency and Power in Asian Regionalism*, Cornell University Press, Ithaca, NY.

Athukorala, P.C. (2011), "Production Networks and Trade Patterns in East Asia. Regionalization or Globalization?", *Asian Economic Papers* 10(1), 65–95.

Azis, Iwan (2012), "Asian Regional Financial Safety Nets? Don't Hold your Breath", *Public Policy Review 8.* Policy Research Institute, Ministry of Finance, Japan, pp. 357–76.

Bhagwati, J. (2008), *Termites in the System: How Preferential Agreements Undermine Free Trade*, Oxford University Press, Oxford.

Chia Siow Yue (2011), "Association of Southeast Asian Nations Economic Integration: Developments and Challenges", *Asian Economic Policy Review* 6(1), 43–63.

Hill, H. and J. Menon (2008), "Back to Basics on Trade", *Far Eastern Economic Review*, June, 44–7.

Hill, H. and J. Menon (2012a), "ASEAN Economic Integration: Driven by Markets, Bureaucrats, or Both?", in M.E. Kreinin and M.G. Plummer (eds), *The Oxford Handbook of International Commercial Policy*, Oxford University Press, Oxford, pp. 357–86.

Hill, H. and J. Menon (2012b), "Financial Safety Nets in Asia: Genesis, Evolution, Adequacy, and Way Forward", ADBI Working Paper 395, Asian Development Bank Institute, Tokyo. Available: http://www.adbi.org/workingpaper/2012/11/12/5330.financial.safety.nets.asia/

Hill, H. and J. Jongwanich (2014), "Emerging East Asian Economies as Foreign Investors: An Analytical Survey", *Singapore Economic Review*, 59(3).

Imada, P. and S. Naya (eds) (1992), *AFTA: The Way Ahead*, Institute of Southeast Asian Studies, Singapore.

Lloyd, P. (2005), "What is a Single Market? An Application to the Case of ASEAN", *ASEAN Economic Bulletin* 22(3), 251–65.

Menon, J. (2007), "Bilateral Trade Agreements", *Asian-Pacific Economic Literature* 21(2), 29–47.

Menon, J. (2009), "Dealing with the Proliferation of Bilateral Free Trade Agreements", *World Economy* 32 (10), 1381–407.

Menon, J. (2014), "Multilateralization of Preferences versus Reciprocity when FTAs are Underutilized", *World Economy*, 37(1), October, 1348–66.

Menon, J. and T.H. Ng (2013), "Impact of Eurozone Financial Shocks on Southeast Asian Economies", *Journal of Southeast Asian Economies* 30(2), 179–200.

Ministry of International Trade and Industry (MITI) (2013), "AFTA", Kuala Lumpur: MITI. Available at: http://www.miti.gov.my/cms/content.jsp?id=com.tms.cms.section.Section_8de83760–7f000010–72f772f7-f5047602

Myint, H. (1972), *Southeast Asia's Economy: Development Policies in the 1970s*, Penguin, Harmondsworth.

Park, Jinsoo, (2013), "Political Rivals and Regional Leaders: Dual Identities and Sino-Japanese relations in East Asian Cooperation", *Chinese Journal of International Politics* 6(1), 85–107.

Plummer, M. and S.Y. Chia (eds) (2009), *Realizing the ASEAN Economic Community: A Comprehensive Assessment*, Institute of Southeast Asian Studies, Singapore.

Rajan, R. and R. Sen (2002), "Liberalization of Financial Services in Southeast Asia under the ASEAN Framework Agreement on Services", CIES Discussion Paper, University of Adelaide.

Severino, R. (2006), *Southeast Asia in Search of an ASEAN Community*, Singapore: Institute of Southeast Asian Studies.

Severino, R. and J. Menon (2013), "The ASEAN Community: An Overview", in S. Basu, J. Menon, R. Severino, and O. Shresta (eds), *The ASEAN Economic Community: A Work in Progress*, ADB and ISEAS, Singapore.

Soesastro, H. (1999), "ASEAN during the Crisis", in H.W. Arndt and H. Hill (eds), *Southeast Asia's Economic Crisis: Origins, Lessons and the Way Forward*, Institute of Southeast Asian Studies, Singapore, pp. 158–69.

Soesastro, H. (2006), "Regional Integration in East Asia: Achievements and Future Prospects", *Asian Economic Policy Review* 1(2), 215–34.

United Nations Department of Economics and Social Affairs (UNDESA) (1974), "Economic Cooperation among Member Countries of the Association of Southeast Asian Nations", *Journal of Development Planning*, No. 7, New York, United Nations.

World Trade Organization (WTO) (2011), *World Trade Report 2011*, WTO, Geneva.

18

The global financial crisis and macroeconomic policy in Southeast Asia

Bhanupong Nidhiprabha

THAMMASAT UNIVERSITY

Introduction

The remarkable record of economic growth achieved by Singapore, Malaysia, Thailand, and Indonesia in the 1980s and early 1990s earned these countries the title of "miracle" economies in the famous World Bank study *The East Asian Miracle* (1993). This and other efforts to account for their success identified macroeconomic stability as a key feature promoting trade, investment growth, and relatively efficient resource allocation. In these four countries, stable nominal exchange rates relative to the US dollar – a key signal to investors, both domestic and foreign – were supported by domestic fiscal and monetary policies that eschewed large public sector deficits and inflation taxes, avoided excessive private sector credit creation relative to GDP growth, and maintained a flexible approach to external shocks that has been praised as "pragmatic orthodoxy" (Corden 1996).

Sadly, the "miracle" did not last for long. The relaxation of controls on international capital flows – especially those of highly liquid portfolio investment and short-term debt – in Thailand, Indonesia, and Malaysia (Singapore's capital account had always been open) diminished the power of monetary policy as a tool to counter inflationary pressures. At the same time, rapidly rising domestic demand (driven by "miracle" rates of income growth) began to push up prices of non-tradables like land, creating debt-financed asset price bubbles, and to raise real wages, reducing the competitiveness of labor-intensive manufactures. These were the drivers of real exchange rate appreciations in the mid-1990s. In the absence of adequate monetary or fiscal policy responses current account deficits widened, setting up an ultimately unsustainable tension between the maintenance of fixed exchange rates and the preservation of international reserves.

The Asian financial crisis of 1997 was a catastrophically large and sudden international response to these imbalances. It wiped out several years of gains from "miracle" growth; it also induced some major macroeconomic policy changes. Most visible among these were moves from fixed to floating (or at least, less tightly managed) exchange rates, and decisions at country level to hoard foreign reserves as insurance against any future crisis. Less obviously, in most countries there was continued progress on microeconomic reform, including tariff and commercial policy liberalization, which further increased the region's exposure to global trade.[1] Most countries also made improvements in financial system governance, for example in prudential regulations, to reduce systemic risk.

At the same time the world economy itself was also undergoing a major structural shift, notably driven by China's rise to prominence as a participant in global trade and investment and in Asian regional production networks. By the 2000s, the fortunes of Southeast Asia's large economies were tied more tightly than ever before to those of the global market.

However, the global market had also become frighteningly unstable. The September 2008 collapse of the US financial firm Lehman Brothers, which with over $600 billion in debt became the largest bankruptcy in US history, was the first domino to fall in a sequence that precipitated global recession – the scale and duration of which had not been seen since the 1930s. This has become known as the global financial crisis, or GFC.

In 2009, GFC reduced demand for exports from Southeast Asian countries, where exports are a major growth driver. Recession in the developed countries led to a contraction in output from Asian countries through export shortfalls. Expansionary and accommodative monetary policy in response to recession in the US and other industrialized economies, through low interest rates and liquidity injections, caused massive capital inflows to Southeast Asia. Although these inflows led to booming stock markets and sustained investment and consumption in some countries, regional currencies also appreciated substantially and this exacerbated the export downturn. Although their growth paths tended to converge over time, Southeast Asian countries experienced dissimilar impacts of the GFC. To see why some countries performed better than others during the crisis, in this chapter we examine factors affecting vulnerability and resilience to external shocks. Factors such as the structure of aggregate demand and the role of macroeconomic policy response must have contributed to the depth and duration of regional downturns after the global economic slowdown.

The next section of this chapter discusses the impact of the GFC on exports and output, followed by an examination of the impacts on the financial sector. Then there is an analysis of business synchronization in Southeast Asian economies before a review of macroeconomic policy responses in terms of fiscal and monetary policy. Exchange rate policy is also examined in light of rapid capital movement. The final section provides concluding remarks.

Impact of the global financial crisis on growth and current accounts

Southeast Asian economies have become integrated with the global economy through trade liberalization and capital account opening. The GFC's impact was delivered through monetary and trade channels. Domestic interest rates and capital flows were directly affected, especially in those countries whose capital markets are most closely connected to world financial centers. The GFC directly impacted the real sector through falling export demand from high-income countries under stress. The 2008 GFC differed from the 1997 Asian financial crisis (AFC), insofar as in 2009, Southeast Asian financial institutions were only mildly affected. In contrast to the 1997 shock, the GFC's impact was more pronounced in the real sector than in the financial sector.

Malaysia and Singapore, the two wealthiest and most open economies in the region, experienced considerable growth fluctuations during the GFC. In 2001, during a mild recession in the USA, their output growth had declined by more than the average of Southeast Asian economies. In 2009, when the GFC-induced recession was at its deepest, output in Malaysia and Singapore also contracted by more than other countries in the region. Yet both countries showed resilience: just one year after the crisis they each underwent a spectacular rebound.

Southeast Asian economies are vulnerable to external shocks from global economic fluctuations. One reason behind differences in output growth is the underlying economic structure exposing each country to external shocks through differences in trade and capital flow linkages. Other than in 2009, Indonesia's growth rate was lower than average for the region. Since 2000, Myanmar's economy has expanded at a higher rate than the regional average, because of a low base income level, an increasingly open economy, and more reliance on market mechanisms.

Whether a country performed poorly or not during the GFC depended in part on the importance of exports in its GDP. Between 2000 and 2011, Singapore, the most open economy in the region, had an average share of exports to GDP of 210 percent. During these years, Myanmar's average share of export to GDP was less than 1 percent. Malaysia and Singapore's volatile output growth and the relatively stable growth of Myanmar's economy are extreme cases. Indonesia, the largest economy in the region, depends less on exports, which accounted for 31 percent of GDP during the 2000s. Indonesia, therefore, is not as vulnerable to export fluctuations as are countries with higher export dependency such as Cambodia (59 percent), Thailand (66 percent), or Malaysia (106 percent).

During the GFC in 2009, Vietnam and Cambodia, whose export dependency ratio was over 60 percent, experienced deep output contractions. Figure 18.1 demonstrates that Southeast Asian economic growth rates were synchronized with the boom and bust caused by global output fluctuations. An exceptionally high degree of globalization implies correspondingly high exposure of the economy to external shocks, and this gives a reason to examine the merits of an export-driven growth strategy. If Southeast Asian economies were to rely more on domestic demand-led

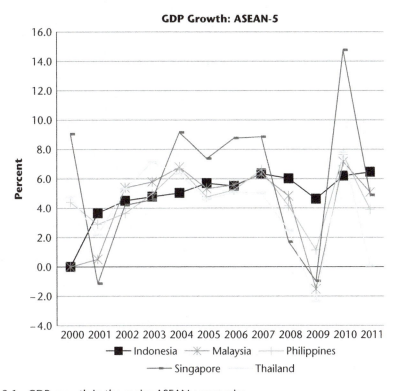

Figure 18.1 GDP growth in the major ASEAN economies
Source: ADB Statistical Data Base.

growth, could they still exploit economies of scale and the competitive environment of an outward-oriented development strategy? The answer is related to the availability of effective macroeconomic policy to lessen the magnitude of business cycles and shorten the length of recessions. After the global economic slowdowns in 2001 and 2009, Southeast Asian economies followed V-shaped recoveries.

World trade volume fluctuates more widely than world output growth. Rapid world economic expansion translates into an acceleration of export and output growth in export-led growth economies. Similarly, a decelerating world output growth results in poor export performance and much lower GDP growth rate in export-dependent countries.

This is what happened in 2001, 2009, and 2011, as seen in Figure 18.2. This figure compares the average export growth rate from 2000 to 2008 and then during the GFC. Synchronized output growth was caused by a similar degree of export exposure to the world market. No Southeast Asian economy was spared the impact of world recessions. But the strong rebound of exports from Southeast Asian economies after 2009 bodes well for the resilience and flexibility of the export sector in response to changing demand conditions.

After the AFC, the region's saving-investment gaps had expanded due to a widespread investment collapse. With wider saving-investment gaps, Southeast Asian economies in general experienced a current account surplus. The GFC, by contrast, reduced exports, thereby lowering the current account surplus in 2008. Enlarged current accounts in Indonesia, Thailand, the Philippines and Singapore were due to output contractions in 2009, which also curtailed import growth (Table 18.1).

A current account surplus need not mean a strong economy. A slow-growing economy would not require rapid growth in imports of capital goods, for example. If demand for imports is income-elastic, a current account surplus might reflect low growth and enlarging savings gaps.

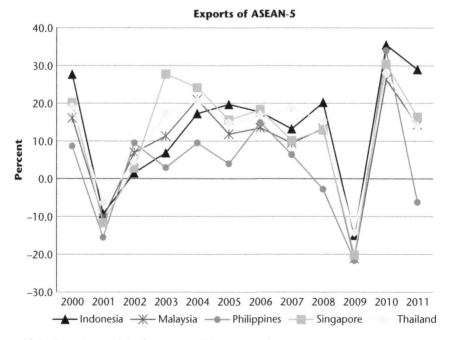

Figure 18.2 Export growth in the major ASEAN economies
Source: ADB Statistical Data Base.

Table 18.1 Post-GFC current account surplus in ASEAN-5 economies (percent of GDP)

	Indonesia	Malaysia	Philippines	Singapore	Thailand
2000–07	2.8	3.1	1.0	18.7	3.0
2008	0.0	5.1	2.1	14.7	0.8
2009	2.0	4.5	5.6	19.0	8.3
2010	0.7	3.4	4.5	21.8	4.1
2011	0.2	3.6	3.1	24.6	1.7

Source: ADB Statistical Data Base.

Table 18.2 Post-GFC current account deficit in CLMV economies (percent of GDP)

	Cambodia	Lao PDR	Myanmar	Vietnam
2002–07	−4.2	−1.4	3.6	−3.3
2008	−10.1	1.5	4.9	−11.9
2009	−8.9	−1.1	3.1	−6.8
2010	−8.0	0.5	3.3	−4.0

Source: ADB Statistical Data Base.

This is true of Thailand and the Philippines, where investment opportunities were relatively low in 2009 and 2010.

Although Lao PDR and Myanmar both experienced current account surpluses prior to the GFC, their surpluses declined in 2009 (Table 18.2). Vietnam and Cambodia have sustained current account deficits for many years. These deficits increased as the world economy slowed at the onset of the GFC in 2007. This widening of current account deficits could have several causes. First, exchange rate policies demand examination, to see if currency overvaluation prevented external adjustment. Second, another reason for a current account deficit is foreign direct investment. When the low-income CLMV countries (Cambodia, Lao PDR. Myanmar, and Vietnam) receive massive capital inflows in the form of FDI, it usually drives up imports of machinery and construction materials. In 2013, Laos experienced a trade deficit for the first time in decades after FDI rose by over 40 percent in 2011 and 2012. This large deficit also put pressure on the Lao currency (the kip) to depreciate, because the country had reached a critically low level of international reserves.

In 2013, a growth slowdown in China led to dismal export performance in the region, including Thailand. When the Thai economy decelerates, exports from Laos to Thailand are adversely affected (Laos' major export to Thailand is hydropower). This subregional economy has been connected by increasing trade intensity during years of local trade liberalization. For this reason, Lao exports are far more vulnerable than most other countries to a downturn in Chinese imports, as seen in Figure 18.3.

The impact of the GFC on ASEAN countries can be observed from Table 18.3. The export slump in 2009 differed sharply from the high export growth from 2000 to 2008. As noted, however, the sharp rebound of exports in 2010 and 2011 augurs well for the resilience of these economies. Imports were affected by the strong world income effects, despite strengthening ASEAN currencies.

Because of high levels of average propensity to consume in low-income countries, fiscal stimulus in such nations will have a stronger impact than in high-income countries such as Singapore or Brunei (Table 18.4).

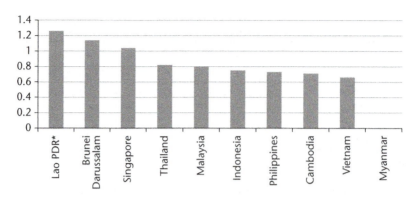

Figure 18.3 Estimated elasticity of exports with respect to China's imports
Source: Author's calculation.
Notes: Elasticity of Lao exports is based on Thailand's export growth. All estimated. Coefficients are statistically significant at 0.01 level of confidence.

Table 18.3 Impact of the GFC on ASEAN export growth, 2009–11

| | Export growth (percent per year) | | | |
	2000–08	2009	2010	2011
Brunei Darussalam	18.4	−32.0	30.2	33.1
Cambodia	13.9	−14.2	29.7	35.8
Indonesia	12.7	−15.0	35.4	29.0
Lao PDR	17.2	−3.6	65.8	6.1
Malaysia	10.3	−21.1	26.5	14.4
Myanmar	20.7	8.8	17.7	3.9
Philippines	4.2	−21.7	34.0	−6.7
Singapore	13.3	−20.2	30.6	16.5
Thailand	13.3	−13.7	28.7	16.0
Vietnam	21.0	−8.9	26.5	34.2

Source: ADB Statistical Data Base.

Table 18.4 Aggregate demand: structural differences and similarities

| | Percent to GDP (Average 2006–08) | | |
	Private consumption	Exports	Tax revenue
Brunei Darussalam	19.2	72.1	33.7
Singapore	38.8	210.4	12.9
Malaysia	44.7	105.7	14.5
Thailand	53.7	66.4	15
Indonesia	62.3	31.2	12.7
Vietnam	65.2	68.5	24.1
Philippines	74.1	42.6	13.6
Cambodia	79.5	59.1	9.8
Myanmar	82.6	0.2	3.9

Source: ADB Statistical Data Base.

Impacts of the global financial crisis on the financial sector

Evidence of the nexus between growth and financial development is abundant. Strong economic growth requires financial resources. In developing countries where direct finance through capital markets is not pervasive, bank credit remains a fundamental source of indirect finance for investors. ASEAN countries other than Singapore are bank-based economies, relying heavily on bank credit expansion for capital accumulation. The ratio of bank loans to GDP is seen as a measurement of progress in financial deepening. Figure 18.4 indicates that Laos and Cambodia are still at the early stages of economic development, by this measure. The bank credit to GDP ratio in both countries is much lower than in the other ASEAN-5 countries.

While the corresponding ratio in Malaysia and Thailand is above 100 percent of GDP, it is considerably lower in Singapore, where direct financing for investors is available in the stock and bond markets. The ratio demonstrates the economy's strength. In bank-based economies, the demand for bank credit increases during a boom, but banks are less willing to lend during a slump. In addition, low output growth generates low demand for bank loans. The impact of the GFC on bank loan activity in Southeast Asia can be observed from Figure 18.4. Except for Singapore, the rising trend of the bank loan–GDP ratio stagnated in ASEAN-5 countries, reflecting a slowdown in economic activity. Even in Vietnam, where bank credits expanded much faster than GDP growth, bank loan growth decelerated in 2008 before resuming a rising trend, which had continued since 2000.

In general, bank performance worldwide was adversely affected by the GFC where banks had a large loan exposure to the export sector. Since peaking during the AFC, non-performing loans (NPLs) in most Southeast Asian economies had declined steadily from 2005 to 2011. In 2009, the rate of decline slowed somewhat, but the NPL to total loan ratio remained well below 4 percent (Figure 18.5). In addition to relatively low exposure to the export sector, Southeast Asian commercial banks had invested little in collateral debt obligations backed by the US subprime loans. Southeast Asian banks remained healthy, therefore, and did not suffer greatly from the GFC.

Singaporean banks experienced the lowest level of non-performing loans due to strong growth in the real sector. Banks in Indonesia and Malaysia were able to reduce NPLs to 2 percent in 2011, because of the strength of both economies. The rate of return on bank equity in strong recovery economies increased considerably after a rapid recovery in line with bank credit expansion.

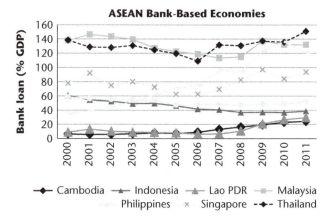

Figure 18.4 Bank loans to GDP, ASEAN economies
Source: ADB.

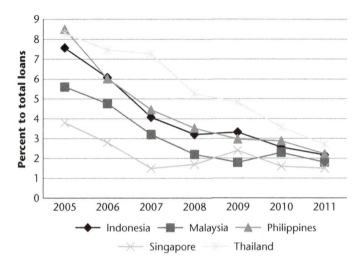

Figure 18.5   Banks' non-performing loans
Source: ADB.

Thailand had the highest rate of non-performing loans among the ASEAN-5 countries (Figure 18.5). Thai banks did not perform well in 2006 and 2007 due to uncertainties from political turmoil. Nevertheless, in general the declining trend of NPLs was unbroken during the GFC. Southeast Asian countries were well prepared as they had undergone extensive financial reforms following the 1997 crisis. In particular – and in contrast with the AFC – improved prudential rules and regulations were in place before the GFC exploded.

A lack of developed capital and bond markets in developing countries has been attributed to the after-effects of the AFC. Evidence of this "original sin" hypothesis can be seen in Figure 18.6. The percentage of stock market capitalization in Singapore and Malaysia is the highest among ASEAN countries. Firms in these economies have alternative means of financing investment projects, relying less on bank borrowing. Other countries in the region, with lower levels of development, exhibit lower values of stock market capitalization. Firms in these economies rely on bank loans more than firms in Singapore and Malaysia. In 2003, there was a rebound from the 2001 world "dotcom" recession. Share prices in Singapore, Malaysia, Indonesia, and Thailand increased in response to the economic upturn.

Note the peaks and troughs of market capitalization between 2000 and 2011. They followed a broadly similar pattern throughout the region. The 2008 GFC severely hit ASEAN stock markets. The cycle's depth was far more accentuated in countries with open capital markets. Likewise, the rebound was also more spectacular in the same countries, again because of their close ties to world capital markets.

In the 2000s, after Southeast Asian countries opened their capital accounts and began reducing tariffs among group members, business cycles became synchronized. Stock price movements in Singapore, Indonesia, Malaysia, the Philippines, and Thailand are increasingly interrelated, since the financial and real sectors of ASEAN-5 have become more firmly integrated. Money market interest rates are also moving more in line and stock market returns in these countries also move together.

Using the Singaporean rate of return on the stock market as a benchmark, in 2006, the correlation of stock returns in Thailand and the Philippine markets was below 0.5, indicating

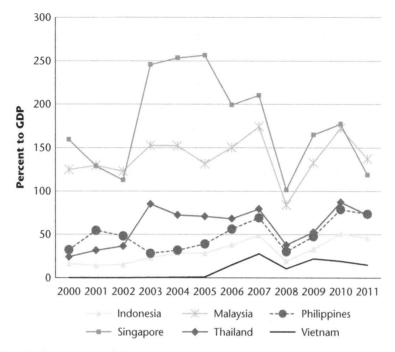

Figure 18.6 Stock market capitalization
Source: ADB.

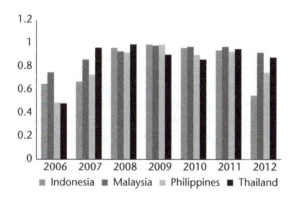

Figure 18.7 Stock market returns: correlation with Singapore
Source: ADB.

that domestic conditions still mattered greatly for investor sentiment (Figure 18.7). At the height of the GFC between 2008 and 2011, however, the correlation coefficients of stock returns among ASEAN-5 countries were above 0.9. Capital inflows from developed and troubled economies alike into Southeast Asia demonstrated how portfolio investors in the USA and Eurozone saw these economies as part of a buoyant region with strong growth potential.

Co-movements of stock prices in ASEAN-5 bode well for the impact of external factors on ASEAN-5 market sentiment. In 2012, correlation coefficients declined in Indonesia and the

Philippines. Domestic factors in those countries exerted influence on the market rate of return. As long as the wealth effect on consumption is weak, consequences of volatile stock markets on private consumption will be minor. A more serious risk is in the fluctuations of the exchange rate resulting from rapid capital inflows and outflows.

One danger of ASEAN capital market integration is that shocks can be transmitted easily in times of boom and bust. Consequently, a lesson from the volatile years since the GFC is that Southeast Asian economies must create instruments to cope with future shocks. If the region is to retain its reputation for "pragmatic orthodoxy", macroeconomic policy responses must be readily available to cope with external shocks caused by overexposure to globalization. This was especially important as the US economy began to resume growth following the GFC. As the US Federal Reserve began to "taper" its stimulus-oriented quantitative easing (QE) monetary policy in late 2013, there was a sharp outflow of portfolio investment from ASEAN. Regional currencies depreciated abruptly. This depreciation favorably affected the export sectors, but depressed regional stock markets.

Business cycle synchronization

Evidence that international capital flows contributed to business cycle synchronization was provided by Kim and Kim (2013). They find that capital movements caused boom–bust cycles in the region. An output boom is driven by increases in consumption and investment following capital market liberalization. If this hypothesis is true, then an output *contraction* might have been expected to occur after the US monetary authority ended its quantitative easing policy, because higher interest rates in the US market would cause massive capital outflow from emerging markets, including Southeast Asia. The beginning of tapering in 2013 did indeed lead to capital outflows; however, these were not large enough to induce recession in Southeast Asia. On the other hand, the simultaneous capital outflows provided additional support to the capital-market theory of business cycle synchronization. In another study Takeuchi (2011) used a dynamic general equilibrium model for eight East Asian developing economies and found that increases in business synchronization are largely attributable to the growing vertical fragmentation (i.e. regional integration) of production and network trade. Allegret and Essahbi (2011) demonstrated that increasing bilateral trade in East Asia resulted in increased long-run business synchronization, while short-run cycles are related to individual country shocks and convergence of macro policy responses to shocks. Moneta and Ruffer (2006) showed that business cycle synchronization in East Asia reflected strong export synchronization rather than consumption and investment dynamics, while oil prices and the yen–dollar exchange rates also play a role in synchronizing activity. Cortinhas (2007) shows a positive correlation between intra-industry trade and business synchronization in ASEAN nations.

From 2001 to 2012, bilateral trade intensity and growing network trade may explain the high correlation of output growth among Singapore and other ASEAN-5 countries (Figure 18.8). Reliance on an export-led growth strategy leads to co-movement of ASEAN-5 growth rates. Distance also determines the volume of trade between countries with common borders. Similar export patterns imply that a positive or a negative demand shock from the world market can affect output growth.

In the group of transition economies, CLMV growth rates are also closely related. The correlation coefficient of output growth rate between Vietnam and Myanmar was 0.94, 0.88 for Vietnam and Cambodia, and 0.84 for Cambodia and Myanmar. Thus, business cycle synchronization is also seen among CLMV countries. Along with Vietnam, Cambodia, Laos, and Myanmar share common borders with Thailand. In the longer run, the business cycle in CLMV must also synchronize with the ASEAN-5.

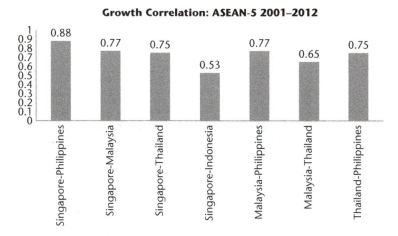

Figure 18.8 Output growth correlation: ASEAN–5
Source: ADB.

Principal component analysis is employed to reduce the dimensionality of GDP growth rates while retaining most of the variation for two groups: ASEAN-5 and CLMV countries. The first principal component with the largest variance accounts for much of the data variability. We define the first principal component as the principal growth components (PGC), as shown in Figure 18.9. The movement of the series represents regional business cycles.

Between 2000 and 2011, the correlation coefficient between the two PGC series was only 0.52. Nevertheless, the two growth cycles moved more closely together after 2007, when the region experienced the effects of the GFC. Southeast Asian economies became more integrated with the world economy through increasing volumes of intra-ASEAN regional trade. From 2000 to 2011, ASEAN-5 countries relied heavily on exports as engines of growth. Using the same principal component analysis to extract common export growth rates from the two regional groups, we find that the correlation coefficient from the principal components of ASEAN-5 export growth and the principal component for ASEAN-5 output growth is 0.94, indicating that export and growth cycles

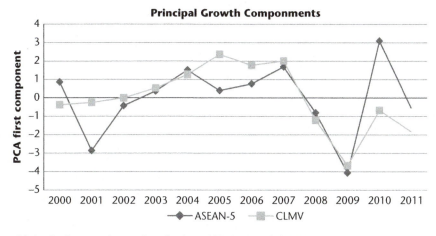

Figure 18.9 Business cycle synchronization: ASEAN–5 and CLMV
Source: Calculated principal components of growth rates.

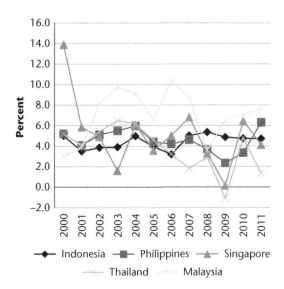

Figure 18.10 Consumption cycle in ASEAN–5
Source: ADB.

are closely related. Thus, boom–bust cycles are related to export cycles. A common commodity export demand shock would lead to a similar pattern of output fluctuations. Using the principal growth component measurements, ASEAN growth cycles are related to CLMV export cycles by a correlation coefficient of 0.6. The ASEAN-5 and CLMV are increasingly interconnected, so that booms and busts in ASEAN-5 can generate a spillover effect to neighboring country exports.

Growth in ASEAN-5 was driven by private consumption (Figure 18.10). The world recession in 2001 was accompanied by a decline in household consumption in Singapore, Malaysia, and Thailand. In 2009, the GFC also hit ASEAN-5 in the form of a reduction in consumer spending. Indonesia and the Philippines did not suffer much from the GFC, as consumption was not severely affected. From a policy point of view, maintaining private consumption seems to be the key to minimizing the impact of export demand shocks during world economic downturns.

The GFC's impact on private consumption was caused by output contraction. With increased uncertainty about jobs, incomes, and asset prices, consumers revised their expected incomes downward. When consumers postpone purchasing consumer durables, excess output capacity rises. Postponement of private investment was due to low capacity utilization of plants and equipment. Indonesia's private consumption did not contract, unlike other ASEAN countries. Since Indonesia has a larger share of consumption expenditure in GDP, Indonesia did not suffer as much as Thailand, Singapore, and the Philippines. And, as noted earlier, the share in the Indonesian economy of trade (and for that matter, foreign investment) is lower than for the other large ASEAN economies.

In the long run, the consumption share in GDP falls as the level of per capita income rises. If a low-income country experiences an export shortfall, it can offset this by stimulating domestic demand through fiscal stimulus. The recession will be deeper in countries where the private consumption share is low, particularly when consumer confidence is subdued. In an economy with a large share of private consumption, the fiscal multiplier will be higher than in high-income countries with a smaller share of private consumption in GDP. In this type of economy, fiscal stimulus need not be massive, provided that consumer confidence remains high. In 2007, when investor sentiment and consumer confidence were low, fiscal stimulus was not as effective as it would have been in a stable political situation.

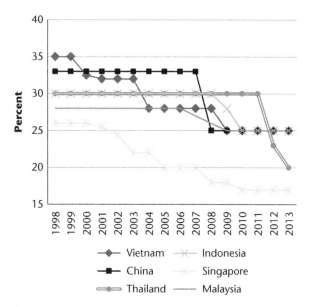

Figure 18.11   Corporate income tax rates in major ASEAN economies

Lipsey and Sjöholm (2011) argue that Indonesia received lower foreign direct investment than other countries in the region because of a poor business environment, inefficient government institutions, and a low level of human and infrastructure capital formation. Athukorala and Swarnim (2011) observe that Malaysia's relative attractiveness for FDI in the region has eroded due to a dualistic investment regime and narrow domestic human capital base. Nevertheless, Malaysia benefits from a complementary FDI relationship with China as a location of high-end activities within global production networks. If FDI is a small proportion of total capital formation, then fluctuations in total investment will depend on factors affecting domestic investment. When FDI is complementary to domestic investment, investment cycles will be dictated by an investment environment shaped by macroeconomic factors.

There is a race for ASEAN countries to cut corporate income taxes to attract FDI (Figure 18.11). Singapore has led the group in cutting its corporate tax rate. Vietnam aggressively reduced taxes from 35 percent in 1998 to 25 percent in 2013. In 2013, Indonesia, Vietnam, Malaysia, and China all employed a corporate tax rate of 25 percent. Thailand followed China in suddenly cutting its corporate tax rate from 30 percent to 20 percent within two years. At this level, Thailand's corporate income tax rate is the second lowest rate in the region, after that of Singapore.

The timing of the tax cut is crucial as it is intended to stimulate foreign and domestic investment at a time of economic slowdown. It remains to be seen whether cutting tax rates can divert FDI, because other fundamental factors also determine FDI flows. Note that the role of automatic fiscal stabilizer will be reduced because of lower tax rates.

Capital formation slowed in 2008 and 2009 when the GFC hit the region, causing investor sentiment to deteriorate and lowering consumer confidence. Collapses of financial institutions, stock market crashes in developed countries, and the intensified Eurozone debt crisis all contributed to delays in investment decisions (Figure 18.12). Investment rebounded in 2010, but the recovery was brief because of the imminent fear of a "double-dip" recession in Europe and the USA. Decelerating output growth in China and India further dampened the investment outlook.

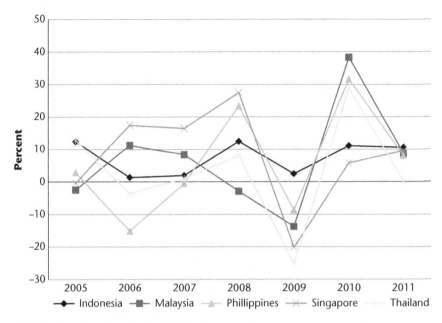

Figure 18.12   Investment cycles in ASEAN–5 economies
Source: ADB Statistical Data Base.

On balance, it appears that the main effect of the GFC on Southeast Asian economies was a large fall in capital formation. If sustained, this fall will ultimately reduce their long-term rate of economic growth. Since all countries in the region have sound reasons to try to maintain the pace of economic growth, it follows that macro policy must be used to stabilize investment fluctuations. An important question is whether low interest rates can revive private investment, and/or whether other policy instruments should also be deployed.

Macroeconomic policy responses to the global financial crisis

In this section, we discuss how Southeast Asian countries use macro policy to deal with recession caused by the global economic slowdown. To compensate for declining exports, fiscal and monetary policy must be employed to stimulate domestic demand. With differences in fiscal space, levels of international reserves, and degree of development in money and capital markets, each country responded differently under certain constraints.

Fiscal policy

If public debt has not reached a critical level, then an expansionary fiscal policy can stimulate private spending to compensate for export shortfalls in times of world economic downturn or recession.

Fiscal spending can be used as a short-term countercyclical policy during crises. Tang et al. (2013) investigated the effectiveness of fiscal policy in ASEAN nations and concluded that government spending has only a weak impact on output. They also found, contrary to expectations, that tax increases have *expansionary* impacts on output, an effect that they attributed to concerns over public finance during the Asian and global financial crises. If Tang et al.'s findings

Table 18.5 Budget deficit after the GFC

Percent of GDP

	2000–08	2009	2010	2011
CLMV				
Cambodia	−1.6	−6.3	−3.1	−4.5
Lao PDR	−3.7	−3.3	−2.2	
Myanmar	−2.4	−4.6	−4.5	
Vietnam	−1.4	−3.9	−4.5	−2.5
ASEAN-5				
Indonesia	−1.2	−1.6	−0.7	−1.2
Malaysia	−4.4	−6.7	−5.4	−4.8
Philippines	−2.8	−3.7	−3.5	−2.0
Singapore	6.4	1.6	7.7	4
Thailand	−1.7	−3.9	−2.4	−1.8

Source: ADB.

are correct, a tax reduction can produce an unconventional impact on output contraction. Green (2010) found that although monetary policy was employed in response to the GFC in Southeast Asia, fiscal expansion was slow to be used. Even if discretionary fiscal policy was too sluggish in reacting to business cycles, automatic fiscal stabilizers can mitigate the impact of global financial crises.

Unlike other emerging market countries where large budget deficits are more typical, Southeast Asian countries with sufficient fiscal space could conduct expansionary fiscal policies to compensate for shortfalls in external demand. Singapore, for example, had a budget surplus before the GFC (Table 18.5). From 2000 to 2008, this surplus was 6.4 percent of GDP on average. However, the surplus declined during the GFC, as the Singapore government used expansionary fiscal policy to raise domestic aggregate demand, so as to compensate for a decline in exports. Similarly, the budget deficit of the Indonesian government was low prior to the crisis, compared to other ASEAN countries. Moreover the Indonesian government did not have to resort to as much fiscal stimulus as Malaysia, the Philippines, and Thailand. The latter three countries are more exposed to trade shocks than Indonesia, and rely less on domestic consumption.

For the transition economies, the GFC led to enlarged budget deficits. Sharp falls in tax revenue coupled with a rise in public spending caused large budget deficits in Cambodia, Vietnam, Lao PDR, and Myanmar (Table 18.5). As in the other ASEAN economies, however, the deficit situation improved as these economies turned around.

Tax revenues rise and fall with output growth, producing some degree of automatic fiscal stabilizers. Vietnam, Thailand, the Philippines, Indonesia, and Myanmar all experienced lower tax revenues in 2009. Apart from Malaysia, Southeast Asian countries were able to collect more tax revenues after the economic recovery in 2010.

Monetary policy

In general, monetary policy is used to achieve stable long-term output growth with price stability. This can be done by avoiding excessive swings of monetary aggregates and keeping their growth rates in line with output growth. Expansionary monetary policy can also mitigate the impact of global slowdowns. As long as the central bank's key policy rate is well above zero, an expansionary monetary policy can be employed to stimulate consumption and investment expenditures to compensate for drops in export demand.

However, countries with less sophisticated financial institutions find it difficult to cope with external shocks by employing monetary policy instruments to respond to changing external demand. Pham and Riedel (2012) have argued that financial sector liberalization precluded Vietnam from pursuing an independent monetary policy to control inflation. A pegged exchange rate and free capital inflows, as well as a lack of monetary policy instruments, complicated the conduct of monetary policy, resulting in Southeast Asia's highest inflation rate. Singapore, by contrast, is an open economy with free flows of trade and capital and well-developed financial institutions. The movement of the SIBOR rate (the benchmark short-term interest rate) is in line with the LIBOR and US federal funds rates.

Although Singapore's key rates match closely with those in global markets, those of other countries in the region are typically higher. The differentials over global benchmark rates reflect country-specific systemic economic and political risk. Accordingly, when a country's interest rate differential declines without a change in the underlying risk factors, it indicates that the monetary policy stance has become more expansionary than in the rest of the world. Since 2002, the money market interest differentials among Southeast Asian nations have narrowed, especially for Indonesia, Malaysia, and the Philippines. With more open capital accounts, it is difficult to pursue an independent monetary policy. Countries face the "trilemma" problem, that with an open capital account they cannot simultaneously determine both domestic monetary policy and the level of the exchange rate.

The actions of some Southeast Asian monetary authorities during the GFC reflect their efforts to find a balance between using expansionary monetary policies to stimulate domestic demand and preventing a collapse of the exchange rate. In 2007, Indonesia, and the Philippines aggressively cut their policy rates (Figure 18.13). Their expansionary monetary policies continued between 2010 and 2012, in response to the global economic slowdown.

As a response to the ongoing GFC, the Bank of Thailand successfully raised its interest rate to ward off inflationary pressure, thereby creating a wider interest rate gap. This in turn led to increased capital inflows and, as a result, the baht strengthened against the dollar, compared to

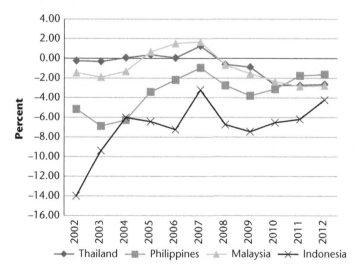

Figure 18.13   Money market rate differentials relative to Singapore
Source: ADB.

Table 18.6 Growth rate of broad money, ASEAN-5 economies (percent per year)

	Indonesia	Malaysia	Philippines	Singapore	Thailand
2005–06	15.6	16.3	15.9	12.8	7.1
2007	19.3	9.5	10.7	13.4	6.3
2008	14.9	13.4	15.4	12.0	9.2
2009	13.0	9.5	7.7	11.3	6.8
2010	15.4	7.2	10.7	8.6	10.9
2011	16.4	14.4	6.5	10.0	15.2

Source: ADB.

other currencies in the region. A stronger domestic currency can dampen inflationary impacts from low interest rate policies intended to stimulate domestic demand.

Indonesia, as mentioned, cut interest rates aggressively at the beginning of the GFC. From 2007 to 2011, Indonesian money supply and price levels grew faster than in other ASEAN-5 countries (Table 18.6). Rising inflationary pressures caused the Indonesian rupiah to depreciate. To counter this, in 2013 Bank Indonesia raised its key policy rate by 25 basis points to 6 percent, ending its loose monetary regime to curb rising inflation, despite weakening global commodity prices and investment activity. However, this induced a "mini-crisis" since through the interaction of monetary and exchange rate policies with domestic distortions – specifically, the policy of fixing nominal fuel prices so as to subsidize consumption and repress inflation. However, currency depreciation widened the gap between foreign and domestic fuel prices, increasing the fiscal burden of the fuel subsidy. Eventually the strain of the subsidy on the government budget became so high that the government had to reduce the subsidy rate. As in all developing countries, inflationary expectations will rise when food prices increase, following more realistic fuel prices. The central bank was forced to raise the key policy rate to contain inflation. There is always a trade-off between price stability and output growth.

In transition economies, financial development occurs with widespread financial services provided by commercial banks. While Singapore, Thailand, Malaysia, Indonesia, and the Philippines controlled monetary growth effectively, Vietnam, Cambodia, Myanmar, and Lao PDR let their money supply grow rapidly (Table 18.7). For fast-growing transitional economies, where the demand for money increases more rapidly than income, inflationary pressure will be mitigated as the velocity of money will not rise. Inflation in Myanmar and Lao PDR remained subdued, as opposed to Vietnam and Cambodia.

Table 18.7 Growth rate of broad money: CLMV economies (percent per year)

	Cambodia	Lao PDR	Myanmar	Vietnam
2005	15.8	7.9	27.3	30.9
2006	40.5	26.7	27.3	29.7
2007	61.8	38.7	29.9	46.1
2008	5.4	18.3	14.9	20.3
2009	35.6	32.4	30.6	29.2
2010	21.3	39.1	42.5	33.3
2011	21.5	25.2	30.5	12.1

Source: ADB.

Notwithstanding the prevalent dollarization in CLMV, monetary growth is much higher than in other ASEAN-5 countries. During transformation from rural to urban regions, the demand for money increases. If an excess supply of money exists as a result of financing budget deficits, inflationary pressures will build. In 2012, property prices in Laos increased by 15 percent as a result of foreign investment in large-scale real estate projects.

As observed by Takagi and Kozuru (2010), output and price correlations have increased in post-crisis Asia. Shocks originating within the region have risen. Increasing interdependence results in co-movements of output and price cycles, but greater regional interdependence does not imply weaker linkages with the rest of the world.

Output cycles are not the only phenomena that have become more synchronized. Inflation trajectories in Southeast Asia also show a similar pattern, decelerating during the slump of 2009 and accelerating during the recovery (Figure 18.14). Those countries simultaneously experiencing booms and busts would also have to withstand pressures from excess demand on price levels. Price stability in Southeast Asian economies depends largely on the ability to control the money supply, which results from exchange rate policies and methods of financing budget deficits. Southeast Asian economies are subject to similar external supply shocks that temporarily threaten price stability. Price stability can be maintained in the long run, provided that aggregate demand can be kept in line with production capacity. If inflation is driven by the demand side, there will be a trade-off between growth and price stability. High output growth must be sacrificed to curb inflationary pressure. If inflation is driven by the supply side such as by energy price shocks, then the output growth and inflation rate would be negatively correlated. Fiscal policy and monetary policy must be coordinated to strike a balance between price stability and output growth.

Exchange rate policy

Although currency appreciation can hurt exports, a strong currency can facilitate importation of capital goods and reduced imported inflation. Exchange rate and monetary policies must strive to achieve an optimal mix so as to strike a balance between export growth and price stability.

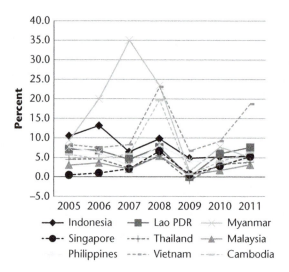

Figure 18.14   Inflation synchronization in ASEAN
Source: ADB.

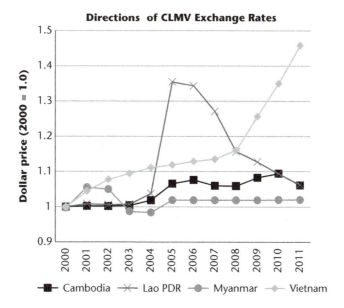

Figure 18.15 Trends in CLMV exchange rates
Source: ADB.

Some Southeast Asian economies that depend on exports of traditional commodities faced a difficulty in allowing their currencies to appreciate during the GFC, since to do so would hamper exports. Myanmar and Cambodia maintained exchange rate stability throughout the GFC (Figure 18.15). The Bank of the Lao-PDR has consistently used a managed floating exchange rate regime to maintain exchange rate stability. Since 2003, it fixed the kip and let it then depreciate by more than 30 percent in 2005. With continued capital inflows, Lao PDR has allowed its currency to appreciate against the dollar and depreciate against the baht of Thailand, its major trading partner.

As Figure 18.15 shows, the Vietnam dong has depreciated more than 45 percent since 2000. This is because it must respond to real exchange rate appreciation caused by high inflation. The rate of depreciation of the dong accelerated during the GFC, making Vietnamese exports more competitive in markets where they compete with other Southeast Asian countries. However currency depreciation also leads to higher imported inflation, which offsets gains in international competitiveness. Partly for this reason, Vietnam has endured the highest inflation rate in the region. A high rate of currency depreciation would not hurt the domestic banking sector if Vietnamese banks did not borrow heavily from abroad in dollars and could attract more foreign investment from neighboring countries. Inflationary expectations are important as they can generate speculation in property and foreign exchange markets. After a steep devaluation, inflation may accelerate if it fuels inflationary expectations. As long as there is a large difference in the official and market rates for the dollar, black market activity persists. In 2012, inflation in Vietnam was 9.2 percent, yet monetary policy was expansionary. To stimulate demand, the State Bank of Vietnam made cuts in key policy rates over six times. In 2012, GDP grew by 5 percent – the lowest growth rate since 1999. In Vietnam, growth is a major priority compared to price stability.

If growth is driven by exports, an economy can lose international competitiveness from domestic currency appreciation. Since 2000, the Malaysia ringgit, Singapore dollar, and Thai baht have appreciated substantially against the dollar, despite intervention by the central banks

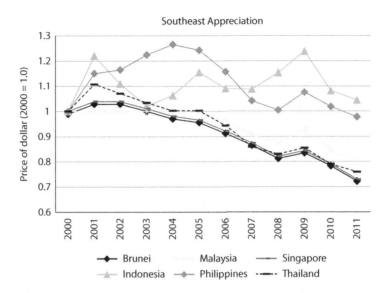

Figure 18.16 Exchange rate appreciation in ASEAN economies
Source: ADB.

(Figure 18.16). While the Philippine peso depreciated from 2000 to 2004, it has since followed a rising trend against the dollar. Indonesia experienced more fluctuations as described above, but even its currency appreciated after the GFC.

During the US mild recession in 2001 and financial turmoil in 2009, domestic currencies of Southeast Asian economies had similarly appreciated against the dollar. This rising trend continued into 2013. During the GFC the currencies of Brunei, Singapore, and Thailand experienced the greatest appreciation, followed by Malaysia. Indonesia experienced the lowest appreciation rate, while the Philippine peso reversed the depreciation trend and eventually regained its original value of 2000. Currency appreciation is a natural consequence of a surplus on the balance of payments. An attempt to resist the trend of currency appreciation can be counterproductive as undervaluing domestic currencies can further complicate macroeconomic management. Often, the fear of appreciation can be unwarranted since exports are more sensitive to the output effect of changing world trade volumes than the substitution effect of currency appreciation.

Currency appreciation did not hurt exports as much as might be inferred from the actual rate of appreciation, because exports also require imported intermediate products. This reflects the long-term structural change in Southeast Asian production in exports from final to intermediate manufactured products. This shift implies that a loss of competitiveness caused by currency appreciation would be proportional to export composition. The lower the share of final manufactured exports among total exports, the greater the burden imposed by a currency appreciation imposed upon competitiveness of exports.

Because of large capital inflows into Southeast Asia in the aftermath of the GFC, currency appreciation cannot be resisted in the long run. Also, while currency appreciation might slow exports, it can also mitigate the impact of imported inflation. This can be seen as a form of financial Dutch disease – the idea that inflows of export earnings (or, in this case, of foreign investment) will lead to rising prices of domestic non-tradables and thus fuel inflation. By resisting the trend of currency appreciation, central banks must intervene in foreign exchange markets. Accumulation of international reserves leads to an expansion of the monetary base, which results in rising price levels in the non-traded sector caused by expanding domestic credit. Adverse consequences of this financial form of Dutch disease had been demonstrated by property bubbles in Southeast Asian countries before the 1997 Asian financial crisis. With increasing flows of capital into Southeast Asia, especially CLMV countries, the same policy mistakes which some ASEAN-5 nations made in the early 1990s might occur again.

Finally, long-term structural changes in the pattern of Asian and global trade are also altering the drivers of Southeast Asian exchange rates. Because of its increasing importance in the global economy, China's output growth increasingly shapes the business cycle of Southeast Asia. The movement of the renminbi affects the direction of Southeast Asian currencies. This can be seen by examining determinants of the real effective exchange rate (REER) index, a measurement of competitiveness provided by the Bank for International Settlements (BIS).

An investigation of REER determinants for ASEAN currencies reveals that they are affected by the dollar, yen, and renminbi. An appreciation of these three currencies causes a depreciation of ASEAN currencies. From 2000 to 2007, before the GFC, movement of the dollar had the greatest impact on the ASEAN REER, followed by the yen, and then the renminbi. An appreciation of the dollar caused an immediate depreciation of ASEAN currencies. After the onset of the GFC, however, the renminbi had the greatest impact on ASEAN currencies, dominating the influence of the dollar and the yen. Depreciation of the dollar and yen caused appreciation of the renminbi, which in turn caused depreciation in ASEAN-5 currencies.

An appreciation of the renminbi causes an abrupt depreciation of the Singapore dollar, due to its greater flexibility relative to other regional currencies. The impact of a change in the movement of the renminbi has a long lag effect; over time, renminbi depreciation leads to losses of competitiveness in ASEAN currencies. Looking to the future, the consequence of this structural shift in the regional and global real economies means that any future slowdown in China's economic growth and/or depreciation of the renminbi relative to the US dollar will require more aggressive stimuli from fiscal and monetary authorities in anticipation of a recession caused by China's business cycle.

Concluding remarks

In 2008, Asian developing countries' growth rates slowed after the Global financial crisis of 2007. With a decline in exports caused by the global recession, economic uncertainty and pessimism further dampened private consumption and investment. Some Southeast Asian economies performed well compared to other countries, given a similar structure of export dependency on the world economy. Their ability to stabilize aggregate demand by means of fiscal stimuli helped maintain the growth despite a sharp fall in exports in 2009. Public debt in these countries is manageable, providing sufficient fiscal space to respond to export demand shocks.

Southeast Asian economies' business cycles are synchronized by impacts of foreign capital flows and supply-chain effects of the global economic slowdown on network trade. Southeast Asian financial sectors have been less vulnerable to external shocks as a result of strengthened rules and regulations by central banks. When key policy interest rates were reduced, Asian bank credit did not expand rapidly because of enlarging saving-investment gaps that started with the collapse of investment after the 1997 financial crisis. Although exchange rates of these countries appreciated against the US dollar, shrinking exports do not adversely affect output growth as long as export shortfalls are compensated by stimulus-driven expansion of domestic demand.

Boom–bust cycles are related to export cycles, which are affected by world economic activity and the policy responses of giant economies. The appreciation of real effective exchange rates of ASEAN-5 countries and subsequent losses of international competitiveness requires policy makers to rethink stabilization strategies by taking into account the increasingly influential role of the

Chinese business cycle. China's exchange rate policy has produced a new environment and this calls for a reassessment of exchange rate policy in the Southeast Asian economies.

Foreign direct investment in the region has increased considerably and will be intensified by Myanmar's newly adopted outward-orientation policy. Whether Vietnam, Cambodia, Lao PDR, and Myanmar can escape the adverse impacts of the Dutch disease depends on the flexibility and effectiveness of countercyclical macroeconomic policy in reining in domestic monetary growth. In response to future global shocks, each country's fiscal and monetary policies must be well coordinated to ensure a rapid revival of domestic demand and therefore a minimal departure from the trend growth path.

In terms of depth of recession and speed of recovery, the local impact of the GFC is pale compared to that of the Asian financial crisis. The high share of consumption in GDP makes it the most important source of volatility, followed by investment, both of which are affected by business sentiment and consumer confidence.

Note

1 Hill (2014) provides a succinct update on the "pragmatic orthodoxy" thesis for Southeast Asia in the 2000s.

Bibliography

Allegret, J.-P.and Essahbi, E. (2011). Business cycles synchronization in East Asian economy: Evidences from time-varying coherence study. *Economic Modelling*, 28, 351–65.

Athukorala, P.-C. and Swarnim, W. (2011). Foreign direct investment in Southeast Asia: Is Malaysia falling behind? *ASEAN Economic Bulletin*, 28(2), 115–33.

Corden, W.M. (1996). *Pragmatic Orthodoxy: Macroeconomic Policies in Seven East Asian Economies*. San Francisco, CA: International Center for Economic Growth.

Cortinhas, C. (2007). Intra-industry trade and business cycles in ASEAN. *Applied Economics*, 39, 893–902.

Frankel, J. and Rose, A. (1998). The endogeneity of the optimum currency area criteria. *Economic Journal*, 108, 1009–25.

Gachter, M., Riedl, A., and Ritzberger-Grunwald , D. (2012). Business cycle synchronization in the Euro area and the impact of the financial crisis. *Monetary Policy and the Economy*, 33–60.

Green, D. (2010) Southeast Asia's policy response to the global economic crisis. *ASEAN Economic Bulletin*, 27 (1), 5–26.

He, D. and Liao, W. (2012). Asian business cycle synchronization. *Pacific Economic Review*, 17(1), 106–35.

Hill, H. (2014). Southeast Asian macroeconomic management: pragmatic orthodoxy? Paper for publication in a special issue of *Masyarakat Indonesia* in honor of Anne Booth, eds. J. Thomas Lindblad and Thee Kian Wee.

Kim, S. and Kim, S.H. (2013). International capital flows, boom–bust cycles, and business cycle synchronization in the Asia Pacific region. *Contemporary Economic Policy: A Journal of Western Economic Association International*, 31(1), 191–211.

Kiseok, H. and Hsiao Chink, T. (2012). Crises in Asia: Recovery and policy responses. *Journal of Asian Economics*, 23(Asia After Crisis), 654–68.

Lipsey, R.E. and Sjöholm, F. (2011). Foreign direct investment and growth in East Asia: Lessons for Indonesia. *Bulletin of Indonesian Economic Studies*, 47(1), 35–63.

Moneta, F. and Ruffer, R. (2006).Business cycle synchronization in East Asia. *Journal of Asian Economics*, 20, 1–12.

Park, C., Adams, C., and Jeong, H. (2011). Asia's contribution to global rebalancing. *Asian-Pacific Economic Literature*, 25(2), 38–51.

Pham, T. and Riedel, J. (2012). On the conduct of monetary policy in Vietnam. *Asian-Pacific Economic Literature*, 26(1), 34–45.

Pradumna Bickram, R. (2007). Economic integration and synchronization of business cycles in East Asia. *Journal of Asian Economics*, 18, 711–25.

Pradumna Bickram, R., Tianyin, C., and Wai-Mun, C. (2012). Trade intensity and business cycle synchronization: East Asia versus Europe. *Journal of Asian Economics*, 23(Asia After Crisis), 701–6.

Takagi, S. and Kozuru, I. (2010). Output and price linkages in Asia's post-crisis: Macroeconomic interdependence. *Singapore Economic Review*, 55(1), 59–81.

Takeuchi, F. (2011). The role of production fragmentation in international business cycle synchronization in East Asia. *Journal of Asian Economics*, 22, 441–59.

Tang, H., Liu, P., and Cheung, E.C. (2013). Changing impact of fiscal policy on selected ASEAN countries. *Journal of Asian Economics*, 24(1), 103–16.

World Bank. 1993. *The East Asian Miracle: Economic Growth and Public Policy*. Oxford: Oxford University Press.

19

Twenty-first-century challenges for Southeast Asian economies

Ian Coxhead

UNIVERSITY OF WISCONSIN-MADISON

Thee Kian Wie

INDONESIAN INSTITUTE OF SCIENCES

Arief Anshory Yusuf

PADJADJARAN UNIVERSITY

Introduction

Southeast Asian economic development is a work in progress. Much has been achieved, and yet in this region only Singapore has managed to sustain a growth rate high enough to break out of middle-income, while some other economies (including Indonesia, the largest) seem destined to remain among the ranks of the lower middle-income countries for the foreseeable future. In most of the region's economies, historical dependence on resource-based production and exports is increasingly being supplanted by activities more reliant on investment goods, technology, and human capital. But the transition remains incomplete and uneven. The continued momentum of structural change is threatened both by internal constraints (lack of infrastructure, urban congestion, and weak educational systems) and external challenges (low-cost competitors in global markets for manufactures, global market instability). In several countries, the political and administrative institutions needed to promote confidence among domestic and foreign investors, to reduce corruption and inefficiency, and to promote stable, fair and sustainable development policies are not convincingly keeping up with the pace of economic growth.

Looking to the future, the region will confront major development challenges. These include: urbanization and the emergence of megacities including Bangkok, Manila, Jakarta, and Ho Chi Minh City; the demographic transition and rising age dependency ratios; environmental risks associated with natural resource depletion and the effects of global climate change; regional economic integration; maintaining or increasing human capital investments; and the global market consequences of fast-growing, large neighboring economies such as China and India. In addition, the region as a whole and its individual states must find efficient means to insure against global economic volatility. Their current strategy of holding large foreign exchange reserves carries low risk and has proven very effective in the latest global financial crisis. However, this strategy is also low-return, so finding a way to "save for a rainy day" that also contributes to sustained economic development is another long-range issue to be confronted. Dealing with these complex tasks while also ensuring that growth satisfies domestic concerns for an equitable distribution of benefits and costs constitutes a first-order policy challenge.

Completing the labor market and workforce transition

Southeast Asian economic growth benefited enormously from the demographic "gift" of a low dependency ratio at precisely the historical moment when it could most productively be put to work (Bloom and Williamson 1998). But fertility rates have fallen, most quickly in the most successfully growing economies. The region's demographic transition is now all but complete, and age dependency ratios are beginning to rise.

Since the 1990s, rising wages and incipient labor shortages, especially in unskilled and informal occupations, have increasingly been cushioned by cross-border migration – just as has occurred in the world's wealthier economies. Thailand, Malaysia, and Singapore are all large importers of mostly unskilled labor from neighboring states. However, the strategy of solving shortages in the national labor force through immigration and guest workers depends on the continued existence of neighbors or nearby countries with dramatically lower levels of living, so as to create incentives for individuals to migrate and to endure the difficulties of life as a migrant worker (and for some the indignities and insecurities of doing so without legal status). As the poorer countries of Southeast Asia catch up in economic growth, the gradual convergence of levels of per capita income over time will naturally reduce incentives for workers to migrate.

Looking to the future, in economies with fewer workers per head of population, there is a premium on labor force *quality* if per capita incomes are to continue growing. Steady economic growth in recent decades has done a great deal to improve the health and nutritional status of Southeast Asian workers, although much yet remains to be done in terms of both individual health and nutrition, and the capacity of delivery systems for health care and social insurance. And perhaps the greatest opportunity for improving labor quality – education – is an area in which few Southeast Asian countries have shown consistently strong performance. Addressing human capital scarcity, and doing so in a way that positions the region's economies to take greatest advantage of evolving global market forces, is one of the greatest challenges for this region, now and in years to come.

Dealing with global economic volatility

Increasing global market integration brings greater rewards but also enhances risks. The extent of these risks, and the proper responses to them, is knowable only to a limited extent because the global economy itself is constantly changing. One indicator of that change is increased global volatility in prices of traded goods and in cross-border capital flows.

Prior to the Asian financial crisis of 1997, volatility in Southeast Asia had two primary sources: domestic political shocks, and terms of trade shocks associated with commodity price volatility linked to business cycles in advanced economies.

In the twenty-first century political volatility has receded as a threat to wellbeing for the majority of Southeast Asians. After decades of authoritarian rule Indonesia, with almost half the region's population, has made a spectacularly successful transition to democratic institutions and orderly regime succession. The Philippines too may finally have escaped the pattern of disorderly and disruptive non-electoral transitions that punctuated the two decades following the overthrow of the autocrat Ferdinand Marcos. Even in Myanmar, the twenty-first century has brought hopeful signs that the military, after many years of brutal totalitarian rule, may be willing to relax its grip on power in favor of an electoral system. Only Thailand is moving in the opposite direction; there, the Bangkok-based elite's unwillingness to accept repeated electoral defeats (in six national elections between 2001 and 2014) brought the military out of their barracks once again in 2014, the dispiriting replay of over a dozen prior coups or coup attempts in the postwar era.

In the remaining nations, one-party governments have proved remarkably resilient, long-lived and stable, whether through a lop-sided electoral process (in Malaysia and Singapore) or through constitutional monopolization of power (Vietnam, Laos, Cambodia, and Brunei). Region-wide, ASEAN as a maturing and increasingly authoritative institution must be given credit for restraining some of the wilder impulses of governments, at least in the sphere of economic policy making, despite its avowed principle of non-interference in the internal affairs of its member states.

In global markets, the terms of trade persist as a source of external shocks causing volatility, but with a greatly diminished role. Increasing industrialization and a correspondingly smaller role of primary commodities in GDP and trade means that global commodity price shocks are no longer the sole and fundamental drivers of economic volatility that they once were. Of course some countries, such as Laos (minerals and hydropower) and Brunei (oil) will remain exceptions for the foreseeable future, and commodity prices still strongly influence macroeconomic events in Indonesia, the region's largest economy. In general, however, manufacturing, and intensified integration in regional and global production networks have overtaken commodity markets as primary trade links to the global market. For the future, export demand shocks emanating from business cycles or macroeconomic shocks in advanced western (including North America) economies will continue to be important, but their impact will be dampened by the increasing importance of intra-Asian trade links, especially as China's economy makes the transition from its current export-driven structure to one more centered on domestic consumption demand. This transition will not happen overnight, however, and in the interim, trade links to China will not provide total insulation against another GFC because of the continuing (if diminishing) importance of western markets as export outlets for overall Asian trade.

In late 2013, a regional macroeconomic temblor caused by the initial "tapering" of post-GFC US federal stimulus policies indicated clearly the rising importance of what may well prove to be the main transmission channel, if not the fundamental cause, of future external volatility in Southeast Asia: global finance and capital markets. The mere announcement in 2013 of a likely end to low interest rates in the US economy was sufficient to send a sharp, if short-lived tremor through stock markets, banking systems, and exchange rates in Indonesia, as well as in other so-called "fragile" economies such as India, Turkey, and South Africa. The deepening international integration of capital markets is an unstoppable phenomenon, even though the pace of integration may slacken from time to time.

Southeast Asian capital markets are for the most part already very open to financial flows. The 1997 crisis revealed enormous regional vulnerability to such shocks, and the response since 2000 has been to self-insure by accumulating large reserves of foreign assets. But given the magnitudes of potential capital flows and the ineffectiveness of capital controls except in the very short run, the decision to self-insure by holding larger reserves is both a very costly instrument (assets held in foreign economies cannot simultaneously be used to build bridges and schools at home) and is in any case an instrument that all countries cannot rely on all the time. Regional risk-sharing arrangements, such as those discussed by Hill and Menon, Chapter 17 in this volume, will become increasingly important.

At a more fundamental level, it is important to emphasize that ongoing change in the relative importance of commodity, trade, and financial/capital market linkages connecting Southeast Asia to the global economy does not eliminate the potential for external shocks, but will alter their nature, duration, and depth, and the set of options for compensating policy responses.

Economic inequality and policy stability

Poverty and severe food insecurity is on the retreat almost everywhere in Southeast Asia. Thanks to progress in agricultural development and income diversification the Malthusian disasters that once haunted the region have not materialized. Achieving food security (at a national level if not for every community) has relaxed one of the most tightly binding constraints on public policy, and thus has expanded the "space" within which relevant economic policies can be designed and evaluated.

Nonetheless, issues of human welfare continue to exert substantial (and in some countries rising) influence over policy formation. Among these, debates over the distribution of gains and losses from growth, and from economic changes, including foreign investment and environmental damages, that may imply differential gains across groups, have risen to prominence (Asian Development Bank 2012). Rising inequality, persistent high inequality, or merely heightened public perception and sensitivity to inequality imposes new constraints on economic policy choices – and may even undermine commitment to existing policies.

By and large, Southeast Asian development has been characterized both by a general trend toward "better" economic policies, and by a willingness to revise policies in response to changing circumstances. This is the "pragmatic orthodoxy" (Corden 1996; Hill 2014) personified in several countries, notably Indonesia, by the rise to prominence of technocratic (as opposed to more narrowly ideological) economic policy advisors (Thee 2003). Yet transitions from established policy can be difficult to negotiate, even if there is widespread agreement on the need for reform. In precarious polities such as Thailand, the Philippines, and Indonesia political parties have responded to rising tensions over inequality with overtly populist programs. These, however, are proving to be very expensive in terms of the opportunity cost of public expenditures.

Indonesia's fuel subsidy program is an important example. This program has absorbed a huge share of public expenditures, with limited effects on poverty and dubious benefits for distribution (Yusuf 2008).[1] Similarly, Thailand's 2011 rice "pledging" scheme, under which the government offered farmers prices up to 40 percent over market for their output, is another. It has been estimated that in 2012–13 this scheme cost the Thai government THB700 billion ($US22 billion), equivalent to an entire year of the Thai government's investment budget (Warr 2014). Like Indonesia's fuel subsidy, the Thai rice purchase program was driven much more by politics than by any strategic vision of economic development.

In the remainder of this section we evaluate trends in inequality, discuss interactions with policy in several countries, and conclude by asking whether rising inequality could seriously impair the capacity of regional governments to maintain the "pragmatic orthodoxy" that has served many of them so well in the past.

Trends in inequality

According to international data sets, inequality has risen sharply in some Southeast Asian countries in the past 10–15 years. Table 19.1 reports summary measures of income inequality for the region. It shows Gini coefficients, the share of income earned by the top 10 percent of the population, and the ratio of the share of the richest 10 percent of households to that of the poorest 40 percent. These are highly aggregative measures and fall far short of capturing inequality in all its dimensions. Nonetheless they reveal some strong trends, especially in the most recent years. Inequality is rising

Table 19.1 Summary measures of inequality for Southeast Asian countries

	1981–85	1986–90	1991–95	1996–00	2001–05	2006–11
	Gini coefficient					
Cambodia			0.38		0.42	0.39
Indonesia	0.30	0.29	0.29	0.30	0.32	0.36
Lao PDR			0.30	0.35	0.33	0.37
Malaysia	0.49	0.47	0.48	0.49	0.38	0.46
Philippines	0.41	0.41	0.43	0.46	0.44	0.44
Singapore*				0.42	0.44	0.45
Thailand	0.45	0.45	0.46	0.43	0.42	0.41
Vietnam			0.36	0.36	0.37	0.36
	Income share of top 10% of households					
Cambodia			33.0		34.9	32.8
Indonesia	24.9	24.7	25.0	25.8	27.1	28.9
Lao PDR			25.8	29.0	27.2	30.3
Malaysia	38.5	36.7	37.4	38.4	28.8	34.7
Philippines	32.7	32.1	34.1	36.5	34.3	33.8
Singapore*				32.8		
Thailand	35.5	35.7	36.8	33.6	33.4	31.9
Vietnam			29.0	29.3	29.7	28.0
	Ratio of income share of top 10% to bottom 40%					
Cambodia			1.2		1.3	1.2
Indonesia	0.8	0.8	0.8	0.8	0.9	1.0
Lao PDR			0.8	1.0	0.9	1.1
Malaysia	1.6	1.4	1.5	1.6	1.0	1.3
Philippines	1.2	1.2	1.3	1.4	1.3	1.3
Singapore*				1.2		
Thailand		1.4	1.4	1.3	1.2	1.2
Vietnam			1.0	1.0	1.0	1.0

Source: World Development Indicators Online, except
* Singapore Department of Statistics *Yearbook of Statistics*, various issues.

in Indonesia, Lao PDR, and Singapore. In Thailand, Malaysia, and the Philippines it has fluctuated (and has recently declined in Thailand and perhaps the Philippines), yet remains persistently high. The data on Cambodia and Vietnam are incomplete and show no clear trends. More recent data for Indonesia show inequality continuing to rise, with the Gini surpassing 41 (Yusuf et al. 2013b), a trend whose persistence over more than a decade has now sparked a broad public policy debate in that country. Similarly Singapore, a country that already boasted more millionaires per capita than any other, has recently recorded a rapid rise in inequality, and this in turn has sparked concerns about social stability and diminished potential for good governance (Bhaskaran et al., 2012).

Why does inequality increase or decline? Traditionally, development economists have looked to secular changes associated with evolving structure of the economy and labor force (Kuznets 1955), though national economic policies and less formal forms of discrimination and exclusion have always played a pivotal role. In recent years, advances in technology and communications have made it possible for skilled or gifted individuals to reap scarcity rents at a global scale (Brynjolfsson and McAfee 2011), and globalization, especially the re-emergence of China as a manufacturing hub, has limited the extent of rises in real wages for low-skill workers in other countries (Wood 1997). Both these trends have tended to increase inequality. At the same time, improved participation in education has led in some countries to rapid increases in the numbers of medium- and high-skilled workers, thereby reducing the skill premium, a key labor market component of earnings inequality. In some other countries, a trend to more inclusive political systems has encouraged policy shifts that favor the median voter – who, in every Southeast Asian country but Singapore, was until very recently both rural and agrarian. The net effects on trends in inequality are contradictory, and vary by country.

In high-inequality economies, all policy decisions are more politically charged. This is most especially true now that political competition is more open in many countries, and contrasts strongly with prior experience in which policy and policy reform programs were administered by an "authoritarian growth-oriented state" (Hill, Chapter 15 in this volume) with the support of a small but influential group of technocrats.

In Southeast Asia, high and/or rising inequality has been just one putative driver of rising tensions; some religious and ethnic fault-lines have also widened. Indonesia experienced a seven-year period of sharply more prevalent and frequent incidents of communal and other forms of violence following the collapse of the New Order regime (Varshney et al. 2004; Bertrand 2008). This was accompanied by a more pervasive sense of a breakdown of social order, or *disintegrasi* (van Klinken 2007). In Thailand, a September 2006 military coup to oust Prime Minister Thaksin spawned ongoing and frequently violent conflict between his supporters ("red shirts") and those whose loyalties lie with the traditional Thai elite ("yellow shirts"). The intensity of this conflict, which is enacted daily on the streets of the capital city, has several times brought daily life and business to a halt, with numerous deaths and imprisonments, and in early 2014 resulted in yet another military takeover of government.

Also in Thailand, violent conflict between secessionists and state forces broke out in 2004 in several southern provinces and continues to the present day. The long-running southern Philippine secessionist campaign continues to ebb and flow, with frequent acts of atrocity and terror not only in the contested region but also in the capital, Manila, and elsewhere, with consequent disruption to social and economic life.[2] The costs of extraparliamentary dissent, conflict, and terror cannot easily be quantified, but have at times clearly reached severe levels in each of these three large Southeast Asian economies. Elsewhere, in Malaysia the reduction of disparities among ethnic groups has been an explicit pillar of development policy ever since a brief but violent outbreak of Sino-Malay sectarian conflict in 1969. Whether the costs of that country's New Economic Policy (1970–90) or its successor plans have been outweighed by gains of faster growth remains moot.

As the region's two largest economies, the cases of Indonesia and Thailand merit somewhat more detailed discussion.

Indonesia

Inequality in Indonesia, the region's most populous country, was historically measured at levels well below those in the region's other large economies. Concern over inequality was a character-istic feature of policy throughout the early decades after independence, as reflected in the national commitment to a "just and prosperous society" (Thee 2001: 177–8). However, inequality rose very sharply in the 2000s: by 2012 it was about one-third higher than in the 1990s, a rate and magnitude of increase with virtually no peacetime precedent in market economies.

What is driving this increase in inequality is a question that may have many answers. However, in general, widening disparity in a developing country's development process is due to underlying inequality in ownership of productive assets, including claims on land and other natural resources, ownership of shares and bonds and human capital (Ahluwalia 1994: 26). Some of Indonesia's most prominent redistributive policies, such as the INPRES program using rents from oil and mineral extraction to promote regional development, have either vanished or been greatly weakened in the post-Suharto era. Other policies intended to promote equality have not achieved their goals – notably, the fossil fuel price subsidy scheme (Yusuf 2008). Prior to recent reforms, this scheme not only distorted fuel prices in ways that hurt Indonesia's poor relative to more affluent vehicle owners, it also had significant impacts on the government's capacity to deliver social services, infrastructure improvements, and other public investments that would improve overall labor productivity.

Another important question is what effect the rise in inequality could have on the Indonesian government's capacity to enact economic policies that promote efficiency and a flexible response to rapidly changing global market conditions. Past Indonesian experience with policies targeting redistribution with growth were not notable for their successes (Thee 2005), although the use of oil export revenues to fund rural and agricultural development and to cushion the effects of a major program of structural adjustment in the 1980s and 1990s provides a more positive example. As the boom in resource exports winds down in the second decade of the twenty-first century, Indonesia will face an ever-tightening need to develop policies that maximize the efficiency of growth without further exacerbating either the reality or the perception of an unequal distribution of the gains.

Thailand

Economic populism associated with the governments of Thaksin Shinawatra (from 2001 until deposed in a military coup in 2006) and his sister Yingluck (until her ouster by non-electoral means in 2014) has created and exacerbated severe internal conflict. This is a consequence of the work in progress that is Thai democracy. Previously, the ruling party/clique/junta could impose its will in economic policy. Dissent was hardly tolerated, there was virtually no electoral contestation. Mechanisms for dissemination of ideas and for initiation of mass action were very limited. Growth was also associated with high and rising inequality. Thailand's move to a more participatory electoral system in the 1990s, and associated steps toward decentralization of some administrative and fiscal powers since the late part of that decade, has greatly empowered the rural electorate, whose gains from earlier growth had been much less great than those of urban/white collar populations. Thai politicians were quick to recognize the shift in power from cities to the rural electorate, giving rise to populism. Thaksin, spotting this sooner than others, rode to power on the back of the rural vote, secured (in part) with promises of cheap health care, loan forgiveness for farmers, and district-level economic development gimmicks. His ousting and exile in 2006, and efforts to limit the momentum of populist economic policies, spawned an unprecedented and ongoing wave of political dissent, pro- and anti-government protests, and sporadic outbreaks of violence and intimidation. These have naturally imposed sharp limits on the capacity and the will of government in the arena of public policy.

The Thaksin years were marked by a decline in inequality, at least as measured by the Gini coefficients and income share ratios summarized in Table 19.1. This may (or may not) be a consequence of the pro-rural populism of the Thaksin regime and its successors. However, numerous commentators have argued that populism in economic policy has had a negative impact on overall economic growth. The decentralization program in particular has come under fire for moving spending authority over key areas such as education, health, and infrastructure out to small subnational administrations without corresponding increases in accountability or transparency, and with little regard to diseconomies of scale or capacity (Warr 2001).

And delivering on other populist programs is measurably costly. As an example, one of the first acts of the military junta that seized power in May 2014 was to deliver the equivalent of billions of dollars in overdue rice subsidy payments to farmers, an act of questionable political wisdom and indubitable fiscal profligacy. As in Indonesia, Thailand must now begin to seek ways to maximize growth dividends from investments and policies whilst remaining highly vigilant against increases in inequality.

Inequality and policy stability: prognosis

The task of designing and maintaining good economic policies for Southeast Asian countries should primarily aim at achieving rapid and sustainable development combined with equity – that is, a steady reduction in the incidence of absolute poverty, preferably with no additional rise in levels of inequality that are already high and have proven records of engendering political strife. The tensions inherent to a real or perceived trade-off between efficiency and equity are well known, and none of the inequality fault-lines described above are new. What *is* new, perhaps, is the extent to which the proponents of different viewpoints or beliefs now have voice in the Southeast Asian political sphere – not merely within the governing elite, but in electoral contests, in traditional and social media networks, and in the streets. It remains to be seen whether "pragmatic orthodoxy" in short-term macroeconomic management and the trend toward greater openness in long-run development policy can be consistent with greater accountability and a more open political competition than was the case in Southeast Asia's recent past.

Environmental risks

The need to cope with resource depletion and global climate change is a challenge of particular importance and urgency in Southeast Asia. Located in the tropics and straddling the equator, Southeast Asia is an important consumer and also producer of environmental damages associated with global economic growth and trade. Comparative advantage in industrial crops such as oil palm, together with weak institutional restraints on land use change, have raised Indonesia to third place among global emitters of greenhouse gases. At the same time, a very large fraction of the region's population, infrastructure, and industrial and agricultural resources are located on river deltas and low-lying coastal zones that are expected to suffer the greatest effects of anticipated sea level rises related to global warming. These global-scale environmental issues, as well as many more occurring at sub-regional or national scale, are of particular concern in a region where in spite of much progress in industrial and advanced service sector growth, natural resource wealth still underpins a large fraction of economic activity, and still provides the fundamental income source for a majority of the poor.

The case of oil palm development exemplifies the complexities of dealing with environmental issues in growing, middle-income economies. Palm oil is used for consumption, household fuel, biodiesel, and as feedstock for oleochemicals. Global demand has boomed in recent years, with expansion of biofuels demand as an alternative to carbon-intensive fossil fuels making up a large share of total growth. As the biggest producers and exporters of palm oil, Indonesia and Malaysia continue to convert land from forests and other uses into oil palm plantations. From 1981 to 2011 the area planted to palm oil in Indonesia and Malaysia grew, on average, by 11 percent and 5 percent per year, respectively. Palm oil and its products made up just 1 percent of Indonesian exports in the early 1990s, but now account for almost 8 percent. Though new plantation development in Malaysia has almost halted, that in Indonesia shows no sign of slowing

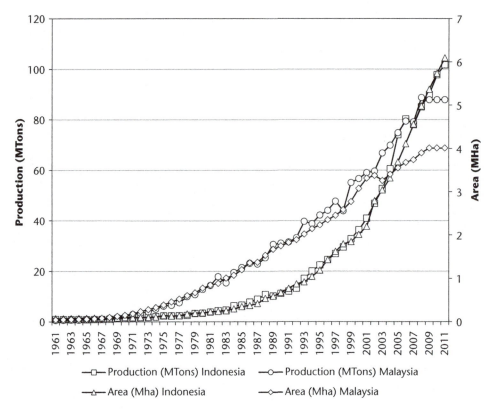

Figure 19.1 Oil palm production and land area, 1961–2011
Source: FAO.

down (Figure 19.1). Further conversion of forests and peat swamps to oil palm threatens the country's international commitment to carbon emissions reduction.[3]

The Indonesian government has introduced some measures intended to slow the rate of deforestation, for example by imposing temporary moratoria on conversion of natural forest areas for oil palm cultivation. However, many argue that the economic incentives to expand palm oil production will undermine the effectiveness of such measures. Based on economic criteria alone, there is a tradeoff: as an illustration, simulations using a dynamic general equilibrium model of the Indonesian economy suggest that a permanent moratorium on palm oil land conversion would result in Indonesian GDP in 2030 falling almost 1 percent below its baseline under current land use practices, as shown in Figure 19.2 (Yusuf et al. 2013a). As generally poorer regions outside Java would be the most heavily affected, efforts to further restrict oil-palm plantation development could face even greater opposition in the name of inter-regional inequality.

The case of oil palm clearly illustrates that deforestation will likely continue to pose a serious threat to sustainable development, in Indonesia as well as other countries such as Myanmar and Laos, that still rely on land-based economic activities to pursue economic growth.

Global climate change is another threat. Southeast Asia is among the world regions most at risk from climate change impacts. The Asian Development Bank has estimated that the various impacts

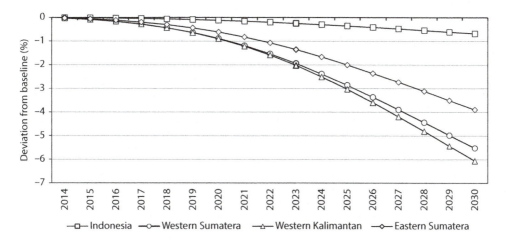

—□— Indonesia —○— Western Sumatera —△— Western Kalimantan —◇— Eastern Sumatera

Figure 19.2 The impact of oil palm land moratorium on the GDP of Indonesia and Indonesia's
oil-palm producing regions (deviation from baseline)
Source: Author's calculation using Indonesian CGE model.

of global climate change could cost as much as 6.7 percent of Southeast Asian GDP in 2100, three
times the global average estimate (ADB 2009). The region is vulnerable to climate-induced
natural hazards such as droughts, floods, typhoons, sea level rise (Yusuf and Francisco 2010).
The Philippines, for example, is highly exposed to cyclones, floods, and landslides. Manila, the
country's capital and a megacity (including contiguous urban areas) of 25 million inhabitants, is the
most vulnerable area in the country and among the most vulnerable cities in Southeast Asia. In
Thailand, the provinces around Bangkok are highly exposed to the threats of sea level rise and
frequent floods. Economic losses due to the 2011 "mega" flood in Bangkok, which brought large
parts of the metropolitan area to a complete halt for up to three months, were estimated at 1,425
billion baht (US$45.7 billion) in a World Bank assessment.[4] Other heavily populated coastal and
deltaic areas, including the north coast of Java, Vietnam's Mekong and Red River deltas, and the
Irrawaddy delta in Myanmar, all face real threats from flooding, storm surges, and related
environmental damage.

The 2013 report of the Intergovernmental Panel on Climate Change[5] suggests that scientists
are more convinced that warming of the atmosphere and ocean system is unequivocal. Many of
the associated impacts such as sea level change have occurred since 1950 at rates unprecedented in
the historical record. A target of 2 degree warming at the end of the century is now very difficult to
attain. Global warming in the future will generate more frequent and more intense climate-related
disasters. The trend of disasters in Southeast Asia has been increasing (Figure 19.3). With an
unavoidable increase in the global temperature, Southeast Asia will be even more vulnerable in the
future.

Broader lessons from the Southeast Asian experience

Macro policy

What generalizable economic policy lessons does Southeast Asia's economic growth and development experience offer to the world? In a prominent pre-crisis analysis, W. Max Corden (1996)
attributed the exceptional growth success of the eight East Asian "miracle" economies to a

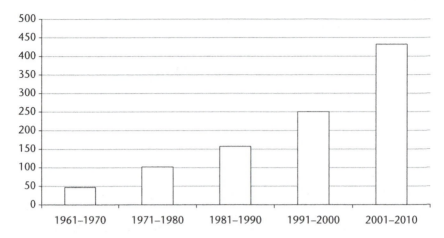

Figure 19.3 The trend of number of climate-related disasters (flood, storm, and landslide) in Southeast Asia

Source: EM-DAT: The OFDA/CRED International Disaster Database (www.emdat.be), Université Catholique de Louvain, Brussels, Belgium.

combination of underlying macroeconomic stability (as measured by low and stable rates of inflation) and a willingness to adjust policies in response to changing external circumstances. Corden called this combination "pragmatic orthodoxy." It is easy to see that these two policy stances helped the East and Southeast Asian economies to take advantage of opportunities for growth and to forestall or minimize the effects of negative macroeconomic shocks. Low and stable inflation is both a reflection of good policy (including, for example, unwillingness to monetize public sector deficits, and a relative lack of nominal price rigidities) and a condition which expands the range of possible policy responses to a shock. Thus even though the causal link from low inflation to growth is not uniquely established, exceptions (high growth with high inflation) are globally rare and usually short-lived. Similarly, the willingness and ability of political and monetary authorities to adjust exchange rates and trade or other policies in response to external shocks has helped East Asian economies to maintain the profitability of tradable sectors in the face of pressures for real appreciation, thereby preserving employment growth and domestic income growth.

Corden's conclusions are if anything reinforced when considering the non-miracle Southeast Asian economies. The Philippines' long history of low and uneven growth has been closely associated with that country's persistent failure to establish macroeconomic stability. And the fluctuating fortunes of the Vietnamese economy since *doi moi* have certainly been correlated with episodes of relative macroeconomic stability and policy flexibility.

What then, of the Asian crisis (which began one year after Corden's study) and subsequent volatility? One very big lesson for the region in 1997 was that a fixed exchange rate target, while providing a convenient nominal anchor for price stability, takes away one valuable tool of adjustment to an external shock (or, for that matter, to a persistent appreciation of the real exchange rate, something that naturally accompanies sustained long-term growth). Moving to a flexible regime adds some much-needed flexibility. However, the (perceived) need in the region to self-insure against future macroeconomic shocks by accumulating large foreign reserve cushions may have taken away another degree of freedom. In the aftermath of the global financial crisis, as in the 1990s, current account deficits are indicators of potential problems, especially when combined with low growth "effort" from each dollar of credit issued (Noble 2013).

Finally, it merits mention that regional middle-income economies must have received a big boost, in terms of macro policy lessons, from their proximity (in both economic as well as geographic senses) to the earlier-developing Northeast Asian economies and Singapore. Lessons from Korea, Taiwan, and Japan on the value of targeting price stability for long-run growth would not have been lost on those charged with forming macro policy in Southeast Asia. This kind of learning is undoubtedly a component of the growth spillovers from Northeast Asia that are so clearly revealed to be a factor in Southeast Asian success.

The central role of labor productivity

Among the more positive lessons, the overwhelmingly dominant one is that in the long run, achieving success in development requires, and is implied by, rising labor productivity. Experience in the region has shown (and experiences in other developing regions have often confirmed, frequently through counter-examples) that barriers to the mobility and efficient allocation of labor reduce aggregate growth and exacerbate tensions over the distribution of the gains from growth. Lowering these barriers, first by creating security among rural and agricultural populations, and second by promoting the integration of internal and international markets, is a necessary means to raise returns to labor, which is the primary income-earning asset of each individual in an economy. The welfare implications of trade liberalization and international market integration, abolition of controls on internal migration, implementation of meaningful land reforms, and more, are almost without exception traced to indicators of human wellbeing through their effects on the market for labor.

Through a combination of geographical accident, good neighbors, and good policies, Southeast Asian countries have succeeded at several points in their modern history in acquiring massive injections of resources that are complementary with labor. This was true of the Green Revolution in the late 1960s and 1970s, which effectively increased the endowment of land available for production of rice, the staple food crop. It was true again for the massive inflow of foreign investment that followed the Plaza Accord, which led to a boom in labor-intensive industrialization. And in a third round still in progress, it is true again of the integration of the region into vertically unbundled production networks, which raise the returns to education, skills, and entrepreneurial nimbleness.

Like the earlier injections of complementary factors, however, the current boom in skill-intensive production will succeed in the long run only if supported by good policies both in the macroeconomy and the microeconomy. Notably, in Indonesia, Laos, and Myanmar, the region's three most resource-dependent economies, this requires managing the effects of natural resource export windfalls and using them to facilitate an appropriate pace of development in infrastructure and logistics systems, so as to ensure competitive opportunities for manufacturing producers.

Dangers of extrapolation

Another broad lesson from the Southeast Asian experience is that predictions about future economic growth and development that are based on extrapolations from a country's past performance or generalization from global data sets are not very reliable. Since the very beginning of its post-colonial experience the region has turned in economic performances that defy predictions by eminent economists. Notably, the region's resource-dependent economies have escaped the worst effects of Dutch disease, in notable contrast to oil and mineral exporters elsewhere in the developing world. And, as noted in Chapter 1, the more pessimistic predictions, whether from

Myrdal in the 1960s or Acemoglu and Robinson in the 2010s, about the inevitability of major policy and growth failures in "soft states," have not, by and large, been realized in this part of the developing world.

Sadli's Law

"Bad times may produce good economic policies, and good times frequently the reverse" is an aphorism attributed to Mohamed Sadli (1922–2008), one of Indonesia's leading economists and architects of the opening of that country's economy in the early years of the New Order (Hill and Thee 2008). Sadli's Law, as it is known in Indonesia, was applied to great effect during several downturns in that country's economic fortunes, most notably at the start of the 1980s, when a world recession drove the prices of energy and commodities deeply down. Since these were Indonesia's major exports, "bad times" took the form of a large negative current account shock. Rather than double down on borrowing, price controls, and other populist measures, the Indonesian government embarked on a far-reaching program of reform in trade and commercial policy, taxation, and other areas of economic life. These reforms laid a solid foundation for Indonesia's period of "miracle" growth and the huge expansion of industrial output, jobs, and exports in the decade prior to 1997.

Sadli's Law provides an excellent axiom for optimal policy strategy in small middle-income economies that are frequently exposed to large external shocks. In the twenty-first century's fast-moving, ever-changing global economy, however, where the capital required to create the jobs that lift individuals out of poverty is highly mobile, the second half of this dictum serves more as a warning. If improving the welfare of the many is an overarching goal, then good times as well as bad must be seized as opportunities to improve policy. As other commentators once observed in a different setting, "Capital is mobile across borders; labor is not. Capital can flee from poor policies; labor is trapped" (Dornbusch and Edwards 1990: 12).[6] Economies whose populations aspire to be lifted from poverty through to middle-income must be constantly striving to maximize efficiency in resource allocation and an equitable distribution of gains.

By the standards of any comparable group of developing countries, and in spite of some clearly recognizable shortcomings, Southeast Asia's efforts in creating and sustaining growth and reducing widespread poverty must be judged a success. Whether their accomplishments thus far, the robustness of their political and economic institutions, and the pragmatic adaptability of their policy regimes will be enough to maintain the pace of development into the future, we can only guess.

Notes

1 Subsidies on fossil fuels are pervasive in Southeast Asia other than Singapore, and three countries (Indonesia, Thailand, and Malaysia) are all within the top 20 worldwide for subsidy rates. In 2011 these countries and Vietnam each devoted between 2.5 percent and 3.4 percent of GDP to spending on fuel subsidies, for a regional total of $US51bn. For additional details see Coxhead and Grainger 2014.

2 In 2004, an Islamist group set off a bomb that sank a passenger ferry in Manila Bay with the loss of 116 lives – the world's worst maritime terrorist attack.

3 Indonesia made a commitment as part of the Copenhagen Accord to reduce carbon emissions 26–41 percent relative to baseline in 2020.

4 http://www.worldbank.org/en/news/feature/2011/12/13/world-bank-supports-thailands-post-floods-recovery-effort

5 IPCC (2013), Working Group I Contribution to the IPCC Fifth Assessment Report Climate Change 2013: The Physical Science Basis, Summary for Policymakers. http://www.climatechange2013.org/images/uploads/WGIAR5-SPM_Approved27Sep2013.pdf

6 The statement is in reference to the so-called "lost decade" of the 1980s in Latin America. Ironically, much of the capital that departed Latin America at that time must ultimately have been repurposed as inward foreign investments in Southeast and East Asia – fleeing, as it were, towards better policies.

References

Ahluwalia, M.S. 1994. "Income inequality: some dimensions of the problem." In Hollis Chenery, M.S. Ahluwalia, C.L.G. Bell, J.H. Duloy, and R. Jolly, *Redistribution With Growth*, Oxford: Oxford University Press.

Asian Development Bank (ADB). 2009. *The Economics of Climate Change in Southeast Asia: A Regional Review.* Manila: ADB.

Asian Development Bank (ADB). 2012. *Asian Development Outlook 2012: Confronting Rising Inequality in Asia.* Manila: ADB.

Bertrand, J. 2008. "Ethnic conflicts in Indonesia: national models, critical junctures, and the timing of violence." *Journal of East Asian Studies* 8(3): 425–49.

Bhaskaran, M., Ho Seng Chee, D. Low, Tan Mik Song, S. Vadaketh, and Yeoh Lam Keong. 2012. "Inequality and the need for a new social compact." National University of Singapore: Lee Kuan Yew School of Public Policy (http://lkyspp.nus.edu.sg/wp-content/uploads/2013/04/SP2012_Bkgd-Pa.pdf).

Bloom, D.E., and J.G. Williamson, 1998. "Demographic transitions and economic miracles in emerging Asia." *World Bank Economic Review* 12(3): 419–55.

Brynjolfsson, E., and A. McAfee. 2011. *Race against the Machine.* Lexington, MA: Digital Frontier Press.

Corden, W.M. 1996. *Pragmatic Orthodoxy: Macroeconomic Policies in Seven East Asian Economies.* Occasional Papers No. 61. San Francisco, CA: International Center for Economic Growth.

Coxhead, I., and C. Grainger. 2014. "The incidence of energy policy reform: fossil fuel subsidies in Southeast Asia." Paper presented at EEPSEA/EAAERE Conference on the Economics of Climate Change in Southeast Asia, Siem Reap, Cambodia, 27–28 February.

Dornbusch, R., and S. Edwards. 1990. *The Macroeconomics of Populism in Latin America.* Chicago, IL: University of Chicago Press.

Hill, H. 2014. "Southeast Asian macroeconomic management: pragmatic orthodoxy?" *Masyarakat Indonesia* 39(2): 459–80.

Hill, H., and Thee Kian Wee. 2008. "Moh. Sadli (1922–2008): economist, minister and public intellectual." *Bulletin of Indonesian Economic Studies* 44(1): 151–6.

Kuznets, S.P. 1955. "Economic growth and income inequality." *American Economic Review* 45(1): 1–28.

Noble, J. 2013. "Spectre of 1990s crisis looms large as debt grows." *Financial Times*, 21 August.

Singapore Department of Statistics. 2012. *Key Household Income Trends, 2012.* www.singstat.gov.sg (accessed 4 September 2013).

Thee, K.W. 2001. "Reflections on the New Order 'miracle.'" In G. Lloyd and S. Smith (eds), *Indonesia Today: Challenges of History.* Singapore: ISEAS, pp. 163–80.

Thee, K.W. 2003. "Introduction." In Thee Kian Wee (ed.), *Recollections: The Indonesian Economy, 1950s–90s.* Singapore: ISEAS.

Thee, K.W. 2005. "Indonesia's first affirmative policy: the *Benteng* program in the 1950s." Reprinted in Thee Kian Wie (ed.), *Indonesia's Economy Since Independence.* Singapore: ISEAS, 2012, pp. 24–37.

Van Klinken, G. 2007. *Communal Violence and Democratization in Indonesia: Small Town Wars.* New York: Routledge.

Varshey, A., R. Panggabean, and M.Z. Tadjoeddin. 2004. "Patterns of collective violence in Indonesia (1990–2003)." Jakarta: United Nations Support Facility for Indonesian Reconstruction, Working Paper 04/03.

Warr, P.G. 2001. "Decentralizing government spending in Thailand." *APEC Economies Newsletter* 5(8): 1–2.

Warr, P.G. 2014. "Thailand's rice subsidy scheme rotting away." Eastasiaforum.org, 14 March (accessed 20 March 2014).

Wood, A. 1997. "Openness and wage inequality in developing countries: the Latin American challenge to East Asian conventional wisdom." *World Bank Economic Review* 11(1): 33–57.

Yusuf, A.A. 2008. "The distributional impact of environmental policy: the case of carbon tax and energy pricing reform in Indonesia." EEPSEA Research report No. 2008-RR1. Singapore: Environment and Economy Program for Southeast Asia

Yusuf, A.A., and H. Francisco. 2010. *Hotspots! Mapping Climate Change Vulnerability in Southeast Asia.* Singapore: Environment and Economy Program for Southeast Asia (EEPSEA).

Yusuf, A.A., A. Komarulzaman, E.L. Roos, and M. Horridge. 2013a. "Regional economic and emissions implication of oil palm development scenarios: a dynamic inter-regional CGE analysis for Indonesia." Paper presented at the 23rd Pacific Conference of the Regional Science Association International (RSAI)/The 4th Indonesian Regional Science Association (IRSA) Institute, July 2–3, Bandung, Indonesia.

Yusuf, A.A., A. Sumner, and I.A Rum. 2013b. "The long-run evolution of inequality in Indonesia, 1990–2012: new estimates and four hypotheses on drivers." Working Papers in Economics and Development Studies No. 201314. Department of Economics, Padjadjaran University.

Index

Please note that page numbers relating to Figures or Tables will be in *italic* print, while references to Notes will be followed by the letter 'n' and note number

ACIA (ASEAN Comprehensive Investment Agreement) 370, 373, 379
Adas, Michael 55n6, 56n30
ADB (Asian Development Bank) 19n10, 183, 186, 416–17
ADBI (Asian Development Bank Institute) 183, 184, 186
AEC (ASEAN Economy Community) 181, 272, 366, 378
AFAS (ASEAN Framework Agreement on Services) 370
AFC *see* Asian financial crisis (AFC, 1997–99)
Africa 109, 110; Sub-Saharan Africa 11, 89, 91
Afroz, R. 126
AFTA (ASEAN Free Trade Area) 181, 182, 192, 195n5, 195n6; patterns of RTA use 185–6; regional integration 366, 369, 372; *see also* ASEAN (Association of Southeast Asian Nations); regional trade agreements (RTAs)
Age Dependency Ratio (ADR) 270
ageing support ratios 224
Age of Commerce 24, 55n2
age pyramids 210, 211
aging of population, challenges of 284, 353–5
agricultural development 89–113; between 1870 and 1930 44–5; agriculture-cum-mining sector 35; climate change and threats to agricultural productivity 110; deforestation vs. agricultural expansion *117*; land consolidation 98–9; linking to food security 107–8; non-staple agriculture, increasing role 110; regional success, prospects for 19n10; "world without agriculture" 93, 97; *see also* food security, Southeast Asia; *under* labor
Agricultural Involution (Geertz) 93
agricultural transformation 97–100
AIA (ASEAN Investment Area) 370, 373, 374, 379
AIC (ASEAN Industrial Complementation) 368
AIJVs (ASEAN Industrial Joint Ventures) 368

AIPs (ASEAN Industrial Projects) 368
air quality 121, 122, 126
Aldaba, R.M. and F.T. 178n11
Allegret, J.-P. 394
Amiti, M. 83n9
AMRO (ASEAN+3 Macroeconomic Research Office) 380
Anand, Sudhir 313
Andrews, James M. 56n32
A-NET test (Advanced National Education Test), upper secondary school (Thailand) 256
anthropometry, in Southeast Asian nations *359*
APEC (Asia Pacific Economic Cooperation) 369
APT (ASEAN Plus Three) 378, 379
APTA (ASEAN Preferential Trading Agreement) 368
Aquino, Corazon 336
ASEAN (Association of Southeast Asian Nations) 5, 15, 18, 114, 153, 296n32, 367, 374, 378; AMRO (ASEAN+3 Macroeconomic Research Office) 380; ASEAN+1 RTAs 181, 182, 184, 185, 186, 193, 194; ASEAN+3 Rice Reserve Scheme 109; ASEAN-5 countries 76, 391, 392, 393, 394, 395, 396, 401, 402, 405; ASEAN-6 countries 185, 195n8, 370; ASEAN Economic Community (AEC) 181, 272, 366, 378; blueprints 286, 378; commercial policy 366–84; creation 181; Customs Code of Conduct 378; demographic factors 201, 204, 216, 218, 220, 225, 226; evolution phases 367–71; extra-regional agreements 377–8; foreign direct investment 374, *375*; Framework on RCEP 378–9; Harmonized Tariff Nomenclatures 378; Inclusion List 369, 370; integration, deepening 373–4; intra- and extra-regional flows 270–1, 272, *375*; intra-ASEAN migration 281; labor 270, 374; member countries 270, 369; merchandise trade 371–3; poverty reduction

304, 305; *see also* regional integration, outward looking; regional trade agreements (RTAs)

ASEAN–China RTA 181, 182, 185, 186, 188, 189, 193, 195n10

ASEAN Comprehensive Investment Agreement (ACIA) 370, 373, 379

ASEAN Declaration on the Protection and Promotion of the Rights of Migrant Workers 374

ASEAN Framework Agreement on Services (AFAS) 370

ASEAN Free Trade Area (AFTA) *see* AFTA (ASEAN Free Trade Area)

ASEAN Industrial Complementation (AIC) 368

ASEAN Industrial Joint Ventures (AIJVs) 368

ASEAN Industrial Projects (AIPs) 368

ASEAN Investment Area (AIA) 370, 373, 374, 379

ASEAN Investment Guarantee Agreement (IGA) 373

ASEAN–Korea RTA 181, 185, 186–7, 193

ASEAN Plus Eight 378

ASEAN Plus Six (APS) 378

ASEAN Plus Three (APT) 378, 379

ASEAN Preferential Trading Agreement (APTA) 368

ASEAN Swap Arrangement (ASA) 379

ASEAN Vision 2020 274

Asian Development Bank (ADB) 19n10, 183, 186, 416–17

Asian Development Bank Institute (ADBI) 183, 184, 186

Asian Drama: An Inquiry into the Poverty of Nations (Myrdal) 6, 9, 93

Asian financial crisis (AFC, 1997–99) 4, 13, 15, 18, 71, 83n11, 338, 367, 418; foreign direct investment 163, 173; and GFC 385–6, 388, 392

Asia Pacific Economic Cooperation (APEC) 369

Association of Southeast Asia (ASA) 368

Association of Southeast Asian Nations *see* ASEAN (Association of Southeast Asian Nations)

Athukorala, P.-C. 9, 17, 65, 142, 143, 151, 152, 153, 156, 157, 159n4, 159n11, 168, 169, 181, 194, 195n3, 258, 371, 397

Australia, regional trade agreements 195n6

automobile industry 121, 126, 146, 153–4, 160n12, 371

Avila, J. 195n5

Azis, I. 341n5

"baby boom" 210–11

Baillu, J. 231

Baker, Chris 55n3

Baldwin, R. 195n5, 341n6

Bangkok, Thailand 30, 49, 203, 208, 277, 351; Declaration 367; *see also* Thailand

Banjarmasin, port of 30

bank-based economies 391

Bank for International Settlements (BIS) 405

Bank Indonesia (BI) 337, 401

Barbier, E.B. 130

Bardhan, P. 329

Basri, M.C. 334

Batam free trade zone (BFTZ) 143, 159n3

Batavia (Jakarta) 49

Bates, R. 330

Bautista, R.M. 335, 341n6

Baxter, James 56n19

Belawan, port of 30

Belize 120

Bennett's Law 100, 106, 108

"Berkeley Mafia" (Indonesia) 329, 333

Bernardo, R.L. 336

Bhagwati, J.N. 182, 330, 333

biodiversity: and forestry 116–19; species under threat *119*

bio-fuels 110

BlackBerry devices 143

Block, S.A. 70

Boediono 341n2

Bonaparte, Sabrina 227n2

Bongaarts, John 209

Boomgaard, Peter 30, 55n5, 55n12, 56n29

Booth, Anne 8, 9, 16, 35, 39n11, 50, 51, 52, 53, 54, 55n5, 55n7, 55n11, 56n18, 56n21, 56n22, 56n23, 56n25, 56n26, 56n27, 56n31, 56n32, 89, 178n8, 245, 249, 260

Bosworth, B.P. 60, 67, 231, 232

Bowring Treaty (1856) 44, 55n3

brain drain 262

Brazil 120

BRICS countries, industrialization 39n9

British Malaya 44, 46, 48, 49, 52, 53, 56n21, 56n31

Brookfield, H. 131n1

Brunei 3, 165, 284, 369, 404, 410

Brunnschweiler, C.N. 132n11

Bryant, R.L. 131n1

BSP (Bangko Sentral ng Pilipinas), Central Bank of the Philippines 337

budgetary allocation patterns 52

Build Operate Transfer (BOT) 371

bureaucracy, economic policy reform 330

Bureau of Economic Analysis (BEA) *152*

Burma 36, 46, 51, 54, 56n25; employment in 47, 48, 55n11; rice production 45, 55n6; and second trade boom 30, 31; trade booms 38, 44; *see also* Myanmar; Rangoon, Myanmar

Busch, J. 125

business cycle synchronization 394–8

Byron, Y. 131n1

Caggiono, Giovanni 49, 55n16

Cambodia: authoritarian regimes 9; as closed economy 72; communist takeover 368; demographic factors 207, 209, 214, 215, 223, 226; development path 6; economic volatility 410; education and human capital 219, 246, 248, 249, 251, 260–1; food security and agricultural development 93, 112n4; foreign direct investment 171; fossil fuel consumption 132n5; and GFC 387, 389, 391, 394, 399, 403; global production sharing 139, 142; growth rate 61, 64; health and aging, dual burdens 351, 354, 361; Khmer Rouge, overthrow of regime 368; land resources and rural environment 120; as low-income economy 66, 81; and Mekong River 126; migration 281, 282, 294n27; poverty reduction 304, 308, 314; regional trade agreements 182; resource endowments and economic growth 128; and second trade boom 30; as smaller economy 3; and structural transformation 97; transboundary issues 126; urbanization 203; see also CLMV countries (Cambodia, Laos, Myanmar and Vietnam)

carbon emissions 122–5

CEB (children ever born) 349, 350, 351

cedula (Philippines) 56n28

CEPT (common effective preferential tariff) 182, 183, 185, 369, 370

CGE (computable general equilibrium) models 182

change in tariff classification (CTC) 189

Chaudhuri, Kirti N. 39n4

Chiang Mai Initiative (CMI) 379, 380

Chiang Mai Initiative Multilateralization (CMIM) 367, 380, 381, 383n8

"Chicago Boys" (Chile) 329

children ever born (CEB) 349, 350, 351

China 10, 28, 29, 32, 98, 102, 115, 390; accession to WTO 151; autarkic policy and Europe 28–9, 258; Cultural Revolution 141; density of population 227n3; education and human capital 248, 258, 259; foreign direct investment 174; global production sharing 151–2; growth rate 3, 63, 65–6, 80–1, 258–9, 260; as major economic power 258, 259; and Mekong River 126; in-migration from 49, 54; population 43, 55n14; as "world's factory" 65, 81

Chinn, Menzie 231, 232

Chirathivat, S. 183, 195n6

Chodorow-Reich, Gabriel 231, 232

Cholon, port of 30

climate change: global 416–17; and migration 273, 294n9; natural resources and environment 122–5; and threats to agricultural productivity 110

CLMV countries (Cambodia, Laos, Myanmar and Vietnam) 272, 369, 370; and GFC 389, 394,

395, 396, 401, 402, 403, 405; regional trade agreements 185, 195n8

closed economies 72, 83n4; see also openness

clove trade 38

CMI (Chiang Mai Initiative) 379, 380

CMIM (Chiang Mai Initiative Multilateralization) 367, 380, 381, 383n8

Cobb–Douglass production function 62, 83n7

coffee trade 24

Cold War 6, 8–9, 367

Collins, S.M. 60, 67

Colombia 330

colonial rule 7, 8, 16, 131n3; and changing role of government 53; and demographic change 48, 49; economic growth and structural change 43–6; and links with international economy 50; "nightwatchman," traditional view of colonial state as 52, 54; post-colonial governments/era 49, 54–5, 116, 178n5, 204, 366, 367, 419; strengthening of, and rising inequality 35–7; weakening of, and falling inequality 38

Columbus, Christopher 22, 23

Comer, B. 331–2, 341n4

command to market economy transition 10

commercial policy 366–84; integration, deepening 373–4; whether Southeast Asia has workable financial safety net 379–81; see also ASEAN (Association of Southeast Asian Nations); regional integration, outward looking

commodities: global market integration 25–6; great commodity exporters' terms of trade boom 31–3; price volatility and export-led collapse 37

common effective preferential tariff (CEPT) 182, 183, 185, 369, 370

communist regimes, collapse 329

Compact Electronics 142

computable general equilibrium (CGE) models 182

Comrade database, UN 159n4

consumer price index (CPI) 306

Copenhagen Accord 420n3

Corden, W. Max 417–18

corruption perceptions 12

Coxhead, Ian 11, 15, 16, 17, 19, 65, 66, 81, 89, 112n1, 117, 118, 131n3, 132n13, 172, 258, 263, 264, 265, 420n1

Cribb, Robert 56n29

"crony capitalism" 130, 335

Cropper, M. 120

CTC (change in tariff classification) 189

Cultural Revolution (China) 141

currency appreciation 404

current accounts, impact of GFC on 386–90

da Gama, Vasco 22, 23

DALYs (disability-adjusted life years) 355, 356, 357

Danang, port of 30
Datt, Gaurav 313
Dayal-Ghalati, A. 231
DEA (developing East Asia) 146, 159n5
De Dios, E.S. 336, 341n2, 341n9
deforestation 117, 118, 119, 416
de-industrialization 34–5, 38, 47
Demographic and Health Survey data 362n2
demographic dividend 217
demographic factors 17, 43, 115; age pyramids
    210, 211; age structure changes, implications
    217–20, *221*, 222; aging of population,
    challenges of 284; ASEAN countries 201, 204,
    216, 218, 220, 225, 226; "baby boom" 210–11;
    changes, from 1870 to 1970 48–9, 55n1;
    Chinese population 43, 55n14; demographic
    transition *see* demographic transition; density of
    population 227n3; elderly, care of 224–5;
    European population and trade booms
    connection 27; forest area vs. population density
    118; growth and development 48, 201, 214–17;
    historical context of population situation in
    Southeast Asia 202–4; International Conference
    on Population and Development, Cairo (1994)
    223, 224; labor mobility 225–6; migration
    209–10, 273, 282; momentum, demographic
    210–12, *213*; mortality statistics *see* mortality
    statistics; policy insights/issues 222–6;
    population aging in developing Asia *239*;
    prospects for future population growth 214–17;
    replacement levels 204, *207*, 209, 211, 223, 226,
    353; Southeast Asian population 48, 201–29;
    trends in vital rates and population growth
    204–9; UN "medium" population projections
    214, *215*, 222, 227n6; urbanization 115, *116*,
    203, 226, 277, 294n4; variation in fertility,
    mortality and population aging 48, 206, 207,
    270, 349–55; *see also* fertility; health and aging,
    dual burdens
demographic transition 10, 18, 96, 204, 218, 236,
    239, 270, 408, 409; epidemiologic transition
    348, 357; European 209; nutrition transition
    348, 357–8; theory 206, 207, 208, 209
depression, economic *see* Great Depression (1930s)
developing East Asia (DEA) 146, 159n5
development in Southeast Asia *see* agricultural
    development; growth and development,
    Southeast Asia
dietary transformation *101*, 102
difference-in-difference models 63
disease patterns, health challenges 355–61
Dobado, Gonzáles 39n10
Doeppers, Daniel F. 227n2
domestic savings rates, determinants and long-term
    projections 230–44; composition of domestic
    saving rate 230; decline in 231, 240; dependent
    variable 231–2; in developing Asia 233, *234–5*,

236–9, *240*; estimation model of determinants
    of rates 231–3; estimation results 237–8;
    financial sector development 232, 236–7, 238;
    interest rates 232–3; life cycle model 231;
    nominal rates 233, 236; past trends in
    developing Asia 233, *234–5*, 236–7; projections
    in developing Asia for 2011–30 238–9, *240*; real
    rates 231–2, 236, *240*; trends over time in
    gross rates *234–5*; variable definitions and data
    sources *241*
"dotcom" recession (2001) 392
"double-dip" recession 397
Drabble, John H. 56n21
"drain" (unrequited export surplus) 51, 56n23,
    56n25
Dutch disease 11, 33, 35, 128, 404
Dutch East India Company (VOC) 23,
    24, 30
Dutch East Indies 32, 33, 34, 37

East Asian Miracle (*EAM*), World Bank 60, 64, 245,
    246, 385
East Asia Summit (EAS) 378
Easterly, W. 19n5
East Timor: food security and agricultural
    development 93, 112n4; as smaller economy 3
economic distance, measures 68
Economic Freedom of the World project
    71, 72
economic growth *see* growth and development,
    Southeast Asia
economic inequality and policy stability: Indonesia
    413–14; inequality trends 411–13; prognosis
    415; Thailand 414–15; *see also* inequalities
economic integration, international 9
economic policy reform 327–43; bureaucracy 330;
    case studies, Southeast Asia 331–8; crisis
    hypothesis 329; definitions 328; donor
    conditionality 330–1; drivers of reform 329–31;
    due diligence 328; issues and context 328–31;
    legislated central bank independence and fiscal
    rules 336–8; Philippines 335–6; and political
    leaders 330; trade liberalization 332–4, 335–6;
    U-turns 327; Vietnam 331–2, 341n4
education 17–18; access to 50, 254–7;
    demographic factors 218, 219, *221*, 227n8;
    growth, globalization and demand for skills
    258–60; higher level 250–1; and human capital
    246–66; inequalities 256–7; investments in
    Southeast Asia 260–2; net enrolment rate
    (NER), primary school 246–7, 248; primary
    253; public education expenditure *252*, 261;
    pupil/teacher ratio in primary education 248,
    253; quality, relatively low nature of 178n8,
    249, 251, *252*, 253–4, 261–2, 267n12; quantity
    246–51; rapid expansion of schooling
    infrastructure 254; schooling, mean years of

248–9, 255, *256*; supply of 246–58; tertiary
  level 251, 257, 262
Edwards, Sebastian 231, 341n2
Eichengreen, B. 65
elderly, care of 224–5
electronics industry, global production sharing
  140, 141, 143, 151–2
El Niño/Southern Oscillation (ENSO) 123, 128
Emerson, Rupert 56n31
employment: diversification (from 1870 to 1970)
  46–8; "by-employment," agricultural 55n12;
  indigenous workers 48, 55n11; manufacturing
  sector 47
Engel curves 104
Engel's Law 100
English (British) East India Company 23–4, 32
Enke, S. 8
ENSO (El Niño/Southern Oscillation) 123, 128
entrepreneurial spirit 8
environment: air quality 121, 122, 126; forestry
  and biodiversity 116–19; fossil fuel consumption
  122–3; greenhouse gases 110, 123; haze 126,
  128, 132n7, 132n9; natural disasters,
  vulnerability to 124, 417; and natural resources
  17, 116–28; particulate matter less than 10
  microns (PM_{10}) 121, 122, 126, *127*, 128, 132n8;
  pollution 115; risks 415–17; road networks 120;
  rural *see* rural environment; sewage disposal 121;
  urban 6, 121–2; *see also* climate change
Environmental Kuznets Curve hypothesis 115
epidemiologic transition 348, 357
EPZs (export processing zones) 189
Erlich, Paul 9
Ertur, C. 68, 69, 74, 81
Essahbi, E. 394
Estevadeordal, A. 62, 63, 84n20
Estrada, G. 195n2
ethical policy 52, 56n29
ethnic minorities 49, 169–70, 204
European trade boom: inter-continental, after
  1500 22–3; and population 27; small gains for
  Southeast Asia from 29–30
Evenson, Robert E. 55n5
exchange rate policy, and GFC 402–5
expenditure surveys 112n6
export processing zones (EPZs) 189
exports 6, 9, 23, 26–7, 28, 34, 46, *390*; collapse 37,
  45; export-led growth (1870–1930) 51; global
  production sharing 139, 143, 146, *149*; great
  commodity exporters' terms of trade boom
  31–3; primary shares *129*, 130–1; rice 109–10;
  and trade boom 23–4

Fairchild (electronics MNE) 143, 159n1
Family Income and Expenditure Survey,
  Philippines 306
Famine 1975! (Paddock) 9

FAO (Food and Agriculture Organization),
  United Nations 91; Food Balance Sheet data
  102; *State of Food Insecurity in the
  World 2012* 90
farm and village communities 6
FDI *see* foreign direct investment (FDI), Southeast
  Asia
Federated Malay States 46, 52, 53,
  56n31
Feldstein, Martin 231
female workers 47
fertility 48, 349–53; decline in 206–12, 218, 223,
  224, 227n5, 227n6, 349, 351; net reproduction
  rates (NRR) 351, 362n4; replacement levels
  204, *207*, 209, 211, 223, 226, 353; Total
  Fertility Rates (TFR) *206*, *207*, *208*, *213*,
  227n4, 270, 349, 351, *352*, 362n4; *see also*
  demographic factors; demographic transition
financial sector, impacts of GFC on 391–4
fiscal policy: and GFC 398–9; in Indonesia 56n27;
  in Philippines 56n27
"flying geese" hypothesis 83n7
Food and Agriculture Organization *see* FAO (Food
  and Agriculture Organization), United Nations
food security, Southeast Asia 16; and agricultural
  development 89–113; agricultural
  transformation 97–100; challenges 108–10;
  changes in food system 92–3; comparative
  indicators *90*; dietary transformation 100, *101*,
  102; essential components 107; food security
  "gap" 91, 112n2; fundamental transformations
  needed to provide 93–102; "macro" food
  security 106; modern food supply chains
  107–8; near-poor, vulnerability 109; rapid
  change in foods systems since 1960 90–3; rice,
  changing role in 102–6, *105*; structural poverty,
  growing importance 109; structural
  transformation 93, *94–5*, 96–7; supermarkets
  16, 93, 99, 100, 107, 108; "10-wheeler" model
  107, 108; volatility of food systems and
  flexibility in food policy 109
foreign direct investment (FDI), Southeast Asia 12,
  17, 65, 162–80; and air transport 167, 168; Asian
  financial crisis 163, 173; attitudes to 162; balance
  of payments data 166; commercial policy 374,
  375; determinants 163, 167–72; distribution of
  FDI to South East Asia 163; effects 174–6;
  European comparisons 167; export-oriented
  171; foreign MNEs, share in Southeast Asian
  manufacturing *166*; geography, role 173–4; and
  GFC 397; industrialization, growth and trade
  174–6; inflows 163, *164*, 170, 171–2, 176, 177;
  institutional change 168–70; intra-ASEAN 270;
  locational advantages 170–1; main sources *165*;
  market-seeking 170; multinational enterprises
  162, 165, 166, 170, 171, 172, 174, 176, 177;
  output 167; policy differences 162–3; political

and macroeconomic stability 172–3; regional integration 372, 374; relative importance 163–4; resource-seeking 171; shares of inflows to Southeast Asia (1970–2011) *164*; source 162, 165; stock of inward 163, *164*; tariff-jumping 178n7; technological change 167–8; and World Bank 167, 168, 171

forestry and biodiversity 116–19; deforestation 117, 118, 119, 416

fossil fuel consumption 122–3, 131n5, 420n1

Foster, Anne L. 56n26

Francois, J.F. 195n2

Freedom to Trade Internationally index 72

free trade agreements (FTAs) 370; ASEAN 182, 186, *187*, 189; bilateral 379; extra-regional 377–8; forms 376; rise of 374, 376–7

Frisch, Max 294n11

FTAs *see* free trade agreements (FTAs)

fuel subsidies 131

Fujii, Takao 232

Furnivall, J.S. 49

gains from trade 35

Garrity, D.P. 120

GDP (gross domestic product): and GFC 387; internal and external growth (since 1970) 70, 71, 72, *78*, *79*, *80*; and particulate matter *127*; poverty reduction 318, 325; real per capita growth and domestic savings rate 232; *see also* growth and development research models; growth in Southeast Asia; spillovers

Geertz, Clifford 93

General Agreement on Trade in Services (GATS) 370

general equilibrium modeling (GEM) 314

Genuine Domestic Savings (GDS) indicator, World Bank 128, *129*

geographical factors: foreign direct investment 173–4; proximity of Southeast Asian economies to those of Northeast Asia 65, 67; regional trade agreements 190, 192; world manufacturing trade, geographic profile *144–5*

GFC *see* global financial crisis (GFC)

GLC (government-linked corporate) sector 374

global economic volatility 409–11

global financial crisis (GFC) 4, 18, 151, 385–407; aggregate demand *390*; and Asian financial crisis 385–6, 388; business cycle synchronization 394–8; capital formation 397, *398*; and exchange rate policy 402–5; exports, estimated elasticity *390*; and fiscal policy 398–9; impact on financial sector 391–4; impact on growth and current accounts 386–90; macroeconomic policy responses to 398–405; and monetary policy 399–402; and stock market 392–3; V-shaped recoveries of Southeast Asian economies 388

globalization 36, 39n3, 273; and education 258–60; first era 43

global production sharing (GPS) 139–61; composition of network products exported 146, *149*; within- and between-country differences *154*, 156; definitions 139; determinants 152–3; domestic value added criterion 156–7; electrical goods 153; electronics industry 140, 141, 143, 151–2; exports 139, 143, 146, *149*; GPS industries at four-digit level of International Standard Industrial Classification 153, 158–9; history 140–3; and manufacturing *144–5*, 146, 153, *154–5*, 156–7, 159n9; and migration 273; multinational enterprises 140, 141, 143, 146, 151, 153, 157; networks 141–2; semiconductor devices 140–1, 142, 143; Southeast Asia and China in production networks 151–2; success of Southeast Asia 139; trade patterns 143, *144–5*, 146, *147–9*, 150–1; value added shares in GPS industries *154*, 156; world manufacturing trade, geographic profile *144–5*

Goh Keng Swee 141

Golay, Frank 56n23

government-linked corporate (GLC) sector 374

Government of Singapore Investment Corporation 165

GPS *see* global production sharing (GPS)

gravity models 65, 67–8

Great Depression (1930s) 37, 43, 44, 45

Great Recession (2008–10) *see* global financial crisis (GFC)

Green, D. 399

greenhouse gases 110, 123, 415

Green Revolution 9, 16, 106

gross domestic product *see* GDP (gross domestic product)

gross enrollment rate (GER) 251, 262

gross fixed capital formation (GCFC) 262

Grove, R. 131n1

growth and development, Southeast Asia: from 1870 to 1970 9, 16, 43–59; from 1970 16, 60–86; from 1980s 3; aggregate growth and poverty 317–19; agricultural development *see* agricultural development; *ceteris paribus* rate 61; deceleration of 80; demographic factors 48, 201, 214–17; determinants 64–7; economic growth in East and Southeast Asia (since 1970) 60–2; and education 258–60; employment, diversification 46–8; food security 93; GFC, impact on 386–9; global context of growth 63–7; government, changing role 52–4; high-performing economies *see* HPAEs ("high-performing Asian economies"); internal and external sources 60–86; international economy, increasing links with 50–1; long-run growth among resource-abundant economies *11*; "miracle" years 10, 13, 15, 16, 385; natural resources and environmental basis of economic growth *see* natural resources; non-agricultural sectors 45, 46; Northeast Asian economic growth, GDP growth spillovers from 65, *79*, *80*; openness 26, 39n5, 62–3, 70, 71, 72, *73*, 75; pessimistic predictions 9–12, 419–20; poverty reduction 303–4, 316, 317–18; rate and pattern 4–5; regional growth 10, *61*, 63–4; research models *see* growth and development research models; and resource endowments 128–31; sectoral growth, and poverty 319–21; whether Southeast Asian economies grow differently 70; spillovers *see* spillovers; structural change and growth (from 1870 to 1970) 43–6, 54; transformation of production and sources of household income 3–4; urbanization 49–50; variety of experiences among countries 3, 5–6, 9–10, 64, 80, 270; "vent-for-surplus" growth 19n8; as work in progress 408; worldwide economic growth *78*, *79*, 114; *see also* GDP (gross domestic product); growth and development research models; Northeast Asian economic growth; Southeast Asian economies; spillovers

growth and development research models: Cobb–Douglass production function 62, 83n7; countries in dataset *82–3*; data 62, 71–2, *82–3*; difference-in-difference models 63; dummy variables 61, 67, 83n3; estimation 70–8; explanatory variables of standard growth model 60; fixed-effects approaches 70, 84n22; gravity models 65, 67–8; maximum likelihood estimates 69, 74, 77, 81, 84n23; model specification 67–70; Ordinary Least Squares analysis 69, 70, 72, 75; results, estimation 72–8; Sachs–Warner index 61, 62, 72, 84n20; simulations, based on econometric results 60–1; Solow model 61, 62, 63, 68, 83n7; spatial autoregressive models 69, 81; spatial weight matrix 69–70; *see also* growth and development, Southeast Asia

growth-poverty nexus: conceptual background 314–17; poverty and aggregate growth 317–18

Guerrero, M.C. 55n7

Gylfason, T. 128, 130

Habibie, Bacharuddin Jusuf (Indonesian President) 341n7

Haiphong, port of 30

handheld products (HHPs) 142

Hansen, V. 19n13, 156

hard disk drive assemblers 141

Hayami, Yujiro *94–5*

haze 126, 128, 132n7, 132n9

health and aging, dual burdens 347–65; challenges of aging of population 353–5; changing disease patterns 355–61; emerging population

challenges 347–65; infectious diseases 357, 362; IPUMS census data 349, 362n1; malnutrition 91, 359, 360; policy insights/issues 361–2; sedentary lifestyles 358–9; Southeast Asian population 347–65; transitions over five decades 347–9; undernutrition 348, 360; variation in fertility, mortality and population aging 349–55; *see also* demographic factors

health facilities, access to 50, 56n35

Heckscher, Eli 36

Held, David 167–8

Henley, David 227n2

Higgins, M. 231

higher education 250–1

high-income countries 239, 246, 261, 270; foreign direct investment 162, 168; and GFC 386, 389, 396; internal and external growth (since 1970) 72, 81; *see also* low-income countries; middle-income countries; *specific countries*

"high-performing Asian economies" *see* HPAEs ("high-performing Asian economies")

Hill, Hal 18, 152, 169, 171, 181, 182, 194, 265, 270, 333, 334, 374, 377, 382n2, 383n8, 383n9, 383n10, 410, 411, 413, 420

Hiratsuka, D. 181, 183, 184

Hirschman, Charles 227n2

Hitachi 170

HIV/AIDS 357

Hong, K. 60, 83n5, 238

Hong Kong 140, 141, 173, 246

Hon Hai Precision Industry 142

Horioka, Charles Y. 231, 232

Houben, Vincent J.H. 55n17

HPAEs ("high-performing Asian economies") 10, 60, 63, 64, 72, 246

Huff, Gregg 49, 55n16, 56n20, 56n31, 169

Hugo, Graeme 227n2

human capital: and education supply 246–58; policy 260–6

Human Development Index 56n34

Hung, Juann H. 231

hunger 91, 92

Hun Sen 340

Hurst, P. 131n4

Hutchcroft, Paul D. 56n30, 336, 341n2, 341n3, 341n9

IGA (ASEAN Investment Guarantee Agreement) 373

IMF (International Monetary Fund) 165, 337, 379

imperata grasslands 120

import-substitution industrialization (ISI) policies 38

independence, political 46, 54–5

India: and agricultural transformation 98; de-industrialization 34; as major economic

power 258; in-migration from 48, 54; population 43; rice production 102
Indochina 36, 45, 51, 52
Indonesia: and agricultural transformation 98, 99; Asian Crisis (1997–99) 13; "balanced budget" rule 336; "Berkeley Mafia" 329, 333; carbon emissions 125; central bank independence 336, 337; and changing role of government 52, 54; and China 65; climate change 123; declaration of independence (1945) 46; de-industrialization 34–5; demographic factors 202, 207, 210, 214, 222, 225; domestic savings rates 230, 236; economic inequality and policy stability 412, 413–14; economic policies and growth (from 1870 to 1970) 45; economic policy reform 329, 332–4; education and human capital 218, 248, 248–9, 255, 256–7, 261, 262, 264–6, 267n12; employment in 47, 48, 55n9, 55n11; ethnic minorities 204; fiscal policy 56n27; food consumption, changing role of rice *111*; food security and agricultural development *96*, 97, 98, 99, 102, 108, *111*; foreign direct investment 163, 166, 167, 171, 172–3, 175; fossil fuel consumption 132n5; and GFC 385, 392; global production sharing 139, 143, 156, 160n12; growth rate 9, 11, 46, 64, 72, 77, 265; health and aging, dual burdens 351, 361; inequalities 37; labor productivity, central role 419; land resources and rural environment 120, 121; as large economy 3, 10; and links with international economy 50–1; as low-income economy 66; migration 275, 284, 285, 294n22; natural disasters, vulnerability to 124; natural resources and agricultural products 9; New Order regime 15, 420; population 55n1; poverty reduction 306, 308, *323*; redistributive policies 414; regional integration 371–2, 374, 383n10; regional trade agreements 184, 185, 186, 188; resource booms and returns to skills 264–6; resource endowments and economic growth 128, 130; rice production 97, 102, *111*; and second trade boom 30, 31; Soeharto era 333, 340; and structural transformation *96*, 97; structural transformation *96*; textile manufacturing 34–5; and trade bust 38; transboundary issues 128; urbanization 203, 272, 276; *see also* Jakarta, Indonesia; Java, Indonesia
INDSTAT database, UNIDO 153
Industrial Coordination Act (ICA), 1975 (Malaysia) 169
industrialization 38, 55n8; of BRICS countries 39n9; de-industrialization 34–5, 38, 47; foreign direct investment 174–6; origins in Southeast Asia 17; as policy goal 45–6
inequalities: economic inequality and policy stability 411–15; education 256–7; engines of

inequality 355; falling, and weakening of colonial rule 38; horizontal 348; Indonesia 37; and price stability 411–15; rising, and strengthening of colonial rule 27, 35–7; trade booms and busts 35–6, 37, 38; trends 411–13; vertical and regional 347, *348*
infant mortality 53, 204, *205*
infectious diseases 357, 362
inflation 400, 401, *402*
Information Technology Agreement (ITA) 189
infrastructure, expenditure on 52, 54, 56n32
Ingram, J. 55n3
institutional change, foreign direct investment 168–70
institutional pessimism 19n10
Intel Corporation (semiconductor producer) 142, 170
Intergovernmental Panel on Climate Change (IPCC) 417, 420n5
International Conference on Population and Development, Cairo (1994) 223, 224
international financial institutions (IFI) 331, 334, 337
International Labour Organization (ILO) 267n4
international migration 277, 279–85; key driving factors 281–2, 284; key trends 279–80; main destinations of international migrants from Southeast Asia 273, *279*; within the region 281; from region to rest of world 284–5; and Southeast Asian population 209–10, 225, 277; trends 282–4, 285; *see also* migration
International Monetary Fund (IMF) 165, 337, 379
International Standard Industrial Classification (ISIC), GPS industries at four-digit level of 153, 158–9
intra-regional trade 27, 44, 177, 270, 370, 371
Ireland 167
Irwin, Douglas 39n3
ITA (Information Technology Agreement) 189

Jakarta, Indonesia 183, 203, 277; *see also* Indonesia
Japan: export drive 46, 55n7, 56n22; foreign direct investment 170, 173–4; growth rate 66, 83n15; Imperial Army 46; multinational enterprises 141; occupation of Southeast Asia by (1942–45) 43; and structural transformation *96*; structural transformation *96*; as technological leader 246; terms of trade exceptionalism 33
Japan External Trade Organization (JETRO) 173
Java, Indonesia 37, 44, 49, 52, 55n1, 202, 351; *see also* Indonesia
Java–Madura 102–3
J-curve transition 10
Jha, Shikha 232
Johnston, R. 126
Jokinen, J. 126

Jomo K.S. 11–12
Jones, Gavin W. 17, 115, 203, 208, 210, 216, 220, 226, 227n8, 267n12, 270, 347, 348, 349, 353, 355

Kahin, George 19n2
Kanbur, S.M.R. 313
Kansu, G. 368
Kaosa-ard, M. 125
Karnow, Stanley 6, 7, 15, 19n3
Kaur, Amarjit 55n17, 56n33
Kawai, M. 181, 183, 184, 195n2, 195n6, 195n7
Khor, Kok-Peng 56n24
Kim, Soyoung 231, 394
Kinugasa, Tomoko 218
Kislev, Y. 55n5
Kitwiwattanachai, A. 195n2
Koch, W. 68, 69, 74, 81
Kohpaiboon, Archanun 17, 151, 159, 168, 169, 178n11, 181, 194, 195n3, 258, 371
Konings, J. 83n9
Korean War 54
Kozuru, I. 402
krismon ("monetary crisis") 15
kristal ("total crisis") 15
Krueger, A.O. 331
Krugman, P. 10, 22, 60
Kuala Lumpur 183, 352
Kumar, S. 181, 183, 188
Kummu, M. 126
Kurihara, Kenneth 47, 55n10
"Kuznets effect," poverty reduction 313

labor 4, 10, 19, 140, 143, 160, 270; abundance 3, 31, 98, 258, 295n25; agriculture/land 18, 27, 35, 36, 37, 93, 96, 99, 303, 320; ASEAN countries 270, 374; costs 13, 156, 157, 160n14, 257, 259; export and import of 273, 279, 283, 284, 295n25, 374; and manufacturing *see* labor in industry and manufacturing; markets 157, 251, 254, 257, 274, 275, 331, 374, 382, 385, 409, 413; migration 274, 275, 279, 282, 284, 285, 286, 287, 295n24, 367; mobility 18, 177, 225–6, 257, 279, 282, 287, 316; policy 361–2; productivity 4, 9, 37, 93, 96, 98, 153, 178n10, 414, 419; scarcity 31, 37, 98, 295n25, 409; semi-skilled or unskilled 173, 258, 266, 281, 286, 316, 320, 325, 409; skilled 65, 251, 254, 262, 263, 265, 266, 286, 287, 374, 378; *see also* migration
labor in industry and manufacturing 9, 15, 34, 38, 118, 325, 368, 376, 419; education and human capital 258, 259, 260, 266; foreign direct investment 162, 169, 173, 174, 177; global production sharing 140, 156, 159n7, 160n14; internal and external growth (since 1970) 60, 64, 65, 66, 80; outsourcing 162, 169, 173, 177

laissez-faire economic policy 141
Lal, D. 329
land resources and rural environment 119–21
Lao Expenditure and Consumption Survey (LECS) 306
Laos/Lao PDR: as closed economy 72; communist takeover 368; demographic factors 202, 207, 209, 214, 215, 223, 226; development path 6; economic inequality and policy stability 412; economic volatility 410; education and human capital 219, 246, 248, 249, 255, 257, 260–1; food security and agricultural development 93, 112n4; foreign direct investment 171; forestry and biodiversity 116; fossil fuel consumption 132n5; and GFC 389, 391, 394, 399, 401; growth rate 61, 64; health and aging, dual burdens 351, 361; labor productivity, central role 419; land resources and rural environment 120; as low-income economy 66, 81; and Mekong River 126; migration 281, 282, 294n22; mining 132n14; natural disasters, vulnerability to 124; poverty reduction 304, 306, 308, *323*; regional trade agreements 182; resource endowments and economic growth 128; and second trade boom 30; as smaller economy 3; and structural transformation 97; transformation 4; urbanization 276; *see also* CLMV countries (Cambodia, Laos, Myanmar and Vietnam)
Latham, A.J.H. 39n7
Latin America 109, 110, 152, 171, 205, 341n1, 421n6
LEDs (light-emitting diodes) 152
Lee, J.-W. 60, 83n5, 231, 238
Lee Kuan Yew 169, 178n5
Lehman Brothers, collapse (2008) 386
Leung, S. 341n4
Lewis, W. Arthur 34
Lian, Chang 16, 112n1
Life World Library (American series) 6
Lim, Teck-Ghee 56n18
Lipsey, R.E. 165, 171, 174, 175, 177, 178n11, 397
loans, non-performing 391, 392
Loayza, Norman 231, 232
local institutions 6
low-income countries 12, 130; education and human capital 257, 261; and GFC 389, 396; health and aging, dual burdens 348, 358; internal and external growth (since 1970) 66, 81; *see also* high-income countries; middle-income countries; *specific countries*
Luhrman, M. 231
Luton, Harry 56n27

MacIntyre, A. 330, 333
Mackie, J.A.C. 333

macroeconomic policy 18, 336; exchange rate policy 402–5; fiscal policy 398–9; monetary policy 399–402; pricing dynamics 360–1; responses to GFC 398–405; twenty-first-century challenges 417–19; see also global financial crisis (GFC)

macroeconomic stability 60, 64, 72; foreign direct investment 172–3

Maddison, Angus 23, *31*, 32, 34, 35, 38, *44*, *53*, 55n4, 55n14, *95*

Makassar, port of 30

Malaysia/Malaya 157; British Malaya 44, 46, 48, 49, 52, 53, 56n21, 56n31; carbon emissions 125; and changing role of government 54; and China 65; demographic factors 202, 204, 206, 209, 210, 212, 215, 220, 225, 226, 227n8; domestic savings rates 230, 236; economic inequality and policy stability 412; economic policy reform 328, 331; economic volatility 410; education and human capital 218, 227n8, 247–8, 251, 253, 260, 265; ethnic minorities 169–70, 204; expulsion of Singapore from Malaya in 1965 169; Federated Malay States 46, 52, 53, 56n31; food security and agricultural development 108, 112n4; foreign direct investment 163, 166, 167, 168–9, 171, 172–3, 175, 176, 397; forestry and biodiversity 118; fossil fuel consumption 132n5; and GFC 385, 386, 387, 391, 392; global production sharing 139, 140, 141, 151, 152, 153, 156; growth rate 8, 11, 46, 64, 72; health and aging, dual burdens 351, 352, 357, 359; labor market 409; land resources and rural environment 120, 121; as large economy 3, 10; migration 281, 282, 284, 286, 294n5; natural resources and agricultural products 9; New Economic Policy 169, 208; openness 72, 75, 366; poverty reduction 308, 314, 317, 322, *323*, 324; regional integration 371, 374; regional trade agreements 184, 185, 186, 188; resource dependence 11; resource endowments and economic growth 128, 130; rice production *105*; and second trade boom 30, 31; and structural transformation 97; transboundary issues 126; urbanization 203, 272, 276; wage–rental ratio (w/r) 36; wheat production *105*; see also Singapore

malnutrition 91, 359, 360

Malthusian limits 9

Manchu authorities, China (1644–1911) 28

Manderson, Lenore 55n15

Manila, Philippines 30, 49, 203, 277, 412; see also Philippines

Mankiw, G.N. 61, 68, 74

manufacturing 47, 115; foreign direct investment *166*, *175*; global production sharing *144–5*, 146, *147–8*, 153, *154–5*, 156–7, 159n9; parts and components in trade flows, South Asia 146,

150; share of network products in *147–8*; textiles 34–5; world manufacturing trade, geographic profile *144–5*; see also global production sharing (GPS)

Manzano, G. 195n5

Marcos, Ferdinand 335, 339

market integration hypothesis 23

Marks, Robert 28, 37

Mason, Andrew 218

Maternal Mortality Ratios (MMRs) 205, 270

Matsubayashi, Yoichi 232

May, Glenn Anthony 56n30

McKinsey and Company 195n5

Medalla, E.M. 341n6

megacities 277

Megawati Sukarnoputri, Indonesian President 338, 341n7

Mekong countries 9, 15, 123, 126; see also Cambodia; Laos; Vietnam

Mekong River Commission (MRC) 126

Menon, Jayant 18, 171, 181, 182, 194, 270, 377, 382n2, 383n8, 383n9, 383n10, 410

Mercosur 382n1

Mertens, Walter 47, 55n10

Metzer, Jacob 56n34

Mexico 120

MFN (most-favored nation) status 151

Middle East 109

middle-income countries 3, *4*, *5*, 13, 15, 17, 93, 239, 251, 272; internal and external growth (since 1970) 65, 81, 83n14; middle-income trap 81, 108, 266; policy reform, political economy 327, 339; twenty-first-century challenges 408, 415, 419, 420

migration 270–99; ASEAN Declaration on the Protection and Promotion of the Rights of Migrant Workers 374; basic key indicators of Southeast Asian countries *271*; challenges and policy implications 285–7; and climate change 273, 294n9; demographic factors 209–10, 273, 282; illegal workers 282, 294n30; internal 209–10, 255–6, 273, 275; international see international migration; key driving factors 281–2, 284; migrant stock matrix (2000 and 2010) *288–9*; migrant to population ratio *290–1*; in-migration to Southeast Asia 48–9; mutual recognition agreements 286, 287; and regional integration 379; regional share of migrant destination *292–3*; remittances 275, 280, 294n10; strategies 122–5; trends 282–4, 285; understanding 274–6; and urbanization in Southeast Asia 272, 276–7, *278*; see also labor; urbanization

Milanovic, B. 39n11

Millennium Development Goals (MDGs) 91

Minebea (Japanese MNE) 142

Ming authorities, China (1368–1644) 28

minimum dietary energy requirement
(MDER) 91
mining 132n14
Mitchell, Kate L. 55n9
MM (European import demand function), trade
booms 25, 26
MMRs (Maternal Mortality Ratios)
205, 270
MNCs (multinational companies) 183, 184
MNEs (multinational enterprises): and ASEAN
countries 371; foreign direct investment 162,
165, 166, *166*, 170, 171, 172, 174, 175, 176,
177; global production sharing 140, 141, 142,
143, 146, 151, 153, 157
Modigliani, Franco 231
Mohamed, Mahathir 170, 222
Moneta, F. 394
monetary policy: expansionary 400; and GFC
399–402
monopolies, European 29, 39n3
Moreno, R. 68, 69, 81
mortality statistics 48, 201, 206, 353; infant
mortality 53, 204, *205*; Maternal Mortality
Ratios (MMRs) 205, 270
Motorola 170
MRAs (mutual recognition agreements) 286, 287,
378, 383n5
Multifibre Agreement (MFA) 173
multinational enterprises *see* MNEs (multinational
enterprises)
multipurpose automobiles 160n12
mutual recognition agreements (MRAs) 286, 287,
378, 383n5
Myanmar: carbon emissions 125; demographic
factors 202, 204, 208, 209–10, 220, 225, 227n5;
development path 6; economic volatility
409–10; education and human capital 248, 249,
255; food security and agricultural development
93, 112n4; fossil fuel consumption 132n5; and
GFC 394, 399, 401, 403; growth rate 13; health
and aging, dual burdens 351, 352, 357, 361; as
isolationist state 369; labor productivity, central
role 419; land resources and rural environment
120; as low-income economy 66; and Mekong
River 126; migration 281, 282; poverty
reduction 304; regional integration, outward
looking 366; regional trade agreements 182;
resource endowments and economic growth
130; and structural transformation 97;
urbanization 276; *see also* Burma; CLMV
countries (Cambodia, Laos, Myanmar and
Vietnam)
Myint, Hla 19n8, 51, 329, 366
Myrdal, Gunnar 6, 9, 19n1, 19n3, 93

Nanking Treaty (1842) 28
Napoleonic Wars (1803–15) 24

National Economics and Social Development
Board (NESDB) 159n9
National Semiconductor (US company)
140, 141, 143
National Statistical Coordination Board
(Philippines) 306
National Statistical Office (NSO), Thailand 306
natural disasters, vulnerability to 124, 417
natural resources: abundance 10–11, 36; and
agricultural products 9; carbon emissions 122–5;
and China 259; climate change 122–5; and
environment 17, 116–28; forestry and
biodiversity 116–19; land resources and rural
environment 119–21; migration strategies
122–5; potential impacts 122–5; resource curse
model 10, 11, 128; resource endowments and
economic growth 128–31; transboundary issues
126–8; urban environment 121–2; urban–rural
gap, closing 121
Nelson, Joan 341n2
net enrolment rate (NER), primary school
246–7, 248
Netherlands Indies 43, 44, 46, 50
net reproduction rates (NRR) 351, 362n4
new economic order 34
New Economic Policy (NEP), Malaysia
169, 208
New Economic Zones 210
Nidec Corporation (Japanese hard disk drive
manufacturer) 142
"nightwatchman," traditional view of colonial state
as 52
Nipon Poapangsakorn 99
Nitisastro, Widjojo 227n2
non-performing loans (NPLs) 391, 392
non-tariff barriers (NTBs) 333, 368
non-tariff measures (NTMs) 189
"noodle bowl" model, RTAs 182, 183
Norlund, Irene 55n9
Northeast Asia 16, 164; economic growth 61, 68,
76; education and human capital investments
245, 250, 257; GDP growth spillover from *79,
80*; proximity of Southeast Asian economies to
those of Northeast Asia 65, 67; *see also* growth
and development, Southeast Asia; growth and
development research models
North Korea 4
NPLs (non-performing loans) 391, 392
NRR (net reproduction rates) 351, 362n4
NTBs (non-tariff barriers) 333, 368
NTMs (non-tariff measures) 189
nutrition transition 348, 357–8
Nye, J.V.C. 340, 341n8

obesity problems 347, *358*, 363n7
ODA (Overseas Development Assistance)
280, 336, 339

OECD (Organization for Economic Cooperation and Development), trade boom (1950s to 1980s) 27
Ohlin, Bertil 36
one-party governments 410
O-NET test (Ordinary National Education Test), lower secondary school (Thailand) 256
openness 26, 39n5, 62–3, 70, 71, 72, 366; gains 63, 83n8; indexes *73*, 75, 84n20, 84n21; *see also* closed economies
opium, trading in 32–3, 56n26
Opium Wars 28
"original sin" hypothesis, and financial markets 392
Ottoman Empire 34
overnutrition 359
Overseas Development Assistance (ODA) 280, 336, 339
Owen, Norman 55n6, 227n2

Paauw, Douglas S. 46, 56n35
Paddock, William and Paul 9
palm oil trade 44, 110, 415, *416*
Pangestu, Mari 330
PAP (People's Action Party), Singapore 169
Papua New Guinea 294n2
Park, Donghyun 230, 231, 232
Park, Seokmin 159n2
Parnwell, M.J.G. 131n1
Parry, M.L. 123
particulate matter 121, 122, 126, *127*, 128, 132n8
Pelzer, Karl 56n18
Penang, Malaysia 30, 151, 153
Penn World Tables 71, 84n21, *233*, *235*, 236
People's Action Party (PAP), Singapore 169
Peper, Bram 227n2
pepper, trade in 24
Petri, P. 195n2
Pham, T.H. 178n11, 400
Philippine Institute for Development Studies 335
Philippines 3, 9, 65, 203, 262; age structure 211, *212*; American policy 52, 56n30; brain drain 262; central bank independence 336, 337; and changing role of government 52, 54; defeat of colonial powers in 46; demographic factors 115, 202, 204, 205, 210, 211, 214, 215, 218, 223, 225; domestic savings rates 230, 236; economic inequality and policy stability 412; economic policies and growth 44, 54; economic policy reform 329, 330, 335–6; education and human capital 219, 248, 249, 251, 255, 257, 260, 262; employment in 47, 48, 55n11; food security and agricultural development 93, 97, 98, 102, 108; foreign direct investment 163, 171; and GFC 389, 392, 396, 399; global production sharing 139, 140, 141, 157; growth rate 5, 13, 64, 72; health and aging, dual burdens 351, 352, 361; migration 275, 281, 283, 284, 285; natural

disasters, vulnerability to 417; natural resources and environment 117, 120, 123, 124, 132n5; in the period 1870 to 1970 46, 50, 51, 53, 55n10, 56n27; poverty reduction 304, 306, 308, 322, 324, *324*; regional integration 372; regional trade agreements 184, 185, 186, 188; resource endowments and economic growth 128, 130; rice production 97, 102; and second trade boom 30, 31; and trade bust 37, 38; *see also* Manila, Philippines
Phillips, James F. 209
Phnom Penh Special Economic Zone, Cambodia 142
Phongpaichit, Pasuk 55n3
Phung, T.T. 16, 81, 112n1, 132n10, 173, 270
physical inactivity 358–9
Pinera, J. 331
PISA (Program for International Student Assessment) 253, 254, 267n5
Plaza Accord (1985) 65, 80, 141, 173
plural society 49
Poffenberger, M. 131n1
policy reform, political economy *see* economic policy reform 18
pollution 115, 120, 121
Pomfret, R. 195n6, 329
poor periphery 32, 33, 34, 35, 36, 37, 38
Population Bomb, The (Erlich) 9
population of Southeast Asia *see* demographics
postcolonial regimes 7
poverty 18; absolute or relative 306; and aggregate growth 317–19; annual rates of reduction *307*, *310*; average rates of reduction *315*; counterfactual projections 321–2, *323*; data sources 306; developing countries/regions *308*; and economic growth 303–4, 316, 317–18; estimation results 305, 318–25; growth–poverty nexus 314–18; headcount measures 306, 308; incidence data 305, 307–10, *311–12*, 313; Indonesia (1980s) 332–4; long-run success of reduction 97; measurement 305–7; national *319*; and natural resources 120–1; near-poor, vulnerability 109; poverty line 306, 317; poverty reduction drivers 303–26; rural/urban distinction 316–17; and sectoral growth 319–21; structural 109; variables 306
Power, J.H. 341n6
"pragmatic orthodoxy" thesis 385, 394, 406n1, 411, 415, 418
Prasad, Eswar S. 231, 232
precious metals 39n1
precolonial economy 8
preferential trade agreements (PTAs) 370, 371, 379
Prevalence of Undernutrition and FSgap 92
Pritchett, L.H. 209
Program for International Student Assessment (PISA) 253, 254, 267n5

protectionism/protectionist tendencies 32, 143, 189, 194, 336, 374
provincial contract system 56n25
PTAs (preferential trade agreements) 370, 371, 379
Punjab region 36

Qian, Rong 231
Quah, E. 128
quantitative easing (QE) monetary policy 394

Radelet, S. 19n7, 60, 67, 83n3, 83n8
Rajapatirana, S. 331
Rama, M. 341n4
Ramos, Fidel V. 335, 336, 337
Ramstetter, Eric 166, 174, 175, 178n4
Rangoon, Myanmar 30, 49; see also Burma; Myanmar
Ravallion, Martin 313
raw material supply 114
Raynankorn, K. 123
RCEP (Regional Comprehensive Economic Partnership) 181, 182, 194, 377; ASEAN Framework on 378–9
real effective exchange rate (REER) index 405
Reardon, Tom 93, 107
recession, global see global financial crisis (GFC)
REDD+ programs 125
Regional Comprehensive Economic Partnership (RCEP) see RCEP (Regional Comprehensive Economic Partnership)
regional growth in Southeast Asia 10, 61; rate comparisons 63–4
regional integration, outward looking 366–84; deepening integration 373–4; whether East Asia has a workable financial safety net 379–81; FTAs, rise of 374, 376–7; merchandise trade 371–3; see also ASEAN (Association of Southeast Asian Nations)
regional production networks 141–2
regional trade agreements (RTAs) 17, 181–97; acquiring knowledge about 190–1, 192;; age of firm 192; ASEAN+1 RTAs 181, 182, 184, 185, 186, 193, 194; ASEAN-6 countries 185; benefits and costs 186, 187, 188; CEPT scheme 182, 183, 185; descriptive analysis of use 185–9; econometric analysis 183, 190–3; enterprise dataset 184–5; export experience in multiple markets 190; firm size 190; geographical location of firm 190, 192; implications 193–4; investigation of use, econometric 190–3; literature on 182–4; mega-regional 181, 194; micro-level data 181, 183; "noodle bowl" model 182, 183; patterns of use 185–6; reasons for not using 188–9; rules of origin (ROOs) 182, 183, 195n4; support 192; technological capabilities, building 190
regional value content (RVC) 189

regression analysis 71, 84n17; fixed-effects approaches 70, 84n22; food security 92; Ordinary Least Squares model 69, 70, 72, 75; probit regression 191, 192
Reid, Anthony 29, 30, 55n2, 227n2
Reisen, H. 231
re-linking 9
replacement levels, fertility reaching 204, 207, 209, 211, 223, 226, 353
Research in Motion (RIM) 143
resettlement programs, Malaysia 210
Resnick, Stephen A. 38
resource curse model 10, 11, 128; see also natural resources
rice: Burma 45, 55n6; changing role in food security 102–6, 105, 111; consumption and production 102–6, 105; export and import of 44, 109–10; Indonesia 111; rural and urban consumption, differences 103; surpluses, threats from 109–10; technological breakthrough in production 9, 92–3; Thai "pledging" scheme 411
Riedel, J. 331–2, 341n4, 400
Robequain, Charles 47, 55n9
Robinson, Warren C. 209
Rodriguez, F. 62
Rodrik, D. 62, 340
ROOs (rules of origin) 182, 183, 195n4, 376
Ross, John A. 209
RTAs see regional trade agreements (RTAs)
rubber trade 44, 110
Ruffer, R. 394
rules of origin (ROOs) 182, 183, 195n4, 376
rural environment: farm and village communities 6; income elasticities 104; and land resources 119–21

Sachs, J. D. 10, 61, 128–9, 132n12, 330–1
Sachs–Warner index 61, 62, 72, 83n4, 84n20, 331, 366
Sadli, Mohamed/Sadli's Law 420
Samsung Electronics 142, 159n2
Samuelson, Paul 36
savings rates, domestic see domestic savings rates, determinants
Schwulst, E.B. 56n31
sectoral transformation 4–5
sedentary lifestyles 358–9
semiconductor industry, global production sharing 140–1, 143
Shanghai Jiao Tong University, ranking of universities by 254
Shein Maung, M.M.T. 56n25
Shepherd, Jack 45, 55n9
Shin, Kwanho 230, 231, 232
Shively, Gerald 17, 120, 124, 132n6, 265, 362

Siam 43–4; and second trade boom 30; and trade bust 38; *see also* Thailand
Siamwalla, Ammar 55n6
SIBOR rate 400
Sicat, G.P. 341n6
Silk Road 19n13
Singapore: and China 65; demographic factors 204, 206, 207, 208, 209, 218, 220, 223; domestic savings rates 230, 236; economic inequality and policy stability 412; economic policies and growth (from 1870 to 1970) 44; economic policy reform 328, 331; education and human capital 247–8, 249, 261, 267n3; expulsion from Malaya (1965) 169; food security and agricultural development 112n4; foreign direct investment 163, 165, 166, 168, 171, 172, 176; fossil fuel consumption 132n5; and GFC 386, 387, 389, 392, 396, 400, 401, 404; global production sharing 139, 140, 141–2, 143, 151, 152, 153; growth rate 46, 64, 72; health and aging, dual burdens 362n3; institutional strengths 12; labor market 409; as large economy 3, 10, 81; migration 281, 282, 284, 286; monetary policy instruments 400; natural disasters, vulnerability to 124; openness 72, 366; port of 30; regional integration 371, 372, 374, 379; regional trade agreements 183; resource endowments and economic growth 130; as technological leader 246; transboundary issues 128; urbanization 49, 203, 276; *see also* Malaysia/Malaya
Singapore–Johor–Riau (SIJORI) 159n3
Sjöholm, Fredrik 17, 165, 167, 169, 171, 175, 177, 178n8, 265, 397, 1741
SMEs (small- and medium-sized enterprises) 184, 195n4
Socio-Economic Surveys (SES), Thailand 306
Soesastro, Hadi 329, 334, 341n5, 366, 382n4
"soft" states 19n1
Solow growth model 61, 62, 63, 68, 83n7
Southeast Asia (Karnow) 6
Southeast Asian economies: composition of Southeast Asian region 270; current trends 13–15; geographic proximity to Northeast Asia 65; whether grow differently as a group 70; growth *see* growth and development, Southeast Asia; high-income *see* high-income countries; long transition 8–13, 89; low-income *see* low-income countries; middle-income *see* middle-income countries 65; migrant Chinese and Indians, role 48; "miracle" economies 60, 83n1, 245, 267n1, 417–18; perception as agrarian and backward 8, 9; recent history (post-World War II) 6–8; semiconductor industry, dominance in 140–1, 142, 143; size 3, 70, 127, 306, 382; whether specifically Southeast Asian economies 16; trade booms and busts *see* Southeast Asian trade booms; trade bust (1914–40), Southeast Asia; transition from primarily rural and subsistence-oriented to urban and trade-oriented 89; V-shaped recoveries, following GFC 388; *see also* HPAEs ("high-performing Asian economies")
Southeast Asian trade booms: first (1500–800) 22–37; second (1815–1913) 30–7
South Korea 46, 50, 173; education and human capital 245–6, 248, 249, 250–1; global production sharing 140, 141; as technological leader 246
sovereign wealth funds (SWFs) 165
"spaghetti bowl" model, RTAs 182
Spate, O.H. 47, 55n9
spice trade 23, 24
spillovers: countries with significantly high growth elasticity from spillovers 78; environmental 114; "flying geese" hypothesis 83n6; foreign direct investment 176, 178n11; and growth 68, 73, 75, 76, 77, 78; within-industry 176; inter-country, influence of 70–1; Northeast Asian countries 65, 79, 80; positive, from FDI 176, 178n11; spatial spillover model 68; technology 176; unconditional, with convergence 72, 74; wage 176; *see also* growth and development research models; growth in Southeast Asia
stability, political and macroeconomic 172–3
Standard International Trade Classification (SITC) 159n4
Stanford Symposium Series on Global Food Policy and Food Security in the 21st Century 112n5
state-owned enterprises (SOEs) 332, 333
Sterling, Arlie 231
Stolper, Wolfgang 36
Straits Settlements, British Malaya 52, 56n31
structural change, and economic growth (from 1870 to 1970) 43–6, 54
structural transformation 4; and food security 93, *94–5, 96–7;* in Japan and Indonesia *96*
Sub-Saharan Africa 11, 89, 91
sugar industry 55n5
Sugimoto, Ichiro *44*
Sugiyama, Shinya 55n7
Sugiyarto, Guntur 17–18, 109, 353
Sukarno, President 169
Sumitomo Corporation, Japan 142
Sundaram, Jomo Kwame 56n18
Sundrum, R.M. *53,* 56n19
supermarkets 16, 99, 100, 107, 108; "supermarket revolution" 93
SUSENAS survey, Indonesia 306
sustainable development challenges 114–15
Swarnim, W. 397

Taiwan 4, 46, 50, 53, 173; education and human capital 245–6, 249; global production sharing 140, 141, 159n4

Takagi, S.] 402

Takahashi, K. 183

Takeuchi, F. 394

Tang, M.G. 336, 398–9

Tanjung Perak, port of 30

tariffs 9, 45, 63, 65, 83n8, 84n20, 143, 190, 195n4, 328, 369, 377; ASEAN Harmonized Tariff Nomenclatures 378; change in tariff classification (CTC) 189; external 381, 382; foreign direct investment 168, 170; high 168, 185; increasing 25, 46; lowering 10, 30, 63, 83n8, 83n9; most favored nation 195n6; non-tariff barriers 333, 368; non-tariff measures 189; preferential 182, 185, 186, 188, 193; tariff-jumping FDI 178n7; zero-rated 183, 195n6, 370; see also common effective preferential tariff (CEPT)

taxation rates 328, 397

Taylor, A.M. 62, 63, 84n20

technocrats 333, 339

technological change: and foreign direct investment 167–8; rice production 9, 92–3

Tecson, G. 335

Temasek Holdings, Singapore 165

Terada-Hagiwara, Akiko 232

Texas Instruments (US company) 140, 141

textiles, trade in 23, 34–5, 47

TFR see Total Fertility Rates (TFR)

Thailand 157; and agricultural transformation 98, 99; Asian Crisis (1997–99) 13; authoritarian regimes 9; carbon emissions 125; and China 65; climate change 123; demographic factors 115, 202, 204, 206, 207, 208, 209, 210, 211, 215, 218, 220, 222, 223, 225; domestic savings rates 230, 236; economic inequality and policy stability 412, 414–15; economic policies and growth (from 1870 to 1970) 44; economic policy reform 328, 331; economic volatility 410; education and human capital 218, 246, 248–9, 251, 253, 255, 256, 260, 262, 265; employment in 47; ethnic minorities 204; food security and agricultural development 93, 99, 108; foreign direct investment 163, 166, 167, 171, 172–3, 175, 178n10; forestry and biodiversity 116, 118; fossil fuel consumption 123, 132n5; and GFC 385, 389, 391, 392, 396, 399, 401, 404; global production sharing 139, 140, 146, 152, 153; growth rate 11, 46, 64, 72; health and aging, dual burdens 351, 357, 359; infrastructure, expenditure on 52–3, 56n32; labor market 409; land resources and rural environment 120, 121; as large economy 3, 10; and links with international economy 51; and Mekong River 126; migration 281, 282, 285,

286, 294n5, 294n24, 294n26, 296n30, 379; natural disasters, vulnerability to 124, 417; natural resources and agricultural products 9; openness 366; opposing factions/conflicts 6, 412; port of Bangkok 30; poverty reduction 306, 308, 322, 324, 324; regional integration 371, 383n10; regional trade agreements 183, 195n6; resource dependence 11; resource endowments and economic growth 128, 130; rice production 97; and structural transformation 97; and trade bust 38; transboundary issues 126; urban environment 121; urbanization 203, 272, 276; see also Bangkok, Thailand; Siam

Thailand–Australia RTA 183

Thaksin Shinawatra 414

Thee, K.W. 341n5

Thimann, C. 231

Thinking Schools, Learning Nation initiative 254

Thompson, Virginia 55n13

"tiger" economies, Northeast 4

Timmer, C. Peter 9, 16, 92, 93, 97, 102, 107, 119

Timor-Leste 171, 215, 223, 294n2

Tong, H. 65

Tonkin 36

total factor productivity (TFP) growth 63

Total Fertility Rates (TFR) 206, 207, 208, 213, 227n4, 270, 362n4; health and aging, dual burdens 349, 351, 352; see also demographic factors; fertility

Toyota 160n12

TPP (Transpacific Partnership) 181, 182, 194, 379

trade booms 16, 22–37; boom–bust cycles 394; ceteris paribus qualification 24; Chinese autarkic policy and Europe 27–9; and colonial rule see colonial rule; declining trade barriers and market integration, not driven by 23–5; de-industrialization 34–5, 38; drivers 25–7; European inter-continental trade boom, after 1500 22–3; factual drivers 27; first boom for Southeast Asia (1500–800) 22–37; great commodity exporters' terms of trade boom 31–3; inequalities, rising 35–6, 37; intra-regional trade 27; market integration hypothesis 23; markups 24, 25; non-competing "exotics" 24; OECD (1950s to 1980s) 27; poor periphery 32, 33, 34, 35, 36, 37, 38; price convergence 24; second boom for Southeast Asia (1815–1913) 30–7; small gains for Southeast Asia from European boom 29–30; theoretical drivers 25–7; wage–rental ratio (w/r) 35, 36, 37, 39n12, 39n13; world trade 22, 23, 26, 31

trade bust (1914–40), Southeast Asia 37–8

trade liberalization 332–4, 335–6

transboundary issues, natural resources and environment 126–8

transition economies 401
Transpacific Partnership (TPP) 181, 182, 194, 379
Trehan, B. 68, 69, 81
twenty-first-century challenges 19, 408–21;
  economic inequality and policy stability
  411–15; environmental risks 415–17;
  extrapolation dangers 419–20; global economic
  volatility 409–11; labor market and workforce
  transition, completing 409; labor productivity,
  central role 419; lessons from Southeast Asia
  417–20; macroeconomic policy 417–19; Sadli's
  Law 420

undernutrition 348, 360
UNEP (United Nations Environmental
  Programme) 123
Unfederated Malay States 52
United Nations Industrial Development
  Organization (UNIDO) 153
United States, semiconductor producers 140, 141
United States Environmental Protection Agency
  (US EPA) 122
Urata, S. 183
urban environment: categorization of an area as
  urban 294n16; versus farm and village
  communities 6; and natural resources 121–2
urbanization: from 1870 to 1970 49–50;
  demographic factors 115, 116, 203, 226, 277,
  294n4; levels in Southeast Asian countries
  (1950–2030) 203; and migration 272, 276–7,
  278; negative and positive impacts 277;
  over-urbanization 286; and prosperity 294n19;
  see also labor; migration

van der Eng, Pierre 27, 28, 30, 31, 35, 38, 39n8,
  45, 55n8
Van Landingham, Mark 227n2
van Zanden, Jan Luiten 34, 37
vegetable oils 358
Vietnam: and agricultural transformation 98; anti-
  export bias 9; climate change 123; command to
  market transition 10; demographic factors 204,
  205, 207, 209, 210, 216–17, 218, 220, 222, 226;
  development path 6; doi moi (renovation) 263,
  332, 366; domestic savings rates 230, 236;
  economic policies and growth (from 1870 to
  1970) 44; economic policy reform 331–2,
  341n4; education and human capital 246, 248,
  249, 251, 255, 256, 261, 262, 263–4, 265; factor
  market distortions and demand for training
  263–4; food security and agricultural
  development 93, 97, 98, 102; foreign direct
  investment 166, 167, 171, 175, 178n4, 332;
  forestry and biodiversity 116; fossil fuel
  consumption 132n5; and GFC 387, 389, 394,
  399, 403; global production sharing 142, 159n2;
  growth rate 5, 61, 64; health and aging, dual
  burdens 351, 361; land resources and rural
  environment 120; as large economy 3; as low-
  income economy 66, 81; and Mekong River
  126; migration 282, 284, 285; natural disasters,
  vulnerability to 124; poverty reduction 304,
  308, 313, 319, 324; regional integration 368,
  369; resource endowments and economic
  growth 128; reunification 368; rice production
  102; and second trade boom 30; and structural
  transformation 97; transboundary issues 126;
  transformation 4, 9; urbanization 203, 276; see
  also CLMV countries (Cambodia, Laos,
  Myanmar and Vietnam)
Viner, J. 182
Vlieland, C.A. 53
VOC (Dutch East India Company)
  23, 24, 30
Voyages of Discovery 22, 28

wage–rental ratio (w/r) 35, 36, 37, 38,
  39n12, 39n13
Wang, Pengfei 232
Ward, P. 124
Warner, A. M. 10, 61, 128–9, 132n12; see also
  Sachs–Warner index
Warr, Peter 11, 18, 19n12, 106, 109, 259, 306,
  314, 325, 326n1, 411, 414
wheat 104, 105
Wignaraja, G. 181, 183, 184, 195n2, 195n6,
  195n7, 361
Williamson, Jeffrey G. 23, 24, 26, 32, 35, 37,
  39n12, 39n13, 89, 409
World Bank 308, 335; East Asian Miracle
  60, 64, 245, 246, 385; and foreign direct
  investment 167, 168, 171; Genuine Domestic
  Savings indicator 128, 129; World
  Development Indicators 71, 94–5, 233, 236,
  265–6
world economic growth, GDP growth spillover
  from 78, 79
world manufacturing trade, geographic profile
  144–5
world trade boom 22, 23, 26, 31
WTO (World Trade Organization): Chinese
  accession 151; Doha Round 194, 379; Uruguay
  trade round 369

Xenos, Peter 227n2

Yamada, Saburo 94–5

Zelek, C.A. 132n6
Zelinsky, Wilbur 227n2

Made in the USA
Monee, IL
09 September 2021